REFRAMING CONTEMPORARY AFRICA

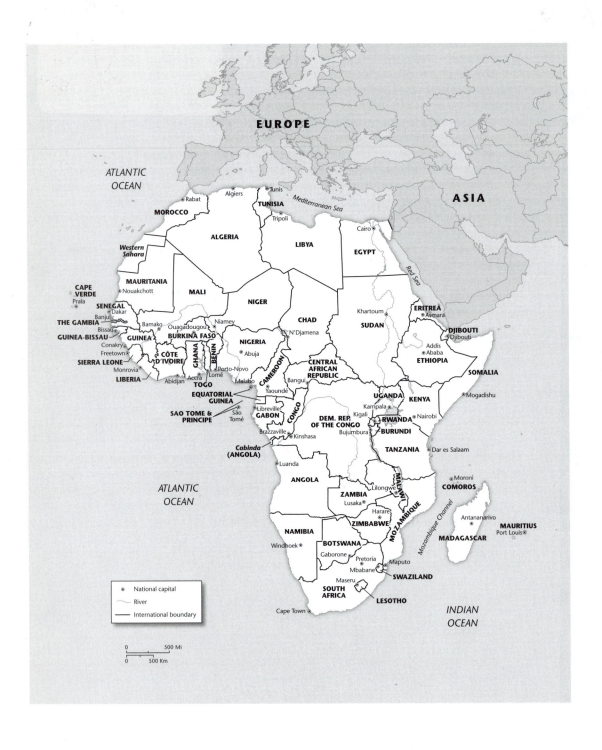

EUROPE

ASIA

ATLANTIC OCEAN

ATLANTIC OCEAN

INDIAN OCEAN

Mediterranean Sea

Red Sea

Mozambique Channel

MOROCCO
• Rabat
Algiers •
• Tunis
TUNISIA
Tripoli •
ALGERIA
LIBYA
EGYPT
Cairo •

Western Sahara

MAURITANIA
• Nouakchott
MALI
NIGER
CHAD
SUDAN
Khartoum •
ERITREA
Asmara •
DJIBOUTI
• Djibouti

CAPE VERDE
Praia •
SENEGAL
• Dakar
Banjul •
THE GAMBIA
Bissau •
GUINEA-BISSAU
Conakry •
Freetown •
SIERRA LEONE
Monrovia •
LIBERIA
Bamako •
Ouagadougou •
BURKINA FASO
Niamey •
N'Djamena •
NIGERIA
• Abuja
GHANA
BENIN
CÔTE D'IVOIRE
Accra •
Lomé •
TOGO
Abidjan •
Porto-Novo •
Malabo •
EQUATORIAL GUINEA
GUINEA
CAMEROON
Yaoundé •
CENTRAL AFRICAN REPUBLIC
Bangui •
Addis Ababa •
ETHIOPIA
SOMALIA
Mogadishu •

SAO TOME & PRINCIPE
São Tomé •
Libreville •
GABON
CONGO
Brazzaville •
• Kinshasa
DEM. REP. OF THE CONGO
UGANDA
Kampala •
Kigali •
RWANDA
Bujumbura •
BURUNDI
KENYA
Nairobi •
Cabinda (ANGOLA)
• Luanda
TANZANIA
Dar es Salaam •

ANGOLA
ZAMBIA
Lusaka •
MALAWI
Lilongwe •
MOZAMBIQUE
COMOROS
Moroni •

NAMIBIA
Windhoek •
BOTSWANA
Gaborone •
ZIMBABWE
Harare •
Antananarivo •
MADAGASCAR
MAURITIUS
Port Louis •

Pretoria •
Maputo •
Mbabane •
SWAZILAND
Maseru •
SOUTH AFRICA
LESOTHO
Cape Town •

⊛ National capital

⟋ River

— International boundary

0   500 Mi

0   500 Km

REFRAMING CONTEMPORARY AFRICA

Politics, Economics, and Culture in the Global Era

Peyi Soyinka-Airewele
Ithaca College

Rita Kiki Edozie
Michigan State University

CQ PRESS

A Division of SAGE
Washington, D.C.

CQ Press
2300 N Street, NW, Suite 800
Washington, DC 20037

Phone: 202-729-1900; toll-free, 1-866-4CQ-PRESS (1-866-427-7737)

Web: www.cqpress.com

Photo Credits: Photo by Sean Connolly (243)

Cover design: Cynthia Richardson
Maps: International Mapping
Composition: C&M Digitals (P) Ltd.

∞ The paper used in this publication exceeds the requirements of the American National
Standard for Information Sciences—Permanence of Paper for Printed Library Materials,
ANSI Z39.48-1992.

Printed and bound in the United States of America

13 12 11 10 09   1 2 3 4 5

Library of Congress Cataloging-in-Publication Data

Reframing contemporary Africa : politics, economics, and culture in the global era / [edited
by] Peyi Soyinka-Airewele and Rita Kiki Edozie.
     p. cm.
   Includes bibliographical references and index.
   ISBN 978-0-87289-407-5 (paperbound : alk. paper) 1. Africa—Politics and government—
21st century. 2. Africa—Economic conditions—21st century. 3. Popular culture—Africa.
I. Soyinka-Airewele, Peyi. II. Edozie, Rita Kiki. III. Title.

   JQ1875.R428 2009
   320.96—dc22

                                                              2009026880

To senior colleague, erudite African scholar, and contributor to this book,

the late professor Oyekan Owomoyela,

whose death in 2007 has not silenced his voice.

Peyi Soyinka-Airewele is associate professor of African and international politics at Ithaca College, New York, with interests in the fields of socio-political memory, the politics of disaster, critical development theory, human rights, and the politics of African Cinema. Her publications include, most recently, *Socio-Political Scaffolding and the Construction of Change,* coedited with Kelechi Kalu; her work on democratic development, collective memory, and cathartic violence has been published in several scholarly journals including the *Journal of African and Asian Studies,* the *Journal of Third World Studies,* and *West Africa Review.* Soyinka-Airewele received her PhD in international studies from the University of Birmingham, U.K. and prior to joining Ithaca College, she taught at Colgate University. She has also served as the International Director of ACT Africa and is currently the president of the Association of Third World Studies. Her current research engages the socio-political discourses of popular African cinema and their fluid interpretations of transforming identities and issues in global and local spaces.

Rita Kiki Edozie is associate professor of International Relations at Michigan State University where she teaches and researches topics in African affairs, comparative politics, democratization, and the international political economy with a focus on development. She is the author of *People Power and Democracy: the Popular Movement against Military Despotism in Nigeria, 1989–1999*; *Reconstructing Africa's Third Wave: Comparative African Democratic Politics*; and has contributed scholarly articles and book chapters to several edited volumes an academic journals. She is a Lilly Teaching Fellow graduate (2007–2008) and describes herself as an "interdisciplinary political-science critical thinking facilitator." Before joining MSU, Kiki earned her PhD in political science from the New School for Social Research in New York City and between 2001–2003 she served as the Deputy Director of the Institute of African Studies at Columbia University's School of International and Public Affairs (SIPA).

CONTENTS

LIST OF TABLES, FIGURES, AND MAPS

Maps

Tables

Figures

CONTRIBUTORS

About the Editors

Peyi Soyinka-Airewele is associate professor of African and International Politics at Ithaca College, New York. She has interests in the fields of sociopolitical memory, the politics of disaster, critical development theory, human rights, and African cinema. She is currently the president of the Association of Third World Studies Inc. (2008–2009) and international director of ACT Africa. Her recent works include *Socio-Political Scaffolding and the Construction of Change*, coedited with Kelechi Kalu (2008) and *Invoking the Past, Conjuring the Nation* (forthcoming, 2009). Her research on democratic development, collective memory, and cathartic violence has been published in several scholarly journals and books, and her current work engages the sociopolitical discourses of popular African cinema and its fluid interpretations of transforming identities and local and global spaces.

Rita Kiki Edozie is an associate professor of International Relations at Michigan State University where she teaches and researches African affairs, comparative politics, democratization, and international political economy with a focus on development. She is the author of *People Power and Democracy: The Popular Movement Against Military Despotism in Nigeria, 1989–1999* (2002) and *Reconstructing Africa's Third Wave: Comparative African Democratic Politics* (2008). Edozie has also contributed scholarly articles and book chapters to several edited volumes and academic journals. She is currently conducting a cross-national examination of the political economy of development trajectories in Africa. From 2001 to 2003, Dr. Edozie served as the deputy director of the Institute of African Studies at the School of International and Public Affairs at Columbia University.

About the Contributors

William Ackah, PhD, is lecturer in community and voluntary sector studies, Birkbeck College, University of London, and the current program director for undergraduate and postgraduate community development programs. Born in London of Ghanaian parents, Dr. Ackah's family roots can be traced to Nkfroful, the birth place of Kwame Nkrumah. His research and publications focus on African diasporic politics and identity in local, national, and global contexts. His publications include "Pan-African

Consciousness and Identity: Reflections on the Twentieth Century" in *Black Identity in the Twentieth Century* (2002) and *Pan-Africanism: Exploring the Contradictions* (1999). He has previously held a number of academic and administrative positions at the universities of Bristol, Edge Hill, and Liverpool. He is currently working on a book on Black community politics in the United Kingdom.

Pius Adesanmi is an associate professor of comparative and African literature at Carelton University in Canada and the director of the Project on New African Literatures (PONAL, www.projectponal.com). He has published "Third Generation African Literatures and Contemporary Theorizing" in *The Study of Africa, Volume 1: Disciplinary and Interdisciplinary Encounters*; "Re-Membering the Present, Prophesying the Past: Colonialism, *Ecriture Engagée*, and Africa's New Intellectuals" in *The Dark Webs: Perspectives on Colonialism in Africa*, "*Things Fall Apart*, the American Classroom, and the Question of Freedom," forthcoming in *New Perspectives on Chinua Achebe*, and "The Subaltern Can Bite: African Women's Writing, the Social, and Transformation in the Postcolony" in *Canadian Review of Comparative Literature*. His current research includes African and Black diasporic literatures in English and French; postcolonial and cultural theory; third world feminist discourses; and African and Black diasporic film, popular culture, and music.

Jude Akudinobi is a lecturer in the Department of Black Studies at the University of California at Santa Barbara. He received a BA in philosophy and English from the University of Lagos, Nigeria; an MA in communication arts from Loyola Marymount University; and a PhD in cinema-television critical studies from the University of Southern California. Dr. Akudinobi's research interests lie in the relationship between culture, media, and society. He has examined the textual and symbolic functions of Africa in the dominant cinema of the 1980s. His feature-length screenplay, *Eze*, uses traditional African institutions to mobilize discourse on the concept of destiny.

Kwabena Akurang-Parry, a Ghanaian poet and historian, is professor of African and world history at Shippensburg University in Pennsylvania. He studied at the Kwame Nkrumah University of Science and Technology, Kumasi, Ghana; the Institute of African Studies, University of Ghana–Legon, Ghana; and Wilfrid Laurier University, Waterloo, Canada. He received his PhD in African history from York University, Toronto, Canada, in 1999. He has published over fifty articles, some of which have appeared in *Slavery and Abolition*, *African Economic History*, *The International Journal of African Historical Studies*, *History in Africa*, *Transactions of the Historical Society of Ghana*, *Left History*, *International Journal of Regional Local Studies*, *African Identities*, *Refuge*, *Ghana Studies*, *African Issues*, *Groniek*, and the *Journal of Cultural Studies*. He is the coeditor of *African Agency and European Colonialism: Latitudes of Negotiation and Containment* (2007). Some of his poems have appeared in *Okike* and *Ufahamu*. His research includes comparative slavery and abolition, colonial rule and African responses, and gender and labor in the Gold Coast (Ghana). He has held teaching posts at Tulane University and York University in Toronto, Canada.

Fantu Cheru is professor emeritus and research director at The Nordic Africa Institute in Uppsala, Sweden. He was a professor of development studies at American University's School of International Service in Washington, D.C. His many publications include *The Silent Revolution in Africa: Debt, Development and Democracy* (1989) and *African Renaissance Roadmaps to the Challenge of Globalization* (2002). He is currently researching remittance and local economic development; globalization, cities, and the politics of water provisioning; and the dynamics of Sino-African relations.

Susan Craddock is associate professor in the Women's Studies Department and the Institute for Global Studies at the University of Minnesota. Her research, public speaking, and publications engage critical issues in women's health, social justice, disease, public health, and the construction of race. She is the author of *City of Plagues: Disease, Poverty, and Deviance in San Francisco* (2004) and *HIV and AIDS in Africa: Beyond Epidemiology*, which she coedited with Ezekiel Kalipeni, Joseph R. Oppong, and Jayati Ghosh (2003).

Anene Ejikeme is an assistant professor of history at Trinity University, San Antonio, Texas. She received her PhD from Columbia University in 2003 after completing research into the history of Catholic women in Onitsha, an important market town in Nigeria. She published "Subterfuge and Resistance: A History of Infanticide in Onitsha, Nigeria" in *Power and Nationalism in Modern Africa: Essays in Honor of Don Ohadike* (forthcoming) and "Let the Women Speak!" forthcoming in *At Issues*, an online journal. She is currently completing "From Traders to Teachers," based in large part on her dissertation, and is investigating the life of the boxer Hogan "Kid" Bassey, the 1957 world welterweight champion. With Dr. Lynette A. Jackson, she is coediting a volume tentatively titled *Black Women Travel*. Prior to coming to Trinity, Dr. Ejikeme taught at Barnard College in New York, where she served as director of the Pan-African Studies Program from 2001 to 2003.

James D. Graham was a professor of history at Oakland University where he dedicated himself to teaching more than a dozen courses in African studies to Detroit-area undergraduates from 1969 to 2003. He contributed a chapter on "Political Development in Historic Africa" and a brief "Historical Overview" of South Africa to Vincent B. Khapoya's introductory text, *The African Experience* (1994, 1998). Initially mentored by historian Jan Vansina at Northwestern University, in 1965 he authored "The Slave Trade, Depopulation and Human Sacrifice in Benin History" for *Cahiers d'Etudes Africaines*, which was excerpted in Robert O. Collins's 1968 edition of *Problems in African History*. His subsequent field research focused primarily on modern Tanzania and included "A Case Study in Migrant Labor" (*African Studies Review*, 1970) and "Indirect Rule: The Establishment of 'Chiefs' and 'Tribes' in Cameron's Tanganyika" (*Tanzania Notes and Records*, 1976, and reprinted in *Colonialism and Nationalism in Africa* by Gregory Maddox et al. in 1993). He published numerous other scholarly articles, book chapters, and book reviews and presented many research papers on Africa's development issues and its vital cultural history.

Siba Grovogui, professor of international relations theory and international law at The Johns Hopkins University, holds a PhD from the University of Wisconsin at Madison. He is the author of *Sovereigns, Quasi-Sovereigns, and Africans: Race and Self-Determination in International Law* (1996) and *Beyond Eurocentrism and Anarchy: Memories of International Order and Institutions* (2006). Dr. Grovogui is currently completing manuscripts on human rights and on the genealogy of the "international." He is also collaborating on a National Science Foundation–funded project on the rule of law under a World Bank–initiated experiment in Chad around an oil and pipeline development project.

Christopher LaMonica is a lecturer in international relations at the University of Victoria–Wellington, New Zealand. His research interests include international relations theory and practice, African politics, and development issues. Dr. La Monica is the cofounder and editor of the new journal *Africana: A Journal of Ideas on Africa and the African Diaspora* (www.africanajournal.org). Some of his publications include *International Politics: The Classic Texts* (2008) and "African Political Thought and International Relations: Challenges and Prospects" in the *Australasian Review of African Studies* (June 2007). He is currently working on a new textbook on international politics entitled *Globalizing International Relations Theory*. His aim is to identify similarities and differences between "non-Western" political thought and the Western classics of IR theory.

Mahmood Mamdani is the Herbert Lehman Professor of Government in the departments of anthropology and political science at Columbia University. He is also the former director of Columbia's Institute of African Studies. He is a former president of the Council for Development of Social Research in Africa (CODESRIA) in Dakar, Senegal. Mamdani's reputation as an expert in African history, politics, and international relations has made him an important voice in contemporary debates about Africa. His book *Citizen and Subject: Contemporary Africa and the Legacy of Late Colonialism* won the 1998 Herskovits Award of the African Studies Association of the United States. In 2001, he was one of nine scholars to present at the Nobel Peace Prize Centennial Symposium. In 2008, he was named one of the top one hundred public intellectuals in the world by *Foreign Policy* and *Prospect*. His recent books include *When Victims Become Killers: Colonialism, Nativism, and Genocide in Rwanda* (2001), *Good Muslim Bad Muslim: America, The Cold War, and the Roots of Terror* (2004), and *Saviors and Survivors: Darfur, Politics, and the War on Terror* (2009).

Célestin Monga is lead economist and advisor to the vice president of the World Bank. A native of Cameroon, he has advanced degrees from MIT, Harvard University, and the universities of Paris-Sorbonne, Pau, and Bordeaux. Dr. Monga has served on the Sloan Fellows Board of Governors at MIT's Sloan School of Management and has taught economics and political science at Boston University and the University of Bordeaux. He was the economics editor of the five-volume *New Encyclopedia of Africa* (2007). His own books have been translated into several languages and are used in colleges and universities around the world. They include *Nihilisme et négritude* (2009), *Un Bantou à Washington* (2007), and *The Anthropology of Anger* (1996).

Makau Mutua is dean, SUNY Distinguished Professor, and the Floyd H. and Hilda L. Hurst Faculty Scholar at Buffalo Law School at the State University of New York. He is the director of the Human Rights Center and teaches international human rights, international business transactions, and international law. Professor Mutua has been a visiting professor at Harvard Law School, the University of Iowa College of Law, the University of Puerto Rico School of Law, and the United Nations University for Peace in Costa Rica. From 2002 to 2003, while on sabbatical in Kenya, he served as chair of the Government of Kenya's Task Force on the Establishment of a Truth, Justice, and Reconciliation Commission. The Task Force recommended a truth commission for Kenya. During the same time, Mutua was a delegate to the National Constitutional Conference, the forum that produced a contested draft constitution for Kenya. He is the author of *Human Rights: A Political and Cultural Critique* (2002) and, most recently, *Kenya's Quest for Democracy: Taming Leviathan* (2008) and *Human Rights NGOs in East Africa: Political and Normative Tensions* (2008). He has also written numerous scholarly articles that explore international law, human rights, and religion.

Iheanyi N. Osondu is an associate professor of geography in the History, Geography, and Political Science Department at Fort Valley State University, Georgia, and has previously taught at institutions in Africa and Europe. Recipient of a 2006 SPACE (Spatial Analysis for Curriculum Enhancement) Instructional Development Award, Osondu's current research involves the use and application of GIS (Geographic Information Systems) in solving environmental problems in Africa. He has worked in the fields of economic and population geography in North America and Africa and has published in the area of housing finance and the informal sector, African migrations, and environmental issues.

Before he died in 2007, **Oyekan Owomoyela** was the Ryan Professor of African Literature and the coordinator of African American and African Studies at the University of Nebraska, Lincoln. He was the author of numerous acclaimed books, monographs, and other critical writings on African literatures and criticism, philosophy, folklore, theater, proverbs, and identity, including *The African Difference: Discourses on Africanity and the Relativity of Cultures* (1996), *A History of Twentieth-Century African Literatures* and *Yoruba Trickster Tales* (2002), and *Culture and Customs of Zimbabwe* (2002). At the time of his death, he was completing his manuscript on African literature, *The Columbia Guide to West African Literature in English Since 1945*, which was published by Columbia University Press in 2008.

Wole Soyinka, poet, playwright, and author of more than thirty-five books, won the Nobel Prize for Literature in 1986, the first African to be so honored. His acclaimed prison memoir, *The Man Died*, was written on toilet paper, cigarette packages, and between the lines of the few books he secretly obtained as a political prisoner in Nigeria in the late 1960s. Soyinka's best known plays include *A Dance of the Forests, The Bacchae of Euripides, The Swamp Dwellers, Kongi's Harvest, The Trials of Brother Jero, Death and the King's Horsemen*, and *The Lion and the Jewel*. His nonfiction books include *The Burden of Memory, The Muse of Forgiveness, The Open Sore of a Continent*, and the beautifully crafted memoir *Ake: The Years of Childhood*. In addition to the Nobel Prize, his many honors include the Enrico Mattei Award for the Humanities, the Leopold Sedar Senghor Award for the Arts, the John Whiting Literary Prize, the Benson Medal of the Royal Society for Literature, and the UNESCO Medal for the Arts. Soyinka has held positions at numerous universities including Cambridge, Yale, Cornell, Harvard, Emory, Ibadan, and Legon, among others. He is professor emeritus of Obafemi Awolowo University in Nigeria, fellow of the DuBois Institute at Harvard University, senior fellow of the Black Mountain Institute at the University of Nevada, Elias Ghanem Professor of Creative Writing in the English department of the University of Nevada, Las Vegas, and the President's Marymount Institute Professor in Residence at Loyola Marymount University in Los Angeles, California. Soyinka has been an outspoken critic of many Nigerian administrations and of political tyrannies worldwide. In 1994, he was designated UNESCO ambassador for the promotion of African culture, human rights, and freedom of expression, media, and communication.

Kendra Sundal is a 2009 graduate of the Department of Politics at Ithaca College. She served as president of the college's Amnesty International student chapter for two years and for one year as head delegate of the Model United Nations team. Born and raised in Madison, Wisconsin, Ms. Sundal's first travel abroad further sparked her interest in global studies and world music. She studied in Ghana for a summer semester, an opportunity that changed her personal and global views on life, livelihood, and what it means to be a woman. She looks forward to returning as soon as possible and would like to extend her gratitude to her parents for supporting all of her endeavors and to the editors for giving her the chance to contribute to this collection. She has the utmost respect for the authors who share these pages.

Okbazghi Yohannes is a professor of international studies at the University of Louisville. His courses include African affairs, international relations, international terrorism, international political economy, the politics of European integration, and the politics of the Middle East. Yohannes has published numerous articles and *Eritrea: A Pawn in World Politics, The United States and the Horn of Africa: An Analytical Study of Pattern and Process, The Political Economy of An Authoritarian Modern State and Religious Nationalism In Egypt, Anatomy of an African Tragedy: Economic, Political, and Foreign Policy Crises in Post-Independence Eritrea* (co-authored), and *Water Resources and Inter-Riparian Relations in the Nile Basin: In Search of an Integrative Discourse.*

Paul Tiyambe Zeleza is a Malawian historian, literary critic, novelist, short story writer, and blogger at *The Zeleza Post.* He is currently president of the African Studies Association, and was recently appointed dean of the Bellarmine College of Liberal Arts at Loyola Marymount University. Prior to this appointment, Zeleza was head of the Department of African American Studies at the University of Illinois at Chicago. Zeleza is widely recognized as one of the leading authorities on African economic history. His book, *A Modern Economic History of Africa,* won the 1994 Noma Award for Publishing in Africa, the continent's most prestigious book award. Some of his notable publications include *The Study of Africa, Disciplinary and Interdisciplinary Encounters, Transnational and Global Engagements, African Universities in the Twenty-First Century, Rethinking Africa's Globalization, Causes and Costs of African Conflicts,* and *Africa and Its Diasporas: Dispersals and Linkages* (2008).

PREFACE

Have you ever found yourself disagreeing with the main book that you have assigned for your African politics or African studies courses? As editors of this volume, we were alarmed by the high number of Africanists who answered this question in the affirmative. Professors of African studies across the spectrum acknowledged that in class—with novice and more advanced students—they found it necessary to contradict the views in their assigned textbooks much of the time. As undergraduate professors of African affairs, we often heard similar complaints from our colleagues about the difficulty of finding books that took Africa seriously—books that presented a comprehensive, accessible, yet satisfying way to approach the continent's contradictions. This very discussion dominated our first meeting at an academic conference on African studies. As we excitedly discovered an intellectual comradeship on a topic that had obviously caused us not a little bit of disconcertment, we realized that the lacunae in existing books were quite obvious: Many of the available texts appeared to silence the plurality of African voices, thereby marginalizing African agent-processes and epistemologies regarding Africa's circumstances. The books were often reductionist and collapsed the complexity and diversity of Africa into a Euro-American panoptic viewpoint; they tended to simplify the study of Africa by relying on obsolete lenses for examining the continent's affairs; they seemed "presentist" in that they often eschewed important historical transformations in their understanding of contemporary African affairs; and, finally, they appeared to be disciplinarily narrow, to ignore more expansive, multidisciplinary perspectives on Africa.

Sometimes the gaps were more basic. We wondered, "Wouldn't it be great to have a map indicating the new global oil reserves in Africa and an explanation of their strategic importance to the world?" and "Why is it that students still have little or no access to materials that help them understand the astronomical growth of the African film industry, the political voice of popular culture, and the way it challenges the Western framing and understanding of Africa?" Peyi had the first brilliant idea when she said, "We need to 'reframe' Africa," and Kiki concurred without hesitation, "let's do it."

This was the genesis of our joint venture on the project, *Reframing Contemporary Africa*. Of course, our intellectual partnership had been foreshadowed by an equally fortuitous encounter in the preceding year between Peyi and Charisse Kino, acquisitions editor at CQ Press. Charisse had been piqued by a report from a sales representative who described a combative meeting with a somewhat frustrated professor of African politics who spelled out just what was needed in a rigorous reading of Africa. When

Charisse contacted Peyi, that rather "combative" professor, to discuss the possibility of developing such a project, Peyi responded so positively to her proposal that the incubator for this text was built overnight. That original project has been transformed, shaped, and enlivened by the integration of new and critical issues and discourses on Africa, such as the U.S. AFRICOM debates and the struggles over postcoloniality as a mode of intellectual framing, as well as by the added punch of a productive editorial enterprise that has incorporated the many experiences, concerns, and vantage points we all bring as teachers, researchers, and students of Africa. Perhaps one of the most distinctive features of this volume is the sense it provides of a wide range of authors, joined in a shared dialogue on how we might interpret the social, economic, cultural, and global realities of African societies.

Reframing Contemporary Africa does just what its title suggests; it recasts critical discourses on African politics, histories, contemporary struggles, and accomplishments. In this volume, we have brought together some of the leading voices on Africa to engage in a lively interrogation of issues pertinent to the study of the continent. Their essays cover African history, politics, economics, security, society, literature, film, health, and more, but they are different from those in other books on African politics. The chapters are unlikely to induce somnolent agreement in all readers—far from it. We have invited our authors, who are all empathetically and critically invested in the continent, to provide richly nuanced, possibly controversial, but indubitably discerning perspectives that will advance our thinking about the African past, present, and future. Their writings provoke debate and understanding not merely of African issues, but also about the West and its framing of Africa and itself.

Our contributors criss-cross disciplinary boundaries, deploying literary, gender, musical, cinematographic, cartographic, sociological, historical, political, and economic analyses. Consequently, the conversations that follow collectively reflect the diversities and complexities of African politics, cultures, and societies. The chapters introduce vital perspectives on the study of Africa; defy intractable images; encourage disquieting encounters with historical and contemporary realities and sociopolitical trajectories; compel an engaging, intense, and challenging confrontation with dilemmas that expose the connections between the domestic and the global; and create a platform for further dialogue and research.

It takes a special set of tools to create new frames such as these. In this book, we employ two important organizing devices. First, we view and present Africa as a comprehensive regional entity and do not subscribe to the normative position that divides the continent between sub-Saharan and North Africa because that only validates a set of problematic geographic, racial, and religious assumptions. The essays take this holistic view of Africa into account. Second, we employ and affirm a wide range of analytical methods, both quantitative and qualitative, using them fluidly throughout the book. The writers embrace the methodological languages of case studies, personal encounters in field research, and empirical and comparative analysis, as they are needed, to facilitate the most vibrant imaging of the continent possible.

The Structure of the Book

Reluctantly, we gave up the tantalizing image of a detailed, vividly realized 4,000-page volume—which the subject surely merits—and settled on somewhat more realistic but no less compelling goals. *Reframing Contemporary Africa* brings together twenty-two essays organized into five thematic sections that capture vital questions, challenges, and realities; stimulate a quest for additional inquiry; and provide the platform for rigorous research. The book's five parts cover an orientation to the discursive and representational strategies involved in the study of the continent; the historical trajectories that enable us to "reread" Africa's past; a reimagining of the continent's politics and political economies; an exploration of its sociocultural dynamics; and an engagement with the most pressing contemporary debates. The editors begin each part of the book with a substantive introduction to introduce readers to the contributors and the scholarly debates to which their essays belong. Readers who are new to the study of African politics will find these to be particularly useful road maps to the chapters that follow. Another of our goals involves our unusual decision to invite an essay by a young student-scholar whose reflections on the discourse on African women is positioned at the critical intersection of a personal and theoretical journey. Her essay is an innovation that follows through on the underlying analytical philosophy of the book, which seeks and embraces a constellation of critical methodologies, voices, and sites for engaging the varied realities of the continent.

Similarly, our multidisciplinary approach presumes that we not rely solely on text to deliver our message. We live in a world in which visual communications underscore and direct the complexities and nuances embedded in the spoken word. That is why we speak through the maps, illustrations, figures, and tables to capture the intricate discourse webs that constitute that place called Africa and locate its political, economic, and cultural affairs in comparative and global perspectives. The cartoonist featured in our book, Khalil Bendib, believes in "cartoons that speak truth to power." So do we; the multiple schemas that we employ will help readers visualize the true scope of Africa and will enhance alternative ways of knowing and understanding the continent.

In Part One, "Critical Perspectives on Africa: Navigating Representation and Reality," we embark on a study of the dominant debates on African identities, landscapes, and histories. Over time, popular media, literature, and academic dialogues have inscribed a problematic idea of African difference into the global imaginary. In the first essay, editors Peyi Soyinka-Airewele and Rita Kiki Edozie interrogate the ideological prisms that reproduce such insidious misrepresentations and that subvert efforts to understand and engage ongoing issues in the continent. Touching on the conventional framing of Africa in popular cinema, literature, news media, and academic texts, they argue for the adoption of alternative schematic methodologies and analytical tools. Their tentative incursion into texts that destabilize our preconceived notions of the African continent is deepened in Mahmood Mamdani's brief but probing examination of the naming and shaping of "Africa" and the ways in which such evolving conversations insistently locate the study of the local in the global imaginary.

The excision of North Africa from what has become popularly known as "sub-Saharan" or "Black Africa" is indicative of the power of inscription as it is configured through ideological, racial, and economic concerns. Both Mamdani and Iheanyi Osondu address the historical, global, and geo-spatial values embedded in certain discursive practices, showing, for instance, how the African landscape has been effectively balkanized via a set of powerful yet subtle markers or "frames" that respond more to outside notions than to African realities and identities. Mamdani's and Osondu's arguments, contextualized as they are by their illuminating exploration of the historical, social, and physical geographies of the continent, serve to offer meaningful new perspectives on Africa.

These writings demonstrate why and how popular constructs of Africa must be engaged from within historical and contemporary contexts. Furthermore, they must be examined as methodologies and mythical contraptions that often map narrowed visions of the continent and sustain the tendency of the West to position itself as the enlightened self to the African Other. In his contribution to this debate,

Oyekan Owomoyela anchors the preceding arguments to an illustrative analysis of the external representation of African gender identities and roles. His essay does not merely disrupt assumptions of African identity, social roles, and relations, but it also opens new lines of inquiry about the West itself—its conflicted value systems as revealed in language and popular discourse.

Part Two, "Political Histories: Rereading the African Past," integrates the past and present through a study of African struggles for the abolition of slavery, the nuanced complexities of African-diasporan relations, and subterranean layers of trauma and violence in the sociopolitical legacies of colonial empire in Africa. Reframing Africa within this globalizing age requires us to query popular assumptions that contemporary globalization is a new phenomenon that marks a clean break with the epoch of colonial imperialism. Our contributors work out a series of new historical approaches and narratives in order to unravel the political, economic, and social challenges facing African societies today. Kwabena Akurang-Parry's research into transatlantic slavery gives voice and background to an important aspect of the harrowing displacements that created the African diasporas. In a focused exploration of abolitionist struggles in Ghana against the continued violence of the transatlantic slavery system, he exposes the limits of conventional discourses on the slave trade.

William Ackah continues this excavation, part of a cyclical discourse on the African diaspora and its connections with the African continent, in his engaging exploration of the relationships between Africa and its old and new diasporas. This timely personal and analytical essay takes its place in one of the most important current transatlantic conversations, which concerns the struggle to define African identity and the meaning of transnationalism. The issues addressed in Ackah's essays raise difficult questions about the relationship between the continent and its traumatically displaced African populations in the New World. Perhaps one of the most recent visible emblems of that taut relationship is represented in the tensions and exuberance surrounding the election and inauguration of President Barack Hussein Obama as the forty-fourth president of the United States of America. African-American son of a White American mother and a Black Kenyan father, President Obama embodies the old and new diasporas and the quest for resolution, healing, and restoration evoked in Ackah's contribution to this book.

Beyond the examination of slavery and its aftermath, Paul Tiyambe Zeleza and Peyi Soyinka-Airewele provide two critical forms of historical work. Soyinka-Airewele's insights into colonial traumas intersect intriguingly with Zeleza's historiography of the African past. Both offer the reader a vital platform for investigating continental and local histories and provide insight into the ways in which African societies, scholars, and leaders have sought to engage and process such histories. Soyinka-Airewele's study of colonialism powerfully links the politics of colonial and postcolonial administrations to contemporary African political affairs—particularly to the many conflicts and crises that the continent has experienced in the postcolonial period. Similarly, Zeleza's generational perspective takes on a dual challenge of writing history: the need to juxtapose collective and personal historical landmarks with the intellectual formulation and rendering of such histories. From the specificity of Soyinka-Airewele's study to the sweeping historical embrace of Zeleza's, these chapters provide timely forms of recounting for postcolonies that have inherited the burden of remembering and addressing a convoluted past.

In Part Three, "Power, Politics and Socio-Economic Struggles," we contend with the continuing struggles of postcolonial recovery and debates on politics and power, democracy, economics, and security. Now is certainly another crucial moment when economic globalization deeply affects social, political, and economic battles in African countries. As a result, the continent is experiencing destabilizing tides of change at a time in which the specter of coloniality continues to mediate its diverse formations.

Fantu Cheru's essay on the African political economy serves to illustrate the impact that economic globalization has had on national and local economies. The socioeconomic problems exacerbated by globalization's uneven outcomes in Africa are reflected in the creation of new political economies such as the continent's Gulf oil fields, the escalation of conflicts within the continent, fluctuations in political leadership, and the growing HIV/AIDS pandemic with its dire impact on African countries. It is all too easy to ignore the intersections of local-national-global dynamics in our analysis of conflicts in Africa, as Siba Grovogui reveals in his analysis of the effect of the pursuit of "international security" on the growing insecurity of the African continent. These same intersections are also uncovered in Susan Craddock's examination of HIV in Africa. While the health crisis has been examined from the diverse insider-outsider perspectives that medical professionals, pharmaceutical agencies, social scientists, and religious and political leaders tend to privilege, Susan Craddock examines the discursive political economies of disease in a hard-hitting exposition of global-local power that shapes health policy and human welfare in Africa. In like manner, Yohannes Ozbaghi's research-based analysis of the frenzied search to rediscover Africa as a fertile reservoir for meeting the energy requirements of the West exposes the emerging political economies and problems associated with the discussions of Africa as the home of the new "Gulf oil states."

These challenges suggest that it is indeed time to turn to the process of retrieval, resistance, and speaking back. Despite the existence of nondemocratic regimes in many African countries, which suggest to some in the West that the African polity is "passive" or "docile," Célestin Monga uncovers evidence of multiple traditions of participatory voice and political engagement that firmly contradict any hint of such passivity. Monga's commentary demonstrates the vibrancy of self-organization and social mobilization required to foster the continent's democratic struggles, and he leads us on a robust examination of the concept and nature of what is termed "civil society" and its place in democratic politics in Africa.

Riding on Monga's navigation of the sociopolitical struggles that inform new frames in African politics, Kiki Edozie expands our deliberations by examining the democratic parameters of politics. Here, she reframes democratic discourses to unearth important issues at the political regime and leadership levels and to present a more varied story of democratization in the continent. Evoking "hybridity" in the evolution of democracy in Africa, Edozie posits the example of the first president of Tanzania, Julius Nyerere, whose discourses and political processes surrounding the "one-party democracy" and its attendant cultural underbelly, the *ujaama* African family," constitute new lenses through which we can see the ritualistic invocations of conventional political discourses embedded in the various intellectual traditions that reify notions of an African backwardness, imitativeness, and authoritarianism.

Together the arguments in this section frame our study of political democratization, conflict, and economic globalization around the recognition of astute and energetic domestic resistance and voice. Readers also gain access to new and emerging African political economies, indigenous and alternative democratic structures, civil societal mobilization, the realities of the global arms trade, as well as to the troubling negotiations between foreign interests and their national and local partners. Such knowledge of the continent assails the commonplace notion in the West that African "politics" refers invariably to political abuse and authoritarian leadership and that traumas of wars emerge almost logically from an indigenous context of placid political ignorance or the pejoratively termed "tribal" identities that presumably sustain ancient animosities and blind fanatic followers.

Part Four, Sociopolitical and Popular Culture and the Social Dynamics of a Contemporizing Continent," introduces timely insights into the influential spheres of the arts and culture in conversations about their transformations and continuities. Pius Adesanmi's masterful piece on literature and the role of the writer in voicing and shaping sociopolitical struggles in African societies erodes the imposed ideas of silence and unidirectional textual control. Moreover, he contextualizes the forms of literary discourses coming from the continent within specific political trajectories, deconstructing literary debates and harnessing trends to specific historical moments of literary resistance, self-retrieval, and identity angst. Jude Akudinobe's fascinating analysis similarly examines the cinematic frames that surround the irrepressible voicing of changing political, social, and popular cultures in Africa as constructed by the continent's filmmakers—from the classical ones to those from the rambunctious Nigerian "Nollywood" and other emerging regional popular cinema industries. Both literary and cinematic frames highlight a continent vibrantly engaging local and global contemporary questions and realities.

The other dimension in our journey around sociocultural issues involves gender discourses, which as Owomoyela notes, constitute one of the primary locations from which African identities have been systematically represented. Therefore, rounding up the conversations on culture, Anene Ejikeme and Kendra Sundal interrogate the construction of African women in the global imaginary. Ejikeme confronts the objective socioeconomic conditions that affect African women, even as she assails the mythic notions of absence and docility with which the West has systematically inscribed African women and simultaneously shored up its concept of self. Her work and that of other African scholars is taken up by young scholar-student Kendra Sundal, who engages the dynamics of women's roles and mobilization as she documents the process of deconstructing her early conceptions of Africa through new experiences and encounters in Ghana. Together, they open a theoretical frame capable of generating new insights and dismantling the divide between African realities and the firmly held imaginaries that stem from historical racial constructions of the African body, identity, and spaces.

Finally in Part Five, "Critical Questions and Challenges in a Globalizing Age," we address selected political, intellectual, and sociopolitical issues that characterize what we refer to as the contemporary "global" era. The highly provocative themes in this section are certain to inspire debates about how to read and respond to African affairs. Nobel Laureate Wole Soyinka addresses millennial challenges for the continent in his scathing denouncement of what he considers the continent's lackluster and ineffective leadership. Makau Mutua, famed human rights scholar, again destabilizes our settled notions of the application of the human rights corpus to African countries. Mutua poses insurrectional challenges to the human rights regime's capacity to be transformed and liberated from its restrictive Western, liberal discursive politics, which confirm the West as savior of the African Other and is alienated from African voices, concerns, and sociocultural and economic experiences.

These two provocative political debates—Soyinka's about intra-African affairs and foreign policies and Mutua's about the narrow conceptualizations of human rights discourses applied to a deeply pluralistic continent—converge in the final essays that resituate the study of Africa. Christopher LaMonica exposes the marginalization of African studies in International Relations theory and addresses the insidious patterns that are created through authoritative academic silencing. In the final essay of the book, we, the editors, conclude our exploration of the continent with a look at the relevance of postcolonial theory to defining and understanding contemporary Africa in an era of globalization. This is perhaps one of the most important accomplishments of *Reframing Contemporary Africa*. That is, we hope to build a vibrant platform for re-envisioning and engaging the African continent through its significance in central debates in the social sciences and continued relevance to the study of the third world, the study of transitional postcolonies, and the West itself.

Acknowledgments

Like many books, this one has emerged out of a voyage sparked by our own experiences as scholars and teachers of African politics and international relations. Classroom encounters with brilliant young scholars eager for illumination on "Africa" in just one semester are a familiar specter to many professors. The baffled faces of students who have just encountered a narrative of Africa different from the one they have previously found in cinema, mass media, or their favorite Internet blogs is a marvel to us. Such experiences motivated us as college professors to keep trying to "get Africa right." This book is the outcome of our desire to bring together in one volume some of the authors who have most powerfully ignited our imaginations about a range of issues and discourses on Africa. These scholars have fueled our passion for travel, research, and scholarship; they have provoked us to explore new arenas of debate and to continue to delve into the histories and transitions of a contemporizing continent and its diverse countries.

As always, we are overwhelmed by our indebtedness to several individuals for the successful publication of this volume. As the foregoing description indicates, this book is truly a collective enterprise by scholars committed to sharing some of their concerns and research on the continent. Our greatest debt is certainly to the contributors to the book who responded graciously to our request to write about the ideas for which they have become so well known in the field. We appreciate their patient responses to endless phone calls and emails over the three-year period during which the project evolved.

We specially honor Professor Oyekan Owomoyela, author of *The African Difference*, who inspired us by his exemplary commitment to completing his contribution to the project in spite of his grave ill health and subsequent death before the book was finally published. We deeply appreciate his support, encouragement, and humility.

CQ Press provided a wealth of editorial guidance that made this publication possible, and we are honored that the press has contracted us as authors of its foray into African studies. To Elise Frasier, our wonderful, patient development editor, we raise several cheers for her editorial insights, ability to understand the ideological and methodological goals and arguments in the book and her close attention to every detail involved in the publication of the book: maps, illustrations, permissions, contracts, and more. We are also grateful for her tireless communications, timely editorial pressure, suggestions, and guidance and for seeing the project through to its successful completion. It is no small measure of her faith in the book that she was referring to a second edition before we were finished with the first.

To Charisse Kino, chief acquisitions editor at CQ Press, our deep gratitude for believing in the potential and need for this book. Charisse has stayed with the project, sharing the task of shaping it and ensuring it lived up to her expectations for a "cutting-edge" book on Africa. Along the way, Kristine Enderle also provided invaluable editorial support and guidance, keeping the pressure on both editors and authors to retain hold of the goals of the book. Indeed, we owe much gratitude to many more of the press's personnel who have contributed to the smooth production of such a comprehensive multifaceted volume.

Kudos to our copyeditor Mary Sebold for her astute grasp of the distinctive authorial and editorial voices represented in this volume, for her capacity to create harmony betwixt the bedlam of individual formatting styles, and dexterity in dealing with what must have seemed like a multitude of ideas and arguments from the book's editors and contributors. We also send a wealth of appreciation to Allyson Rudolph, Steve Pazdan, and Erin Snow for making a complex editing, production, and marketing process appear so seamless and for ensuring the book ends up in the hands of the readers for whom we have written. Finally, we offer a special note of thanks to the cartographers at International Mapping Associates, who translated our various ideas and instructions into the excellent illustrations that vividly capture Africa's historical and contemporary socioeconomic realities.

No body of scholarship as voluminous, comprehensive, diverse, and controversial as this one would succeed without the intellectual rigor of academic peer review. As editors, compiling and cohering the disparate ideological and disciplinary perspectives of twenty erudite scholars of Africa was not a task that we could have achieved alone. In addition to the book's anonymous peer reviewers, we are indebted to professors Olufunke Okome and Tukumbi Lumumba-Kasongo for their roles in shaping this intellectual product and for sharpening our book's collective expression of the continent's complexity in a way that is conducive to a diverse readership.

We also greatly value the many forms of support we received from our colleagues and the endless questions, criticisms, and perspectives from our students at Ithaca College and Michigan State University. In particular, we would like to thank Peyi's students in the Africa through Film course at Ithaca College; they read, critiqued, and responded warmly to the book even in its formative draft stage. Their comments and feedback helped to shape the final product. Special thanks also to Peyi's former student, Sean Connolly, for generous permission to use the photograph of the HIV billboard taken during his stay in Ghana, and to Andrew Woodson and Lyn Bartkowiak, Kiki's student research assistants at MSU, who helped with light research and editorial fact checking for the undergraduate reader.

Finally, our hearts' warmest appreciation go out to our families for their willingness to engage our passions and debates about Africa and for their patience and love as we carved out and stole time from them to complete this book. Our professional lives constantly affect those closest to us, and so we are grateful for their support in providing the opportunities for extra time and space away from their lives to pull off this feat. Special bouquets of gratitude from Peyi to her husband and foremost supporter, Aloja Airewele; to her children, the indomitable trio, Olutale, Oseoba, and Yolore Airewele; and to her parents Olayide and Wole Soyinka for their irrepressible political voices; and from Kiki to her mother, the late Monica Edozie; to her father, Chief John Uzo Edozie; and to her wonderful children, Kelechi, Goz, and Uba Anyadiegwu.

As always, we are indebted to many more people, whom we have not mentioned, for their constructive criticisms and ideas. Lastly, we acknowledge our responsibility as writers for the final contents of this volume.

Part I

DISCOURSES ON THE REPRESENTATION OF AFRICA

The first set of chapters in this book converges in a bid to provide a provocative introduction to Africa's current landscape. We present the study of Africa as a vigorous encounter, not merely with histories and socioeconomic and political constructs, but also with ongoing discourses that redefine and make specific contributions to why and how we study the Other. Our first section sets the tone for the volume through invigorating perspectives on the representation and realities of the continent—its histories and alternative futures—and the current discourse and state of the discipline. In essence, they prime the reader to move beyond a passive reading of facts to a desire to engage Africa in all its complexities.

In the first chapter of the introductory section, "Reframing Contemporary Africa: Beyond the Global Imaginary," Soyinka-Airewele (coeditor of *Socio-Political Scaffolding and the Construction of Change*, 2009) and Edozie (author of *Reconstructing the Third Wave of Democracy: Comparative African Democratic Politics*, 2008) turn a searchlight on the dominant languages and discourses that have impacted the representation of African countries and peoples. Through the exploration of selected illustrations in media, scholarship, and popular cinema, such as Jamie Uys's *The Gods Must Be Crazy*, they provide a landscape for understanding dominant trends in representation through which the reader can develop an empowering frame of analysis for analyzing and critiquing the rendering of African histories, debates, and realities. Soyinka-Airewele and Edozie argue that there is some urgency to the process of self-retrieval amid the struggles for political self-determination, collective well-being, and socioeconomic and political change in the continent. As a way to introduce the volume's point of view, the authors of the first chapter suggest that the challenge is to generate and employ *frames* around Africa that will help to resituate, connect, and explain complex, contemporary realities, as well as the political, social, intellectual, and economic histories of African countries.

Consequently, they call for a layered approach that engages paradox and contradictions in the study of the African continent and that opposes the one-dimensional imaginary of corruption, ignorance, and oppression, which is ritualistically associated with analyses of African countries. Insisting that scholars are involved not merely in analysis that lends itself to the production of new knowledge, but also in acts of inscription, the authors of this chapter invite an engagement in the study of Africa that interrogates not only African realities, but also the motives and positioning of those who seek to study the continent.

Indeed, the furor that accompanied Martin Bernal's[1] multivolume tome, suggestively titled *Black Athena: The Afroasiatic Roots of Classical Civilization*, and that generated Mary Lefkowitz's[2] irate

---

[1] Martin Bernal is professor emeritus of Ancient Eastern Mediterranean Studies at Cornell University, New York.

[2] Mary Lefkowitz is professor emerita of Classical Studies at Wellesley College, Massachusetts.

response certainly suggests that those wishing to study the African continent must continue to engage the motivations, fears, and interests that underscore Africa's representation and give rise to an almost feral resistance to evidences of African impact on the development of the modern world. Bernal, in line with some of the research by leading Senegalese scholar Cheikh Anta Diop, claims that ancient Greek civilization was heavily influenced by the Babylonians, Phoenicians, and Egyptians, as is apparent in the writings of classical historiographers before the racially driven revisionisms of eighteenth- and nineteenth-century Europe. His position was expectedly countered by other classical scholars, whose initial objections were heavily overlaid with a sense of intuitive aversion to the very notion that Greek civilization might be "out of Africa"; hence, Lefkowitz's meteoric emergence from Wellesley College as a public figure, sought after for public appearances, hastily organized symposia, and, ultimately, anthologies written with other vocal opponents—*Not Out of Africa: How "Afrocentrism" Became an Excuse to Teach Myth as History* (1997)[3] and *Black Athena Revisited* (1996), coedited with her Wellesley colleague Guy MacLean Rogers.

In the second chapter of the present volume, "Reconfiguring the Study of Africa," critically acclaimed scholar and public intellectual Professor Mahmood Mamdani sets some parameters for the task of reframing African studies within the academy. Mamdani is the former director of Columbia University's Institute of African Studies, the Herbert Lehman Professor of Government at Columbia, and a former president of CODESRIA, based in Dakar, Senegal. His books, including *Citizen and Subject* (1996) and *When Victims Become Killers: Colonialism, Nativism, and the Genocide in Rwanda* (2002), have become the reference points for critical postcolonial discourses on Africa. In his brief contribution, Mamdani argues that the study of Africa has inherited critical flaws since "historically, African Studies developed outside Africa, not within it. It was a study *of* Africa, but not *by* Africans." The context of this development was colonialism, the Cold War, and apartheid, and Mamdani reminds us that this period shaped the organization of social science studies in the Western academy.

Thus, the continued racialization of the African studies curriculum, of which Mamdani speaks, and the structural and discursive prejudices that inform the naming and framing of the African continent are deeply embedded in the structural practices of the academy regarding the field of African studies. These structural practices include the balkanization of the continent into a "darkest" sub-Saharan Africa, "Arab" North, and "apartheid" South Africa. Further to his blistering critique of such flawed tendencies, Mamdani offers a substantive agenda that addresses the racialized colonial legacies and the dilemmas they create for scholars and students of Africa.

The transitions of naming and framing Africa discussed by Mahmood Mamdani are then taken up by Iheanyi Osondu, who investigates the flawed geographical and physical assumptions of such

---

[3] Enthused reviewers of Lefkowitz's *Not Out of Africa* posed incendiary questions that were quite disconnected from the mass of cautious arguments raised by Bernal in his book, for instance, were Africans the true inventors of democracy, philosophy, and science, rather than the ancient Greeks? In *Black Athena Revisited*, contributors argue that Bernal's claims are exaggerated and unjustified. Professor Bernal has responded to these critics in *Black Athena Writes Back: Martin Bernal Responds to His Critics* (London: Duke University Press, 2001). Bernal bolsters his thesis with new information, citing additional archaeological, linguistic, and anthropological findings that demonstrate historical and contemporary racial politics that have fueled what Bernal describes as academic hypocrisy birthed in the "cult of Europe." Bernal aims a blistering critique at academics who only recently and begrudgingly acknowledged Egypt's contributions to Western civilization and who still deny any connection between ancient Egypt and modern or historic Black Africans.

frames and further excavates the motives underlying the ways of seeing and defining the African continent. Osondu, a professor of geography, provocatively assaults the new balkanization of the African continent by Western scholars, media, development agencies, and the global policy community. In his chapter, "Not 'Out of Africa'? Sifting Facts from Fiction in the New Balkanization of Africa," he critically examines the growing edifice of discourses on "sub-Saharan" Africa and draws attention to the absurdity and illogicality of the increasingly popular practice of excising North Africa from the African landmass and merging it with the region ill-termed the "Middle East."

Osondu takes off from the debate between Martin Bernal and his many critics to tease out the crises of representation of Africa's geographies and the refusal to recognize associated realities of African identities, cultures, and development—historical and contemporary. Engaging the accompanying racist discourses on Africa, Osundu suggests that there is a deficit of integrity and an abundance of self-interest that may stem from resentment of the rich historical evidence pointing to Egypt's contributions to Greek and, consequently, Western civilization. Finally, he provides or redirects us toward appropriate mapping language for exposing African physical and political geographies outside of the racially driven discourses of our time.

In the last contribution to this section, the late professor Oyekan Owomoyela writes on "The Myth and Reality of Africa: A Nudge Toward a Cultural Revolution." Owomoyela's extensive writings include *The African Difference: Discourses on Africanity and the Relativity of Cultures* (1996), *A History of Twentieth-Century African Literatures* (1993), and *Yoruba Proverbs* (2005). His research has been brought to bear on his insightful analysis of the construction of myths of the African identity, and he delivers a biting critique of Western imaging of the African "difference" in issues of masculinity, gender discrimination, and women's oppression.

Professor Owomoyela locates his controversial arguments within a substantive exposition on the context and logic of culture, which defines some of the complexities of gender relations. He takes on both African and non-African commentators for what he condemns as specious handling of the struggles of decolonization. He also explores constructs of difference, not only in discourses on African sexism, but also in echoes of Orientalism that speak in literary depictions of the African past, knowledge, institutions, and ceremonies. Beyond a mere critique of Eurocentric constructions, Owomoyela helps the reader to resituate meaning and logic in societal realities, such as the significance of aspects of funereal ceremonies, especially when derided in the African context while naturalized in Western ones (for instance, Irish). Always provocative, as in the discussion of wife inheriting, Owomoyela, nevertheless, seeks to present a thoughtful reasonableness to custom.

While such a quest for the signifiers of societal traditions are often dismissed as echoes of a defensive cultural chauvinism, Owomoyela's call for a cultural revolution is telling when he says, "we have a duty in our time to challenge the widespread misconstruction of African institutions and ethos in order to ensure that we do not bequeath a besmirched image of Africa to posterity by default. . . . The second conclusion is that the routine and automatic pathologization of Africanity does a disservice not only to Africa, but also to the human community at large, inasmuch as it forecloses the possibility of the enrichment of the common human stock with African input."

Together, the contributors to the introductory section of this book provoke us to adopt new mapping methods for our voyage around the African continent.

Chapter 1

REFRAMING CONTEMPORARY AFRICA
Beyond Global Imaginaries

Peyi Soyinka-Airewele
Rita Kiki Edozie

One of the most rewarding aspects of studying Africa is the encounter with literature and conceptual debates that simultaneously provoke, reveal rich nuances, reflect African intellectual discourses and sociopolitical realities, provide a framework for grappling with vast regional diversities and contradictions, and disturb the complacency of our settled notions of the continent. The fifty-three countries that make up Africa's Northern, Southern, Eastern, Western, and Central regions draw the scholar into a maelstrom of vivid living histories, political debates, and urban and rural cultural and social dynamics that define and yet defy simple explanations of their complex realities. In this chapter, we start with a voyage around the politics of representation of African identities and spaces; next, we engage the organizing devices and concepts of *schematic frames* and *imaginary significations* that underlie popular discussions of the continent; and finally, we review some critical intellectual and theoretical traditions that have been employed in the study of Africa by interrogating the visions of the continent they have bequeathed and the implications of such sights and (mis)understandings for those who wish to study African countries today.

Introduction: Representation of African Identities and Spaces

> *Those who teach and study Africa today must learn to problematize the issue of representation in order to locate and unpack the economic, political, personal, and other motivations that might underlie any particular image of Africa (Grinker and Steiner 1997, xxvi).*

In the aftermath of the terrorist bombings of September 11, 2001, and the terrifying reminder of human vulnerability, the undying Western identity problematic resurfaced through sharpened definitions of racial, national, cultural, and religious identities, and a reinvestment of meaning to the world of the known and the unknown, the "civilized" and the "uncivilized" (Soyinka-Airewele 2002). At the same time, it gave new meaning to the continuing struggles to contest the meanings and impact of imposed political, racial, and socioeconomic dichotomies. Unfortunately, the ensuing avalanche of interest in understanding the global Other cannot be said to have dented the myths and images of atavism and absence with which Africa, a region of abundant historical, socioeconomic, and political vibrancy and accomplishments, has historically been framed. It is not hard to discern some of the roots of that persistent ignorance: notions of European racial, social, technological, economic, and cultural exceptionalism; the substantive legacies of imperial

On Being Black and African

Source: © Khalil Bendib, The Pen is Funnier than the Sword: Cartoons That Speak Truth to Power. www.bendib.com. Reproduced with permission.

Note: This cartoon shows the infamous slaying of Amadou Diallo, an unarmed immigrant from Guinea, by the New York Police Department Street Crime Unit. As he stood in the doorway of his apartment in the Bronx, just after midnight on February 4, 1999, the 22-year-old West African died in a hail of forty-one police bullets fired by four plainclothes police officers who later claimed they thought Diallo's wallet was a gun. The police officers were acquitted of murder, sending into motion widespread protests and a lawsuit. The United States Justice Department decided in January 2001 that federal civil rights charges were unwarranted, but just before the case went to trial, the police department finally reached an out-of-court settlement with the family and lawyers five years after the incident.

conquest; and the continuing dynamics of global power and interests partly shape the ideologies, political economies, and linguistic methods used in imagining and defining the African continent.

Accordingly, Ella Shohat and Robert Stam have thrown the provocative challenge of "unthinking Eurocentrism" at those disquieted by the continuing realities of a global core, which persists in viewing the world from a "flattened landscape" that ignores the diversities and problems within its own sphere, constructs the world's realities in opposition to its own ideals, and flattens the external landscape through homogenization, while highlighting the presumed inadequacies and limitations of that external landscape through sweeping generalizations.[1]

---

[1] Ella Shohat and Robert Stam, *Unthinking Eurocentrism, Multiculturalism and the Media*, is a seminal work, invaluable for its incisive exposure of the nature of Eurocentrism and its proposal of new polycentric ways of seeing the world.

Since marginalized states are indelibly touched by the consequences of the choices, values, and priorities of the media, geopolitical, and academic core, perhaps one of the most important contributions of any collection of writings on the African continent is the deliberate presentation of frameworks for validating and rendering visible the multiple sociocultural, intellectual, political, transnational, and other prosaic realities that are typically delegitimized by that global core (Soyinka-Airewele 2002). In talking about *realities* of the everyday and the prosaic, we refer, for instance, to the effervescent sociocultural presence and role of writers, musicians, and popular cinema; to political economies that include enduring local and transcontinental networks of market women and other entrepreneurs, as well as the hegemonial presence of global capital; and to the political spaces that reflect the power and force of indigenous monarchies, the state, and citizen agency and resistance.

Consequently, our goal in this chapter is to explore preliminary issues in the representation of the African continent within news media, cinema, literature, and scholarship; to understand some of the ideologies and interests that influence such *maps;* and to present alternative, debated frameworks. Above all, we hope to provoke and energize a broader desire to engage the African continent in all of its variegated realities. Such an approach would lend itself, as the various contributors to this volume undertake to do, to the construction of multiple discursive centers that support the unveiling of various strata of sociopolitical, economic, and cultural life in African countries. The racial and ideological notions and invested interests, which have shaped the language on Africa for so long, are troubling reminders that, more than ever, we cannot afford to trade the contemporizing authenticity of a historically global African world for fraudulent constructs of homogenizing notions and popular reductionist liberties that have long lost their ability to shroud the ghouls of ignorance that birthed them.

It is no longer plausible to assume that Africa can be inscribed or studied from a site of unfettered or pure vision that is untroubled by the very act of representation itself. Beer reflects that tension in her reflections on the concept of representation:

> We favour currently the word "representation" because it sustains a needed distance between experience and formulation. It recognises the fictive in our understanding. It allows a gap between how we see things and how, potentially, they might be. It acknowledges the extent to which ideologies harden into objects and so sustain themselves as real presences in the world. The objects may be books, pictures, films, advertisements, fashion. . . . Representations rapidly become representative—those empowered to speak on behalf of their constituency: the authentic voices of a group. That is where the trouble starts when the claim is representing women: Are we offering and receiving formulations of an abiding group; offering accounts of a person, or a group of people, conceived as stable? (Beer 1989, 63–64).

In her writing on "African women" or specifically "Nigerian women" and, even more specifically, as she carefully reminds us of the so-called characterization of "Nigerian market women," Ufomata ruminates on the dilemmas of representation and the quest for authenticity, or the faithful relaying of local realities by both "insider" and "outsider" scholars:

> I am aware of the implications of the methods I adopted in terms of the role of my own voice. I am not a market woman, and I write in English, a language that is not commonly spoken in the market. . . . I believe that my portrayal of market women presents the view of an insider, the most authentic possible through the eyes of another person. After all, as a Yoruba adage says, "the only reason a deaf person is vilified in front of his or her child(ren) is the certainty that the message will be delivered." As much as possible, I tried to represent the views of the women objectively. Like others, I realize that, "Speaking both for and as a woman (rather than 'like' a woman), is the problem of women's writing" (Jacobus 1989, 55; Ufomata 2000).

Indeed, the gulf that exists between the worlds of the scholar and the realities of those about whom they write is not necessarily a function of racial difference, as Soyinka-Airewele also reminds us:

> Some years ago, I had the much awaited opportunity to conduct research situated at a richer interface of "scholar-practitioner" realities, an opportunity that would involve displacement, to an area of protracted conflict, of sharply opposed mythico-histories and deep political polarizations in an African country. Surely, not a particularly difficult undertaking, since I had the advantage of personal and linguistic familiarity with the location. Not for me the "fish out of water," "displanted" and "out of its elements" experience, so chillingly defined in Roget's handy thesaurus. Nevertheless, in the first week of fieldwork, I had the distinctly disturbing experience of being categorized as a *safari intellectual* by a good friend and senior colleague, despite the fact that I had once lived and taught in this same community. Interestingly, the heated debate that ensued, on his part, bespoke a legacy of anger and frustration at the incompetence and superficiality of Western Africanists, irrespective of cultural belongings, who jaunted into town and made their reputations by recoding ill-understood local issues for the oft-arcane world of western academia.[2]

An assessment like this implies that the enterprise of studying African countries has often resembled a refined Hobbesian impulse—short lived, self-centered, impatient with collaboration, and certainly somewhat brutish. This is not acceptable in a continent that disdains the deep-seated tendency in Western media and academia to view and use the region as a laboratory with pliable theory-supporting subjects.[3] It is apparent that we must, therefore, continue to ask questions about who is speaking and what informs and filters their perspectives. Martin and Clifford rightly remind us that ". . . representations of Africa generally tell us far less about those who are being represented than they do about the preoccupations and prejudices of those engaged in the act of representing" (Grinker and Steiner 1997, xxvi).

Representing Africa in Popular Media

In October 2004, the *National Geographic Magazine* issued this retraction titled "Revisiting the Elephant Hunters of Tanzania":

> We let you down: In the July 2004 issue, we published a story about elephant hunting by the Barabaig people in Tanzania. Soon after, a few of you pointed out that there are letters and numbers on the tusk shown on page 78—faint but unmistakable in the printed magazine, yet not visible in the prints we used while preparing the article. We now know that the photographer, Gilles Nicolet, borrowed the tusks from the Tanzanian Department of Wildlife and gave them to the hunters to hold. They are not, as the picture caption says, tusks taken by the Barabaig "from an elephant found dead in the bush." The caption was based on information provided us by Nicolet—information that he insisted was true under tough questioning from us, until after the story was published and we confronted him about the numbers. . . . We later learnt that the two photographs on page 85—which the caption identifies as showing a hunter reclaiming his spear from an elephant and then removing the tusks—were actually taken several years earlier in Cameroon.

---

[2] Peyi Soyinka-Airewele, "Navigating 'Realities,' Illusions and Academic Impulses: Displaced Scholars at Large," *GSC Quarterly* no. 6 (Fall 2002).

[3] ibid.

National Geographic's "apology" for this "unwitting" violation was crafted to painstakingly protect the magazine's claims to its time-honored "accuracy," "honesty," "rigor," and "bond of trust" with its readers. Consequently, it disclaimed any responsibility for photographer Gilles Nicolet's odious falsification. However, a more critical reading of this incident invokes very disquieting questions that should have been taken up by Bill Allen, the magazine's editor. Why, for instance, did Nicolet assume that an image of African hunters holding spears and tusks supposedly taken from a dead elephant and of a hunter's hand embedded in the bloodied flesh of an elephant would be so appealing to the editors of the magazine and its many readers? Why was it so unacceptable to convey the reality that the tusks had been borrowed from Tanzania's department of wildlife? Did Nicolet anticipate that revealing this fact would create a dangerous "de-exoticism" of the African continent by permitting the magazine's readership to glimpse a continent that had institutions of social organization like those of the rest of the world? After all, the existence of a department of wildlife is conclusively indicative of modern political and socioeconomic organization, officialdom, bureaucratic procedure, and legality, as well as the existence of distinct lines between humans, fauna, and flora.

We must be willing to probe into the pressures, intellectual traditions, and myths that would impel a photographer to falsify and insert old images from Cameroon—a country lapping the waters of the Bight of Benin, a bay of the Atlantic Ocean on the vast western coast of the world's second largest continent—into a story on Tanzania, a country on the eastern coastline of the continent, bordering the Indian Ocean. What really is the dominant notion of a homogenous unspecific "Africa," of blackness and primitivism, to which those marketing their writings, scholarship, films, and images are expected to conform? And would the *Geographic* prove willing to move toward a critical self-examination of its own historic preferences and tendencies in the portrayal of the African continent and its peoples? Nicolet's was a deliberate act of deception, but its central logic points us to an all-too-common desire to imagine "Africa" from within particular frames. It was from a weary, yet irate acknowledgment of such tendencies in literature, film, media, and scholarship that award-winning Kenyan writer Binyavanga Wainaina's satirical primer "How to Write About Africa" offered the following infamous tips for budding writers of Africa:

> Never have a picture of a well-adjusted African on the cover of your book, or in it, unless that African has won the Nobel Prize. . . . If you must include an African, make sure you get one in Masai or Zulu or Dogon dress. In your text, treat Africa as if it were one country. It is hot and dusty with rolling grasslands and huge herds of animals and tall, thin people who are starving. Or it is hot and steamy with very short people who eat primates. Don't get bogged down with precise descriptions. . . . Make sure you show how Africans have music and rhythm deep in their souls, and eat things no other humans eat. . . . Taboo subjects: ordinary domestic scenes, love between Africans (unless a death is involved), references to African writers or intellectuals, mention of school-going children who are not suffering from yaws or Ebola fever or female genital mutilation. . . . Avoid having the African characters laugh, or struggle to educate their kids, or just make do in mundane circumstances. . . . African characters should be colourful, exotic, larger than life—but empty inside, with no dialogue, no conflicts or resolutions in their stories, no depth or quirks to confuse the cause (Wainaina 2006).

Blinkered writing on Africa is clearly not necessarily spawned of apparently hostile, conservatively racist voices as Wainaina reminds his readers:

Establish early on that your liberalism is impeccable, and mention near the beginning how much you love Africa, how you fell in love with the place and can't live without her. . . . Blame the West for Africa's situation. But do not be too specific. Broad brushstrokes throughout are good. . . . Describe, in detail, naked breasts (young, old, conservative, recently raped, big, small) or mutilated genitals, or enhanced genitals. . . . Remember, any work you submit in which people look filthy and miserable will be referred to as the "real Africa," and you want that on your dust jacket. Do not feel queasy about this: you are trying to help them to get aid from the West (ibid.).

Finally, in a sharp reminder of the language of bestiality with which Africans are likened to or contrasted with the denizens of the animal kingdom, Wainainna proposes that

animals, on the other hand, must be treated as well rounded, complex characters. They speak (or grunt while tossing their manes proudly) and have names, ambitions and desires. They also have family values: *see how lions teach their children?* Elephants are caring, and are good feminists or dignified patriarchs. So are gorillas. Never, ever say anything negative about an elephant or a gorilla. Elephants may attack people's property, destroy their crops, and even kill them. Always take the side of the elephant. Big cats have public-school accents. Hyenas are fair game and have vaguely Middle Eastern accents. Any short Africans who live in the jungle or desert may be portrayed with good humour (unless they are in conflict with an elephant or chimpanzee or gorilla, in which case they are pure evil) (ibid.).

Despite its own obvious broad brushstrokes, Wainaina's piece cannot be dismissed simply as a caustic exaggeration. Evidence points to continuing efforts to create and maintain a discourse around the African continent that fixes it in global opposition to all that is civilized, advanced, and thinking. Such forms of framing do not always emerge from a benign "ignorance" of facts, but sometimes from more deliberate distortions. In "Telling Africa's Past in Literature: Whose Story Is It Anyway?" Oyekan Owomoyela (2002, 221) insists that the mass of fabrications and misrepresentations of Africa's past are at a critical historical juncture, especially after the European colonizing enterprise during which "Europeans felt it best to write their own histories of the continent." His scathing assault on the Othering of Africa calls to mind the writings of John and Jean Comaroff who argue that European discourses on Africa make it clear that the continent has been established as the dark stage of savagery, cannibalism, and backwardness into which "white men" write themselves. The representation of African identities thus emerged out of a relationship of "opposition and inequality" in which, by historical imperative, Europe stood to Africa as "civilization to nature," "savior to victim," "actor to subject" (Comaroff 1997, 691). Hence, the tendency we see in Gilles Nicolet's photographic mirage of Barabaig elephant hunters is predated by an epoch of less subtle calls to inscribe Africa as the zone of "dark backwardness," irrespective of all social, political, and economic evidence to the contrary.

With some apprehension perhaps that our imaginations might falter in transforming African reality into the desirable realm of the primeval, many have elected to play a more determined role in the construction of a time-bound, primal Africa. Jamie Uys's cult film *The Gods Must Be Crazy* was received by thousands in Japan, France, Venezuela, Sweden, England, the United States, and several other countries as a genial, "unsophisticated, slapstick culture-clash comedy," and it continues to be presented in many institutions as a "sophisticated" commentary on cultural relativism and a self-critique of Western modernism. (Three more Hong Kong feature films followed a sequel.) Keyan Tomaselli's description of the film captures its main elements. "Social harmony in a remote Bushman (San) clan supposedly based in the Kalahari desert is disrupted by a Coke bottle which falls out of the sky, discarded by a passing pilot. For Xi's clan, the Coke bottle is firstly, 'one of the strangest and most beautiful things they have seen.' Second, it becomes 'a real labor saving device'; third, they learn that it can make music. Finally it is recognized as 'the evil thing' which has brought dissension and competition between individuals within the clan" (Tomaselli 1998).

The film goes on to show how the clan makes a decision to remove the source of the conflict by returning the bottle to the gods. In his journey to achieve this goal, Xi encounters a zoologist, his "colored" helper, and a white woman who wants to teach far away from the city rat race. Interlaced through this narrative are buffoonish black guerrillas intent on overthrowing the banana republic government (see Tomaselli 1998).

It is important to underscore the vast popularity of this film, an appeal well captured in the London *Guardian*'s obituary for Uys in 1994:[4]

> Jamie Uys, who has died of a heart attack aged 74, was the first South African film director to gain international recognition with the serendipitous box-office success of *The Gods Must Be Crazy* (1981). During the darkest-before-the-dawn days of apartheid, this unsophisticated, slapstick culture-clash comedy drew audiences everywhere. It became the highest-grossing foreign movie ever in France where it showed for months, outdoing *An Officer and A Gentleman* and *Tootsie,* ran a year in Portugal, and broke all records in Malaysia. The Queen Mother is supposed to have seen it three times. Explanations for the universal appeal of this story of a Bushman's contact with "civilization" would be its artlessness, its reliance on visual comedy, its animals, its underlying ecological message and, above all, the natural playing of the Bushman himself. "I spent three to four months looking at and taking pictures of Bushmen in Namibia, Botswana and the northern Cape," explained Uys. "I wanted to see every Bushman in the whole world before I chose my man. I came back with 40 to 50 photographs. He just stood out." He was Nixau (pronounced with that unique Xhosa clicking sound), a hunter along the Namibia-Botswana border. "I knew from the start that to make a contract with him would not be easy. Money means nothing to him," Uys commented. "Most of the money he earned is still in a trust fund. To Nixau, making the film, like everything else the whites did, was a game."

Here again, we are presented with an image of an artless and simple people, apparently portrayed as they exist in reality. To the contrary, well-documented research and the direct, filmed testimony of Uys's star actor N!xau,[5] provide depressing evidence of purposeful deception by Uys in seeking to perpetuate the notion of an African people immured in timeless tradition. Gugler's critical analysis of the film has a telling subtitle, "The World According to Apartheid" (2003, 71), and he reveals that filmmaker Uys lied repeatedly in interviews. He claimed to have traversed the Kalahari landscape looking for the perfect "native" to play !Xi and finally found N!xau, who had only ever seen one white man in his entire life and whose language had no concept of work or money (Gugler 2003, 73). In fact, Marshall's documentary released earlier shows the filming of *The Gods Must Be Crazy* in the Tshumkwi camp

---

[4] Bergan Ronald, "One Man's Reality Before the Dawn in South Africa. Obituary: Jamie Uys," *The Guardian*, February 2, 1996.

[5] *N!lai: The Story of a !Kung Woman.* Documentary directed by John Marshall. Distributed in the U.S. by Documentary Educational Resources. Length. 59 minutes, 1979. Note that commentators spell N!xau as "Nixau," "N!kau," or "Nikau."

established by the apartheid South African authorities, where much of the !Kung had been living in debilitating conditions. N!ai who plays !Xi's wife had actually lost her adult son in this camp. Uys's "Bushman" hunter star, N!kau Kganna, was never the hunter claimed by Uys in public interviews but had grown up as a herd boy on a farm in Botswana and had then worked as a cook in the Tshumkwi school where he was "discovered by Uys" (Gugler 2003, 74).

Uys's high-profile cinematic swindle reduces *National Geographic's* Gilles Nicolet to an amateur. While Uys repeatedly informed the world that N!kau had no use for or understanding of money, researchers have made it clear that, in fact, while N!kau was all too familiar with the uses of money, "he was paid a mere pittance, 2000 Rand, then about $1,700, for *The Gods Must be Crazy,* which made a fortune; the film cost $5 million and earned $90 million in its first four years. Even after these record earnings, and after N!kau had become a national hero in Japan, he had to settle for 5,000 Rand and a monthly retainer of 200 Rand for the lead role in the sequel *The Gods Must be Crazy II* (Gugler, 2003, 74). *In Darkest Hollywood* (1993) closed its segment on *The Gods* with an interview with N!kau, who insists that Uys actually had him dress in a loincloth and then imitate the customs of a Bushman. "I did not think it was right to do something that was not true," he said. "The right thing is to show things as they are."

Consequently, we can hardly settle for Vincent Canby's airy dismissal of his own struggles with the film's patronizing nuances and disturbing political silences:

> *The Gods Must Be Crazy* is an innocuous enough tale about the comic conjunction of two wildly different cultures as represented by one Kalahari bushman, whose tribe hasn't yet reached the Stone Age, and by bumbling, neurotic whites and blacks who, in one way and another, cannot cope with contemporary civilization. I think it's safe to guess that Mr. Uys is certainly neither a racist nor an apologist. Nobody with the sense of humor that he displays in *The Gods Must Be Crazy* could be. Nobody who would take the time to choreograph the kind of elaborate sight gags that are the reason to see this film could support the sort of self-interest officially sanctioned by the South African government. Such narrowness of vision is antithetical to the creation of laughter (Canby 1984).

This disingenuous claim is quite unsupportable given that racism and "self-interest" are most compatible with the pervasive commentaries on the African Other that often pass for comedy. Hollywood is littered with numerous comedies that maintain ideological, racial, or economic interests in framing African societies along such familiar pathways. In fact, slapstick and broad humor, as Gugler maintains, "are so persuasive that many Western viewers fail to perceive the underlying ideology," and in *The Gods Must Be Crazy,* "we are initiated into the world view of apartheid" (2003, 71). Indeed, the African types that Uys propagates are best understood in the context of the apartheid government's effort to vigorously market to the world in the late 1980s its violent policies for the "idyllic" separation of races through forcible movement of the Black majority to marginal lands marked as Bantustans (black homelands).[6] In the context of the film, this violent displacement of a resistant Black population is reconstituted as the racist regime's benevolence in permitting "tribal" and peaceful Africans to return "unwanted goods of civilization" (the symbolic Coke bottle) to the Whites and peacefully return to their harmonious wilds or desert, as the case might be. This, of course, is how filmmaker Uys distorts and

---

[6] Bantustans are so-called Black (derogatorily "Bantu") homelands, forcibly created by the apartheid regime to serve as pseudo-independent Black colonies and reservoirs for labor and to maintain the myth of independence for the displaced Black majority citizens of South Africa.

subverts the African voice—both through the character !Xi, who refuses to accept any monetary reward for his heroic acts, and the actor N!kau, who presumably also had no use for money. Again, these misrepresentations of reality fed into the ongoing global and national concerns and conversations about social justice and restitution for the ravages of apartheid.

Despite his film's much-vaunted nonpolitical nature, Uys has created a powerful commentary on the independence struggles in South Africa and neighboring countries through insidious typologies of an "African" nature and reality. Beyond the "traditional" African of the "Bush," Gugler shrewdly observes that there are three other unmistakable types: the "good" Africans, who sing and welcome the coming of the Whites; the "incompetent" Africans, who run their own countries and bring them to ruin; and the "bad" Africans, symbolized by the guerillas led by an outsider, who in name and looks uncannily resembles Sam Nujoma, leader of the liberation movement SWAPO, and Fidel Castro (Gugler 2003, 74–5). Thus, Uys adopts and conveys the apartheid South African government's discourse on its independent neighbors (especially Zimbabwe), on Marxists, and on internal dissidents and, in so doing, erodes their voices with devastating humor.

Uys does not quite trust in his viewers' acceptance of the exotic, "unknowable" Otherness of the African and decides to help that latent imaginary along by overlaying the !Kung language with extra clicks to enhance the sense of its incomprehensible distance from "normal" languages.[7] While many Western reviewers continue to insist on consuming the film as a harmless, apolitical treatise on culture, and as a film that is positively supportive of the rights of Africans to hold on to their innocent primeval existence, the South African government exhibited no such reservation about the service Uys rendered to the cause of apartheid. Although he had produced films for three decades, it was after the success of this film that he received the highest South African civil decoration in 1983. The citation read in part, "And most especially for having given the example . . . of faith in the future of our country and our people"[8] (Tomaselli 1986, 26; Gugler 2003, 76). The ire of African commentators is understandable:

When it comes to Africa, one can afford to indulge in approximations, generalizations, even illiteracy. Africa's overall image is so negative that only the most pessimistic types of discourse conform to the logic that governs understanding of the continent. Publications as "prestigious" as the *Financial Times, Der Speigel,* or *Time,* can publish cover stories and surveys built upon falsehoods and factual errors without stirring up a storm of protest, no doubt because "experts" on Africa know that rebuttals will not damage their professional reputations. . . . Having been brutally involved in sociopolitical turmoil in my country, Cameroon, and having worked and traveled extensively in various other African countries, where I became connected to different social networks, I felt frustrated by most of the literature on the determinants of a successful process of democratization, the exact role of civil society in the current changes, and the political behavior of African people. The more I read, the more frustrated I became, because I could

---

[7] Toby Alice Volkman's 1988 "Out of South Africa: The Gods Must Be Crazy" notes that while the !Kung language has clicks, these sounds were added to increase the exoticism of the language. Cited in Josef Gugler's *African Film: Re-Imagining a Continent*, 73, Volkman's paper is one of thirteen essays that examines the moral rights of the subjects of documentary film, photography, and television. Such image makers—photographers and filmmakers—have come under increasing criticism for portraying subjects in a "false light," appropriating their images, and failing to secure "informed consent." They peculiarly question the moral obligations of minorities who image themselves and the producers of autobiographical documentaries. See Larry Gross et al., *Image Ethics: The Moral Rights of Subjects in Photographs, Film, and Television* (New York/Oxford: Communication and Society, Oxford University Press, 1991).

[8] Gugler translated this commentary by Tomaselli from the French. See Keyan Tomaselli, 1986. "Le rôle de la Jamie Uys films dans la culture Afrikaner," *CinémAction* 39 (1986): 24–33.

perceive in the political historiography of Africa the same contempt and disconnection I described, neither the academics nor the journalists were able (or willing) to capture what was the very essence of the social phenomena and the political movements that I had witnessed for years: the determination of people at the grassroots level to engage in the political arena, at any cost, in order to bring about some positive changes in the way they had been ruled for several centuries (Monga 1996, 38–39 and viii–ix).

Myers and colleagues have produced some of the most instructive research to illuminate this crisis of representation.[9] U.S. news media "elected," they argue, to cast their coverage of the civil war in Rwanda and Bosnia in two different frameworks, despite the following striking similarities between the wars: Both conflicts emerged in relatively small, rural, agriculturally oriented, and densely populated states; were marked by appalling atrocities; produced comparable estimates of war-related deaths; and were obstinate in their duration, despite some external intervention. The theaters, political histories, and the progressions of the conflicts also indicate remarkable commonality, with similar legacies of Western imperialism's cultivating and exploiting internal strife, roles of ethnic identities in fomenting the struggles, and terrains and strategies of warfare (Myers et al. 1996). Yet against this background, there was a startling discrepancy in the international press coverage of these wars.

The application of computer-assisted discourse analysis to reporting on Rwanda and Bosnia during a four-year period revealed extreme discrepancies in the amount of coverage (a total of 560 reports referring to Rwanda and 14,114 referring to Bosnia) and in the language of civil war, ethnicity, and tribalism. Although there was near-total absence of "tribal" terminology in the Bosnian stories, it comprised the explanatory core of the Rwandan articles. Myers and colleagues found that only 1 percent of the occurrences of the word "tribal" in the Bosnia articles referred to Bosnian tribalism; the other instances referred to tribes in Rwanda and other parts of Africa. "Typical of such references might be a sentence beginning with phrases such as 'ethnic warfare in Bosnia or for that matter tribal war in Rwanda. . . .'" The characterization of the Rwandan conflict as tribal warfare opened the floodgates for other macabre journalistic depictions. As these writers deplored, "Rwanda's war was simply centuries-old tribal savagery" or an orgy of blood and terror "unbounded by any rationality other than some sort of ritualistic, primitive logic." Ten articles in a two-week period in 1994 described events in Rwanda as an "orgy" of violence and revenge (Myers et al. 1996, 33). Yet in the Bosnian case, despite extensive documentation of repeated gang rape and mutilation of Muslim women, only one of the more than 14,000 articles during the four years of Myers's study used the term "orgy." The selective cultural association is revealing: an "orgy" is defined in *Webster's* "as a secret ceremonial rite . . . usually characterized by ecstatic singing and dancing, drunken revelry or an excessive indulgence in an activity" (Myers et al. 1996, 33). In contrast to such representational prisms, Edozie has attempted to reconstruct the Rwandan genocide in its proper political and regional contexts through a close examination and re-presentation of the dilemmas around national ethnicities, democracy, and conflict in tandem with a consideration of neighboring Burundi (see Edozie 2008).

Unfortunately, media feed rarely reflects such nuanced analysis. A *Newsweek* article on the first Liberian civil war (which ended in 1996) titled "Africa: The Curse of Tribal War" insisted that "an ancient plague, whose outbreaks are often bloody episodes like the one in Liberia, continues to afflict the people of sub-Saharan Africa." The writers of the article referred to the "wild profusion" of languages, religions, and ethnic groups in Africa and claimed "such unparalleled cultural diversity brings with it a

---

[9] This is discussed at length in Soyinka-Airewele, *Invoking the Past, Conjuring the Nation*, forthcoming 2009.

constant risk of conflict and bloodshed."[10] (See Campbell 1997, 57.) The reader is expected to uncritically accept the association of Africa with the language of the primitive ("tribal war"); time-bound societies ("ancient"); disease ("plague"); savagery ("bloody episodes"); the irrational, unknowable, and supernatural ("curse"); and nature ("wild profusion"). The prewar landscape in Liberia reveals a very different reality—a modern society beset by a sharply divided and oppressive sociopolitical system created with the assistance of the American Colonization Society through which the United States repatriated and resettled willing, freed slaves in the African continent where they could not incite the slaves of the "New World." Far from being an ancient African "plague," the violent implosion in Liberia was inevitable, given the structure of hierarchies legislated in favor of the resettled Americo-Liberians and an increasingly resentful indigenous African population.

The world of scholarly writing on Africa is not immune to fictive lenses and philosophies. Yet we are unlikely to effectively address the crises of scholarship on Africa until we acknowledge the need for added depth and breadth in explorations of the continent. For a typical American student, the first college-level Introduction to American Politics course is contextualized by possibly thirteen years of multiple layers of formal and informal study, access to media, and a robust awareness of popular culture, political issues, and diversities in social, cultural, and economic realities. By contrast, few Western-based scholars have a context from which generalizations, misrepresentations, and scholarly errors on Africa can be challenged. Thus, the illusion is maintained that before colonialism was a void and after colonialism, the immolation of a self-destructing continent, as Schwab (2001) fancifully describes the region today.

The tendency to succumb to a tidy way of classifying Africa is quite pervasive, as evidenced in one study of Africa, which featured a continental map with countries labeled apparently to characterize the country's dominant realities. Thus, South Africa is "apartheid," and Nigeria is "corruption"; other African nations are reduced to single-word depictions that borrow heavily from Western social science discourse on Africa: "bureaucracy," "dependency," "civil society," "personal rule," "socialism," "state collapse," "Islam," "class," "legitimacy," "race," "ethnicity," "irredentism" (that, in the Horn of Africa), "predatory rule," and so on.[11] Such labels are generally considered objectionable when defining the complex "essence" or "identity" of the nations of the global core—for instance, the United States, France, Japan, and Canada—and should be even more unacceptable when describing countries in Africa with their deeply variegated and transitioning political systems, urban-rural divides, and sociocultural and geographical diversities. There is also an urgent need to reconstruct African politics so that we can examine the appropriate impact and varied responses to the democratization that has occurred in Africa since the 1990s. It is no longer adequate to merely fashion politics in Africa in a simple authoritarian regime versus liberal democratic dualism. The complexity of democracy is in its variegated consequences and presentation of challenges to Africa's new polities (Edozie 2008b).

Beyond the characterization of politics in Africa, the reification of oppositional images of Western *self* and African *Other* (through language that inscribes difference in similar social constructs—between, for

---

[10] Cited in Campbell (1997). The use of the word "plague" clearly represents the construction of ethnicity in Africa and the politics and issues that might be connected to "ethnic" identities as a pathological condition, a disease. As Ngũgĩ wa Thiong'o stressed, there must be a search for a liberating perspective from which the mental universe imposed on Africa can be revised. Only in such a reconstruction can the continent coldly and consciously view its relationship to itself and the rest of the world and seek self-definition. (See Ngũgĩ wa Thiong'o in *Moving the Center: The Struggle for Cultural Freedoms*, Oxford: James Currey, 1993).

[11] See cover map in Alex Thomson, *Introduction to African Politics* (New York, Routledge, 2004).

instance, Halloween, psychics, and tarot-card readers versus African tribal superstitions and beliefs; designer cosmetics versus native face paint; bikini-clad women versus half-naked African maidens; and Hollywood's in-vogue "labio-vaginal sculpting" versus "African female genital mutilation"—help maintain a sense of logic regarding structures of global hierarchy and unspoken convictions of racial difference and cultural superiority. Tragically, they evolve into structures of seeing that silence the historical legacies of Africa's leading contributions to technology, architecture, medicine, algebra, the arts, socio-political and commercial organization, and global networking, which informed the development of societies in Europe and elsewhere, as Cheikh Anta Diop (1974),[12] Martin Bernal (1987), and other leading historians have made clear. In tandem with such silencing, there is a similar reluctance to acknowledge that the historical and contemporary experiences of Euro-America provide evidence of problems similar to those confronted by Africa today, albeit to different degrees in the continuing challenges of poverty and socioeconomic marginalization, political corruption, police brutality, identity tensions and violence, and contradictions in struggles for women's equality and political participation, among other things.

Schematic Frames and Imaginary Significations

Inevitably, studying Africa, perhaps more than any other global region, requires we make decisions about the appropriate frames to employ to gain the ideal ideological sites from which to view the continent and the methodologies to use in our pursuit. In defining the parameters that guide our goal of *reframing and re-presenting,* we begin the conceptual voyage with Obioma Nnaemeka's striking reminder of an Igbo philosophy, in her musing on the multiplicity of the perspectives represented in discourses around Black and African feminisms. "As my ancestors philosophized: *adiro akwu ofu ebe enene nmanw* (one does not stand in one spot to watch a masquerade). As with the dancing masquerade, vantage points shift and one must shift with them for the maximization of benefits" (1998, 3).

We offer here a few thoughts provoked by this eloquent reflection on the way the sites from which we view ultimately define the sights we receive. Nnaemeka's reminder of the shifts in our vantage points alludes to the notion of *frames* that we use in this book as textual structures that shape how we see, what we see, and how we process our visions. Like a photographer who adjusts his shutter to gain particular shots within his frames, one's location and repositioning may be imperative for acquiring shots that capture the shifting movements of the subject. The camera's frames define, illuminate, maximize, and transform each shot and their contribution to the emerging image. "For those unfamiliar with the concept of masquerades, it is important to note that in many parts of Africa, masquerade performers do not merely entertain their audiences, they play a vital role in the social, spiritual, and cultural life of their societies. Often disguised flamboyantly to represent ancestors, animals, or ordinary human beings, their musical and dramatic rendering of narratives of societal histories, popular legends, and stories conveys and affirms social values, religious beliefs, or a political ethos and utilizes dance as a commentary on life, wisdom, and special knowledge." (Soyinka-Airewele, 2009).

---

[12] Cheikh Anta Diop, *The African Origins of Civilization: Myth or Reality*, edited and translated by Mercer Cook (New York: Lawrence Hill, 1974).

Consequently, our concept of *reframing* Africa as used in this book extends Nnaemeka's interpretation of the dance of the masquerade in various ways.[13] "In the first place, the masquerade is typically not confined to a stage in a theater but, instead, utilizes the living geographical and communal spaces, streets, city squares, and palace compounds the dancers choose. They define their message, how and where it is uttered, with audiences that move and shift in response to the dance of the masquerade. The student of Africa must hold first a sharpened awareness of a continent that is vastly different from the popular media notion of a confined dark and immobile entity, a historical fossil to be dissected within museum glass cases, entombed for cultural voyeurs and anthropological forays. We are confronted with a dynamic swirl of constantly contemporizing societies and their transforming social, political, and economic populations, landscapes, and realities. Like the audience of masquerades, the reader cannot define the voice—where or how it is spoken. This is of particular importance to the Western observers who often bemoan, to the ire of their hosts, their unsuccessful search for the real Africa, as against the Africa that strangely appears much like other places in the world with roads, bridges, televisions, traffic problems, congested cities and bustling towns, businesses and traders, politics, cinemas, and music" (Soyinka-Airewele, 2008).

Second and most significant is that "within the context of many African societies, masqueraders are not the carnival-type entertainers with which many Westerners might be familiar. Rather, they serve as interlocutors and repositories of memory, influence, knowledge—engaging, critiquing, and provoking values and concepts in a constantly modernizing milieu."[14] The continuing tendency to imagine Africa as a source of entertainment, through the foibles of Hollywood's Tarzan-like or naïve natives in whose lives the noble and enlightened outsider is invested either as development agent, democracy tutor, or civilizing force, is a fallacy that has long outlived any capacity for toleration. Haile Gerima, director of *Sankofa,* an unforgettable cinematic treatise on memory, enslavement, and the bonds between the African continent and its diaspora, spoke for many when he declaimed that "African culture in film should not be made to satisfy only the exotic curiosity of the developed countries. We are not exotic fixtures. Our cultures have values. Our intellectual property has value. . . . If I make a movie it is because I also want to empower my voice" (Uhadike 2002, 260–266).

The third aspect of our use of Nnaemeka's philosophical masquerade concerns its symbolism within a spatial dimension, through a cloaked entity of which the outer layers often appear to convey, obstruct, or limit apprehension of the inner performer. As Soyinka-Airewele argues, "the disguising of the inner performer accentuates the message conveyed, perhaps with parallels in the symbolisms of certain masking and religious traditions in the West. The masquerader does not dance to celebrate Otherness, but often to engage through spheres that might be as distinct as spirit is to earth. The spiritual is humanized as much as the human is spiritualized, revealing the impossibility of simplistic distinctions between the society as a material calculus and the inner ethos of values, beliefs, and systems in which the society itself is anchored from life to the Beyond. Thus, the cloaking of the performer is not merely designed to cajole the audiences into a sense of difference between one human and another (either the human audience and the human performer or the Western and African audience), but also to demonstrate how one society—its political leadership and citizens—are most comprehensible through reference to their access to those from whom

[13] Soyinka-Airewele, "Insurgent Transnational Conversations," 2008.
[14] ibid.

they would otherwise be alienated, who through the disguised performer, belong, engage, and are engaged."[15] This reading of masquerades is very much at variance with the one in Western scholarship and media in which masquerades are a stock symbol of the African difference, of an Otherness that presumably separates the continent with cultural performers alienated and inaccessible, watched by a bemused audience that cannot hear their voices because they lack the capacity to speak intelligibly. Mbembe in the seminal *On the Postcolony* put some meaning to the determined framing of an African *Other*:

> It is in relation to Africa that the notion of "absolute otherness" has been taken farthest. It is now widely acknowledged that Africa as an idea, a concept, has historically served, and continues to serve, as a polemical argument for the West's desperate desire to assert its difference from the rest of the world. In several respects, Africa still constitutes one of the metaphors through which the West represents the origin of its own norms, develops a self image, and integrates this image into the set of signifiers asserting what it supposes to be its identity . . . whether in everyday discourse or in ostensibly scholarly narratives, the continent is the very figure of "the strange. . . . In this extremity of the Earth, reason is supposedly permanently at bay, and the unknown has supposedly attained its highest point. Africa, a headless figure. . . . quite innocent of any notion of center, hierarchy, or stability is portrayed as a vast dark cave where—the rift of a tragic and unhappy human history stand revealed: . . . in short, a bottomless abyss where everything is noise, yawning gap and primordial chaos" (Mbembe 2001, 2–3).

The construction of such a fantasy, of course, shocks with the profoundness of its extreme alienation from the realities with which most Africans know their own "normal" communities and societies. Mbembe argues that since, in principle, everything Africa says is translatable into human language, this alleged inaccessibility regarding Africa "must flow not from the difficulty of the undertaking, not from what therein is to be seen and heard, not from what is dissimulated. It flows from there being hardly any discourse about Africa for itself. In the very principle of its constitution, in its language and in its finalities, narrative about Africa is always pretext for a comment about something else, some other place, some other people. . . . Thus, there is no need to look for the status of this discourse; essentially, it has to do at best with self-deception and at worst, with perversion" (2001, 3).

This book adds to the varied responses to Mbembe's acerbic question, just what is going on? by grappling analytically with a range of issues—from discourses on representation and naming, to the contemporary political economies, sociopolitical cultures of literature and cinema, and gender dynamics and contradictions. The frames revealed by the masquerade and by this book ultimately criticize the sites of thought about which Mbembe has also argued that "whether dealing with Africa or with other non-European worlds, this tradition long denied the existence of any 'self' but its own. Each time it came to peoples different in race, language and culture, the idea that we have, concretely and typically, the same flesh . . . became problematic" (2001, 2). That is, the "theoretical and practical recognition of the body and flesh of 'the stranger' as flesh and body just like mine, the *idea of a common human nature, a humanity shared with others,* long posed, and still poses, a problem for Western consciousness" (2001, 2).

Such a seemingly harsh diagnosis is at the heart of our objective—reframing contemporary Africa. This ambitious task does not suggest that we have conjured and are presenting entirely new evidence, information, and paradigms. But each topical contribution provides illuminating evidences, contexts, and understandings

---

[15] ibid.

that have the capacity to challenge and transform dominant schematic frames, or what have been called *imaginary significations*, that is, invented notions that paradoxically become essential to sustaining the world the West imagines for itself and the roles and practices it adopts towards others (Mbembe 2001, 2). More specifically, our use of the concept of "frame" borrows deliberately from the field of media studies, a field that increasingly seeks to study the overwhelming role of the media in constructing the Other and in normalizing such imaginary significations. Entman and Rojecki's critique of the racial dimension in American media concludes that the Black image in the White mind is acquired primarily through media images and not personal encounters and that these images support and shore a sense of difference, conflict, and hierarchy (Entman and Rojecki 2000). Starting with a discussion of the mental processes by which imaginaries are created, they posit that we "more often approach life with assumptions that lead us to confirm expectations rather than to inscribe fresh interpretations of daily experience upon a blank mental slate. This tendency toward mental inertia is the joint product of cognitive economy and of cultural influence" (2000, 48). Mental shortcuts such as *schemas* and *frames* constitute the framework for sustaining cognitive economy. A schema, argue Entman and Rojecki, is "a set of related concepts that allow people to make inferences about new information based on already organized prior knowledge" (2000, 48). This permits the association of, at a local level, "welfare" with "lazy," "Black person," "single mother," etc., and, at a global level, "Africa" with "tribes," irrespective of the pervasive evidence of African global trade networks, growing industry, and extremely large, bustling cities where socioeconomic activities far exceed those of many small-scale Western cities.

Frames are quite similar to schemas, except that they are often deemed to "reside within media texts and public discourse. Frames highlight and link data selectively to tell more or less coherent stories that define problems, diagnose causes, make moral judgments, and suggest remedies. When we say a news report "framed" a drive-by shooting as a gang war story, we mean it selected certain aspects of the event that summoned an audience's stored schematic understanding about gang members. The story may have included visuals illustrating turf consciousness, exaggerated attachment to symbolic clothing, hand signaling, weapons, and aimless loitering. By highlighting this gang "frame," the report obscures other possible mental associations such as, perhaps, the shooter's absent father, unemployment or low wages, and clinical depression. The gang frame makes these more sympathetic connections less available to the audience (Entman and Rojecki 2000, 49).

In the *Anthropology of Anger*, Célestin Monga's analysis of the failures of some of the dominant instruments of Western political science analysis concludes that "in recent years, the continent has become the El Dorado of wild thought, the best place for daring intellectual safaris, the unregulated space in which to engage in theoretical incest, to violate the fundamentals of logic, to transgress disciplinary prohibitions; in short, to give oneself over to all forms of intellectual debauchery—with impunity and in good conscience" (1996, 39). Schematic frames are evident in responses to some of the forms of intellectual debauchery that Monga deplores. Peter Schwab's book dramatically titled *Africa: A Continent Self-Destructs* (2001) features a bloody skull on its front cover and attracted heated responses from reviewers on a book Web site.[16] One reader enthusiastically endorsed the book for "telling it like it is" and explained that "like many Americans, I scan the news of the third world more than I read it. So I opened this book in part to see if the sweeping generalizations about sub-Saharan Africa

---

[16] Amazon.com book reviews, www.amazon.com.

I'd come to believe, more through osmosis than analysis, were true or needed revision. The conclusion, unfortunately, is that it's even worse than I thought. Corruption, disease, political instability, economic chaos, genocide are all part-and-parcel of Africa four decades after independence (give or take a few years, country to country)."[17] This reader's candid self-assessment of his osmotic method for thinking about Africa is an apt illustration of Entman and Rojecki's arguments about how the "Black African" image emerges in the Western imaginary.

It is true that many African countries are undergoing grave economic and political crises, with attendant severe social privations, but when such ongoing problems are selectively harnessed to anecdotal evidence and excerpts from works of fiction by African novelists, they add up to a devastating schema of the continent, which lacks context and historicity. Students of Africa must question frames that diminish the reality of the vast disparities found across the continent, generalize the African condition, and depend on imaginary signifiers. For instance, some other readers were able to deploy a range of critical thinking traditions to understand the limitations of Schwab's conclusion about Africa. One such reader offered this commentary:

> Schwab is a master of sweeping statements like . . . this one: "In Africa, clean water is an oxymoronic concept" (p. 75). Reading *Africa: A Continent Self-Destructs,* one rapidly gets the impression that all Africans lead lives of constant suffering, forever at the mercy of armed thugs, deadly pestilence and malnutrition. This, of course, is absolute bunk. . . . Schwab's argument is a little like saying "The horrors of Kosovo are a striking illustration of how Europe is falling apart." It's a stretch, to say the least. Unfortunately, Schwab is hardly unique among Africa specialists in making such broad and empty generalizations. *Africa: A Continent Self-Destructs* concludes that Africa has broken down, perhaps beyond repair. Schwab finds nothing salutary in African culture, viewing it only as an obstacle to progress: "unless the negative vitality of tradition and tribalism is vitiated, the future of globalization in sub-Saharan Africa remains bleak indeed" (p. 139). The final chapter title is "Will Africa Survive?"—as if continents, or societies, could die.[18]

As the reviewer argues above, it is not that such problems as water scarcity or political persecution that Schwab describes are imaginary; it is that they are his choices for defining the continent and that he tends to ignore the other critical realities that explain how a majority of Africans go about their daily business outside the limelight of war or other media-worthy events. Unfortunately, the everyday, prosaic, and mundane business of "normal" life is rejected in favor of the construction of a powerful imagery that becomes the map through which students of Africa attempt to read and navigate its sociopolitical dramas. In the words of Grinker and Steiner, "just as observation is a form of control, so too is the process of writing and representing what has been observed" (1997, 18).

We deliberately use the notion of schematic frames within the different *reframed* issues covered in this book. Although the popular non-photographic use of "framed" is most common in negative representation, as in a "frame-up," he was "framed," and so on, we choose to recognize the use of frames as an inevitable part of any process of studying, viewing, and seeing. The distinctive flavor of this book lies in its recognition of the conscious and subconscious extant "framings" of Africa and the role of analysis in providing alternative frames (reframing) that allow the student to shift, as the audience of the masquerade,

---

[17] Amazon.com book reviews, www.amazon.com.

[18] See readers' reviews of *Africa: A Continent Self-Destructs,* www.amazon.com.

to relocate within the context of a discourse, or the methodology of study because of a dawning awareness that they have missed critical shots, sights, and sites that would have helped them to understand the issues encountered in discourses about Africa, including those around contemporary problems such as democratic transitions, HIV/AIDS, conflict, and human rights dilemmas. Frames are embedded both in how we see things and how we represent them and several scholars have highlighted the structures that delimit such frames. "Our views are largely determined by the structures of observation. Each view frames an object or image that negates our liberation, for when we look *at* something we always, necessarily, look *from* somewhere else. . . . Pure vision is an illusion" (Grinker and Steiner 1997, 282).

Spotless vision is indeed an illusion, and we do not pretend to supply such comprehensively chaste visions of Africa in this book. Such an undertaking would actually reduce the enormity of the felt experiences and subjectivities that—like the subjectively experienced traumas of colonialism in our chapter on colonialism in this volume—are vital to understanding the region. *Reframing Contemporary Africa,* therefore, reflects the dilemmas of authorial and editorial choices. Like the photographer selecting shots that together build a desired outcome, each contributor and the editors have attempted to add value, refreshingly and provocatively to the study of the continent. The disparate frames necessarily differ in relationship to the different topics, to the authors' styles, perspectives, and goals, but together they open conversations and invite debate on closed or silenced subjects; create new understanding of social, political, and economic problems through a vigorous, contextualized analysis; add new issues to the debate and discourse on Africa; and challenge extant representations, ideologies, and constructs.

Reframing Africa: Conceptual Journeys and the Search for Liberating Methodologies

So far, in this opening chapter, we have spoken about a corpus of intellectual thinking about Africa that exposes and presents counter-narratives to the popular discourse on contemporary Africa. We now turn our attention to some of the broad theoretical traditions that have informed scholarship on African countries with a view to determining their continuing relevance to the study of the continent. These traditions, in particular, the *Euro-centered–liberal* tradition and the *Critical* traditions, have been influential in defining the present, envisioning the future, and determining the prescriptions that are used in developing specific policies and institutions today. We have purposely said "Euro-centered–liberal" tradition to distinguish the word "liberal" from its usual meaning in Western societies—"the opposite of conservative." In fact, what is typically described as the liberal tradition in global analysis tends to incorporate the position of the conservative core in the West.

The outworking of these traditions and their varied manifestations in African politics and society has been explored and reflected extensively in the literature. (See for instance, Harbeson et al. 1994 and Schraeder 2000.) In Schraeder's informative study, he notes that the liberal, or Euro-centered liberal, paradigm has dominated the study of Africa through its assumptions that the progress and "development" of the newly independent African countries of the 1960s must proceed along the path of liberal democracies and free market economies adopted by their former colonizers and other Western societies. Despite the various divergences within the tradition and the shifts from the optimistic texts of the 1960s and 1970s to the pessimistic trends of the 1980s and 1990s, a disturbing thread links these Euro-centered liberal voices—the notion that the West provides a model for "modernizing change" in Africa. Such a perspective continues to be a powerful idea despite the obvious error of historicity: It ignores the actual roots of Western economic growth and vibrancy, including the fact that the industrial revolution and its economic offshoots were embedded in the systems of slavery and global imperialism that spurred the global ascendancy of European and other Western powers. Schraeder chronicles the birth of this intellectual tendency:

> In 1995, David A. Apter captured the sentiments of an entire generation of Africanist scholars within the liberal tradition when he underscored the "tremendous sense of excitement" associated with carrying out field research in the soon-to-be-independent African country of Ghana. For Apter and his contemporaries, the African continent represented an intellectual challenge which, similar to that faced by the Western explorers of the 18th and 19th centuries, offered the possibility of making discoveries that could ensure both fame and fortune within their given academic disciplines. Unlike the earlier explorers, however, the scholars of the 1950s carried with them an intellectual blueprint for understanding the development of Africa that became known as modernization theory (Schraeder 2000, 24).

The concerns of these modern explorers ranged from prescriptions for stability and political order in Africa (Zolberg 1966), policy analysis (Rothchild and Curry 1979), and democratic experimentation (Bratton and van de Walle 1997). This rank of analysts includes Samuel Huntington, whose problematic formulations on global cultural difference in his 1996 *Clash of Civilizations and the Remaking of World Order* followed his dire calls for institutionalization and observations on the difficulty of modernization in the "less developed world" (1968). As is well known, modernization theory permitted the normalization of the well-propagated notions of African backwardness for liberals who felt themselves invested in achieving positive global change and who pushed an agenda that eventually worked in tandem with the economic and strategic goals of international economic institutions, financial agencies, Western governments, and nongovernmental organizations. Their disparate agendas brought social, economic, and other goals into cohesive statements in which the African Other would emulate and move through stages of growth (including the eradication of internal problems that they insisted were at the root of the continent's malaise, poor leadership, poor ethics, etc.) till it finally attained the ultimate prize of modernization through the accoutrements of urbanized, free market, industrialized, and democratic statehood. The failures of such a culturally misinformed ideological paradigm, with its narrow understanding of historicity, its willful manipulation of African societies, incapacity to understand ongoing discourses around decolonization, and continued dependence on global superpower interest and resource exploitation, during and after the Cold War period, were not surprising. They were evident in the decades of splintering "Western liberal" policies and treatment by International Monetary Fund (IMF), World Bank, and world trade prescriptions that entombed African countries in a rising spiral of social, economic, and political crises.

Opposition to such a liberal framing of reality, problems, and solutions led not only to reformist efforts at internal change, but also to a much broader groundswell of support for a multidimensional, oppositional paradigm loosely described by several scholars, including Schrader (2000), as the "critical tradition." In contrast to the image of a vibrant Africa, emerging through the model of Western societies, scholars and policymakers, energized by the critical tradition, found voice in vigorous opposition to liberal paradigms and insisted through a changing range of models, that it would be the formation of socialist-style states that would free Africa for transformative development in the aftermath of formal colonialism. Although their roots derived from various affinities for or connections with Marxist ideals, several of the scholars and political leaders ultimately identified with the critical tradition did not formally espouse classical Marxism but a socialist vision for Africa, often based on culturally embedded social values.

Perhaps one of the most powerful intellectual trends to gain a foothold in African universities and among its scholars and activists was dependency theory. University students in many of Africa's capitals in the late 1970s, 1980s, and 1990s would certainly have been exposed to this body of literature, often called "structural economics," which in fact galvanized and helped to consolidate a language of protest that swept many African societies in opposition to IMF and World Bank policies on trade liberalization and privatization of social services. In contrast to the penchant of liberal scholars to insist that the source of crises was the lack of a civilizing, modernizing, and liberalizing culture in Africa, dependency theorists variously located the crises in a logical outworking of a historical and structural problem that generated exploitative relationships between countries of the global core, consisting of the former colonizers, and countries of the global margins, which consisted primarily of the formerly colonized, formally independent, yet still subservient and marginalized countries of Africa, Asia, the Middle East, and Latin America. Relations between these sets of countries, they proposed, could never be equal or fair within the continuing terms of relations and would only continue to generate rising social, economic, and political disabilities. That is, rather than tend toward development, continued relations between the West and the Rest would only tend to the development of underdevelopment (Schraeder 2000, 48). The excitement generated by the wildly influential treatise of Walter Rodney (*How Europe Underdeveloped Africa* 1972) continued to be evident in research by James Blaut (1992), Inikori, and numerous other researchers who provided evidence that Africa was proceeding along lines of growth similar to those Europe followed before the violent reversals caused by slavery displacement and colonialism.

These were not mere academic discourses. Several of Africa's political elite and postindependence leaders embarked on alternative struggles for a socialist statehood, while other more nationalist leaders sought to incorporate such socialist ideals within the agricultural, educational, health, cultural, and other sectors of their newly independent states. Presidents Kwame Nkrumah of Ghana, Sekou Toure of Guinea, Julius Nyerere of Tanzania—all intellectuals—sought to shape states based on differing forms of socialist or Marxist sociopolitical organizing ideals, which were variously described as "African consciencism," "African socialism," "Ujaama" systems, etc. The end of the Cold War and the seeming ascendancy of the global market imperative would appear to have struck a death toll on these ideals, but a paradox exists in Africa as elsewhere: while liberal markets dominate in practice, and most policy makers pledge allegiance to the agencies that sustain such systems, the language and demands of popular activism and political plaints is within the critical tradition, even though there is a palpable sense of pessimism that such radical changes, including the call for a new international economic order, would ever occur.

If the dominant schools of thought that shaped the study of Africa have encountered such critique or destabilization, what then should guide our search for answers? A constantly evolving web of intellectual schools has taken up the debates around the study of the African "postcolony" (itself a debated term). Structuralism, for instance, with its emphasis on analyzing the continent as a complex, globally comparable system of interrelated parts linking internal and external components, resonated with its dependency or structural economics dimensions and helped to explain the crisis in the continent. However, criticisms of the rigidity of the school amid political anxieties about change, new feminisms, changes in colonial formations, and resistance to communist coherence in Europe in the 1960s led to the emergence of yet another intellectual tradition, "post-structuralism," whose thinkers tend to be categorized by others rather than self-designated. As a child of social destabilization itself, post-structuralism was molded as a tool for destabilizing the reading of texts, for creating alternative and sundry perspectives, and for identifying fictional constructs that had hitherto assured us of our identities as readers of texts. Thus, as a collective, post-structuralist thinkers would seek to question our conceptualization of "self" as a distinct and consistent entity, insisting rather that we read the self as the product of conflicted and contradictory identities, including race, class, ethnicity, gender, religion, and age. It is an intellectual school that has certainly become increasingly influential in contemporary readings of history and is disturbingly in evidence in a growing chasm in Africanist scholarship, in part, because of its suggestion that the perception of meaning must take preeminence over the task of discerning or identifying an original authorial or textual intent. In essence, post-structuralism urges that texts cannot and should not be limited to singular meanings or purposes and that it is the reader who constructs the signified, or the meaning, from a signifier using many perspectives that might actually be discordant, emerging, if need be, from contradictory theoretical arguments and providing new meanings through the consideration of a range of variables involving reader, author, and text.[19]

How do these ongoing debates affect the study of Africa? We started this chapter with an explanation of popular imaginaries and schematic frames for seeing Africa and the sites from which we view. These conceptual methodological frames determine how scholars search, process, and convey continental realities. The struggle of African societies against the mishandling of discourses on social and political identities, the exploitation of their landscapes, values, and institutions can be enriched or hampered by the evolving methodologies of intellectual inquiry.

Three decades ago, in his 1976 lecture series, Michel Foucault succinctly summarized the general impetus of the post-structuralist movement as involving, since the 1960s,

> the immense and proliferating criticizability of things, institutions, practices, and discourses; a sort of general feeling that the ground was crumbling beneath our feet, especially in places where it seemed most familiar, most solid, and closest to us, to our bodies, to our everyday gestures. But alongside this crumbling and the astonishing efficacy of discontinuous, particular, and local critiques, the facts were also revealing something . . . beneath this whole thematic, through it and even within it, we have seen what might be called the insurrection of subjugated knowledges (Foucault 1976).

Such a penchant for deconstructing and destabilizing meaning and for interrogating the reader and the text has in many ways liberated the space for contrary thinking constrained by the cultural Othering and rigidities of the liberal school and the multiple institutions, policies, and crises the school spawned in Africa. On the other hand, there is a strong feeling among many scholars that the school has also generated a crisis of permissibility, particularly in the arts and humanities as scholars read, redefine, and distort literary, visual, and cultural arts and artifacts with little appreciation for how such readings facilitate the continuity of willful cultural dispossessions in a continent grappling with postcolonial self-retrieval, self-definition, and ownership. Indeed, it opens up space for the voicing of subjugated knowledges but calls into being a larger debate among several African scholars on whether the emergence of

---

[19] See for instance, Peter Schraeder, *African Politics and Society: A Mosaic in Transformation*, 2nd ed. (Belmont, CA: Wadsworth Publishing, 2003).

the "post-" theories—postmodern, poststructural, and postcolonial—simply represent Western license for new hegemony and inscriptions of the African continent.

Niyi Osundare, poet and writer, made clear his position:

Either as a result of the politics of their provenance or an inherent crisis in their modes and methods of analysis and application (or both), "mainstream" Western post-structuralist theories have demonstrated little or no adequacy in the apprehension, analysis and articulation of African writing and its long and troubled context. This essay is not intended to push an exclusivist, essentialist viewpoint that "our" literature cannot be apprehended by "their" theory. But it is the case that the ethnocentric universalism of contemporary theoretical practice; its reification of theory into some oracular Western canonical monologue, its fetishization of text and disregard for the deeper reaches of referentiality, its replacement of theory itself with masochistic theoreticism—all these crises have produced a kind of radical conservatism, an anti-hegemonic hegemony which distance Western theory from the fundamental peculiarities of non-Western peoples (2002, 54).

Theories matter, he agrees. "They provide a neat, handy background aid to methodological and analytical procedures. They foster and enhance a reflective globality on issues while sharpening that predictive and speculative capability which facilitates the marriage of imagination and knowledge. As post-structuralist theories are beginning to accept, thanks to the New Historicism, all theories are positional, contingent, connected, even partisan. In their originary, epistemological, and analytical presumptions, the 'major' literary theories in the world today are exclusivistically Western and oracular. They have yet to demonstrate adequate capability for coping with issues and events in other parts of the world" (ibid., 54).

Consequently, as we consider the application of frames, schemas, and theoretical perspectives on the study of contemporary Africa, it is important to remember that resistance by African scholars is not merely to theoretical organizing devices, but also to the notion of a grand "master theory" of the post-colonies emerging from the celebrated Western centers. Thus, Mamdani (in chapter two of this volume), Osundare (2002), and Achebe (1989), alike, exhort an interrogation that does not reinscribe the colony within the same dichotomies and binaries of the fundamental racisms and ethnocentrisms that often creep unrecognized into the work of deconstructionist scholars, whose interrogative literary readings, for instance, rarely prevent the importations of the same historical blindness that reinforces the notion of an African Otherness. For instance, Niyi Osundare contends that it is almost impossible to find Western critics of Conrad's *Heart of Darkness* who demonstrate an ability or willingness to understand the African or to "sympathize with him/her as a victim of a Eurocentric discursive and cognitive violence," because understanding the African in this context would require the dismissal of "critics who practice 'historicism without history' and the quest for critics fore-grounded in a thorough and comprehensive understanding of both text and context, specifically, African historiography (a task Zeleza undertakes in this book). Conrad's mis-creation of African savagery, of a space unspoken by howling natives lacking language, has been described as a 'practical, incontestable demonstration of this dehumanization and absencing' of the African in Western writing on Africa. In spite of Chinua Achebe's (1989) powerful critique of Conrad's *Heart of Darkness,* a review of late twentieth-century Western critics concludes that most have sustained a process of 'preferred visions' that continue Conrad's silencing and negation of Africans" (Osundare 2002, 51–54).

Our final stop on this conceptual voyage around the framing of Africa is at *postcolonialism,* a grow-ing coalescence of literature and critical perspectives. Saurabh Dube gives us a sweeping sense of its growing influence within writings about the developing world:

Over the past two decades, a variety of critical perspectives have questioned the place of the West as history, modernity, and destiny. First, recent years have seen vigorous challenges to univocal concep-tions of universal history under the terms of modernity. Imaginatively exploring distinct pasts forged within wider, intermeshed matrices of power, these works have queried the imperatives of historical progress and the nature of the academic archive, both closely bound to aggrandizing representations of a reified Europe (Amin 1995; Banerjee Dube 1999; Chakrabarty 2000; Dube 1998; Fabian 2000; Florida 1995; Hartman 1997; Klein 1997; Mignolo 1995; Price 1990; Rappaport 1994; Skaria 1999; see also Axel 2001; Mehta 1999; and Trouillot 1995).

Second, close to our times, dominant designs of a singular modernity have been increasingly inter-rogated by contending intimations of heterogeneous moderns. Such explorations have critically considered the divergent articulations and representations of the modern and modernity that have shaped and sutured empire, nation, and globalization. As a result, modernity/modernities have been, themselves, revealed as contradictory and contingent processes of culture and control, as checkered, contested histories of meaning and mastery—in their formation, sedimentation, and elaboration . . . (Chatterjee 1993; Cooper and Stoler 1997; Coronil 1997; Comaroff and Comaroff 1997; Dube forthcoming; Ferguson 1999; Gilroy 1993; Gupta 1998; Hansen 1999; Prakash 1999; Price 1998; Taussig 1987; see also Appadurai 1996; Escobar 1993; Harootunian 2000; Piot 1999; and Rofel 1999).

Third and finally, for some time now critical scholarship has contested the enduring binaries—for example, between tradition and modernity, ritual and rationality, myth and history, and East and West—that have shaped influential understandings of pasts and key conceptions of cultures . . . (Asad 1993; Bauman 1992; Comaroff and Comaroff 1992; Errington 1998; Gray 1995; Lander 2000; Mignolo 2000; Said 1978; Rorty 1989; Taussig 1997; see also Lowe and Lloyd 1997; Dube, 2002: 197–8; and Scott 1999).

Such scholarship increasingly appears to dominate many emerging Western intellectual discourses, certainly in relation to the study of the African continent and postcolonies of Asia and Latin America. This is not surprising. The most recent wave of violent struggles for political independence was in Africa, and the continent's celebration of the 1993 collapse of apartheid, the brutal white separatist rule in South Africa, reminds us eloquently that colonialism is a raw and recent reality. Consequently, Osundare explained his discomfort with the very concept of postcolonialism as a handle for defining African experiences in this manner:

"Post-colonial" is a highly sensitive historical and geographical term which calls into significant atten-tion a whole epoch in the relationship between the West and the developing world, an epoch which played a vital role in the institutionalization and strengthening of the metropole-periphery, center-margin dichotomy. . . . We are talking about a term which brings memories of gunboats and mortars, conquests and dominations, a term whose accent is blood stained. We are talking about a term whose "name" and meaning are fraught with the burdens of history and the anxieties of contemporary reality (2002, 42).

Like Biodun Jeyifo and other critics of postcolonial studies, there is protest over a "naming" that can be misread as not merely producing a sense of passing for a still painfully present past, but also endowing "its principal morpheme 'colonial' with an originary privilege" in that the word "colonial" appears to carry the voice of the beginning, suggesting it is the moving force and the significant point of departure (ibid., 45–46).

Such critics are well aware of Gilbert and Tompkins's reminder in *Post-Colonial Drama: Theory, Practice, Politics,* that the term "postcolonialism—according to a too-rigid etymology—is frequently misunderstood as a temporal concept, meaning the time after colonialism has ceased, or the time following the politically determined Independence Day on which a country breaks away from its governance by another state. Not a naïve teleological sequence which supersedes colonialism, postcolonialism is, rather, an engagement with and contestation of colonialism's discourses, power structures, and social hierarchies" (1996, 2). So it is perhaps what some deride as its "phatic" sense of itself as a naming force, bestowing identity and authoritative referencing and definition on an otherwise blurred continent, that evokes resistance from a number of African scholars, writers, and activists to the critical perspectives offered in postcolonial studies. Is it the case then, as these scathing critics insist, that as a frame for understanding Africa, the "problem concerns the politics of the genealogy of theory, specifically of post-colonial theory, its perceived imperialism and ethnocentrism, its rigidified location and attitudinally located way of seeing that embeds itself with the same ease and complacency with which Western theories have taken over the global literary and intellectual arena, the way they inscribe themselves as though the world were a *tabula rasa*?."[20]

A careful reading suggests that at the core is a resistance to what is experienced as a continued imperial incursion, an appropriation of Foucault's "subjugated knowledges" that should have been freed by these very insubordinate forms of intellectual inquiry and practice. Unfortunately, the troubled histories of conceptual journeys of the West around the African continent tempt scholars to jettison frameworks that might offer congruence with ongoing African-based scholarly traditions, with their indigenous modes of intellectual inquiry and critique that might not bear the label of "postcolonial" but, in fact, do share many concerns and practices, including the question of the continuing influences of the colonial in the colonizer and the colonized; questions of cultural identity, resistance, reclamation, and redefinition in colonized societies; the quandary of national identity in the postcolony; the structures, institutions, literatures, and other texts that sustain or challenge and transform the images, relations, hierarchies, and identities of the colonized and the colonizer. These internal struggles around memory and identity(ies) are themes that have occurred and continue to occur with much frequency in the memoirs, literary works, oral literature, and public discourses in African societies and presage the contemporary labels bestowed on similar critical readings termed "postcolonial" theory, postcolonial literature, and criticism.

As emerging scholarship critiques a range of popular Western imaginaries about Africa, such challenges are embroiled in debates about the extent to which a focus on the redefinition of self becomes an exercise that evades the harsh scrutiny of internal realities and conditions. Arif Dirlik, for instance, contends that "in its preoccupation with Eurocentrism, postcolonial criticism has also refused to confront an increasingly audible revival of traditions that—while perhaps serving as antidotes to Eurocentrism—nevertheless present serious problems of their own, as the values they espouse are neither necessarily progressive nor

---

[20] Niyi Osundare's trenchant criticism of postcolonial thought goes in many directions. His biting critique is echoed in presentations by numerous other African writers, philosophers, and social scientists.

to the benefit of the peoples they purportedly represent" (2002, 613). His point is well taken and certainly speaks to a danger that accompanies many critiques of Eurocentric paradigms. However, Dirlik's criticism does not speak to the robust, self-aware engagement and critique of internal and external traditions by contributors to this book. The compelling strength of the arguments by Wole Soyinka, Anene Ejikeme, Pius Adesanmi, Célestin Monga, and other contributors is located in their capacity to hold multiple realities in tension as critical and intersecting parts of the African trajectory.[21] Thus, their eye on the past produces a logical relaying of larger truths and intersections in a manner similar to Titi Ufomata's negotiation of her engagement with the colonial:

> I am not suggesting for a second that oppression or inequity did not exist in the traditional system prior to colonialism. Such a claim would be false. There was significant subordination of women to indigenous social structures that rendered them unequal in family, lineage and state matters. There is the issue of inheritance among several African societies, for example. One has to remember however, that the basis of subordination, for example wives to daughters of a family or wives to husbands does not parallel the idea of gender subordination pervasive in the literature. While a woman can be discriminated against as a wife, she has important rights as a daughter or sister. Secondly, the English language and history have served to masculinize things in such a way that even women's accomplishments are masked. . . . Many records of female rulers exist in Yorubaland. Only recently, the Regent of Ado, a major town in Ekiti State of Nigeria, was a woman. There were a lot of women in the traditional Oyo political structure and the positions were quite significant (Ufomata, 2000).

The question then seems to concern the depth to which individual authors can burrow in the liberating spaces created by the tradition. Dirlik himself suggests that these spaces offer potential for much rigorous work. "By far the most important contributions have been those that have brought cultural questions into discussions of political economy, opening the way to a more holistic understanding of colonialism. Of these approaches, perhaps the most salient has been the critique of claims to nation and national identity. Postcolonial criticism has revealed the impossibility of any clear-cut cultural distinction between colonizer and colonized, showing how the cultural formations of one are incomprehensible without reference to the cultural formations of the other" (Dirlik 2002, 612–613). This compelling notion of a duality of currents between the domains of coloniality is simplified in Steinmetz's description of the constitutive imperative and impact of the margins on the colonizing core. We cite him at length by way of emphasizing the possibilities opened up for reenvisioning Africa and the world through this cross-critical reframing:

> While "postcolonial studies" has been taken to mean many things, it is identified above all with the claim that colonialism has been as much about Europe and Europeans as about the colonized. . . . Postcolonial analysts are not the first to examine the impact of colonies on Europe. . . . Economic historians and historical sociologists discussed the contribution of gold and silver from the American colonies to the emergence of capitalism in Europe. Other historians analyzed the impact of colonial products such as sugar, tobacco, pepper and spices, coffee and tea, and rubber on European culture. . . . Indeed, one of the most vibrant areas of postcolonial thinking has involved the reinterpretation of canonical works of European literature that are not ostensibly concerned with colonialism at all. Writers like Gayatri Spivak and Edward

---

[21] These scholars do not necessarily identify as postcolonial thinkers. We merely reference their works, which present concerns, perspectives, and methodologies found in much postcolonial criticism.

Said have analyzed texts by "noncolonial writers" (Jane Austen, Mary Shelly, Charlotte Brontë, Baudelaire, Kafka, Shakespeare) as constituted by the colonial margin. Others have explored the ways in which the intertwining of core and periphery has shaped other aspects of European culture.... The new colonial studies have also started to disrupt entrenched ways of thinking about processes that are not colonial in any conventional sense. Historians have begun rewriting the history of intra-European state formation in the medieval and early modern periods as a colonial process, even though it was not construed as such by the actors at the time. The influx and growing awareness of postcolonials within the core societies is forcing Europeans to think about the long-term ramifications of colonialism for their own societies. Most dramatically, this shift can be understood as a "historical decentering" and a "reversal of colonial history" in which the center-periphery axis is destabilized and the "master's language" is transformed into a form of creole (Steinmetz, 2003).

Conclusion

Inikori's award-winning research (*Africans and the Industrial Revolution in England,* 2002) on the impact of African resources on European economies remains an important reminder of the vital importance of this trend in intellectual analysis. His research destabilizes and provides the data and evidences that challenge settled Eurocentric imaginaries of Africa and the West and offers a most beguiling anchor for new work by African and Africanist scholars, that is, the use of this large body of critical traditions as a means of speaking back, interrogating and not merely refuting and defining the West itself via its intersections with and interventions on the African continent. As we conclude this initial voyage around theorizing Africa, it is clear that the evolving contours of postcolonialism may offer critical pathways for future incursions in "reframing" Africa and the West. Clearly, there is need for what we call a fluid, polycentric thrust in studying the African continent, one that adopts some of the central concerns and tools of what is perhaps more cautiously termed studies of "coloniality" in which we reference Mignolo's (2000) work on the *space where the reconstitution of subaltern knowledge and border thinking takes place.* Therefore, we reenter this conversation on frames with renewed vigor in the concluding chapter of the book, having allowed the reader the opportunity to engage in provocative, substantive discussions of a range of contemporary social, economic, cultural, and political issues and problems that provide an informed landscape from which to demand certain requirements of a workable frame and methodology.

As the various contributions to this book systematically destabilize the totalizing ways of reading history, identity, conflict, disease, culture, and the arts in African countries, we bring these concerns together in our concluding consideration of the value of a robust and gutsy form of theoretical criticism that meets the demand for new strategies of resistance and change at the local and global levels and supports the struggle to transform both the objective indicators of crises on the continent while embracing the struggle for "voice," "representation," and "agency" of colonized peoples from internal and external forces of oppression and exploitation. Such a frame offers a rigorous interrogation, which, as Ali Rattansi has noted, allows for the investigation of the mutually constitutive role played by colonizer and colonized, center and periphery, the metropolitan and the "native" in forming, in part, the identities of both the Western powers and the non-Western cultures that they forged (1997).

Reframing Contemporary Africa does not reify the validity of so-called African perspectives and voice as though they were irreproachable but supports a nuanced and transformative analysis of African political, economic, and cultural practice. As we show in the preface to this volume, the essays collectively expose global-national-local nexus in problems of governance, political instability, and the deterioration of social conditions in many African countries. Such realities are analyzed with an acute understanding of context and historicity and with an obligation to introduce silenced voices through a language of discourse and analysis that embraces a critique of global reductionism without evading uncomfortable issues of local agency. Such a language of analysis generates a capacity, for instance, to confront and expose human suffering without consigning those who suffer into nameless wastelands of an African Otherness or suppressing the reality of their own capacities and complex, even conflicted, political and social positioning or identities.

Scholars are, thus, engaged not merely in analysis that lends itself to the production of new knowledge, but also in acts of inscription, be they alien observers, differentially situated citizens, or authoritative brokers of memory and history,[22] and it is our hope that these goals and methodologies have converged in a provocative, intellectual production that confronts problematic discourses and realities in an ethical quest for justice, sociopolitical change, and peace in Africa.

REFERENCES

Abrahamsen, Rita. *Disciplining Democracy, Development Discourse and Good Governance in Africa*. London: Zed Books, 2000.

Achebe, Chinua. "An Image of Africa: Racism in Conrad's Heart of Darkness," in *Hopes and Impediments: Selected Essays*. New York: Doubleday, 1989, 1–20.

Ahmed, Ismail. "Understanding Conflict in Somalia and Somaliland," in *Comprehending and Mastering African Conflicts: The Search for Sustainable Peace and Good Governance*, edited by Adebayo Adedeji, 236–256. London: Zed Books, 1999.

Airewele, Peyi and C.U. Ukeje. "Gender Diplomacy at the Crossroads: Foreign Aid, Women and Development in Nigeria," in *Nigerian Women in Society and Development*, edited by Amadu Sesay and Adetanwa Odebiyi, 199–230. Ibadan: Dokun Publishing House, 1998.

Allen, Bill. "From the Editor/A Special Message. Revisiting the Elephant Hunters of Tanzania," *National Geographic* (October 2004).

Anderson, Benedict. *Imagined Communities: Reflections on the Origins and Spread of Nationalism*. London: Verso, 1983.

Angelou, Maya. *All God's Children Need Traveling Shoes*. Toronto: Random House, 1986.

An-Na'im, Abdullah A. *Cultural Transformation and Human Rights in Africa*, edited by London: Zed Books, 2002.

Appadurai, Arjun. *Modernity at Large: Cultural Dimensions of Globalization*. Minneapolis: University of Minnesota Press, 1996.

Asante, Molefi K. *The Afrocentric Idea*. Trenton, NJ: Africa World Press, 1987.

Attanasio, Paul. 1984. "A Review of The Gods Must Be Crazy." *Washington Post,* November 5, 1984. http://uweb .txstate.edu/~rw04/film/history/hollywood_film/gods_attanasio_review.htm.

Bakari, Imruh, and Mbye B. Cham. *African Experiences of Cinema*. London: British Film Institute, 1996.

Baradat, Leon. *Political Ideologies, Their Origins and Impact*. 6th ed. Upper Saddle River, NJ: Prentice-Hall, 1997.

Beer, Gillian. "Representing Women: Re-presenting the Past," in *The Feminist Reader: Essays in Gender and Politics of Literary Criticism*, edited by Catherine Belsey and Jane Moore. London: Macmillan, 1989, 68–80.

Bergan, Ronald. "One Man's Reality Before the Dawn in South Africa; Obituary: Jamie Uys," *The Guardian,* February 2, 1996.

---

[22] Peyi Soyinka-Airewele, *Invoking the Past, Conjuring the Nation*, forthcoming 2009.

Bernal, Martin. *Black Athena: The Afroasiatic Roots of Classical Civilization.* Vol. 1, *The Fabrication of Ancient Greece 1785–1985.* New Brunswick, NJ: Rutgers University Press, 1987.

Blaut, J.M. *The Debate on Colonialism, Eurocentrism, and History.* Trenton, NJ: Butterworth-Heinemann, 1992.

Blaut, J.M. T*he Colonizer's Model of the World, Geographical Diffusionism and Eurocentric History.* New York/London: Guilford Press, 1993.

Bratton, Michael and Nicholas van de Walle, eds. *Democratic Experiments in Africa: Regime Transitions in Comparative Perspective.* Cambridge University Press, 1997.

Butchart, Alexander. *The Anatomy of Power: European Constructions of the African Body.* New York: St. Martin's Press, 1998.

Campbell, A. "Ethical Ethnicity: A Critique." *The Journal of Modern African Studies* 35, no. 1 (1997): 53–79.

Canby, Vincent. "Film View: Is 'The Gods Must Be Crazy' Only a Comedy?" *New York Times,* October 28, 1984.

Chabal, Patrick and Jean-Pascal Daloz. *Africa Works: Disorder as Political Instrument.* Bloomington: Indiana University Press, 1999.

Chakrabarty, Dipesh. *Provincializing Europe: Postcolonial Thought and Historical Difference.* Princeton, NJ: Princeton University Press, 2000.

Chatterjee, Partha. *The Nation and Its Fragments: Colonial and Postcolonial Histories.* Princeton University Press, 1993.

Chazan, N., P. Lewis, R. Mortimer, D. Rothchild, and S.J.Stedman. *Politics and Society in Contemporary Africa.* 3rd ed. Boulder, CO: Lynne Rienner, 1995.

Clapham, Christopher. *Africa and the International System: The Politics of State Survival.* Cambridge University Press, 1996.

Comaroff, John and Jean Comaroff. *Ethnography and the Historical Imagination.* Boulder, CO: Westview Press, 1992.

Cooper, Frederick and Ann Laura Stoler. *Tensions of Empire: Colonial Cultures in a Bourgeois World.* Los Angeles: University of California Press, 1997.

Davis, Peter. *In Darkest Hollywood: Exploring the Jungles of Cinema's South Africa.* Johannesburg: Ravan Press; Athens, OH: Ohio University Press, 1996.

Diop, Cheikh Anta. *The African Origins of Civilization: Myth or Reality?* edited and translated by Mercer Cook. New York: Lawrence Hill, 1974.

Dirlik, Arif. "Historical Colonialism in Contemporary Perspective," in *Public Culture* 14, no. 3 (2002): 611–615.

Dube, Saurabh. "Introduction: Colonialism, Modernity, Colonial Modernities," *Nepantla: Views from South* 3, no. 2 (2002): 197–219.

Du Bois, W.E.B. *The World and Africa.* New York: International Publishers, 1965.

——. 1903. *The Souls of Black Folk.* Waking Lion Press: 1903. Reprint 2006.

Dussel, Enrique. *The Invention of the Americas: Eclipse of "the Other" and the Myth of Modernity,* translated by Michael D. Barber. New York: Continuum, 1995.

Edozie, Kiki. "Rwanda-Burundi's National Ethnic Dilemma: Democracy, Deep Divisions and Conflict Re-represented," in *Ethnicity and Socio-political Change in Africa and Other Developing Countries: A Constructive Discourse in State Building,* edited by Santosh Saha. Lanham, MD: Lexington Books, 2008a.

——. *Reconstructing the Third Wave of Democracy: African Democratic Politics.* Lanham, MD: University Press of America, 2008b.

Entman, Robert and Andrew Rojecki. *The Black Image in the White Mind: Media and Race in America.* University of Chicago Press, 2000.

Escobar, Arturo. *Encountering Development: The Making and Unmaking of the Third World.* Princeton University Press, 1993.

Eyoh, Dickson. "African Perspectives on Democracy and the Dilemma of Postcolonial Intellectuals," *Africa Today* 45, no. 3/4 (Jully–December 1998): 281–306.

Fanon, Frantz. *The Wretched of the Earth,* translated by Constancy Farrington Harmondsworth. London: Penguin, 1967.

——. *Black Skins, White Masks,* translated by Charles Lam Markmann. London: Pluto Press, 1986.

Foucault, Michel. *Society Must Be Defended,* translated by David Macey; edited by Mauro Bertani and Alessandro Fontana. New York: Picador, 2003.

Furedi, Frank. *The Silent War.* New Brunswick, NJ: Rutgers University Press, 1998.

Gilbert, Helen and Joanne Tompkins.. *Post-Colonial Drama: Theory, Practice, Politics.* London and New York: Routledge, 1996.

Gilroy, Paul. *The Black Atlantic: Modernity and Double Consciousness.* Cambridge, MA: Harvard University Press, 1993.

Gordon, April and Donald Gordon. *Understanding Contemporary Africa.* Boulder, CO: Lynne Rienner Publishers, 2003.

Grinker, R.R and C.B. Steiner. *Perspectives on Africa: a Reader in Culture, History, and Representation.* Oxford: Blackwell Publishers, 1997.

Gugler, Josef. *African Film. Re-Imagining a Continent.* Bloomington: Indiana University Press, 2003.

Harbeson, John and Donald Rothchild. *Africa in World Politics, Post–Cold War Challenges.* Boulder, CO: Westview Press, 1995.

Harbeson, John and Donald Rothchild. *Africa in World Politics: The African State System in Flux.* Boulder, CO: Westview Press, 2000.

Harbeson, John, D. Rothchild, and N. Chazan. *Civil Society and the State in Africa.* Boulder, CO: Lynne Rienner Publishers, 1996.

Herbst, Jeffrey. *States and Power in Africa.* Princeton University Press, 2000.

Hilliard, Constance. *Intellectual Traditions of Pre-Colonial Africa.* Boston, MA: McGraw-Hill, 1998.

Hooks, Bell. *Feminist Theory: From the Margins to the Center.* Boston: South End Press, 1984.

Huntington, Samuel. *The Clash of Civilizations and the Remaking of World Order.* New York: Simon and Schuster, 1996.

——. 1968. *Political Order in Changing Societies.* New Haven: Yale University Press.

In Darkest Hollywood: Cinema and Apartheid. Documentary written, directed and edited by Daniel Riesenfeld and Peter Davis. Produced by Villon and Nightingale (USA) and distributed by Villon Films, 1993.

Inikori, Joseph E. *Africans and the Industrial Revolution in England: A Study in International Trade and Economic Development.* Cambridge University Press, 2002.

Jackson, John G. *Introduction to African Civilizations.* New York: Kensington Publishing, 1994.

Jacobus, Mary. "The Difference in View," in *The Feminist Reader: Essays in Gender and the Politics of Literary Criticism,* edited by Catherine Belsey and Jane Moore, 42–62. London: Macmillan, 1989.

Khapoya, Vincent. *The African Experience: An Introduction.* 2nd ed. Upper Saddle River, NJ: Prentice-Hall, 1998.

Kolawole, Mary Modupe. *Womanism and African Consciousness.* Trenton, NJ: Africa World Press, 1997.

Lefkowitz, Mary and Guy MacLean Rogers. *Black Athena Revisited.* Chapel Hill, NC: University of North Carolina Press, 1996.

Lefkowitz, Mary. *Not Out of Africa: How Afrocentrism Became an Excuse to Teach Myth as History.* New York: Basic Books, 1996.

Levett, Ann, Kottler, A. Burman, and Erica and Ian Parker. *Culture, Power and Difference: Discourse Analysis in South Africa.* Cape Coast: University of Cape Coast Press, 1997.

Lewis, Peter. *Africa: Dilemmas of Development and Change.* Boulder, CO: Westview Press, 1998.

Mbembe, Achille. *On the Postcolony.* Los Angeles, CA: University of California Press, 2000.

Mengisteab, Kidane. *Globalization and Autocentricity in Africa's Development in the 21st Century.* Trenton, NJ: Africa World Press, 1996.

Mignolo, Walter D. *Local Histories/Global Designs: Coloniality, Subaltern Knowledges, and Border Thinking*. Princeton University Press, 2000.

Monga, Célestin. *The Anthropology of Anger, Civil Society and Democracy in Africa*. Boulder, CO: Lynne Rienner Publishers, 1996.

Myers, Garth, T. Klak, and T. Koehl, "The Inscription of Difference: News Coverage of the Conflicts in Rwanda and Bosnia," *Political Geography* 15, Issue 1, January 1996: 21–46.

Nandy, Ashis. *The Intimate Enemy: Loss and Recovery of Self under Colonialism*. Delhi: Oxford University Press, 1983.

N!ai: The Story of a !Kung Woman. Documentary directed by John Marshall. Distributed in the United States by Documentary Educational Resources, 59 minutes, 1979.

Nnaemeka, Obioma. *Sisterhood, Feminisms and Power in Africa: From Africa to the Diaspora*. Trenton, NJ: Africa World Press, 1998.

Osundare, Niyi. *Thread in the Loom: Essays on African Literature and Culture*. Trenton, NJ: Africa World Press, 2002.

Owomoyela, Oyekan. *The African Difference, Discourses on Africanity and the Relativity of Cultures*. New York: Peter Lang Publishing and Witwatersrand University Press, 1996.

Rattansi, Ali. "Postcolonialism and Its Discontents," *Economy and Society* 26, no. 4. (November 1997): 480–500.

Reno, William. *Warlord Politics and African States*. Boulder, CO: Lynne Rienner, 1999.

Rothchild, Donald and Robert L. Curry, Jr. *Scarcity, Choice and Public Policy in Middle Africa*. Berkeley: University of California Press, 1979.

Said, Edward W. *Orientalism*. New York: Pantheon, 1978.

Sargent, Lyman. *Contemporary Political Ideologies: A Comparative Analysis*. Orlando, FL: Harcourt and Brace, 1999.

Schraeder, Peter J. *African Politics and Society: A Mosaic in Transformation*. 2nd ed. Belmont, CA: Wadsworth Publishing, 2003.

Schwab, Peter. *Africa Self-Destructs*. Basingstoke: Palgrave Macmillan, 2001.

——. *Designing West Africa: Prelude to 21st Century Calamity*. Basingstoke: Palgrave Macmillan, 2004.

Scott, David. *Refashioning Futures: Criticism after Postcoloniality*. Princeton, NJ: Princeton University Press, 1999.

Shohat, Ella and Robert Stam. *Multiculturalism, Postcoloniality, and Transnational Media*. New Brunswick, NJ: Rutgers University Press, 2003.

Soyinka-Airewele, Peyi. "Western Discourse and the Socio-Political Pathology of Ethnicity in Africa," in *The Issue of Ethnicity in Africa*, edited by E.I. Udogu, 167–186. Aldershot Hampshire: Ashgate Publishers, 2001.

——. "Navigating 'Realities,' Illusions and Academic Impulses: Displaced Scholars at Large," *GSC Quarterly* no. 6 (Fall 2002).

——. "When Neutrality Is Taboo: Reconstituting Institutional Identity and Peace-building Paradigms in Africa: The Nigerian Ife/Modakeke Case," *African and Asian Studies* 2, no. 3 (2003): 259–305.

——, "Insurgent Transnational Conversations: Globalization and Identity in the Nollywood Complex," presented at the Transnational Africa Symposium, Bowdoin College, December 2008.

Spivak, Gayatri, "Can the Subaltern Speak?" in *Marxism and the Interpretation of Culture*, edited by Nelson and Grossberg. Urbana, IL: University of Illinois Press, 1988.

——. *In Other Worlds: Essays in Cultural Politics*. New York: Routledge, 2006.

Steinmetz, George. "Culture and the State in State/Culture," in *Historical Studies of the State in the Social Sciences*, edited by George Steinmetz, 1–49. Ithaca, NY: Cornell University Press, 1999.

——. *The Implications of Colonial and Postcolonial Studies for the Study of Europe*. Council For European Studies: Columbia University, 2003. http://www.ces.columbia.edu/pub/Steinmetz_feb03.html.

The Gods Must Be Crazy. Film written and directed by Jamie Uys. Produced by Boet Trotskie (South Africa). Distributed in the United States by Swank Motion Pictures. 90 minutes, 1980.

The Gods Must Be Crazy II. Film written and directed by Jamie Uys. Produced by New Realm, Mimosa and C.A.T. Film (South Africa). 108 minutes, 1989.

Thomson, Alex. *Introduction to African Politics.* New York: Routledge, 2004.

Tomaselli, Keyan, "The Gods Must Be Crazy," http://ccms.ukzn.ac.za/index.php?option=com_content&task=view&id=217&Itemid=43, 1998.

Ufomata, Titi. "Women in Africa: Their Socio-Political and Economic Roles," W*est Africa Review* 2, no. 1 (2000).

Ukadike, Nwachukwu Frank. *Questioning African Cinema: Conversations with Filmmakers.* Minneapolis: University of Minnesota Press, 2002.

Volkman, Toby Alice. "Out of South Africa: The Gods Must Be Crazy," in *Image Ethics: The Moral Rights of Subjects in Photographs, Film and Television,* edited by Larry Gross et al., 236–247. New York/Oxford: Communications and Society, Oxford University Press, 1988.

Wainaina, Binyavanga. "How to Write About Africa," *Granta 92: The View from Africa.* Jan 15, 2006. http://www.granta.com/extracts/2615.

Williams, Patrick, and Lauren Chrisman. *Colonial Discourse and Postcolonial Theory.* New York: Columbia University Press, 1994.

Wisner, Ben, Camilla Toulmin, Rutendo Chitiga and Mary Robinson. *Towards a New Map of Africa.* London: Earthscan Publications, 2005.

Wright, Stephen. *African Foreign Policies.* Boulder, CO: Westview Press, 1998.

Zolberg, Aristide R., *Creating Political Order: The Party States of West Africa.* Chicago University Press, 1985.

Chapter 2

COMMENTARY
Reconfiguring the Study of Africa

Mahmood Mamdani

Few of us have the privilege of naming ourselves. Typically, others name us. Africa was a Roman name—the name by which Rome called its southernmost province, what we today call North Africa. The next big shift in the meaning of Africa came with the slave trade. The trans-Saharan and trans–Indian Ocean slave trades identified with Arabs, while the trans-Atlantic slave trade identified with Europeans. In the imaginations of those who debased humanity in Africa through the slave trade, Africa became identified socially with Negro Africa and physically with sub-Saharan Africa. Instead of the bridge it had been between lands to its north and south, the Sahara was now seen as a great civilizational barrier.

Arabs called the land to the south of the Sahara "bilad al-sudan," the land of the Black people. As the Atlantic slave trade gathered steam, Europeans followed suit. In *The Philosophy of History*, Hegel divided Africa into three parts: "European Africa," which included the Mediterranean lands of North Africa; "the land of the Nile," by which he meant Egypt, Nubia, and Ethiopia, all "closely connected with Asia"; and, finally, "Africa Proper," the source of slaves, debased in the European imagination as "the land of childhood . . . lying beyond conscious history . . . enveloped in the dark mantle of Night."

The Hegelian notion of "Africa Proper" as sub-Saharan Africa was modified in the era of colonialism and the Cold War. The more "apartheid South Africa" came to be seen as an exceptional experience, the more Africa came to be identified racially and geographically: racially with Negro (Bantu) Africa and geographically with middle Africa, the land the Sahara and the Kalahari. This is the notion of Africa that came to be inscribed in the academy, not only in Europe, but also in the United States and, indeed, in apartheid South Africa.

Even today, the academic preoccupation of institutes of African studies in the United States is not with the African continent, but with sub-Saharan Africa. If the end of colonialism did not pose this question sharply, then the simultaneous end of the Cold War and apartheid certainly underlined the necessity to review a tradition that originated in the period of slavery and was institutionalized under successive doses of colonialism, the Cold War, and apartheid. It is worth recalling that the first significant departure from this tradition came in the postcolonial African academy. Founded by social science faculties inside Africa, the Council for the Development of Social Research in Africa (CODESRIA)

Source: From Mahmood Mamdani, "Reconfiguring the Study of Africa," *SIPA News*, Spring 2000, Volume XIII, no. 2. p. 2.

defined itself as a continental organization committed to reflecting on the very historical experience that had come to define the contours of postcolonial Africa. With the end of apartheid, the reorganized Human Science Resource Council (HSRC) of South Africa followed suit.

The new period poses a double challenge to the institutional study of Africa. The first stems from the legacy of slavery, colonialism, and apartheid, and is one that has crystallized the institutional boundaries of African studies as different from the geographical boundaries of Africa. The second stems from the legacy of the Cold War, which shaped a tradition of area studies that tended to treat the geographical boundaries of continental "areas" into boundaries of knowledge.

I would like to suggest a tentative answer to this double dilemma. The first part involves redefining the institutional boundaries of African studies to coincide with the geographical boundaries of continental Africa and surrounding islands. The second part requires treating these boundaries as shifting in time and porous at any point in time. By reconsidering boundaries, we would stop taking geography as a permanent artifact, a historical given. Instead, we would see it as a historical product that continues to be fluid.

If the end of the Cold War has set the stage for a single global process (globalization), then one needs to beware before turning it into a one-sided preoccupation that dispenses with the local in the name of the universal. Since globalization can only be perceived, defined, and, indeed, shaped from a local vantage point, the recognition of global trends should be reason not to downplay area studies as local knowledge. Rather, it should lead to making the boundaries of areas sufficiently permeable to problematize the relationship between the local and the global.

Chapter 3

NOT OUT OF AFRICA?
Sifting Facts from Fiction in the New Balkanization of Africa

Iheanyi N. Osondu

The African continent has come a long way since the Berlin conference of November 15, 1881, when conflicting European powers sat down in Europe and demarcated Africa to suit their imperial interests. The conference participants fully divided the continent into 50-odd colonies, without reference to existing boundaries of states, empires, cultures, or over 1,000 ethnic nationalities. Driven by fractious internal class and socioeconomic tensions, spiraling violence of competitive empire building, and fear of the emerging American power, every major colonial authority sought to pursue narrow economic interests on the African continent. "Great" Britain, for instance, desired a Cape-to-Cairo territory, while other countries, such as France, Belgium, Germany, Portugal, Spain, and Italy, haggled over geometric boundaries.

Europe's seemingly "civil" conference on balkanization masked its violent campaign of conquest, which made possible the colonization of the continent. From the sustained wars with the Asante Kingdom of present-day Ghana and the Zulu nation of South Africa to Italy's humiliating defeat in its attempt to violently dominate Ethiopia, it must be remembered that the subjugation and control of African territories was neither peaceful nor easy. It is not surprising that against this background of a forced use of Africa as a prime source of natural resources and as a market for Europe's expanding industrial products, the African continent has been dubbed "the dark continent," "the white man's burden," "a sick baby," and now "a continent of transition" (Stock 2004). Such images, which define Africa in terms of its land and resources, were shaped largely by Europe's attempt to justify its ambitions and claims on African territory. The stock of popular images includes the widely held imaginaries of primitive Africans pillaging their environment through peasant agriculture and rapid population growth; ethnic violence and decay; and notions of deserts, jungles, and uncontrollable environments that require the bounty of Western control.

The prevailing communication of Africa as a continent in crisis and warfare (Stock 2004) continues to be central to the Western struggle to reenact the arbitrary division and control of African territory. It is important to emphasize here that these deeply embedded assumptions and stereotypes about Africa not only stand in the way of effectively learning about the continent, but also have been the basis for ill-conceived academic research and development policies (Stock 2004).

Nevertheless, it is not these views that are the focus of this paper but the increasing absurdity of the ways in which scholars, the popular media, and development and policy actors increasingly misrepresent the political and human geography of Africa. The twin processes of colonial balkanization and misrepresentation obviously did not terminate with the struggle for political liberation by African countries. Numerous authors, such as Marston, Knox, and Liverman (2002), have adopted a problematic, ritualized invocation of differentiation in the misleading, if not meaningless, terms "sub-Saharan Africa" and "Africa South of the Sahara." All African countries, except the five predominantly "Arab" states of Morocco, Libya, Tunisia, Algeria, and Egypt, are typically and now unquestioningly dubbed "sub-Saharan Africa."

Bradshaw, White, and Dymond (2004); Hobbs (2007); and Lydia and Alex Pulsipher (2008) even included Sudan, a country with an African majority and an Arab minority, in their classifications of "North Africa" and "Middle East Asia." It is very interesting to note that the Pulsiphers observed that North Africa and Southwest Asia, as a single region, have been subjected to misrepresentation and unwarranted generalization—both typical by-products of colonialism. Despite their observation, the authors still set out to misrepresent and merge North Africa with parts of Asia. Is this then a mistake, the pursuance of a deliberate policy, or just another example of the tendency to join the bandwagon of analytical and terminological laxity in the study of Africa?

So far, only de Blij and Muller (2007) have attempted to clarify the use of "sub-Saharan Africa." They admit that the use of "Africa South of the Sahara" is not satisfactory but recognize that the convenient name "sub-Saharan" Africa has come into use to signify not physically "under" the great desert but directionally "below" it. There is need to establish, in an objective manner, the way or ways directionally the rest of Africa is "below" North Africa. In addition, one might ask in which directional way "south" is below or north, directionally "above" in a horizontal pattern or layout. This is like saying that Canada is above the United States or that Scotland is above England. Yet it is correct to say that Canada and Scotland are north of the United States and England, respectively. But regarding Africa, the underlying assumption is that one is above and the other, below or, put succinctly, in a relationship of superiority and inferiority. Moreover, it is important to take scholars of Africa to task by asking just what exactly is convenient about the use of the term "sub-Saharan Africa," except perhaps as a nomenclature that does not present the regional human geography of North Africa as African?

It should be noted that de Blij et al. (2007) acknowledge that the African landmass is indivisible. Nevertheless, the authors "partitioned" the human geography into two. Even Marston et al. (2008) admitted that dividing Africa into two regions is artificial, but they still did it because in their imaginations, the northern part of the continent is dominated by an Arab and Islamic culture and the southern, by a predominantly Black and Christian population. This and the preceding assumptions are misleading. There is a substantial Christian population in Egypt and Ethiopia and a large Muslim population in the rest of Africa. Moreover, when did race become the ideal factor in defining the human geography of any area? One might also query why the African continent has been the only one subjected to such a ritualized subdivision.

Interrogating the Notion of "Sub-Saharan"

There are four possible meanings of the prefix "sub-." According to *Merriam-Webster's* (1998), it can mean "under," "below," and "beneath," as well as "subordinate to," "secondary to," "next lower than," or "inferior to." According to de Blij (2007), "sub-Saharan Africa" is used to mean directionally "below" the Sahara Desert. Are we to infer, therefore, that the region is inferior or lower in rank or value to the "Sahara" and the countries above it? This application is very misleading. It is not obvious from its numerous uses in other American textbooks, such as Marston, Knox, and Liverman (2002, 2008), which of the possible meanings of the prefix authors attach to their use of "sub-Saharan." However, the weight of usage of the term in media, scholarship, and the work of international development agencies suggests clearly that, in the popular imagination, most potent is the sense of a racially, economically, and socially differentiated region that is subordinate, secondary to, lower than, or inferior to that of its North African "kindred." Note that, apart from the five predominantly "Arab" countries, there is a country sandwiched between Mauritania and Morocco called "Western Sahara." Does "sub-" refer to under, below, beneath or inferior to Western

Sahara? Equally important to note is that many of the present inhabitants of Egypt, Libya, Tunisia, Morocco, and Algeria have complex perspectives on their identities as both Africans and Arabs.

Moreover, it is equally worth noting that in textbooks such as those of de Blij et al. (2007) and Clawson et al. (2007), "sub-" applies unambiguously to the region below Morocco, Tunisia, Libya, and Egypt. Each of these countries is partly covered by the Sahara Desert. Therefore, where does de Blij et al. (2007) fix the boundary of sub-Saharan Africa? What is directionally "below" it?

More interesting is the fact that these countries are simultaneously disengaged from the African land-mass on which they are located and unashamedly merged with the Middle East because of their "majority Arab populations." Authors such as Marston, Knox, and Liverman (2008) and Hobbs (2007) have not addressed the large non-Arab populations in each of them. What, for example, of Berber, an Afro-Asiatic language spoken by 40 percent of the people in Morocco, 30 percent in Algeria, and smaller percentages in surrounding countries? The Berber language survived the Arab onslaught and colonization in places such as the hilly areas of the Atlas Mountains (Bradshaw et al. 2004). At the same time, it is important to realize that the "Middle East" (another misnomer) is populated not only by Arabs, but also by Jews, Persians, Kurds, and Turks. Therefore, the use of an ethnic group in redefining Africa along racial, socio-economic, and such lines is not only flawed, but also not fully representative of the facts.

The large population of Berbers, approximately 3 million scattered across North Africa, call them-selves "Amazigh." Their history in North Africa is very diverse and extensive. Berbers had contacts with ancient Romans, Greeks, and Phoenicians before the arrival of the Arabs and modern Europeans, and Berber culture and language predate them. Berber belongs to the Afro-Asiatic (formally called "Hamito-Semitic") language family, with Hausa, Fulani, Mossi, Hebrew, Arabic, and Maltese. Hausa and Fulani are widely spoken in the savannah regions of West and Central Africa. Geographically, Berbers live mainly in Morocco, Algeria, Tunisia, Libya, Egypt, Mauritania, Niger, Mali, and Burkina Faso. In other words, they extend from the Mediterranean coast to West and Central Africa. Therefore, to assume that only people of Arab descent inhabit North Africa is a fallacy. On the other hand, to presume that because many Berbers converted to Islam they became Arabs is to turn history upside down. If they are Arabs because they are Muslims, what becomes of Arabs who are Christians or members of other faiths?

There are millions of non-Arab Muslims in Africa and, indeed, all over the world. Indonesia is perhaps the most populated Muslim country, but no one has ever suggested merging it with Middle East Asia due to religion. And not all inhabitants of Middle East Asia are Muslim. Hence, the use of religion as an excuse to join North Africa and the Middle East can only be described, at best, as intensely myopic.

It is true that immediately after independence, all Maghrebi countries tried to pursue a policy of "Arabization," which aimed at replacing French with Arabic as the dominant language of education and literacy. Under this policy, the Berber language was suppressed. But recent events have seen the revival of Berber in education and a move toward recognizing it as a national language in Morocco and Algeria. Human geography, of course, is more than a discourse on religion, and the human geography of Africa is very distinct from any study of the spread of Islam. Therefore, religion, and particularly Islam, cannot be used as an excuse for a "cut-and-paste" exercise in African geography.

If culture and, in this case, language are used as the yardsticks for arbitrary scholarly mergers of North Africa and Middle East Asia, it is worth remembering that Kiswahili is a language that emerged as a result of Arab-African interaction through centuries of trade in East Africa. None of these authors has consid-ered merging East Africa with the Middle East because of its African-Arab linkage. This, however, assumes that all of the Middle East is Arabic-speaking, which it is not. Furthermore, if language is a factor in African human geography, one wonders why, elsewhere, Québec, a French-speaking province

Map 3.1   Human Geography and the Failure of Racial/Cultural Balkanization of Africa

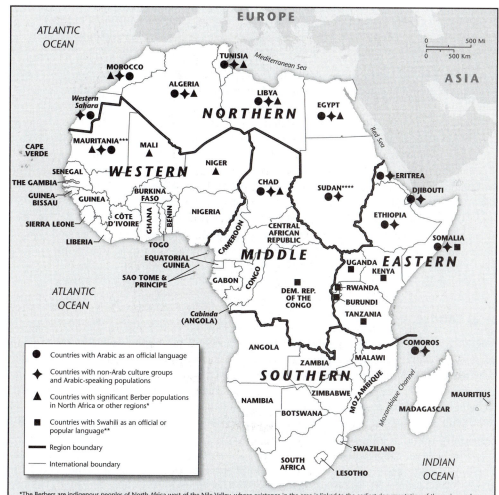

*The Berbers are indigenous peoples of North Africa west of the Nile Valley, whose existence in the area is linked to the earliest documentation of the region and predates Arab military expeditions and invasion of the Maghreb.

**Swahili is an indigenous African language spoken for several centuries by the Swahili people of Eastern Africa. It is not, as many assume, a blend language formed from Arabic and local languages. However, comparable to English's use of Latin and Greek, modern Swahili utilizes a remarkable amount of loanwords from various languages and, in particular, from Arabic, an indication of the historic integration of Arabic-speaking peoples within the cultural milieu of the eastern African sub-region.

***Mauritania is in Northwest Africa and is often alternately defined as part of Northern Africa. It is the only country in geographical West Africa that is not a member state of the Economic Community of West African States (ECOWAS).

****The Sudan is in Northeastern Africa and is often classified as a part of Eastern and not Northern Africa.

Sources: The regional classifications in this map are based on multiple sources: The United Nations Economic Commission for Africa Sub-regional Offices: http://www.uneca.org; United Nations Statistics Division, http://millenniumindicators.un.org/unsd/methods/m49/m49regin.htm; the African Union: http://www.africa-union.org; The Economic Community of West African States: http://www.ecowas.int; and the South African Development Community: http://www.sadc.int.

of Canada, is not merged with Europe, or South Africa with Europe, because of its Dutch-speaking population. In addition, why not merge people of Spanish descent in South America with Spain? Indeed, is there any reason not to merge English-, Spanish-, and Portuguese-speaking countries in regional studies if language should be used to categorize or to measure similarity in human geography?

Although Stock (2004) argued that the North African countries of Libya, Tunisia, Morocco, Algeria, and Egypt have stronger cultural and historical ties to the Mediterranean and Southwestern Asia, it should be noted that geography is holistic, and regional geography is more inclusive than cultural geography. It is a novelty to use "stronger cultural ties" as a basis for merger rather than comparison, for where else in the world have geographers used language to create a "region"? Are there no strong cultural ties between Spain and her former South American colonies or between France and Québec?

Furthermore, Marston et al. (2008) observed that North African countries that border the Mediterranean Sea—Morocco, Algeria, Tunisia, Libya, and Egypt—have more in common with the Middle East than with the countries that lie south of the Sahara. This is not an absolute truth because historical evidence shows that Arab, Berber, and other ethnic nationalities in Africa, such as the peoples of the ancient West African kingdoms of Mali and Ghana, had contacts with one another through trade and scholarship. Timbuktu, an ancient city in present-day Mali, was noted for scholarship and was famous for trade in gold and salt. Authors fail to say that southern Europe, especially countries like Spain and Portugal, should be included in this newfound regional grouping. Why carve out North Africa and not all areas that came under Muslim-Arab conquest, domination, and influence and, thus, share some sociocultural heritage? Muslim jihadists conquered southern Europe, and their imprint remains till today in art, religion, and culture.

Physical Landscapes

The geography of Africa is fairly straightforward, or at least not as complex as that of other continents, such as Asia. However, Africa is so diverse that even educated outsiders confuse or lose sight of its variety when discussing its geography. Geologically, Africa is the richest continent, although it is the least industrialized. Africa's diversity can be seen in its many ethnic groups and nationalities. Over 1,000 languages are spoken, and there are many religious beliefs and types of art and music. Hence, it is very difficult to generalize about Africa, although various myths and misconceptions about it still exist, especially among those who know her least.

The continent covers approximately 11,668,545 square miles, which account for 20.4 percent of the land area of the earth and about 6 percent of its total surface. All the adjacent islands add 12 million square miles. Presently, there are 46 countries on the African mainland; there is a total of 53 African countries if island groups and nations are included. In 2004, Africa's population was estimated to be 885 million, which is approximately 14 percent of the world's total population. Hence, Africa is the second-largest continent in the world, next in size to Asia. Africa extends approximately 5,000 miles from the northernmost point at Cape Ben Bekka in Tunisia on the Mediterranean coast to Cape Agulhas at the southernmost tip of the Republic of South Africa. The width of Africa, from the west-most point at Cape Almedes to the east-most tip at Cape Hafun, is about 4,700 miles.

Africa lies across the equator, which almost bisects it. It is separated from Europe by the straits of Gibraltar in the Mediterranean Sea (near Tunisia) at about 37° 21′ north. The Sinai Peninsula, at the northern end of the Red Sea (cut by the construction of the Suez Canal) separates Africa from Middle East Asia. To the west, Africa extends to 17° 32′ west at Cape Almades by the Atlantic Ocean, and to the east, it extends to Cape Hafun on the Indian Ocean, 51° 26′ east. Southwards, Africa extends to 34° 52′ south. Africa is the only continent crossed by both the equator and the prime meridian.

Considered part of Africa are the islands of Madagascar, one of the world's largest island countries, separated from the mainland by the Mozambique Channel. Other relatively small African island nations include Mauritius, Réunion, the Seychelles, Comoros, São Tomé and Principe, Guinea Bissau, Equatorial Guinea, and the Canary Islands (still colonized by Spain).

Contrary to the way people unfamiliar with Africa refer to her, Africa is a continent, not a country. Hard to believe is the fact that Africa can accommodate within its size the whole of Europe, China, New Zealand, Argentina, India, and the United States (see Map 3.2 below).

With regard to its physical characteristics, the African continent is a single, easily identifiable landmass with its contiguous island nations. Africa is often described as a "plateau continent" (de Blij 2007) with an average elevation of about 3,000 feet above sea level, except in the Somali and Djibouti lowlands and the lowlands on either side of the Mozambique Channel and the narrow coastal plains and river valleys. There are, however, areas of higher elevation, above 3,000 feet. Prominent among them are the Atlas Mountains in the northwest that run from Morocco to Tunisia, the Tibesti Plateau in southern Algeria, and the Ahaggar Plateau in northern Chad. In West Africa, there are the Guinea Highlands (or the Fouta Djalon mountains), the Cameroon Mountains (4,070 feet) on the Adamawa highlands along the southern border between Nigeria and Cameroon, and the Jos Plateau in north-central Nigeria. In northeast Africa, the Ethiopian highland is prominent.

In East Africa, the east African highlands include Mount Elgon (4,321 feet), Mount Kenya (5,199 feet), and Mount Kilimanjaro (19,341 feet). Mount Kilimanjaro is the highest mountain in Africa. Although it is situated along the equator, the snow-capped summit is spectacular and attracts mountaineers from all over the world. However, recent aerial photographs of the mountain show that the snow is gradually melting, perhaps due to global warming. Other areas of high elevation in Africa include the Bieu Plateau, found mainly in southwestern Angola and northern Namibia, and Drakensberg Mountain in southeastern South Africa, whose peak reaches 3,482 feet above sea level.

Apart from the highlands, there are also lowlands that present spectacular features. Examples are the Somali-Djibouti lowland, lowlands on either side of the Mozambique Channel, and those along narrow coastal plains and river valleys. The lowest point in Africa, Djibouti's Lac Assal, is 512 feet (156 meters) below sea level. There is also the great East African Rift Valley, with its deep and elongated lakes and beautiful scenery. This type of elevation, though, is not synonymous with the "Middle East," which is not a plateau, if one considers the Dead Sea Valley (1,286 feet below sea level), the lowest point on the earth. Even Wegner's theory of continental drift did not present the African block as part of the Middle East. Rather, Africa formed the core—the solid block—that is very much central to his thesis.

Therefore, to cut and paste parts of Africa in order to create a reconceptualized region is a disquieting tendency that demands deeper investigation. In the absence of a meaningful physical connection between North Africa and the Middle East—one that transcends evidence of the latter's essential geological and physical location—the logic of "similar physical environment" cannot be used to wed these regions. Such reasoning is as clumsy and untenable as the racial and cultural rationales.

Human geography cannot be constricted to a narrow notion of cultural geographies because it involves study of the distribution of people and their activities (Bradshaw 2004) or their interactions with the environment, not just their history, language, and ethnicity. Human geography deals with the world as it is and might be made to be (Fellmann, Judith Getis, and Arthur Getis 2005). It is that aspect of geography that unifies the physical and human activities in a region and, consequently, should create better-informed citizens of a globalizing world. It should not be a harbinger of inscriptions of difference and artificial divisions underwritten by hidden racial, cultural-nationalistic, and economic discourses of hierarchization that do disservice to scholarship and reality.

There are issues regarding the geography of Africa that demand a closer examination. For example, the physical geography of Africa is usually treated without moving the northern part, or the Maghreb,

Map 3.2   The Relative Size of Africa

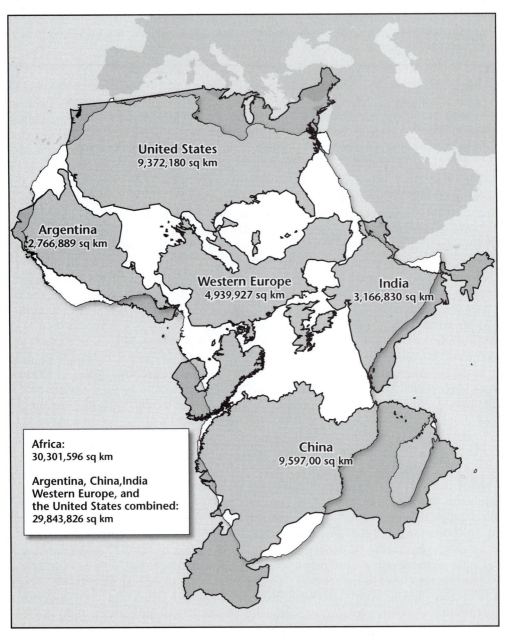

United States
9,372,180 sq km

Argentina
2,766,889 sq km

Western Europe
4,939,927 sq km

India
3,166,830 sq km

China
9,597,00 sq km

Africa:
30,301,596 sq km

Argentina, China,India
Western Europe, and
the United States combined:
29,843,826 sq km

Map 3.3　Physical Map of Africa

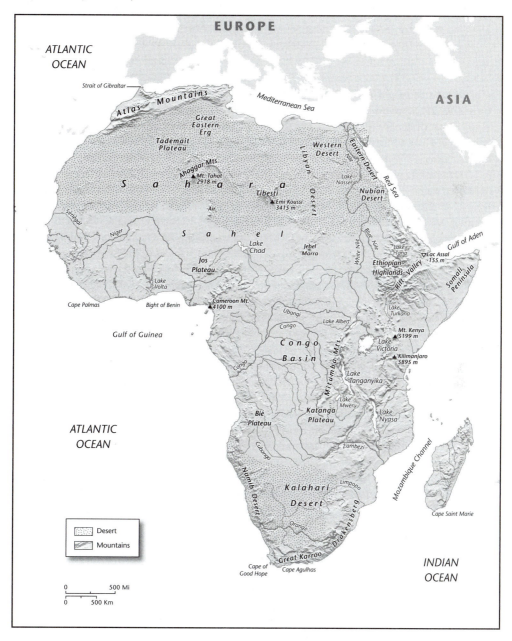

EUROPE

ATLANTIC
OCEAN

ASIA

Strait of Gibraltar

Atlas Mountains

Mediterranean Sea

Great
Eastern
Erg

Tademait
Plateau

Western
Desert

Libyan Desert

Eastern Desert

Nile

Lake
Nasser

Red Sea

Ahaggar Mts.
▲ Mt. Tahat
2918 m

S a h a r a

Air

Tibesti
▲ Emi Koussi
3415 m

Nubian
Desert

S a h e l

Senegal

Niger

Jos
Plateau

Lake
Chad

Jebel
Marra

White Nile

Blue Nile

Lake
Tana

Ethiopian
Highlands

Rift Valley

Gulf of Aden

▽ Lac Assal
-155 m

Somali
Peninsula

Lake
Volta

Cape Palmas

Bight of Benin

Cameroon Mt.
▲ 4100 m

Gulf of Guinea

Ubangi

Congo

Lake Albert

Lake
Turkana

Mt. Kenya
▲ 5199 m

Congo

Congo

Basin

Mitumba Mts.

Lake
Victoria

▲ Kilimanjaro
5895 m

Lake
Tanganyika

Bié
Plateau

Katanga
Plateau

Lake
Mweru

Lake
Nyasa

ATLANTIC
OCEAN

Cubango

Zambezi

Mozambique Channel

Namib Desert

Kalahari
Desert

Limpopo

Drakensberg

Orange

Cape Saint Marie

Great Karroo

Cape of
Good Hope

Cape Agulhas

INDIAN
OCEAN

Desert

Mountains

0   500 Mi

0   500 Km

into Asia (Grove 1989; Adams W.M. et al. 1999). However, if, as Marston et al. (2008) noted, a chapter on Africa would be too long, surely it would be better to focus on specific sub-regional studies, that is, to adopt an approach similar to that used for Asia, rather than merge North Africa with the Middle East for reasons that cannot withstand serious academic scrutiny, except, of course, if one is going by nineteenth-century Western philosophic views of Africa.

Historic Perspective

Such a practice of arbitrary demarcations might be traced back to the nineteenth-century German philosopher Georg Wilhelm Friedrich Hegel, who wrote *The Philosophy of History* in which he declared that Africa was not part of history. Hegel died a long time ago, but his spirit still seems to roam "the hallways, and institutions and haunt the syllabi, instructional materials, and journals of Euro-American philosophy." According to Taiwo (1978), "the chilling presence of his ghost can be felt in the eloquent absence and the subtle and not so subtle exclusions in the philosophical exertions of Hegel's descendants" (ibid).

Hegel insisted there was no meaningful African world and that Africa was not a part of the historical world because it lacked any serious movement or development (1956). Furthermore, he contended that any African historical movements occurred in the northern part of the continent, which "belongs to the Asiatic or European world." Viewed through these disturbed frames, Hegel saw Carthaginian history as an important transition in civilization, but he classified Carthage as a Phoenician colony, a part of Asia, not Africa. And he considered Egypt in reference to the passage of the human mind from its Eastern to its Western phase, without its belonging to the African spirit (see Taiwo, 1998).

Hegel (1956) added that what was properly understood as Africa was the unhistorical, undeveloped spirit, still involved in the conditions of mere nature. That is to say, Hegel presented Africa as only the threshold of the world's history. If Hegel could be pardoned for being ignorant of African history and geography, what excuses have modern geographers? According to Taiwo (1998), there are many ways in which Euro-Americans continue the Hegelian exclusion of Africa. For example, the use of such difficult to define and defend phrases as "Africa South of the Sahara," "Sub-Saharan Africa," "Black Africa," is in many ways reflective of Hegelian instance that areas designated as "Africa Proper" must be deemed to be less important to the rest of the world. Are twenty-first-century writers continuing to peddle somewhat disguised Hegelian sentiments?

Because the use of these superfluous phrases is increasingly commonplace, one wonders if it is unconnected to the acrimonious debate on the epidermal character of ancient Egyptian civilization. This debate was sparked by the research and writings of Martin Bernal (1987) and Cheikh Anta Diop (1974). Bernal, professor emeritus of Ancient Eastern Mediterranean Studies at Cornell University, ignited a furious debate in the North American academic community with his explanation of the historiography of Egypt and North Africa and claims that classical civilization in ancient Greece was not indigenous but founded on Afro-asiatic and Semitic cultures. Bernal's Revised Ancient Model is rooted in classical historiography and, specifically, in classical historians' unambiguous recognition of an Egyptian and Phoenician cultural heritage. Bernal contrasts this model with what he has termed the Aryan Model, which is rooted, to some extent, in eighteenth- and nineteenth-century racist revisionisms that posit Indo-European speakers entering the area from the north and an older, indigenous population of non-Indo-European stock as the main cultural source of classical Greece.[1]

Senegalese historian and anthropologist Cheikh Anta Diop, author of numerous texts including *The African Origin of Civilization: Myth or Reality* (1974), had already suggested that archeological and

---

[1] See Martin Bernal's review of Leftkowitz's critique at: http://brynmawr.edu.

anthropological evidence supported his views that pharaohs were of negroid origin (Diop 1989). His groundbreaking work was heavily criticized by the Western academic world, but he consistently held the view that Africans should not be boxed into a rigid corner that classified them as existing somewhere south of the Sahara. He maintained that Africans varied widely in skin color, facial shape, hair type, height, and a number of additional factors, just as other normal humans did. Diop (1974) seriously castigated European scholars who argued for a separate evolution of human types and denied the African origin of *Homo sapiens*.

Diop's argument, which placed Egypt in the cultural and genetic context of Africa, was greeted with wide condemnation, but recent DNA mappings of human genes have proved him right. In addition, Diop's analysis centered on the definition of who is a true "Black" person; he insisted on a broad interpretation similar to that used in classifying European populations as "White." He was of the opinion that his critics used the narrowest possible definition of "Black" in order to place various African groups, such as Nubians, into a European, or Caucasoid, racial zone. Using the "true Negro" approach, he contended that peoples who did not meet the stereotypical classification were mixed with outsiders, or split off and assigned to Caucasoid clusters. Moreover, Diop claimed that his critics were very hypocritical in stating that the Egyptian race was not important to define when they did not hesitate to introduce race under new guises. For example, Diop was of the view that the introduction and use of terms like "Mediterranean" and "Middle Eastern" and the statistical classification of all who did not meet the "true" Black stereotype as some other race were attempts to use race to differentiate among African peoples.

His assessments seem to be true of contemporary social scientists whose efforts to carve out North Africa from the rest of the continent appear to be linked to some disquiet at the evidence of the impact Africa had on the emergence of ancient European civilizations. Confronted by similar evidence of hitherto ignored histories of intellectual, technological, and sociopolitical development in African countries, which cannot be as conveniently carved out and credited to other regions, there has been a tendency to silence, ignore, or attribute such historical accomplishments to mythical European figures.

Is the excision of North Africa an effort to counter the Afrocentric sentiments raised by Martin Bernal and Cheikh Anta Diop, who asserted that Western civilization originated from African peoples who created libraries and universities long before most Europeans had achieved such things? Because there is evidence that the merger of North Africa and Middle East Asia is misleading, human geography appears to have lost its true value and become a tool for prejudicial academic interpretations of the real world.

Conclusion

The cut-and-paste approach to defining the African continent is clearly untenable. As noted earlier, the Sahara Desert is a very large territory and not a single line or a regional boundary. Even if the thesis of an Arab-dominated North Africa is accepted, it should be remembered that there are people of Arab and European descent "below" the Sahara Desert. Where then do these identities and groups fit in this scheme of subdividing Africa into two regions based on race and ethnicity? Using Arab domination of North Africa as a basis for this regional divide is quite unacceptable. Moreover, as Marston et al. (2008) noted, the geographical racial, ethnic, and religious basis for dividing Africa into two world regions is artificial, and it oversimplifies both the cultural and historical distinctiveness of the two regions, their overlap, and their great diversity. It is interesting to see that standard atlases do not create this regional divide, which certain textbook writers have adopted. Perhaps authors such as Ramsay (1999), Edge (2006), Grove (1993), and Adams et al. (1999) have diverted from the mainstream cut-and-paste balkanization of Africa because they have lived in Africa and have extensive working knowledge of the continent. In an age of technology and information systems, it is time to reject the present-day recreation of the Berlin conference, which subverts African realities. The pursuit of academic excellence should be over and above recycled Hegelian prejudices.

REFERENCES

Adams, W.M, A.S. Goudie, and A.R. Orme. *The Physical Geography of Africa*. Oxford University Press, 1999.

Bergman, E.F. and W.H. Renwick. *Introduction to Geography: People, Places, and Environment*, 8th ed. Upper Saddle River, NJ: Pearsons/Prentice Hall, 2008.

Bernal, M. Black Athena: *The Afroasiatic Roots of Classical Civilization*. Vol. 1, The *Fabrication of Ancient Greece 1785 -1985*. London: Free Association Books; New Brunswick, NJ: Rutgers University Press, 1967.

———. Review of *Not Out of Africa: How Afrocentrism Became an Excuse to Teach Myth as History*, by Mary Lefkowitz. *Bryn Mawr Classical Review*, April 5, 1996. http://bmcr.brynmawr.edu/1996/96.04305.html.

Bradshaw, M., G. White, and J. Dymond. *Contemporary World Regional Geography: Global Connections, Local Voices*. New York: McGraw-Hill, 2004.

Clawson, D.L, D.L Johnson, V. Haarmann, and M.L. Johnson. *World Regional Geography: A Development Approach*. Upper Saddle River, NJ: Pearsons/Prentice Hall, 2007.

de Blij, H. M and A.B. Murphy. *Human Geography: Cultures, Society, and Space*, 7th ed. Hoboken, NJ: John Wiley and Sons, 2003.

——— and P.O. Muller *The World Today: Concepts and Regions in Geography*, 3rd ed. Hoboken, NJ: John Wiley and Sons, 2007.

———, A.B. Murphy, and E.H. Fouberg, *Human Geography: People, Place, and Culture*, 8th ed. Hoboken, NJ: John Wiley and Sons, 2007. .

——— and R.M. Downs. *College Atlas of the World*. John Wiley/ National Geographic, 2007.

Diop, C.A. *Presence Africaine*. 1964.

———. *The African Origin of Civilization*. Chicago: Lawrence Hill, 1974.

———. *The Cultural Unity of Negro Africa: The Domains of Patriarchy and Matriarchy in Classical Antiquity* London: Karnak House, 1989.

Edge, Wayne. *Global Studies: Africa*, 11th ed. Dushkin/ McGraw-Hill Sluice Dock, 2006.

Fellmann, J.D, A. Getis, and J. Getis. *Human Geography: Landscapes of Human Activities* New York: McGraw Hill Higher Education, 2005.

Grove, A.T. *The Changing Geography of Africa*, 2nd ed. Oxford University Press, 1993.

Hegel, G.W.F. *The Philosophy of History*, translated by J. Sibree. New York: Dover Publications, 1956.

Hobbs, J.J. *Fundamentals of World Regional Geography*. Florence, KY: Brooks/Cole, 2007.

Lefkowitz, M. *Not Out of Africa: How Afro-centrism Became an Excuse to Teach Myth as History*. New York: Basic Books, 1996.

Lefkowitz, M. and G.M. Rogers, eds. *Black Athena Revisited*. Chapel Hill: University of North Carolina Press, 1996.

Marston, S.A., P. Knox, and D. Liverman. *World Regions in Global Context*, 3rd edition. Upper Saddle River, NJ: Prentice-Hall, 2008.

Merriam-Webster's Collegiate Dictionary, 11th ed. Springfield, MA: Merriam-Webster, 2005.

Oxford New Concise World Atlas New York: Oxford University Press, 2003.

Pulsipher Lydia, M. and Alex Pulsipher Alex. *World Regional Geography: Global Patterns, Local Lives*, 4th ed. New York: W.H. Freeman, 2008.

Ramsey, Jeffres F. *Global Studies: Africa*, 8th ed. Dushkin/ Mcgraw-Hill Sluice Dock, 1999.

Rowntree, L., M. Lewis, M. Price, and W. Wyckoff. *Diversity Amid Globalization: World Regions, Environment, Development*, 2nd ed. Upper Saddle River, NJ: Prentice Hall, 2003.

Stock, Robert. *Africa South of the Sahara: A Geographical Interpretation*, 2nd ed. New York: The Guildford Press, 2004.

Taiwo, Olufemi. "Exorcising Hegel's Host: Africa's Challenge to Philosophy." *African Studies Quarterly* 1, no. 4.

Chapter 4

THE MYTH AND REALITY OF AFRICA
A Nudge Towards a Cultural Revolution

Oyekan Owomoyela

The Persistence of Africa's Pariah-hood

Half a century into the era of African independencies and by the end of the first decade of the new millennium, the place and fortune of the continent and its people in the contemporary world remain as contested as they were in the days of high colonialism. Africa is prominently in the news in its accustomed pose, that is, as the epitome of qualities the shedding of which would confer civilization. Two specific instances serve as illustration. In May 2007, Nigeria, whose onetime characterization as the Giant of Africa has lately been ironically derided, witnessed the transfer of power from one civilian president to another. It was an event that would normally call for celebration as the successful and routine enactment of one of the affirmative rituals of enlightened public life, especially inasmuch as the country had not been able to manage the feat in more than half a century of independence. Instead, the exercise confirmed Nigeria as a reveler in the perversion in which it had mired itself. The international community joined the outraged civil groups within the country in condemning the elections as unworthy of a modern nation. Nonetheless, it embraced their outcome presumably because, after all, it was all happening in Africa, and, again, presumably (and with appropriate apologies to some atypical African countries) it would be unrealistic to expect any better of the continent. On the same day that saw the inauguration of the new Nigerian president, the president of the United States, George W. Bush, in an unrelated development, announced economic sanctions against the government of Sudan for continuing—in defiance of international condemnation—its genocidal campaign against its own citizens in Darfur.

Such events seem to lend credence to views in circulation that Africa is speedily reverting to the habits the colonizers cited as motivating their civilizing irruption into African history and serve as evidence that the termination of their salvational intervention was premature.

The Determinism of Colonization

The ensuing discussion, which is envisioned within the context I have described above, deliberately conceives of colonization as the moment that signaled the radical disruption of African history and development. Although its duration was far shorter than that of the other visitation on Africa authored by Europe—the pernicious trans-Atlantic slave trade that preceded it—unlike its predecessor, colonialism left no part of the continent untouched. It is also fair to contend that while the scourge of colonization was not confined to Africa, its impact on the contemporary fortune of its victims remains corrosive, virulent, and the most recent.

The celebrated Nobel laureate V. S. Naipaul exemplifies the tendency to fixate on Africa as the height of perversion (see Owomoyela 2002, 495). The title story in his *In a Free State*, for instance, is unrestrained in its vilification of Africans as stinking and wantonly bestial, perhaps even worse than the wild dogs that menace Linda and Bobby during their evening walk—ill-trained dogs that have gone rabid after being abandoned by their erstwhile owners, the departed colonizers (Naipaul, 188–189). Tony Moore's cover illustration for the Penguin edition of the book superbly captures the spirit of the work: it depicts two African men running through the countryside in step, stark naked, and posed to show their genitalia to best advantage. For that scurrilous depiction of Africans, the Booker Prize Foundation awarded Naipaul its prestigious fiction prize in 1971, thus signaling to ambitious writers that fame and fortune await authors adept at recycling testimonies to the Otherness of Africans. The message has not been lost on aspiring writers, African and non-African alike.

The African American journalist Keith B. Richburg is another non-European (at least ethnically speaking) powerfully impressed by Africa's supposed odiousness and odoriferousness. On arrival in Nairobi as the bureau chief of the *Washington Post*, he was, like Naipaul, assaulted by "the smell. . . . that's Africa" (Richburg 1998)[1] and after three years at his station, during which he had the unpleasant experience of witnessing the worst of the Tutsi massacre of 1991, he returned home thanking God that his ancestors had been captured and transported as slaves to America and, thus, were redeemed from the native savagery of Africans. "Thank God my ancestor got out, because, now, I am not one of them [Africans]. . . . In short thank God that I am an American" (Richburg 1998, xviii).

Aborted Postcolonialism and a Presumption of Perversity

In such studies as Frantz Fanon's *The Wretched of the Earth* (1968), Edward Said's *Orientalism* (1979), Valentin Mudimbe's *The Invention of Africa* (1988) and *The Idea of Africa* (1994), and Christopher Miller's *Theories of Africans* (1990), to mention only a few, scholars have detailed the pillorying to which colonizing and civilizing agents subjected Africans and African cultures simply because of the felt necessity to indict the victims in order to legitimize their rape. If the colonial enterprise objectified Africa and its cultures in grossly pejorative misrepresentations, which it did, a measure of Africa's uncharacteristic location within postcolonialism is not the mitigation of the misrepresentations but, among other things, their augmentation by non-Western (and sometimes African) collaborators. Moreover, the impression is rife that things African are somewhat unwholesome, and, as such, their castigation requires no justification. The implications are unfortunate.

Let us imagine, as an analogy, a man on trial for certain offenses. The tribunal is quite disposed to be magnanimous because its members believe that the accused has had a rough and deprived upbringing. They are also disposed, however, to believe that the charges against the accused are quite valid, being consistent with what is widely known about him and established patterns of behavior in the applicable circumstances. As far as the tribunal is concerned, therefore, the best course open to the accused would be to admit his guilt and sue for leniency and the opportunity to reform. Let us imagine, then, that he adamantly refuses to plead guilty, *because he is, in fact, innocent of the charges,* and insists on explaining why those who assume his guilt are wrong. As we can imagine, the more he strives to convince the tribunal, the more he is liable to alienate its members, who would consequently become increasingly certain that he is absolutely incorrigible, unredeemable, and deserving of a draconian lesson.

---

[1] Keith Richburg, *Out of America: A Black Man Confronts Africa* (Harvest/HBJ Books, 1998).

Withholding Traditional Vindication

Versions of the tribunal's reaction to the accused man's protestations usually emerge in discussions of African cultural institutions and practices, in particular (but not exclusively) in those pertaining to religion and gender. To illustrate: In a scholarly comparison of the gendered properties of a Western language (in this case English) and an African one (in this case Yoruba), the proffered conclusions seem to brush aside the logical in favor of settled assumptions.[2] The credibility of the scholar involved, moreover, would seem unassailable, inasmuch as he is a native speaker of Yoruba and one whose expertise in linguistics centers on a comparative study of that language and English.

In the study in question, Yisa Yusuf cites Edward Sapir's assertion that language mirrors the values of the culture associated with it and points out that, in light of that assertion, English "ignores and obscures women by using masculine terms (e.g., 'he,' 'man,' and 'chairman') specifically to refer to males and females generically or broadly to refer to human beings in general" (7). Furthermore, he adds, the practice in English usage of placing the masculine term before the feminine in such formulations as "he or she," "man and woman," "brothers and sisters" (with the notable exception of a few like "ladies and gentlemen"), attests to the notion that "the female are an appendage to the male (and less significant than them)" (7). Moreover, in English practice, a man bears the title "Mr." regardless of his marital status, while an unmarried woman is distinguished from a married one by the use of "Miss" for the former and "Mrs." for the latter. In English naming conventions, a woman drops her natal surname upon marriage and assumes her husband's, whereas a man does not change his name, and a couple's children bear the father's surname rather than the mother's. As additional evidence, Yusuf remarks, "while 'master' is a generally elevated term, 'mistress' is a synonym of the thoroughly degrading word 'prostitute'[3] (8). All this validates, in his view, Alma Graham's conclusion that "women are 'assigned to a semantic house of ill fame'" (8). "The examples of linguistic sexism given above," he concludes, "reflect the fact that mother tongue English-speaking societies are sexist . . ." (8).

Yusuf proceeds from that conclusion to develop contrasts between English and Yoruba in a manner that shows the latter to stark advantage. Firstly, unlike their English counterparts, Yoruba pronouns are not gender-specific: the same pronoun ó for example translates as "he," "she," or "it"; secondly, children do not bear surnames in Yoruba practice, only their given names; thirdly, women do not change their names upon marriage, a married woman being "described (not labeled) as the wife of X, while the husband may equally be described as the husband of Y." Given the foregoing evidence, Yusuf concludes that "Yorùbá naming practices, like its pronoun system, are unlike those of English, non-sexist" practices (11). The widespread adoption of the sexist English model in Nigeria, he argues, resulted from the pressure that the colonialists applied through the educational and health care institutions they operated: they insisted that children registering in schools and clinics do so with surnames (i.e., the fathers' names) and demanded that women seeking care at clinics register under their husbands' names. "With time,"

---

[2] The intention in this essay is not to construe Nigeria as synonymous with Africa. I believe, however, that the Ghanaian writer Ama Ata Aidoo had a point when she made Sissie (the heroine of *Our Sister Killjoy*) say in response to a question from her German friend Marija, "Nigeria not only has all the characteristics which nearly every African country has, but also presents these characteristics in bolder outlines" (52). The same caveat applies, with the necessary modifications, to my repeated resort to Yoruba examples.

[3] A mistress is more often used in reference to a "kept woman," secret lover, or a man's long-term sexual partner, especially when he is married to another woman.

he adds, "it has become necessary or expedient in many cases to give children surnames at birth and for wives to adopt their husbands' names" (21).

Further, according to Yusuf, in some governmental institutions, women who retain their maiden names after marriage are refused benefits and privileges normally available to married women, and since such women usually lack the means to buck the system, they are forced "to succumb to patriarchal pressure by adopting their husbands' names" (22). Yusuf offers another quite interesting and telling observation: "Ironically, in Nigeria, it is so-called rural or uneducated women who more commonly avail themselves of the protection of this shield [which Yoruba practice offers to women regardless of their marital status], and it is the so-called educated, elite, or professional women who more generally let down their guards with respect to protective naming." Especially noteworthy, he adds, is the insistence by professional women, like doctors and professors, on adding "Mrs." to titles, such as "Dr." and "Professor" (23).

Yusuf's presentation is, on its face, a defense of traditional African cultures (specifically here with reference to the Yoruba of Southwest Nigeria) against the routine charge that they are inveterately sexist or misogynistic. Before we examine his position in greater depth, it is pertinent to note that evidence of sexist language in a culture does not necessarily define the nature or dimensions of gender relations in that society, nor does the apparent absence of sexist terms in the naming conventions of a language denote gender equality or an absence of patriarchal hierarchies and relations. Unfortunately, presumably because uppermost in his consideration is the championship of women against masculinist oppression, he unexpectedly negates his positive representation of Yoruba culture as more enlightened with regard to gender than most Western commentators concede. Referring back to the opinions of Sapir and Whorf that language is a "symbolic guide to culture" and that altering it correspondingly alters its user's apprehension of reality, he declares, "Both of these deductions . . . are false," adding:

> Traditional Yorùbá thought is sexist in a wide range of ways. For example, in spite of the gender equality in Yorùbá, it is sexistly [sic] thought abnormal, nauseating and, in fact, humiliating *by some of its native speakers* for a woman to lead or perform a superseding feat in comparison to a man. . . . Moreover, though women were not labeled in relation to their husbands, it used to be a widely accepted practice for a widow to be inherited by a male member of the family of her dead husband like the deceased's property (11; emphasis added).

The question immediately arises: to what extent can one fairly generalize about the central values of a culture, *any* culture, on the basis of the beliefs or prejudices of *some* of its members? But more serious issues demand our attention, and to them I will return presently. My presumption-of-guilt analogy is applicable here because although Yusuf is painstaking in providing evidentiary bolster for his discussion of Sapir's and Whorf's theses and how they apply (or do not apply) to English and Yoruba, by contrast, he offers only declarations, without adducing supporting evidence or argument, that Yoruba society (despite what its linguistic conventions suggest) is sexist, that many Yoruba speakers are nauseated by women who excel in comparison with men, and that the practice of inheriting the wives of deceased relatives is indicative of the culture's perception of wives as their husbands' property. The reason for the omission is, I believe, that assurance that the writer's credentials as a Yoruba scholar would suffice to stamp his pronouncements on the subject as reliable. He does illustrate his case for Yoruba sexism with some proverbs from the culture, but then he cites a number of equally sexist proverbs from the English language. Thus, on his evidence, English culture is, in addition to being characterized by sexist vocabulary, also rich in proverbs that denigrate women. On the other hand, key terms in the Yoruba language are seemingly nonsexist, although the culture has sexist proverbs. Yet Yoruba culture, not English culture, draws Yusuf's reprimand.

The readiness to excoriate Africans for sexism is also manifest in Firinne Ni Chreachain's citation of a rather startling statement Ousmane Sembene, the Senegalese dean of African filmmakers, made to her in an interview. Her catchy, one might even say "sensationalist," caption for the published account of the exchange is, "If I were a Woman, I'd Never Marry an African" (1992). A number of African film-makers, especially Francophone filmmakers, have been renowned for their championship of the cause of women, typically by representing African women as victims of assorted forms of abuse at the hands of African men. Representative of their works in this regard are such films as Gaston Kaboré's *Wend Kuuni* (1982), Sembene's *Niaye* (1964) and *Xala* (1974), and Cheick Oumar Sissoko's *Finzaan* and *Guimba* (1990). Ni Chreachain's title immediately suggests, therefore, that Sembene was warning women away from African men because he believes them to be unsuitable as husbands.

The declaration Ni Chreachain attributes to him arouses curiosity about Sembene's point. A careful reading of Ni Chreachain's interview, however, resolves these questions. While Sembene's well-placed concerns for gender equality and women's rights are beyond question, he evidently did not anticipate that his words would be cited out of their context, which was really not a discussion of gender matters. He was lamenting the social and cultural transformations that took hold in Africa during the colonial period and that persist in the postcolonial era. In his youth during colonial days, he said his father used to retire after a hard day's work, with its often humiliating encounters with the White world, to the warm embrace of the family and its usually cozy storytelling sessions. The closeness and togetherness of the family were therapeutic, he added, and the storytelling inculcated traditional values in the young. In postcolonial Senegal, he said, that experience has unfortunately become passé, lost forever to television and cultural imports from America. The traditionally self-sufficient Wolof society, he complained, is now materially "on its knees, waiting for America to provide." He continued,

> Never, ever, ever, in the space of ten years, have I felt so humiliated by my society as now. They [mean-ing Americans] give us "gifts": a few thousand dollars worth of rice—mere chicken-feed. A society can't live on handouts. A society that has its own culture can confront all sorts of calamities and adversities with its head held high. I always say, if I were a woman, I'd never marry an African. Women should marry real men, not mentally deficient ones" (244).

To Sembene, in other words, Africa, postcolonial Africa, is like a deficient man, not a "real man" who can provide for himself and for his family and who would not stoop to seeking handouts from others. To Ni Chreachain's comment and question, "That's very hard. Do you mean Africans in general, or just a particular class? Can young people, for instance, be blamed for being victims of this type of hegemony?" Sembene answers, "It's not the fault of the young people: they are reflections of my own short-comings. What I find humiliating is the incompetence of those who make speeches in the name of a people whom they sell into prostitution. . . ." The postcolonial leaders of his country, in his view, have prostituted the people (and themselves) to outsiders in return for contemptuous and contemptible charity.

The interview with Sembene ranged over a variety of issues, including migrancy, for example, on which the interviewee had much to say, but the words he employed to express his frustration with Africa's postcolonial leaders resonated most powerfully with Ni Chreachain, arguably because they corroborated a stereotypical image of African men.

As I will now show, just as Sembene's words and intention were not accusatory of African men as misogynists, we can search for a better understanding of the practice Yusuf reads as disparaging to women. It must be stated that while there is evidence of patriarchal social relations and women's oppression in every African society from Egypt in North Africa to the Cape of South Africa, such hierarchies certainly share much in common with the realities of women's lives in Europe and other parts of the world. But, more important, what I argue here is that in contrast to the tendency to assume that Africa has produced an atavistic and obdurate form of male chauvinism in contrast to enlightened Western societies, a more careful analysis reveals layers of philosophical, cultural, religious, and linguistic dimensions to gender relations that contradict popular notions of uniformly retrogressive gender relations in Africa.

Despite its many problematic dimensions and outcomes, the arrangement described as wife inheriting (whereby the male survivors of a deceased man "inherit" his wives) was originally designed, in part, as a practical device to ensure that bereaved women were not left bereft of care. Yusuf is not alone in mistaking the rationale of the tradition (which, by the way, is not uncommon among African cultures): the famous Francophone novelist Mariama Bâ had earlier misrepresented the Wolof version of it in her celebrated work, *So Long a Letter* (1989, 57; see Owomoyela 1996, 137). There are certainly numerous social arrangements that have lost some of their original meanings and value or become subject to myriad manipulations in the varied transitions that have accompanied our contemporary age. But it is imperative that we isolate and evaluate the context and logic behind the emergence of such customs before using them to impose generic signifiers on the contemporary societies from which they evolved. It is also important that we avoid the temptation to lump fifty-three countries, which are themselves differentiated by religion, political systems, and social conditions, under assumptions of particular gender constructs. In light of that, it must be noted that the linguistic signifiers in Yoruba language do not necessarily represent the realities of Herero in Namibia, Sukuma in Tanzania, or Berber in Libya. Similarly, a Harare professional woman's experience of wife inheriting, as an exploitative imposition and a nod to male domination, might well be at variance with that of a woman from a small agrarian community that has maintained a battery of additional indigenous laws designed to protect women and children affected by such a tradition.

Gender and Postcolonial Pessimism

Kwame Anthony Appiah's discussion of postcolonialism and postmodernism characterizes the prefix "post-" in both as a "space-clearing gesture" (149). The essay centers around the 1987 show titled *Perspectives: Angles on African Art* (organized by Susan Vogel, curator at the Center for African Art in New York) and much of it concerns the question of voice and who has the opportunity to pronounce on African art. This question is important in the discourse of postcolonialism if only because one of the strategies through which colonialism effected its debilitating impact on the colonized was by appropriating their voice, silencing them, and thus preventing them from counter-colonialist distortions of their cultures and images. In Robert Young's conception of postcolonialism's utility,

> if you are someone who does not identify yourself as western, or as somehow not completely western even though you live in a western country, or as someone who is part of a culture and yet excluded by its dominant voices, inside yet outside, postcolonialism offers you a way of seeing things differently, a language and a politics in which your interests come first, not last (2).

He elaborates that postcolonialism focuses its interest on the marginalized and those—for example, refugees and migrants (114)—whose cultural identity has fallen victim to the forces of global capitalism. In the two views (Appiah's and Young's), then, postcolonialism is a space-clearing project that enables hitherto suppressed or marginalized knowledges to find expression and that provides a forum for the "Other" to come to voice and recover from the tarnish its image had accrued in the silence of colonization. Significantly (for my purpose in this essay), Young's further elucidation of postcolonialism is germane:

> The framework of postcolonial politics is such that gender constitutes one of its enabling conditions. The inseparable centrality of gender politics to postcolonialism can be simply illustrated by contrasting it to the phrase "women in third-world politics" . . . The masculist assumption there is that there is a ready-made constituency, third-world politics, and that women can be adequately catered for by seeing how they operate within it (114–15).

The observation is useful in a number of ways: it acknowledges the centrality of gender to the postcolonial discourse, and it indicates (in the last sentence) why the important subject of gender could become a minefield that the wary might prefer to avoid.

Herein lies one explanation for the observation Appiah once made that in Africa "postcoloniality has . . . become a condition of pessimism" (155). Africa's experience of postcolonialism is thus ambiguous, to say the least. By that I mean that, while its history of colonialism qualifies it to claim the recuperative dividends of postcolonialist interventions, its customary depiction (as well as that of its cultures), from a dominant Western perspective, has had the consequence of interdicting its enjoyment of those dividends.

Postcolonialism is productive, one can confidently assert (at least with reference to Africa), to the extent that it is in concert with feminism, an assertion that finds corroboration in the operations of several professional organizations in which the influence of women's mobilizations makes feminism, or women's interests (since not all African women embrace the designation), arguably the most determinate consideration of their politics and programming. Recognizing perhaps the potential for an exacerbated gender conflict to derail the recuperative aspirations of Africa's postcoloniality, the Malawian poet Felix Mnthali penned a controversial plea to "my sister" in his poem "Letter to a Feminist Friend." It begins:

> My world has been raped
> looted
> and squeezed
> by Europe and America

Now, he continues, the satiated women of Europe and America have turned on their own menfolk, castigating and castrating them all "from the cushions of a world / I have built!" He asks why they should be allowed to come between him and his "sister":

> *You and I were slaves together*
> uprooted and humiliated
> Rapes and lynchings . . .

No, he says, we must not allow that because "too many gangsters / still stalk this continent. . . ." He then concludes:

> When Africa
> at home and across the seas
> is truly free
> there will be time for me
> and time for you
> to share the cooking
> and change the nappies—
> till then,
> first things first!

—Ogundipe-Leslie, 498–99

The celebrated African feminist Molara Ogundipe-Leslie quotes the poem in its entirety as the epigram for her rejoinder, "Nigeria: Not Spinning on the Axis of Maleness," her contribution to *Sisterhood Is Global: The International Women's Movement Anthology* (1984). In the piece, Ogundipe-Leslie avoids Mnthali's arguments that European women (obviously meaning feminists) were assaulting an African world already battered by Europe and America and that all Africans should present a united front to the external threat, after defeating which they could turn to internal squabbles, but instead she critiques Mnthali for using masculine personal pronouns to claim that it was *his* world that was raped and that *he* built that world. She then turns to what she describes as a statement "irritatingly typical of male supremacists everywhere: to wit that other issues abound which are more urgent than the liberation of women." She adds, "Somehow, miraculously, you can liberate a country and later turn your attention to the women of that country. . . ."

Those who feel that Mnthali includes all Africans among those he wishes to rescue from European persecution have, in turn, critiqued Ogundipe-Leslie's argument. They have argued that Mnthali was not trivializing the issues that African women have raised against men but was simply using the literary device of minimization, or understatement. His resort to the trope of dishes and nappies has been read to suggest that the issue between African women and their men is not insurmountable but amenable to easy resolution once the external oppression is defeated. It does not suggest that old ideas about the gendered assignment of roles with regard to dishes and nappies are inviolate. At the very least, the debate makes plain the vibrant contestations around gender equality and oppression, which contrast with the typical image of female passivity and silenced subservience. Several scholars have also argued for a careful examination of gender relations in precolonial Africa, stressing the evidence of deteriorating conditions for women as a result of the structures, legislations, and notions of women's place imposed by European colonists. Such changes gave men various advantages over women, which men in the new states of Africa have inherited. This does not indicate that gender relations in precolonial Africa were universally equitable or void of exploitative traditions such as prevailed globally. But important to note are the ways in which the contact with a presumably civilizing West also played a critical role in the deterioration of women's voice, roles, and rights in many parts of the continent.

The Pervasive Disparagement of Africanity

The tendency to dismiss traditional African knowledge is not confined to gender matters, nor is it limited to Europeans and other Westerners. For example, despite his admirable championship of the use of African languages as a means of celebrating and revitalizing African cultures, Ngũgĩ wa Thiong'o[4] seems to undermine his own position in his monumental *Wizard of the Crow* (2006). Elaborating on the contents of *Magnus Africanus: Prolegomenon to Future Happiness, by the Ruler,*—The Ruler's prescription for the education of Aburria's youth—Ngũgĩ writes:

> Teachers would be strongly encouraged to impart to schoolchildren the virtues of the past, of unquestioning obedience. Instead of using the word *past,* they would talk about African modernity through the ages, and they should talk of the leading figures in Africa's march backward to the roots of an authentic unchanging past as the great sages of African modernity (622).

And on the day The Ruler's opus was published, "he issued a special decree that traditional African healers would no longer be called sorcerers, diviners, or witch doctors. Henceforth, they would be called specialists in African psychiatry, in short, afrochiatrists, and they would be allowed to call themselves *Doctor*" (622). Here, one hears echoes of claims that traditional Africans considered their universe to be unchanging, "finished," or, as Naipaul would say, "completed" (Crocodiles, 92), and the derision of "ethnophilosophy," "ethnohistory," and the like. Ngũgĩ's dismissal of what he calls "Afrochiatry" feels somewhat reminiscent of Marcien Towa's outrage that Africans presume to describe their deistic beliefs and associated practices as religions and their ratiocinations as philosophy, thus insulting the Western institutions and practices so designated. The derision of Afrochiatry is also kin to the ribbing to which Naipaul subjected Georges Niangoran-Bouah's discipline of "drummologie" and especially to Naipaul's version of African cosmology in "The Crocodiles of Yamoussoukro," according to which Africans possessed such things as "aeroplanes, cars, rockets, lasers, satellites," not in the ordinary, visible world, though, but "in the world of the night, the world of darkness" (Ngũgĩ 174).

Neither Naipaul's nor Ngũgĩ's dismissal of their respective targets follows upon an analysis of their claims or procedures; indeed, the notion of Afrochiatry is no less plausible than what might be termed "Eurochiatry," a.k.a. "psychiatry," or the study, prevention, and treatment, as developed and practiced in the West, of mental illnesses and emotional and behavioral problems. One of the most palpable signals for an automatic aversion to Afrochiatry is the prefix "Afro-," which is, like "ethno-," a presumed marker of inferiority and illegitimacy in the Western scheme. A serious investigation will obviously uncover marked similarities in and differences between the work of mental health practitioners using indigenous methodologies in African countries and that of those practicing Western-derived methods of psychiatric practice, whether in Africa, Europe, or any other region. But it is troubling that we fail to uncover the assumptions that underlie the *automatic* mockery of notions of mental health practices developed within the African continent, despite evidence that, increasingly, psychiatrists trained in Western methodologies are seeking to derive instruction for community-based care, diagnosis, and treatment from "traditional medicine" practitioners in Africa, Asia, and other regions. The slew of collaborative ventures, conferences, and changes in care regimes suggests that so-called Afrochiatry has

---

[4] Ngũgĩ wa Thiong'o.

been legitimized beyond Ngũgĩ's parody. Of course, it would be unwise to ignore the main target of Ngũgĩ's ire—the manipulative leadership eager to subvert and silence, to emulate and seek to legitimize social agents by investing them with Western properties and associated terminologies.

Perhaps our larger concern should be with ensuring we move away from knee-jerk reactions and simplified quests for change that avoid a more reflective engagement with context, meanings, and outcomes. For instance, Ghanaian philosopher Kwasi Wiredu's critique of traditional African funerary rituals, in which he lambasted the ceremonies that often "involve large alcohol quaffing gatherings" as sheer irrational wastefulness (1984, 155–56), might well express his concern about the impact of such financial waste on those left behind. Indeed, when contrasted with the long-term impact of loss of a breadwinner on widows and children and the widespread absence of insurance and social security benefits, his dismissal of wastefulness appears well placed. However, those seeking to understand how these ceremonies are placed within societal context of survival and recovery must go beyond an image of a witless group of sodden alcoholics drowning their sorrows to examine the larger structure and philosophy surrounding funeral ceremonies in such societies.

In many such societies, funeral ceremonies incorporate some critical elements for managing grief and bereavement. The communal elements of support and long-term mutual grieving, as well as convivial celebration in the case of the elderly who have left behind a legacy of heirs, seem indicated in the capacity for emotional recovery. In some instances, the departed is invoked during the ceremony or their physical presence, commanded, as in the Yoruba *egúngún* (masquerades). The notion of a continuing and more powerful presence of the departed might be instrumental in protecting the bereaved from avaricious exploitation and in endowing often-vulnerable heirs with some life-sustaining support from peer, religious, or gender-based associations. When the financial outlay far outweighs the emotional or psychological benefits, there is a case to be made for change, but it is counter-productive to simply dismiss or ignore the efficaciousness of communal support ceremonies and rites of birth, marriage, and death without a careful examination of the reasons why they have been embraced and sustained over time.

Correcting Misrepresentations, Recovering Beneficial Ways

The foregoing observations serve as the basis for my contention that but for the unwarranted perception of the constituents of African culture(s) as being of dubious rational or moral value, they would quite legitimately constitute a quarry from which the repertoire of ideas beneficial to humanity could be profitably augmented.

To mine such a quarry of ideas does not require a wholesale endorsement or adoption of constructs that might be unsuitable in a changing age or context. But it would provide a realm of possibility for reconsidering how gender justice might evolve in specific contexts. Consider, for example, the notion of equitable division of labor and apportioning of economic resources and proceeds between husband and wife as described by the pioneering sociologist of the Yoruba, N.A. Fadipe. According to the scheme, responsibilities are divided between the spouses, as they were in the predominantly agrarian societies in traditional Yoruba land where the woman marketed the produce and received a commission from the proceeds (88). Hers exclusively were, for instance, the palm kernels that she shelled and sold to European traders (88). (The kernels were as much an important source of oil as the pericarp from which palm oil is derived.) Husband and wife also split equally the earnings from the dye materials that the indigo plants yielded (88–89). In Fadipe's words, man and wife did not necessarily form a mutually complementary productive unit. The wife was free to follow her own trade independently of the husband, and it was an obligation on the part of the husband to supply her with the means of doing this. Her earnings were her own exclusive property, although the husband was obliged to feed her and give her a separate room. She had, however, to provide herself with clothing (88).

Clearly this is not applicable to many women in Africa today, but it is a reminder of the multiple mistakes made by modern nongovernmental organizations that unintentionally created projects that left the proceeds of work firmly in the hands of male members of the society even when the work was conducted by women. With increased awareness of and attention to some underlying indigenous methods of women's mobilizations, work, and methodologies of rights protection, there are signs that new struggles can be based on an acknowledgment of existing structures and philosophies rather than the notion of an African void. Examples abound of women who have excelled in different endeavors in contemporary times and in recent memory and who are, and were, celebrated by men and women alike. These include Madam Tinubu and Beere Ransome-Kuti, who in Wole Soyinka's *Aké: The Years of Childhood* led the women's revolt against taxation in Abeokuta during World War II (195–230) and Efunseta Aniwura, reputedly the most renowned woman[5] in Ibadan history and the subject of both a play and a movie in her honor by Akinwunmi Isola (see Smith 2005).

With perhaps more consistency than many other world regions, Africa has produced highly influential female leaders, from ancient Egypt to South Africa, including queens, chiefs, priestesses, and warriors. As far back as the eighth century, for instance, the Berber prophetess Kachina led the resistance to the Arab invasion. The female prophetess Nehanda of Zimbabwe led her people in resistance to British imperialism under Cecil Rhodes during the late nineteenth century, and Queen Mother Yaa Asantewa fought against British colonial conquest in the Asante kingdom of present-day Ghana. The early twentieth-century example of the Aba Riots, or Women's War, among the Igbo of Nigeria made plain the ability of women in various parts of the continent to use associative power based on genderized social formations to protest foreign or domestic decisions that impacted them negatively.

The point here is not that African societies are immune to the male-dominated political and social arenas of other global regions, but that there is a basis and historicity for African women's agency and voice, which, in turn, can and should be plumbed for the benefit of the continent and the world. The existence of influential female leaders in historic or contemporary arenas, again, does not presuppose the absence of oppressive gender relations, but it should give ample pause to those who presume that Africa presents a given landscape of misogynous patriarchal realities that contrasts unfavorably with Western progress in this area. Indeed, writing about the status of women vis-à-vis men in *Gelede: Art and Female Power among the Yoruba*, Henry and Margaret Drewal reiterate the observations P.C. Lloyd published a couple of decades earlier, to wit:

> It is not inconsequential that the market is a major setting of social and economic activity involving primarily women. Trading is probably the most common profession among women in Yoruba society. Indeed the market is controlled by women, its administrative head, the *Ìyálóde*, holds a position on the king's council of chiefs. Women are economically independent, and through trading they can acquire greater wealth and higher status than their husbands (Drewal and Drewal 1990, 10).

---

[5] Efunseta's mode of economic and political power and control would probably allow her to be described somewhat as a "terror."

Because there is no evidence that high achievement and renown imperiled the social relations or marital status of all the women cited above, surely a more careful scrutiny of the religious, cultural, political, social, and other contexts that bore such contradictory evidence of women's roles is required by those wishing a more meaningful understanding of the continent.

A Usable Example of African Enlightenment

Chinua Achebe's rejection, in his famous "manifesto" in "The Novelist as Teacher" (1976, 59), of Western claims to a redemptive mission in Africa is well known, its import being, of course, that Africans have much that is worth embracing and may be, in many cases, more desirable than what the Europeans imposed. Let us consider as an example a central feature of Yoruba jurisprudence, which is encapsulated in the proverb, *A kì í ti kóòtù bò ká sòré.* The saying, which states simply that one does not return from a law court and resume a friendship, is a reference to the adversarial nature of Western litigation. Two adversaries in a court case hardly continue a prior friendship because one side usually wins at the expense of the other. A Yoruba sage might employ the proverb to advise a person in a dispute that instead of taking it to a modern, Western-style court, he or she should seek a settlement in a traditional forum. There, the emphasis would not be on simply assigning guilt and innocence and, accordingly, assessing the penalty or restitution. Guilt would be determined, of course, and any necessary and commensurate redress mandated, but there the matter would not rest. The overarching consideration for the adjudicators would be that life goes on after even the most divisive of quarrels. The emphasis in their adjudication would, therefore, be more on arbitration and conciliation. In urging the latter on the two sides, the sages would probably cite two related proverbs, the first of which would remind the two sides that while *ahón àtehín a máa jà* (even the tongue and the teeth sometimes quarrel), the lesson of the second, *a kì í rí arémájà; a kì í rí ajàmárèé* (there is no friendship without quarrel; there is no quarrel without reconciliation), must be taken to heart.

Belief in the superior efficaciousness of such a juridical approach to the punitive, adversarial preoccupation of Western-style adjudication prompted Mark Drumbl's commentary on the international community's application of the latter in the trials that followed the Rwandan genocide of 1994. In "Punishment, Postgenocide: From Guilt to Shame to Civis in Rwanda," he argues that

> the key variable that should determine policy responses to genocide is the social geography of the postgenocidal society. . . . It means that trials and imprisonment will not be necessarily the methods of choice to rebuild the rule of law in postgenocidal societies. Rather, the importance to attach to trials, punishment, retribution, redistributive reparations, forgiveness, public inquiries, amnesties, truth commissions, lustration, reconciliation, and other approaches within the constellation of postgenocidal policies depends on the social geography of the postgenocidal society in question (1225).

My argument is that, in this instance, some of the juridical alternatives in certain African societies (as the notion of restorative justice advocated by Archbishop Desmond Tutu for post-apartheid South Africa) might prove more productive in some situations than the methods of the adversarial Western legal system because they seek to repair social ruptures and restore harmonious coexistence in the group. It is true that even in the West, there are traditions of restorative justice beginning to tug at the dominant legal methods, with some lawyers seeking training in reconciliatory law, and it is equally certain that in many African societies, the legal system is not necessarily oriented toward reconciliation nor is such an approach necessarily indicated in every case. The focus of the argument here remains the same: there is a danger in the tendency to imagine that African countries are void of critical traditions and legislative and other structures that could help global society reframe, or at least rethink, its approach to handling critical issues around social, economic, and political organization.

In my opinion, two conclusions at least are warranted. One is that we have a duty in our time to challenge the widespread misconstruction of African institutions and ethos in order to ensure that we do not bequeath a besmirched image of Africa to posterity by default. Such a duty does not entail a denial of the exploitation, oppression, and grave sociopolitical and economic problems in the continent. However, it recognizes such crises not as indicative of a peculiar African difference, but as located in a concrete past and present, as part of the continuing realities of our global community, the interactions between external and internal constituents, and the struggle over power and its use. The second conclusion is that the routine and automatic pathologization of African identity does a disservice not only to Africa and Africans, but also to the human community at large, inasmuch as it forecloses the possibility of the enrichment of the common human stock with African input. The change I advocate is, therefore, for the benefit of Africa and humanity.

REFERENCES:

Achebe, Chinua. "The Novelist as Teacher." *Morning Yet on Creation Day*. Garden City, NY, 1976.
————. *No Longer at Ease*. New York: Anchor, 1994.
Aidoo, Ama Ata. *Our Sister Killjoy, or Reflections from a Black-Eyed Squint*. Harlow, Essex: Longman, 1977, 2006.
Appiah, Kwame Anthony. *In My Father's House: Africa in the Philosophy of Culture*. New York: Oxford University Press, 1992.
Bâ, Mariama. *So Long a Letter*. Harlow: Longman, 1989.
————. *Scarlet Song*. Harlow: Longman, 1998.
Drewal, Henry John and Margaret Thompson Drewal. *Gelede: Art and Female Power among the Yoruba*. Bloomington: Indiana University Press, 1990.
Drumbl, Mark. "Punishment, Postgenocide: From Guilt to Shame to Civis in Rwanda," *New York Law Review* 75 (October 2000): 1221–1326.
Fadipe, N.A. *The Sociology of the Yoruba*. Ibadan: Ibadan University Press, 1970.
Fanon, Frantz. *The Wretched of the Earth*. New York: Grove Press, 1968.
Johnson, The Reverend Samuel. *The History of the Yorubas: From the Earliest Times to the Beginning of the British Protectorate*. Lagos: C.M.S. (Nigeria) Bookshops, 1921.
Miller, Christopher L. *Theories of Africans: Francophone Literature and Anthropology in Africa*. University of Chicago Press, 1990.
Mudimbe, V.Y. *The Invention of Africa: Gnosis, Philosophy, and the Order of Knowledge*. Bloomington and Indianapolis: Indiana University Press, 1988.
————. *The Idea of Africa*. Bloomington and Indianapolis: Indiana University Press, 1994.
Naipaul, V.S. *Among the Believers: An Islamic Journey*. New York: Vintage, 1982.
————. "The Crocodiles of Yamoussoukro," in *Finding the Center: Two Narratives*. London: Andre Deutsch, 1984.
Ngũgĩ wa Thiong'o. *Wizard of the Crow*. New York: Pantheon, 2006.
Ni Chreachain, Firinne. "If I Were a Woman, I'd Never Marry an African." *African Affairs* 91, no. 363 (April 1992): 241–247.

Nzenza-Shand, Sekai. *Songs to an African Sunset: A Zimbabwean Story.* Melbourne: Lonely Planet Publications, 1997.

Ogundipe-Leslie, Molara. "Nigeria: Not Spinning on the Axis of Maleness," in *Sisterhood is Global: The International Women's Movement Anthology,* edited by Robin Morgan, 498–504. New York: Anchor, 1984.

Okome, Mojubaola Olufunke. "African Women and Power: Reflections on the Perils of Unwarranted Cosmopolitanism." *Jenda: A Journal of Culture and Women Studies,* http://www.jendajournal.com/jenda/v011.1/okome-.html, ISSN 1530–5686, 2001.

Owomoyela, Oyekan. *The African Difference: Discourses on Africanity and the Relativity of Cultures.* Johannesburg: Witswatersrand University Press; New York: Peter Lang, 1996.

———. "The Mata Kharibu Model and Its Oppositions: Conflicts and Transformations in Cultural Valuation," in *The Transformation of Nigeria: Essays in Honor of Toyin Falola,* edited by Adebayo Oyebade, 483–509. Trenton, NJ: Africa World Press, 2002.

Richburg, Keith B. *Out of America: A Black Man Confronts Africa.* San Diego: Harcourt Brace, 1998.

Said, Edward W. *Orientalism.* New York: Vintage, 1979.

Smith, Pamela J. Olúbùnmi. *Efúnsetán Aníwúrà, Ìyálóde Ìbàdàn and Tinúubú, Ìyálóde Ègbá: Two Yorùbá Historical Dramas.* Trenton, NJ: Africa World Press, 2004.

Soyinka, Wole. *Aké: The Years of Childhood.* London: Rex Collins, 1981.

Wiredu, J.E. "How Not to Compare African Thought with Western Thought," in *African Philosophy: An Introduction,* edited by Richard A. Wright, 149–162. Lanham: University Press of America, 1984.

Young, Robert J.C. *Postcolonialism: A Very Short Introduction.* Oxford: Oxford University Press, 2003.

Yusuf, Yisa Kehinde. "Language: Mirror, Weapon and Shield." Inaugural Lecture Series 187. An Inaugural Lecture Delivered at Oduduwa Hall, Obafemi Awolowo University, Ile-Ife, on February 14, 1906. Ile-Ife: Obafemi Awolowo University Press, 2006.

Part II

THE POLITICAL HISTORIES OF AFRICA

In the second section of the book, scholars tackle the political histories of the continent, offering us a brilliant rereading of the African past. The U.S. K–12 debates over the "origins of civilizations" support the importance of historical discourse as a tool for the construction of politics. While viewed by some negatively as "the culture wars," in effect, the debates really represent the struggle by third world peoples for the inclusion and correct interpretation of their histories in the mainstream public agenda. Africa also is in a constant struggle for the inclusion of its histories in world history, on the one hand, and, on the other, the reinterpretation of African politics over an epistemological tradition that has been dominated by colonial ethnographers and more recently by non-Africans. Indeed, while it is now accepted, based on archival and DNA evidence, that the continent of Africa is the location of the origins of humanity, a historical rendition of Africa's past has yet to match this crucial fact.

New historical scholarship seeks to restore the sense of African political identity taken from African peoples through colonization and slavery, thus serving to present an understanding of the tremendous variety of human experience in the past. The success of such an undertaking rests in part on its deliberate inclusion of a comparativist global approach that contextualizes the African past alongside an effective rendering of the world, especially the European world, and one that does not leave the reader with the idea of a fossilized and unchanging African history against (the familiarity of) Western modernizing transformation. Here, we aim to create a clear awareness of a constantly contemporizing continent's historical dynamics, which are best perceived through the lenses of equivalent developments and conditions in the rest of the world.

Histories of Africa often veer between selective discussions of small-scale societies or of precolonial African states and empires famed for extraordinary accomplishments in long-distance trade, exploration, architecture, medicine, and scholarship, and for military, cultural, and political sophistication. African and Arab scholars have long published substantive works describing African expeditions to the western side of the Atlantic Ocean, including descriptions of the exploration of the New World by the Mali Empire around 1312. The chronicles of Jenne, Gao, Ghana, Kanem Bornu, Great Zimbabwe, the Nubian and Egyptian empires, and many others, clearly attest to such outstanding precolonial development over thousands of years preceding European control. However, the devastating horrors of the trans-Saharan and trans-Atlantic trade in enslaved Africans have created debates about the nature of social organization, class, and rights within these powerful African states. They have also raised questions about the nature of colonial violence, local resistance or complicity, postcolonial struggles for independent statehood, and the nature of the old and new Diasporas formed through such a turbulent past.

Paul Tiyambe Zeleza, in "Towards the Globalization of African History: A Generational Perspective," provides an intimate and compelling journey into African histories and the study of those histories through disciplinary frames. Zeleza is widely recognized as one of the leading authorities on African economic history. His book, *A Modern Economic History of Africa*, won the 1994 Noma Award for Publishing in Africa, the continent's most prestigious book award.

Zeleza provides a framework for exploring the African past and aruges that historians have handled African history either as one continuum interrupted only slightly by colonialism or as defined largely by the colonial experience. The latter understandably emerges from two different orientations, or positions. The first represents the view of colonialists who believed the European incursion was the marker for any serious consideration of African history. The second represents the young African nationalists whose focus on the colonial period derived from a passionate anger and determination to expose the impact of imperialist, colonialist, nationalist, Marxist, and feminist histories.

He insists, "African historians must take seriously the challenge of placing African history in world history." As Zeleza reminds us, such a task has already been advanced by Joseph Inikori who, in keeping with earlier works by Walter Rodney and Eric Williams, has challenged Eurocentric apologists for the slave trade by demonstrating "convincingly in his award-winning book, *Africans and the Industrial Revolution in England*, that international trade based on the Atlantic slave system was pivotal to the world's first industrial revolution in England between 1650–1850." Thus, he entices the reader into seeking a deeper understanding of Africa and its diasporas, establishing Africa's vantage point as a "central player" in the dramas of global history. Rather than prescribing a closed or completed sense of history, Zeleza suggests we are actually on the cusp of an intellectually exhilarating and invigorating journey into new historiographical work to be conducted by those in the new generation who take up the challenge.

In the following chapter, Kwabena Akurang-Parry simultaneously captures the enormity of the transatlantic slave system and its devastating impact on Africans displaced in the diaspora and the continent, as well as the unsung role of African abolitionists in the struggles to permanently eliminate the Atlantic slave system. Kwabena Akurang-Parry is a poet and historian and coauthor of *African Agency and European Colonialism: Latitudes of Negotiations and Containment* (2007). His work to restore historical agency through a serious engagement with documentation is testament to the silences that have informed the traditional hegemonic reading of African histories. Akurang-Parry does not attempt to speak for Africa as much as expose the vibrancy of agency and mobilizations that speak to this much-ignored aspect of slavery systems in the New World. His chapter, "Remembering the Unforgotten History of Enslavement and African Contributions to Abolition in Africa," rethinks the staple conclusion that abolition in Africa was the work of European and American institutions and agents, and provides an epistemic basis for the study of transoceanic epochal abolitionism by applying theory and empiricism to the framing of African agency in Africa's own liberation and its contributions to global abolitionism.

Akurang-Parry's study of African resistance to slavery provides an important complement to the work of Joseph Inikori, whose keenly researched comparative examination of servile social categories in medieval Europe and precolonial Africa has answered many questions about the social institutions in the precolonial world. On the basis of much evidence, he concludes that the societies of medieval Europe were closer in all respects to those of precolonial Africa and that the New World slave societies that were specifically organized for the large-scale production of commodities for an evolving capitalist world market were new forms of slavery.[1] His study of slavery and serfdom in England and Russia up till the second half of the nineteenth century is pre-dated by a body of literature on the spread and nature of slavery across Europe, where Portugal, England, Greece, and Spain practiced domestic slaveholding and trading; the Sicilian region in Italy, Naples, Venice, Crete,

[1] Inikori, Joseph E. "Slaves or Serfs? A Comparative Study of Slavery and Serfdom in Europe and Africa," in *The African Diaspora*, Isidore Okpewho, Carole Boyce Davies, and Ali Al'Amin Mazrui, eds. (Bloomington: Indiana University Press, 1999).

and other parts of Greece, and the Spanish kingdom of Valencia were well known centers of slave trading activities supported by numerous seaports that dealt in human captives, including that of the Russian Black Sea. However, scholars of European history define servile categories in medieval Europe to include a study of serfdom, slaves, and other dependant categories.

In this context, Inikori's powerful contribution to the literature is located in his insistence that the terminological laxity in defining all dependent and servile categories in Africa as symbolizing slaving societies is a deliberate form of socio-political and racial Othering that serves to provide exculpation for the horrors of transatlantic slaving. Inikori notes that students of European history often define serfs as *non-slave* dependent people who possess the means of production of their own land large enough to provide a potential income that could support a household (with children and old members), have enough free time to produce for themselves, are allowed to retain for their own use some of the income earned, and whose residences are physically separated from their lords' estates. On the basis of the evidence of social organization in precolonial African societies, he concludes that both slaves and serfs, properly defined, can be encountered in African societies at some point in time and in specific regions and that the majority of the servile population were serfs and not slaves if the terminology applied to Europe is applied equally to such African societies.

Inikori's evidence includes societies in which the people described as slaves by scholars had so much freedom that it would not be appropriate even to call them serfs. For instance, in the Puna and Kuni societies of modern Congo, "slaves" labored the same way as their free counterparts, they could hold any office in society, and they were usually married to free spouses from the lineage of their masters. Inikori notes that in scholarship on Africa, whenever there is a "dependent cultivator" situation, scholars are quick to label all such African peoples as slaves, despite the fact that often these workers owned their own land and could provide for their families. Additionally, "intergenerational mobility" among slave populations in Africa—the tendency for the children of slaves to become free persons—meant that the slave class in Africa often could not reproduce itself, largely because children of slaves normally did not remain in slavery. They either become free or became serfs.

Apart from the clove plantations of East Africa, controlled by Arab slaveholders, most of what scholars have called slave plantations in Africa were serf villages. Consequently, since the slavery experienced by Africans in the Americas introduced a new form of human commodity use, Inikori concludes that the eagerness of western scholars to use "slave" terminology regarding servile groups in precolonial Africa, but not in medieval Europe, emerged from the need of slave traders and colonialists to perpetuate the savage image of Africans and defend their colonizing enterprise against abolitionists in the 18th century. Akurang-Parry's innovative research in this book, however, shifts our attention from this ongoing debate to the exciting acknowledgement of the existence and substantive involvement of the African intelligentsia and populace in resisting and abolishing slavery in the continent and Diaspora.

Peyi Soyinka-Airewele, coeditor of the current volume and author, with Kelechi Kalu, of *Socio-Political Scaffolding and the Construction of Change* (2008), tackles the colonial and postcolonial question of Africa head on in chapter 7, "Colonial Legacies, Ghosts, Gulags, and the Silenced Traumas of Empire." She begins by invoking the tragic events that led to the assassination of the first and only freely democratically elected leader of the Democratic Republic of the Congo, Prime Minister Patrice Lumumba, whose heroic, brief, and tragic rule reminds us of the insidiousness of colonial violence and its legacy in facilitating the continued political, economic, and socio-cultural issues that grip contemporary African affairs. Linking Africa's recent political past with its present, Soyinka-Airewele asserts that the colonial experience evokes a certain discomfort due to the fact that political independence occurred only fifty years ago for some and in the last two decades for others, including Mozambique, Angola, Zimbabwe, Namibia, and South Africa.

There is no doubt about the truth of her assertion. President Barack Obama's July 2009 speech to the Ghanaian parliament in Accra inspired a distinctly negative reaction in many Africans. The president seemed to imply that Africa's underdevelopment had less to do with colonialism and neocolonialism and more to do with corruption, ethnicism, and Africans' colonialist victimhood mentality.[2] Contrarily, for Soyinka-Airewele, Africa's colonial past is indeed linked to its postcolonial present in ways that indict colonialism. In today's African "postcolonies," she writes, there is an acute awareness that efforts to change are entrapped in structures, identities, and relations molded by forces and agencies of the colonial past.

In excavating the complexities of the colonial conquest of Africa, Soyinka-Airewele's contribution presents a unique historical reconstruction of the African precolonial landscape. Highlighting the work of James Graham,[3] Soyinka-Airewele illustrates the conquest of the continent as having occurred on socially, economically, and politically developed terrain, which had well-established relations with foreign powers. She quotes Graham to explain the rationale and intention behind colonialism. The European invasion interrupted the development of large-scale political economies in Africa. During this period, Africans' interests and opinions were disregarded.

Significantly, Soyinka-Airewele identifies three kinds of colonial violence and attributes them with the course of contemporary African politics: Epistemic violence employs pernicious forms of racial imperialism to construct colonial relationships with the colonized. Physical violence includes a range of atrocities, from scorched-land policies, mass executions, concentration camps, large-scale pogroms, and well-documented, egregious forms of torture that continue to traumatize the memories of contemporary Africans. The third type, colonial violence is European colonists' construction of an intensely antidemocratic, violent, deeply racist, hierarchical, and exclusionary state from which Africa's current leadership emerged.

Given this damning indictment of colonialism's impact on Africa, whither the postcolony in 2010, ponders Soyinka-Airewele. She is optimistic. Citing the main character from Ferdinand Oyono's *Houseboy*,[4] she concludes that Africa's postcolonial future is with Africans who seek to change the colonial structures that inhibit change.

Finally, in an intimate and poignant discussion of "The Intersection of African Identities in the Twenty-First Century: Old and New Diasporas and the African Continent," William Ackah asks and answers the question, what is Africa to me? as a way to explore what it means to be an African in the diaspora in the twenty-first century. Author of *Pan-Africanism—Exploring the Contradictions: Politics, Identity and Development in Africa and the African Diaspora* (Ashgate, 1999), Ackah illustrates the ways that new encounters, parallels, and divergencies of experience between the old and new diasporas are affecting new relationships between Africans and Africans in the diaspora. Connecting the trauma of rupture with the construction of identities, cultures, and new political economies in Africa, Ackah concludes that, in the twenty-first century, the dichotomy between old and new diasporas, respectively based on the enslavement process and postcolonial migrations, will become less relevant as new points of convergence and difference in the diaspora stem from the personal stories that diverse diasporan Africans from Thailand to Trinidad tell about their experiences of dispersal at home.

---

[2] Stephen Gowans, "Obama's Africa Speech: Lies, Hypocrisy, and a Prescription for Continued African Dependence" http://gowans.wordpress.com/2009/07/17/obama%E2%80%99s-africa-speech-lies-hypocrisy-and-a-prescription-for-continued-african-dependence/ July 17, 2009, accessed 10/13/2009.

[3] James D. Graham is a special contributor to *Reframing Africa*. His work includes "Political Development in Historic Africa," in Vincent B. Khapoya's *The African Experience* (1994, 1998).

[4] Ferdinand Oyono, *Boy!* Trans. John Reed. London and New York: Macmillan, 1966.

Chapter 5

TOWARDS THE GLOBALIZATION OF AFRICAN HISTORY
A Generational Perspective: Commentary

Paul Tiyambe Zeleza

As I advance in age, the temptation to reflect on my own past as an African intellectual becomes more tempting. In this essay, I would like to reminisce about African history as encountered by students, researchers, and teachers of my generation. As we all know, the past is never entirely about the past; it is always framed through the prism of the present with an eye to the future. Hence, the title of my essay: "Towards the Globalization of African History."

In discussing the development of African historiography, or any academic field for that matter, it is important to note that the economies and cultures of knowledge production are an integral part of complex, sometimes contradictory, but always changing institutional, intellectual, ideological, and individual dynamics and predilections that unfold at interlocking national and transnational, or local and global levels. The production of disciplinary histories serves to commemorate the founders, socialize newcomers, and establish boundaries and guideposts for the future. I am particularly fond of such histories for institutional reasons, as a past academic administrator who was paid to keep track of where African studies was going; for intellectual reasons, given my fascination with both the history of ideas and the history of knowledge-producing institutions; and for personal reasons, as an African scholar based in the global North who is forced to communicate with different intellectual communities and negotiate multiple intellectual traditions on both sides of the Atlantic.[1]

I begin the paper with autobiographical sketches as a way of taking disciplinary stock, of reflecting on the long, tortuous journey that the discipline of African history has traveled over the past few decades. I will then discuss the institutional dynamics of African historiography and the phases that the field has undergone, which reflect the changing fortunes of African universities—the centers of production, dissemination, and consumption of academic history. This will be followed by an examination of the intellectual dimensions—the ideas, theories, and analytical paradigms—in African historiography. Needless to say, the interpretive frameworks or perspectives developed in African historiography over the past half century have been greatly influenced by the prevailing ideological hegemonies and tendencies. I would like to close with a few thoughts on future directions of the field and a research agenda for world history.

---

[1] For a detailed examination of the disciplinary, interdisciplinary, and international contexts of African knowledge production, see Paul Tiyambe Zeleza, *The Study of Africa*; vol. 1, *Disciplinary and Interdisciplinary Encounters*; vol. 2, *Transnational and Global Engagements* (Dakar: Codesria Book Series, 2006–2007).

A Brief Institutional History of African Historiography

I went to university in my home country, Malawi, in 1972 and graduated four years later with a major in history and English, then spent a year as a teaching assistant before proceeding for a master's degree in African history and international relations in England from 1977 to 1978, and finally ended up in Canada for my doctorate between 1978 and 1982. My trajectory as a student was fairly typical of my generation: Many of us did our bachelor's degrees in Africa's newly established, postindependence universities; the University of Malawi was merely seven years old when I enrolled. Then we found ourselves trekking for our graduate studies to Western Europe or North America, where we were trained in newly established African studies programs by newly minted Africanist scholars, who belonged to the same cohort as the relatively young and eager lecturers who taught us back home. We differed from the generations immediately before and after us: The former were pioneers in the establishment of African history as a respectable academic field, and they did most of their training in the 1950s and 1960s in overseas institutions because higher education was still in its infancy during these turbulent years of decolonization. Those who came after us in the 1980s and 1990s could receive their entire education on the continent, although they confronted universities undergoing the crises of structural adjustment. This is to suggest that, as students, my generation was educated during the golden years of African universities and African historiography.

In an intriguing comparative analysis of the development of African history at six universities in Africa, Britain, and the United States between the 1950s and 1990s (University of Ghana, the University of Dar es Salaam, the University of Cape Town, the School of Oriental and African Studies [SOAS], Northwestern University, and the University of Wisconsin–Madison), Esparanza Brinzuela-Garcia has identified three phases, what she calls the formative years, the golden era, and the decades of crisis.[2] The formative years, the period from the late 1940s to the early 1960s, were characterized not only by staffing and curricular challenges as the disciplinary architecture of the field was being laid, but also by the excitement of building a new interdisciplinary field, all underpinned by the rise and eventual triumph of African nationalism. During the golden era, from the mid-1960s to the late 1970s, the discipline matured; as new universities were founded across Africa, vibrant historiographical schools emerged, African studies programs grew in the United States and Britain, the range of African history courses expanded, and undergraduate and graduate student enrolments increased rapidly. No sooner had African history become consolidated than the third phase set in, from the 1980s to the 1990s, when the discipline's institutional standing began eroding due to budgetary constraints tied to the collapse of the welfare state in the global North and the developmentalist state in the global South and the rise of neoliberalism. African countries and universities were hit especially hard.

The institutional changes were tied to new ideological and intellectual currents. History and historians increasingly fared less well as the nationalist fervor of the 1950s and 1960s gave way to the developmentalist preoccupations of the 1970s and the deflationary structural adjustment prescriptions of the 1980s and 1990s. The effect of all this was that African historiography became ideologically and theoretically fragmented. More important, perhaps, is the sad fact that African universities lost their lead in the production of African historical knowledge and became increasingly subordinated to Northern

---

[2] Esparanza Brinzuela-Garcia, "The History of Africanization and the Africanization of History," *History of Africa* 33.1 (2006): 85–100.

institutions, to their detriment and the development of the entire discipline. Also, research focus shifted from the *longue durée* of African history to contemporary, twentieth-century history (the colonial and postcolonial eras).

I can vouch for these trends from my experience as a student and a young lecturer. In my student days, Africanist historians from Western Europe and North America were not taken seriously until they had cut their academic teeth teaching in African universities. And I recall the days when publishing in African historical journals was mandatory for Africanists. For example, no one studying Kenya, to use the country on which I did my PhD research, was taken seriously without publishing in the *Kenyan Historical Review,* which last appeared in 1978. Today, there are Kenyanists who hardly go to Kenya let alone interact with Kenyan historians. On the other hand, in the 1960s and 1970s African graduate students eagerly returned home to take up positions in the expanding universities, assured not only of middle-class comforts and respectability, but also eager to write their beloved ethnic groups, nations, and continent into the empirical and theoretical disciplines and to strip them of their Eurocentric blinders and conceits. When I finished my doctorate in 1982, the idea of working in North America appeared absurd, so I went to teach in Jamaica for two years, then Kenya for six years.

From the 1980s, these trends were reversed as African universities became less attractive to Northern Africanists worried about the tightening job markets at home as White male–employment privilege was eroded by an affirmative action that increasingly brought White women and racial minorities to American campuses. At the same time, growing numbers of Africans educated in the global North opted to stay there. One of the few empirical studies on the rates of return of African PhDs trained in North America between 1986 and 1996, conducted by Pires et al., shows that variations were engendered by different patterns of economic growth and the state of political stability in specific African countries, the relative size of immigrant populations in the host countries, nature of sponsorship, discipline, and age of the graduate students.[3] The likelihood of return was higher for those in the older age cohorts, for those in the life sciences compared to those in the humanities, including history.

As for the temporal focus of my generation's historical research, we were clearly more enamored of colonial than precolonial history. Nationalist historians of the generation of Ade Ajayi, Bethwell Ogot, Adu Boahen, and Cheikh Anta Diop were wont to reduce colonialism to an episode, a digression, a footnote, which altered African cultures and societies only slightly, and to emphasize continuity in Africa's long history. They were clearly reacting against imperialist historiography, according to which colonialism marked the beginning of history in Africa. My generation of historians, schooled by the nationalist historians, never doubted the historicity of Africa but was enraged by the continued dehumanization of Africans.

Not surprisingly, we focused our intellectual energies on unraveling the structures and processes of oppression and exploitation that engendered this. Capitalism and colonialism became our chief culprits. So we largely abandoned research on (although we, of course, taught) the histories of Africa before the European contact. Instead, the depredations of Africa's integration into the world system, from the slave trade to colonialism to neocolonialism, loomed large in our constructions of African history. The iconic representation of this historiographical tendency was Walter Rodney's *How Europe Underdeveloped*

---

[3] Adelino Serras Pires, *A Memoir of Adventure and Destruction in Deepest Africa* (New York: MacMillan, 2001).

Africa.[4] We were critical of both imperialist and nationalist historiographies, but we failed to realize the depth of our intellectual debts to the Eurocentric and Afrocentric paradigms: Like the former, we were preoccupied with the European intervention and impact and, like the latter, with African agency and adaptations.

Intellectual Trends in African Historiography

During the past thirty-two years since I started studying African history seriously as a student in Malawi, Britain, and Canada, and later as a teacher in Jamaica, Kenya, Canada, and, for the past eleven years, the United States, it seems to me the field has undergone four major trends in terms of the dominant theoretical paradigms.[5] African historiography is, of course, much older going back to the very origins of the discipline. It has been suggested that African historiography has undergone three broad phases, each of which embodied various tendencies.[6] The first is the pre–fifteenth-century era dominated by three successive and coexisting traditions: The Christian tradition, as represented by St. Augustine, the great theologian from present-day Algeria, who articulated perhaps the first philosophy of history in *The City of God* and saw history as inevitably universal and metahistorical in that it entails movement toward divine providence. The ecclesiastical histories of Christian Africa extend to Ethiopia, where chronicles such as *Kebra Negast* (Glory of Kings) were produced to proclaim dynastic glory in a religious idiom.

The second tradition is the Islamic, as represented by Ibn Khaldun from present-day Tunisia, whom many regard as one of the greatest historians of all time and whose history of the world provided the first serious challenge to providential history. His work postulated a cyclical theory of history, anticipated modern historical methodology, and influenced interpretations of Maghrebi history well into the twentieth century. It is to Khaldun that we owe one of the earliest surviving fragments of the history of the Mali Empire. Muslim scholars from North Africa and West Africa produced numerous works on West African societies, among them the famous *Tarikh al-Sudan* and *Tarikh al-Fattash,* both produced in Timbuktu in the seventeenth century, and the *Kano Chronicle* and the *Gonja Chronicle,* produced in modern-day Ghana in the eighteenth century. In East Africa, there are similar chronicles, such as the *Kilwa Chronicle.* It is not an exaggeration to say that comprehension of Arabic and Ajami writings (writing using Arabic script) is fundamental to understanding African history and historiography. Out of this conviction, a few years ago, I started taking Arabic classes. I haven't made much progress.

---

[4] Walter Rodney, *How Europe Underdeveloped Africa* (Washington, D.C.: Howard University Press, 1982).

[5] The literature on African historiographies is vast. For a sample see, Frederick Cooper, "Africa and the World Economy," *African Studies Review* 24, no. 2/3 (1981): 1–86; R. Hunt Davis, "Interpreting the Colonial Period in African History," *African Affairs* 72, no. 289 (1973): 383–400; Mamadou Diouf, *Historians and Histories: What For? African Historiography Between State and the Communities* (Amsterdam and Calcutta: Sephis and CSSSC, 2003); Toyin Falola and Christian Jennings, eds., *Sources and Methods in African History: Spoken, Written, Unearthed* (Rochester, NY: University of Rochester Press, 2003); Bogumil Jewsiewicki, "African Historical Studies: Academic Knowledge As 'Usable Past' and Radical Scholarship," *African Studies Review* 32, no. 3 (1989): 1–76; Bogumil Jewsiewicki and David Newbury, *African Historiographies: What History for Which Africa* (Beverly Hills, CA: Sage, 1986); John Lonsdale, "States and Social Processes in Africa: A Historical Survey," *African Studies Review* 31, no. 2/3 (1981): 393–422; and Paul Tiyambe Zeleza, *Manufacturing African Studies and Crises* (Dakar: Codesria Book Series, 1997).

[6] Paul Tiyambe Zeleza, "Development of African History," in *Encyclopedia of Twentieth Century African History*, edited by Paul T. Zeleza and Dickson Eyoh (London and New York: Routledge, 2003), 143–149.

The third tradition is what I call the "griot." Griots—known by different names in various societies—were highly trained custodians of oral traditions and narratives. Their recollections sought to link the past and the present, construct collective worldviews and identity, educate the youth, express political views, and provide entertainment and aesthetic pleasure. The production of oral traditions often involved performance based on a participatory ethic. From Thomas Hale's fascinating history, it is clear griots had many other functions besides being genealogists and historians; they were also advisers to rulers, patrons, and other members of society and were spokespersons, diplomats, mediators, interpreters and translators, musicians, composers, teachers, exhorters, warriors, witnesses, praise-singers, and ceremony participants during namings, initiations, courtships, marriages, installations, and funerals. In West Africa, griots first emerged at least a thousand years ago, and, since then, their role has changed.[7]

During the second period, from the fifteenth to the nineteenth centuries, two new historiographical traditions emerged alongside the three identified above, which continued to exist and develop and engaged the new traditions in complicated ways. I call these new traditions the "Eurocentric" and the "vindicationist" traditions. Many of the early European writers visiting African coastal regions did not set out to produce histories as such, although their works were later used as historical sources. But several self-consciously historical works were produced. From the late eighteenth century throughout the nineteenth, the volume of European travel literature grew rapidly. Some of the travel writings sought to incorporate historical accounts. Much of this work was unapologetically Eurocentric, especially as the Atlantic slave trade expanded and the need to justify it grew. Some scholars have stressed that many Portuguese writings, for example, were based on unreliable sources, were interpreted out of context, or were full of literary embellishments and fantasy because renaissance historiography put greater emphasis on telling a story well, in an erudite fashion, and on literary embellishments, than on relating the facts or adopting a critical approach to sources.

Africa was increasingly portrayed as "primitive," and as the drums of imperialism began beating, its salvation was seen to lie in European overlordship or outright conquest. Eurocentrism was given philosophical imprimatur in Hegel's *The Philosophy of History* in which he declared, categorically, that Africa "is not a historical continent; it shows neither change nor development" and that the portion that showed historical light, according to his judgment, namely, North Africa, was not really a part of this benighted continent.[8] Thus was born the racist truncation of Africa into the sub-Saharan cartographic contraption. In the meantime, North Africa was encapsulated into the Orientalist paradigm, dissected so brilliantly by Edward Said in his book *Orientalism*, the foundational text of postcolonial studies.[9]

In reaction, Western educated scholars in West Africa and the African diaspora began producing histories that emphasized African civilizations and achievements. The vindicationist tradition found a powerful voice in Olaudah Equiano's *The Interesting Narrative of the Life of Oluadah Equiano*.[10] Even more scholarly and combative were the works of the great Liberian scholar Edward Blyden, whose trilogy—*A Vindication of the African Race, The Negro in Ancient History,* and *Christianity, Islam, and*

---

[7] Thomas Hale, *Griots and Griottes: Masters of Words and Music* (Bloomington and Indianapolis: Indiana University Press, 1998).

[8] G.W.F. Hegel, *Phenomenonology of Spirit* (Monial Barnasidas, 1998).

[9] Edward Said, *Orientalism* (New York: Vintage Books, 1978).

[10] Olaudah Equiano, *The Interesting Narrative of the Life of Olaudah Equiano: or, Gustavus Vassa, The African* (New York: Norton, 2001 [1793]).

the Negro Race—set the tone for much twentieth-century nationalist and Pan-Africanist thought and historiography.[11] Besides these large civilizational histories, national histories were also published by West African intellectuals, such as Samuel Johnson's influential and classic *History of the Yoruba*.[12] From the diaspora came the writings of Alexander Crummel and, in the early twentieth century, those of W.E.B. Dubois, most memorably his *The World and Africa*,[13] and those of W.L. Hansberry, who conducted lifelong research on the image of Africa and Africans held by classical Greco-Roman writers.[14] These histories defended the humanity and historicity of Africans. I recall the electrifying impact some of these works had on me when I first read them as an undergraduate student.

The third period emerged in the twentieth century and was characterized, in the colonial and postcolonial academy, by four traditions, what I call the "imperialist/Eurocentric" tradition; the "nationalist" tradition; the "radical" tradition, incorporating Marxist, dependency, feminist, and environmental approaches; and the "post-" traditions—postmodernism and postcolonialism. Each of these approaches differed in their interpretations and methodology and in the type and way they used sources. Imperialist and nationalist historiographies represented almost diametrically opposed views of African history; to the former, African history began with the arrival of Europeans and was a narrative that turned colonialism into a decisive moment, while to the latter, African history stretched for millennia, and colonialism was a parenthesis.

Consequently, imperialist historians mostly discussed, in positive light, the policies of colonial governments and the activities of colonial auxiliaries, from European merchants to missionaries to settlers. When Africans appeared in their narratives, they condemned their societies and cultures or chronicled their Westernization or modernization. Those who resisted colonial conquest or colonial rule were depicted as atavistic, while those who collaborated or accepted the colonial regime were praised for their foresight and wisdom. In fact, in-depth study of African societies was largely left to anthropology, which with its functionalist-positivist paradigms and ethnographic present, exonerated, if not extolled, colonialism. The methodological forte of nationalist historiography lay in its discovery of new sources of data. Oral tradition, historical linguistics, natural sciences, and historical anthropology joined written and archaeological sources prized by Eurocentric historiography as valid sources for historical research and reconstruction.

While imperialist historiography ignored North Africa, it found an auspicious home in apartheid South Africa. The English-Afrikaner divide among the ruling White minority found expression in the historiographical divide between largely liberal English historians and nationalist Afrikaner historians.[15] From the 1920s, when liberal historiography became dominant in the English-speaking universities, the country was seen through the prism of race and culture, and its history was interpreted as a series of racial and cultural interactions between the Afrikaners, Africans, and British in the context of a changing and modernizing economy. In this historiography, Afrikaners became the eternal villains

---

[11] Edward Blyden, *A Vindication of the African Race, The Negro in Ancient History* (New York: 1862 [1857]) and *Christianity, Islam, and the Negro Race* (Edinburgh; University of Edinburgh Press, 1967 [1887/1888]).

[12] Samuel Johnson, *History of the Yoruba* (CSS, 1997).

[13] W.E.B. Dubois, *The World and Africa* (International Publishers, 1979).

[14] W.L. Hansberry, *Africa and the Afro-American Experience: Eight Essays* (Washington, D.C.: Howard University, 1981).

[15] For succinct analyses of South African historiographies see, H.M. Wright and Alan Cobley, "Does Social History Have a Future? The Ending of Apartheid and Recent Trends in South African Historiography," *Journal of Southern African Studies* 27, no. 3 (2001): 618.

behind the development of apartheid, while the English, ignoring the role of British capital in the construction of South Africa's racial capitalism, were portrayed as enlightened. Africans, for their part, appeared generally innocent or were portrayed with undisguised paternalism, their Herculean struggles against settler colonialism left unacknowledged. In the meantime, nationalist Afrikaner historians concentrated on chronicling the travails and triumphs of the Afrikaner nation, pitted against the imperialist English and "primitive" Africans.

But the production of historical knowledge was not an imperial monopoly even in the darkest days of colonialism. This is because colonialism and its various projects were always contested. The perennial struggles over the organizations of the colonial economy, politics, and culture created spaces for the production of anti-imperialist historical knowledge by the "traditional" historians, Western-educated historians, and Islamic historians. In short, the griots did not die, nor did the Islamic schools and scholars disappear. The children who went to the colonial schools later turned into anticolonial historians. There were also colonial critics in the imperial metropoles themselves. The relationships between these groups were complex and contradictory and varied from place to place and changed over time. Their methods, audiences, and objectives also differed in some cases and overlapped in others.

Independence created favorable conditions for the production of nationalist historiography as national universities were established, research funds became available, historical associations were formed, journals launched, and publishers scrambled for the latest research findings. Famous schools emerged, most prominently the Ibadan school, which denounced the shortcomings of missionaries and colonial governments and launched an influential series, and the Dar es Salaam school, which popularized dependency approaches. Nationalist historians chronicled the rise and fall of Africa's ancient states and empires, long-distance trade, migrations, and the spread of religions, and they critiqued colonial policies, celebrated the growth of nationalism, and reincorporated Egypt and North Africa into the mainstream of African history. They gave the fragile new states historical identity and a legitimizing ideology.

The nationalist perspective influenced historical writing in Europe and North America, where oral and other sources were increasingly used. African history itself was incorporated into university history syllabuses, and specialized African studies centers mushroomed, beginning with a lectureship in African history at SOAS in 1948 and the establishment in 1962 of the *Journal of African History,* developments that were replicated across Western Europe, the former Soviet Union, and its client states in Central and Eastern Europe, as well as in the United States, where African studies and history, long confined to the Historically Black Colleges and Universities (HBCU), finally entered the segregated corridors of the historically White universities, beginning with Northwestern, where the Program in African Studies was established in 1948 to address national security concerns. Before long, African studies, as chronicled in Zeleza's two-volume study, *The Study of Africa,* had spread to Canada, the Caribbean, and Asia.[16]

From the 1970s, the nationalist school began to face challenges. Critics charged that nationalist historiography focused on the "voices" of the ruling classes, rather than those of the "masses." They also pointed out that nationalist historiography was too preoccupied with showing that Africa had produced organized polities, monarchies, and cities, just as Europe had. So African scholars wrote African history by analogy and subsumed it to European history, failing to probe deeper into the historical realities of African material and social life before colonial rule. As for the colonial period, nationalism was made

---

[16] Zeleza, *The Study of Africa.*

so "over determining" that only feeble efforts were made to provide systematic analyses of imperialism, its changing forms, and their impact, not to mention the processes of local class formation and class struggle. These critiques were widespread by the time I entered graduate school, and we took enormous pride in attacking nationalist historiography.

It was in this context that Marxism became increasingly popular as a paradigm of social science research and that I wrote my dissertation on "Dependent Capitalism and the Making of the Kenyan Working Class During the Colonial Period," a title that wears its influences loudly.[17] Marxist influence grew with the triumph of radical liberation movements in the early 1970s and the adoption of Marxism as a developmentalist ideology by several African political parties and states and by Western intellectuals who were dissatisfied with bourgeois liberalism and Western imperialism in the Third World. The Marxist historians examined the processes of production, social formation, and class struggle, as well as the complex mediations and contradictory effects of imperialism in modern Africa.

Marxist historiography, broadly defined, came in different theoretical and national configurations. There were many Marxisms and Marxists, some of the labels worn by choice; others, by association, either in self-congratulation or derision. Some of the Marxist-inspired work was schematic, doctrinaire, and pretentious. Theoretically ambitious scholars tried desperately to fit Africa into linear Marxist modes of production and, when that did not work, to invent their own tropicalized modes. Or they saw the encounter between Africa and Europe as an articulation of modes of production. Nevertheless, some of the work was rich and enlightening. Particularly impressive were the studies on labor and workers, agriculture and peasants, and the changing structures of Africa's incorporation into the world economy.

Hardcore Marxists often did not regard dependency theorists as fellow travelers. Indeed, there was much theoretical and ideological bloodletting between the two, but they shared more affinities than differences in their emphasis on exploitative economic structures and processes. The Marxists preferred to concentrate on the internal dynamics of African societies, while the dependistas were more interested in the external dynamics. Many, of course, combined both approaches as I tried to do. Before long, radical historiography broke into the settler laagers of southern Africa, where a new breed of radical historians challenged liberal historiography. They began to demystify the Portuguese myth of lusotropicalism and racial tolerance and to map out the growth of the South's racial capitalism, although some seemed more inclined to emphasize class than race.

Despite some of the fine work the various approaches inspired, there was one glaring omission—their coverage of gender and women's history. The underrepresentation of women could be found virtually in all the major historical texts written up to the 1980s, as I chronicled in a survey of dozens of continental, regional, national, and thematic histories.[18] From the turn of the 1970s, feminist historians began to challenge women's marginalization in African historiography, a challenge buoyed by the growth of the women's movement. Some African feminists relentlessly attacked the epistemological hegemony of Western feminism, criticizing the very foundational categories of Western feminist scholarship, those of "gender," "woman," and the "body," arguing that these categories must be subjected to critical analysis and the need to privilege the categories and interpretations of African societies. Perhaps the most

---

[17] Paul Tiyambe Zeleza, "Dependent Capitalism and the Making of the Kenyan Working Class During the Colonial Period" (PhD Dissertation, Dalhousie University, 1982).

[18] Paul Tiyambe Zeleza, "Gender Biases in African Historiography," in *Engendering the Social Sciences in Africa*, edited by Ayesha M. Imam, Amina Mama, and Fatou Sow (Dakar: Codesria Book Series), 81–115.

famous interventions were those made by Ifi Amadiume[19] and Oyeronke Oyewumi,[20] whose books *Male Daughters, Female Husbands* and *The Invention of Women: Making African Sense of Western Gender Discourses*, respectively, soon achieved canonical, if highly controversial, status.

From the 1980s, there was an explosion of feminist-inspired histories, many of which simply sought to restore women to history—to record women's activities and experiences in the conventional themes of African historiography—and some to engender African historiography as a whole. The early feminist histories focused mainly on women leaders; the impact of religion on women; the role of women as slaves, peasants, and traders; the changing forms of marriage and kinship; and the constructions of gender and sex roles. Some of this work concentrated on the precolonial era, but much was on the twentieth century in which the impact of colonialism featured prominently. They examined how different groups of women were affected by the imposition of colonial rule and by the combination of colonial and indigenous patriarchal ideologies. By far, the topic that attracted the most attention was that of women's resistance to colonialism and women's participation in nationalist struggles. For the postcolonial period, much of the research was conducted within the women-in-development paradigm, which later gave way to the women-and-development and gender-and-development frameworks. I jumped on the bandwagon with a book on women in the Kenyan labor movement, recasting my neo-Marxist work.[21]

More recent work has focused on issues of sexuality, constructions of gender identities, and colonial representations.[22] According to Zine Magubane, African sexuality and its control and representations were central to ideologies of colonial domination.[23] In colonial discourse, female bodies symbolized Africa as the conquered land, and the alleged hyper-fecundity and sexual profligacy of African men and women made Africa an object of colonial desire and derision, a wild space of pornographic pleasures in need of sexual policing. Sexuality was implicated in all forms of colonial rule as an intimate encounter that could be used simultaneously to maintain and erode racial difference and as a process essential for the reproduction of human labor power for the colonial economy. Both demanded close surveillance and control, especially of African female sexuality. Feminist studies on the construction of gender identities and relations have helped spawn a growing literature on the creation and transformation of colonial and postcolonial masculinities. It looks at how masculinities were produced and performed in different institutional contexts—from the state, church, and school, to the workplace and the home—each with its own gender regime and power relations and in different locations, rural and urban.[24]

---

[19] Ifi Amadiume, *Male Daughters, Female Husbands* (London: Zed, 1987).

[20] Oyeronke Oyewumi, *The Invention of Women: Making African Sense of Western Gender Discourses* (Minneapolis: University of Minnesota, 1997).

[21] Paul Tiyambe Zeleza, *Labor, Unionization and Women's Participation in Kenya: 1963–1987* (Nairobi: Friedrich Ebert Foundation, 1988).

[22] See, for example, the following influential texts, Anne McClintock, *Imperial Leather: Race, Gender, Sexuality and the Colonial Contest* (New York: Routledge, 1995); and Frederick Cooper and Ann Laura Stoler, eds., *Tensions of Empire: Colonial Cultures in a Bourgeois World* (Berkeley, CA: University of California Press, 1997).

[23] Zine Magubane, "Sex and Sexuality," in *Encyclopedia of Twentieth-Century African History*, edited by Paul Tiyambe Zeleza and Dickson Eyoh (London and New York: Routledge, 2003), 481–484.

[24] See, for example, Lisa A. Lindsay and Stephan F. Miescher, eds., *Men and Masculinities in Modern Africa* (Portsmouth, NH: Heinemann, 2003); and Lahoucine Ouzgane and Robert Morrell, eds., *African Masculinities: Men in Africa from the Late Nineteenth Century to the Present* (New York: Palgrave Macmillan, 2005).

For its part, environmental history began to reshape the way various periods and phenomena in African history were understood as dynamic processes involving complex interactions between humans and habitat, nature and society, and history and geography. Physical environment and human activity interact in such a way that people's creativity and thought produce places as much as places produce people's cultures and identities. Ideologies of power affect the landscape deeply and vice versa. Several environmental approaches can be identified.[25] There were the merrie Africa and apocalyptic perspectives in which the nationalist and imperialist historians battled it out. To the former, Africa before the colonial fall was a tropical Garden of Eden, and they blamed the colonial intervention for undermining age-old and sound environmental management capacities. The latter celebrated the beneficial impact of European environmental knowledge, management, and policies upon the allegedly environmentally unsound African agrarian and pastoral practices.

Influenced by postcolonial ideas, many environmental historians increasingly stressed the complexity and contradictions of environmental change and the variability of outcomes, that environmental transformations generated during different historical moments, including colonialism, were both negative and positive, they were not always intended, and they were simultaneously products of creative and failed adaptations. Interrelated work has dwelt on African environmental ideas, ideologies, movements, and conflicts.[26] Included are environmental feminists, who seek to decipher the gendered perceptions and constructions of environmental changes and adaptations. Many of the newer perspectives have not been initiated by historians (some are quite suspicious of them), but the days of environmental blindness and binaries are now happily gone.

The 1980s and 1990s also saw the rise of the fourth set of approaches and paradigms inspired by the rise of the "posts," approaches that shared a distrust of the "metanarratives" of nation, class, and sometimes gender, and the positivism and dichotomies of modernist history. They insisted on the hybridity, contingency, decenteredness, ambivalence, and the centrality of discourse in historical experience. History and historians have had a complex and problematic relationship with the "posts," one characterized by advocacy, ambivalence, and antagonism. To many African and Africanist historians, the claims of the "posts" often sound both familiar and strange. They are familiar to these scholars because they have spent their entire careers deconstructing Western and modernist claims to truth, to the universal, and to chronicling the clashes and convergences of cultures and the loss of certainties. The "posts" seem strange to the same historians because many of them believe passionately, bred as they were with

---

[25] For succinct summaries of African environmental historiography, see William Beinart, "African History and Environmental History," *African Affairs* 99 (2000): 269–302; and William Y. Osei, "Environmental Change," in *Encyclopaedia of Twentieth Century African History*, edited by Paul Tiyambe Zeleza and Dickson Eyoh (London and New York: Routledge, 2003): 188–194. For two influential early texts, see David Anderson and Richard Grove, eds., *Conservation in Africa: People, Policies and Practice* (Cambridge University Press, 1987) and Helge Kjekshus, *Ecology Control and Economic Development in East African History* (London: Heinemann, 1977).

[26] An influential figure on indigenous environmental management capacities is Paul Richards, *Indigenous Agricultural Revolution: Ecology and Food Production in West Africa* (London: Unwin, 1985). James Fairhead and Melissa Leach, *Misreading the African Landscape: Society and Ecology in a Forest Mosaic* (Cambridge University Press, 1996) offer a compelling and controversial critique of conventional environmental historiography by arguing that human activities during the course of the twentieth century in parts of West Africa contributed to improved environmental conditions rather than degradation. For a relatively recent collection on the social dynamics of African environmental history, see, William Beinart and JoAnn McGregor, eds., *Social History and African Environments* (Athens: Ohio University Press 2003).

the enduring dreams of African nationalism—self-determination, development, and democratization—in the necessity of progress, in the possibilities of historical agency.[27]

To the antagonists, the "posts" were dismissed as the latest in a long line of disempowering theories and discourses that came at a time when Africans, who had long been silenced, had begun to act as the subjects rather than objects of history. They were suspicious of the globalist ambitions of "post" theorizing and cultural critique and its deflationary discourse on Africa, which seemed to glibly dismiss African difference and world significance by trying to absorb it into the West's self-indulgent modernity, with what Kwaku Korang calls its monocentricism, monolingualism, monologism, and monovision.[28] On the other hand, the accommodationists, with their cosmopolitan internationalism, sought to Africanize the "posts," to find an African habitation for them, based on the conviction that Africa is inescapably immersed in the West's material and cultural economy and assimilated into its cognitive and discursive hegemony, thanks to the imperial-colonial intervention. Some historians in post-apartheid South Africa and in Francophone Africa seized on the "posts" with alacrity, either in gestures of intimate familiarity with Western intellectual fads or for refuge from dealing with the structural deformities of the postcolonies and postapartheid South Africa.

Korang advocates Kwame Appiah's more nuanced posture—that the "posts" ought to facilitate both Africa's interrogation of the world and its interrogation by the world. The "posts" should translate African difference for the world, not the difference of the exceptionalism of the nationalists, but the difference of the same. Africa is an integral part of modern, transnational culture, and Africa and the West have mutually constituted each other.[29] Appiah seeks to rehabilitate an ethical universal, a modernist humanism that is negotiated between world cultures that are contaminated and inscribed with each other. The power of the "posts" lies in the extent of their ability to promote such a project, to bring together the Africa-for-the-world and the Africa-for-itself. To achieve this, requires, Korang insists, that the accommodationist position be vigilantly self-aware, protected by the armor of a healthy rejectionism.

I tried to understand the "posts" and other new paradigms, such as globalization, by writing a series of papers and a book, which left me more confused than ever. It would seem to me that, beneath all the theoretical babble, the impact of the "posts" on historiography has been more one of theoretical intent than one of actual practice. This is largely because the institutional constraints, demands, imperatives, procedures, and practices of historiographical production—teaching, training, research, publishing, and employment—remain wedded to the Rankean method. The "posts" may have discredited teleologies, but that does not suggest that history is meaningless or that historical change and movement are fictional.

I have tempered my old antagonism to the "posts" as I have come to appreciate how congenial they have proved to feminist and ethnic studies. They have encouraged the study of historically despised or marginalized groups, the construction and constitution of identities, the understanding and representation of situations and events, and the importance of language and literary sensibility to historical writing. But historians

---

[27] For a more detailed analysis of the relationship between the "posts" and history see, Paul Tiyambe Zeleza, *Rethinking Africa's Globalization*. vol. 1, chap. 5. *The Intellectual Challenges* (Trenton, NJ: Africa World Press, 2003).

[28] Kwaku Larbi Korang, "Useless Provocation or Meaningful Challenge? The 'Posts' Versus African Studies," in *The Study of Africa*. vol. 1, *Disciplinary and Interdisciplinary Encounters*, edited by Paul Tiyambe Zeleza, (Dakar, Senegal: Codesria Book Series, 2006), 465–490.

[29] Kwame Anthony Appiah, *In My Father's House: Africa in the Philosophy of Culture* (New York: Oxford University Press, 1992).

were not blissfully unaware of these things before. Indeed, since the nineteenth century, when the discipline emerged in its current form, new methodologies, topics, and approaches have continuously arisen and have been incorporated into historiography. This shows the strength, not the infirmity, of history.[30]

Towards a New Global History of Africa and Humanity

The immense achievement of African historiography over the past half century is not in doubt. The apotheosis of the African historiographical revolution was the publication of two rival compendiums, each in eight volumes, namely, the *UNESCO General History of Africa* and the *Cambridge History of Africa*.[31] Jan Vansina calls the UNESCO project "a unique venture in twentieth century historiography." It is, he continues, "the most impressive venture of this century, not only because of its size or complexity, but because it involved authors from the most diverse origins belonging to all the schools of thought then active in international academic circles."[32] The *General History* brought together the largest group of historians ever assembled to work on a research project, and besides the volumes themselves, it generated numerous symposia and the publication of invaluable archival guides, which will have a lasting impact on African historiography. The project was born out of Pan-Africanism, for it was at the founding meeting of the Organization of African Unity that UNESCO was asked to undertake the project, which was launched in 1965 and completed in 1993.

Nevertheless, African historiography has yet to rid itself entirely of the epistemic erasures, omissions, fabrications, stereotypes, and silences of imperialist historiography.[33] The struggle to liberate African history will have to continue resting on a double intellectual maneuver: provincializing Europe, which has monopolized universality, and universalizing Africa beyond its Eurocentric provincialization. This requires not only continued vigilance against Eurocentric conceptions of history and categories of analysis, but also vigorous reconstructions of history that re-center African history by deepening and globalizing it in its temporal and spatial scope. It is a mark of the marginal position African history still occupies in the circles of Eurocentric scholarship that in a recent survey of world historiography by Daniel Woolf, Africa is short-shrifted in two and half pages out of more than fifty pages in which the "Western tradition" occupies center stage. The "African Past," as it is subtitled, appears belatedly under the last rubric in the chapter, "Twentieth Century Developments and New Paths," a section duly opened with reference to the notorious dismissals of African history made by G.W.F. Hegel and his British intellectual descendant, Hugh Trevor-Roper.[34]

---

[30] Paul Tiyambe Zeleza, "The Troubled Encounter Between Postcolonialism and African History," *Journal of the Canadian Historical Association* 17, no.: 89–129. Also see the tempered discussion of postcolonialism by Ania Loomba, *Colonialism/Postcolonialism* (London and New York: Routledge, 1998).

[31] *UNESCO General History of Africa* (Berkeley, CA: University of California Press, 1981–1993); and *Cambridge History of Africa* (New York: Cambridge University Press, 1977–1985).

[32] Jan Vansina, "Unesco and African Historiography," *History in Africa* 20 (1993): 350.

[33] This is the angry indictment of Jacques Depelchin, *Silences in African History: Between the Syndromes of Discovery and Abolition* (Dar Es Salaam: Mkuki na Nyota Publishers, 2005). For a commentary on this book and the historiographical issues it raises, see Paul Tiyambe Zeleza, "Banishing the Silences: Towards the Globalization of African History," Paper presented at the 11th General Assembly of the Council for Development of Social Science Research in Africa (CODESRIA), Rethinking African Development: Beyond Impasse, Towards Alternatives, Maputo, Mozambique, 6–10 December 2005.

[34] Daniel Woolf, "Historiography," in *New Dictionary of the History of Ideas*, edited by Maryanne Cline Horowitz (New York: Charles Scribner's Sons, 2005), 1: xxxv–xxxviii.

This survey demonstrates quite powerfully the propensity to cast Europe, conveniently camouflaged from time to time by that imagined signifier of appropriation—the West—as the central player in global history and to reduce other world regions to minor players in the human drama. Not surprisingly, we are offered another truncated Africa, the Africa of what V.Y. Mudimbe famously called the "colonial library," the Africa of Western derision, a caricature constructed from European epistemic fantasies deeply entrenched in Europe's social imaginary of its ultimate and most intimate "Other."[35] African intellectual historians must reclaim Africa's historiography scattered in the various libraries, especially in the "ancient library" and the "Islamic library," and must vigorously decolonize the "colonial library" to challenge its linear and narcissistic narratives by pointing out the contributions of thinkers and writers of African descent, from the theologians of early Christianity, such as St. Augustine, to the theoreticians of American modernity, such as W.E.B. Dubois, who are often appropriated into an ever-rising and everlasting Western civilization.

No amount of historiographical conceit can hide the fact that Europe has not always been the dominant part of the world, or Europeans the most numerous members of the human species. The rise of Europe to global dominance is fairly recent: Until the mid-eighteenth century, the Muslim world was dominant in much of the Afro-Eurasian world. And in recent times, global power has been shifting gradually from Euroamerica to Asia, led by Japan, China, and India. But power alone cannot be the measure of history in all its complexities and ramifications; to equate history to power is to write impoverished histories of victors of war and genocide, colonialism and imperialism, of those whose glories have exacted heavy ethical costs for the value of human life and high entropic costs for the viability of the planet itself.

African historians must take seriously the challenge of placing African history in world history. The field of world history has grown rapidly in the last few decades, but African historians are poorly represented. Until more African historians are engaged in researching, writing, and teaching world history, Africa will continue to be treated as a peripheral part of human history, and world history will necessarily remain incomplete, deprived of Africa's vantage point as one of the central players in the human drama. World or global history, which comes in all manner of transcontinental, transregional, transnational, and comparative configurations, helps to bring into question the construction and utility of conceptual categories used in Western historiography that are often applied uncritically to the histories of Africa and Asia.[36] The popularity of world history has been influenced quite considerably by the emergence of globalization studies and diaspora studies.

Diaspora studies offer African historians a key avenue to globalize African history and contest European appropriations of global history. The African diaspora has been studied from three vantage points: the slave trade, the Black Atlantic, and the globalization paradigms. Studies of the slave trade have focused on its causes, courses, and consequences. Historiographical dispute has centered on the trade's demographic and economic impact on Africa and Euroamerica. Joseph Inikori has advanced the work, begun by Eric Williams and Walter Rodney, against Eurocentric apologists of the slave trade to demonstrate convincingly in his award-winning book, *Africans and the Industrial Revolution in England,*

---

[35] V.Y. Mudimbe, *The Invention of Africa: Gnosis, Philosophy, and the Order of Knowledge* (Bloomington and Indianapolis: Indiana University Press, 1988); and *The Idea of Africa* (Bloomington and Indianapolis: Indiana University Press, 1994).

[36] Jerry H. Bentley, "Myths, Wagers, and Some Moral Implications of World History," *Journal of World History* 16, no. 1 (2005): 51–82, sees "ecumenical world history" as a way of transcending the ideologically driven, totalizing, and teleological histories of both the right and the left.

that international trade based on the Atlantic slave system was pivotal to the world's first industrial revolution in England between 1650 and 1850.[37]

Gilroy's Black Atlantic paradigm suffers from its disdainful excision of Africa as the silent presence in the formation of Atlantic cultures and the primacy it gives to the Anglophone diasporas, ignoring the much larger Spanish- and Portuguese-speaking diasporas.[38] Nevertheless, when the book was first published in 1993, it opened new analytical possibilities that recast old conceptions of the Atlantic world as some kind of Eurogenic creation. The studies that have been produced since then on the emergence and development of an integrated, if unequal, Atlantic world have helped to restore the African and African diasporic contributions to the construction of the Americas, modern Europe, and Africa itself to their rightful place. It is important to remember that until the mid-nineteenth century, the majority of people migrating from the so-called Old World to the New World were Africans and not Europeans. As Sheila Walker puts it: "the demographic foundation of the Americas was African, not European. . . . In the necessary process of recreating themselves in their new milieu, these Diasporan Africans invented and participated in the inventing of new cultural forms such as languages, religions, foods, aesthetic expressions, and political and social organizations."[39]

It was partly because of a growing conviction of the importance of African diaspora studies to Africa's global historical presence that I embarked on a project on the history of Africa and its diasporas.[40] The project seeks to map out the dispersal of African peoples in all the major world regions—Asia, Europe, and the Americas—compare the processes of diaspora formation within and among these regions, and examine the ebbs and flows of linkages—demographic, cultural (including religion and music), economic, political and ideological, intellectual and educational, artistic and iconographic—between these diasporas and Africa over time. The sheer volume of literature on the subject has been a source of inestimable intellectual pleasure and some trepidation for me. I spent six weeks in June and July 2006 on my first field visits to Venezuela and Brazil of a projected three years of visits to all the major African diaspora centers across the globe.

A project such as this has immense intellectual and policy relevance: It can help deepen our understanding of the complex histories and constructions of African diasporas and their equally complex, sometimes contradictory, and always changing engagements with Africa. It is especially critical at this juncture as the African Union, other continental agencies, and national governments seek to build more productive relationships between themselves and their diasporas.[41] Also, as global African migrations increase, the challenges of integrating new African diasporas into the host countries increase, as has been seen across Europe (for example

---

[37] Joseph Inikori, *Africans and the Industrial Revolution in England: A Study in International Trade and Development* (New York: Cambridge University Press, 2002); Rodney, *How Europe Underdeveloped Africa;* and Eric Williams, *Capitalism and Slavery* (Chapel Hill: University of North Carolina Press, 1944).

[38] Paul Gilroy, *The Black Atlantic: Modernity and Double Consciousness* (Cambridge: Harvard University Press, 1993).

[39] Sheila S. Walker, ed., "Are You Hip to the Jive? (Re)Writing/Righting the Pan-American Discourse," in *African Roots/ American Cultures: Africa in the Creation of the Americas,* edited by Sheila S. Walker (New York: Rowan and Littlefield, 2001), 2–3.

[40] For an outline of the project, which is funded by a $200,000 grant from the Ford Foundation, see Paul Tiyambe Zeleza, "Rewriting the African Diaspora: Beyond the Black Atlantic," *African Affairs* 104, no. 1 (2005): 35–68.

[41] In 2004 and 2006, the African Union organized two important conferences to discuss relations between Africa and its diasporas—The Conference of Intellectuals from Africa and the Diaspora (CIAD I and CIAD II). CIAD I was held in Dakar, Senegal, and CIAD II, in Salvador, Brazil. The proceedings of the two conferences can be found at http://ocpa.irmo.hr/ resources/docs/Intellectuals_Dakar_Report-en.pdf (CIAD I) and http://www.africandiasporastudies.com/downloads/alica_ CIAD_II_article.pdf (CIAD II).

in the uprising in France in 2005), and so do the challenges of integrating them into the communities with long-established historic African diasporas, as is evident in the Americas (especially in the United States).[42] Thus, diaspora studies enable us to insert Africa into global history and rewrite the histories of the various regions to which Africans were dispersed whether voluntarily or by force. The Africans who went to Portugal and Spain and ruled for eight centuries during the Andalusian period went voluntarily,[43] while those who were shipped to the Americas during the era of the Atlantic slave trade were coerced. Both left an indelible mark on the history of Europe, Africa, and the Americas. The effects are still with us and are central to understanding the history of Euroamerica, the whitened West.

If we carry the idea of African migrations to its logical conclusion, Africa's centrality in world history, in the history of humanity, becomes even more obvious. As Colin Palmer has noted, there are at least six waves of migrations from Africa, three that occurred in what historians call prehistoric times (beginning with the great exodus that began about 100,000 years ago from the continent to other continents) and three in historic times, including those associated with the Indian Ocean trading system with Asia, the Atlantic slave trade to the Americas, and the contemporary movement of Africans and peoples of African descent to various parts of the globe.[44]

Conventional history covers only the last 5,000 years, a flash in the span of human evolution and existence on this planet. It is now abundantly clear that Africa is the original homeland of our species, *Homo sapiens*, and the place from which the world's populations scattered across the globe. It was archaeology that first suggested the out-of-Africa thesis, and the Human Genome Project has provided conclusive genetic evidence of our commonality. Humans worldwide share 99.9 percent of their genetic blueprint. There are larger genetic differences among Africans than between Africans and Eurasians.[45] Two clear conclusions can be drawn from these studies: First, it is now certain that the notion of biological races is a myth, albeit a dangerous one that has wrought incalculable damage on human beings, not least for people called "Africans," and, second, that Africa is at the heart of human history. It is the continent where humans have lived longest, where they underwent and made many of the fundamental transformations and innovations that characterize modern humans and social life.

Convinced that it is essential to understand the emergence and development of human history from the inception of modern humans to the present, some scholars have established the field known as biohistory. While conceding that historians' wariness of biology can partly be attributed to the sad

---

[42] For an examination of these relations, see Paul Tiyambe Zeleza, "Diaspora Dialogues: Engagements Between Africa and Its Diasporas," from a conference on The New African Diaspora: Assessing the Pains and Gains of Exile, Africana Studies, Binghamton University, Binghamton, USA, April 7–8, 2006.

[43] The African dimensions of Moorish and Muslim rule in Spain and Portugal are often lost through the racialization of Africa as "Black" and the racialization of Islam as "Arab," propositions that the Moroccan scholar Anouar Majid, *Unveiling Traditions: Postcolonial Islam in a Polycentric World* (Durham and London: Duke University Press, 2000) and *Freedom and Orthodoxy: Islam and Difference in the Post-Andalusian Age* (Stanford University Press, 2004) has persuasively debunked. He argues that in so far as "the domain of African Islam extended as far north as Spain," al-Andalus could be considered "essentially an African kingdom in Europe," *Unveiling Traditions*, 77.

[44] Colin Palmer, "The African Diaspora," *Black Scholar* 30, no. 3/4 (2000): 56–59.

[45] See Donald Johanson, "Origins of Modern Humans: Multiregional or Out of Africa." ActionBioScience. May 2001. Available at http://www.actionbioscience.org/evolution/johanson.html retrieved November 11, 2005. Johanson 2001; Ning Yu et al., "Larger Genetic Differences Within Africans Than Between Africans and Eurasians," *Genetics* 161 (May 2002): 269–274; and R.C. Lewontin, "Confusions About Human Races," Social Science Research Council, April 2005. Available at http://raceandgenomics.ssrc.org/Lewontin/ retrieved November 11, 2005.

legacies of social Darwinism and the misguided determinisms of sociobiology and evolutionary psychology, Robert McElvane vouches for biohistory, insisting that it is different in that it "seeks to illuminate aspects of history through a better understanding of human nature—the fundamental traits and predispositions that all humans share and that make us alike. . . . Biohistory, moreover, does not see human history as a Darwinian struggle. Instead, it contends that history consists, to a considerable extent, of the interplay between humans' biological inheritance and the social environments in which the creatures with that inheritance have lived over the past 10,000 years or so."[46]

Long conceptions of human history offer African historians an immense opportunity to recenter Africa in global history and deepen everyone's understanding of African history. It is, indeed, a failure of historical imagination to concentrate on the last 5,000 years of recorded history, let alone subsume world history to the trajectory of European history since the rise of European global hegemony two and half centuries ago. The difficulties of reconstructing human history since the emergence of modern humans are immense. Traditional historical methods based on written and oral sources are of little use because they do not exist beyond that time span. Archeology is invaluable, and the low levels of investment in archeological work in Africa should be of great concern. Also critical are the fields of paleontology, evolutionary biology, ecology, epidemiology, anthropology, and historical linguistics. Few historians possess literacy in these disciplines, but their benefits cannot be doubted.

A fascinating example of a long-term history of Africa that recasts Africa's place in world history can be seen in Christopher Ehret's *The Civilizations of Africa: A History to 1800,* which I use to teach ancient African history in a first-year class.[47] The book covers the period from 16,000 B.C.E. to 1800 C.E., broken into distinct periods. It takes African history seriously and offers a bold reinterpretation of its periodization and the development of four civilizational clusters in Africa. This allows the author to discuss Africa as a whole without making untenable generalizations or resorting to racialized narratives. Ehret places Africa at the heart of the human story and examines Africa's contribution to developments of global importance—from food production and religion to metallurgy and commerce—and the complex connections between the continent and Eurasia and the Americas.

Another Africanist historian, Patrick Manning, has vigorously sought to bring insights from African history into world history, to break the boundaries of regional and thematically parochial histories, and to explore the problem and patterns of interaction in world history.[48] Writing world history has tended to involve identifying and analyzing historical phenomena on a worldwide scale, that is, interactions between people organized in, or more often seen by historians as belonging to, bounded cultures, civilizations, and continents. Many of the difficulties faced by world historians have centered on the conceptual difficulties of defining what constitutes the "world" and "interaction." The "world" of most world or global histories—some distinguish between the two—remains trapped in the myopia of Eurocentric historiography, and the "interactions" tend to be confined to a few variables (usually long-distance commerce, mass migration, and empire building), the activities of a few agents, limited periods, and a few geographical zones. Manning favors a broader and, in my view, more compelling vision of world history, one that encompasses exchanges of a wider range of material and expressive cultures and social and political

---

[46] Robert S. McElvaine, "The Relevance of Biohistory," *The Chronicle of Higher Education* 49, no. 8 (2002): B10.

[47] Christopher Ehret, *The Civilizations of Africa: A History to 1800* (Charlottesville: University Press of Virginia, 2002).

[48] Patrick Manning, "The Problem of Interactions in World History," *The American Historical Review* 101, no. 3 (1996): 771–782.

institutions, focuses on "different groupings of human agents for different types of linkages among societies," considers "the changing character of cross-cultural interaction from period to period," both in terms
of the "character of the interaction as well as changes in the results of interaction," and transcends evolutionary stages constructed on analysis restricted to the Afro-Eurasian landmass, or a few zones within
it, by including "the Americas and the Pacific before 1500." In his *Navigating World History,* Manning
offers an ambitious and persuasive guidebook on how to produce more expansive world history. He
recommends interdisciplinarity and literacy in the humanities and the natural, behavioral, and social sciences; innovative research methods and analytical paradigms; and deep appreciation of the complex and
changing connections within the global human community.[49]

In many ways, these studies echo the findings and preoccupations evident in the *UNESCO General History
of Africa,* the supreme compendium of historical knowledge produced by the generation of nationalist historians. They are all part of the arduous task of rescuing both African history and world history from the burdens and blindfolds of Eurocentric historiography. This project begun by the nationalist historians needs to
continue, even as we discard some of their outdated questions and answers, enriched as we are by new historical sources, methods, and theories that have emerged over the last three decades or so. The challenge now,
as I see it, is to recenter African history by deepening and globalizing it in its temporal scope and spatial scale—
taking the place of Africa in human history seriously. That is perhaps the primary contribution my generation
of historians can make and pass on to the generation coming of age and to the generation being trained now.
Africa has always been central, and will remain so, to its peoples and to humanity, whose cradle this ancient
continent is, where much of its history on this remarkable planet resides.

I feel our work—my generation's historiographical work—has only just begun, and I find that intellectually exhilarating and invigorating. Perhaps it is the delusion of age, but I was told that when I turned
fifty, I had a right to occasional delusions.

---

[49] Patrick Manning, *Navigating World History: Historians Create a Global Past* (New York: Palgrave MacMillan, 2003).

Chapter 6

REMEMBERING THE FORGOTTEN HISTORIES OF ENSLAVEMENT AND AFRICAN CONTRIBUTIONS TO ABOLITION IN AFRICA

The Case of the Gold Coast (Ghana)[1]

Kwabena Akurang-Parry

Since the 1970s, the study of slavery and its abolition in Africa has been at the forefront of African history. Thematic preoccupations that inform such studies have included Islam and the trans-Saharan trade; African contributions to the making of the Atlantic community; demography and gender; the "legitimate" trade, colonial rule, and abolition; and emancipation and the nature of post-slavery societies.[2] The most studied of the themes are the nature of slavery and Euro-American roles in the demise of slavery in colonial Africa. Overall, the corpus of literature has excluded African ideologies of antislavery and contributions to abolition.[3] Indeed, various controversial theories and paradigms have informed the epistemic layers of African history; hence, it is surprising that historians of slavery and abolition in Africa have not even hypothesized or theorized the possibilities of African contributions to the global abolition of slavery.

Primarily, this chapter, a case study, briefly looks at the nature of slavery in the Gold Coast (Ghana) during the precolonial era and colonial period in the late nineteenth century. More significantly, the chapter deals extensively with the processes of abolition of slavery in the Gold Coast, especially the role of African agents illustrated by the ways that James Hutton Brew, the editor of the Cape Coast–based

---

[1] Portions of this work have appeared in Kwabena Akurang-Parry, "'We Shall Rejoice to See the Day When Slavery Shall Cease to Exist'": *The Gold Coast Times* and African Abolitionists in the Gold Coast," *History in Africa* 31 (2004): 19–42.

[2] The literature is vast. See, for example, *The End of Slavery in Africa*, edited by Suzanne Miers and Richard Roberts (Madison, WI: University of Wisconsin Press, 1988); Patrick Manning, *Slavery and African Life* (Cambridge University Press, 1990), 157–164; Martin Klein, *Slavery and Colonial Rule* (Cambridge University Press, 1998); Paul Lovejoy and Jan Hogendorn, *Slow Death for Slavery, The Course of Abolition in Northern Nigeria, 1897–1936* (Cambridge University Press, 1993); and Suzanne Miers and Martin Klein, eds., *Slavery and Colonial Rule in Africa* (London: Frank Cass, 1999).

[3] Richard Rathbone, "Some Thoughts on Resistance to Enslavement in West Africa," *Slavery and Abolition* 6 (1985): 11–22; Winston McGowan, "African Resistance to the Slave Trade in West Africa," *Slavery and Abolition* 11 (1990): 5–29; Ismail Rashid, "Escape, Revolt, and Marronage in Eighteenth and Nineteenth Century Sierra Leone Hinterland," *Canadian Journal of African Studies* 34 (2000): 656–683; Kwabena O. Akurang-Parry, "'A Smattering of Education' and Petitions as a Source Material: A Study of African Slave-Holders' Responses to Abolition in the Gold Coast, 1874–75," *History in Africa* 27 (2000): 39–60; and Akurang-Parry, "'We Shall Rejoice,'" 19–42.

Gold Coast Times newspaper, crusaded for abolition. His campaigns for abolition in the Gold Coast are broadly framed as a representation of the African intelligentsia's packaging of abolitionist ideology, which served as their composite response to the British colonial abolition of slavery in the Gold Coast at the onset of colonial rule.[4] Additionally, this chapter principally rethinks the staple conclusion that abolition in Africa was the work of European and American institutions and agents. It argues, among other things, that there were African abolitionists in the Gold Coast and that their abolitionism predated the British colonial abolition inaugurated in 1874/75. Stressing African agency and what I conceptualize as the "osmotic Atlantic community," I argue that evangelical Christianity, humanitarianism, economic determinism, and slave revolts—all significant watersheds of antislavery in the Atlantic communities of Europe and the Americas—also occurred in the Atlantic rim of the Gold Coast and throughout West Africa. I use the concept of osmotic Atlantic community here to refer to the diffusion of antislavery ideologies emanating from specific points on the Atlantic rim to other sectors along and beyond it. In sum, antislavery ideologies sprouted in specific areas of the Atlantic community and diffused exponentially with consequent intermittent and differential results. This is similar to what George Shepperson calls the "triangular trade of ideas" in the region of the Atlantic community.[5]

Slavery and Abolition

States in the region of what broadly became known as the Gold Coast during Portuguese exploration of the West African coast in the late fifteenth century included the area occupied by Ga-Adangbe, Krobo, Fante, southern Ewe, Ahanta, Nzema, and Akuapem. The adjacent interior sector between the coast and the powerful Asante Kingdom of the eighteenth and nineteenth centuries, which became known in the nineteenth century under British colonial sway as the "Protectorate," included the Akyem, Sefwi, Wassa, Assin, Kwahu, Akwamu, Denkyira, Krepi, Agona, and parts of the mid-Voltaic Ewe states. Prior to 1901, the boundaries between the colony and the protectorate remained nebulously defined.

---

[4] For the processes of abolition in the Gold Coast, see, for example, Gerald M. McSheffrey, "Slavery, Indentured Servitude, Legitimate Trade and the Impact of Abolition in the Gold Coast, 1874–1901," *Journal of African History* 24 (1983): 349–369; Claire C. Robertson, "Post-Proclamation Slavery in Accra: A Female Affair," in *Women and Slavery in Africa*, edited by Martin Klein and Claire C. Robertson (Madison: University of Wisconsin Press, 1983), 220–245; Raymond Dumett and Marion Johnson, "Britain and the Suppression of Slavery in the Gold Coast Colony, Ashanti and the Northern Territories," in *The End of Slavery in Africa*, edited by in Suzanne Miers and Richard Roberts, 71–116; Peter Haenger, *Slaves and Slave Holders on the Gold Coast* (Basel: Schlettwein, 1997); Trevor R. Getz, *Slavery and Reform in West Africa: Toward Emancipation in Nineteenth-Century Senegal and the Gold Coast* (Athens, Ohio: Ohio University Press, 2004); Kwabena O. Akurang-Parry, "The Administration of the Abolition Laws, African Responses, and Post-Proclamation Slavery in Colonial Southern Ghana, 1874–1940," *Slavery and Abolition* 19 (1998): 149–166; Kwabena O. Akurang-Parry, "Slavery and Abolition in the Gold Coast: Colonial Modes of Emancipation and African Initiatives," *Ghana Studies* 1 (1998): 11–34; Kwabena O. Akurang-Parry, "Rethinking the 'Slaves of Salaga': Post-Proclamation Slavery in the Gold Coast (Colonial Southern Ghana), 1874–1899," *Left History* 8, no. 1 (2002): 33–60; Kwabena O. Akurang-Parry, "To Wassa Fiase for Gold: Rethinking Colonial Rule, El Dorado, Antislavery and Chieftaincy in the Gold Coast (Ghana), 1874–1895," *History in Africa* 30 (2003): 11–36; Kwabena O. Akurang-Parry, "Aspects of Women's Agency and Activism in the Gold Coast (Colonial Ghana), 1874–1899," *The International Journal of African Historical Studies* 37, no. 3 (2004): 463–482; and Kwabena O. Akurang-Parry, "Making a Difference in Colonial Interventionism in Gold Mining in Wassa Fiase, Gold Coast (Ghana): The Social and Political Activism of Two Women, 1874–1893," in *Mining Women: Gender in the Development of a Global Industry, 1670–2005*, edited by Jaclyn J. Gier and Laurie Mercier (New York: Palgrave Macmillan, 2006), 40–57.

[5] George Shepperson, "Notes on Negro American Influences and the Emergence of African Nationalism," *Journal of African History* 1 (1960): 299.

The processes of state-formation of all these states predated the Atlantic slave trade in the fifteenth century. During the eighteenth and nineteenth centuries, these autonomous states came under formal Asante domination at one time or another. All the states directly or indirectly were influenced by the Atlantic slave trade, and in the aftermath of abolition, they also engaged in "legitimate" trade from the 1830s forward by using servile labor, among other methods, to produce cash crops, including cocoa, that were exported mostly to Europe.

Slavery was a worldwide phenomenon; therefore, in addition to Africa, it existed in various parts of the world, in different forms. The 1290 derivation of the word, *Sclave,* points to the enslavement of Central Europeans by the Spanish and Portuguese. Slavery has early records in the Bible, and almost every civilization, including ancient Greece, ancient Rome, and the Islamic Caliphates, have practiced it. African involvement in modern "chattel slavery," the sort trans-Atlantic slave traders practiced in what became broadly defined as the Gold Coast, is contested. Historians of Africa have acknowledged that some Africans were active participants in the slave trade with Europeans and Americans; however, these same scholars persuasively argue that this fact in no way suggests that slavery was unique to African cultures or that Africans are responsible for the horrendous tragedy of the trade. Alternatively, some of these scholars state unambiguously that the chattel slavery of the modern trans-Atlantic slave trade was initiated and dominated by European and Americans.[6]

Thus the Gold Coast region and adjacent areas, on the eve of colonial rule and abolition in the 1870s, had local servile populations that were a part of the economy. At this time, slavery occurred under the auspices of incipient British presence along the coast. At the high noon of colonial rule from the 1880s to the early 1920s, slavery and debt bondage, in addition to colonial forced labor practices, expanded as sources of labor for producing cash crops, mining, and building infrastructure, such as roads.[7] Slaves were exploited for their labor in various capacities: Slaves worked as cooks and cleaners, engaged in child care, went on errands, produced food, and fetched firewood and water. Some slaves engaged in specialist labor as artisans, crafts people, soldiers, traders, etc., in the service of the host-kinship group and larger community.

Compared to slavery in Europe and the Americas, slaves in the Gold Coast and other parts of Africa experienced degrees of assimilation into host-kinship families. Manumission in the Gold Coast was more common than it was in the Americas. Oral history shows that on the eve of colonial rule in the 1870s, manumission had become a normative institution: For instance, first–generation-born slaves and their descendants were invariably free, though with degrees of continued positions of servility within the political economy of the host-kinship group and the community at large.[8]

---

[6] Joseph Inikori, review of *The Atlantic Slave Trade*, by Herbert Klein, *Hispanic American Historical Review* 82, no. 1 (2002): 130–135.

[7] See, for example, Kwabena Akurang-Parry, "Colonial Forced Labor Strategies for Road-Building in the Gold Coast (Southern Ghana) and International Anti-Forced Labor Pressures, 1900–1940," *African Economic History* 28 (2000): 1–25; and Kwabena O. Akurang-Parry, "'With a Load on His Head and Nothing in His Hands': The Opposition of the Gold Coast (Ghana) Press to the Compulsory Labor Ordinance, 1895–ca.1899," *Transactions of the Historical Society of Ghana* New Series, 4 and 5 (2000–2001): 83–104.

[8] See, for example, interview with Oheneba Kwasi Akurang, Mamfe-Akuapem, March 13, 1994; and interview with Nana Afua Oye, Suhum, June 17, 1997 (PhD diss., Kwabena Akurang-Parry).

Exploitation of slaves may have been common, but slaves had normative rights, sometimes established as state ideologies. For example, among the Akans of the Gold Coast, slaveholders were normatively barred from sexually abusing their female slaves and had to account for the accidental deaths of their slaves.[9] Such normative ideologies changed over time; what is more important from a critical standpoint is that tenets of state ideologies have not always manifested in practice. In sum, slavery in precolonial Africa was not as harsh and exploitative as the forms of slavery that developed from the 1830s forward, the era of massive export cash crop production that consequently peaked during the period of formal colonial rule starting in the early 1880s.

The empirical paradigms and theoretical perspectives that inform the study of servile groups in the Gold Coast derive from two main opposing historiographies. One is based on R.A. Rattray's ethnographic study of Asante slavery conducted in the late 1920s. Rattray's study illustrates that slavery in Asante was benign and kinship-based in the sense that slavery was a conduit for expanding the population of kin-groups or lineages.[10] His perspective on the mildness of slavery has been perpetuated by Marion Johnson and Raymond Dumett, who have argued that there were different kinds of servile institutions, including domestic slavery and pawnship, or debt-bondage, and that all were mild and kinship-based. They also argue that emancipation was not cataclysmic and that the desertion of slaves in the early colonial period did not disrupt servile labor because debt-bondage was easily available.[11] Furthermore, they challenge the view that the emancipation policy of the colonial government derived from capitalist motives. Accordingly, the prevailing slave mode of production in the colonial period was not used to sustain labor for the burgeoning colonial capitalist economy. Additionally, they assert that slaves were assimilated into "host kinship groups"[12] and challenge the assertion that 10,000 slaves left their masters in Akyem Abuakwa alone.[13] In terms of the impact of abolition, they refute the view that emancipation undermined the structures of indigenous political institutions. In summation, they posit that "the ending of slavery in the Gold Coast . . . must be one of the quieter social revolutions of the late nineteenth and twentieth centuries."[14]

Dumett and Johnson's conclusions are contrasted with the position of Gerald McSheffrey. Based primarily on missionary sources, McSheffrey examines the period from 1874 to 1901 and concentrates on the eastern part of the Gold Coast, especially, Akyem Abuakwa. He concludes that slavery in the Gold Coast was harsh and that emancipation of slaves from 1874 to 1875 had a sudden and profound impact on the local economy and society. He argues further that economic change led to the intensive use of slave labor and worsened social stratification.[15]

---

[9] See ibid. See also R.S. Rattray, *Ashanti Law and Constitution* (New York: Negro Universities Press, 1969).

[10] ibid.

[11] Dumett and Johnson, "Britain and the Suppression of Slavery," 100–105.

[12] ibid., 107–108. See also Robertson, "Post Proclamation Slavery," 227.

[13] Dumett and Johnson, "Britain and the Suppression of Slavery," 91.

[14] ibid., 108.

[15] McSheffrey, "Slavery," 354–368.

Theorizing the Efflorescence of Abolitionist Ideas in the Gold Coast

There are a number of nuanced and sometimes overarching theoretical perspectives on the role of Africans in abolition. For instance, Joseph C. Miller has cogently argued that "African history stands solidly on three legs [Africa, Europe, and the Americas], and Africans join others around the world as intelligible participants in themes central to European history."[16] For his part, Lamin Sanneh has instructively asserted, "Africans were no exception to the rule of righteousness, a rule opposed to any compromise with slavery and its supporting structures."[17] In their introduction to *The End of Slavery in Africa,* Richard Roberts and Susan Miers explain that "abolition in Africa was part of the same worldwide set of changes in the organization of production that emanated from the spread of the world capitalist economy."[18]

With regard to slave resistance as an agency of abolition, Susan Miers and Martin Klein, writing about Africa, have concluded that "in fact, slaves themselves were usually important actors in their own liberation. In many parts of Africa, they took the initiative and fled in large numbers."[19] These are formidable conclusions that offer rich possibilities for rethinking African agency in the abolition and emancipation of slaves. That slave flight weakened slave regimes and served as an agency of freedom in Africa is incontrovertible. What needs rethinking is the preponderant notion that slave flight occurred mostly in the colonial period. It needs to be stressed that during the early years of colonial rule, the colonial authorities, for the most part, were not willing to push for effective abolition.[20] Thus, colonial rule may have provided fertile ground for resistance, but it was the slaves who took matters into their own hands to emancipate themselves. Therefore, studies of abolition should not overemphasize the role of European agents and should include an assessment of the contributions of enslaved Africans to abolition.

Indeed, a stimulating empowering editorial in the *Gold Coast Times* issue of August 20, 1874, neatly encapsulated the abolitionist position of the African intelligentsia on the pending British abolition of slavery inaugurated on November 3, 1874.[21] Among other things, the editorial plaintively echoed, "We shall rejoice to see the day when slavery shall cease to exist on the Gold Coast in any shape or form."[22] The collective, encompassing "we" represented the microcosmic views of the African intelligentsia, the opinion leaders and a pressure group in the Gold Coast. The abolitionist ideology of the African intelligentsia illustrates that the agencies of humanitarianism, Christian charity, economic

---

[16] Joseph C. Miller, "History and Africa/Africa and History," *American Historical Review* 104 (1999): 31.

[17] Lamin Sanneh, *Abolitionists Abroad: American Blacks and the Making of Modern West Africa* (Cambridge, MA: Harvard University, 1999), 156.

[18] Richard Roberts and Susan Miers, "The End of Slavery in Africa," in *The End of Slavery in Africa*, edited by in Miers and Roberts, 55.

[19] Susan Miers and Martin Klein, "Introduction," in *Slavery and Colonial Rule in Africa*, edited by Miers and Klein, 7.

[20] ibid., 4–7.

[21] *The Gold Coast Times* (Cape Coast), August 20, 1874, 50. For a critical descriptive account of Governor George Strahan's inauguration of abolition at Cape Coast and subsequently in Accra and the Eastern districts, see *Gold Coast Times*, November 30, 1874, 53; and for the text of Governor Strahan's speech, see, for example, Strahan to Carnarvon, November 3, 1874, Encl. in No. 11 in Further Correspondence Relating to the Abolition of Slavery on the Gold Coast, Parliamentary Papers, 1875, C. 1139 (hereafter C. 1139); and *The African Times*, (London), Dec. 31, 1874, and Jan. 1, 1875, 2–3.

[22] *The Gold Coast Times*, August 20, 1874, 50.

determinism, and slave resistance shaped the osmotic Atlantic community during the period of epochal abolitionism.

The paucity of sources makes it difficult to determine when the abolitionist ideologies of Brew and the African intelligentsia developed in the Gold Coast. Larry Yarak's study of Afro-Europeans in Elmina shows that a considerable number of wealthy Afro-Europeans did not have slaves, suggesting that antislavery may have gained ground in the Gold Coast beginning in the 1820s.[23] Additionally, John Parker's work illustrates that by 1861 there was a connection between the Basel Mission's antislavery policy and the existence of antislavery sentiments in the Ga region.[24] By extrapolating from the evidence, it becomes clear that the leading African intellectuals of the day, including Brew, were aware of the epochal abolitionism of the eighteenth and nineteenth centuries.[25] For example, in August 1874, the Gold Coast–based correspondent of *The Scotsman* noted the "comparative ease by which slavery might be abolished."[26] The correspondent further affirmed that "the people expect it [slavery] to be put to an end, and will be astonished if it be allowed to go on."[27] Thus, the evidence strongly confirms that African antislavery in the Gold Coast predated the imposition of colonial rule that led to the inauguration of abolition in 1874/75.

The evidence shows that the efflorescence of African abolitionist ideology in the coastal states was affected by British imperial responses to developments in Asante. Throughout the nineteenth century, especially on the eve of colonial rule in 1874/75, the coastal states had to deal with the military might of Asante. In sum, the failure of the coastal states to contain Asante partly contributed to the British invasion and defeat of Asante in 1873/74. Consequently, abolition became a part of the paradoxical British imposition of colonial rule on the coastal states, their very allies, in the aftermath of the war of 1874/75.[28] The coastal states, especially the Fantes, did not oppose abolition and the British parliament and newspapers had recommended the pretext of using the war as a reciprocal obligation for shaping British colonial policies, including abolition.[29]

Furthermore, on the eve of colonial rule and abolition, some of the local intelligentsia (the opinion leaders) were tied to the political apron strings of the British Empire. The leaders of the Gold Coast intelligentsia had seemingly placidly explained that "this country"—the Gold Coast—had been ruled by the "British nation" for "three centuries."[30] Exegetical readings of anticolonial criticisms in the Gold Coast newspapers, mostly reformist in bent, exemplify some of the intelligentsia's belief that they

---

[23] Larry Yarak, "West African Coastal Slavery in the Nineteenth Century: The Case of Afro-Europeans of Elmina," *Ethnohistory* 36, no. 1 (1983): 44–60.

[24] John Parker, "Ga State and Society in Early Colonial Accra, 1860s–1920s" (PhD diss., University of London, 1995), 123–124; and John Parker, *Making the Town: Ga State and Society in Early Colonial Accra* (Portsmouth, NH: James Currey, 2000), 95.

[25] See *African Times*, March 1, 1875, 33; and *Gold Coast Times*, October 20, 1874, 51.

[26] *African Times*, August 29, 1874, 16.

[27] ibid.

[28] Akurang-Parry, "'Smattering of Education.'"

[29] For editorial columns, see, for example, *African Times*, August 29, 1874, 29; June 30, 1874, 70; and March 1, 1875. For the letters to the editor, see, for example, *African Times*, December 31, 1874, and Jan 1, 1875, 3. In one case, the letter to the editor was signed by "One Who Served Throughout the Late Campaign"—Anglo-Asante war of 1873–74.

[30] Strahan to Carnarvon, January 3, 1875, Encl. in No. 1 in Further Correspondence Relating to the Abolition of Slavery on the Gold Coast, Parliamentary Papers, 1875, C. 1159 (hereafter C. 1159).

belonged to the British Empire.[31] Thus, the African intelligentsia's support for abolition may be due partly to the complex relationship between the coastal states and the British.[32]

Another reason for the rise of abolition in the Gold Coast was the degree of cultural and educational linkages between England and the Gold Coast. David Kimble and Ray Jenkins have provided information on a considerable number of Africans from the Gold Coast who visited and studied in England in the nineteenth century. They suggest that Gold Coast Africans became agents of cultural nationalism and Pan-Africanist ideologies.[33] But there is also reason to argue that Brew and others, who had studied in Britain prior to abolition in the Gold Coast, were imbued with abolitionist ideologies then prevailing in the osmotic Atlantic community.[34] This conclusion is borne out by African scholars' contributions to the discussions that informed the British colonial abolition in the Gold Coast: They made references to perspectives on abolition and emancipation current within the larger osmotic Atlantic world. For example, the *African Times*, commenting on an article that appeared in the *Daily News* (London) regarding the Gold Coast abolition petitions, revealed that

> the memorials of the native Chiefs [of the Gold Coast] to the Queen and to her representatives at the Gold Coast are evidently of European origin. They clothe native feelings in civilized ideas and arguments. These documents might very well have proceeded from a conference of American or West Indian planters when emancipation impended over the slave-owners of the Southern States or Jamaica.[35]

The perspective on similarities is certainly an exemplification of the cross-pollination of ideas within the osmotic Atlantic community, and it is a strong empirical example of the ways that antislavery had spread in the Atlantic world.

Furthermore, the African intelligentsia had access to articles on abolition and emancipation elsewhere that appeared regularly in the *African Times*. It should be stressed that the *African Times* was read by the African intelligentsia throughout the West African region. A letter to the editor of the *African Times* written by "An African" and headlined, "Case of Gross Injustice at Cape Coast in the Gold Coast," stated that

> for four years and more you have been the brave champion of Africans; have defended them against oppression and acts of injustice they, from time to time, have received at the hands of their European rulers in Africa. The *African Times* has become a household name to all intelligent

---

[31] This view is strongly suggested by Ray Jenkins, "Gold Coasters Overseas 1880–1919," *Immigrants and Minorities* 4 (1985): 5–52.

[32] Akurang-Parry, "'Smattering of Education.'"

[33] David Kimble, *A Political History of Ghana, 1850–1928* (Oxford, 1963), 92, says that roughly "200 Gold Coast Africans had received higher education or traveled overseas" in the nineteenth century. Also Jenkins, "Gold Coasters Overseas," 5–6, gives an account of 140 Africans who visited Britain from ca. 1880 to 1919 and asserts that considering the Gold Coast population of 895,330 in 1901, these numbers were a "modest proportion."

[34] ibid., 43–52.

[35] *African Times*, March 1, 1875, 33. For a fuller account of the memorials and petitions, see Akuramg-Parry, "'A Smattering of Education.'"

Africans, a name near and dear to them; your office an institution that they reverence and worship.[36]

Indeed, the *African Times* received a spate of letters to the editor from the Gold Coast and the whole West African region. Considering the readership and the areas covered by the newspaper, a strong claim can be made that West Africans were exposed to abolitionist ideologies prevailing in the late nineteenth century. For instance, the December 23, 1862, issue culled an article from the *New York Principia* called "President Lincoln's Emancipation Proclamation."[37] Similarly, in 1865, a news item regarding emancipation in the United States was titled "The Africans in the United States."[38] Other generic themes in the *African Times* included the vestiges of slavery, slave insurrections, and the Royal Commissions of Inquiry in the Caribbean.[39] Also, the African intelligentsia had access to information regarding antislavery crusades of the African Aid Society that appeared regularly in the *African Times*. Additionally, from its inception in 1862, the *African Times* consistently argued for abolition in the West African region, including Lagos, Dahomey, Liberia, Badagry, Ambas Bay, and Fernando Po.[40]

In sum, the antislavery ideologies championed by the *African Times* were assimilated by the West African intelligentsia. Consequently, some of them, in their own way, propogated the anti-slavery ideologies espoused in the columns of the *African Times*. The evidence strongly shows that the Africans were involved in the ideological currency and historical relevance of abolition.[41] Indeed, an 1874 editorial of the *Gold Coast Times* regarding compensation adequately captures the African intelligentsia's insights into global abolitionism:

What has become of the spirit that emanated from your Wilberforce, your Clarksons, your Buxtons? Is it dead? And has your race degenerated? What has become of that England which at the present century was the wonder and terror of the globe? Has she descended so low that she must impoverish a whole nation just for the purpose of carrying out a pet idea . . . ? It is clear the same spirit no longer pervades

---

[36] *African Times*, August 23, 1866, 16. On page 22 of the same issue, an African, responding to Colonel E. Conran's disparaging reply to a petition submitted to the colonial authorities by Accra merchants regarding a colonial expedition to the Voltaic districts and the declining trade due to slavery and violence, noted that the European authorities in the Gold Coast did not respect the *African Times*, although the African intelligentsia and Africans in general did. In 1865, the African intelligentsia of Sierra Leone paid tribute to the *African Times*. See the *African Times*, December 23, 1865, 64.

[37] *African Times*, December 23, 1862, 69.

[38] *African Times*, June 23, 1865, 59. The author explained that despite emancipation, African Americans were not raised to the position of social equality.

[39] See, for example, *African Times*, June 23, 1866, 136; the *African Times*, November 23, 1865, mentions on page 50 and 52 the insurrection in the eastern districts of Jamaica (Morant Bay) on October 10, 1865. They described how Jamaican slaves had sought to kill Whites and mulattos.

[40] See, for example, *African Times*, November 22, 1862, 53.

[41] *The Gold Coast Aborigines*, November 5, 1898, reported Ottobah Cugoano's "reflections on the Slave Trade, and the Slavery of Negroes" and noted that, "he raised his voice to spread abroad the spirit of religion and prove from the Scriptures that the stealing, sale, and purchase of men and their detention in a state of Slavery are crimes of the deepest die. . . . To steal men, to rob them of their liberty is worse than to plunder them of their goods." Of course, this is about a latter period, but it points to the undeniable fact that the African intelligentsia kept abreast of developments associated with abolition.

the foremost men . . . they will trucke and haggle over . . . what their fathers expounded in the attainment of that which they profess to abhor.[42]

The quotation certainly mirrors important aspects of the epochal abolitionism, including the issue of compensation, the struggles between the southern and northern states of America over slavery, and the ways that humanitarianism and antislavery, championed by abolitionists, led to abolition. It also confirms Shepperson's conclusion that "the heydays of abolitionism may have left imprints on early African nationalism," and that African nationalists "learned much from the pressure-grouping techniques of the British and American abolitionists."[43]

The impact of the epochal abolition of the eighteenth and nineteenth centuries on African political thought, articulated by Shepperson, also sowed the seeds of abolition in the Gold Coast and elsewhere along the West African coast. Tracing the development of the epochal abolitionism, Shepperson focused on the emancipatory works of diasporic Africans and the ways that their ideas impacted continental African emancipatory ideologies.[44] Some of the diasporic African intellectuals mentioned by Shepperson were Frederick Douglass, Martin R. Delany, and Alexander Crummel.[45] These stalwart intellectuals and avid antislavery activists engaged not only in antislavery, but also preached Pan-Africanist ideologies in their quest to stamp out the racialized politics of inferiority imputed to Africans in the course of the trans-Atlantic slave trade and abolition debates. Shepperson wrote that "much of the work of the emerging African political thinkers of the abolitionist epoch centers on the issue of racialism."[46]

With regard to West Africa, Shepperson's views are borne out by the political activism of James Africanus Beale Horton, whose writings were informed by antislavery and Pan-Africanist ideologies.[47] According to Shepperson, by the 1850s, the "'Negro heritage' influence of abolitionism particularly as reflected in the writings of Edward Blyden, was affecting the very nomenclature of leading African political thinkers."[48] More recently, Sanneh has comprehensively focused on the roles of diasporic Africans in abolition in West Africa. Sanneh argues that the diasporic Africans who settled Sierra Leone and Liberia, having been influenced by the religious and humanitarian fervor of abolitionism, joined in struggles for abolition in West Africa.[49] Thus, the abolitionist fervor of the diasporic Africans stimulated the African intelligentsia to stake similar abolitionist positions in the Gold Coast.[50]

Ideally, prosopographic studies of the African intelligentsia as abolitionists have much to recommend them. But due to the paucity of sources, specific case studies also offer illuminating insights. In 1863, during the Anglo-Asante war scare, Samuel Greenich, a West Indian soldier with the Fourth West Indian

---

[42] *The Gold Coast Times*, October 20, 1874.

[43] Shepperson, "Abolitionism and African Political Thought," *Transition* 3, no. 12 (1964): 26.

[44] ibid., 22–26.

[45] See also Sanneh, *Abolitionists Abroad*.

[46] Shepperson, "Abolitionism," 23.

[47] ibid.

[48] ibid., 24.

[49] Sanneh, *Abolitionists Abroad*.

[50] For contact between the Gold Coast and their Sierra Leone counterparts, see Jenkins, "Gold Coasters Overseas," 10.

Regiment who had arrived on the Gold Coast on July 1, 1863, had the following, revealing "Last Verse of [a] Song" published in the *African Times* issue of September 23, 1863:

> To banish slavery from the land,
> We go a willing a sturdy band,
> And banners green,
> Our Colours to Coomassie [Kumasi] proud
> We'll carry through Ashantee's crowd;
> Advance, 4th West, and shout aloud
> God Save our Queen.[51]

Certainly, this was tinged with the propagandist ethos that underscored the British quest to conquer Asante. Greenich came from a society where emancipation had been granted, and the fact that he had spent barely three months in the Gold Coast should support the contention that individuals, including foreigners, in the Gold Coast were imbued with abolitionist ideology that may have facilitated the flowering of abolitionism in the littoral communities.

Closely associated with the contributions of diasporic Africans was the role of the African agents of the church. In comparison, E.A. Ayandele, writing about southern Nigeria, shows that James Johnson (Holy Johnson) in the course of his work with the Church Missionary Society in Yorubaland in the late 1870s exhibited strong abolitionist sentiments:

> James Johnson's attitude was quite different. . . . In his letters and journals since assumption of his office he had never spared any words to inform the Church Missionary Society about the cruelties and inhumanities of this institution, giving details of the sufferings of slaves, the prices they fetched from market to market and his hopes that one day these oppressed people would be liberated.[52]

Indeed, Ray Jenkins has argued that Gold Coasters "shared a common experience of acculturation with other West African coastal communities."[53] His views, in addition to extrapolation from the evidence, suggest that the Gold Coast African elites partook in the antislavery sentiments that had been espoused by others. Brew's antislavery crusade, for example, falls under this purview.

The activities of the Christian missions in the nineteenth-century Gold Coast have become a happy hunting ground for historians: Were the missionaries noble altruists or agents of cultural benightedness and colonial rule?[54] Historians agree that the Christian missions were instrumental in the demise of slavery in the Gold Coast but tend to overlook the contributions of the African agents, who did more

---

[51] *African Times*, September 23, 1863, 59.

[52] E.A. Ayandele, *Holy Johnson, Pioneer of African Nationalism, 1836–1917* (London, 1970), 128–129.

[53] In "Gold Coasters Overseas," Jenkins explains on page 10 that although the Gold Coasters "were not expatriates or returnees" their "shared cultural experience" was influenced by other "lateral" ties, including the direction of shipping routes and trade patterns, administrative integration, and links provided by the Christian missions and trading companies.

[54] For a discussion of the literature on the role of the Christian missions, see, for example, Kwabena O. Akurang-Parry, "'A Campaign to get Fetishes Destroyed': The Basel Mission's Pupil Recruitment and Missionization in the Gold Coast, 1850–1877," *Groniek Historisch Tijdschrift* 151 (2001): 157–161.

than their European counterparts to expand the church.[55] For example, much has been written about Rev. David Asante, a stalwart African Basel missionary, and his antislavery struggles against the Akyem Abuakwa rulers during the last quarter of the nineteenth century. Scholars have stressed Asante's political intransigence, but none has ably concluded that Asante's work was defined by the Christian notion of antislavery. Critical readings of Asante's accounts of slavery and the slave trade in Akyem and elsewhere in the Gold Coast, based on his missionary travels, illustrate his avowed distaste for slavery.[56] Above all, the extant historical record, both oral and written, shows that Theophilus Opoku and, indeed, many others of similar evangelical persuasion, starting in the 1860s, contributed more than their European counterparts to the seeding of antislavery in the areas of active evangelization in the Gold Coast, including the Fante coast, Akyem Abuakwa, Ga-Adangbe, Akuapem, Krobo, and Anum.

Like the comparative literature, economic problems of the time, stemming from slavery, also help explain the emergence of antislavery in the Gold Coast. Starting in 1862, a number of local correspondents of the *African Times* wrote about slavery in the Gold Coast and the need to abolish it.[57] As noted, Roberts and Miers have asserted that abolition in Africa was equally affected by the global changes in capitalist organization of production.[58] Overall, Gold Coast merchants and cash crop producers came to the realization that the predatory underpinnings of slavery and slave trading were jeopardizing trade and agricultural ventures in the Gold Coast,[59] as a correspondent of the *African Times*, writing from Keta, noted in 1863.

This was particularly true of the region described in the correspondents' reports as the eastern district, a trading enclave coterminous with the Dahomian slave ports of Whyda and Abosume. [60] The eastern district was the nucleus of the palm oil trade and burgeoning cotton plantations. Additionally, in the aftermath of the Anglo-Asante war from 1873 to 1874, predatory activities, including pawning, panyarring, and consequent population displacement occurred in the region between the protectorate and Asante.[61] These two developments explain why the newspaper correspondents called upon the British government and the British authorities in the Gold Coast to intensify abolition activities in the eastern districts.[62] What is not clear is the nationality of the correspondents, but given that the region had a large number of African and Euro-African traders, it is very likely that members of either group served on the team of newspaper correspondents who wrote about the persistence of slavery and the

---

[55] See, for example, Haenger, *Slaves and Slave Holders*.

[56] See, for example, ibid.

[57] See, for example, a series of letters to the editor in the *African Times* issue of November 22, 1862, 51–52.

[58] Roberts and Miers, "End of Slavery in Africa," 55.

[59] See, for example, *African Times*, November 22, 1862, 51–52; March 23, 1863, 99; October 23, 1863, 44; June 23, 1866, 158; July 23, 1866, 5; August 23, 1866, 23; and October 23, 1866, 45.

[60] The eastern district included the "countries" of Accra, Akuapem, Krobo, Shai, Osu, Doku, Asutuare, Akwamu, Akim, "along the banks of the River Volta to Ada," and Keta. See *African Times*, January 23, 1863, 87.

[61] For a fuller account, see above and Kwabena Akurang-Parry, "'What is and What is not the Law': Imprisonment for Debt and the Institution of Pawnship in the Gold Coast, 1821–1899," in *Pawnship, Slavery, and Colonialism in Africa*, edited by Paul E. Lovejoy and Toyin Falola (New Brunswick, NJ: Africa World Press, 2001), 427–447.

[62] See, for example, Akurang-Parry, "Rethinking the 'Slaves of Salaga.'"

need for abolition. These activities, which jeopardized trade, forced the African intelligentsia to stake antislavery positions, calling upon the colonial authorities to seek antidotes to the problems of slavery, pawnship, and panyarring.[63]

Furthermore, humanitarianism and altruism have been touted and universalized for the Euro-American sectors of the osmotic Atlantic community. Humanitarianism also occurred in the Gold Coast and undoubtedly the littoral of West Africa as a whole. The simple, unvarnished fact is that as much as the case has been made for Americans and Europeans, Black Africans had realized the inhuman vagaries of slavery and sought to end it. The abolitionist epoch occurred in the context of Atlantic history, and as a number of historians, including Miller and Sanneh have posited, Africans recognized the inhumanity of slavery.[64] Oral histories and traditions support the argument that Africans had similar notions of altruism, charity, and philanthropy.[65] Only historians who want to deny the contributions of Africans to abolition would maintain that humanitarianism remained the exclusive preserve of Europeans and Americans during the period of epochal abolition. Overall, by the second half of the nineteenth century, abolitionist thought had percolated not only into the thinking of the Gold Coast African elite, but also into that of ordinary Africans who bore the ravages of slavery and other forms of bondage.

The *Gold Coast Times:* Agency of Abolitionism

The *Gold Coast Times,* founded in 1874,[66] was edited and published by James Hutton Brew at Hamilton House, Cape Coast.[67] Brew, a Fante, was a fourth-generation descendant of an Irish merchant, Richard Brew, who had spent thirty years on the Fante coast.[68] James Hutton Brew was a legal advocate for the Kings and Chiefs (traditional rulers) on numerous occasions. He was the author of the Gold

---

[63] See, for example, Further Correspondence Respecting the Affairs of the Gold Coast, Parliamentary Papers, 1886, C. 4906 (hereafter 4906). For a fuller account, see Akurang-Parry, "Rethinking the 'Slaves of Salaga.'"

[64] Miller, "History and Africa/Africa and History," 156.

[65] See, for example, Interview with Oheneba Kwasi Akurang, Mamfe-Akuapem, March 13, 1994; and Interview with Nana Afua Oye, Suhum, June 17, 1997.

[66] See editorial, *Gold Coast Times*, March 31, 1875, 70. By the 1870s, the West African press had become a platform for political activity. The history of the West African press can be traced to the first decade of the nineteenth century, when newspapers were published as government gazettes. The first newspaper, the *Sierra Leone Gazette*, was issued in 1801. For a historical account of the West African press, see, for example, K.A.B Jones-Quartey, *History, Politics, and the Early Press in Ghana* (Accra, 1975); Fred Omu, *Press and Politics in Nigeria, 1880–1937* (London, 1978); and Leo Spitzer, *The Creoles of Sierra Leone: Responses to Colonialism 1870–1945* (Madison, 1974).

[67] In the first issue of the *Gold Coast Times*, Brew wrote that "we have embarked on this undertaking without any previous experience of the dangers and troubles attendant upon Editorship; but, since we have mustered sufficient courage to test them, any apologies on our part would be out of place. Once engaged in an enterprise we hold it our duty not to turn back. . . ." See *Gold Coast Times*, March 28, 1874, and May 22, 1875, 4. Also see Jones-Quartey, "Thought and Expression," 72.

[68] See Margaret Priestley, "The Emergence of an Elite: A Case Study of a West Coast Family," in *New Elites of Tropical Africa*, edited by P.C. Lloyd (London: Oxford University Press, 1966), 87–99; and Margaret Priestley, *West African Trade and Coast Society: A Family Study* (London, 1969). Richard Brew engaged in the Atlantic slave trade in the second half of the eighteenth century and became influential along the Fante coast.

Coast abolition petitions that sought to rectify Governor George Strahan's misguided abolition policy.[69] Margaret Priestley asserts that

> after 1874 . . . Brew's main purpose was to secure the recognition of African right. . . . He exerted pressure on the colonial administration through organized channels. Indeed, for the first twenty-five years of its existence, the Gold Coast Colony had no more forceful critic than James Hutton Brew.[70]

The *Gold Coast Times* covered events throughout the Gold Coast and circulated in the region between Elmina in the east and Keta in the West. Patronized by the African intelligentsia, the *Gold Coast Times* had correspondents in most of the coastal towns, and letters to the editor came from several communities along the coast. The *Gold Coast Times* also covered events in Africa and Europe, especially England, and culled information from West African and British newspapers. While the editorials dealt with anticolonial themes, it is apparent that the objective was reformism, not revolution; that is, the newspaper sought to better conditions in the Gold Coast but did not seek the demise of colonial rule.[71] However, critical readings of the *Gold Coast Times*, especially composite perspectives on slavery and forced labor in the Gold Coast, illustrate revolutionary takes on colonial policies that informed such institutions.[72]

The editorials of the *Gold Coast Times,* written by Brew, encapsulated the African intelligentsia's abolitionist ideology. If we accept that the African intelligentsia formed the readership, then Brew's editorial views represented them. Overall, the African intelligentsia was a heterogeneous group. Described as the new, social, and Western-educated elite, the African intelligentsia may be divided into two groups: One group was Western educated and "local," mostly Fantes, Akuapems, and Ga-Adangbes. The other group, members of the African Diaspora, namely African-Caribbeans and African-Brazilians, had, from the 1830s, settled the coast between Elmina and Accra, and the immediate interior regions of Akuapem.[73]

Abolitionist Ideologies on the Eve of Abolition

The Cape Coast–based correspondent of *The Scotsman* noted in August 1874 that "the people expect it [slavery] to be put to an end, and will be astonished if it be allowed to go on."[74] "People," as used here, refers to the generality of the Gold Coast population in the littoral towns. Also in October 1874, the *Gold Coast Times* published some comments made by the Gold Coast–based correspondent of the *Standard* (London) in which the writer stated, "the question of domestic slavery is creating considerable

---

[69] See, for example, *Gold Coast Times*, November 30, 1874; and *African Times*, March 1, 1875, 30. For a fuller account, see Akurang-Parry, "'A Smattering of Education.'"

[70] Priestley, *West African Trade*, 166.

[71] See *Gold Coast Times*.

[72] See, for example, "'With a Load on His Head'": 83–104; and Akurang-Parry, "Colonial Forced Labor Strategies" 1–25.

[73] See, for example, Priestley, "West Coast Family"; and Priestley, *West African Trade*. For a summation of the conceptual framework, see Akurang-Parry, "'Smattering of Education.'" For a more recent account, see Roger S. Gocking, *Facing Two Ways: Ghana's Coastal Communities Under Colonial Rule* (Lanham, 1999).

[74] *African Times*, August 29, 1874, 16.

excitement just now throughout the Protectorate." The *Gold Coast Times* then noted that the correspondent "advises the Government to take the bull by the horns and abolish it at once and for ever."[75] The excitement over pending abolition in the protectorate shows that the discussion of abolition had not only occurred in the colony, the hub of the African intelligentsia's intellectual and political activities, but also in the backwater regions of the protectorate.

Given the lack of cogent evidence, it is difficult to pinpoint the exact nature of the excitement in the protectorate, but extrapolation from the evidence shows that at least sections of the littoral populations were excited about the impending abolition.[76] A close reading of some of the opinion pieces in the Gold Coast newspapers shows that the peoples of the coastal states, especially the Fantes, with their access to various Atlantic influences, tended to see themselves as more "civilized" than the interior peoples, notably the Asantes.

Indeed, more substantive and comprehensive accounts of the abolitionist ideology and position of the African intelligentsia can be found in the *Gold Coast Times*. These appeared in the form of a series of reports and editorial comments perhaps mostly written by the founder-editor, Brew. On October 24, 1874, the editorial stated that

> a grand durbar is about to be held during the course of this month by Governor Strahan . . . the Kings and Chiefs have already assembled here [Cape Coast]. Whatever may be the motive, whatever the cause, there are a great many questions to be discussed, difficulties which must be solved one way or the other. . . . [77]

This is a strong indication that the African intelligentsia had readily recognized the future problems of abolition. Nevertheless, the African intelligentsia was also willing to surmount difficulties entailed in the process in order to champion a successful abolition. That the African elite propogated worldwide abolitionist views is illustrated by their ability to distill the colonial state's manumission and compensation policies. Commenting on the approaching meeting to discuss abolition in the Gold Coast, the editorial of the *Gold Coast Times* pinpointed the main objective of the meeting by saying that

> the slave question is uppermost in the minds of all; and the general opinion is that it is principally, if not solely on account that the Kings and Chiefs have been assembled here. If it is so we may rest assured that the government have [sic] found a solution of [sic] this great difficulty—a solution we trust, that will admit of no misunderstanding, and which will not leave scope for the existence of slavery in any shape degree or form.[78]

The editorial went on to warn that if the impending abolition policy "falls short of this";[79] that is, if the policy were not vigorously geared to total abolition of slavery, devoid of "misunderstanding," then the problem (slavery) had better been left untouched. It added, "It is a question which must be dealt with

[75] ibid.

[76] See Kwabena Akurang-Parry, "Ritual, Rumor and Colonialism in Asante and the Gold Coast: The Case of the Alleged Human Sacrifice of 200 Girls by Asantehene [King] Mensa Bonsu in 1881–1882," in *Empires and Slavery in the Atlantic World: Essays in Honor of Robin Law*, edited by Toyin Falola, forthcoming.

[77] *Gold Coast Times*, October 20, 1874.

[78] *Gold Coast Times*, October 20, 1874.

[79] ibid.

completely and thoroughly, so as not to lead to misapprehension in the minds of the ignorant, and admit of evasion by the more intelligent of the community."[80]

The dichotomous allusion to "ignorant masses" and "more intelligent of the community" was to advise the colonial government to implement an abolition policy that would be clear to everyone. Equally, it was a message for the slaveholding class who might exploit ambiguities and loopholes in a lax abolition policy in order to perpetuate slavery.

Perhaps the most forceful statement of all summing up the African intelligentsia's views on the subject merits quoting at length in order to capture the exact mood of the times:

> What our views on the subject are, we have again and again expounded. We shall rejoice to see the day when slavery shall cease to exist on the Gold Coast in any shape or form, when all shall be free; anything short of this will be but trifling with the question, and will but be deferring the inevitable; nevertheless, with all this we contend that the slave-holders are entitled to compensation, and if they are not indemnified it will be simply because the government will have resolved to make might right where right—i.e. justice—would be detrimental to their pecuniary interest.[81]

This quotation clearly affords a number of formidable interpretations. First, it bears out the idea that discussions and opinions bordering on abolitionist sentiments had occurred long before the British authorities contemplated abolition in the Gold Coast. Second, the normative use of "we" and "our" refer to both the generality of the African intelligentsia and abolitionist viewpoints expressed in the *Gold Coast Times*. Third, it shows that compensation remained an important issue. Fourth, it illustrates that the African intelligentsia believed that the demise of slavery was inevitable, and, hence, they emphasized abolition. Last, it shows overt abolitionist enthusiasm for freedom over bondage.

Exemplifying their enthusiasm, the African intelligentsia campaigned to influence the colonial government to define the geographical extent of the Gold Coast in order to make abolition effective. In October 1874, the *Gold Coast Times,* writing about the impending meeting between Governor Strahan and the chiefs at Cape Coast in preparation for abolition, advised that

> whatever may be the motive [of abolition], whatever the cause . . . There are problems which must meet with a solution of some kind; questions affecting the political status of the Colony not less than that of the Kings and Chiefs who have been convened here and their peoples. The one which strikes us, first and foremost, is the extent and limits of the so-called Colony. We say *so-called* [sic: italicized] because in our idea it does not yet answer to its designation. The extent of British jurisdiction must be clearly and distinctly defined.[82]

The newspaper continued that the colonial government must make it clear if the Gold Coast Colony included what was then known as the protectorate. Also, the editorial argued that "it will not be safe any longer not to define the extent of British jurisdiction; it must be thoroughly effective and authoritative."[83] It concluded that a well-defined boundary of the Gold Coast Colony would clearly

---

[80] ibid.

[81] ibid.

[82] ibid.

[83] ibid.

help to demarcate the extent of British jurisdiction and help officials to know where exactly to implement the abolition ordinances.[84]

In fact, in the course of the Anglo-Asante war from 1873 to 1874, the British Parliament debated the geographical extent of the Gold Coast.[85] The debate raised two issues. The first one was whether the Gold Coast should be defined as the areas adjacent to the forts and castles, that is, where British influence had extended since the Bond of 1844. The second one was whether the Gold Coast should be extended to include areas beyond the forts and castles—the region between the coast and Asante, known as the Protectorate. In June 1874, the parliamentary under secretary for colonies, J. Lowther, stated that the Gold Coast was the land occupied by government buildings.[86]

Thus, the British government had made a distinction between bona fide British territory within which slavery would not be allowed to exist and the territory commonly called the Protectorate, where the colonial government could not care less about the prevalence of slavery.[87] Two months later, Lord Carnarvon, the secretary of state for colonies, delimited the Gold Coast to "extend only to the forts, or at most, to so much of the lands immediately adjacent as may be required for defensive, sanitary, or other purposes essential to the maintenance of the British position on the Coast. All beyond that area is foreign country."[88]

A close reading of Lowther and Carnarvon's respective ideas suggests that the colonial government's administration of the abolition ordinances would be marginal in the regions bordering the colony. In the aftermath of abolition, the *Gold Coast Times* continued to demand that the geographical extent of the Gold Coast Colony and adjoining territories should be properly defined in order to make abolition effective.[89] The *Gold Coast Times* culled from the *Standard* (London), which had elucidated that "if we desire the luxury of abolishing slavery on the Gold Coast we must pay for it, not only in money, but in acceptance of full responsibilities of sovereignty over the territory."[90]

This concern, raised before abolition was effected, was used as a protest against Governor Strahan's abolition policy.

Post-Proclamation Abolitionist Viewpoints

The African intelligentsia's abolitionist ideology and their views on British abolition were further exemplified by their response to Governor Strahan's inauguration of abolition. Overall, the African intelligentsia insisted that Governor Strahan had done very little to pave the way for a successful abolition. The *Gold Coast Times* denounced Governor Strahan's speech, saying, "We must confess that we were sadly disappointed thereat" and concluding that

---

[84] ibid.

[85] See *African Times*, March 30, 1874, 51–53; and June 30, 1874, 68–70.

[86] *African Times*, June 30, 1874, 69.

[87] ibid.

[88] Quoted by the *Standard* (no date) and culled by *Gold Coast Times*, March 31, 1875, 70. See also *African Times*, July 20, 1874, 9.

[89] There is no consensus among scholars regarding the extent of active British jurisdiction in the Protectorate. For instance, Roger Gocking has argued that "by this time [mid-1880s] the legal distinction between the colony and the Protected Territories was breaking down." See Gocking, *Facing Two Ways*, 115.

[90] *Standard* (no date) culled by *Gold Coast Times*, March 31, 1875, 70.

a vast amount of time, trouble, and money could have been saved by placarding so many copies of the speech, or by an Ordinance rendering the holding, selling and buying of slaves penal, and the holding and taking of pawns in payment of debt criminal. The speech, as it stands, is good in its way, but that it solves or has solved the great problem, we fear cannot be said.[91]

The editorial noted that Governor Strahan did not make any lasting impression on the assembled indigenous rulers with his "reading over . . . so many lines of written matter."[92]

Mirroring the interest of the African intelligentsia, the *Gold Coast Times* enunciated their visceral attachment to the British Empire,[93] plaintively reporting that

whoever drafted out the speech has not much to be proud of; the rant probably was worthy of the occasion and was much as might be acceptable to a number of ignorant natives. But it should have been borne in mind that whatever was uttered on the occasion was spoken to the world. . . . Hearing and knowing that the British Government were [*sic*] about giving the deathblow to slavery here, all nations and peoples have been on the alert, watching closely the measures they would adopt for its abolition.[94]

Thus, the African intelligentsia concluded that the speech was uninformative and, more important, one that could not fulfill the hopes of using the form abolition took in the Gold Coast as a blueprint for abolition elsewhere. This powerful critique of Governor Strahan's speech unequivocally shows the African intelligentsia's yearning for a successful abolition. In fact, the *Gold Coast Times,* questioned the efficacy of Governor Strahan's speech.

The *Gold Coast Times* argued that nascent informal British rule was based on "a paternal government," with "a high hand"; therefore, Governor Strahan should not have approached abolition with "these half-measures especially in the period of formal colonial rule." Rather, he should have passed an "ordinance at once abolishing slavery and discharging all pawns, instead of finesseing [*sic*] over the point."[95]

Another concern of the African intelligentsia was that abolition was inaugurated without any law or ordinance backing it. That is, the inaugural meeting on November 3, 1874, had occurred before any legal document effecting abolition was made available to the public. As a result, the *Gold Coast Times* reported that

the Government are [*sic*] now preparing an Ordinance[96] to that effect, and that Governor Strahan's speech was merely to give the people a warning of that which is to be done . . . the speech will no more have the desired effect unless backed by law than an edict issued prohibiting the sale of the necessaries

---

[91] *Gold Coast Times,* November 30, 1874, 59.

[92] ibid.

[93] See, for example, Akurang-Parry, "'A Smattering of Education.'"

[94] *Gold Coast Times,* November 30, 1874, 59. See also Akurang-Parry, "'A Smattering of Education.'"

[95] *Gold Coast Times,* November 30, 1874, 59.

[96] I have argued that historians of slavery in the Gold Coast have overlooked this flaw in the abolition process and that most scholars writing about the subject have concluded that there was legal backing for the inauguration of abolition on November 3, 1874. See "'A Smattering of Education.'"

of life. The question is of too great importance—of vital importance—to the peoples of the Colony for them to take any notice of whatever was uttered by Governor Strahan if nothing more is going to be done . . . if you are determined to put an end to slavery and the pawning of people, make laws and do not speechify.[97]

The pivotal argument is that, lacking a law to back it, Governor Strahan's speech and, for that matter, abolition would be taken lightly despite the fact that the "question is of too great importance."[98] The critical position espoused by the *Gold Coast Times* was picked up by the London-based *African Times,* which echoed, "Was it after all, only a vain and empty boast with no intention on the part of the Governor . . . to insist on obedience?"[99] In the end, the *Gold Coast Times* stated that as result of the ineffectiveness of the speech and the fact that there was no law backing it, "people" had interpreted abolition "in their own way such as will suit their own ideas of affairs."

About one month after the inauguration of abolition, and perhaps due to the massive desertion of slaves, the African intelligentsia called into question the lack of assistance for freed slaves in their transition from bondage to freedom. The *Gold Coast Times* explained that freed slaves would be a "pariah of society,"[100] noting that they were "branded" and would remain as outsiders, "until they find their emancipation an incubus on them" and were "resold" eventually.[101]

Thus, the African intelligentsia had concluded that, lacking social and economic choices and opportunities, freed slaves would revert to forms of bondage and dependency. They issued this statement about one month into abolition, and it was prophetic: the lack of policies to assist government-freed and deserting slaves posed a barrier to emancipation in the Gold Coast.

Conclusion

This chapter, a case study of abolition in the Gold Coast, addresses the issue of African contributions to abolitionism in the Gold Coast prior to and during the early stages of abolition. It is patently clear that the *Gold Coast Times,* patronized by the African intelligentsia, blazoned abolitionist thought. Abolitionism was articulated by a section of the African intelligentsia who had certainly used local ideas and also borrowed from the forces of change that had shaped agencies of abolition in Europe and the Americas. Thus, the watershed of the African intelligentsia's abolitionist thought was a mixture of local factors and concentric movements of ideologies within the nodal points of the osmotic Atlantic community. The evidence of the African abolitionist ideology is not only based on their mere utterances, but also on their compelling recommendations. Indeed, had the Colonial Office and Governor Strahan listened to some of what the African intelligentsia had to say and, for instance, developed freed slave villages, the course of abolition in the Gold Coast would have been different.

---

[97] *Gold Coast Times,* November 30, 1874, 59.

[98] ibid.

[99] *African Times,* December 31, 1874, and January 1, 1875, 8.

[100] This view was also expressed in the *Western Echo,* December 19, 1885. The founder-editor of the *Western Echo* was James Hutton Brew.

[101] *Gold Coast Times,* November 30, 1874, 59.

Chapter 7

COLONIAL LEGACIES:
Ghosts, Gulags, and the Silenced Traumas of Empire

Peyi Soyinka-Airewele

Introduction: History Will One Day Have Its Say

My beloved companion,

I write you these words without knowing whether you will receive them, when you will receive them, or whether I will still be alive when you read them. Throughout my struggle for the independence of my country, I have never doubted for a single instant that the sacred cause to which my comrades and I have dedicated our lives would triumph in the end. But what we wanted for our country—its right to an honorable life, to perfect dignity, to independence with no restrictions—was never wanted by Belgian colonialism and its Western allies, who found direct and indirect, intentional and unintentional support among certain high officials of the United Nations, that body in which we placed all our trust when we called on it for help.

They have corrupted certain of our countrymen; they have bought others; they have done their part to distort the truth and defile our independence. What else can I say? That whether dead or alive, free or in prison by orders of the colonialists, it is not my person that is important. What is important is the Congo, our poor people whose independence has been turned into a cage, with people looking at us from outside the bars, sometimes with charitable compassion, sometimes with glee and delight. But my faith will remain unshakeable. . . .

I want my children, whom I leave behind and perhaps will never see again, to be told that the future of the Congo is beautiful and that their country expects them, as it expects every Congolese, to fulfill the sacred task of rebuilding our independence, our sovereignty; for without justice there is no dignity, and without independence there are no free men.

Neither brutal assaults, nor cruel mistreatment, nor torture have ever led me to beg for mercy, for I prefer to die with my head held high, unshakeable faith and the greatest confidence in the destiny of my country, rather than live in slavery and contempt for sacred principles. History will one day have its say; it will not be the history taught in the United Nations, Washington, Paris or Brussels, however, but the history taught in the countries that have rid themselves of colonialism and its puppets. Africa will write its own history, and both north and the south of the Sahara it will be a history full of glory and dignity.

*Do not weep for me, my companion. I know that my country, now suffering so much, will be able
to defend its independence and its freedom. Long live the Congo! Long live Africa!
Patrice*[1]

Congolese prime minister Patrice Lumumba's riveting last testament to his wife was penned in a death cell shortly before his brutal murder in January 1961, as a victim of a chilling web of global intrigues and complicities involving the Belgian government, the U.S. Central Intelligence Agency, and local conspirators. Democratically elected the first prime minister of the newly independent Congo in June 1960, Lumumba's defiant anti-imperialism soon swept him from the triumphal heights of popular support and adulation into a horrifying tale of international "liquidation plots," torture, and brutal execution less than a year after a heady inaugural speech that incensed the Belgian monarch.

Ludo de Witte (2001) and other scholars have provided a magisterial accounting of the global convulsions evoked by Lumumba's struggle against empire, his desperate efforts to define the fate of the formally liberated Congo, to prevent its balkanization at the behest of global capital, and to resist the power of the international neocolonial coalition that ultimately orchestrated his downfall and assassination. The official apology issued by the Belgian government following a commission of inquiry decades after Lumumba's assassination has not stilled the questions raised by this ghost of the early postcolonial past.

How is one to relate Africa's colonial past to issues that challenge its incumbent postcolony? For some, Lumumba's story speaks to the invidious machinery of colonial authoritarian violence that continues to haunt contemporary Africa—a history well captured in several books, including Adam Hochschild's *King Leopold's Ghost: A Story of Greed, Terror, and Heroism in Colonial Africa* (1999) and Caroline Elkins's *Imperial Reckoning: The Untold Story of Britain's Gulag in Kenya* (2005a). For others perhaps, his biography foreshadows the discomfiting question of the continuities and tensions of empire, of complicities between local and global forces, of unconcluded questions of global accountability. For Achille Mbembe, the postcolony relates colonial power to contemporary subjectivities in African political processes in ways that indict the African postcolonial state's ability to transcend its bestial, obscene, and grotesque colonial roots (Mbembe 2001).

More than any other region, the African postcolony evokes discomfiture in the accounting of colonialism, due perhaps to the fact that its political independence is of very recent provenance. Formal independence occurred in tandem with the civil rights movement of the 1960s in the United States and was perhaps only concluded with the 1994 inauguration of South Africa's first Black president, Nelson Mandela, the harbinger of liberation after centuries of a virulently racist colonized state. The colonial question in Africa is constantly contemporized by the economic crisis in the continent and global representations of the Black identity. For citizens of the postcolony, the discourse of history is not only complicated by the frustrations that have attended dreams of a progressive social, economic, and political future and by apparent leadership failures, but also by an awareness that current struggles for change are stymied by structures, identities, and relations molded by agencies of the colonial past. For the older generation, there are also suppressed accounts of trauma and loss, and their effects have not been addressed in the aftermath of colonialism.

---

[1] Ludo de Witte, "Letter to Pauline Lumumba," in *The Assassination of Lumumba* (London and New York: Verso, 2001).

On the other hand, for the postcolonial generation in the West—the contemporary legatees of the power of the colonizing centers—African colonial history often evokes discomfort, guilt, and the burden of memory. Not surprisingly, many observers have felt safer neutering the discussion of empire by a clinical treatment of the subjects of benefit and loss and cultural transitions. Within such methodological cages, the tumultuousness of empire can be tamed and confined to a specific time frame, and its violence can be anesthetized through a dispassionate analysis of the destabilizing colonial remapping of the continent, its languages, its democratic traditions, and its economies.

Lumumba's poignant letter is a disturbing invitation to embrace a more murky study of coloniality. The impact of colonial violence, personal and collective trauma, colonial institutions and structures, and constructed historical relations that weave colonizer and colonized into tangled webs of empire can be seen clearly today in many African countries. Those influences and institutions of colonialism—the ghosts and gulags—reach deeply into the past while holding the continent a casualty of their continuing influence.

Televised interviews with Lumumba's executioners have brought a chilling reminder of the tangible presence of empire and its power even today. In Thomas Giefer's documentary, *Une mort de style coloniale: Patrice Lumumba, une tragédie africaine* (2000), Belgian officers chortle gleefully as they proudly regale the world with reminiscences of their role in the torture, murder, and dismemberment of the Congolese prime minister. For Colonel Claude Grandelet of the Katangan Army, Roger Leva of the Katangan Military Police, Commander Verdickt, Colonel Moliere, and others of the Belgian secret services, remorse seems an unknown value.

Like complicit representatives of the United Nations, the U.S. CIA, and Congolese conspirators, they face the cameras, secure in their knowledge of service to Western empire and protected by a nation whose reluctant apology is nullified by the absence of punishment and the open flaunting of the prurient conscience of its agents. "For us," they now explain proudly, "the business began after his execution. We cut the bodies [of prime minister Lumumba and two of his ministers] up into pieces, we burned them and we also had huge quantities of acid, like you have in car batteries, so most of each body was dissolved, and then the rest, we burned them, but we had to do all this without the blacks seeing, in the middle of the forest—that was a problem too."

The interviewer probes unsuccessfully for signs of transformation in the imperial mindset: "What was your reaction?"

"Oh I said good riddance, what else would you expect me to say?"

"Was it a solution to your problems?"

"Yes."

"You were happy?"

"Happy is not the word. Busy—you were busy. Here's one problem gone—now what's the next problem?"

But the repeated peals of laughter from the Belgians belie this statement. One happily displayed his personal souvenir of photos and two of Lumumba's teeth to the cameras and in barely controlled fits of merriment informed the viewers that "there are even people who believe he will return, but the man will have to come back with two front teeth missing I think, ha ha ha."

"Did you feel any pity for him?"

"Why should I? I have no pity for him, he insulted our king" (Giefer 2000).

Imperial structures and tensions cast a long shadow in the African continent. Alan Cowell's thoughtful commentary on a recent contentious public trial in Kenya in May 2009 was most appropriately titled, "Wrestling with Ghosts of Colonialism." When Cholmondeley—"son of the fifth Baron Delamere, scion of Kenya's residual White aristocracy"—was arraigned in court in Nairobi, charged with murdering a Black poacher, Cowell observes that

> . . . it was inevitable that this juxtaposition of bloodshed and privilege across the racial divide would provoke comparison with other misbehavior by his forebears stretching back decades. It was inevitable, too, that as his trial unfolded and he was sentenced earlier this month to eight months in prison on manslaughter charges—in addition to the three years he had already served awaiting trial—the contrast between the gravity of the crime and the seeming leniency of the punishment would ignite protests that white privilege had survived far beyond the moment in 1963 when Kenya first raised aloft its banner of independence. And most of all, the outcome seemed to hold up to blacks and whites alike the fractured mirror through which each perceives the other—literally as "the other," uneasy partners thrust together by history and still struggling to lay to rest the troubled ghosts of their uneven tryst. (Cowell 2009)

The fissures in Kenyan public sentiment surrounding the case bore witness to the lingering tensions in addressing the present past, as Cowell acknowledges:

> For some among Kenya's dwindling white minority—30,000 in a land of more than 35 million—the punishment handed down to the 40-year-old Mr. Cholmondeley (pronounced CHUM-lee), despite his protestations of innocence, was taken as confirmation that the sins of the colonial past would forever be visited on successive generations. For Masai protesters in the courtroom, recalling the way colonial intruders took their land a century ago, the leniency reflected a double standard. A year before the death of the poacher, Robert Njoya, in May 2006, Mr. Cholmondeley had been accused of shooting to death a Masai game warden, Samson Ole Sisina, though the charge was dropped on the order of the attorney general.
>
> "Who next?" read one placard held aloft by a courtroom protester. "Butcher of Naivasha," said another, referring to the town close to the Delameres' 19,500-hectare, or 48,000-acre, estate, called Soysambu, 88 kilometers, or 55 miles, north of Nairobi. With some gallows humor, and in reference to the whites who indulged tastes in drugs and partner-swapping on the shores of Lake Naivasha in the 1930s—the so-called Happy Valley set—wags in Nairobi began talking of the Trigger Happy Valley set. But there was, too, another lesson: independent Africa has been remarkably generous toward its erstwhile colonial rulers, offering a pact with one very simple rule. "The white community has survived by laying low, keeping their mouths shut," one settler, Michael Cunningham-Reid, told the *Guardian* newspaper of London. But, decades later, how do Africa's stubborn postcolonial minorities define their niche among people who did not invite their presence in the first place? (ibid., 2009)

Africa today does not offer the scholar the luxury of imagining a closed and neatly captioned colonial epoch. It neither offers the ease of a concluded past, nor an alienated history. The countries that epitomize the African postcolony embody the contradictions of formal independence—of indigenous agency, identities, and cultures subsisting in the transmuted presence of colonial empire, which persists, not as a vestigial social, institutional, and political-economic ghost, but, in several countries, as tangible cultures, monuments, hierarchies, and institutions.

Colonialism in Africa: A Basic Frame

European colonial claims to "civilizing missions" and representations of a primitive savage African identity are at odds with the documented reality of Africa's precolonial histories. Historians from across the world have made copious contributions to our understanding of the historical context within which Europe began its various engagements with African societies. They include Basil Davidson (1995), Jan Vansina (1978), Adu Boahen (1989), Toyin Falola (2001, 2005), John Iliffe (2007), Joseph Harris (1998), Willis N. Huggins and John G. Jackson (1969), Mahmood Mamdani (1996, 2001), Cheikh Anta Diop (1974), and Martin Bernal (1987). Such intensely researched, carefully documented works are widely available and cover a wealth of diverse archeological, linguistic, and other evidences preceding the transatlantic slave trade and colonial expansion of Europe into Africa. The evidence demonstrates the extensive political, social, and economic development of precolonial African societies and their far-reaching international relationships and influences on Europe, the Middle East, Asia, and even the Americas. The historical documentation of precolonial Africa provides a fascinating account of extensive trade; industrial, intellectual, and social development; religious globalism; famed rulers; and societies organized with all the pomp familiar to the European nations that sought to engage them in formal commerce, communications, diplomatic relations, and alliances. These historical realities are much at variance with the later discourse of "civilizing missions" that was evoked to justify the conquest of the same empires, states, kingdoms, and small stateless societies.

Precolonial Context

Historian James Graham has compiled an exhaustive accounting of political developments in Africa preceding and during the interruption of African statesmanship by the transatlantic slave trade and later by Europe's infamous "scramble for Africa" (c. 1880–1900), a hiatus that surpassed the turbulence earlier generated by the Arab invasions because it led to the substantive removal of Africans from international political history, the disruption of domestic political power, and a severe and lasting economic, social, and cultural impact. To fully understand the nature of colonial epistemic and structural violence, we must contextualize it within the reality of the historic political structures and developments in Africa. I turn to Graham's (1998) abridged account of historic Africa for conjuring the forms of the societies that were formally annexed by conquering Europeans in the late nineteenth century (see Box 7.1).

The Scramble for Africa

The "scramble" for Africa was arguably a quest for absolute and direct political control of Africa's enormous natural resources, burgeoning markets, and political economies. By the early 1800s, after two centuries of an ever-expanding Atlantic slave trade, much of the continent was under the influence of rival European commercial interests often in direct competition with each other as the trade in captives transformed into competition over access to land and natural products, such as palm oil, cocoa, cotton, and groundnuts needed for the growing industries of Europe and the New World. In 1787, Britain had established its first West African colony, Sierra Leone, as a home for freed slaves, and in 1822, the American Colonization Society founded Liberia. Its capital city, Monrovia (named after U.S. president James Monroe) was selected as the initial settlement for freed slaves, who might have fomented antislavery violence among other slaves had they remained on American soil. Such settlements generated tensions between those native to the region and the settlers who came to dominate the political and

Box 7.1 Revisiting Development in Ancient and Medieval Africa by James Graham

Ancient Times

The annals of numerous ancient African civilizations are well documented and increasingly well known. During the early prehistory of Africa, the Rift Valley ancestors of modern human beings gradually evolved and began to settle more permanently in villages (initially in the Nile River Valley) to develop the political foundations of ancient civilization. The Old Kingdom of Ancient Egypt (c. 3100–2180 BCE) developed Africa's earliest large-scale political economy, blending local and regional societies into one powerful Nile Valley nation, ruled by successive pharaohs. Citizens rendered enough tribute to support the building of massive pyramids and other public works and to maintain large and specialized state bureaucracies.

The earliest of ancient Egypt's architectural masterpieces, now known as the Step Pyramid, was designed by Imhotep (c. 2700 BCE) in honor of Pharaoh Zoser, whom he served. In addition to his considerable and creative skills as an architect, Imhotep is widely remembered for his ancient studies in astronomy, medicine, mathematics, and philosophy; one of his best known proverbs, handed down through the ages, is said to have been "Eat, drink and be merry, for tomorrow we shall die." The great pyramid at Giza (481 feet high, 755 feet on each side at the base) was constructed for Pharaoh Khufu (c. 2600 BCE). It is now estimated that Egyptian citizens cut, hauled, and carefully fit together more than two and a half million 5,000-pound blocks of limestone rock for over twenty years to erect this massive, powerful, and enduring monument. Such awe-inspiring monuments attest to a more complex and widespread political and religious system than had ever existed previously, a system so successful that it still excites our imagination today.

Following years of fragmentation and change in Egypt's Old and Middle kingdoms, a succession of warrior pharaohs reunited the ancient Egyptian nation; invaded and conquered other ancient civilizations in Kush, Assyria, Palestine, and elsewhere; and established the earliest multinational empire in ancient Africa. Although Egypt's New Kingdom (c. 1600–1100 BCE) expanded to become an empire under military leadership, its most widely known pharaohs were those who sought to develop commerce, communications, construction, and the arts. One such noted pharaoh was Queen Hatshepsut, who ruled as coregent during the reigns of three imperial pharaohs (c. 1500 BCE) and who is now recognized as one of the most successful female rulers in early ancient Africa.

Later, when another New Kingdom ruler, Akhenaten, became pharaoh (c. 1375 BCE), he proclaimed the revolutionary idea of monotheism—that there was only one God. He built an exemplary new city and promoted new "classical" standards in ancient artwork, as typified by the famous sculpted head of his wife, Nefertiti. Pharaoh Ramses II (c. 1290–1220 BCE) devoted most of his sixty-seven-year reign to maintaining peace, expanding international trade, and undertaking extensive building projects throughout the Nile Valley. Foreign invasions from the Middle East and southern Europe later transformed the trajectories of ancient Egyptian development, while other African civilizations also established large-scale political and economic structures during ancient times.

Ancient Egyptians coexisted with various Kushite kingdoms (southward, along the Nile River) throughout their dynastic history (c. 3100–1100 BCE), after which the Kushites reorganized, conquered Egypt (c. 750–660 BCE), and established extensive ironworks in their reconstituted empire at Meroe (c. 600 BCE–350). Meanwhile, near the southern coastline of the Red Sea, ancient writings refer to the Queen of Punt (c. 1500 BCE) and Makeda, the fabled Queen of Sheba (c. 950 BCE), as

(continued)

Box 7.1 (continued)

well as to King Ezana of Axum (c. 350), who adopted Coptic (Egyptian) Christianity as a state religion.

Elsewhere, impressive sculptures from ancient Nok and Jenne (c. 500 BCE–200), suggest that other ancient civilizations also existed long ago, near the Niger River. Ancient trade routes across the Sahara linked such West African civilizations, through Mauritania, to Carthage's lucrative commercial empire in the Maghreb of northwest Africa (c. 600–150 BCE) and excited the envy of Rome's early rulers. Toward the end of the Carthaginian wars, Roman ships and soldiers attacked, looted, burned, and completely destroyed the ancient city of Carthage, imposing what has come to be known as an uncompromising "Carthaginian Peace" on the inhabitants, who reestablished their cultural presence with St. Augustine (d. 430 in imperial Rome) as well as later (in the Maghreb).

Medieval Times

Even though different sects of ancient Christianity had developed in Egypt, the Maghreb, eastern Sudan, and Ethiopia, the beginnings of Africa's medieval history were much more broadly associated with the initial expansion of Islam (c. 640–740), as new cultural influences and identity configurations began to emerge. Indeed, the most renowned of Africa's medieval empires consolidated and rose to the highest stages of international influence with Islam as their imperial religion. From their home base in the Maghreb, for instance, North Africans established the Fatimid Dynasty in Cairo (c. 970–1170), where they founded al-Azhar, the first modern university in the medieval world. The Almohads (c. 1150–1250), succeeding an Almoravid dynasty of Mauritania, unified the entire Maghreb and Southern Iberia into an Islamic empire that produced some of the most advanced architecture and scientific thought in early medieval times. The subsequent fragmentation of the Almohad Empire, into different autonomous regions, led to the emergence of cities like Tripoli, Tunis, Algiers, Tangier, and Marrakesh as regional urban centers of government (in the core areas of the modern African countries of Libya, Tunisia, Algeria, and Morocco).

By about 1150 in Ethiopia, the first of a new line of emperors (known as the Zagwe Dynasty) began to reunite various local kings and Christian monasteries under a single ruler, or "king of kings." In 1270, this Zagwe Empire was taken over by a new dynasty of Christian Abyssinian rulers, who claimed royal authority by virtue of being direct descendants of ancient Israel's King Solomon and Sheba's Queen Makeda. Like ancient Axum's King Ezana, Abyssinia's medieval Solomonic kings claimed that their descent from Israel's King David made them cousins of Jesus, and they also reestablished official ties with Egypt's ancient Christian (Coptic) Church. Abyssinia's medieval Christian Kingdom then expanded into a Highland Empire, at least until the last years of the long regency by Empress Helena (1487–1522). In 1520, a dynamic coastal ruler named Ahmed Gran acquired muskets (from Ottoman Muslims) and declared an Islamic holy war against Christian Abyssinia. For about twenty years, Ahmed Gran's coastal Muslims fought against Christian kings of the interior and conquered much of the Ethiopian Highlands. In 1542, however, musketeers from Abyssinia's Portuguese allies (who maintained Christian solidarity and diplomatic relations with Abyssinian rulers until 1608 when they split over doctrinal differences) helped Ethiopia's Christian kings to regain control over their mountainous domains.

South of Ethiopia, along East Africa's Indian Ocean coast, venturesome seafarers from the Arabian Sea had been settling in many Swahili towns, some of which developed into prosperous city-states, between 1100–1500. Based primarily on their exports of gold and ivory from the interior, a common

Bantu-based language and culture, Islamic and South Asian contacts, and splendid coral-rock architecture, medieval Swahili city-states such as Mogadishu, Pate, Mombasa, Zanzibar, Kilwa, Mozambique, and Sofala were among the wealthiest, most commercial, and cosmopolitan civilizations of East-Central Africa.

Meanwhile, the largest and most famous empires of medieval Africa arose in the western Sudan, where the (Mande-speaking) Soninke Kingdom of Ghana and the (Islamic) Almoravid movement in Takrur each consolidated and came to control large portions of the westernmost caravan routes across the Sahara Desert (c. 700–1100). It was only after Takrur's Almoravids emigrated northward (to conquer the Maghreb) and rival Mande kings joined to challenge Ghana's imperial dominance along the Upper Niger River during the twelfth century that Mali's legendary warrior-prince Sundiata coopted, conquered, and consolidated twelve neighboring Mande kingdoms (including Ghana) into one multinational Islamic Empire (c. 1235–1260).

The richest and most famous of all Mali's Emperors was Mansa Musa (c. 1307–1330). During 1324–1325, Mansa Musa's imperial caravan lingered in Cairo (where he distributed so much gold as to deflate its international value) before proceeding on his holy pilgrimage to Mecca (where he was confirmed as the caliph of West Africa). On his return trip, Mansa Musa recruited Islamic sages, architects, and scholars from Egypt and the Maghreb to help staff Mali's leading universities in ancient Jenne and legendary Timbuktu, along the Niger River Bend. During the thirteenth and fourteenth centuries, Mali's empire grew to encompass many commercial, multicultural cities (civilizations) and kingdoms, all of which (and many more) were subsequently (after Mali's fifteenth-century fragmentation) absorbed into the third and largest successive empire of Africa's medieval Western Sudan. Established by the Gao Kingdom near Timbuktu, it became widely known as the Songhay Empire (c. 1460–1590).

Under Songhay's founding emperors, Sunni Ali and Askia Muhammad Toure (c. 1460–1530), the magnificent architecture of Sankore University (in Timbuktu) came to symbolize the uplifting spirit of learning, while the empire's extensive military and administrative control over their far-flung production and trade of both gold and salt resources brought legendary wealth to Timbuktu, Jenne, and other imperial cities. Drawing on such robust revenues, Askia Muhammad financed his own grand pilgrimage to Mecca (1494–1496), where (like Mansa Musa 170 years earlier) he was proclaimed the caliph of West Africa. During the early 1500s, after Portuguese seafarers built their massive stone fortress (El Mina) on West Africa's "Gold Coast" (undermining Songhay's trans-Saharan trade), a papal emissary from Rome named Leo Africanus wrote that there were "many doctors, judges, priests and other learned men" who lived in Timbuktu, where "various manuscripts and written books" were imported from the Maghreb and "sold for more money than any other merchandise." Noting that the Songhay government in Timbuktu had "a magnificent and well furnished court" and that the city's inhabitants were "exceedingly rich," Leo Africanus also observed that there were "a great store of men and women slaves" in Songhay. Some of these war captives rose through government and military bureaucracies, by virtue of meritorious work, to achieve high positions of administrative responsibility—as, indeed, did Muhammed Toure, when he rose by military merit to become a general (*askia*) and, ultimately, a most exalted emperor and caliph of West Africa.

In addition to these wealthy Islamic empires of the Western Sudan, many kingdoms and city-states emerged endogenously in other parts of medieval Africa. In what is now Nigeria, for instance, Benin, Yoruba, Hausa, and Ibo city-states were important centers of commerce and civilization, long before European explorers and sea captains had "discovered" them—or their classically sculpted bronze figures

(continued)

Box 7.1 (continued)

(many of which were later looted by colonial armies, ending up in European museums). Meanwhile, in central Africa, federated kingdoms such as Luba and Lunda emerged, thriving on internal African trade of local copper, iron, and gold resources. To the south of Central Africa's copper belt, the Shona Kingdom of Zimbabwe was producing gold for international commerce as early as 1100. As the Indian Ocean sea trade increased along with international demand for gold, medieval Zimbabwe also flourished (c. 1250–1450); its massive stone ruins, extensive craft work, and imported luxury items (from as far away as China) have provided archaeologists and historians with material evidence of the splendor in which their rulers lived.

*   *   *   *   *

Although contemporary Africa is often portrayed (by modern media) as an "underdeveloped" continent, mired in its own "poverty, ignorance, and disease," we know that medieval African city-states, kingdoms, and empires were as developmentally sound and advanced as any other civilizations of that era (among Europeans, Asians, or Native Americans). Then, beginning about 500 years ago, as Walter Rodney has trenchantly argued (in *How Europe Underdeveloped Africa*, Howard University Press, 1981), "underdevelopment" came to be used as a *comparative* term in modern discourse—i.e., Africa's "underdevelopment" can historically be seen as the underside of Europe's "development," like "two sides of the same coin." By dominating international terms of trade, capital accumulation, technological change, and racialist attitudes, Europeans launched the Commercial, Scientific and Industrial revolutions (c. 1500–1870). Then, supported by African gold and slave labor, they finally established enough control over world trade, finance capital, and military technology (e.g., gunboats, mortars, repeating rifles, and maxim guns) to divide, conquer, and colonize the "Dark Continent" (which they knew so little about) between about 1870 and 1920.

This Early Modern Period of African History—associated with the infamous Atlantic slave trade (c. 1500–1870) and Europe's brutal "Scramble for Africa" (c. 1870–1920)—is far too complex (if seen from the perspective of the Africans who struggled so courageously and persistently to sustain their independence and dignity) to summarize here. During the devastating centuries of slave raiding in West-Central Africa, for instance, Kongo's King Affonso (1506–1543) sent heartfelt letters to his diplomatic and "brother king" in Portugal, protesting the wanton disruptions and cruelty of the Portuguese slavers who were "trading" in his lands (which, in fact, led to a tragically premature dissolution of the Kingdom of Kongo). A century later, after the Portuguese had built and come to inhabit another of their great stone fortresses, at the nearby port of Luanda (in Angola), Matamba's famous Warrior-Queen Nzinga devoted her whole adult life (1624–1663) to fighting the depredations of yet another generation of Portuguese slave traders. This kind of ongoing heroism among so many African resistance leaders, through four centuries of conflict with European intruders, eventually gave rise to such forward-looking Pan-Africanist pioneers as those who organized the last independent multinational confederations to effectively oppose the implementation of colonial rule. An inspiring leader of two such confederations in the Western Sudan (1875–1898) was Samori Toure (both a modernizer and a unifier) who developed innovative military tactics, adopted Islam as a unifying ideology, promoted schools and literacy, developed centralized administrative structures and industrial workshops, and sought alliances with other West African leaders in fighting against French and British invaders before he was captured in 1898.

In short, the endogenous development of early modern Africa was interrupted (during the past 500 years) by persistent foreign intrusions, continuing pressures to obtain captives for the Atlantic slave trade and, ultimately, Europe's full-scale invasion, subjugation, and colonization of the continent.

social hierarchies of their new homes and resulted in disastrous wars in postcolonial Liberia and Sierra Leone (Khapoya 1998, 98–100).

The specifics of the "scramble for Africa" provide glaring proof that the ethnocentric claims of "civilizing Africa" or Kipling's "white man's burden" had little to do with the commercial, political, and economic logic that drove the quest for formal control of African territories. The establishment of the "Congo Free State" by Belgium's King Leopold, who sought to rule over the massive Congo (Zaire), and counterclaims by other European monarchs provide ample proof that greed ruled the day. In response to King Leopold's stake, the French and Portuguese grabbed the neighboring lands around the mouth of the Congo River during the early 1800s, and then Germany made hasty claim to three different strips of West Africa's coast. Britain responded with a frenzied consolidation of its commercial interests around the Niger River Delta and elsewhere, while France quickly dispatched its armed forces to West Africa and, later, to North Africa and other regions.

The colonial land grab was certainly facilitated by superior military equipment that resulted from the Industrial Revolution and wealth from slave plantations and mines in the New World, but it was anchored in a virulent racism against the colonized Africans, who were increasingly visualized as debased subjects, slaves in the New World, and occupants of conquered territories. This was the racial vista of the colonizers, administrators, missionaries, explorers, and European citizens who stood to gain from conquest, pacification, settlement, and control.

Despite the fact that many African states struggled to preserve indigenous institutions that enabled some autonomy and resistance to European domination, Graham (1998) argues that, "European colonialism in Africa interrupted important continuities in the development of large-scale political economies throughout the continent. Because of their racialist attitudes, colonial administrators often pursued policies that totally disregarded African interests or opinions and that removed colonized Africans as active participants in shaping their own history" (ibid., 110).

European rule in Africa was formalized at the infamous Berlin conference of 1884–1885, when rival European monarchs met and elected to settle their armed competition over the continent's resources through formal annexation agreements. Some scholars have sought to rationalize the colonization of Africa as emerging from an "exploratory European" spirit and quest to discover the global Other, a religious missionary zeal, and an ethnocentrism that led colonizers to believe they were indeed humanizing the African world. However, the documented evidence on the state of historical development of Africa at the time, the intensity of the economic rivalry between the European states for resources and manpower in the continent, and the subsequent inhumane violence linked to the extraction of resources for European benefit—all prove that colonization was merely a sordid quest for direct political and military control of the human and material resources of the colonies. Colonization involved an extension of imperial control to fit the needs of the newly industrialized European powers and, thus, the official "Partition of Africa" recognized various territories of influence and control, with Britain and France controlling approximately two-thirds of the continent. The consensus was to parcel out the spoils of war, as evidenced in the agreement to immediately deprive Germany of its colonies after the First World War under the League of Nations mandate (ibid., 112).

Resistance, Containment, and the Postcolonial Legacy

Resistance to colonial expansion was widespread and often prolonged, as in the northeast "Horn of Africa," where the Somalian confederation of clans under Said Mohammed (1895–1920) formed

Table 7.1 European Control of Africa

Imperial power	Period	
	Pre–World War I (percentage)	Post–World War I (percentage)
France	36	37
Britain	30	34
Belgium	8	8
Germany	8	0
Italy	7	7
Portugal	7	7
Uncolonized	4	7
Total	100	100

Source: Vincent Khapoya, *The African Experience*, 1998, 112.

a coalition that continued to resist colonial authority in British, French, and Italian Somaliland, as well as in Ethiopia's Ogaden region, into the 1920s. Menelik II (1889–1912) was extremely successful in creating the nineteenth-century confederation of Ethiopia and in modernizing the national army, so Ethiopians were able to repeatedly repel Italian invaders and ultimately avoid being colonized (Graham 1998, 108). "Menelik II exploited European rivalries skillfully enough to gain international diplomatic support and to arm his soldiers with up-to-date weapons. He also promoted literacy and modern infrastructure, building the foundations for a permanent capital in Addis Ababa and a centralized government in Ethiopia" (ibid). Despite such vibrant resistance, virtually the entire African continent was ultimately subdued and made subject to various colonial institutions.

Whether by direct or indirect political control or company rule (which gave latitude to merchant companies to govern the colonies through extremely brutal and repressive forms of exploitation), certain features manifested repeatedly in Europe's African colonies—the expropriation of land; exploitation and use of forced labor; adoption of extreme modes of repression and punishment of resistance, including concentration camps or colonial gulags; the introduction of cash crops and mono-cultural economies; imposition of unjust and repressive taxation that forced citizens off their lands; use of indentured labor from Asia to minimize local resistance and create new social and racial hierarchies; the transfer of mineral wealth from African colonies to Europe; the direct official suppression of industrialization; and the elimination of preexisting transnational and regional cooperation and trade.[2]

It is impossible to document the egregious structural, physical, and epistemic violence that accompanied colonial control of the continent. However, the ubiquitous instability in so many postcolonial African countries owes much to the tangible and intangible structures—our gulags and ghosts—that were instrumental in Europe's realizing its "civilizing mission" to the continent.

The contemporary Kenyan crisis, Anderson affirms, was shaped by the complexion of its racial politics. Its people were "locked within the limits of a racial hierarchy that placed Europeans on top of

---

[2] For a discussion of some of the economics of colonialism, see Vincent Khapoya, *The African Experience*, 2nd ed. (Upper Saddle River, NJ: Prentice-Hall, 1998), 134.

Asians, and relegated the African majority very firmly, to the bottom of the pile" (Anderson 2005, 10). The colonial territory included approximately 5 million indigenous Kenyans denied a political voice and dispossessed of their lands, 97,000 Asians who arrived largely as indentured servants to serve the interests of colonial Britain in the early twentieth century, and about 27,000 White British settlers (ibid.). Similarly, colonial racialization and administrative polarization in Rwanda ultimately ignited the genocide of 1994. In the aftermath of independence, across the continent, the postcolony exhibited signs of political authoritarianism, instability, and socioeconomic crisis that appear to be, in part, progeny of the profound destabilization, authoritarian power relations, hierarchies, and institutions of the colonial past.

A Layered Portrait: Colonial Cultures of Violence

I borrow here from Ayotte and Husain's (2005) probing examination of the rhetoric of the veil in Western discourses on Afghanistan to create a way of presenting colonial culture in Africa as constituted in epistemic, physical, and structural forms of violence. We might well agree that the pursuit of human security is one of the primary goals of citizens faced with the intensification of economic, health, infrastructural, educational, and political disabilities of their countries, and that the conditions, institutions, hierarchies, and philosophies that constrain human dignity, personal and collective development, freedom, and rights effectively limit human well-being and security in Africa.

Therefore, although it has become increasingly unfashionable to speak of the colonial, our study of the political, economic, and social challenges confronting contemporary Africa must account for the sundry ways in which at least three forms of colonial violence in Africa have created and perpetuate conditions of material harm. That is, the pervasive Eurocentric discourses about the continent create an epistemological context for inflicting substantive harm, while the physical and structural violence of colonialism creates situational and relational conditions for distinct harm manifest in outbreaks of social and political violence, deepening impoverishment, economic disparities, trauma, turbulent mobilizations for justice, land claims and disputations, the alienation of subjects from leaders, the emergence and persistence of authoritarianism despite citizen resistance and mobilization, and new forms of identity conflicts. Although there are clear distinctions among epistemic, physical, and structural violence, they enjoy a complicitous kinship that will be explored subsequently.[3]

Epistemic Violence and Colonial Discourses

Representations of Africans and peoples of African origin have been overwhelmingly found to be pernicious forms of racial imperialism that serve to construct colonial relationships with the colonized subjects. The images reinforce the logic of a world order that transforms the African subject into a primordial type, a victim, or savage in need of "saving" by the West and its institutions. It is this paternalism, all too familiar to those who have heard the wearying rhetoric of a "civilizing mission," that constitutes "epistemic violence, the construction of a violent knowledge of the third world *Other*,"[4]

---

[3] Kevin Ayotte and Mary Husain have written an excellent interrogation of these forms of violence in Western framing of veiling in Afghanistan, and I borrow their frames to examine neocolonial violence in Africa. See Kevin J. Ayotte and Mary E. Husain, "Securing Afghan Women: Neocolonialism, Epistemic Violence, and the Rhetoric of the Veil," *NWSA Journal* 17, no. 3 (Fall 2005): 112–133.

[4] Ibid.

and erases Africans as subjects in international relations. Images of the savage African, the cannibalistic native, or the bloodthirsty Kenyan Mau Mau (the Kikuyu resistance) provided fodder for efforts to mask marauding colonial activities in Africa, as benevolent paternalism. So seductive are the tendencies to construct idealistic facades for the most avaricious imperialist ventures that popular discourse is yet to fully acknowledge that the language of "civilizing missions" cannot be sustained against the evidence of colonial culture and violence.

The "process of narrating and interpreting the African past," Grinker and Steiner argue in their penetrating examination of perspectives on Africa, "has long been an intellectual struggle against European assumptions and prejudices" (1997, xxiii). Prejudices are nothing new, nothing surprising; what is startling for the new scholar of African history is the remarkable contrast between historical reality and some of the most frequently cited assumptions that have been woven into contemporary views of the continent. As the wave of independence began in the 1960s, the "Oxfordian" historian Hugh Trevor-Roper started making waves with his infamous opinion that while there might possibly be some African history to teach in the future, "at present, there is none: there is only the history of the Europeans in Africa. The rest is darkness . . . and darkness is not the subject of history."[5] A decade after that feckless statement, Graham Clark insisted that during the Late Pleistocene much of Africa "remained a kind of cultural museum in which archaic traditions continued . . . without contributing to the main course of human progress."[6] The contrast with reality is quite staggering, and Grinker and Steiner put it in stark terms:

> Contrary to this view, however, research in paleontology and archeology has shown that the first micro-lithic technology emerged in Africa and that cattle domestication and pottery may have been indigenous African development. We also often forget that the earliest complex states emerged on the continent of Africa, in what is today Egypt (McIntosh and McIntosh 1983). If we cast our sights back to the evolution of humanity, we find that human-made tools appear in Africa at least 2.6 million years ago, long before they appear in Eurasia. (Grinker and Steiner 1997, xxiv)

It is of course, fairly easy to ignore the significance of such evidences along with the knowledge that scientists generally cite Africa as the birthplace of humankind, since the "earliest available evidence of our hominid ancestors was unearthed in the Afar region of Ethiopia, and in the Rift Valley of northern Kenya and Ethiopia . . . ." (White, Suwa, and Asfaw 1994 and Leakey et al. 1995, cited in Grinker and Steiner 1997). But an even more stunning avalanche of scientific, archeological, and other written evidence demonstrates incontrovertibly that as Graham's record of historic Africa shows, "from prehistory onward, Africa has remained a vital and central force in building the world we live in" (Grinker and Steiner 1997, xxiv).

European claims to a benign paternalism are not merely symptomatic of cultural ignorance, misinformation, or lack of sensitivity to the African Other. On the contrary, these are insidious representations that are rooted in the colonial encounter and are currently utilized to rhetorically encapsulate the

---

[5] Cited in Roy Grinker and Christopher Steiner, "Introduction: Africa in Perspective," in *Perspectives on Africa: A Reader in Culture, History, and Representation*, ed. Roy Grinker and Christopher Steiner (Oxford: Blackwell Publishers, 1997).

[6] Like several other scholars of the colonial academy, Graham Clark claimed much scientific authority for his clearly flawed opinions. See ibid.

African continent in forms of knowledge that serve to legitimize and rationalize Western economic control, military interventionism, and political interference, as can be seen in the recent creation of the "imperial" U.S. military command for Africa discussed elsewhere in this book. It was Western media that first transformed the villagers and civilian protestors fighting against oil companies in Nigeria's devastated oil producing regions into "terrorists." The creation of a new outback for the "war against terror" ultimately rationalized the egregious "anti-terrorism" violence of the Nigerian government, intensified the infusions of arms and violence on all sides, validated U.S. military partnering, and masked the root causes of structural violence in Nigeria's oil region.

Epistemological violence bred in the colonial epoch is embedded in ongoing social conflicts, political turbulence, and even in health care dilemmas. Former South African president Mbeki was rocked by the widespread perception that his government was ineffectual in handling the soaring HIV/AIDS crisis in South Africa. His questioning of the relationship between the HIV virus and the AIDS syndrome generated an unprecedented level of global vilification, as well as a more positive local activism that led to a legal judgment requiring the government to provide antiretroviral therapy to people living with AIDS. While the mobilization by AIDS activists was a much-needed tool of social change, there is no doubt that the ghosts of apartheid haunted the president's stance:

> I don't think anyone can give a simple explanation for why our AIDS program has failed. . . . But the race issue is huge. It's like we eliminated apartheid but it left behind this huge well that none of us knew how to tear down or get around.[7]

As Charlayne Hunter-Gault, a well-respected human rights journalist noted, Mbeki's attitude stemmed from two critical issues: the first is his belief that the crisis of post-apartheid South Africa is overwhelmingly one of poverty and that an urgent frontal effort to address poverty will generate a more effective response not only to AIDS, but also to all of the "debilitating and deadly diseases threatening the recovery of the continent, including malaria, heart disease, diabetes, diarrheal diseases, and non-AIDS related tuberculosis" (Hunter-Gault 2006, 33). But, more astutely, she notes that it is apparent that President Mbeki's position was deeply rooted in fear invoked by the ghosts of racist discourses that had shored the colonial apartheid state for so many years.

> In a heated parliamentary exchange with opposition members of Parliament, who accused him of being an "AIDS denialist," Mbeki said he would not keep quiet while "others whose minds have been corrupted by the disease of racism accuse us, the black people of South Africa . . . [of] being, by virtue of our Africanness and skin colour, lazy, liars, foul-smelling, diseased, corrupt, violent, amoral, sexually depraved, animalistic, savage and rapists." (ibid., 33–34)

While for much of the watching world, the question of HIV/AIDS might constitute merely a health crisis, South Africa's debates made it clear that health and the human body are enclosed in broader sociopolitical constructs evident in the sentiments of a president who openly declared his prayerful hope that South Africans of all races would soon "dare to drag racism from the hushed conversations and

---

[7] Morna Cornell, director of the AIDS Consortium, a South African nonprofit counseling project, cited by Jon Jeter, reporter for the *Washington Post*, in Charlayne Hunter-Gault, *New News Out of Africa: Uncovering Africa's Renaissance* (Oxford University Press, 2006).

murmurs and silences into the arena of public discussion" (ibid.). In Jeter's insightful attempt to make sense of the government's failure to address the AIDS pandemic, he concluded that while the issue was complicated, his inquiry drove him to the "raw and deep wound left by the racial caste system of apartheid." His insights are worth recording at length:

> After decades of seeing friends and relatives jailed, poisoned and even sterilized by whites, the ANC shut clinics that could have been useful in treating and counseling patients infected with HIV, largely because the facilities were heavily staffed with white doctors, according to people involved in AIDS policy. After negotiating an uneasy co-existence with the white minority, the new leaders' initial efforts to address the epidemic were slowed and even sabotaged by white civil servants inherited from the apartheid era. . . . The ANC's return to open politics coincided with a seismic shift in the spread of HIV. Largely isolated to white, gay men when it first appeared in the country in the early 1980s, the virus had by 1990 begun affecting primarily black heterosexuals.

"It was doubly stigmatized," said Mark Gevisser, a South African journalist who is writing a biography of Mbeki. "It went from being the 'Gay Plague' to the 'Black Death' and it really reinforced the stereotype of the super sexualized, irresponsible black male. This is the stigma that the exiles came home to." As the ANC and then-ruling National Party engaged in tense negotiations for a transition to majority rule, the apartheid regime used fear of AIDS to undermine the popularity of their adversary. Fliers with crude depictions of black men began to appear in the black townships, warning that virus-carrying exiles were importing HIV to the country.

"That definitely put us on the defensive," said Smuts Ngonyama, an ANC spokesman. "We, on the one hand, understood that this was a disease that we needed to deal with. But we also resented the National Party's demonization of us as promiscuous . . . and terrorists bringing death and disease home to our people. They were aggressively selling this stigma so we couldn't stand on the moral high ground" (cited in ibid., 35–36).

The relationships between epistemic, physical, and structural forms of violence in the postcolony are thus laid bare even in discussions of disease. Discursive gambits that represented the African in vile racial configurations were harnessed to the gruesome, politically sanctioned physical and militarized attacks against apartheid's opponents.[8] Perhaps President Mbeki's unfortunate wariness was that of a colonized subject well aware of how the discourse of war against a disease could easily metamorphose into the validation of diverse forms of violence against those framed as carriers of the disease. In Somalia, for instance, Maren observed that rhetorical patterns of ethnocentric compassion could easily morph into corporeal or physical violence. In 1992, the discursive languages of aid agencies in Somalia mutated with startling speed into U.S. military intervention in a manner reminiscent of the relationship between the discourse of humanitarian deliverance of women behind the veil to the bombings of Iraq and Afghanistan. Reflecting on this transmutation, Maren soberly observes:

---

[8] Scholars continue to argue for a direct link between European colonial racism and the perpetuation of violence in the postcolony. For instance, French and Belgian colonial racism and the institution of divisive policies based on the racialization of political identities were clearly implicated in the spiraling tensions and anger that culminated in the Rwandan genocide.

One day, we were looking at photos of beefy marines rescuing big-eyed starving babies. The next day, it was equally compelling images of Cobra attack helicopters strafing Mogadishu streets. Suddenly, the humanitarian intervention had become a military assault. The skinny Somalis who had so recently been seen as victims had become the enemy. [Indeed] . . . the violent events that occurred in 1993 were not an aberration; they were in fact foreign aid carried out to its logical conclusion. The desire to help had—as it almost always does—become the desire to control. (Maren 1997, 217–218)

Beyond "Epistemological Registers": Gulags and the Corporeality of Colonial Violence

The violent legacy of colonialism is one of the most critical issues facing contemporary African countries. The atrocities of colonialism in Africa are well documented, such as the scorched land policies, mass executions, concentration camps, large-scale pogroms, and egregious torture. Examples of colonial mayhem and carnage include that of the Germans during the Herero and Nama wars, the French in Algeria, Belgians in the Congo "Free" State, the Portuguese in Angola and Mozambique, the British in Kenya, and the Dutch settlers in Southern Africa.

Ghosts of the Congo

The Congo had long been key to Europe's involvement with Africa (Fabian 2003). When the sixteenth-century ruler of the Kongo, King Affonso I, son of an African monarch converted to Christianity by the Portuguese, became desperately troubled by the slaving activities of the Portuguese who were depopulating his kingdom and even seizing members of the royal family, he wrote an eloquent missive to the Portuguese King, insisting that the Kongo was only interested in the peaceable work of missionaries and teachers. His royal entreaty was ignored; the Atlantic slave trade only gathered steam and two centuries later, Belgium, a small European country, was able to formally annex the vast territory of the Congo. Belgian King Leopold II's subjugation of the Congo, the resource rich colony that he claimed as his private fiefdom in 1885, is a horrifying chronicle of colonial administration. The Belgian monarch, a cousin of Queen Victoria, enjoyed the blessings of many of his European compatriots and the U.S. president Chester A. Arthur, but by the early twentieth century, accounts of the unmitigated bestiality of his "civilizing mission" to the Congo had begun to disturb many Europeans, who were obviously quite reconciled to violence against the Black Other. Leopold employed a mercenary army, the Force Publique, to destroy the local economy by burning villages, eliminating prior means of livelihood, driving Africans into forced labor in mines and rubber plantations, and punishing them through dismemberment and mass executions.

Adam Hochschild's *King Leopold's Ghost* brings alive this disturbing colonial and precolonial history. Beyond the vivid and grisly facts of the conversion of a large society into a massive rubber plantation, most compelling are the connections Hochschild makes between the violent precolonial intrusion of Portuguese slave traders; the brutal colonialism of Belgium; the conspiracy against and execution of the Congo's radical, nationalist postcolonial leader Patrice Lumumba; and the ruthless leadership of postcolonial president Mobutu Sese Sekou, whose role in the death of Lumumba was engineered by European and American powers interested in the Congo's abundant wealth. Mobutu's close ties to the West and the crisis of the postcolonial state are entrenched in the power structures constructed in the colonial period.[9]

---

[9] Tukumbi Lumumba-Kasongo provides an informative reading of the Belgian-Zaire ties in his article "Zaire's Ties to Belgium: Persistence and Future Prospects in Political Economy," *Africa Today* 39, no. 3 (1992).

King Leopold's enslavement of citizen-subjects in colonial rubber territories relied on a commitment to physical and structural violence, such as piling the severed hands of men, women, and children into baskets to terrorize the population. The heinous crimes of Belgian colonial administration were not unique in the annals of European colonialism, but a vigorous global campaign against Leopold managed to awaken an aspect of the Western moral imagination. The opposition was partly spearheaded by two African Americans: George Washington Williams, the first major campaigner who was disdained because he was Black, and William Sheppard, an African American Presbyterian missionary, whose firsthand accounts and photographic records drove the campaign, as well as European observers such as E. D. Morel and Roger Casement, a British consul.

We can understand Hochschild's astonishment about the widespread contemporary amnesia (including his own) regarding the Congo. Most visitors to the famed Winter Palace, Leopold's extravagant monument to his former Congo fiefdom, seem comfortably unaware that the park is testament to some of the most grievous forms of colonial exploitation. Paradoxically, it also sustains the logic of colonial violence through images and artifacts that perpetuate the myth of a Belgian crusade to civilize the barbaric, cannibalistic Congolese (Rahier 2003).

Kenyan Gulags

In British-ruled Kenya, Mamdani reminds us that "a battery of laws underwrote settler privilege at the expense of native lives. Herded into reserves, peasants were forbidden to grow the most lucrative crops, taxed so they would work at any pay, and had their movements constantly tracked. The landless became 'squatters' on settler farms, laboring for a third of the year in return for a plot to cultivate and permission to graze cattle. By 1940, there were 150,000 squatters—one in every eight Kikuyu" (Mamdani 2005). Forcibly "repatriated" between 1946 and 1952, squatters were able to organize in just one location, Olenguruone, where they forged some unity by taking an oath (a *muma*, later corrupted by the British into Mau Mau), which was traditionally meant for male elders, but was then administered to men, women, and children. As the oath taking spread to cities in the Kenyan region of the East Africa Protectorate, the British declared a state of emergency on October 9, 1952. Within six months, they had isolated and detained some 50,000 Mau Mau fighters without trial, treated every Kikuyu who was not a loyalist as a confirmed oath-taker, and set entire villages on fire. With their houses and property burnt, more than a million Kikuyu were forced into some 800 barbed-wire villages between June 1954 and October 1955 (ibid.).

Accounts of the Mau Mau guerilla insurgency in colonial Kenya mesmerized Westerners in the 1950s. They read, with horrified fascination, lurid stories about obnoxious oath-taking African criminals who terrorized the British colonial communities. Settlers had arrived in what was then the British East Africa Protectorate fired up by advertisements in the colonial press that offered unrestricted wealth and profiteering, vast estates, Black servants, and a life of nobility unavailable back home. By the twentieth century, the occupation of the region was consolidated, in part by thousands of indentured servants from Britain's Asian empire. They endured punishing work on the railroads and ultimately constituted a racial and social layer beneath the White settlers. Settler narratives and the "testimonials" of colonial administrators in Kenya swept the global imaginary, and the Mau Mau came to symbolize, much as the fabricated tales of a homicidal Chaka, King of the Zulu, the supposed bestial nature of the colonized African.

Even today, popular Western mythologizing of the armed resistance continues to conjure notions of the wholesale torture and slaughter of civilian British settlers. The historical reality is quite startling, Mamdani (2005) and Elkins (2005a) remind us. Less than a hundred colonial settlers (approximately thirty-two in Anderson's 2005 account) lost their lives in the prolonged waves of colonial violence that left tens of thousands of Kenyan Mau Mau dead, brutalized hundreds of thousands in concentration camps, and transformed much of the colony into a prison governed by racial violence. The repeated demands of insurgents fighting for *ithaka na wiyathi,* or the return of their land and freedom, did little to engender public support for African liberation in Britain. Indeed, the demands for freedom only intensified the violently militarized responses from the British. Over a two-year period, colonial forces, supported by the Royal Air Force, fought a drawn-out offensive against approximately 20,000 Mau Mau guerrillas, who lacked sophisticated equipment and finances. Concurrently, they directed a lengthier campaign against some "1.5 million Kikuyu who were believed to have taken the Mau Mau oath and had pledged themselves to fight for land and freedom" (Elkins 2005a, xvii, xi–ii).

"The battlefield for this war," reports Caroline Elkins, a respected scholar of Kenyan colonial history, "was not the forests but a vast system of detention camps, where colonial officials reportedly held some eighty thousand Kikuyu insurgents" (ibid., xi–xii). Elkins's scrutiny of the data led her to conclude that the number of Africans held in the British gulags in Kenya was between 160,000 and 320,000. She somberly testified, "I now believe there was in late colonial Kenya a murderous campaign to eliminate Kikuyu people, a campaign that left tens of thousands, perhaps hundreds of thousands dead. Mau Mau has been portrayed as one of the most savage and barbaric uprisings of the twentieth century. But . . . I ask that we reconsider this accepted orthodoxy and examine the crimes perpetrated by colonial forces against Mau Mau, and the considerable measures that the British colonial government undertook to conceal them" (ibid., xvi).

The intensity of such violence generated a vast body of critical literature, such as the haunting novels and acerbic scholarship of the famed Kenyan author Ngũgĩ wa Thiong'o. Unfortunately, the substantial research did not quite succeed in transforming the popular Western romance with the myth of a valiant Europe battling the forces of atavism and savagery on the "dark continent." The continuing efforts to remind the world of historical facts were given a boost with the publication of the well-documented works by Elkins and David Anderson. Elkins has argued that while the colonizers' savagery in Africa was not unusual in global history, what was happening in Africa in the late nineteenth century was, in many respects, different. In her opinion, this process had a proto-industrial logic, infused with racism—that was unprecedented in its virulence, even though present to varying degrees in earlier cases of indigenous eradications. This virulence, Elkins suggests, combined with an ideology of how to rule over and exploit African resources and labor, led to a form of colonialism in Africa that, while mirrored in some respects in other twentieth century European possessions around the globe, was far more extreme.[10]

Historians and political scientists have noted the manner in which direct and indirect forms of colonial administration created lasting legacies that are implicated in the continuing turbulence and impoverishment of the continent. Perhaps one of Elkins's most important contributions in *Imperial*

---

[10] For an extensive treatment of this argument, see Caroline Elkins, "Race, Citizenship, and Governance: Settler Tyranny and the End of Empire," in *Settler Colonialism in the Twentieth Century: Projects, Practices, Legacies,* ed. Caroline Elkins and Susan Pedersen (New York: Routledge, 2005b), 203–222.

Reckoning (2005a), is the utilization of the concept of gulags and concentration camps, images linked vividly in the West with violence, racism, injustice, and silencing in the construction of an imagined statehood. "Concentration camps" evoke a grisly realism at variance with the euphemism of "detention camps," preferred by the British. Not only did Europe construct artificial "tribal" identities, governing institutions, and legal customary codes, they imposed a hostile state on their conquered territories in order to enforce the compliance of the governed. The epistemic and structural violence of colonialism is well conveyed in the following raw narratives that depict the racial imagination of the colonial state.

> In the settler imagination . . . they were indistinguishable in local thought and expression from the animals that roamed the colony. From the early days of the Emergency, this attitude became accepted orthodoxy for much of the Administration. Frank Lloyd, who was later knighted for his formidable service in Britain's empire, was stationed in Kenya's Central Province for the entire Emergency. He thought Mau Mau was "bestial" and "filthy"—an "evil movement" that was "extremely vile and violent." "Mau Mau had to be eliminated at all costs" he later recalled, "something had to be done to remove these people from society." . . . During a brief stop in Nairobi in the spring of 1954, journalist Anthony Sampson likewise observed what he later called the "dehumanization of the enemy" by local settlers and colonial officials. "I heard it everywhere I went," he said. "How many Kukes had to be gotten rid of, how many Kukes did you wink today. [It was] almost like they were talking about big game hunting." The historical record is littered with lengthy descriptions from settlers and colonial officials of Mau Mau as "vermin," "animals," and "barbarians," . . . Like other predatory animals, they were "cunning," "vicious," and "bloodthirsty." (cited in ibid., 49)

Widespread use of torture and physical violence by the colonial administration in Kenya, foreshadowed the methods that would be used in Nazi concentration camps. The brutality of conquest and "pacification" was designed both to break African resistance and to create local cadres to sustain the political, administrative, and economic processes essential for the sustainability of a settler economy. Violence was, therefore, not an aberration but in the very nature of the colonial state and its settler population.

> In the Rift Valley, for example, one settler who operated his own screening camp was known as Dr. Bunny by the locals. It was his experimental prowess when it came to interrogating Mau Mau suspects that earned the doctor his notorious nickname: the Joseph Mengele of Kenya. One settler remembers her brother, a member of the Kenya Regiment and a pseudogangster, boasting of Dr. Bunny's exploits, which included burning the skin off live Mau suspects and forcing them to eat their own testicles. Another former settler and member of the local Moral Rearmament Movement also recalled Dr. Bunny's handiwork. He, too, remembered skin searing along with castration and other methods of screening he would "prefer not to speak of." (ibid., 67)

Margaret Nyaruai, a young woman at the time of Mau Mau, was taken to the screening hut on the estate of her settler employer near Kabauru not long after the start of the Emergency. There she was beaten by a white man whom the Kikuyu had nicknamed Karoki, or He Who Comes at Dawn, and by the young settler turned British colonial officer nicknamed YY. While being screened, Margaret was asked: "Questions like the number of oaths I had taken, where my husband went, where two of my stepbrothers had gone (they had gone into the forest). I was badly whipped, while naked. They didn't care that I had just given birth. In fact, I think my baby was lucky it was not killed like the rest. . . . Apart from the beatings, women used to have banana leaves and flowers inserted into their vaginas and rectums, as well as have their breasts squeezed with a pair of pliers, after which, a woman would say everything because of the pain . . . even the men had their testicles squeezed with pliers to make them confess! After such things were done to me, I told them everything. I survived the torture, but I still have a lot of pain in my body even today from it." Margaret's confession did not earn her release. Instead, Karoki forced her to labor without pay on his estate throughout most of the emergency. From time to time the screening teams, hungry for any information, continued to interrogate her, often thrusting hot eggs into her vagina to force her to talk (ibid., 67–68).

Like Cross, other police officers offered accounts of brutality. In one case, Peter Bostock wrote that it was "quite common to shoot prisoners 'while [they were] trying to escape'" and that one officer had said proudly that he "got nine of the swines [sic] in that way." After recalling various acts of terror, Bostock then went on to report, "I can truthfully say that only one act of cruelty towards a Kikuyu ever revolted me during my service in the Police. With two other Europeans I was questioning an old man. His answers were unsatisfactory. One of the white men set his dog at the old fellow. The animal got him to the ground, ripped open his throat, and started mauling his chest and arms. In spite of his screams, my companions [i.e., fellow police officers] just grinned. It was five minutes before the dog was called off. I can still hear that old man's screams" (ibid., 86).

Special Branch there had a way of slowly electrocuting a Kuke—they'd rough up one for days. Once I went personally to drop off one gang member who needed special treatment. I stayed for a few hours to help the boys out, softening him up. Things got a little out of hand. By the time I cut his balls off he had no ears, and his eyeball, the right one, I think, was hanging out of its socket. Too bad, he died before we got much out of him (British settler cited in ibid., 87).

The enormity of the abuses conducted during Europe's humanization of the "dark continent" is quite disturbing, particularly since such narratives are rarely acknowledged in discussions of colonialism in Africa. The silence in contemporary academic and social discourses and the continued invocation of the colonial civilizing myth are partly a result of deliberate policy efforts at misinformation, as Elkins discovered during her field research.

I came to learn that the colonial government had intentionally destroyed many of these missing files in massive bonfires on the eve of its 1963 retreat from Kenya. . . . After years of combing through what remains in the official archives, I discovered that there was a pattern to Britain's cleansing of the official records. Any ministry or department that dealt with the unsavory side of detention was pretty well emptied of its files, whereas those that ostensibly addressed detainee reform, or Britain's civilizing mission, were left fairly intact. . . . Even the most assiduous purges, however, often fail to clean up all the incriminating evidence. . . . Today, when reflecting on the number of Mau Mau suspects killed from the start of screening in late 1952 to the end of detention in 1961, de Souza says: "By the end I would say there were several hundred thousand killed. . . . This was a form of ethnic cleansing on the part of the British government, and there is no doubt about that in my mind. (ibid., xii–xiii, 89)

Structural Violence and the Fetishizing of the Democracy-Authoritarianism Nexus

Clearly, what colonialism sought to create in the African continent was not democracy. What Europe constructed was an intensely antidemocratic, violent, deeply racist, hierarchical, and exclusionary form of leadership. Today, media reports of Africa are awash in numbing accounts of human suffering, economic failure, and sociopolitical instability. It is not difficult to understand the frustrations of citizens who had fought hard against colonial domination and now continue to challenge the post-independence governments that maintain the authoritarian systems of power, marginalization, and violence crafted under erstwhile colonialists. But efforts to interrogate the historical structures on which postcolonial states are built are often countered by reminders of the ineffectiveness of "blame," or the futility of anticipating any accountability from the global core. A more influential issue is the pervasive anger directed at postcolonial leaders, who now embody the failures in the continent and constitute the tangible representatives of a global imperialism that has functioned from the colonial to the globalization era to keep millions of Africans in poverty. Nonetheless, there has been widespread African discourse for many years about the need to dismantle the foundation and logic of the postcolonial state in order to address the roots of contemporary institutional and political anomie. Such conversations have included strident calls for "national constitutional conferences" that would permit a collective pooling of visions on restructuring the ideological framework of the state and generating a new institutional apparatus for challenging the legacies of structural violence that resist ongoing struggles for change. What then do we mean by structural violence?

It is important to recognize that the analysis of structural violence addresses the conditions that inflict diverse material damage on individuals and are likely to shorten life expectancies dramatically. Ayotte and Husain, like Farmer (2003), draw attention to issues such as inadequate education and health care, exploitative employment conditions, and endemic poverty and argue that "rather than allowing these conditions to remain unexamined as a neutral part of the landscape, attention to structural violence imputes agency and, hence, responsibility to social, political, and economic actors" for the maintenance of structural conditions that cause harm (Ayotte and Husain, 126).

The ruthless physical violence of colonialism led to the death of millions of Africans, but it was complemented by the deliberate use of a range of social and economic policies that generated and maintained devastating forms of oppression. Addressing structural violence in the postcolony is a complicated undertaking. Embedded deeply within the interstices of the global economy, it functions through the same logic of resource exploitation, competition, economic efficiency, and growth on which colonialism was anchored. No wonder that in defying efforts to erase their voices, marginalized peoples have consistently articulated their lived experiences of violence as "disposable" people, consigned to brutal death and egregious suffering due to forces of inequality and exclusion that make them vulnerable and unheard.

We have been denied the most elemental education so that others can use us as cannon fodder and pillage the wealth of our country. They don't care that we have nothing, absolutely nothing, not even a roof over our heads, no land, no work, no health care, no food, and no education. Nor are we able freely and democratically to elect our political representatives, nor is there independence from foreigners, nor is there peace or justice for ourselves and our children.[11]

---

[11] These stark words resound in the manifestos of many of the movements that fought against colonial rule in Africa, yet they were spoken regarding the Zapatista Movement in Mexico—evidence of the global nature of structural violence and its relationship to external control, expropriation, inequality, and marginalization. Cited in Paul Farmer, *Pathologies of Power: Health, Human Rights, and the New War on the Poor* (Berkeley and Los Angeles: University of California Press, 2003), 93.

Paul Farmer, well known medical practitioner, HIV/AIDS specialist, and vocal advocate for the marginalized, has also captured some core components of structural violence from the viewpoint of a doctor working in Haiti. Farmer notes that gender, race, ethnicity, and socioeconomic factors define structural violence and that the combination of these "various social 'axes' is imperative in efforts to discern a political economy of brutality" (Farmer 2003, 43; Schneider 2006). With regard to gender for instance, "the power differential [among gender identifications] has meant that women's rights are violated in innumerable ways," and females have been documented to suffer and endure more than males, especially in poorer nations where "the disadvantage of women may even apply to . . . health care, nutritional support and elementary education" (Farmer 2003, 44).

The question is whether women's suffering derives from atavistic cultural traditions, as declaimed in popular Western discourse, or from other structural roots? The representation of women's suffering in Africa has long fit into the racial discourses of Western imperialism. By vilifying African societies as pernicious patriarchal systems, African women were cast as unenlightened, subjugated objects whose liberation would derive ultimately from Western civilization. Yet the literature is replete with accounts of colonial administrations confronted by defiant African women leaders, who led struggles against foreign powers in Nigeria, Ghana, Dahomey, etc. The female mobilizations of the nineteenth century have long historical antecedents, predated, for instance, by Queen Nzinga of Angola's resistance to Portuguese slavers in the seventeenth century. In the economic sphere, the vibrant involvement of African women in the marketplace, local industries, and even trans-regional trade has been well documented. Thus, Anene Ejikeme (2008), Ifi Amadiume (1987), Oyeronke Oyewumi (1997), Judith Van Allen (1976), and several other scholars have concluded that in the European colonies in Africa, women were forcibly removed from roles of political, social, and economic agency in order to satisfy European gendered constructs of good submissive womenfolk. Specifically, colonialism inflicted special forms of structural violence against African women by destroying their institutions, economic and political spaces, and socioeconomic and political roles and rights.

Farmer again affirms that "racial classifications have been used to deprive many groups of basic rights and therefore have an important place in considerations of human inequality and suffering," and multiple examples exist across the African continent, including in the apartheid and post-apartheid periods in South Africa, where "*poverty* remains the primary cause of the prevalence of many diseases and widespread hunger and malnutrition among black South Africans" (ibid., 44–45). The same occurs in affluent nations, such as the United States, with startling differences in life expectancy, proneness to disease, and economic disparities among the races. The legalization of racial and ethnic differences and the construction of a political economy based on invented difference came to a height in the violent racialization of Africa that occurred during the colonial period, as Mamdani (1966, 2001) and others have amply demonstrated in analyzing the Rwandan genocide, the crisis in Zimbabwe, Sudan, South Africa, and Kenya.

Structural violence is not necessarily spawned only by colonial or imperial imperatives. Nevertheless, the forms of epistemic and physical violence that found expression in colonial rule in Africa, the logic of economic dispossession and inequality of power, and the silencing and domination that are the very nature of colonialism lead us to some unavoidable conclusions: that the recent experience of colonialism in Africa in all its political, social, and economic configurations generates a context of structural violence that is reinforced by global hierarchies and institutions and can only be addressed by a more prolonged and focused transformative struggle than suggested by the initial euphoria of formal independence.

Entrenched Political Axis of Violence

In analyzing the crisis of the postcolonial state, we must understand the role of state power, colonial and post colonial, in shaping the dynamics of the system and then consider the forces often arrayed in opposition to the state, mimicking its violence and perpetrating cycles of impunity. When the postcolonial state demonstrates its inherited capacity to exercise force with impunity, there is transference of cultures of violence within the public space. The resulting instability is much in evidence during electoral politics and the liberalization of the public space as the structures of violent containment by authoritarian regimes are loosened. Indeed, Robbins insists that since definitions of the state, "revolve around its claim to monopoly on the instruments of death and violence . . . violence remains one of the main tools of nation-building [and] the modern nation-state is essentially an agent of genocide and ethnocide" (Robbins 2002, 103, cited in Soyinka-Airewele 2004).

R.J. Rummel has examined the evidence that the state is indeed the main conveyor of violence, whether in quelling conflicts or pursuing power and citizenry acquiescence and soberly concludes that at least 170 million men, women, and children from 1900 to 1987 have been "shot, beaten, tortured, knifed, burned, starved, frozen, crushed, or worked to death; buried alive, drowned, hung, bombed or killed in any other of the myriad ways governments have inflicted death on unarmed, helpless, citizens and foreigners. The dead could conceivably be nearly 360 million people. It is as though our species has been devastated by a modern Black Plague. And indeed it has, but a plague of power not germs" (cited in ibid.).

The question of nation building, which typically occupies center stage in the policy objectives of most African states today, has to be carefully reexamined if the transitional state is to address the structural legacies—political, economic, and social—of colonial violence within the polity in any meaningful way. Unfortunately, the institutions of the authoritarian colonial state and its progeny are not easily redressed, and radical reformers who wish to address the past in a comprehensive manner are likely to encounter vigorous internal and external opposition from those who are invested in the hierarchies that support their power (ibid.).

No wonder several liberation scholars and theologians, including Gustavo Gutierrez for instance, insist that the social and economic rights of the poor can only be achieved by breaking the "market forces" that "sculpt the outlines" of our modern constructs of social goods, including medicine, education, political participation, and economic wealth and by acknowledging that "the poor are a by-product of the system in which we live and for which we are responsible. They are the oppressed, exploited proletariat . . . hence the poverty of the poor is not a call to generous relief action, but a demand that we go and build a different social order."[12]

Finally, as demonstrated in the murder of President Patrice Lumumba, erstwhile colonizers and global superpowers have often retained the prerogative to interfere at will in the affairs of independent African states. The French, Belgian, and British governments consistently meddled in the economic and political affairs of their former African colonies since the first throes of independence, providing support to client states and friendly regimes. Several scholars consider the French-Belgian intervention in the build up to the Rwandan genocide to be one of the more infamous interventions, and the French government has been charged by many of its own citizens and international human rights activists with complicity with the Hutu government responsible for the genocide.

---

[12] See Jon Sobrino and others in ibid., 9, 142–143.

Colonial Cultures: Continuities and Change

Cultures create forms of affirmation about the logical organization of social life, and while institutions can be dismantled, they often linger on, constituted not in buildings but in political, philosophical, and economic constructs. Colonialism bequeathed an edginess to life in the postcolony, with tensions of empire that reflect in layered dissensions over modernity, what is desirable and ideal, and over identity and alternative futures. More concretely, the colonization of Africa has generated economic systems subordinated to a global economic imperium, instigated debates over the privileging of particular languages, adoptions of legal and educational systems, struggles over the place of indigenous and external knowledge systems, and political processes. As Cowell noted in his telling narrative of the postcolonial state, across the continent—particularly in eastern and southern Africa where imperial powers sent their citizens as settlers—the decades following the independence wave of the 1960s offered the vista of the extension of White privilege, embodying the scholarly discourse on neocolonialism and the continuation of empire.

> In Zambia, whites hewed a cricket pitch from the encroaching savannah at a village called Ngwerere outside the capital, Lusaka; played polo in a town called Mazabuka; and some offered croquet and pink gins on manicured lawns. Even in Zimbabwe, where the president, Robert Mugabe, has now chased most of the 4,500 white farmers off their estates, his campaign to give expropriated land to landless peasants (or, more usually, to his cronies) gathered pace only after, in his view, whites turned against him by backing his political adversaries. And yet, colonialism was built on huge imbalances and staggering chutzpah by an uninvited elite. In 1890, for instance, the so-called Pioneer Column was sent by the British arch-colonialist Cecil John Rhodes to the territories north of the Limpopo River that came to bear his name—Rhodesia—hoping to find an African Eldorado of gold and diamonds. When those dreams fizzled, land became the prize, as in other places, such as Kenya and South Africa. It is barely surprising, thus, that claims to lost land provide such political tinder in many places and touch such deep veins of resentment among those, like the Masai at Mr. Cholmondeley's trial, who still hanker for the return of ancestral terrain. (Cowell 2009)

The tensions are only deepened by the central claim by White settlers to their economic indispensability in postcolonial Africa, even in South Africa, the most recently independent African nation, whose White minority controls enormous wealth acquired in what was the "continent's biggest, most vivid, most tangled and certainly most epochal struggle" in its diverse histories of racist colonial imperialism. Notwithstanding, or perhaps because of such continued economic influence, the turbulent liberation campaigns of the postcolony still tend to trigger in South Africa and certainly in other settler-type African countries a "jittery reflex" that Cowell agrees is discernable at the interface of minority privilege and majority power.[13]

---

[13] Alan Cowell, "Wrestling with Ghosts of Colonialism," *New York Times*, May 23, 2009, www.nytimes.com/2009/05/23/world/africa/23iht-letter.html?pagewanted=print.

He notes that South Africa's White minority traces its history to the first Dutch settlers in the seventeenth century, long before Victorian Britain's colonialism of South Africa. Whites constitute the biggest minority—almost 10 percent of a population of 49 million—and the richest. Despite decades of brutal apartheid rule, racial reconciliation was the cornerstone of the first post-apartheid administration, led by Nelson Mandela. Reconciliation went into retreat somewhat under his successor, Thabo Mbeki.

Some of Ngũgĩ wa Thiong'o's poignant insights into colonial cultures start with his experience of a profound paralysis that prevented his writing *A Colonial Affair*, a book he was commissioned to write about the social life of European settlers in Kenya. He struggled to find the right tone in capturing the world of British colonial settlers in Kenya—a world his agent had described as having "forever vanished." Ngũgĩ wa Thiong'o eloquently identified the problem. "The difficulty," he admitted, "lay in more than my uncertainty as to whether or not 'their world' had really vanished. An account of their social life would have to include a section on culture, and I was by then convinced that a Draculian idle class could never produce a culture. For the settlers in Kenya were really parasites in paradise" (1997, 616). Sitting in detention, the famous author of numerous fictional works on colonial Kenya pondered the many acts of violence of the European settlers. Foremost was the image of the paternalistic, aristocratic vanguard of a new colonized Africa for whom the continent meant big game hunting and living it up on the backs of myriad field and domestic slaves:

Coming ashore in Mombasa, as was clearly shown by the photographic evidence in the 1939 edition of Lord Cranworth's book, *Kenya Chronicles*, was literally on the backs of Kenyan workers. "No one coming into a new country," he writes, "could desire a more attractive welcome. We were rowed ashore in a small boat and came to land on the shoulders of sturdy Swahili natives." This was in 1906. By 1956, Sir Evelyn Baring, the governor, could still get himself photographed being carried, like a big baby, in the arms of a Kenyan worker. Thus, by setting foot on Kenyan soil at Mombasa, every European was instantly transformed into a blue-blooded aristocrat. An attractive welcome: before him, stretching beyond the ken of his eyes, lay a vast valley garden of endless physical leisure and pleasure that he must have once read about in the *Arabian Nights* stories. The dream in fairy tales was now his in practice. No work, no winter, no physical or mental exertion. (ibid., 613)

But as he contemplated the harrowing narratives of dispossession, the legalization of violence, torture, concentration camps, and summary executions—all to maintain colonized fiefdoms—wa Thiong'o, one of a cadre of leading intellectuals who fell afoul of the post-independence government, soon changed his mind about the cultures of colonialism:

I thought about this in my cell at Kamiti prison and suddenly realized I had been wrong about the British settlers. I should have written that book. For the colonial system did produce a culture. But it was the culture of legalized brutality, a ruling-class culture of fear, the culture of an oppressing minority desperately trying to impose total silence on a restive oppressed majority. This culture was sanctified in the colonial administration of P.C., D.C., D.O., Chiefs, right down to the askari. At Kamiti, we called it the Mbwa Kali culture. Culture of silence and fear: the diaries and memoirs of the leading intellectual lights of the old colonial system contain full literary celebration of this settler culture. (ibid., 616)

It is here that wa Thiong'o invites us to understand his angst about the continuance of administrative and legal violence, of inequities and structural hierarchies manifested in the flux of cultures that surged in the postcolony at the time of independence. His stinging indictment of the early post-independence leadership that silenced the pen and left him in prison is written from a historically located, intimately experienced, and yet analytically intense perspective. Wa Thiong'o obviously had no intention of protecting the postcolonial government from culpability for its devastating malfunction; indeed, his prison diary is a reflection on that failure. But he illuminates clearly the crisis of perpetuation of a colonial culture that has embedded its authoritarian norms, sociopolitical institutions, and values in its subjugated landscape.

Thus, the acts of animal brutality described by wa Thiong'o and later by several other scholars were not, he insists, "cases of individual aberration, but an integral part of colonial politics, philosophy and culture. Reactionary violence to instill fear and silence was the very essence of colonial settler culture" (ibid., 618). The successful imposition of the colonial ruling elite with its excesses, nondemocratic politics, imitative cultures, economic and political dependencies, contradictions, wastefulness, and feudal formality are captured by Ngũgĩ in an acute scrutiny of the post-independence leadership—from their European aristocratic clothing and language to their political institutions.

The perpetuation of a colonial culture does not deny agency to Africans; it does not nullify the capacity for change and for resistance, for articulating new visions for transformation. And such visions and active mobilizations for achieving them abound liberally in every society on the continent. They testify ultimately to the imperial failure to manufacture consent. Continuities with the colonial past do not in any way suggest mindless societies fascinated by beguiling colonial images, nor do they infer that citizens passively submit to authoritarian rule, colonial or postcolonial. The colonial cultures of which we have been speaking, derive their power from *pragmatic* survival in the new dispensation: First, they already subsist in the same power structures that violently integrated military, economic, and political forces during the colonial period. Second, the difficulty of rapidly creating countervailing institutions capable of dismantling colonial inequities, hierarchies, and power allow colonial cultures to persist in the postcolony. Third, the imposition of Eurocentric statutory and customary laws in the colonial period structured identities and groups, protected the state from public accountability, and thus, impacted rights and access in the postcolonial system. Fourth, they exert pervasive influence through the political handover transactions by the colonial administrators who sought to assure a continuity of colonial power. And finally, the present is hostage to the past partly because the postcolony remains vulnerable to interventions and interference by global powers that control its economic fortunes.

Certainly, the continent has had many ideologically motivated champions of freedom and change, but many like Patrice Lumumba were allowed but a brief taste of political leadership. For others, the allure of power and their witting or unwitting entanglement with colonial fiat crumbled their resistance to the convenience of authoritarian governance.

> Unfortunately, it is the repressive features of colonial culture—Hardinge's sword and bullet, as the only insurance of continuing their life-style—that seem to have most attracted the unqualified admiration of the compradors. The settler with the *sjambok* lording it over a mass of "pulling and pushing nigger boys" that figure so meticulously preserved on the walls of "The Lord Delamere" in the Norfolk Hotel, seems the modern ideal for the post-colonial ruling class. How else can it be explained that the 1966 [Kenyan] laws of detention, sedition and treason, reproduce, almost word for word, those in practice between 1951 and 1961 during the high noon of colonial culture? (ibid., 622)

Reining in power and violence is difficult to achieve anywhere in the world. The rapid enactment of the American Patriot Act that allowed the U.S. government to restrict people's personal freedoms was purportedly designed to empower the government to pursue internal and external enemies. The Act has severely eroded constitutional rights, but it has gone unobserved by many of the nation's citizens, although scores of scholars, activists, and media commentators have stridently and ineffectively denounced it. In a somewhat similar vein, the inability of indigenous peoples in the Americas to reclaim material goods, voice, and place, once dispossessed by colonial rule, is not an indicator of their complacency. It is a continuing tragedy that has been assimilated into the democratic structures that insulate the majority of Americans from the corporeality of violence and that manufacture their consent to the epistemic and structural violence of colonialism in North America. The structural violence that defines the place of Native Americans in the settler state and maintains their invisibility and subordination remind us of the crisis of the African postcolony.

Conclusions: Beyond the "Colonial" Victim Construct

The process of remembering recent colonial violence is more than a mere litany of grief and blame. As I have argued before, a major challenge confronting African countries is the task of reconstituting stable polities in the aftermath of resistance struggles. In Rwanda, the government of President Paul Kagame repealed colonial laws mandating the inscription of ethnic identity on national identity cards to help prevent the polarization that had led to the cataclysmic events of 1994. Kagame's action was no novelty; it was outdone by some other African governments. Burundi, for instance, dramatically outlawed using culturally identifiable names introduced under colonialism. If nothing else, such desperate measures by governments reveal the challenge of refashioning nations in the aftermath of violence (Soyinka-Airewele 2004).

Relatively recent wars of liberation were fought by Algeria, Angola, Eritrea, Guinea Bissau, Kenya, Mozambique, Namibia, South Africa, Western Sahara, and Zimbabwe (Turshen 1998, 6), and in the postcolonial period, rapidly spiraling violent struggles in Algeria, Angola, Burundi, Chad, Congo (Kinshasa), Djibouti, Ethiopia, Gambia, Liberia, Mali, Mozambique, Niger, Nigeria, Rwanda, Senegal, Sierra Leone, Somalia, South Africa, Sudan, Tanzania, and Uganda generated over 8 million refugees by 1996, constraining security (Turshen 1998; Adejumobi 2001, 149, cited in Soyinka-Airewele 2004).

If the goals of African governments include instituting new modes of empowerment, democratically navigated claims and entitlements, political responsiveness and accountability, reclamations of citizenship, and reinstitution of rights, justice, and reconciliation, then we must address the ways in which the historic deployment of violence by various imperial interests has affected the public arena and those who inhabit it. According to Nordstrom, such violence maims cultures and jars their very foundations; destroys crucial networks, frameworks of knowledge, and people's sense of reality; ruins social institutions and infrastructure; and jeopardizes identities based on place and community (Turshen, 1998, 18–19).

> The colonial government clearly had time on its side. Detention camps are a waiting game; given enough time, they will eventually transform human beings into something they never imagined possible. When reflecting on his experience in the Soviet gulag, Gustaw Herling concluded that "there is nothing . . . a man cannot be forced to do by hunger and pain." Having spent months or years in the Pipeline, former detainees expressed sentiments that were strikingly similar. "There is only so much a man can bear," Phillip Macharia said, recalling why he confessed his oath. He had been detained for nearly two years, spending most of his time at Iagra, living in filthy clothes, and listening to British colonial propaganda day in and day out. "I felt as though I could no long persevere with life. I had been beaten; I watched others being tortured and killed. I just couldn't take it anymore." For Phillip, the breaking point came when he and some other detainees were caught by guards reading a scrap of newspaper. As a punishment they were forced to put toilet buckets on their heads and run to the site where they were to be dumped and cleaned. "We had excrement and urine running down our faces and backs; all the while the guards were beating us with their clubs to make us go faster. A few days later I was taken to the screening, and this time I confessed my oath to get out of the hell I was living in."

There were others in the Pipeline for whom—in the words of Tzvetan Todorov, who wrote extensively on moral life in concentration camps—"staying human [was] more important than staying alive." Random acts of kindness, or "ordinary virtues" as Todorov calls them, are found throughout the annals of Britain's gulag. There are recollections from former detainees of men giving their day's food ration and blankets to those who were so ill and weak they were near death (Elkins 2005a, 179–181).

In Ferdinand Oyono's novel, *Boy*, like Sembene's film, *La Noire de*, we are invited to recognize and understand the many ways in which colonized subjects have sought to reshape, restrain, and resist the pressure of colonial power. In Oyono's skillful handling of the domestic relationship between a White colonial administrator and his unfaithful wife, the houseboy (as colonial settlers were prone to call their domestic servants), Toundi, captures in his diary the tragedy of colonialism not only as a system of brutality, but also as one full of ridiculous pretensions and unfounded claims of European superiority.

In Dagan, the European quarter and the African quarter are quite separate. But what goes on underneath those corrugated-iron roofs is known down to the smallest detail inside the mud-walled huts. The eyes that live in the native location strip the whites naked. The whites on the other hand go about blind. There was not a soul unaware that the wife of the Commandant was deceiving her husband with M. Moreau, the prison director and our greatest terror (Oyono 1966, 71).

The satire and humor are devastating, but despite Toundi's sense of self, voice, and dreams and his ability to dissect White colonial society, he apparently underestimates the violence of the structures that uphold White identity and his place within that construct of race and power. Toundi stays after his boss, the commandant, discovers his wife's infidelity, and she becomes enraged with Toundi for trifles. Because he could not accept that his boss would allow him to be tortured and unjustly murdered, he remains, after the cook and worldlier maid warn and, indeed, beg him to flee for his life. Through the maid, Kalista, Oyono urges, "If I were in your place," she said, "I'd go now before the river has swallowed me up altogether. . . . I was saying though, that because you know all their business, while you are still here, they can never forget about it altogether. And they will never forgive you for that. How can they go on strutting about with a cigarette hanging out of their mouth in front of you—when you *know* . . . If I were in your shoes, I swear I'd go right away. . . . I wouldn't even wait for my month's wages" (ibid., 119). Toundi ultimately pays dearly for this faith in his boss.

In a heartrending scene in which Toundi is brutally whipped by another colonized subject, Oyono attempts to reframe the capitulation of those whom wa Thiong'o castigated for basking in admiration of the colonizer. As he bears the agony with determined stoicism, the African constable begs him to weep, so he can stop administering a punishment that seems as agonizing to the constable charged with inflicting it as to the one undergoing it. "'Scream, for God's sake,' he yelled in the vernacular, 'cry out. They'll never let me stop while you won't cry. . . . ' He counted twenty-five, then he turned around to the whites. 'Give me the whip,' said Gullet. He brought down the hippopotamus-hide lash across the constable's back. The constable gave a roar of pain. 'See, that's how I want him whipped. Start over again!' Mendim rolled up the sleeves of his khaki jacket, his lips twisted in pain. 'Scream, scream,' he begged as he went to work on me again.' . . . The whites went off. I could hardly have expected to spend the night in Mendim me Tit's house. He is dozing in front of me, his mouth open, huddled in an old armchair like an old overcoat. 'I think I've done something today that I shall never be able to forget or make up for . . . he said to me when the whites had gone.' His great eyes grew dim with tears. 'Poor Toundi . . . and all of us,' he moaned" (ibid., 135). Through the constable, Oyono seeks the voices and emotions of some of those who were complicit in maintaining the violence of colonial politico-economic control, moving beyond the assumption that they were simply motivated by a desire to partake in their master's bread.

Today, the West has adopted the language of "new charitable humanitarianism" as the accepted mode for discussing "Africa's problems." The crisis in the postcolony seems sufficiently removed from the structures of colonial empire in which they were incubated. Presumably, the trail ends with the failed and misguided policies enacted by some self-interested post-independence leaders who have kept a watching world enthralled by their vacuous attempts to corral national tensions. If the trail ends at those doors, then apparently the obligation of the world is only to extend the beneficence of its postcolonial gains through a contract that maintains the economic, legal, and political power structures, which like those of the colonial period, reinforce the delegitimization of Africans and normalize the profound suffering in the postcolony.

> The resurgence of charity is at once a symptom and a cause of our society's failure to face up to and deal with the erosion of equality. . . . Our popular culture provides us with no shortage of anesthesia. I can refer to "our" popular culture because, increasingly, the beneficiaries of inequality share a transnational culture in which elements of both work and leisure are regimented by tastes cultivated in affluent societies. This is not to argue that local cultures are unimportant; nor would I argue that resistance to dominant cultures is insignificant. But many posit a soul-numbing equation between conspicuous consumption and modern existence, a formula said to lead millions to intellectual and moral oblivion. There are, of course, more subtle means of manufacturing consent: [as the] modes of explaining the world, including social inequalities and the violence they engender, are also undergoing a form of globalization. . . . (Farmer 2003, 154, 176)

The quest for justice, stability, and liberation in Africa will consequently be a long and turbulent one that involves renewed efforts to demythologize colonial history and arrive at a more critical epistemology, discovering in the process that "evil not only is present in the hearts of powerful individuals who muck things up for the rest of us, but is embedded in the very structures of society, so that those structures, and not just individuals who work within them, must be changed if the world is to change."[14]

References

Amadiume, Ifi. *Male Daughters, Female Husbands: Gender and Sex in an African Society*. London: Zed Books, 1987.

Anderson, David. *Histories of the Hanged: The Dirty War in Kenya and the End of Empire*. New York: W.W. Norton, 2005.

Austen, R. "Africa and Globalization: Colonialism, Decolonization and the Postcolonial Malaise." *Journal of Global History* 1, no. 3 (2006): 403–408.

Ayotte, Kevin J., and Mary E. Husain. "Securing Afghan Women: Neocolonialism, Epistemic Violence, and the Rhetoric of the Veil." *NWSA Journal* 17, no. 3 (2005):112–133.

---

[14] Farmer following Paulo Freire, *Pathologies of Power*, 143.

Bernal, Martin. *Black Athena: The Afroasiatic Roots of Classical Civilization (The Fabrication of Ancient Greece 1785–1985, Volume 1)*. New Brunswick, NJ: Rutgers University Press, 1987.

Boahen, Adu A. *African Perspectives on Colonialism*. Baltimore, MD: Johns Hopkins University Press, 1989.

Burton, Andrew, and Michael Jennings. "Introduction: The Emperor's New Clothes? Continuities in Governance in Late Colonial and Early Postcolonial East Africa." *International Journal of African Historical Studies* 40, no. 1 (2007): i-iv.

Cowell, Alan. "Wrestling with Ghosts of Colonialism," *New York Times*, May 23, 2009. www.nytimes.com/2009/05/23/world/africa/23iht-letter.html?pagewanted=print.

Curtin, Philip, Steven Feirerman, Leonard Thompson, and Jan Vansina. *African History*. Boston, MA: Little Brown, 1978.

Davidson, Basil. *Modern Africa: A Social and Political History*. Essex, England: Longman Group and Basil Davidson, 1995.

de Witte, Ludo. *The Assassination of Lumumba*. London and New York: Verso, 2001.

Diop, Cheikh Anta, and Mercer Cook. *The African Origin of Civilization: Myth or Reality*. Chicago: Lawrence Hill, 1974.

Ejikeme, Anene. "Let the Women Speak! And Listen," January 17, 2008. www.pambazuka.org/en/category/comment/45464.

Elkins, Caroline. *Imperial Reckoning: The Untold Story of Britain's Gulag in Kenya*. New York: Henry Holt, 2005a.

———. "Race, Citizenship, and Governance: Settler Tyranny and the End of Empire." In *Settler Colonialism in the Twentieth Century: Projects, Practices, Legacies*, edited by Caroline Elkins and Susan Pedersen, 203–222. New York: Routledge, 2005b.

Fabian, Johannes. "Forgetful Remembering: A Colonial Life in the Congo." *Africa* 73, no. 4 (2003): 489–504.

Falola, Toyin, ed. *Africa, vol. 1: African History Before 1885*. Durham, NC: Carolina Academic Press, 2001.

———, ed. *Africa, vol. 2: African Cultures and Societies Before 1885*. Durham, NC: Carolina Academic Press, 2001.

———, ed. *Africa, vol. 3: Colonial Africa 1885–1939*. Durham, NC: Carolina Academic Press, 2001.

———. *The Dark Webs: Perspectives on Colonialism in Africa*. Durham, NC: Carolina Academic Press, 2005.

Farmer, Paul. *Pathologies of Power: Health, Human Rights, and the New War on the Poor*. Berkeley and Los Angeles: University of California Press, 2003.

Fletcher, Yael Simpson. "'History Will One Day Have Its Say': New Perspectives on Colonial and Postcolonial Congo." *Radical History Review* 84 (2002): 195–220.

Graham, G. James. "Political Development in Africa." In *The African Experience: An Introduction*, 2nd ed., edited by Vincent B. Khapoya. Upper Saddle River, NJ: Prentice-Hall, 1998.

Giefer, Thomas. *Une mort de style coloniale: Patrice Lumumba, une tragédie africaine*, 2000; 16 min., 10 sec.; www.dailymotion.com/video/x937y9_patrice-lumumba-une-tragedie-africa_news.

Grinker, Roy, and Christopher Steiner. "Introduction: Africa in Perspective." In *Perspectives on Africa: A Reader in Culture, History, and Representation*, edited by Roy Grinker and Christopher Steiner, xvii–xxx. Oxford: Blackwell Publishers, 1997.

Harris, Joseph. E. *Africans and Their History*. New York: Penguin Books, 1998.

Hochschild, Adam. *King Leopold's Ghost: A Story of Greed, Terror, and Heroism in Colonial Africa*. New York: Mariner Books, 1999.

Huffman, Robert T. "Colonialism, Socialism and Destabilization in Mozambique." *Africa Today* 39, no. 1–2 (1992): 9.

Huggins, Willis N., and John G. Jackson. *An Introduction to African Civilizations, with Main Currents in Ethiopian History*. New York: Negro Universities Press, 1969.

Hunter-Gault, Charlayne. *New News Out of Africa: Uncovering Africa's Renaissance*. Oxford University Press, 2006.

Iliffe, John. *Africans: The History of a Continent*. Cambridge University Press, 2007.

Jackson, John G. *Introduction to African Civilizations*. New York: Citadel Press, 2001.

Khapoya, Vincent B. *The African Experience: An Introduction*, 2nd ed. Upper Saddle River, NJ: Prentice-Hall, 1998.

Lumumba-Kasongo, Tukumbi. "Zaire's Ties to Belgium: Persistence and Future Prospects in Political Economy." *Africa Today* 39, no. 3 (1992).

Mamdani, Mahmood. *Citizen and Subject: Contemporary Africa and the Legacy of Late Colonialism*. Princeton University Press, 1996.

———. "Preliminary Thoughts on the Congo Crises." *Social Text* 17, no. 3 (1999): 53–62.

———. "Beyond Settler and Native as Political Identities: Overcoming the Political Legacy of Colonialism." *Comparative Studies in Society and History* 43, no. 4 (2001): 651–664.

———. *When Victims Become Killers: Colonialism, Nativism, and the Genocide in Rwanda*. Princeton University Press, 2001.

———. "Colonial Legacies." Review of *Imperial Reckoning: The Untold Story of Britain's Gulag in Kenya*, by Caroline Elkins; *Histories of the Hanged: The Dirty War in Kenya and the End of Empire*, by David Anderson; *The Africa House: The True Story of an English Gentleman and His African Dream*, by Christina Lamb. *Washington Post*, July 3, 2005, www.proquest.com.

Mandela, Winnie. *Part of My Soul Went With Him*, New York: W.W Norton, 1984.

Maren, Michael. *Road to Hell: The Ravaging Effects of Foreign Aid and International Charity*. New York: Free Press, 1997.

Mbembe, Achille. *On the Postcolony*. Berkeley and Los Angeles: University of California Press, 2001.

Muiu, M. "'Civilization' On Trial: The Colonial and Postcolonial State in Africa." *Journal of Third World Studies* 25, no. 1 (2008): 73–93.

Ogot, B. "Britain's Gulag." Review of *Histories of the Hanged: The Dirty War in Kenya and the End of Empire*, by David Anderson, and *Britain's Gulag: The Brutal End of Empire in Kenya*, by Caroline Elkins. *Journal of African History* 46, no. 3 (2005): 493–505.

Osaghae, Eghosa E. "Colonialism and Civil Society in Africa: The Perspective of Ekeh's Two Publics." *Voluntas* 17, no. 3 (2006): 233–245.

Oyewumi, Oyeronke. *The Invention of Women: Making an African Sense of Western Gender Discourse*. Minneapolis, MN: University of Minnesota Press, 1997.

Oyono, Ferdinand. *Boy!* Translated by John Reed. London: Macmillan, 1966.

Rahier, Jean Muteba. "The Ghost of Leopold II: The Belgian Royal Museum of Central Africa and Its Dusty Colonialist Exhibition." *Research in African Literatures* 34, no. 1 (2003): 58–84.

Ranger, Terence. "Europeans in Black Africa." *Journal of World History* 9, no. 2 (1998): 255–268.

Rodney, Walter. *How Europe Underdeveloped Africa*. Washington, D.C.: Howard University Press, 1981.

Schneider, Leander. "Colonial Legacies and Postcolonial Authoritarianism in Tanzania: Connects and Disconnects." *African Studies Review* 49, no. 1 (2006): 93–118.

Sembene, Ousmane. *La Noire de*. VHS. Distributed by New Yorker Video. 1966.

Soyinka-Airewele, Peyi. "Subjectivities of Violence and the Dilemmas of Transitional Governance," *West Africa Review*, no. 6 (2004).

Turshen, Meredith. "Women's War Stories." In *What Women Do in Wartime*, edited by Meredith Turshen and Clothilde Twagiramariya, 1–26. London: Zed Books, 1998.

Van Allen, Judith. "'Aba Riots' or Igbo 'Women's War'?: Ideology, Stratification and the Invisibility of Women." In *Women in Africa: Studies in Social and Economic Change*, edited by Nancy J. Hafkin and Edna G. Bay, 59–86. Palo Alto, CA: Stanford University Press, 1976.

wa Thiong'o, Ngũgĩ, "Detained: A Writer's Prison Diary." In *Perspectives on Africa: A Reader in Culture, History, and Representation*, edited by Roy Grinker and Christopher Steiner, 613–622. Oxford: Blackwell Publishers, 1997.

Chapter 8

THE INTERSECTION OF AFRICAN IDENTITIES IN THE TWENTY-FIRST CENTURY
Old and New Diasporas and the African Continent

William Ackah

Countee Cullen, in his famous poem, "Heritage" (1925), posed the question, "What is Africa to me?" It was both a personal question and a question for generations like his who were descendants of those forcibly removed—as he eloquently put it—"from the scenes his forefathers told." In this chapter, I want to pose the same question to explore what it means to be an African in the diaspora in the twenty-first century. Africa in the historical imagination has meant many things to different people. For the survivors and descendants of the Atlantic slave trade, it has been the site of hope, pain, trauma, and, ultimately, restoration as the scenes the forefathers told have faded, resumed, and changed over time.

Yet are things that different for the postcolonial or new African diaspora, whose hope is a renaissance? The new African diaspora has had to face the pain and trauma of postcolonial conflict, as well as environmental and economic degradation, and has had to engage in reworking the dreams and visions of the independence freedom fighters to generate ideas at home and abroad.

In consideration of this volume's theme—reframing contemporary Africa—I will illustrate the ways that new encounters, parallels, and differing experiences are leading to a reconstruction of relationships between old and new diasporas. I will particularly use examples from politics, media, and popular culture to explore the intersection of African diasporic identities in the global era. I want to locate the sites and drivers of globalized African identities and argue that, in the twenty-first century, the dichotomy between old and new diasporas based on the enslavement process and postcolonial migrations will become less relevant. There will be a need to explore and research new points of convergence and difference in the diaspora, points that still stem from asking the old question, what is Africa to me?

Defining Diaspora

The usage and understandings of the word "diaspora" have exploded in recent times. It was once primarily confined to describing the experiences of the Jewish people, who throughout history have experienced exile and removal from what they considered their homeland. Those who had been scattered to various places around the world, it was argued, still had memories of "home" expressed in religious, cultural, and economic practices and, ultimately, political movements. They continued, and continue, to forge an identity abroad linked to an idea of home. From being applied to the Jewish experience, the idea of diaspora has been widened to other communities, such as the Armenian, Palestinian, and Cuban. Safran, in his often utilized definition of diaspora, has a six-themed template for defining the word. Among the themes are the dispersal from an original place of origin to two or more different regions, the retention of an idea of an original homeland, and a sense of not being accepted in the places to which the people relocated (see Safran 1991, 83–84 for all six themes). Some scholars find Safran's conception of diaspora too rigid. They argue that the relationships between communities abroad and their homelands can be much more uncertain. Diasporas can have strong relationships with their places of origin, but these relationships can also over time loosen and revive, depending on circumstances.

Communities abroad, as well having attachments to a homeland, develop cultural, economic, and political practices that relate to the places where they settle, and this, too, is a strong influence on the trajectory of a given diaspora. Hence, a fixed definition cannot capture the complexity and unfolding nature of diverse diasporan experiences. Thus, for some, a more useful way of conceiving of diasporas is as relational, yet fluid communities across time and location. "Diasporas [have] roots and routes" (Gilroy 1993; Clifford 1997).

But where do African diasporas fit into these conceptions of diaspora? It could be argued that newer diasporas, with specific language and ethnic ties to specific places in Africa, could match Safran's criteria. In contrast, older African diasporas in the West, stemming from the enslavement process, have much looser direct ties and a more generic African heritage. They may not fit Safran's definition but, instead, match the idea of diaspora put forward by Clifford and others. Before exploring and challenging whether these dichotomies between new and old diasporas still work as a means of conceptualizing different African heritage communities' relationships to the continent, outlining the relationships and characteristics that shape so-called new and old African diasporan identities and identifications with Africa is worthwhile.

Old African Diaspora and Africa

In essence the African diaspora is as old as humanity itself. Evidence suggests that human life began in Africa; hence, the movement of the first humans out of Africa to various parts of the world should rightly be considered the beginnings of the African diaspora. More common in the popular imagination is the idea that the old African diaspora originated in the horrors of the enslavement process. Africans have been subject to two of the worst forced removals of populations in world history, namely, the trans-Saharan and trans-Atlantic slave trades. Both saw millions of Africans forcibly removed from their homes and communities and forced to endure terrible hardships and degradations. The trades resulted in Africans being transported to far-flung places, mainly to Asia and Arab lands in the case of the trans-Saharan trade and to the Americas in the case of the trans-Atlantic (Harris 1982; Gomez 2005). This work will focus attention on the descendants of the trans-Atlantic trade and their subsequent relationship with Africa.

Atlantic slavery was a four-hundred-year process, which was initiated by the Portuguese, but eventually involved most of the major European powers, including Britain and France. It transformed the known world, creating new nations and communities in the Caribbean and North and South America. Estimates vary hugely as to the numbers affected by the enslavement process; however, between 10 and 20 million Africans were shipped across the Atlantic. That number does not include those who did not survive the voyage or those who remained but had their economic, social, and cultural lives ruined by the wholesale removal of the most productive individuals from the continent (Reynolds 1985).

For those who did make it across the Atlantic—to Brazil, Jamaica, Haiti, Argentina, and the United States, to pick a few destinations from many—there unfolds a remarkable history of people; events; and cultural, economic, political, and religious transformations that still reverberates today across most fields of human endeavor (Segal 1995). Such is the multidimensional nature of the impact of the enslavement process and subsequent struggle for freedom and dignity by Africans in the diaspora. Through examples, I want to outline the role of Africa in the process of identity formation for the old African diaspora.

Africa and Identity in the Old African Diaspora

Identity formation in the old African diaspora is multidimensional. Ideas of Africa, even within diasporas that reside within the bounds of one country, such as the Jamaican and U.S. diasporas, have never been singular or uncontested. It is not possible to answer the what-is-Africa-to-me? conundrum for such a range of people.

Among those individuals taken from Africa to the Americas, the primary allegiance would have been to an ethnic identity, not Africa generally. Unlike some African diasporan communities, over time and as more descendants of the first Africans were born in the diaspora, identification with specific ethnicities and locations in Africa waned and was replaced by a more general African identity. W.E.B. DuBois, the brilliant African American intellectual and activist, identifies this changing relationship well:

> From the fifteenth through the seventeenth centuries, the Africans imported to America regarded themselves as temporary settlers destined to return eventually to Africa. Their increasing revolts against the slave system, which culminated in the eighteenth century, showed a feeling of close kinship to the motherland and even well into the nineteenth century they called their organizations "African" as witness the "African unions" of New York and Newport and the African Churches of Philadelphia and New York. In the West Indies and South America, there was even closer indication of feelings and kinship with Africa and the East (W.E.B. DuBois 1957 in J. Clarke 1991, 135).

African identity was important to those diasporan Africans who lived in the enslavement era. Aspects of African culture and identity were and are still clearly discernible among diasporan Africans who lived in the Caribbean and South America, where slave populations heavily outnumbered other groups. For example, variants of African traditional religions, such as Santeria, Candomble, and Vodun, are still followed in Cuba, Brazil, and Haiti. The extent to which the descendants of enslaved Africans have retained a sense of African culture and identity has been the focus of immense scholarly debate and continuing research (Herkovits 1958; Frazier 1963; Holloway 1991; Gomez 2005).

Specific identification with specific places in Africa has been replaced by a more generalized identification with the continent. A key feature of the old diasporan experience, whether based in societies where they were a majority or minority, was that these Africans were brought up in societies where they were subordinated and subjugated because of their heritage. Ideas of who they were and of their self-worth were inextricably linked to the concept of Africa. This produced a range of reactions, from outright denial of African heritage to wholehearted embrace of African identity (Richburg 1998). The old African diaspora no longer has a united view of its identity in relation to Africa.

Some of the most powerful religious and political movements in the African diaspora have emerged out of the struggle to form an African identity to provide those living under racist domination and subjugation a sense of self-worth. Marcus Garvey's Universal Negro Improvement Association (UNIA) was probably the most important movement of this type (Lewis 1987; James 1998). Here was an economic, political, cultural, and religious diasporan movement that had uplifting African people as its central platform. Its founder, a Jamaican printer by trade, who developed his vision in London from 1912 to 1914 and made his reputation in the United States in the 1920s, influenced the Black world from South America to Africa. He created possibly the largest mass movement in the history of the African diaspora, yet he never set foot on Africa himself. Given the economic and political circumstances diasporan and continental Africans found themselves in, the formation of UNIA and its achievements were remarkable. It was an important platform and a key influence on the racialized Black experience, which found expression in such movements as Rastafarianism and Afrocentricity. It also affected the thinking of future African continental leaders, such as Kwame Nkrumah, a pivotal Pan-African figure of the twentieth century (Nkrumah 1957).

Garveyism exemplifies a theme that underlies the old diaspora. Garvey argued that positive notions of Africa and African heritage were tied to Black experience and identity in the diaspora (Garvey 1969). His ideology is particularly a strand in the English-speaking African diaspora among prominent Black activists and intellectuals interested in powerful and influential African states like Ethiopia and Egypt. The histories of these countries were used to valorize what Africans were and what they could be. In the French-speaking African diaspora, there has also been reference to the past, or non-European, conceptions of Africa in order to enhance African identity. The Negritude movement of the 1930s rejected Western paradigms and embraced "traditional African values" (Keselfoot 1974).

DuBois in his most often-quoted statement raises another aspect of African identity:

One ever feels his twoness, an American, a Negro; two souls, two thoughts, two unreconciled strivings; two warring ideals in one dark body, whose dogged strength alone keeps it from being torn asunder (DuBois 1969, 45).

By articulating the pressures of racialized subordination and the horrors of White supremacy, DuBois called into question, for the old diaspora, what it meant to be an African in the world. This sense of duality and striving to be accepted as an African and fully fledged, equal human being has created unique diasporan experiences. It is the duality that has been responsible for the marked creative impact that the diaspora has had after slavery on Western art, music, and many other fields of culture. Racism, issues of identity, and ideas of Africa echo throughout the syncopated drum beats, jazz riffs, carnival dances, paintings, and written expressions of creative artists in the African diaspora. Looking both ways at the same time, living in the now, visioning past horrors and pre-horrors, and gazing into the future for brighter prospects for "Africans at home and abroad" has been a key theme of the nineteenth- and twentieth-century African diasporan experience.

Another theme has been to ignore Africa or reject it. The daily media images of a ravaged Africa, accompanied by a racist cultural dialogue that only perceives the continent as the "dark" place, has led some members of the diaspora to consciously downplay affiliations with Africa. In the 1990s, the so-called king of pop Michael Jackson, in his album *Dangerous*, claimed that if you wanted to be his lover, it did not matter if you were Black or White, yet his redesign of his own phenotype seemed to suggest the opposite. In effect, being part of the diaspora meant being absorbed by the wider society and forgetting about identification with Africa. In South America, the disappearance of many African communities and the appearance of a melting pot in places like Brazil have made some old diasporan communities unaware of or unconcerned by their African heritage.

What is left of the diasporan African experience? Is there still a unifying theme in the midst of its diversity? Does it possess an Africanity or African personality that has an affinity with the experience of diasporan Africans who never experienced enslavement? It is to this group that our attention now turns.

The New Diaspora and Africa

The new African diaspora is, for the most part, postcolonial. Although there had always been small numbers of continent-born Africans who during the enslavement and colonial eras traveled out of Africa as students, traders, and professionals, the post–Second World War movement of Africans within and outside Africa was new, and it took place during the unfolding of African liberation. In 1957, Ghana became the first state in sub-Saharan Africa to gain its independence from the British, and over the course of the remainder of the century, through political protest, struggle, agitation, and war, Africans liberated themselves from the yoke of European colonialism. The period also saw Africans liberate themselves from the White racist minority settler regimes in Zimbabwe and South Africa.

The context for new African migration within and outside the continent was shaped by over fifty separate nation-states trying to forge their ways. Their existence postindependence has been well documented: economic stagnation, political instability, military rule, Cold War politics, ethnic tension, wars, and epidemics have blighted many of the positive achievements of liberation and have resulted in many Africans leaving their countries to seek opportunities elsewhere (Koser 2003). Hence, on one level, the causes of the new African diaspora are totally different from those of the old, whose members left Africa in shackles. Once in diaspora, old and new migrants found themselves in places where they were perceived as unequal.

Africa and Identity in the New African Diaspora

Given the recentness of the migration of the new diasporans, their identity and identification with Africa is specific, rather than generalized. (A major source of individual African states' gross domestic products is the remittances sent home by family members living in the diaspora.) While identity and self-worth are important, they are based not on a racialized sense of self from the past, but on being with familiar people and communities in new and sometimes hostile places, as they are for many new diasporan communities. So new diasporan African communities in Europe, North America, and the Middle East establish ethnic associations and religious organizations where they meet, eat, and speak in their native languages and establish political and cultural ties with their homelands (Akyeampong 2000).

Interestingly, with many of these communities, depending on numbers, whereabouts, and circumstances, there is a flexibility regarding identity. Thus, in London, a Ghanaian can be a Nzema and belong to the Nzema association. The same person can attend a Ghanaian-led church and listen to Ghanaian radio stations to adopt a Ghanaian national identity, and can watch Africa-focused television and go to a Pan-African music venue to adopt a continental identity.

A consequence of this type of diasporan experience is, for example, evident in the Ghanaian diaspora in Europe in places like Holland, Germany, Italy, and, especially, in the United Kingdom. In these places emerge publishing, Internet, and transfer services that facilitate ongoing dialogue between the diaspora and the country of origin. Other services help these communities establish "roots" as well as "routes" that include stores that sell African food and other products, places of worship, and, in some cases, ethnic support organizations that receive subscriptions and state funding and provide advice and guidance to new migrants (Peil 1995; Akyeampong 2000).

New African diasporas may experience the "twoness" struggle, but the ambiguity of the relationship between their homelands and diasporas may stem more from their homeland experiences rather than from their struggles to gain acceptance in the diaspora. For example, Africans escaping war in places like Somalia, the Congo, or Rwanda may have ambiguous feelings, which will undoubtedly impact their lives in the diaspora. Personally, I have seen Africans, who have had to flee countries in very trying circumstances, bemoan the quality of government and berate the state, but they have not lost interest in African affairs or abandoned their identification with the homeland in favor of a diasporan identity (Omar 2007). This may change over time and for the third and fourth generations; theirs may well be a different story, as a British-born journalist of Ghanaian parents attests in his autobiography, which describes ambiguities similar to those expressed by DuBois (Eshun 2005).

Among poor migrants, the "twoness" reveals itself in the daily struggle to maintain existence by undertaking degrading, low-paid work in the Middle East or Europe, while trying to support family members in Africa. In a sense, the battle for economic viability is the means by which one can secure one's identity, as opposed to fighting for racial equality. Rejection or denial of African heritage is not a common feature among new African diasporans. Individuals and groups who have experienced oppression in Africa because of their gender or because of their religious or cultural practices may, on moving to another place, reject the culture or faith that lead to the oppression that they suffered. However, a more generalized rejection of African identity, after acquiring new citizenship, and an unwillingness to be identified with a repressive homeland is not so common. Even African sports stars who have adopted another country's vest for citizenship purposes are known to maintain close allegiances and ties to their countries of origin (Vieira 2005).

The new diaspora is also a worldwide phenomenon, with Africans not just moving to countries of former European colonizers. Being free and from independent states, they have been able to venture far and wide and, for the most part, retain strong connections with the African continent. Whether this will remain true over time remains to be seen, and whether long term the new will mirror the old or follow different trajectories is something that will be explored later.

Problematizing the Old and the New

Thus far, we have tried to define old and new African diasporas—enslavement and postcolonial identification with a generalized Africa in the old versus tangible links with specific places in the new. The old diaspora looked to an Africa of the past to gain self-worth in the present, while the new diaspora struggles to survive in an alien environment and support the people it has left behind.

This way of looking at the diasporan experience over time creates a false dichotomy between old and new. That is not to say that there are not differences between, for example, African Americans descended from slaves and Africans in America from postindependence African states. But are these differences as significant as those between, for instance, Haitians and African Americans? Might not Haitians, in spite of enslavement, have a closer bond with new African diasporas than with African Americans? When does an individual or group stop being new? Is it when a concern for a specific African experience is replaced by a more generalized and romanticized vision of Africa?

If so, Leopold Sedar Senghor, a new African diasporan who was not only the first president of Senegal, but also a key figure of the Negritude movement (an artistic movement of the French African diaspora that espoused particularly romanticized visions of Africa), should actually be considered a member of the old diaspora. In contrast, Frantz Fanon, the Martinique-born psychiatrist who rejected romantic visions of an African past and who devoted the best part of his life to the real-life liberation of Algeria, should be considered part of the new diaspora. And what are we to make of Ayaan Hirsi Ali, the Somali born Muslim, who denounced her heritage as she became the darling of right-wing racists in Holland and a leading political figure in Dutch politics for a time? (Ali 2007). Gender, class, locale, and experience have always cut across the racialized vision of a united Black continent. This does not take into account the Asians, Whites, and other races with African connections who would argue that they have legitimate cause to be part of the African diaspora.

What accounts for the sense of shared meaning and differences between African communities? This is not a particularly easy question to answer (Appiah 1992). At the dawn of the twentieth century, DuBois said the color line was the defining characteristic of the lived experience of people of color. In many senses, Pan-African struggles for the liberation and dignity of Black peoples, implicitly and explicitly, worked around a notion of racialized solidarity, Africanity, African Personality—call it what you will—but the color line was there in the midst of all the differences and contradictions of what it meant to be an African.

Now that enslavement is over, segregation and colonialism are no more: now that a new African diasporan has led the United Nations (Kofi Annan), an old African diasporan has been the secretary of state of the most powerful nation on earth (Condoleezza Rice), and a combination of the new and old (Barack Obama) is the president of the United States, we are asked to consider whether the old–new dichotomy is relevant.

Towards an Experiential Understanding of African Diasporan Experience in the Twenty-First Century

If I were to characterize myself according to the descriptions outlined above, I would be classed as a new African diasporan. My parents came to London from Ghana in the mid-1960s, and I was their firstborn. While I went to school in London, however, Africa was invisible, and Africans did not exist as complex, rational human beings. Rather, the only modes available for Black identity were Jamaican or African American. I knew I was not White; the host society made it abundantly clear that birth did not equal equality or belonging. I searched for valorization and self-worth in positive notions of Blackness wherever I could find them (Ackah 1999).

Hence, I have a fondness for West Indian cricket and the music of Bob Marley and Gil Scott Heron. It was through their music that I became aware of the idea of a Black diaspora and ultimately of Pan-Africanism and Africa as a visible place. It was, however, an Africa seen through the lenses of Black diasporan identity. Later, as the shoots of multiculturalism were rising in the school classroom, I was introduced to the works of Chinua Achebe and Ngũgĩ wa Thiong'o and Africans who spoke about their own experiences in their own languages. They were not experiences I was familiar with, but they were pieces in my own jigsaw in terms of understanding where I came from, who I was, and where I was going.

But what does my personal experience have to do with diasporan trajectories of the twenty-first century? What I want to illustrate is that future intersections of the African diaspora lie in the multitude of diaspora stories as much as in abstract theorizing about globalization or political economy, as important as these ideas may be.

Although the African diasporan experience and emergent identities are diverse and wide-ranging, I would like to suggest that what joins old and new diasporas is the nature of their experiences. What I mean by this is that although Africans in the diaspora have not been governed by a single political philosophy or a singular religion and are not racially homogenous or united by language, from Thailand to Trinidad, when an African has lived in the land, that multifaceted, hard-to-define, somewhat mystical, and intangible Africanity is there. We may argue about it and question its relevance in relation to Africa's economic well-being and the political life of the continent, but the simple fact that we do that says that Africa still means something even in the postmodern, fragmented, globalized, multiple-identity world of the twenty-first century.

I think this is a tribute, in many ways, to the old diaspora story of struggle against slavery and oppression, an all-embracing story with its own literature, music, academia, and cultural momentum, which many people still use to define their past and current experience. Even in my childhood case, it was not strictly my own twentieth-century experience that mattered; it was the lens through which the diaspora and Africa were by and large seen that mattered.

All around the world, there has been an almost silent revolution taking place. New African diasporans are occupying many positions in academia in the States. Diasporans are doctors treating patients in the Caribbean and Europe. They are African soldiers in Israel; African traders in China, Taiwan, and Malaysia; and businesspeople and leaders of new African communities abroad. Yet at present, the story of these people and their lives is not an all-encompassing diaspora story—not a universal Black story like those of Malcolm X, Kunte Kente, Rosa Parks, Bob Marley, Beyoncé, or Queen Nzingha—by which Africans come to be known and even emulated. Perhaps because many new African diasporan communities are still establishing themselves and are operating at the lowest economic rungs, they still have first-generation sentiments, and their real investments of resources, creativity, and energy are in their homelands, not in the diaspora.

There are suggestions that this new wave of migration may bring about new diasporan concerns and interests that will become all-inclusive. In the cinema, Forest Whittaker, the African American actor, won an Oscar for his performance of Idi Amin in *The Last King of Scotland,* a contemporary and controversial representation that reached a worldwide audience. Nelson Mandela is a modern icon for all Africans across the globe, and South Africa could be, with its wealth and influence, the place in Africa where cultural forms and political ideas form part of a new diaspora story. Such a story could weave its way into the fabric of Jamaicans, African Americans, Afro-Brazilians, Nigerians, Kenyans, Indian Siddis, Black French, Black British, and South Africans living around the world.

The ways in which the African diasporan experience travels the world and is shared by disparate groups are complex. I have argued elsewhere that African American cultural production, riding on the wings of U.S. imperialism, powerfully influences global Black trends and the intersection of the old and new (Ackah 1999, 90–102).

Here, I want to suggest that religious expression, for better or worse, is another point of intersection. Islam has been a major force in Africa for many centuries, and African diasporan Muslims have been at the forefront of developing and modernizing Spain and other parts of Southern Europe, beginning in the eighth century. The new African Muslim diaspora, although fragmented ethnically and nationally, has a potential that has yet to be realized or really assessed. Africa, in the twenty-first century, also may become the Christian continent, such is the speedy growth of the faith there. It has also transported Christianity across the diaspora through African-derived churches and Christian communities (Ter Haar 1998; Olupona and Gemignani 2007).

Ironically, some of these African churches are similar to African American churches, with powerful charismatic leaders and a strong emphasis on music, worship, and the experiential as means of coping with or forgetting the burdens of trying to make ends meet in the diaspora. At the moment, these faith experiences, new and old, seem to run parallel to each other, with little interaction between groups, but because faith is a powerful motivating factor in Africa and the diaspora, both old and new, it could lead to an intersection of identities and themes, particularly as Western societies become increasingly secular and less tolerant of faith-based voices.

The unpredictably of the diaspora is its strength and Achilles heel. The fact that it reinvents itself and is so diverse means that it is rich in resources. On the other hand, solidarity and concerted political action can never be guaranteed. The TransAfrica Forum, a diasporan social movement of old and new Africans, campaigns and lobbies on a number of contemporary issues affecting African people all over the globe, showing the potential of diasporan action. On the other hand, Dinaw Mengestu in his evocative novel *Children of the Revolution* depicts a new African diaspora, one with fading negative memories of political despotism on the continent and unrealized hopes in the diaspora. In its own way, Mengestu's novel is as important as the work of the TransAfrica Forum. They are both African diasporan stories that need to be told and embraced. It is in the acceptance of coexisting new, multiple Africanities that I hope and believe the intersection of old and new will take place in the twenty-first century.

REFERENCES

Ackah, W. *Pan-Africanism: Exploring the Contradictions, Politics, Identity and Development in Africa and the African Diaspora*. Brookfield, VT: Ashgate, 1999.

Appiah, K. *In My Father's House*. London: Methuen, 1992.

Akyeampong, E. "Africans in the Diaspora: The Diaspora and Africa," *African Affairs* 99 (2000): 183–215.

Ali, A.H. *Infidel*. New York: Free Press, 2007.

Clarke, J.H. *Notes for an African World Revolution: Africans at the Crossroads*. Trenton: Africa World Press, 1991.

Clifford, J. *Routes: Travel and Translation in the Late Twentieth Century*. Cambridge: Harvard, 1997.

Cullen, C. "Heritage" in *The Portable Harlem Renaissance Reader,* edited by D.L. Lewis, 244. New York: Penguin, 1994. (Poem originally published in 1925.)

DuBois, W.E.B. *The Souls of Black Folk*. New York: Signet, 1969.

Eshun, E. *Black Gold of the Sun: Searching for Home in England and Africa*. London: Hamish Hamilton, 2005.

Frazier, E.F. *The Negro Church in America*. New York: Schocken, 1964.

Garvey, A., ed. *Philosophy and Opinions of Marcus Garvey*. New York: Atheneum, 1969.

Gilroy, P. *The Black Atlantic: Modernity and Double Consciousness*. London: Verso, 1993.

Gomez, M.A. *Reversing the Sail: A History of the African Diaspora*. Cambridge University Press, 1997.

Harris, J.E., ed. *Global Dimensions of the African Diaspora*. Washington, D.C.: Howard University, 1982.

Herkovits, M. *The Myth of the Negro Past*. Boston: Beacon, 1941.

Holloway, J.E. *Africanisms in American Culture*. Bloomington: Indiana University Press, 1991.

James, W. *Holding Aloft the Banner of Ethiopia: Caribbean Radicalism in Early Twentieth-Century America*. New York: Verso, 1998.

Keselfoot, L. *Black Writers in French: A Literary History of Negritude*. Philadelphia, Temple University: 1974.

Koser, K., ed. *New African Diasporas*. London: Routledge, 2003.

Lemelle, S., and R.D.G. Kelley, eds. *Imagining Home: Class, Culture and Nationalism in the African Diaspora*. London: Haymarket, 1994.

Lewis, R. *Marcus Garvey, Anti-colonial champion*. London: Karia, 1987.

Nkrumah, K. *Ghana, The Autobiography of Kwame Nkrumah*. London: Thomas Nelson, 1957.

Olupona, J.K., and R. Gemignani, eds. *African Immigrant Religions in America*. New York University, 2007.

Omar, R. *Only Half of Me British and Muslim: The Conflict Within*. London: Penguin, 2007.

Peil, M. "Ghanaians Abroad," *African Affairs* 94 (1995): 345–367.

Richburg, K.B. *Out of America: A Black Man Confronts Africa*. New York: Basic, 1997.

Reynolds, E. *Stand the Storm: A History of the Atlantic Slave Trade*. New York: Schocken Books, 1985.

Safran, W. "Diasporas in Modern Societies: Myths of Homeland and Return," *Diaspora* 1.1 (1991): 83–89.

Segal, R. *The Black Diaspora*. London: Faber and Faber, 1995.

Ter Haar, G. *Halfway to Paradise*. Cardiff: Cardiff Academic Press, 1998.

Vieira, P. *Vieira My Autobiography*. London: Orion, 2006.

Part III

POWER, POLITICS, AND SOCIOECONOMIC STRUGGLES

Due to Africa's late decolonization, discourses on political conflict, leadership failure, disease, and underdevelopment still tend to dominate the political and economic analysis of African politics. It is now commonplace to refer to Africa as a place in crisis, a state of affairs oftentimes presented too simplistically and framed in the behavioral tradition of comparative politics by which the continent's leaders are scolded for being corrupt, illiberal, or premodern and given menacing labels. Considered in perpetual economic turmoil, the continent is berated for its "poor" ranking on the UN development scale and its lack of economic growth compared to the Asian Tigers. Africa's failure of leadership and the persistence of its cultures and traditions are often blamed for creating what is considered the world's most underdeveloped region. Former British prime minister Tony Blair once called Africa a "scar" on the world, despite his obvious humanitarian intentions towards the continent.

While we advocate critical initiatives in response to Africa's structural and other debilitating problems, our approach to political and economic development is not sanguine about the Washington Consensus because it imposes governance and economic reform policies on Africa that deny the continent economic and political sovereignty. What is more, many peoples, groups, identities, and other political agents have responded in complex, often dissident, ways to normative and externally derived political processes forced on the continent.

The authors of Part III examine diverse reactions to politics, economics, and change by investigating the political-economic challenges faced by various African countries. In this section, we highlight the problematic nature of a "development discourse" that reinforces inequities in global power relations. We avoid simplistic and reductionist notions of African development, according to which structural adjustment policies are the only economic reform measures governments need to undertake to spur development. Moreover, we do not limit our understanding of development to "income" and "wealth creation"; rather, we study development holistically, including social sectors and global economic power structures that mediate the development prospects of the continent.

In this section, we also problematize issues pertaining to politics, governance, and democratization in Africa. For example, while we acknowledge the tremendous democratic transformations Africa has undergone, we do not confine our examination of political democracy to a myopically conceived, linear, global progression of democracy from a Western center, and we do not restrict the notion of "democratic development" in the continent to liberal democracy. Instead, we offer a rich survey of the development of political and democratic ideas, institutions, and processes that have emerged within the continent.

We consider current African international security relations under an international political economy rubric to avoid the normative analysis that constructs Africa as a "collapsed state." This description we view as a heuristic device that invokes and deliberately provokes a structural, functionalist, anthropological characterization of Africa as full of chaotic, disorganized, Hobbesian, "state-less" societies forged in the 1800s. To underscore and expand our international political-economic theme, we also include chapters on transformations in the oil industry and energy sector along the Guinea coastline and on the political economy of the AIDS crisis in Africa. In essence, Part III serves to represent politics, power, and socioeconomic struggles across the continent in ways that expand the study of the "economic" and "political" and show relationships between them.

We begin this section by using the concept of civil society to appraise current changes in Africa's political landscape. Cēlestin Monga, a Cameroonian political economist, scholar, and author of *The Anthropology of Anger* (Monga 1996), offers an important commentary on the continent's politics, power, and socioeconomic struggles. He resuscitates the classical ideas of de Tocqueville and reexamines other Western civil society theorists, such as Jurgen Habermas and Robert Putnam, to analyze the reconstructivist surges of African civil societies. To provide the appropriate scope and functions of civil society, Monga asks what legitimizes citizen advocacy organizations. He also considers the moral principles and values of civil society while attempting to measure its contributions to social capital, harmony, and democratic consolidation.

Rita Kiki Edozie's chapter challenges us to think differently about the political process and political culture of Africans. In the coming decade, we will no longer be able to pigeonhole African political systems or reduce them narrowly to patrimonial regimes. The author of *Reconstructing the Third Wave of Democracy* (2008), Edozie argues that democracy has arrived in Africa and suggests that correct analysis of democratization in the continent is key to our understanding of contemporary African politics. In her examination, she includes the precolonial foundations of African culturalist interpretations of democracy, as well as the liberal and social democracies that were transferred to African contexts during the waning years of colonialism. By presenting what she refers to as Africa's postcolonial experience with democracy, she attempts to demonstrate how contemporary African democracies cannot be viewed dualistically, that is, merely as democratic or authoritarian.

Instead, Edozie claims that these nascent African political systems are hybrid regimes that experimentally mix several genres of democracy. Africa's relative underdevelopment has also contributed to the vibrant and lively history of socialist democracy and the derivation of populist struggles in the incumbent democracies. Tanzania's one-party democracy, Botswana's dominant-party democracy, Nigeria's multinational federalist democracy, and South Africa's nonracial democracy are some of the cases Edozie uses to explore Africa's democratic trajectories.

Siba Grovogui, author of *Sovereigns, Quasi Sovereigns, and Africans: Race and Self-Determination in International Law* (1996), considers the effect of international security structures that exacerbate the continent's conflicts. Grovogui's previous writings have countered the simplicity and reductionism of failed-state theories that dominate international relations analyses of Africa. In his chapter, Grovogui takes on similar themes. For example, in his examination of the plight of the Taureg in Mali and Niger, Grovogui argues that postcolonial proxy Cold Wars, colonially driven development models that emphasized security and order, and, most perniciously, post–September 11 "war on terror" policies (disguised as human security development assistance) are external mechanisms that undermine the sustainable peace and secure development of a self-determined Africa. Reframing African security relations, with the goal of reducing conflict and fostering peace, can only be obtained, according to Grovogui, if the continent is free to consciously draw from African indigenous knowledge and practices to build security and development institutions.

In the next chapter, by presenting the many facets of the African international political economy, Fantu Cheru, the author of *African Renaissance: Roadmaps to the Challenge of Globalization* (2002), reveals the deep global economic structures that simultaneously inhibit and foster reframing contemporary Africa. Cheru's daunting statistics and political-economic analysis explain why Africa has had a generally negative experience with globalization compared to China and India. The core of the problem lies in the continent's incapacity to restructure its bottom-tier global economic status because of policies of the world's richest economic powers. Cheru argues that former colonizers imposed limitations on Africa during the colonial period, and their legacy is preeminent in the contemporary African political economy.

One-size-fits-all, externally imposed, neoliberal economic policies, unfair trade, limited foreign direct investment (FDI), and aid dependency are the dynamics that mitigate against self-determined national development in African countries, according to Cheru. If Africa is to be reframed in the twenty-first century, argues this scholar of development, Africans themselves must develop at the national and continental levels to successfully navigate the cold currents of economic globalization.

According to Okbazghi Yohannes, author of *The United States and the Horn of Africa* (1997), the international political economy of hydrocarbon resources and their shaping of petrostates in the African Gulf of Guinea are critical issues in the present-day global era. He charts a path for Africa by presenting the radical transformation in orientation of these states, which include Nigeria, Cameroon, Gabon, Angola, Senegal, Ghana, Ivory Coast, Equatorial Guinea, Chad, and Sao Tome and Principe. While examining the role that oil and energy has played in these countries and Africa generally, Yohannes calls for a coherent counter-hegemonic narrative, installation of countervailing institutions, and provision of intellectual infrastructure and leadership regarding the geopolitics of oil. Presenting history and a contemporary analysis of the "new scramble for Africa over oil," Yohannes demonstrates that ever since the integration of Africa into global capitalism half a millennium ago, the continent's place in the international division of labor, as a producer and supplier of primary resources, has remained constant. "The discovery and exploitation of hydrocarbon resources in recent decades have added complexity to the continent's historically determined assignment with long-term implications," such as the tug-of-war for oil between an overstretched hegemon, the United States, and its rising competitor, China. According to Yohannes, "the articulation of a counter-hegemonic narrative should start from a thorough understanding that the problem in resource-rich West African states is not resource abundance; it is systemic and political."

In a previous book, Susan Craddock, author of *City of Plagues: Disease, Poverty and Deviance in San Francisco,* implied that disease did not discriminate but helped those who did (2000). In the current volume, Craddock's chapter on the political economy of AIDS in Africa rings a similar bell. She quotes the former UN special envoy on AIDS in Africa, Stephen Lewis, who said, during the Sixteenth International AIDS Conference in Toronto, that Washington practiced "incipient neocolonialism" in telling African nations how to fight AIDS and that "no government in the western world has the right to dictate policy to African governments around the way in which they respond to the pandemic" (BBC 2006). Here, Craddock reframes the discourse about AIDS in Africa by examining some of the controversies that AIDS has generated. Of significance, she claims, are Western responses that limit Africans' freedom to address the crisis. To make her argument, Craddock examines two of the most contested issues: prohibitively priced antiretrovirals and the "sexualized" nature of the funding for combating HIV and AIDS.

Chapter 9

CIVIL SOCIETY AND SOCIOPOLITICAL CHANGE IN AFRICA
A Brief Theoretical Commentary

Célestin Monga

What better way to begin an inspection of the politics, power, and socioeconomic struggles of Africans than by examining the phenomenon of civil society and its role in reshaping the continent's political institutions. Throughout Africa, people are invading the political arena to get leaders to take into account their will, and they express their ambitions through mobilization and activism. This manifestation of civil society in Africa offers students of African politics new areas for reflection, where avenues, themes, and dimensions of political participation can be viewed from many perspectives. The signs of the rebirth of civil society, however, raise questions about the validity of the analytical tools and frameworks for interpretation—which ones are adaptable to the African context and incorporate local culture. Thus, reflecting on civil society as an appropriate theoretical framework is important for reframing African politics.

Let me refer you to an interesting tale that has been at the core of mainstream civil society and democratic theory since de Tocqueville published his *Democracy in America* more than 170 years ago. It can be summed up in one sentence: societies thrive politically when they are able to build strong, nurturing social capital through a vibrant civil society. The tale builds on a series of impressionistic and bold statements made by de Tocqueville in his work: "There is only one country on the face of the earth where the citizens enjoy unlimited freedom of association for political purposes. This same country is the only one in the world where the continual exercise of the right of association has been introduced into civil life and where all the advantages which civilization can confer are procured by means of it."[1] Similar observations were made, though with less popular success, by Thomas Paine during the American Revolution.[2] They have inspired several generations of social scientists who have tried to document the key role of civil society in political theory.[3] One of the well-known proponents of this now-dominant thesis in political science and sociology is Robert Putnam, who claims that "effective and responsive institutions depend, in the language

---

[1] A. de Tocqueville, *Democracy in America*, vol. 2

[2] Paine considered civil society to be "a natural condition of freedom" and the last line of defense against state despotism. See J. Keene, *State and Civil Society* (London: Verso, 1988).

[3] For a review of the literature in English, see J.L. Cohen and A. Arato, *Civil Society and Political Theory* (Cambridge: MIT Press, 1992); J. Alexander, *The Civil Sphere* (New York: Oxford University Press, 2006).

of civic humanism, on republican virtues and practices. All of these scholars were right: Democratic government is strengthened, not weakened, when it faces a vigorous civil society."[4]

Many studies in the social sciences have concluded that the main reason for the perceived failure of the Third Wave of Democracy in the African context is the weakness or lack of civil society organizations. As a result, African civil society has become a major topic of study. Landmark publications have been released in recent years, and international and academic institutions have even established formal links with civil society organizations. Kofi Annan, former United Nations secretary-general, has noted that although the UN "once dealt only with governments. By now, we know that peace and prosperity cannot be achieved without partnerships involving governments, international organizations, the business community and civil society. In today's world, we depend on each other."[5]

Indeed, an examination of the sociopolitical situation in most African countries since the famous National Conference (which ended the socialist regime in Benin and, like Nelson Mandela's freedom, came in early 1990) reveals the preeminent role of previously neglected social mechanisms and public opinion in the continent. Civil society is once again coming alive as people become more aware of belonging to defined groups and increasingly express the desire to create interest groups in civil and political arenas. From human rights activists to small businessmen, from unemployed youths of the suburbs to the intellectual and religious elites, there is hardly a social group that has not felt the need for its members to communally articulate their daily concerns.[6] In both public and private companies the void due to the absence of structures of collective organization—notably, unions, works committees, employers associations—is being filled by a multiplicity of increasingly dynamic informal groupings, even if these are often established along Weberian lines of sex, age, kinship, and religion.

For Africans, these groupings are a way of reclaiming the right of self-expression, long confiscated by the official institutions of power. In establishing their members as full participants in the political game, these groups have expanded the arena of association, stealthily influencing the ongoing multifaceted transformation. By blurring the rules of the game, they represent a disruptive force in the sociopolitical environment. It's my view that civil society will represent an important vehicle for restructuring African politics and power relations. The actions of new elements of societies' interaction with and impact on political institutions will act as an important new framing phenomenon for the continent as new voices, perspectives, and styles of leadership hold sway in the continent's emergent democracies.

Africans have a longstanding tradition of an indigenous form of civil activism based on the continent's culture, arts, social organizations, and individual and collective behavior within the public sphere. The current quest for freedom in the continent is deeply entrenched, and recent sociopolitical events are simply

---

[4] R.D. Putnam, Robert Leonardi, and Raffaella Y. Nanetti, *Making Democracy Work: Civic Traditions in Modern Italy* (Princeton University Press, 1993), 182.

[5] K. Annan, Speech at the 2005 World Summit General Assembly, September 14, 2005. The UN's Department of Public Information now has a special section for civil society issues. Arguing that "the growth of civil society has been one of the most significant trends in international development," the World Bank has also created a special Web site that provides information on its evolving relationship with civil society organizations around the world. Many academic institutions have done the same thing. Pioneering institutions in this domain are the London School of Economics Centre for Civil Society and the Johns Hopkins University Center for Civil Society, which "seeks to improve understanding and the effective functioning of not-for-profit, philanthropic, or 'civil society' organizations throughout the world in order to enhance the contribution these organizations can make to democracy and the quality of human life."

[6] Ansley Hamid has referred to this description of civil society in the Caribbean in his book *The Ganja complex: Rastafari and Marijuana* (Lanham, MD: Lexington Books, 2002).

the natural results of the dynamics of the above traditions. It is this strength of civil society that will strongly affect the democratic structure of African countries over the next decades. Throughout Africa, people are invading the political arena in an attempt to get their will finally taken into account by the leaders. Ethical ambition is expressed through explosions of anger expressed through civil society. The real issue lies in the fact that these popular movements lack appropriate leadership. The new civil society "representatives" are beginning to acquire the competence to build institutions that take into consideration the cultural realities and power relationships among the major social actors. It is these factors that finally determine the dynamics of the democratic project.

Yet a closer examination of the empirics of political evolution shows that despite its popularity, civil society has not yet really yielded either democratic consolidation or economic well-being.[7] In fact, even in so-called advanced democracies (North America, Western Europe, Japan) where civil society is supposed to be much stronger than in developing countries, lack of confidence in and mistrust of government are high. In twelve of the thirteen countries for which data are available, trust in representative institutions and politicians is in decline.[8]

Moreover, civil society remains an elusive concept. For one, there is little consensus among researchers on how to define it rigorously. Also, some creative authoritarian regimes have attempted (often successfully) to hijack the concept: by creating their own civil society groups, they have often been able to surreptitiously subvert the rules of the political game. Furthermore, globalization has not only strengthened the winds of political change across the world but has also strengthened the already influential role played by Western non-governmental organizations (NGOs) whose philosophy, agenda, and legitimacy are now questioned in the various regions of Africa.

Significantly, as I reflect upon the goals of the current volume, which seeks to present reconstructivist avenues for addressing African affairs and the question of civil society, I ask if Western social scientists of the past, who have sought to analyze African reality, have examined Africans' ways of conceiving freedom. Daily, in order to transform its states and societies, African civil society and various new powers face an intense relationship.

All these issues raise questions: What if de Tocqueville was wrong? What if the philosophical assumptions underlying his approach to civil society and democracy were inconsistent with an effective theory of freedom? In an era where various kinds of non-governmental organizations—including infamous ones such as the Ku Klux Klan, al-Qaida, Uganda's Lord's Resistance Army—claim to represent civil society, what criteria should be used to define it? What motivations give legitimacy to citizen advocacy organizations that represent various segments of society? What moral principles and values should be considered in establishing such criteria? Even if the definition of such criteria were straightforward, how would one rigorously measure adherence to it by political, religious, and business organizations? How would one measure their contribution to social capital, social harmony, and democratic consolidation? In places where some citizen organizations promote their political agenda through "immoral" means, is there such thing as a negative social capital? What are the proper scope and functions of civil society?

----

[7] See E. Gyimah-Boadi, ed., *Democratic Reform in Africa: The Quality of Progress* (Boulder, CO: Lynne Rienner, 2004). See also M. Bratton and N. van de Walle, *Democratic Experiments in Africa: Regime Transitions in Comparative Perspective* (New York: Cambridge University Press, 1997); and C. Monga, *Measuring Democracy: A Comparative Theory of Political Well-Being,* Working Papers Series, 2 vols. (Boston University, African Studies Center, 1996).

[8] See R.D. Putnam, S.J. Pharr, and R.J. Dalton, "Introduction," in *Disaffected Democracies: What's Troubling the Trilateral Democracies,* ed. S.J. Pharr and R.D. Putnam (Princeton University Press, 2000). Their data confirm the intuitions already laid out in M. Crozier et al., eds., *The Crisis of Democracy* (New York University Press, 1975).

While presenting current transformations in African politics with the goal of reframing the ideational realm in the continent through Africa's own civil associational agency, this commentary attempts to address the questions that I have outlined above by reexamining the intellectual foundations of the civil society debate. I will discuss the origins of this concept and some of its current applications. Applying theory to African contexts, I will argue that the confusion over the semantics has led to conflicting uses of the word, which is now claimed even by organizations that oppose the democratic ideal and produce what I call negative social capital. I will conclude by recommending a framework for understanding civil society's role in the process of democratic consolidation, not as the generator of freedom, but simply as the platform for debates and eventually the vector for sociopolitical changes.

Civil Society: A Semantic and Ethical Deficit

Civil society has generated as much enthusiasm as skepticism. One major reason for this is the heavy burden placed on it by some of its most vocal advocates who present it as a key prerequisite to sustainable democratization processes without fleshing out precisely its link with normative theories of liberal democracy.[9] This creates an atmosphere of confusion in which the realities and myths of civil society are intertwined. To reframe the debate in a constructive way, it may be useful to start by discussing briefly some of the challenges posed by the semantics of civil society. Such a discussion highlights one fact: with all its virtues, civil society is also the place where negative social capital—defined as instances where social groups pursue radically different norms and values and work at cross-purposes, often toward's unethical ends—can be generated.

What exactly is civil society? What criteria should the organizations classified under that label meet? Trying to define a term that is used today in many different disciplines and contexts and has a complex and still evolving conceptual history is a complicated task. The term "civil society" was *en vogue* in Western Europe in the eighteenth and nineteenth centuries and generally referred to all institutions, formal and informal, between the family and the state, as Hegel put it.[10] Considering the link between civil society and the state as one of mediation and interpenetration, he stressed three characteristics of the concept: legality, plurality, and association. Laws and self-mobilization were supposed to allow for the institutionalization and long-term reproduction of civil society.

While such a framework may have seemed appropriate in the context of Western societies because the *law* actually meant something, it was clearly not very pertinent in societies under authoritarian political regimes. In most of eighteenth and nineteenth centuries, informal or underground organizations later known as civil society groups often emerged against existing laws and social norms.[11]

Hegel's elegant but vague framework did not explain under which social conditions citizens from various backgrounds get involved in voluntary associations to critically discuss and act on public issues that they consider relevant to their lives. Habermas's relatively recent exploration of the "public sphere" offers a more convincing set of ideas for the analysis of civil society.[12] It highlights the fact that the existence of a public sphere adequate to a democratic polity usually depends both on the level of participation of the citizenry in a rational-critical debate, the quality of the discourse, and the subsequent ethical standards

---

[9] Cohen and Arato is a notable exception.

[10] G.W.F. Hegel, *Elements of the Philosophy of Right* (Cambridge University Press, 1991).

[11] See E.A. Isichei, *A History of African Societies to 1870* (Cambridge University Press, 1997).

[12] J. Habermas, *The Structural Transformation of the Public Sphere: An Inquiry into a Category of Bourgeois Society* (Cambridge, MA: MIT Press, 1989).

that emerge from these often informal channels of conversation. This brings up two observations: First, inclusion of all social groups into the public sphere is a prerequisite for the production of positive social capital[13] and the sustainability of the democratic process. While it may bring a "degeneration" of the quality of the public discourse dominated by scholars or professional politicians, it gives a sense of legitimacy to the society at large. Second, including everyone into the social market for ideas, attitudes, and public policies increases the risk of giving voice to non-democratic and non-ethical forces (negative social capital). Still, bringing them out in the open is in fact a lesser evil: it improves transparency in the struggle for power by all kinds of social forces, and sheds light on their unconstructive ideas and harmful activities, and encourages democratic forces to build the types of alliances needed to win.

The obvious question that comes to mind here relates to the transferability of the concept. Should we agree with Habermas's contention that the bourgeois public sphere is a "category that is typical of an epoch" and that "it cannot be abstracted from the unique developmental history of that 'civil society' (*bürgerliche Gesellschaft*) originating in the European High Middle Ages; nor can it be a transferred, ideal typically generalized, to any number of historical situations that represent formally similar constellations"?[14] Habermas's prudent view raises the traditional epistemological problem arising from the transfer of sociological concepts across space and time. While his analysis of civil society was restricted to the European bourgeois political life of the seventeenth through the mid-twentieth centuries, his conclusions are of normative relevance to the discussion of social transformations anywhere. He does not prescribe a ready-to-use framework to be imposed upon social scientists everywhere, and his two general principles for studying the bourgeois public sphere have offered a great deal of richness to discussions of civil society in other contexts.

The first principle from his analysis is the openness of civil society—its "transforming" power: the European public sphere gained relevance by ceasing to be a bourgeois, *masculinist,* and elitist platform where educated men made decisions about social standards, values, politics, and public affairs. It opened itself up to women and to interlocutors of all walks of life. Status differentials were then bracketed so that people could deliberate as if they were social equals. It was "a kind of social intercourse that, far from presupposing the equality of status, disregarded status altogether."[15] Societal equality was no longer a necessary condition for political democracy.[16] Even the places where these rational-critical debates were held proliferated across Europe and became much less formal. They ranged from open meetings in public places to private homes or even coffee shops.[17]

---

[13] J.S. Coleman defined social capital as "people's ability to work together in groups"; see "Social Capital in the Creation of Human Capital," *American Journal of Sociology Supplement*, no. 94 (1988): S95–S120. F. Fukuyama defines the concept more broadly to include "any instance in which people cooperate for common ends on the basis of shared informal norms and values." See "Social Capital and Development: The Coming Agenda," *SAIS Review* XXII, no. 1 (Winter–Spring 2002): 23. I prefer to define it here as people's ability to work together voluntarily in groups toward's freedom, democratic consolidation, and other ethical goals. This allows for the distinction between positive and negative social capital.

[14] Habermas, xvii.

[15] ibid., 36.

[16] See N. Fraser, "Rethinking the Public Sphere: A Contribution to the Critique of Actually Existing Democracy," in *Habermas and the Public Sphere*, ed. C. Calhoun (Cambridge, MA: MIT Press, 1992): 109–142.

[17] According to Calhoun, London had 3,000 coffee houses by the first decade of the eighteenth century; each had its regulars. Conversations in these little circles covered affairs of state administration and politics. In Germany, table societies drew together academics and laymen. In France, salons located in private homes brought together aristocrats and other social groups. See "Introduction," in C. Calhoun. About the claim to full accessibility, it must be stressed that the so-called revisionist historiography suggests a much darker picture of the bourgeois public sphere than the one described by Habermas. Women of all classes and ethnicities were excluded from political participation, and plebeian men were excluded on the basis of property qualifications. See N. Fraser.

A second principle is people's willingness to discuss all sorts of topics, including those over which church and state had hitherto exercised a virtual monopoly. These principles allowed for a less idealistic approach to democratic consolidation: the myth of common, shared interest that supposedly guides the design and implementation of political rules and public policies was abandoned as people realized that reasonable political outcomes emerge from negotiated compromises among competing social interests.

That acknowledgment has been the cornerstone of sustainable democratization processes throughout the Western world. But they have done little to restrain the debate on what should be the proper scope and functions of civil society. Some authors have tried to differentiate civil society from political society (political parties, political institutions such as parliaments, etc.) for the reason that their true aim is to control the state and gain power. Others sought to exclude the economic society of firms and trade unions from civil society, arguing that they represent an extreme form of capitalism, which has become a totalitarian threat to all spheres of social activity.[18]

Going back to Hegel's initial, generic insight, Cohen and Arato suggest that civil society be the "sphere of social interaction between economy and state, composed above all of the intimate sphere (especially the family), the sphere of associations (especially voluntary associations), social movements and forms of public communications."[19] But they are quick to circumscribe civil society more narrowly. They argue that it would be misleading to consider all social life outside the administrative state and economic processes to represent civil society because "the actors of political and economic society are directly involved with state power and economic production, which they seek to control and manage."[20] That distinction is a bit naïve, as almost no group would pass such a stringent test: everywhere, all actors in the realm of public participation in voluntary associations, the media, professional groups and lobbies, trade unions, and the like have hoped to either control power or at least influence it in the sense of their particular interests.

Still, that basic framework was adopted in the Charter of the United Nations (UN). It noted that the UN's Economic and Social Council "may make suitable arrangements for consultation with non-governmental organizations which are concerned with matters within its competence. Such arrangements may be made with international organizations and, where appropriate, with national organizations after consultation with the Member of the United Nations concerned" (Article 71). Though the term "non-governmental organization" was never itself defined in the Charter, successive resolutions of the Economic and Social Council have tended to highlight two basic characteristics of that notion: first, separation and independence from the structures and processes of government;[21] second, their aims and purposes that are not primarily for profit.

In fact, the UN itself has struggled to maintain consistency in its literature on the topic. After it issued a report on civil society in 2004, a group of influential international NGOs wrote back to the Secretary General complaining that the definition used was too broad, as it assimilated "fundamentally different

---

[18] See P. Rosanvallon and P. Viveret, *Pour une nouvelle culture politique* (Paris : Seuil, 1977). See also A. Gramsci, whose theory of hegemony also builds the distinction between political society (political institutions) and civil society (the non-state or private sphere, including the economy). He recognizes that his conceptual categorization does not hold in practice because political and civil society overlap. *Letters from Prison* (New York: Columbia University Press, 1994).

[19] Cohen and Arato, ix.

[20] ibid.

[21] While this distinction between governments and NGOs may seem straightforward, the question could be raised in some contexts where ruling entities are reflect the philosophy and implement the agenda of specific non-governmental organizations. This was the case for instance in Iran after the 1979 revolution or in Afghanistan under the Taliban. It is also the case in Somalia today.

groups." They expressed the view that, "though the term 'civil society' is notoriously vague, and although the issue of whether [the UN] description also covers business entities is highly contested, we would argue that it certainly does not cover parliamentarians—in view of their direct participation in the structures and processes of government."[22] Not surprisingly, the writers of the letter did not question the legitimacy of their own international NGOS, whose agendas have often been questioned, especially in the African context.[23]

The European Commission initiated in the 1990s a "civil dialogue," which was a first attempt by the European Union to give the institutions of society—and not only governments and businesses—a voice at the policy-making tables in Brussels. Yet the criteria to meet for any particular organization to be invited to such a dialogue remained fuzzy. In fact, the very broad definition recently offered by the London School of Economics Centre for Civil Society to guide research activities and teaching sums up well the conventional wisdom and the confusion:

> Civil society refers to the arena of uncoerced collective action around shared interests, purposes and values. In theory, its institutional forms are distinct from those of the state, family, and market, though in practice, the boundaries between state, civil society, family, and market are often complex, blurred, and negotiated.

Civil society commonly embraces a diversity of spaces, actors, and institutional forms, varying in their degree of formality, autonomy, and power. Civil societies are often populated by organizations such as registered charities, development non-governmental organizations, community groups, women's organizations, faith-based organizations, professional associations, trade unions, self-help groups, social movements, business associations, coalitions, and advocacy groups.[24]

Reexamining Civil Society in Africa

Defining civil society has been even more problematic in the African context. The main reason is the inherent inadequacy of using tools designed for understanding the workings of Western democracies to analyze situations elsewhere in the world. The extreme diversity of situations and political traditions from one area to another—and sometimes even within the same country—further complicates the task. Sociologists in the Maghreb, for example, tend to include only the parties and associations that, despite their divergences of opinion on many issues, share the same values of human rights and individual freedoms.[25] Such a definition excludes movements laying claim to Islam, even if they have a dominant role in society.

---

[22] See the Report of the Panel of Eminent Persons on United Nations–Civil Society Relations, *We the Peoples: Civil Society, the United Nations and Global Governance* (A/58/817), released on June 21, 2004; and the Letter to the UN Secretary General, September 1, 2004, www.un-ngls.org/10901joint.pdf.

[23] Cilas Kemedjio, "Remembering Globalization: Fragmented States, the Deferred Global Civil Society, and the Globalized Humanitarian Misunderstanding" (paper presented at the International Conference on Transnationalism: The Impact of Transnational Processes on the Nation-State and National Cultures. Organized by the Royal Institute of Interfaith Studies, June 19–21, 2001). See also conference abstracts in *Bulletin of the Royal Institute of Interfaith Studies* 3, no. 2 (Autumn/Winter 2001).

[24] The Centre stresses that this definition should not be interpreted as a rigid statement See www.lse.ac.uk/collections/CCS/what_is_civil_society.htm.

[25] A. Zghal, "Le concept de société civile et la transition vers le multipartisme," in *Changements politiques au Maghreb*, ed. M. Camau (Paris : Editions du CNRS), 191–205.

The reluctance of many social scientists in North Africa to consider religious organizations as an integral part of civil society should not be attributed simply to current events—the resurgence of religious fundamentalism and its rejection of Western-type liberal democracy. The roots of the mistrust are deeper. In fact, the skepticism over the democratic virtues of religious groups may originate from the differentiated ways in which Islam, Christianity, and Judaism have dealt with political power over time. According to sacred texts, Moses, who led the children of Israel from bondage to the Promised Land (of which he only had a glimpse) never exercised political power. Jesus, too, was crucified and never had the chance to rule any kingdom. By contrast, Prophet Muhammad achieved political victory in his lifetime. He conquered the Promised Land and was the sovereign political figure of his state. "As such, he promulgated laws, dispensed justice, levied taxes, raised armies, made war, and made peace. In a word, he ruled, and the story of his decisions and actions as ruler is sanctified in Muslim scripture and amplified in Muslim tradition."[26]

Because the original Islamic state was officially religious in its essence and ruled as such by its founder, there was no need for secularism—understood as separation of religion and political authority—except in Mustafa Kemal Ataturk's Turkey and in the six Soviet republics with predominantly Muslim populations. For over a thousand years, Islam provided the only officially recognized set of rules for the regulation of public and social life. This may explain why some political scientists and sociologists in Muslim countries in North Africa even today are hesitant—if not opposed—to integrating religious groups into civil society. As Lewis points out, "in the Islamic context, the independence and initiative of the civil society may best be measured not in relation to the state, but in relation to religion, of which, in the Muslim perception, the state itself is a manifestation and instrument."[27]

In other parts of Africa, researchers have been willing to include religious groups in their definition of civil society because of their generally positive legacy in the struggle for freedom of the nineties.[28] Despite their influence, religious organizations do not, at least for the moment, claim to have determining roles on the course of political events, with the notable exception of the Lord's Resistance Army in Uganda.[29] Religious organizations comparable to the Islamic movements that exist in Algeria, Tunisia, Egypt, or Morocco have not manifested themselves in other African countries with large Muslim populations such as Mali, Niger, or Burkina Faso, though things appear to be evolving in that direction in the northern states of Nigeria where religious conflicts have resulted in large casualties in recent years. In Senegal, the very influential leader of the Mouride community has for many years dominated the country's power game but has so far chosen not to have his organization involved directly in politics.[30]

---

[26] B. Lewis, *What Went Wrong? Western Impact and Middle Eastern Response* (New York: Oxford University Press, 2002), 101.

[27] ibid., 112.

[28] Several French-speaking countries, such as Benin, Gabon, Congo, Congo/Zaire, Chad, Niger, and Togo, avoided civil wars in 1990 and 1991 because of the mediation of respected religious leaders. See C. Monga, *The Anthropology of Anger: Civil Society and Democracy in Africa* (Boulder, CO: Lynne Rienner, 1996).

[29] Founded in 1986 as the successor to Alice Lakwena's guerila group, Holy Spirit Movement, the Lord's Resistance Army (LRA) has called for the overthrow of the Ugandan government and its replacement with a regime run on the basis of the Ten Commandments. More frequently, however, the LRA's current leader, Joseph Krony, who claims to have supernatural powers and receive messages from spirits, has spoken of the liberation of the Acholi people whom he sees as oppressed by the "foreign" government of Uganda. See U.S. Department of State, *Patterns of Global Terrorism 2003* (Washington, D.C., 2004). For an analysis of the social and historical contexts that gave rise to the LR and the use of spirituality by its founders, see T. Allen, "Understanding Alice: Uganda's Holy Spirit Movement in Context," *Africa: Journal of the International African Institute* 61, no. 3 (1991): 370–399.

[30] M. Magassouba, *Sénégal: demain les mollahs?* (Paris : Karthala, 1985).

The complexity of the semantics of civil society makes it unrealistic to come up with a definition that would be valid in all places and at all times. For the purpose of analyzing sociopolitical transformations in Africa today, civil society needs to be understood as a flexible concept that includes all organizations and individuals whose actions strengthen social identities and the rights of citizenship—often in opposition to those in power—whose natural tendency is to repress such identities and rights. Civil society refers to all social and political movements formed on a voluntary basis and aiming to produce social capital.

Clearly, the specific organizations to be included in such a framework would necessarily vary from one place to another. Some of them work within the prevailing value system to expand the boundaries of collective freedom and strengthen the democratic ideal in the polity. Others only focus on their microscopic and often egoistic objectives. They all contribute in different (and sometimes conflicting) ways to enlarging social participation. In the era of globalization, they all benefit or suffer from the external influence of foreign NGOs or institutions (Figure 9.1).

Despite its advantages—most notably not having to prescribe a pre-determined and generic definition of civil society to all contexts—such a minimalist approach does not immunize one from the next difficult challenge, which is to assess the commitment to democratic ethics by all these organizations. Conventional wisdom about what constitutes civil society and its role in fostering political change does not address the difficulties of identifying clear mechanisms through which civil society can help strengthen political accountability. Across Africa in particular, the upsurge of civil society has contributed to changing not

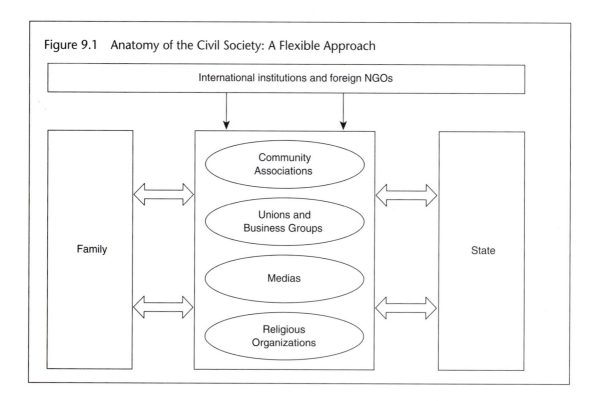

Figure 9.1   Anatomy of the Civil Society: A Flexible Approach

just the existing political order, but also the prevailing value system—if not the surrounding moral order. Civil society organizations have contributed both to the quest for freedom and sometimes to the weakening of democratic ideals.

Social Capital and Civil Society

Belonging to civil society groups provides people with multiple social identities that often determine the level and nature of their participation to the political discourse. This raises several questions: What are the true objectives of these civil society groups? How do they operate? How consistent are their stated and hidden goals with the national project of building and sustaining democratic institutions? What type of means do they have at their disposal to achieve their goals? What is the relationship between self-proclaimed "apolitical" NGOs and political parties with clear ideological agendas that compete fiercely for power? What type of connections do they entertain with business interests and financial lobbies, both local and foreign? What kind of support do they gain from international civil society groups that may not be constrained by national law and regulations?

These questions may complicate the assessment of the way civil society groups operate, but they help us understand why some of them may not focus on consolidating democratic processes as it is often assumed. In fact, in places where they have become too powerful, some authoritarian leaders have even created their own "independent" NGOs. A well-known case was that of President Mobutu Sese Seko of then Zaire (Democratic Republic of Congo). Forced in 1991 by a social uprising to concede to a national conference to rewrite the rules of the political game (including the appointment of an independent prime minister and new government, and the adoption of a new constitution and electoral timetable), he was able to slow down the process of democratic transition by infiltrating the civil society movement: it is estimated that over half of the newly created NGOs who sent delegates to the national conference were actually his supporters.

Moreover, because civil society leaders are often political entrepreneurs, some NGOs are hijacked by and serve as Trojan horses for people who are motivated by the quest for political power. True, this particular argument is sometimes used by authoritarian leaders who oppose the kind of political awareness that civil society groups may bring to the people. This was most notably the case in Cameroon in 1991 when President Paul Biya arbitrarily banned a large number of civil society organizations that were seen as spreading "subversive ideas"—including a local affiliate of Human Rights Watch. That strategy has not been used only by African authoritarian leaders. In recent years, the battle over control of so-called apolitical NGOs has made headlines in many different places: Palestinian Authority President and leader of the Fatah Mahmoud Abbas has banned religious charities in the West Bank, accusing them of serving as underground political affiliates to rival organization Hamas.

Over the past decade, media organizations and NGOs of various types have been banned in Vladimir Putin's Russia for arbitrary reasons. Even in the United States, a well-known Islamic charity has been indicted on terrorism charges, prompting the attorney general to announce that "a U.S.-based charity that claims to do good works is charged with funding the works of evil."[31] While some of the crackdown operations on civil society groups are often motivated by purely partisan or political reasons,

---

[31] Statement by U.S. Attorney General John Ashcroft on July 27, 2004. The charges included conspiracy, providing material support to a foreign terrorist organization, tax evasion, and money laundering. The forty-two-count indictment, returned by a federal grand jury in Dallas, Texas, alleged that the Holy Land Foundation for Relief and Development provided more than $12.4 million to individuals and organizations linked to Hamas, from 1995 to 2001. The U.S. government froze the charity's assets in December 2001.

it is also undeniable that some organizations that pretend to work under the civil society umbrella do not adhere to national laws and regulations. Far from contributing to the emergence of a collective social compact, their actions can actually generate negative social capital.

The hijacking of civil society by oppressive and totalitarian groups everywhere and the disaffection with the myths of democracy in many places, including the so-called established Western democracies, have shed a crude light on the shortcomings of de Tocqueville's political theory. It now seems that all human societies are uncivil by nature and capable of producing simultaneously the kind of positive social capital needed to sustain democratic consolidation and some negative social capital that constrains human freedom. This raises some difficult questions about how to assess civil society's role in sociopolitical transformations and its contribution to the process of democratic consolidation: How do we disentangle pro-democratic activities by civil society groups from routine power struggles by political entrepreneurs who hide behind civic or charitable organizations to pursue an often unethical agenda? In sum, what principles should be taken into account when monitoring the production of social capital in uncivil societies?

Answering these questions may very well represent a utopian intellectual agenda, as the conceptual differentiation between "pro-" and "anti-"democratic civil society groups is illusory when put into practice. Besides the fact that it is impossible to measure the degree of ethical commitment of any civil society group, most of them operate on several levels: they fight for positioning and power and can, therefore, generate negative social capital, even when they are genuinely involved in great democratic ideals. Western political scientists have been struggling to label community organizations such as Hezbollah a terrorist group,[32] while hundreds of thousands of people in Lebanon have always considered it the main employer and only provider of welfare in their neighborhoods. The same is true for Islamic charities that fund schools in Pakistan or Indian madrassas, which are described both as threats to democratic principles and sole providers of basic public services in poor communities.[33]

In fact, a close analysis of the ethical content of the jihad of an international NGO such as al-Qaida, as opposed to its purported political intent, reveals that it differs profoundly from such groups as Egypt's Muslim Brotherhood and Indonesia's Jemaah Islamiyah, which aim to establish fundamentalist Islamic states. With its decentralized structure and emphasis on moral rather than political action, al-Qaida may actually have more in common with multinational corporations, antiglobalization activists, and environmentalist groups, and organizations that are self-proclaimed defenders of social justice.[34] In metaphysical terms, the jihad discourse may appear extreme, but it delegitimizes the idea that certain civil society groups may have a monopoly over morals and ethics. The same kind of ambivalence is found in analyses of controversial civil society organizations throughout Africa.[35]

---

[32] See J.P. Harrik, *Hezbollah: The Changing Face of Terrorism* (New York: I.B. Tauris, 2005). For a much more nuanced analysis, see A. Saad-Ghorayeb, *Hizbu'llah: Politics and Religion* (London: Pluto, 2002).

[33] See S.H. Ali, "Islamic Education and Conflict: Understanding the Madrassahs of Pakistan" (paper presented at the U.S. Institute of Peace, Washington, D.C., June 24, 2005); Y. Sikand, *Bastions of the Believers: Madrasas and Islamic Education in India* (New Delhi: Penguin India, 2005).

[34] F. Devji, *Landscapes of the Jihad: Militancy, Morality and Modernity* (Ithaca, NY: Cornel University Press, 2005).

[35] See, for instance, M.E. Pommerole, "Universal Claims and Selective Memory: A Comparative Perspective on the Culture of Opposition in Kenya," *Africa Today* 53, no. 2 (Winter 2006): 75–93.

Conclusion

The concept of civil society has enjoyed much success in the social sciences in recent years—especially because of the role that it supposedly played in the rise of the Third Wave of Democracy. Yet mainstream democratic theory has struggled to define it convincingly and to outline its functions in the collective quest for freedom. The reason is that the concept originated from the Hegelian, one-dimensional view of history and carried the heavy baggage of ethnocentrism associated with the Enlightenment. Not surprisingly, many researchers from the non-Western world have adopted radically different approaches to civil society, often by opposing relativist definitions of civil society to what they perceived as a tyranny of universalism.

Going beyond the objectivism that underlines the views from both sides, this chapter has attempted to offer a more flexible framework to civil society and an analysis of the mechanics of freedom. It concludes that civil society's role in fostering sociopolitical changes cannot be denied. But the argument here differs from the mainstream theory of democratic consolidation on at least two important points: First, civil society plays an important role in diffusing social norms and social values but not necessarily in generating them. Moreover, some civil society groups might actually work against the diffusion of freedom and the process of democratic consolidation. The production of social capital, which is the final outcome of the struggle between these forces, is often uncertain.

Second, civil society is neither monolithic in the values that it endorses and advertises, nor is its march towards a democratic horizon a linear one. In de Toqueville's America of the 1830s, slavery was in full force as a system of brutality and coercion, denying millions of people the right to citizenship. While the abolitionist movement that emerged in the early 1830s was vocal and insistent upon an immediate end to slavery, other civil society organizations, such as the one later known as the Ku Klux Klan, dominated political and associational life.

Yet de Tocqueville could describe America as "the government of a democracy [that] brings the notion of political rights to the level of the humblest citizens."[36] Such statements may well have been signs of an extraordinary dose of naiveté or cynicism on his part. They could also simply reflect the fact he missed the fundamentally uncivil nature of all human societies and the limited role that associations and other non-governmental organizations actually play in the process of social change.

As for Africa, it is hoped that a reciprocal contract between the state and civil society be defined as the vehicle through which democratic renewal will occur. Africa's social fabric is being strengthened in a variety of ways not least by helping the independent mass media play a more effective role in nation building. In essence, however, the leaders of African civil society should be allowed the means of avoiding the errors, delays, and catastrophes that marked the democratic process in the West.

REFERENCES

Annan, K. Speech at the 2005 World Summit General Assembly, September 14, 2005.

Devji, F. *Landscapes of the Jihad: Militancy, Morality and Modernity.* Ithaca, NY: Cornell University Press, 2005.

Habermas, J. *The Structural Transformation of the Public Sphere: An Inquiry into a Category of Bourgeois Society.* Cambridge, MA: MIT Press, 1989.

Hamid, Ansley. *The Ganja Complex: Rastafari and Marijuana.* Lanham, MD: Lexington Books, 2002.

Hegel, G.W.F. *Elements of the Philosophy of Right.* Cambridge University Press, 1991.

---

[36] de Tocqueville, vol. 2, chapter 7.

Isichei, E.A. *A History of African Societies to 1870.* Cambridge University Press, 1997.

Lewis, B. *What Went Wrong? Western Impact and Middle Eastern Response.* New York: Oxford University Press, 2002.

Kemedjio, Cilas. "Remembering Globalization: Fragmented States, the Deferred Global Civil Society, and the Globalized Humanitarian Misunderstanding." Paper presented at the International Conference on Transnationalism: The Impact of Transnational Processes on the Nation-State and National Cultures. Organized by the Royal Institute of Interfaith Studies, June 19–21, 2001. See also conference abstracts in *Bulletin of the Royal Institute of Interfaith Studies* 3, no. 2 (Autumn/Winter 2001).

Magassouba, M. *Sénégal : demain les mollahs?* Paris : Karthala, 1985.

Monga, Célestin. *The Anthropology of Anger.* Boulder, CO: Lynne Rienner, 1996.

Putnam, R.D. Robert Leonardi, and Raffaella Y. Nanetti. *Making Democracy Work: Civic Traditions in Modern Italy.* Princeton, NJ: Princeton University Press, 1993.

de Tocqueville, A. *Democracy in America,* vol. 2.

Zghal, A. "Le concept de société civile et la transition vers le multipartisme." In *Changements politiques au Maghreb,* edited by M. Camau, 191–205. Paris : Editions du CNRS.

Chapter 10

NEW FRAMES IN AFRICAN DEMOCRATIC POLITICS
Discourse Trajectories

Rita Kiki Edozie

Neither scholars nor international policy analysts pay much attention to the theoretical dimensions of "democracy," or especially to the word's definition by the peoples who will supposedly benefit from a democratic form of government. In their survey assessing Africans' "support" for democracy, Bratton and Mattes[1] report that when asked whether Africans thought "democracy [was] good," a majority of respondents in five African countries replied that democracy was, indeed, the best form of government. However, even the authors admit that their survey revealed little about democracy's complex meaning to a diverse population of Africans. The authors are right to conclude that, as in most areas of the world, democracy continues to evoke strong reactions—support, rejection, contradiction, and misunderstanding.

Julius Nyerere's almost twenty-five-year political regime reflects this dispute over the meaning of democracy in provocative ways. Defying the authoritarian label that was so easily conferred on Africa's post-nationalist regimes, Nyerere and a vast majority of Tanzanians considered their country a "democracy." In arguing for Africa's own way to democracy, Nyerere's Ujaama system called for an indigenized form of democracy and found no need for Africans to be "converted" to socialism or "taught" democracy.[2] In his own attempt to reconfigure the postcolonial liberal democratic state he inherited from Britain into what he referred to as a "one-party democracy," the late Tanzanian president developed ideas and practices regarding democracy that illustrate the many meanings of "democracy."

A rigorous inquiry into democratic ideas and democratic theory is rarely conducted in the study of African politics. By implication, some scholars have complained about this. Célestin Monga, in his book *The Anthropology of Anger*, argues for a new approach to defining democracy—one that projects not the values of those performing the analysis but one that represents the values of those experiencing the democracy.[3] Marcin Krol has similarly warned that if democracy is not to become "non-democracy" in the non-West, it is the Western democratic models transplanted into the late-democratizing non-Western world that must change and be adapted to the regions to which they are transferred.[4] In a 1999

---

[1] Michael Bratton and Robert Mattes, "Support for Democracy in Africa: Intrinsic or Instrumental?" *British Journal of Political Science* 31, no. 3 (2001): 447–474.

[2] Julius Nyerere, "Ujamaa: The Basis of African Socialism," in *Government and Politics in Africa*, ed. Okwudiba Nnoli (Harare: AAPS Books, 2000).

[3] Célestin Monga, *The Anthropology of Anger* (Boulder, CO: Lynne Rienner, 1996).

[4] Larry Diamond and Marc F. Plattner, eds., *Economic Reform and Democracy* (Baltimore: Johns Hopkins University Press, 1995).

study of African politics, Patrick Chabal challenged his readers to think about the ways that political power and representation have defined the evolution of contemporary African democracies.[5]

This chapter will illustrate Africans' construction and reconstruction—aka reframing—of democratic ideas by interpreting democracy and why and how this system of government differs from country to country, region to region, and even regime to regime. Liberalism, socialism, African culturalism, and consociationalism (ethnic power sharing) are ideological platforms on which democracy has been socially constructed since the continent's independence-era nationalism and decolonization. More recently, in the 1990s, ideological constructions of democracy in Africa have been subsumed into a new kind of post–Cold War pragmatism. In this respect, African democracies nominally categorized as liberal democracies are once again reinterpreting the meaning of democracy and readjusting their practices in developmental contexts. As a result, in an age of ongoing democratic transitions, political regimes in Africa cannot be classified as either distinctly liberal, socialist, or culturalist. They exhibit attributes of all.

In examining the idea of democracy in Africa, I will resuscitate Richard Sklar's "hybrid" interpretation of democratization to provide evidence for the ways in which the continent's experience with modern democracy have illustrated regimes' and civil societies' considerable efforts to construct the democratic idea in diverse contexts. Doing so will reveal how such ideas have included those of Western "liberalism," developed by way of Africans' complex interactions with colonialism and decolonization. The chapter will demonstrate ways in which democratic ideas in Africa have been reconstructed and readjusted by Africa's postcolonial nationalist leaders and civil societies, who experimented with alternative forms of liberal democracy to accommodate cultural circumstances, such as Africa's ethnic pluralism. These ideas represented an expansion and deepening of democratic thought during the 1990s, a period of post-nationalism and globalism. During this period, a reactivation of associational movements and organizations redirected democracy's trajectory towards populist, new political economy discourses.

Consistent with the theme of the current book, this chapter will reframe African politics by embarking upon an interpretive analysis of politics in Africa, historically and conceptually, and will build upon theoretical knowledge and understanding that is endogenous to the existing structures and historical experiences within and between African countries. It will do so to dispel inaccurate core assumptions about democracy and politics in the continent and direct readers to a reconstruction that appropriately analyzes the region's democratic theory and practice. Here, I will reframe Africa by reacting against the trends of "Afro-pessimism," a term that Okwudiba Nnoli (2000) defined as an unbalanced, negative interpretation of political processes in African politics. I will insert the debate about democratization into the representational discourse about "Africa" that dominates contemporary African politics.

Reframing African Politics and the Postcolonial Method

Despite significant transitions to democracy in Africa since the 1990's, mainstream analyses of African politics continue to define the continent as corrupt, illiberal, personalistic, traditional, and inefficient. The most damning negative label applied to Africa's new democracies is "authoritarian." Elsewhere, I have characterized this labeling as a remnant of the dark cloud of Afro-pessimism that still hangs over the heads of those who analyze African politics. In quoting Stephen Stedman (Stedman 1993), Richard Werbner illustrated this pessimism when he asserted that the debate on Afro-pessimism was ruled by an intellectual movement in

---

[5] Patrick Chabal, *Africa Works: Disorder as Political Instrument* (Bloomington, IN: Indiana University Press, 1999).

which analysts create generic models of African governments that include "lame leviathans," "swollen states," "kleptocracies," and "vampire states" (Werbner 2004, 2).

Let us turn to another example of "Afro-pessimism" in a leading 2004 article that questioned the relevance of the "postcolonial" moment in Africa. The author examines the political trajectory of African states from the terminal colonial period to the millennium.[6] From providing evidence for his contention that the postcolonial moment has passed for Africa and that postcolonial theory remains irrelevant to contemporary African political processes, the author proceeds with his interpretation of the development of African statehood. He argues that the African state (politics) was decanted by the 1980s from colonialism into a patrimonial autocracy of decay. The state's even more serious erosion occurred by the 1990s due to its inability to economically and politically reform. The ineffectiveness of African statehood, according to this view, further opened the door for even greater crisis by way of civil conflicts and the informalization of politics in the contemporary era.[7]

This theory of African statehood and politics is premised on merely one perspective on the African state, one that privileges the negative features of African political processes and posits them as normative theory. There are other ways to examine the same processes of statehood in the continent, ways that avoid feeding the pathological African failed-state political theory (Edozie 2008). Reframing the analysis of African politics is one step in that direction. To my mind, scholars and policymakers theoretically and empirically impose an externally driven construct of democracy on the African continent. Such an imposition has been fraught with problems in implementation.

New intellectual insights derived from postcolonial theory offer a reframed analysis of democracy and politics in Africa because they expose the processes of democratization in the continent neither in simplistic, linear, liberal ways nor in terms of unidirectional, nativist, Africanist essentialism.[8] Afro-pessimism has had its day, asserts Werbner (2004) in arguing that the time has come for a reevaluation of the prospects for Africa. He begins his own reevaluation in his book on the Kalanga state crafters of modern Botswana[9] by saying that the country's democratic state-society represents only one African case study in a stream of hopeful, informed, and crucial postcolonial transformations in Africa (Werbner 2004, 3).

Like Werbner's, my own analysis of democracy in Africa also presents a counter-narrative of modern democratic politics by reimagining the continent's political processes along lines of postcolonialism. Such an agenda allows new strategies for understanding African societies at the local and national levels while not losing sight of the disempowering effects of contemporary global imperial practices.[10] We can examine democratization through Africa's complicated interaction with postcolonial democratic institutions, processes, and ideas.

The postcolonial method uniquely allows us to understand dilemmas in achieving democratization and how African state-societies have negotiated and continue to negotiate their ways through complexities that have grown out of colonization and decolonization during the post–World War II period. According to the

---

[6] Crawford Young, "The End of the Post-Colonial State in Africa? Reflections on Changing African Political Dynamics," *African Affairs* 103 (2004): 23–49.

[7] ibid., 23.

[8] Pal Ahluwalia, *Politics and Post-Colonial Theory: African Inflections* (New York: Routledge, 2001).

[9] Richard Werbner, *Reasonable Radicals and Citizenship in Botswana: The Public Anthropology of Kalanga Elites* (Bloomington, IN: Indiana University Press, 2004).

[10] Bill Ashcroft, "Globalism, Post-Colonialism and African Studies," in *Post-Colonialism: Culture and Identity in Africa,* ed. Pal Ahluwalia and Paul Nursrey-Bray (Commack, NY: Nova Science Publishers, 1997).

postcolonial vanguard scholars,[11] an important methodological core of the postcolonial method is to avoid the circular debates over "colonialist" transcendence or reversal in postcolonial regions; postcolonial theory deliberately eschews discussions about endings and beginnings of the African condition. Thus, Bill Ashcroft argues that while the postcolonial method acknowledges colonialism's link to Africa's contemporary democratic processes, Africa's future is not contained by it (Ashcroft 1997). As in other societies, Africa also exists in complex interaction with colonialism, undoing and redrawing its contingent boundaries in dynamic ways.[12] Africa's experience with democratic politics must be understood within this purview.

It is, therefore, worth re-representing postcolonial and contemporary African politics as "democratic" politics. Doing so reveals new trends in Africans' experience of politics. By injecting African agency into democratic processes, postcolonialist democratic theory leads scholars to document and analyze Africans' multiple, varied responses to modern democracy.

Democratic Practice in Africa: The Contours of Hybridity

Despite the dominant role played by the Western world in the construction of modern democratic thought, the notion that democracy is solely a "Western" idea that can only be practiced successfully within the confines of a pluralist, liberal democracy is increasingly being challenged by the non-Western world. In presenting how "Asian values" nurtured Asian democratic development, the former president of Singapore, Lee Kuan Yew, argued that a generational and hierarchical Confucian Asian culture offered important epistemological determinants for a different democracy in Asia. Culture was used to justify the adoption of the successful Japanese dominant-party model and present it as an Asian democracy. Other regions, including Africa, have challenged the Western idea of "liberal democracy" in a similar fashion.

For example, some scholars of Islamic thought, such as the Sudan's late Mahmoud Taha, have referred to the Quran and the Hadith to illustrate that classical Islamic thought and democracy are compatible.[13] Africans have found democracy among its pluralist societies prior to colonialism and scholars refer to it as the African "palavar" democracy in which political communities built democratic institutions based on community dialogue and equal representation of adults in decision making.

Richard Sklar is one Africanist who has explored the complex meaning of democracy in Africa. In a 1983 classic discourse on the subject, he examined what he referred to as the syncretic and hybrid nature of democracy in the continent. Sklar rejected the commonplace notion that democracy in Africa is merely a political system's transition from authoritarian rule to a linear and ideal liberal democracy. Instead, he underscored that Africa is a veritable workshop for democracy (Sklar 1983). To him, Africans had created a twenty-year-old, modern democratic system by using trial, error, and correction to test and improve new political mechanisms. Sklar refers to democracy in Africa as a process of "developmental democracy,"[14] whereby Africans have continued since independence to experiment with and adjust their democratic political systems to reflect

---

[11] Gyan Prakash, *After Colonialism: Imperial Histories and Postcolonial Displacements* (Princeton University Press, 1995); Partha Chatterjee, *The Nation and its Fragments: Colonial and Postcolonial Histories* (Princeton University Press, 1993); Bill Ashcroft, *Post-Colonial Transformation* (New York: Routledge, 2001).

[12] Gyan Prakash, *After Colonialism*.

[13] Rita Kiki Edozie, "Sudan's Identity Wars and Democratic Route to Peace," in *Perspectives on Contemporary Ethnic Conflict: Primal Violence or the Politics of Conviction?*, ed. Saha Santosh (Lanham, MD: Lexington Books, 2006), 225–250.

[14] Richard Sklar, "Democracy in Africa," *The African Studies Review*, XXV, no. 3/4 (September/December 1983): 11–24.

the different socioeconomic and cultural environments they find themselves in. African democratic regimes have been at once liberal and social, participatory and consociational, oligarchic and *democratica*.[15]

Sklar presents African regimes as "hybrids" and suggests that it is important to move beyond the contest between "Western" and "indigenous" values. As in other regions of the world, ideas about democracy in modern Africa are debated, disputed and are constantly constructed and reconstructed by regimes in countries with different historical experiences. In short, democracy has adapted to myriad democratic ideas, including Western liberalism, African culturalism, and third world socioeconomic contexts, which have tended to foster a brand of democratic socialism.

For example, the endogenous democratic ideas of African nationalist leaders and civil society movements (associational organizations and working-class movements) must be considered with liberal democratic development in the continent. Ghana's president Kwame Nkrumah was often believed influenced by Pan-African "liberalism," which he combined with socialism. Seretse Khama, the first president of Botswana, developed a style of liberalism that only appeared to be adapted from British liberalism; in actuality, it was influenced by Khama's aristocratic Tswana background. Nigeria's nationalist leaders— Nnamdi Azikiwe, Obafemi Awolowo, and Ahmadu Bello—differed ideologically but were committed to the concept of liberal democracy. Senegal's Leopold Senghor's "Negritudism" also combined liberal democratization with African determination, as Nyerereism combined culturalism and socialism.

Sklar has also argued that African democracies, like democracies elsewhere, are not pure (Sklar 1999) and, as a result, may exhibit elements of *democratica* and oligarchy. Just as democratic discourse in Africa should not be viewed as an essentialized Western and indigenized African dichotomy, democracy in the continent should not be seen as a simple democratic and authoritarian dualism. Unlike Sklar, mainstream scholars label many of the continent's newly established democratic political systems as authoritarian regimes. Such classification blurs complexity and nuance, so we cannot distinguish modern democratic experiences beyond the liberal democracy that Africans have encountered. Examples of other genres of modern democracy include social democracy, guided democracy, and consociational democracy (Pinkney 2002). President Julius Nyerere called his twenty-five-year hybrid regime a "one-party democracy" and, thus, rejected the authoritarian label that contemporary Western democratic theorists assigned the Tanzanian political system.

More controversial are African military regimes, which have not been merely authoritarian. A close analysis shows that many of them have been vanguardist: they have advocated a form of "guided democracy" for their developing societies. African military regimes led coups against elected democracies in the name of democratic renewal. As long as military governments proclaimed their goals as transitory to democracy, African civil societies often supported and interacted with them (Edozie 2002). The guided democratic regime was first formulated under former Indonesian president Suharto, who called his leadership a true nationalism that represented the "general will" of postindependence Indonesia. With time, postcolonial republics would foster conditions that would nurture democracy in their countries. Nigeria, Ghana, and the Gambia's vanguardist militaries are important cases to examine.

Socialist and populist conceptions of democracy have also meant a lot to African states and societies. The specter of socialism and communism in Africa derived from a socioeconomic context in which rapid modernization and aggressive globalization have occurred. Income inequality and increasing urban and rural poverty continue to speak to the importance of "social democracy" and

---

[15] This is the original Greek/Athenian term for democracy, understood today as a populist form of democracy such as direct democracy.

other popular conceptions of democracy, such as culturalist and indigenous Africa. Africa's ethnic pluralism, wherein ethnicities' goals for self-determination prevail over class and individuality to promote democratic mobilization and political participation, leads to a different meaning of democracy. Africa's ethnic pluralism encourages the practice of direct "African-style" communal democracies and provokes consociational ideas about democracy, so that multi-ethnic differences can be mediated. Nigeria, Ethiopia, Kenya, and Burundi have come the farthest in adapting consociational democratic ideas and practices.

As is the case elsewhere in the world, the meaning of democracy in Africa is geo-spatial, i.e., democracy's meaning is constantly changing and adapting to internal and external structural influences over time. For example, ideas about democracy in Africa have been redefined since the 1980s and 1990s as a result of the global restructuring that has occurred in the post–Cold War era. By the 1990s, with the Third Wave of Democracy, African political thought began to reflect an ideological shift towards a much more intense examination of African democratic theory and practice. Characterized by Pieter Boele van Hensbroek[16] as a new democratic turn, the period provided important implications for a renewed social construction of democracy.

New actors began to speak on behalf of Africa as nationalist presidents lost ground to opposition leaders, new and resuscitated social movements, human-rights activism, and international donor agencies (van Hensbroek 1999). As democratic ideas led to the reestablishment of liberal democracy across the continent, people switched from a discourse on "democratic struggles" and "transition to democracy" to discourses on the challenges of democratic consolidation, and they engaged in a deep, more substantive introspection into rights and freedoms.

Table 10.1, below, charts the various democracies Africans have experienced in the twentieth century. There are four major ideological prisms—liberal, social, cultural, and non-liberal democratic—through which to analyze Africa's socially constructed democratic ideas. These democratic ideas have progressed over four stages of African contemporary democratic development—the 1950s period of nationalist democracies, the 1970s post-nationalist period of guided democracy, the 1990s Third Wave of Democracy struggles, and the contemporary global era in which incumbent democracies operate. While African countries—and within them their different regimes—have variously embodied the features of one or more of the democratic ideas listed in Table 10.1, some countries and their regimes are well known for practicing specific forms of democracy. Table 10.1 (discussed in more detail later) categorizes countries by their most recognizable genre of democracy, qualified by historical regime type. For example, Nyerere's regime in early postindependence Tanzania is known for its one-party democracy, which is associated with the culturalist palaver democratic idea. It is important to note that the focus here on contemporary democratic formulations does not ignore the indigenous democratic form mentioned earlier.

Ideas in Practice I: Liberalism and Liberal Democracy in Africa

By the 1990s Third Wave, liberal democracy had come to be associated with the term "democracy." Few analysts of democracy in Africa, however, have explored the development of liberal democracy in African environments. Instead, they have focused their analysis on criticizing the lack of liberalism in African and non-Western political development (Zakaria 1997). They point to the undemocratic

---

[16] Pieter Boele van Hensbroek, *Political Discourses in African Thought, 1860 to the Present* (Westport, CT: Praeger, 1999).

Table 10.1   The Contours of Democratic Ideas and Practices in Africa: Regimes and Country Cases

	HISTORICAL PERIOD			
DEMOCRATIC IDEOLOGY	Nationalist Postcolonial Liberal Democracies 1950s–1960s	Post Nationalist, Developmental Experiments 1970s–1980s	Third Wave Democratic Struggles 1990s	Current Third Wave Democratic Regimes
Liberal Democracy	**Decolonization** S. Leone Senegal Kenya Zambia Botswana DR Congo Sudan Malawi Gambia	**One-Party Regimes** Zambia Malawi Tanzania Rwanda Burundi	**Pro-Democracy Movements** Kenya Zambia Malawi Senegal Benin South Africa Nigeria	**Free Democracies*** Botswana S. Africa Senegal Ghana Mali Cape Verde Mauritius Sao Tome and Principe
Socialist Democracy	**Decolonization** Ghana Tanzania Benin Ethiopia Congo-Braz.	**Marxist/Leninist Regimes** Sudan Somalia Congo-Braz. Burkina Faso (1983)		
Culturalist Democracy Palavar/Precolonial	Tanzania	Uganda (1986)		
Culturalist Democracy Consociational	Nigeria		Ethiopia Sudan Burundi	
Hybrid, Non-Liberal Developmental Democracies				All other African Third Waves that are considered partially free or "not free"

* See Freedom House

behavior of elected politicians and the dearth of individualism and civil mobilization as obstacles to the development of democracy in Africa (Hyden 1983). Contrary to the assumption that liberalism is nonexistent in African political development, is the fact that liberal ideas have emerged endogenously in some countries and regimes. This is to say that liberalism and the ideas that are associated with

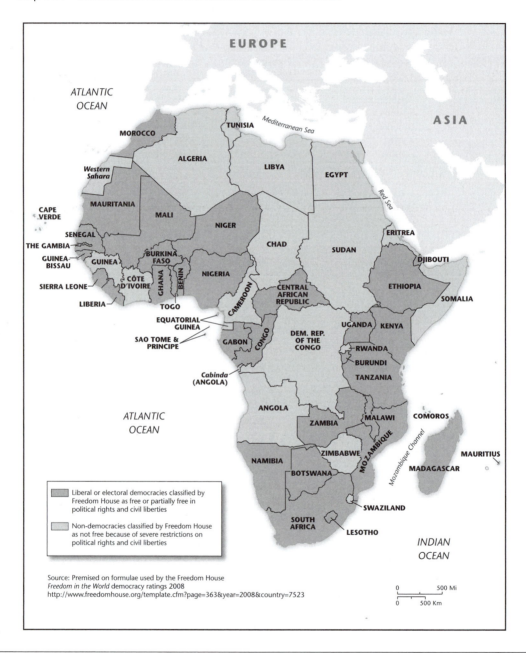

Map 10.1   Electoral and Liberal Democracies in African Politics

EUROPE

ASIA

ATLANTIC
OCEAN

Mediterranean Sea

MOROCCO

TUNISIA

Western
Sahara

ALGERIA

LIBYA

EGYPT

Red Sea

MAURITANIA

CAPE
VERDE

MALI

NIGER

CHAD

SUDAN

ERITREA

DJIBOUTI

SENEGAL

THE GAMBIA

GUINEA-
BISSAU

GUINEA

BURKINA
FASO

NIGERIA

ETHIOPIA

SIERRA LEONE

CÔTE
D'IVOIRE

GHANA

BENIN

CAMEROON

CENTRAL
AFRICAN
REPUBLIC

SOMALIA

LIBERIA

TOGO

EQUATORIAL
GUINEA

SAO TOME &
PRINCIPE

GABON

CONGO

DEM. REP.
OF THE
CONGO

UGANDA

KENYA

RWANDA

BURUNDI

TANZANIA

Cabinda
(ANGOLA)

ATLANTIC
OCEAN

ANGOLA

ZAMBIA

MALAWI

COMOROS

Mozambique Channel

ZIMBABWE

MOZAMBIQUE

MAURITIUS

NAMIBIA

BOTSWANA

MADAGASCAR

SWAZILAND

SOUTH
AFRICA

LESOTHO

INDIAN
OCEAN

Liberal or electoral democracies classified by
Freedom House as free or partially free in
political rights and civil liberties

Non-democracies classified by Freedom House
as not free because of severe restrictions on
political rights and civil liberties

Source: Premised on formulae used by the Freedom House
Freedom in the World democracy ratings 2008
http://www.freedomhouse.org/template.cfm?page=363&year=2008&country=7523

0   500 Mi

0   500 Km

it—individualism, human rights, liberty, citizenship, the separation of powers, universal suffrage, free political association, and freedom—have been adapted to varying degrees in the ferment of African democratic development.

The core philosophy of liberal democracy is liberalism, which is generally characterized as a doctrine devoted to protecting the rights of the individual to pursue life, liberty, property, and happiness.[17] In Africa, liberalism has influenced the ideas adapted by African nationalists during the decolonizing period, the structural ideas of liberalism that emerge from the liberal democratic state, and the pro-democratic struggles forged by the resuscitated civil society in the 1990s. One can trace the emergence of liberal democratic thought in Africa beginning with the establishment of the modern, representative, liberal, political democracy that was a direct descendant of decolonization and African independence in the 1940s.

Liberalism's ideas influenced African democratization as a result of the world's Second Wave of Democracy (Huntington 1993), which marked the beginning of the end of Western colonial rule and produced a number of new liberal democratic African states. The end of worldwide imperial French and British rule led to a period of colonially administered self-governance. This was a period that would introduce Africans to liberal democratic governance, with its emphasis on minimalist institutions, civic nationalism, and majoritarian rule. As a result of this history, the structure of the modern African state was fashioned on classical liberalism, which sought to secure the representation of individuals and groups and to protect them from others and from state oppression.

Through this experience, an African nationalist elite, educated in the Western tradition, assimilated liberal ideas to reconstruct platforms for achieving political freedom from colonialism. Once independence had been won, the values of liberalism began to permeate the social milieu of the leading nationalists and inspire consolidation of the new African democracies. The idea of liberal democracy required that the postcolonial African state recognize the rights of "citizenship" to give Africans a certain reciprocity of rights and duties to their new political communities. Former colonized African subjects became citizens in a liberal democracy and ideally were set to enjoy equality before the law and constitutional safeguards to protect their rights. Yet democratization in this context had taken place against the background of a poorly developed civil society and underdeveloped economies that remained patterned on the colonial monopoly economy and on deeply divided heterogeneous, pluralist ethnic communities in which there was only a nascent understanding and partial penetration of liberal ideas. Liberal democracy was seen as divorced from the vast cultural terrain of the various new societies. It was no wonder that liberalism and liberal democracy constituted an experiment that would take more than forty years to mature across the continent.

The process by which Britain and France had attained liberal democracy two centuries earlier was not to be easily replicated in Africa. An important principle for liberal democracies is the idea that there is "reciprocity of power" between governments and subjects. In the West, this reciprocity emerged as a result of a growing dependence on the cooperation of subject populations in European absolutist states. These states had developed sophisticated national systems of regulation. Yet the establishment of modern republicanism in Africa during the post–World War II era was to be different. The exhaustion of traditional forms of legitimation (religion and community) and the gradual autonomous emergence of civil society, which created a marketplace for labor power and capital in order to foster the separation of the economic and political spheres, were processes that were for Africa only beginning to be advanced within a very different international power structure.

---

[17] Marc F. Plattner, "From Liberalism to Liberal Democracy," in *The Global Divergence of Democracies*, ed. Larry Diamond and Marc F. Plattner (Baltimore: Johns Hopkins University Press, 2001), 78–92.

Liberal democracy had other limitations in Africa. The structure of liberal democracy and its association with privilege, economic inequality, and individualized civil liberties and political rights remained alien in African contexts. The existing sociopolitical organization of African societies encouraged the formation of cultural and community self-determination, or group rights, not merely articulation of individual or working class interests. Resulting contradictions perverted the liberal democratic experiment in Africa and led, in many cases, to its breakdown, rather than to its consolidation and expansion. At most, liberalism existed as a partial construct among African nationalist elites and the urban working classes. Rhetoric on contested elections and constitutional safeguards was not sufficient to sustain liberal democratic states in culturally plural societies. It is no surprise that the "liberal" expression of democracy was pushed aside for experimentation with alternative "non-liberal" democratic ideas.

Over time, there emerged deepening legitimacy problems in the non-democratic regimes that followed the breakdown of liberal democracy and the unprecedented global economic growth of the 1960s and 1970s. The urban middle class greatly expanded in many African countries. These processes gave rise to revival of liberal democratization in the 1990s, or the Third Wave of Democracy (Huntington 1992). However, Africa's 1990s liberalization and redemocratization would not have been possible without the underlying liberal democratic institutions and ideas that had persisted, despite the restrictions on democracy during the period of liberal democratic reversal. All over Africa, these "fragments of democracy" were present in trade union movements, voluntary associations, and nascent political parties that, by the 1990s, served as platforms for the return of liberal democracy (Heilbrunn 1995).

There is a lot of debate concerning how to categorize Africa's incumbent redemocratized state-societies. Even though many of these regimes are liberal democratic regimes with liberal democratic institutions, constitutions that uphold political rights and the civil liberties of their citizens, and vibrant civil societies, many doubt whether these regimes are indeed socially and culturally liberal. Moreover, while these regimes may not be ideal liberal, representational democracies of the Western pluralist genre, many have Freedom House ratings that are equivalent to those of Western pluralist democracies like the United States, France, and the United Kingdom. Freedom House categorizes Ghana, South Africa, Cape Verde, Senegal, Mali, and Botswana as "free," liberal, pluralist democracies and gives them democracy rankings similar to those of advanced industrial democracies.

Liberal democracy has been more successful in some African countries than in others. Botswana, one of the only two postcolonial liberal democracies in Africa not to collapse after independence, is an African country in which liberal democracy has been successful. To explain Botswana's success with liberal democratic governance,[18] studies have looked at the "liberal" leadership of Seretse Khama during the 1960s transfer of power and have contrasted the liberal governance style of the Botswana Democratic Party (BDP) with that of the Botswana People's Party (BPP), the radical Pan-African party. Khama, a prince of the Tswana monarchy (Kgotla), and the BDP represented a style of political rule that was characterized by Khama's ability to balance tradition with modernity in a way similar to the gradualist liberal governance mechanisms achieved by the British monarchy in the eighteenth century. Khama governed with a cohesive group of modernizing elites and bureaucrats who maintained a commitment to "liberal economic developmentalism" and the gradual development of a relationship between the state and civil society.

Like Botswana, Mauritius is a democracy that has not failed since its independence in 1968, and it may have more of a successful liberal democracy than Botswana because of the dynamism of Mauritius's

---

[18] Michael Crowder, Jack Parsons, Neil Parsons, Louis Picard, John Holm, and Patrick Molutsi.

electoral institutions through which government turnovers have been achieved after stable, regular, multi-party elections. A handover to an oppositional party regime has not occurred in Botswana, so despite its successful liberalism, it may still be described as having a dominant-party regime in the BDP. In Mauritius, both the first and second parties to lose power through elections have peacefully handed over power to the winners. Like Botswana, Mauritius's high level of economic development may explain its success with liberal democracy.

Both countries share the title of "Africa's little tigers." However, compared to Botswana's semi-presidentialism, which has possibly led to the country's dominant partyism and strong executive, Mauritius's liberal democracy has a very different institutional design, which includes parliamentary structures and an alternative electoral system. During the country's decolonization, the Banwell Commission recommended a "first-three-past-the-post" plurality system, which Mauritian nationalists accepted because they saw it as effective in mediating and accommodating a diverse, multi-ethnic society (Brautigam in Joseph 1999). It is this multi-cultural liberalism that has led to the democratic stability and economic success of Mauritius.

The principles of liberalism have also played dominant institutional roles in the political development of other African countries—Gambia until the 1990s, Kenya's two-party regime until 1969, Senegal since 1981, Nigeria's early regimes (and the country's experiment with American-style federalism), South Africa since 1949 (especially the regimes since the 1990s), and Liberia before the 1980s Doe coup. It may seem ironic to discuss the Gambia and Nigeria in the context of liberalism and liberal democracy given the tenuous state of these countries' current liberal democracies, which, in both cases, were discontinued in the postcolonial period and revived in the 1990s. However, until a military coup in 1994, the Gambia was heralded for its successful and continuous liberal democracy. For almost thirty years, from 1965 to 1994, since the founding of the independent Gambian nation, Gambians accepted the British-derived competitive party politics as the ideal mode of state power (Edie, 2000). After independence in 1957, the Gambia maintained a multi-party liberal democracy, governed by the dominant People's Progressive Party, and Dawda Jawara, who held the presidency from 1970 to 1994. However, again, as in Botswana, Dawda Jawara's adherence to liberal-style competitive politics and his skill in coalitional party politics contributed to the ascendancy of the People's Progressive Party, while the Gambian opposition parties were never able to overturn the elections and come to power. This was an important factor that led to the breakdown of the country's liberal democracy.

Nigeria has a rich tradition of constitutional liberty, and scholars have remarked on the country's liberalism. Modern Nigerian politics developed in a liberal democratic framework from 1957 to 1960, during the period of colonial self-government from 1960 to 1966 in the First Republic after independence, from 1979 to 1983 in the Second Republic, briefly in 1998 in the Third Republic, and since 1999 in the Fourth Republic. Nigeria's three nationalist leaders—Chief Awolowo, Dr. Nnamdi Azikiwe, and Alhaji Sir Tafawa Balewa—articulated liberal democracy in distinct ways. In 1957, Balewa announced that the British system of democratic government was part of the Nigerian heritage.[19] Awolowo argued that the best form of government was democracy because of its basic freedoms of conscience, expression, assembly, and association.[20] Similarly, Dr. Azikiwe pronounced that Nigerian governance was established upon a belief in democracy—government by discussion, consent, and the majority.[21]

---

[19] Alhaji Sir Abubakar Tafawa Balewa, *Nigeria Speaks: Speeches Made Between 1957 and 1964* (University of Lagos Press, 1966).

[20] Obafemi Awolowo, *The Problems of Africa: the Need for Ideological Reappraisal* (London: Macmillan, 1977).

[21] Nnamdi Azikiwe, *Zik: A selection from the Speeches of Nnamdi Azikiwe* (Cambridge University Press, 1961), 97–99.

Nigeria's liberalism is best expressed not so much in the country's liberal democratic institutions, which fail constantly, but in the country's practice of federalism, a liberal style of government predicated on the division and restraint of powers. Federalism in Nigeria gave rise to a staunchly independent judiciary that has protected the rights of Nigerian citizens and the country's constituent gubernatorial states and local communities. Nigeria's constitutional federalism makes the country distinct in Africa (Sklar 1983). Moreover, despite the suspension of liberal democratic rule in Nigeria, the country's military regimes may be said, by and large, to have maintained the conditions of a "plural" society (Edozie 2002) because police state methods and totalitarianism did not characterize Nigerian politics under military rule. Even after military takeovers in 1966 and in 1983, constitutional principles continued in force. Indeed, federalism was established and expanded by the military regimes (Nwabueze 1992).

Ideas in Practice II: Socialism, Populism, and Participatory Democracy

Socialism has significantly guided democracy in African contexts because socialist ideas and institutions have often been by-products of limited liberal democracy in underdeveloped economies. The tension between liberalism and democracy is central to democratic theory: the former (liberalism) excludes the primacy of socioeconomic equality, and the latter (democracy), through the principle of universal suffrage, embodies the notion of political equality. In Africa, as elsewhere in the developing world, freedom and equality have clashed. During the 1960s, given the global specter of communism, even among advanced industrial democracies, social democratic regimes ("welfare states"), not liberal democracies, dominated. Concerned more explicitly with equality and social justice, social democrats see society as a potentially organic whole with common interests and see the state as an engine for resource redistribution through public ownership and provision of extensive welfare (Pinkney 2003).

During the 1960s, 1970s, and 1980s, several African states established socialist democracy; in doing so, many incorporated into their governing platforms the revolutionary idea of democracy reflected in the Marxist-Leninist vanguard and communist ideology. Ghana under Kwame Nkrumah and Guinea under Sekou Toure adopted this form of democracy: they asserted that in their socialist states, citizens' political and economic rights were protected to the extent that all were equal before the law and that the state existed to execute the will of the people. Socialist conceptualizations of democracy became popular in the late 1960s as they replaced nascent liberal democracies. Rejecting liberal democracy, these postcolonial states adopted "one-party democracy," using it as a basis for promoting the socialist idea of democracy. Social democracies were preferred over non-liberal democratic systems because they fostered greater civic nationalism (equality) in highly plural, underdeveloped societies. Between the late 1960s and the early 1980s, liberal democratic regimes were ousted, one by one, by liberal regimes in the name of socialist democracy.

In presenting the idea of an "African" socialism, Julius Nyerere argued that socialism, like democracy, was an attitude rooted in African principles of equality. Declaring Tanzania a "one-party democracy," Nyerere rejected the competitiveness and division of liberal democracy and capitalism and promoted the idea of a Fabian social democracy. In Zambia, Kenneth Kaunda, who construed democracy as democratic participation in all spheres of life, established a "one-party participatory democracy." No single individual or group of individuals had a monopoly on political, economic, social, or military power.

In other African states, radical military regimes, in alliance with leftist organizations, seized power to displace the nationalist, liberal democratic ruling elite; they would use socialist ideology to try to transform their societies. In most cases, Marxist-Leninist platforms ousted liberal democracy in the name of "socialist democracy." Benin's 1972 "revolution," through the military coup of Mathieu Kerekou, proclaimed socialism for Dahomey (present-day Benin) in order to eradicate what he considered as the "exploitation of man by man" (Mathurin C. Houngnikpo 2001). Jerry Rawlings's coup against Ghana's liberal democratic nationalist regime was executed in the name of radical socialist democracy. Rawlings's Marxist regimes in the 1970s were social democracy in practice, and they fostered social mobilization as a means of democratic empowerment. In his 1983 political orientation speech, the Marxist president of Burkina Faso, Captain Thomas Sankara, proclaimed his August Revolution in the name of the Burkinabe people's deepest aspirations for democracy, liberty, and independence from neo-colonialism (1983 Orientation Speech). Sankara viewed the mass demonstrations in May 1983, which brought his National Revolutionary Council (NCR) to power, as the open support of "a whole people, and in particular its youth" for his revolutionary ideals.

In Ethiopia, the Dergue, the military and workers party, forged a coalition to oust Haille Selassie's feudal monarchy. The popular upsurge that began in February 1974 culminated in the Ethiopian revolution and was followed by the removal of feudal forms of economy and land nationalization in the name of the "people." By 1987, the regime had promulgated a constitution and established itself as the People's Democratic Republic of Ethiopia (PDRE) and a socialist democracy. In the Sudan, from 1969 to 1983, Colonel Jaafar Nimeiri established a Marxist-Leninist platform with a single party under the guidance of the Sudanese Socialist Union (SSU). This was to be a union of working people, who sought to eliminate the influence of sectarianism by stripping sectional parties of their tribal and religious base and establishing a secular socialist national identity over the entire country. In October 1969, revolution in Somalia was similarly launched by the military under Major General Mohammed Siad Barre and the Somali Marxist intellectuals. In the name of "socialism" and economic development (*handiwadaag* in Somali), the political regimes of the country also reflected socialist democratic ideas.[22]

Despite the failure of socialism and Marxist-Leninist ideas, evidenced by the fall of the former Soviet Union and the 1990s revival of democratic liberalism and the laissez-faire market, the idea of socialist democracy has survived in Africa and has been transformed: while socialist democracies are not practiced by political regimes, socialist ideas remain strong among African civil societies. Fragments of social democracy shadow many of the continent's incumbent liberal democracies. Unlike liberal democracy, the popular socialist conception of democracy does not limit the practice of democracy to the political sphere alone. Rather it expands democracy's meaning to include ways in which a state-society's resources are used and equitably distributed. The continued salience of populist genres of democratic expression in Africa's millennium may be explained by the continued limitations that the incumbent liberal democracies are experiencing in their capacity to provide economic and social welfare benefits to underdeveloped and unevenly developed African societies.

Discussion of the relationship between democracy and the economy has only just begun to be effectively examined in Africa. Scholars are now beginning to establish a heuristic distinction between liberal democracy and popular or social democracy. Africans have begun to underscore this distinction to avoid confusing what they have perceived as the long human struggle for democracy and equality (socialism/populism) with its particular historical form—Western liberalism with its attention to individualism. (Issa Shivji 1991a, 255). Liberal democracies broke down, and continue to falter, so quickly in postcolonial Africa because of the tension between liberal democracy and popular democracy. The liberal democratic state's focus on limited government (governance) and "electoral democracy" (political and civil rights) eschews substantive aspects of democracy, including economic, social, and cultural rights. Attention to governance and rights glosses over the fact that Africans want not only freedom, but also social and economic security (Forsyth and Rieffer 2003).

---

[22] John Markakis and Michael Waller, *Military Marxist Regimes in Africa* (London: Frank Cass, 1986).

With its own focus on socioeconomic structures, equality, and self-determination, the "socialist" conception of democracy remains alive during the Third Wave of Democracy because of the shortcomings of liberal democracies in relation to Africa's underdeveloped economies. Populist mobilization by African social movements for broad-based economic rights is prevalent among the democratic regimes of South Africa, Nigeria, and Guinea. These countries have experienced nationwide strikes in popular sectors. The liberal democratic regimes are incapable of absorbing populist pressures. Africa's liberal democracies are, therefore, better classified as "exclusionary" democracies: they allow for "formal" or electoral democracy, but because of the high incidence of poverty, the liberal regimes have difficulty responding in substantive and meaningful ways to the demands for public welfare from Africa's majorities (Abrahmsen 2000).

Ideas in Practice III: African Culturalism, Identity, and Consociational Democracy

With a culturalist logic, Africans reach into their precolonial pasts to define "democracy." An increasing acknowledgment that African state-societies are ethnically and religiously plural also influences culturalist constructions of democracy in the continent. Multiculturalism and its attendant challenges to democracy have always directed the continent's social construction and democratic practice.

Regarding precolonialism and democracy, there is a growing opinion among Africans and scholars of Africa that a deeper meaning and practice of democracy than the liberalism or socialism borrowed from the West can be found in the rich culture and traditions of Africa. Senegal's Leopold Senghor complained that Europeans spoke to Africans as if Africans did not have their own conception of democracy before European conquest of the continent. Contrarily, Senghor argued that African democracy was founded on *palabre* by which one has the right to speak and take the floor to express opinions.[23] Pieter Boele van Hensbroek (1999) refers to *palabre,* now resurgent in Africa, as a neo-traditionalist discourse of democracy based on a shared African identity and culture. Scholars, such as Wamba-dia-Wamba, who support this idea of democracy argue that rejection of Western liberal democracy is not rejection of "democracy" but a call for democracy's enrichment with African values and institutional forms that could lead to greater participation by the majority of African communities who embrace these values.[24]

Neo-traditionalists argue that liberal democratic politics contradict "African culture." For example, in positing the precolonial notion of "African democracy," Ghanaian scholar Kwesi Wiredu perhaps made the best scholarly case for a reconstruction of the idea of democracy based on African values against a "Western" liberal democracy when he identified the merits of the nonparty democracy (Eze 1997). Wiredu showed that even though African political systems did not have multiparty institutions, they did have democratic institutions for representation and meaningful dialogue towards effective and inclusive decision making. Comparing African traditional democracies with liberal Western democracies, Wiredu argued that African democracies valued fostering "consent" to achieve consensus, unlike majoritarian democracies that tended to arrive at consensus through competition. In African democracies, while parties did not exist, lineage and kinship groups served as representative bodies of good governance.[25]

---

[23] Irving Leonard Markovitz, *Léopold Sédar Senghor and the Politics of Negritude* (New York: Atheneum, 1969), 195–196.

[24] Ernest Wamba-dia-Wamba, "Beyond Elite Politics of Democracy in Africa," *Quest* 6, no. 1 (1992).

[25] Kwasi Wiredu, "Democracy and Consensus in African Traditional Politics: A Plea for a Non-party Polity," in *Postcolonial African Philosophy: A Critical Reader,* ed. Emmanuel Chukwudi Eze (Cambridge, MA: Blackwell, 1997), 303–312.

In African democracy, the state was seen as a "communocracy," or a "village democracy," whose kinship institutions rested on the needs of the total society. This system represented a means for national mobilization and identity representation. It further served as a system of mutually beneficial role reinforcements and as a constitutional principle that regulated the political processes required to uphold functional democratic representation in attributing and controlling the exercise of power in African states and societies.[26] This practice was found in many parts of traditional Africa and successfully enhanced popular participation in governance. Household heads and adult males were admitted to village councils and had effective voice in deliberations in their individual and representative capacities. However, there were also provisions for individuals, who otherwise would not have been able to participate formally in decision making, to air their views in public gatherings organized in village squares.

In his famous treatise on precolonial Kenyan political systems, Jomo Kenyatta, Kenya's first president, in his book *Facing Mount Kenya* argued that prior to the advent of the Europeans, the Gikuyu (Kikuyu) system of government was based on true democratic principles (Kenyatta 1959). In describing African democracy, Kenyatta's book describes the Kikuyu *itwika* (revolution) as a radical transition from autocracy to democracy. *Itwika* led to the establishment of the Kikuyu democracy. Each village was represented by a governing council, or *njama ya itwika*, and a constitution—a social contract of sorts—that included the principles of freedom for the people to acquire and develop land under a system of family ownership. It also included universal tribal membership and a consensual sub-village council led by elders (*kiama*).[27]

Contemporary Africanist historians have also drawn on Africa's precolonial, acephalous communities to illustrate similar representations of democracy. Botswana is an oft-cited case. The precolonial Tswana political community (*morafe*) was governed by the *kgotla*—a traditional assembly where all free adult males deliberated over political, social, religious, legal, and economic matters of public concern.[28] Botswana's *kgotla* system was a "tribal democracy" because it allowed all the Tswana people to express their aspirations and values.[29] Burundi's pre-German/Belgian political system had a similar democratic structure, the *bashigantahe,* an institution that formed the democratic core of Burundian society. Acting as a parliament, it advised the monarchy and was open to all capable subjects regardless of their social standing.[30]

Tanzania's Julius Nyerere did the most to incorporate the neo-traditional idea of African democracy into modern democratic practice through his 1967 Arusha Declaration and the establishment of the Ujaama one-party democracy. Nyerere argued if the nation identified with one party, the foundations of democracy would be firmer than they could ever be with two or more parties each representing only a section of the community.[31] Nyerere's one-party democracy sought to "Africanize" democracy by recapturing and modernizing the precolonial cultural system and incorporating it into the modern democratic system. For example, in successfully persuading Tanzanians to vote for replacing Tanzania's British-transferred liberal, multiparty democracy with a one-party African democracy, Nyerere argued that extended "family-hood" (*ujaama*) ought to form the basis of a modern African democratic system.[32]

---

[26] Onigu Otite, ed., *Themes in African Social and Political Thought* (Enugu, Nigeria: Fourth Dimension Publishers, 1978).

[27] Jomo Kenyatta, *Facing Mount Kenya* (New York: Vintage Books, 1962).

[28] Olufemi Vaughan, *Chiefs, Power, and Social Change: Chiefship and Modern Politics in Botswana, 1880s–1990s* (Trenton, NJ: Africa World Press, 2003).

[29] Isaac Schapera, *Handbook of Tswana Law and Custom* (London: Oxford University Press, 1938).

[30] Rene Lemarchand, *Rwanda and Burundi* (London: Pall Mall Publishers, 1970).

[31] Julius Nyerere, *Freedom and Development* (Oxford University Press, 1973), 63.

[32] Nyerere, "Ujamma—The Basis of African Socialism." In *Government and Politics in Africa*, edited by Okwudiba Nnoli. Harare: AAPS Books, 2000.

Nyerere's brand of democracy sought to avoid the conflictual, competitive nature of liberal multi-partyism. He believed that it was the people (community and family) embodied in the nation-state, not the individual with needs, passions, tastes, and fantasies, who were to forge the modern African democracy. In Tanzania, Senegal, Zambia, and Malawi and across much of the new postcolonial Africa, the one-party democracy emerged as African democracy in which society was depoliticized. United in the party, the masses were mobilized to create and erect the foundations of the state and the nation.[33]

Uganda's regime held on to the principle of African democracy in the spirit of culturalism until a February 2006 election when Yoweri Museveni's National Resistance Movement (NRM) established the "0-party" democracy based on the principles of Nyerere's "African-centered" democratic values. Twenty years before reestablishing multiparty elections in 2006, in justifying his 20-year ban on liberal democracy, President Museveni asked, "what is crucial for Uganda now is for us to have a system that ensures democratic participation until such a time as we get, through economic development, especially industrialization, the crystallization of socioeconomic groups upon which we can then base healthy political parties."[34]

Another way to understand Africans' renewed interest in the cultural meaning of democratization is the continent's tendency to practice consociational forms of democracy, or ethnic power sharing. This concept of democracy is most popularly associated with political scientist Arend Lijphart, who recommends consociational power-sharing institutions for societies with a high degree of segmental autonomy, or cultural pluralism (Lijphart 1977, 25). In Africa, colonialism forcibly brought together precolonial nations, which, in the postcolonial nation, became reduced to "tribes and ethnicities" under the modern nation-state. However, in this context, as Nigerian historian Ade Ajayi has argued, postcolonial liberal democratic regimes, which sought to homogenize and nurture single nations out of many, caused the mobilization of counter-resistance "self-determination" movements that viewed democracy as a political platform for establishing cultural-group rights, as opposed to citizenship rights.

Some of Africa's most forceful postcolonial self-determination struggles have been made in the name of "democracy." These included the Biafran struggle in Nigeria (1967–1970), the Southern Sudanese struggle in the Sudan (1958–2003), the Eritrean struggle in Ethiopia (1945–1992), the North-South split in Chad, the Katanga struggle in the Democratic Republic of the Congo, andthe Rwandan genocide (1990–1993)—all conflicts caused by cultural and ethnic misunderstandings. The late John Garang, who for twenty years led the Southern Sudanese struggle, characterized the movement he led as a "self-determination" democratic struggle for national democratic inclusion (Garang 1987). The Eritrean self-determination struggle against the Ethiopians also began as a democratic one for autonomous inclusion of the Eritrean nationality before it became strictly secessionist. Because of these realities, Africa's multi-ethnic state-societies require democratic institutions that foster inter-ethnic accommodation and cooperation. They need democratic arrangements to mediate between diverse subnationalities and ethnicities. That is why consociational democratic policies, such as ethnic power sharing, proportional representation, and federalism, are popular genres of democracy in Africa.

For Africa's contemporary democratic polities, self-determining democratic struggles and consociational democracy have been resuscitated in "identity" politics and "power-sharing" agreements. In

---

[33] Robert Fatton, *The Making of a Liberal Democracy: Senegal's Passive Revolution, 1975–1985* (Boulder, CO: Lynne Rienner Publishers, 1987).

[34] Yoweri Museveni, *Sowing the Mustard Seed: The Struggle for Freedom and Democracy in Uganda* (London: Macmillan, 1997).

incumbent African democracies, the postcolonial idea and practice of "civic nationalism" is gradually giving way to a "multinationalism" that is leading to new consociational democratic political practices in the continent. For example, Ethiopian democrat Meles Zenawi restructured state-society relations, so the country could weaken the 2,000-year-old Solomonid-Amharic hegemonic grip on the state. The 1993 Ethiopian democratic revolution sought to reconfigure Ethiopia into an ethnic federal democracy in which power would be decentralized along the country's several ethnic regions.

Consociationalism had important implications for South Africa. During the country's democratic transition in the early 1990s, Arend Lijphart advised negotiating parties to adopt consociationalism to accommodate contending "identities"—the ANC's Black majority, the Zulu nationalists, and the White minority. Though the ANC favored a liberal majoritarian, democratic regime, its government did adopt some form of consociationalism at the local level, for the Zulu especially, and at the party level for the National Party, which represented the White minority.

The 2004 Sudanese Comprehensive Peace Agreement also adopted consociational mechanisms to include the Southern Sudan in a multi-ethnic "new Sudan" that is at least temporarily "binational" and that allows for the "self-determined" rights of the non-Muslim Southerners in a new power-sharing federal polity (Edozie in Saha, ed., 2008). Nigeria's post–civil war federalist initiatives were also designed to deal with ethnic diversity. Federalism, for Nigeria, would recognize ethnic autonomy and balance cultural pluralism with a multinational[35] central government. A "federal character" and rotational presidency are just some of the Nigerian innovations.

Burundi, one of Africa's newest democracies, perhaps represents the best case of a contemporary African consociational democracy. Burundians in 2005 chose former Hutu rebel leader Pierre Nkurunziza in ethnic power-sharing elections. Despite a series of violent conflicts over the course of the country's democratic development, former president Pierre Buyoya's consociational experiment forced Hutus and Tutsis to share power in 1988 and fostered the democratic successes that Burundi enjoys.

Contemporary African Democratic Ideas: Melting Pot Versus Pragmatic Liberal Developmentalism

As the world—and Africa is no exception—re-democratizes, the phenomenon called "democracy" will continue to be constructed and re-constructed. Democratic institutions, processes, and discourses will be adapted to the unique sociocultural contexts of each country. By analyzing the construction of democratic ideas and the formulation of democratic values that inform Africans' interpretation of democracy, one can conclude that African democracy is not limited to liberal democracy in the Western sense, and it is not "illiberal." To the contrary, it is a hybrid.[36]

According to the melting-pot interpretation of democracy in Africa advanced by Robert Pinkney (Third World) and Richard Sklar (Africa), Africa's contemporary democracies incorporate elements of socialism, liberalism, and African culturalism. This hybridity is characteristic of other Third World democracies. Socioeconomic and sociocultural contexts and history inform different liberal democratic ideas in these regions. Since the 1990s, more than half of Africa's polities re-established democratic regimes. Yet while

---

[35] Nigeria is made up of several precolonial nationalities, including the Yoruba, Hausa-Fulani, and Igbo. "Multinational" acknowledges the separate identities of these peoples who live together in a strong, federated nation.

[36] Harvey Glickman, "Frontiers of Liberal and Non-Liberal Democracy in Africa," *Journal of Asian and African Studies* 23, nos. 3–4, (1988): 234–254.

many of these incumbent democratic regimes subscribe nominally to liberal democratic ideas, including political rights, liberties, participation, and inclusion through regular multiparty elections, in actuality nonideological (neither liberal nor socialist) watchdog parties dominate them. As a matter of fact, these regimes behave more like classical liberal regimes of the Rousseau genre than contemporary pluralist democracies practiced in the advanced industrial world. This is because in African countries, developmental circumstances continue to compel their democratic regimes to nurture the public good and, therefore, behave like guided democracies rather than liberal representative democracies.

While Africa's incumbent liberal democracies preside over greater political participation and pluralism than in the past, the regimes continue to behave developmentally: they are mostly focused on nurturing a collective nationalistic public good for the purpose of healing nations, uniting their diversities into harmonious wholes, and achieving economic development. Incumbent African democracies exhibit characteristics similar to those of their transitioning world counterparts. Like their Third World counterparts, Africa's incumbent democracies may be best described as majoritarian: democracy serves the masses as a whole through a "social contract," as opposed to amalgamation of individual, competitive interests in a liberal democracy.[37]

The idea of "developmental democracy" (Sklar 1983) continues to characterize African state-society attempts to grapple with democratic practice that suit their conditions. The contradictions inherent in most of the continent's democracies, their adaptation of socialist democracies manifest in populist struggles, and their recognition of cultural diversity are ways in which Africans find meaning in the concept of democracy.

Democracy in Africa cannot be simply discerned by categorizing the continent's political systems into simple dichotomies: liberalism (democracy) versus illiberalism (authoritarianism). Indeed, one might even observe that the inclination to adapt liberal democratic ideas to suit African conditions has staved off authoritarianism rather than prevented or restricted democracy (Sklar 1999).

Examine, for example, the hybrid ideas and somewhat non-liberal practices of some of Africa's incumbent liberal democracies, such as South Africa's under Thabo Mbeki, which invoke a Pan-Africanist renaissance ideology to promote a style and process of democratization that will resuscitate African values and alleviate poverty. Similarly, Nigeria's Olusegun Obasanjo often called for African pragmatism in mediating between and reconciling the country's northern Islamists and Christian secularists. Moreover, while imposing stability and security, Rwanda's Paul Kagame claims an original Rwandan democracy based on traditional Rwandan and liberal democratic values.

Having established a democratic system of government—an "ethnic federalist decentralized" democracy—the county's democratic transition leader, Meles Zenawi, in practice, restricts political and civil freedoms to achieve national identity and security. One of the most interesting examples of Africa's incumbent hybrid democracies is Benin's. In 1994, the country's President, Mathieu Kérékou, seemed to refashion his "socialist democracy" as a "populist democracy," but he merely constructed a democratic agenda to contend with Nicophore Soglo's liberal democratic regime. Kerekou, an "acclaimed" former "dictator," defeated pro-democracy hero Soglo because, in practice, Benin's democratic constituents rejected Soglo's brand of liberal democracy through which he introduced draconian neo-liberal economic reform programs.

---

[37] Crawford Brough Macpherson, *The Real World of Democracy* (Toronto: CBC Enterprises, 1983).

Conclusion

The ideas of African democracy will continue to be drawn from African experiences rooted in various ideologies. Democracy will have varying implications for different states, societies, communities, and citizens. Africans have established liberal democratic regimes, but they have constructed alternative social and cultural versions of liberal democracies to replace unsuitable features of Western democracy. Be that as it may, in some cases, perverse adaptations of democracy by Africa's states and societies have sacrificed liberty. Well-intentioned guided democracies have become paternalistic, corrupt, and restrictive in advancing the democratic rights required of a substantive democracy. As we reframe African politics as democratic politics, we must consider Africa's diverse, socially constructed experiences with democracy.

REFERENCES

Ahluwalia, Pal. *Politics and Post-Colonial Theory: African Inflections.* New York: Routledge, 2001.

Ashcroft, Bill. "Globalism, Post-Colonialism and African Studies." In *Post-Colonialism: Culture and Identity in Africa,* edited by Pal Ahluwalia and Paul Nursrey-Bray. Commack, NY: Nova Science Publishers, 1997.

Awolowo, Obafemi. *The Problems of Africa: The Need for Ideological Reappraisal.* London: Macmillan, 1977.

Azikiwe, Nnamdi Zik. *A Selection from the Speeches of Nnamdi Azikiwe.* Cambridge University Press, 1961.

Balewa, Alhaji Sir Abubakar Tafawa. *Nigeria Speaks: Speeches Made Between 1957 and 1964.* University of Lagos Press, 1966.

Bratton, Michael. "The 'Alternation Effect' in Africa," *Journal of Democracy* 15, no. 4 (October 2004): 147–158.

Brautigam, Dwight D. "The 'Mauritius Miracle': Democracy, Institutions, and Economic Policy." In *State, Conflict and Democracy in Africa,* edited by Richard Joseph. Boulder, Colo.: Lynne Reinner, 1999.

Chabal, Patrick. *Africa Works: Disorder as Political Instrument.* Bloomington, IN: Indiana University Press, 1999.

Diamond, Larry and Marc F. Plattner, eds. *Economic Reform and Democracy.* Baltimore: Johns Hopkins University Press, 1995.

Edie, Carlene J. "Democracy in the Gambia: Past, Present, and Prospects for the Future," *Africa Development* XXV, no3/4 (2000).

Edozie, Rita Kiki. "Sudan's Identity Wars and Democratic Route to Peace." In *Perspectives on Contemporary Ethnic Conflict: Primal Violence or the Politics of Conviction?,* edited by Saha Santosh, 225–250. Lanham, MD: Lexington Books, 2006.

Fatton, Robert. *The Making of a Liberal Democracy: Senegal's Passive Revolution, 1975–1985.* Boulder, CO: Lynne Rienner, 1987.

Forsyth, David P., and Barbara Ann Rieffer. "U.S. Foreign Policy and Enlarging the Democratic Community," *Human Rights Quarterly* 22, no. 4 (2000).

Garang, John. *John Garang Speaks.* Edited by Mansour Khalid. London, KPI, 1987.

Glickman, Harvey. "Frontiers of Liberal and Non-Liberal Democracy in Africa," *Journal of Asian and African Studies* 23, no. 3–4 (1988): 234–254.

Heilbrunn, John R. *Markets, Profits, and Power: The Politics of Business in Benin and Togo.* Bordeaux: Institut d'Etudes Politiques de Bordeaux, 1996.

Houngnikpo, Mathurin C. *Determinants of Democratization in Africa: A Comparative Study of Benin and Togo.* Lanham, MD: University Press of America, 2001.

Huntington, Samuel P. *The Third Wave: Democratization in the Late Twentieth Century.* Normal: University of Oklahoma Press, 1991.

Hyden, Goran. *No Shortcuts to Progress: African Development Management in Perspective.* Berkeley: University of California Press, 1983.

Kenyatta, Jomo. *Facing Mount Kenya.* New York: Vintage Books, 1962.

Lemarchand, Rene. *Rwanda and Burundi.* London: Pall Mall Publishers, 1970.

Lijphart, Arend. *Democracy in Plural Societies: A Comparative Exploration.* New Haven: Yale University Press, 1977.

Macpherson, Crawford. *The Real World of Democracy.* Toronto: CBC Enterprises, 1983.

Markakis, John and Michael Waller. *Military Marxist Regimes in Africa.* London: Frank Cass, 1986.

Markovitz, Irving Leonard. *Léopold Sédar Senghor and the Politics of Negritude.* New York: Atheneum, 1969.

Monga, Célestin. *The Anthropology of Anger.* Boulder, CO: Lynne Rienner, 1996.

Museveni, Yoweri. *Sowing the Mustard Seed: The Struggle for Freedom and Democracy in Uganda.* London: Macmillan, 1997.

Nwabueze, B.O. *Military Rule and Constitutionalism in Nigeria.* Ibadan: Spectrum Law Publications, 1992.

Nyerere, Julius. *Freedom and Development.* Oxford University Press, 1973.

———. "Ujamaa: The Basis of African Socialism." In *Government and Politics in Africa,* edited by Okwudiba Nnoli. Harare: AAPS Books, 2000.

Otite, Onigu, ed. *Themes in African Social and Political Thought.* Enugu, Nigeria: Fourth Dimension Publishers, 1978.

Pinkney, Robert. *Democracy in the Third World.* Boulder, Colo.: Lynne Reinner Publishers, 2003.

Plattner, Marc F. "From Liberalism to Liberal Democracy." In *The Global Divergence of Democracies,* edited by Larry Diamond and Marc F. Plattner, 78–82. Baltimore, MD: Johns Hopkins University Press, 2001.

Prakash, Gyan. *After Colonialism: Imperial Histories and Postcolonial Displacements.* Princeton University Press, 1995.

Edozie, Rita Kiki. "Rwanda-Burundi's 'National-Ethnic' Dilemma: Democracy, Deep Divisions, and Conflict Re-Represent." In *Ethnicity and Sociopolitical Change in Africa and Other Developing Countries: A Constructive Discourse in State Building,* edited by Santosh C. Saha. Lanham, MD: Lexington Books, 2008.

Schapera, Isaac. *Handbook of Tswana Law and Custom.* London: Oxford University Press, 1938.

Shivji, Issa. *State and Constitutionalism: An African Debate on Democracy.* Harare, Zimbabwe: SAPES Trust, 1991.

Sklar, Richard. "Democracy in Africa," *The African Studies Review* XXV, no. 3/4 (September/December 1983): 11–24.

van Hensbroek, Pieter Boele. *Political Discourses in African Thought, 1860 to the Present.* Westport, CT: Praeger, 1999.

Vaughan, Olufemi. *Chiefs, Power, and Social Change: Chiefship and Modern Politics in Botswana, 1880s–1990s.* Trenton, NJ: Africa World Press, 2003.

Wamba-dia-Wamba, Ernest. "Beyond Elite Politics of Democracy in Africa," *Quest* 6, no. 1 (1992).

Werbner, Richard. *Reasonable Radicals and Citizenship in Botswana: The Public Anthropology of Kalanga Elites.* Bloomington, IN: Indiana University Press, 2004.

Wiredu, Kwasi. "Democracy and Consensus in African Traditional Politics: A Plea for a Non-party Polity." In *Postcolonial African Philosophy: A Critical Reader,* edited by Emmanuel Chukwudi Eze, 303–312. Cambridge, MA: Blackwell, 1997.

Young, Crawford. "The End of the Post-Colonial State in Africa? Reflections on Changing African Political Dynamics," *African Affairs* 103, no. 23–49 (2004).

Zakaria, Fareed. "The Rise of Illiberal Democracy," *Foreign Affairs,* November/December 1997.

Chapter 11

YOUR BLUES AIN'T MY BLUES[1]
How "International Security" Breeds Conflicts in Africa

Siba Grovogui

The ideas of national independence, postcolonial emancipation, and African dignity generated a great deal of optimism after World War II. This initial optimism has given way to harsh realities: political repression, civil strife, and declines in health, economy, and environment. How did the optimistic scenarios of decolonization give way to total insecurity and impoverishment in the contemporary global era? How did endemic civil wars come to prevail where once the future looked so bright? As often happens, the symptoms are easier to identify than a diagnosis. Indeed, the symptoms are unmistakable. The descent into the abyss began when authoritarian rulers equated national unity and political stability with unquestioned submission to their imposed political and economic orthodoxies. Political repression ensued against opposition parties and anyone who demanded transparency and accountability in the management of the affairs of state. Where ruling coalitions had once been solicitous of all, single-party states turned to repression when it became difficult to deliver political consensus and economic prosperity. Under these conditions, the state could no longer claim credibly to rule on behalf of the nation. Wary populations withdrew support and, therefore, legitimacy from the state. In some cases, this erosion of domestic legitimacy led to civil wars and ethnic conflicts that produced millions of refugees and diseased communities.

I begin the current inquiry with the supposed symptoms of the African crisis because they have led to fantastic suppositions and conclusions. This is particularly true of those who would attribute the failings of the postcolonial order solely to the corruption of public institutions and the unscrupulousness of African leaders.[2] The first supposition leads to the conclusion that the Westphalian regime of sovereignty was ill suited to postcolonial African states and that the "international community" (from which Africa is excised) was ill advised to grant sovereign equality to African states in the first place.[3] According to this thesis, the immunities granted to postcolonial leaders under the rule of sovereignty-as-enclosed-territory allowed dictators and authoritarians[4]

---

[1] This title is inspired by Bebe Moore Campbell's *Your Blues Ain't Like Mine* (New York: Ballantine Books, 1993).

[2] Jean-Francois Bayart, "Africa in the World: A History of Extraversion," *African Affairs* 99 (2000): 217–267.

[3] Pierre Englebert, "The Contemporary African State: Neither African nor State," *Third World Quarterly* 18, no. 4 (1997): 767–775.

[4] Robert H. Jackson and Carl G. Rosberg, *Personal Rule in Black Africa* (Berkeley, CA: University of California Press); Robert Kaplan, "The Coming Anarchy," *Atlantic Monthly*, February 1994, 44–76; Stephen Krasner, "Realism, Imperialism, and Democracy," *Political Theory* 20, no. 1 (1992): 38–51; Christopher Clapham, *Africa and the International System: The Politics of State Survival* (Cambridge University Press, 1996).

to repress and embezzle with impunity at the expense of their own populations.[5] Despite the fact that this argument is incoherent, it is often advanced as justification for so-called humanitarian interventions in Africa.

I do not dispute the symptoms of the so-called African condition, but I do question the diagnosis according to which "Africa" has fallen under the weight of its own politics, cultures, and traditions. This diagnosis is fraught with analytical errors, ideological confusions, and historical omissions. It assumes that the departing colonial powers bestowed upon the successor postcolonial states a certain institutional coherence reflected by constitutional orders that purposefully aspired to domestic legitimacy and international credibility. It also assumes that the postcolonial state had the aptitude and capacity to create and maintain a secure environment for the nation and defend itself against competing entities. In fact, the symbolic fit between the postcolonial state and the "nation" was invariably assumed but could not be realized under the instituted constitutional orders. Postcolonial constitutions were invariably derived from historically and geographically contingent circumstances that had no bearing on domestic African institutions and practices. In the main, they were not resonant with "native" processes and systems of production, distribution, and consumption. Nor were they intended to promote and sustain forms of life, economy, and politics that made sense in their particular temporal and spatial African contexts. In short, the identities and subjectivities affected under the postcolonial constitutional order seldom corresponded with the expressed desires, values, and interests of the social bodies that composed it.

This situation is the context of security and insecurity. Yet disciplinary representations of security and insecurity have remained confusing. The confusion did not arise solely from the failure of the postcolonial state to clearly stipulate the purpose of social life, the goal and object of security, and the boundaries of intervention in the event of insecurity. Analysts failed to consider the life-forms implicated in the conception of security. They interrogated the relationships between state and citizens, but few ventured in their investigations beyond the Westphalian common sense regarding the traditional duties of the state: to secure border and to protect the lives, rights, and liberties of individuals. This emphasis was misleading because the subjects and objects of protection were not universal. Nor were the conception of security and its attendant legal obligations derived from inclusive debates about life and its modalities in the spaces of their enactment. More often than not, the conceptions of security did not reflect the exigencies of social life (for instance, solidarity and justice) and their reproduction through systems of production, distribution, and consumption. This situation was compounded by the fact that the extent and requirements of security are not the exclusive by-product of domestic processes. They have emanated at times from an international system dominated by the concerns of hegemonic powers that may or may not coincide with the preoccupations of postcolonial citizens. In this latter regard, for instance, the Sahelian states of Mali and Niger have recently clashed with their nomadic populations over specific forms of control of population and borders mandated by the United Nations Security Council as part of the internationalization of the so-called war against terrorism, after September 11, 2001. The related measures exacerbated an ongoing degradation of the environment due to drought in Mali and the extraction of uranium in Niger.

---

[5] Robert H. Jackson, "Juridical Statehood in Sub-Saharan Africa," *Journal of International Affairs* 46, no. 1 (1992a): 1–16; Robert H. Jackson, *Quasi-States: Sovereignty, International Relations and the Third World* (Cambridge University Press, 1992); and Stephen Krasner, "Structural Causes and Regime Consequences: Regimes as Intervening Variable," *International Organizations* 36 (Spring 1982): 185–205.

The illustrations for the above come from political contests in Mali (and to some extent Niger). These two states are inhabited by sedentary and nomadic populations whose relationships to space, land, and state necessarily differ due to their distinct if not contradictory requirements of life. As a result, they have maintained uneasy coexistence, punctuated by agreements on and contestations over land tenure systems, the spatial allocations of authority, and resources. The obtained social landscapes and life-forms have produced distinct notions of authority and legitimacy of the state. Contestations and disagreements over the organization of state and society have led to violent confrontations between the states and their nomadic populations. So, too, have external mandates, particularly the colonial state and today's hegemonic powers acting through the United Nations, been equally constraining structures to domestic entities in Mali and Niger. Specifically, their suggested modes of control have provoked nomads into rebellion more than once. Related events illustrate the problematic of security as it relates to the protection of the constitutional order, the regulation of life, access to resources, and, therefore, the possibility of life.

The discussions allude to relations between, on the one hand, the introduction of liberal forms of property, land tenure systems, and the disintegration of systems of solidarity and, on the other hand, the eruption of near-civil war at the time of drought, when mobility and access to natural resources become ever more indispensable to the survival of nomads. The discussions also revisit past institutions of resource management and cohabitation in the zones of transition between the Sahel and the Sahara. Finally, it is argued that the Cold War actualized an ethos of permissiveness in Africa and that the threatened populations responded in kind with violence of their own against the state and its symbols. These discussions are intended to highlight competing structures of authority and related questions of legitimacy and state capacity beyond Mali and Niger. The particulars are by no means exhaustive accounts; nor are they intended adjudication of past conflicts, their causes, and resolutions. I merely wish to underscore, firstly, the contexts in which the organization of security by the state and the international system imperils certain populations; and, secondly, the lessons and manners in which past institutions could be selectively mobilized for solutions to today's conflicts. In any case, the actualization of security depends principally on the legitimacy of both particular conceptions of it and the structure of authority underlying them. In this light, insecurity may be the outcome of the breakdown of legitimacy, authority, and their related ideologies of security and not necessarily a function of state capacity to impose itself.

Countering Hegemony and Being Trampled Upon

The first moment of insecurity and violence in postcolonial Africa coincided with decolonization or, more accurately, the transfer of power from former colonial powers to politically independent African states. This moment was the culmination of three epic events: the revolt of the formerly colonized against the West, the desire to democratize the international order, and the search for domestic constitutional orders that responded to the needs of the citizenries. African colonies were not alone in this pursuit. China, Indonesia, India, Pakistan, Indochina, and many other countries were involved in related post–World War II struggles against colonizing imperial systems built by and around European colonial powers and their settled outposts in the Americas, Australia, and elsewhere. Japan, which played a significant role in the imperial adventure, was also a target of anti-imperialist and anticolonial struggle. The anti-imperialist revolt was the most important event of the twentieth century because it liberated many millions more people from tyranny than did the collapse of the Soviet empire—the second most significant political event of that century.

Political independence allowed Africans to dream of an alternative moral order. This time, the struggle and its outcome were more muddled. Decolonization, it must be remembered, was founded upon three predicates: *nationhood* and African *dignity;* social *justice* and a "return to the source," or greater reliance on African cultural and intellectual resources; and *racial equality* and a distinct African perspective on world affairs. At independence, it was not uncommon for African leaders to aspire to unify fragmented nations around the principles of solidarity, equality, and mutual respect. Although they held contrasting perceptions of African identity, the majority of African leaders shared the view that private life and public authority could be molded into new forms of government reflecting indigenous material cultures, social relations, and spiritual values. They also held that political unity was necessary for forging nations out of disparate religious, linguistic, and cultural groups. As ideologies, these beliefs led to reliance on centralized welfare states as means to counter the evils of fragmentation that had manifested themselves in many instances prior to independence (in Congo Leopoldville) or soon after (with the 1963 military coup in Togo and the 1965–1969 Nigerian civil war). These events were evidence that certain forms of political contests bore dangers for the new Africa states. The centralized state emerged as the most effective instrument for distributing the spoils of national independence: schools, hospitals, bridges, and soccer fields, among other things.

This period of postcolonial African history did not last long. The economic crisis of the 1970s robbed even well-meaning and sincere African leaders of the capacity to deliver on their promises. So, too, did misguided economic plans contribute to the onset of the coming miseries. From forced villagization in Tanzania to the forced collective farms of Guinea-Conakry, few Afro-socialists seem to find the right recipes for development.[6] By contrast, Western politicians and theorists placed misguided faith in the inequitable liberal capitalist orders of such diverse states as Liberia, Côte d'Ivoire, and Kenya.[7] As it happened, these states also underwent economic stagnation. The crisis, its mismanagement, and the resulting social tensions brought to the fore politically tolerable, but morally deficient dimensions of decolonization—the political usurpation of the wills and desires of the majorities by minorities of elites. While anticolonialism had been a generalized phenomenon, African leaders had not been sufficiently solicitous of the majorities of their constituencies during the transfer of power from colonial administrations to postcolonial governments. This exclusion of citizens was particularly glaring during the drafting and adoption of postcolonial constitutions.

This oversight of the majority of citizens' interests everywhere was intrinsic to the transfer of power, which occurred typically as the outcome of negotiations between colonial European ruling elites and their postcolonial African counterparts. As a result, the risk always existed that the institutions of postcolonial governance and the processes that ensued would not capture the imaginaries of life, politics, and society of domestic constituents. During the period of initial decolonization, the most significant moment of betrayal came to light after economic collapse when African rulers relied for survival on the utility and instrumentalities of state violence. Regardless of their ideological commitments, leaders frequently invoked the state and national interest to evade questions of legitimacy and accountability. A few decades into national independence, the state could monopolize and deploy violence credibly and at will. Before long, however, the state could not deploy violence without drawing comparison with the colonial state

---

[6] Goran Hyden, *Beyond Ujamaa* (Portsmouth, NH: Heinemann, 1980); see also James C. Scott, *Seeing Like the State* (New Haven: Yale University Press, 1999).

[7] Crawford Young, *Ideology and Development in Africa* (New Haven, CT: Yale University Press, 1982).

and, thus, encountering resistance. This bode ill for all parties because nonstate actors could muster the resources, external financial support and, therefore, sufficient materials and organizational structures to mount counter-hegemonic "national" projects. The only question was whether the counter-hegemonic project would cause the state to radically rethink the constitutional order or face collapse under armed assault.

Constitutional deficiency alone does not account for the absurdity and excessive violence that followed the collapse of the state. African states were also caught up in global relationships of hegemony typified by the Cold War. While the Cold War and its attendant strategies instilled stability at the core of the international system, particularly within and among the two competing European blocs, they stripped postcolonial states of the capacity to envisage an alternative international order. The emergent states were confronted with a simple policy option—a "necessary choice" between two politico-military and socioeconomic camps. In Africa, the 1960–1964 Congo crisis and the 1954–1962 Algerian war dashed continental hopes for an international order hospitable to local and national interests. Specifically, the assassination of Patrice Lumumba and the economic and cultural clauses of the Évian Franco-Algerian accord signaled that, although the former colonial powers had accepted the inevitability of decolonization, they were equally determined to maintain their hegemonic positions within the postcolonial order. This signal was reinforced by the North Atlantic Treaty Organization's (NATO) support for Portugal's reluctance to relinquish control of Guinea Bissau, Cape Verde, Angola, and Mozambique.

It is significant that the obstinacy of the fascist regime in Portugal in retaining power in its colonies in Africa—Angola, Mozambique, and Guinea and Cape Verde—followed the institution of apartheid in South Africa and the Unilateral Declaration of Independence that instilled a White minority regime in Southern Rhodesia led by Ian Smith. Both White minority regimes professed to be strong Western allies and a bulwark against communism in Africa. While the Black majority in Rhodesia forced Ian Smith to relinquish power, the apartheid regime was incorporated in Ronald Reagan's policy to "roll back" communism. The Reagan regime not only allied South Africa with its policy of subverting the Angolan and Mozambican communist governments, it also rewarded South Africa in the latter's attempt to retain political and economic influence over the mandate territory of South West Africa (now Namibia). In this context, the two rival superpowers institutionalized their "balance of terror" into exportable fragments that would play out in the local "theaters" of the former Portuguese colonies and in Namibia. There, as in Congo and Algeria previously, NATO allies supported near-sadistic, anticommunist militias whose purpose was to subvert the process of decolonization.

This scenario was part of the larger Reagan Doctrine, which itself was a logical extension of U.S. containment policy. From 1948 to 1989, this policy formed the genetic structure for the production and distribution of violence and its means. Under the rubric of the Cold War, it established the context of permissiveness and licentiousness with which violence was brought to bear for political ends. Rival superpowers took turns in absolving allied states of their responsibility for violence by lending legitimacy to violence under competing ideological schemes. While giving political credence to ideological allies, the United States and the Soviet Union also provided material support to nonstate actors whose principal aim was the military defeat of their declared enemies. This is not to say that such groups had no legitimate grievances against their particular states and individual rulers. It is to say that violence—wanton and indiscriminate—found its place as the primary mode of political opposition with the assistance and guidance of "global players."

Cold War alliances did not serve the interests of the majority within postcolonial states. Instead, they elevated to prominence a class of politicians and elites who depended on military violence, political fanaticism, and ideological intolerance to survive. As a result, although the global Cold War ended without direct military engagement between the superpowers or their respective European blocs, it created an ethos of violence as the principal mode of policing lesser powers by the so-called great powers. Specifically, the superpowers directly provided the means of violence, including landmines, cluster bombs, and tracking devices. The superpowers also christened terror tactics as legitimate tools of combat. The above contradicts Robert Kaplan[8] and other Western theorists of the failed state thesis, according to which a certain vulgarization of violence in Africa today is the result of fierce domestic competition over power and dwindling resources.

In fact, the maiming of civilians and the recruitment of child soldiers did not originate in the 1990s. These activities came to prominence in Mozambique in the 1980s when the anticommunist Resistência Nacional Moçambicana (Renamo) sought to unseat the then Marxist government in Maputo. Renamo received material support from apartheid South Africa and private U.S. Cold War warriors. So-called Cold War hawks in the Reagan administration remained largely indifferent to Renamo's actions, despite condemnations from the U.S. State Department.[9] The sadistic reduction of villagers into slave laborers initiated in the 1990s by the Revolutionary United Front (RUF) in Sierra Leone was not new either. It began with Jonas Savimbi, leader of the anticommunist União Nacional para a Independência Total de Angola (Unita) and an occasional visitor to the Reagan White House. Unita placed a military vice on diamond-rich regions of Angola, allowing Savimbi and his militias to enrich themselves and fund their insurgency against the Marxist government in Luanda. Although ragtag groups in West Africa may use the same strategy today, it had been the hallmark of an African Cold War warrior who was proclaimed a freedom fighter by Ronald Reagan.

The above suggests that today's "bad" behaviors and practices are not constitutive of an "indigenous" African scourge. Their internalization came about only because the so-called great powers guaranteed or christened their success through direct material and political support. In other words, the theater of violence may be Africa, but, thankfully, the actors are few and do not have wide support within society. Significantly, the forms of today's political violence differ markedly from others in recent African history. For instance, anticolonial wars of independence varied normatively and qualitatively from today's anti-system violence. Military activities associated with the former did not deliberately target civilians. Nor did they aim strategically for strict military victory. These struggles were not military per se, and their leaders were not professional soldiers and militiamen. The struggles also had larger sociocultural aims in that they sought to assemble political societies and their base communities under the rubric of the nation. Likewise, precolonial, intercommunal confrontations were largely moderated and regulated by the desire for justice, accommodation, and collective survival. As we show later in the context of the Sahel, the terms of conflicts and violence in precolonial political contests were largely understood such that the total destruction of the adversary was seldom an aim. Rival armies and militias preserved the ability of vanquished societies to sustain life.

---

[8] Robert Kaplan, "The Coming Anarchy," *Atlantic Monthly,* February 1994.

[9] "Renamo Denies Charges; Allegations Called 'Disinformation,'" *Washington Post,* January 24, 1988.

In examining violence in today's Africa, therefore, one must distinguish between three separate concerns: the first is whether the anticolonial imaginary was ever plausible and, if so, whether the postcolonial constitutional collapse may be linked to a deviation from the original imaginary that mobilized masses of Africans for decolonization. The first concern is separate from the second: whether there is a connection or not between, on the one hand, disillusion and rejection of the discredited postcolonial state and, on the other, the current instrumentalization of violence and its elevation as proper political idiom. The third and last concern is the question of the imputability of acts of violence to their perpetrators. Unfortunately, these three issues are frequently lumped together in a bid to redirect African politics toward support for notions of security and securitization that have little relevance to either the everyday of most Africans or the long-term strategic interests of postcolonial entities.

In what remains, I argue that, once again, today's conceptions of global security, particularly in the era following the terrorist incidents of September 11, 2001, in the United States, are dangerous for the postcolonial African society, culture, and life. The tragic U.S. events have led to changes in U.S. assistance to African states. These include the resurrection of "practices previously associated with police aid during the Cold War."[10] Hence, from Senegal on the southwestern edge of the Sahel to Somalia and Kenya to the southeast, the United States has initiated new "police assistance programs" to local governments. Among them, the Trans-Sahara Counter-Terrorism Partnership is driven by a "terrorist-threat" ideology of security intended to bolster the capacity of local governments to fight terrorism. The accompanying policy instruments may or may not be flawed, but the pursuit of the global strategy will result in unwelcome changes within the concerned states.

The new global policies have already spilled over into the Sahelian states of Mali and Niger, which in the 1990s had made peace with their Tuareg populations. The conflict in Mali began in the 1970s when, under the dictatorship of Moussa Traoré, the nomadic Tuareg suffered severe hardship during exceptional droughts that destroyed a large part of their livelihoods, especially their herds. Feeling abandoned by their state, thousands of young Tuareg took refuge in southern Libya. In the 1980s, they began a struggle for recognition by and autonomy from the central government. The government ignored their social and economic grievances. This led to a conflict that lasted until March 27, 1996. The conflict ended under the leadership of Alpha Omar Konaré, the post-dictatorship, democratic government of Mali. The agreement, which was symbolized by the Flame of Peace ceremony in Timbuktu,[11] allowed the integration of the Tuareg within the body politic. Now, it seems, new antiterrorist security states have the military means and "international" support to alter past agreements and to unilaterally impose their wills on dissident populations. The same scenario applies in Niger, where Tuareg have long faced multiple dangers, including an environmental disaster linked to the exploitation of uranium (a strategic resource!) by the French conglomerate Areva. Here, too, the state has adopted national security measures

---

[10] Alice Hills, "Trojan Horses? USAID, Counterterrorism and Africa's Police," *Third World Quarterly* 27, no. 4 (2006): 629–643.

[11] European Centre for Conflict Prevention, with IFOR and the Coexistence Initiative of the State of the World Forum, "People Building Peace: How the Touareg Rebellion Came to an End"; see also Robin E. Poulton and Ibrahim ag Youssouf, "A Peace of Timbuktu: Democratic Governance, Development and African Peacemaking" (New York and Geneva: United Nations, 1998).

Map 11.1 External Resource Interests and Involvement in African Conflicts

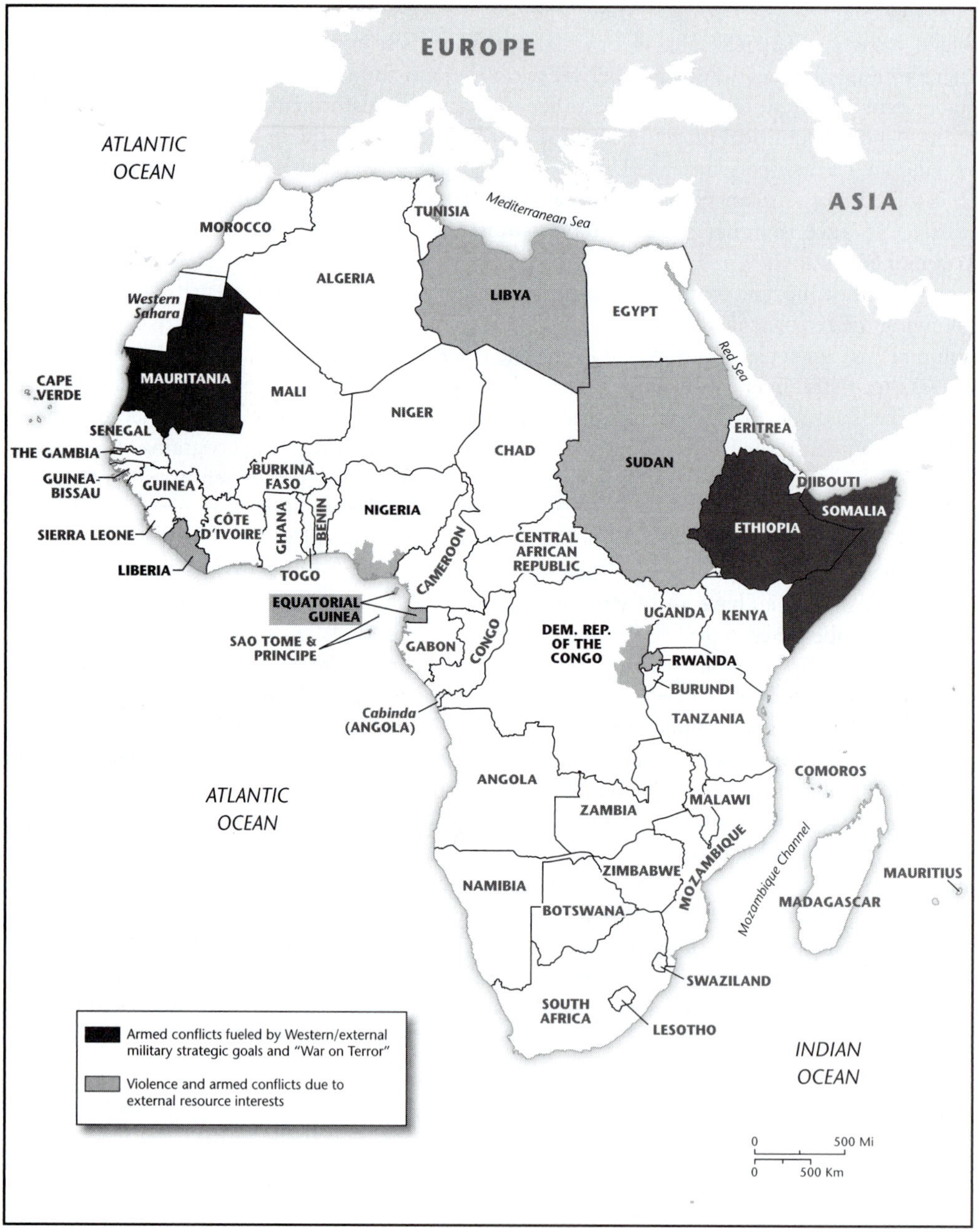

EUROPE

ATLANTIC OCEAN

ASIA

Mediterranean Sea

MOROCCO

TUNISIA

ALGERIA

LIBYA

EGYPT

Western Sahara

Red Sea

CAPE VERDE

MAURITANIA

MALI

NIGER

CHAD

ERITREA

SUDAN

DJIBOUTI

SENEGAL

THE GAMBIA

GUINEA BISSAU

GUINEA

BURKINA FASO

SOMALIA

SIERRA LEONE

CÔTE D'IVOIRE

GHANA

BENIN

TOGO

NIGERIA

CAMEROON

CENTRAL AFRICAN REPUBLIC

ETHIOPIA

LIBERIA

EQUATORIAL GUINEA

SAO TOME & PRINCIPE

GABON

CONGO

DEM. REP. OF THE CONGO

UGANDA

KENYA

RWANDA

BURUNDI

TANZANIA

Cabinda (ANGOLA)

ATLANTIC OCEAN

ANGOLA

ZAMBIA

MALAWI

COMOROS

MOZAMBIQUE

Mozambique Channel

MAURITIUS

ZIMBABWE

NAMIBIA

BOTSWANA

MADAGASCAR

SWAZILAND

SOUTH AFRICA

LESOTHO

INDIAN OCEAN

Legend:
- Armed conflicts fueled by Western/external military strategic goals and "War on Terror"
- Violence and armed conflicts due to external resource interests

0   500 Mi
0   500 Km

that allow the repression of rebellious Tuareg and the indefinite imprisonment of journalists who adver-tise their plight.[12]

These cases serve to highlight crucial relationships between political violence (of particular sorts) and ideological representations of insecurity—an acute internal physical or psychological experience or sentiment of imminent or real external affliction. It is often argued in discourses surrounding the "global war on terrorism" that the aim of the accompanying security measures is to remedy or prevent afflictions, experiences, and sentiments of violence resulting from the actions and activities of terrorists, who practice "terror" (an objective affliction) and "terrorism" (the resulting experiences and senti-ments). Less evident are the effects of global security measures on the capacities of the citizenries of lesser powers (for instance, those of Mali and Niger) to maintain meaningful lives. This concern will inform the remainder of this essay; it is central for those embarking on a reconstructivist agenda for Africa and, thus, requires exploration of the constitutive practices and institutions of the global war on terrorism as it pertains to specific populations, in this case, to the Tuareg of Mali and Niger.

Modernizing Insecurity: Development, Drought, and Civil War

Although the Sahel is afflicted by cyclical droughts, all observers agree that the drought of the 1970s was exceptionally harsh. The physical harshness of the environment was compounded by the social and psychological effect of abandonment by the state. Indeed, it is common sense that for centuries the nomadic and agrarian peoples of countries bordering the Sahara desert—Senegal, Mauritania, Niger, and Mali—had developed grazing, traditional storage, irrigation, trade, and import mechanisms to lessen the impact of famine. Tuareg had learned to cope with climatic changes through migration, resource management arrangements with less vulnerable southern farming communities, and dependable modes of solidarity. These institutions and practices had been decimated under various modernization projects beginning in the colonial and postcolonial eras. This added to the inability of Tuareg to cope with the 1970s drought, leading to the sentiment of imminent abandonment by the state—and their neighbors.

In Mali, conflict erupted in the 1970s and 1980s in the Fifth Administrative Region, currently located where the semi-autonomous state of Macina once stood. The region assembles more than eight different groups, from the delta Fulani agro-pastoralists (ex-Macina) to Sahel Fulani transhumant pastoralists to Moors and Tuareg livestock traders. Here, for centuries, resident populations knew and complied with the rules of an institution called the *dina*.[13] Again, it is difficult to generalize about any society and its past, and it is not my intention to reproduce the past. This brief allusion to the *dina* is therefore intended to show that prior to colonialism and national independence, the communities of today's Mali had developed insti-tutions for the management of resources.[14] From the fourteenth century onward, Peulh (Fulbe) herders, particularly the Tuculors who conquered villages at the periphery of the dryland of the Sahel, experimented

---

[12] For illustration of the treatment of the press and journalists who report on the Tuareg rebellion in Niger, see "Moussa Kaka," Reporters Sans Frontières, www.rsf.org/article.php3?id_article=23911.

[13] See FAO Corporate Documents Repository, "Community Forestry: Herders' Decision-Making in Natural Resources Management in Arid and Semi-arid Africa," 1978.

[14] John W. Bennett et al., "Land Tenure and Livestock Development in Sub-Saharan Africa," *Aid Evaluation Special Study*, no. 39 (Land Tenure Center, University of Wisconsin-Madison for U.S. Agency for International Development, May 1986), 90–91.

with the *dina* as means of rationalization of resource use and integration of captive populations into a general economy dominated by the captors' values. It is evident from its origin that some practices, including raids and enslavement, associated with the *dina* were variously resisted by conquered communities and ran counter to modern ethics of development. On the other hand, the *dina* system brought order and a functional economy to a region prone to drought, limited resources, and conflict over resources. In this region, the *dina* gave rise to coordinated management of land and land improvement techniques, systems of grazing reserves, deferment schemes of grazing, and water and fishing development.

When it operated, the *dina* system served as the basis for conceptions of production and distribution, solidarity and entitlements, and justice and ethics. Contrary to what has often been claimed, the *dina* did not merely give rise to "pasture-control systems based on ownership of wells and general territorial claims based on the contest of arms, treaty, and tribute."[15] It emerged from centuries-old collaboration and contestations that led different groups, under the initiative of the Moors and Tuareg, to elaborate systems of solidarity and justice. The *dina* took a long time to implement, and it is not my intention to claim that all Fulani adhered to it[16] or that it was equally advantageous to all. For instance, the *dina* helped "the Toucouleurs in their forays into the periphery of the Empire."[17] It also suffered strains due to structural constraints and processes of social change. Thus, I do not contend that the *dina* system must be reintroduced in its totality or as it was practiced centuries ago, but I do maintain that it represents ancient reflections on life and, as such, has had significant influence on the life and social relations that developed in the Sahel prior to colonialism and the modernization projects that ensued.

Several social and environmental factors contributed to the decline of the *dina*, but none was more significant than the colonial system.[18] First, French colonial authorities introduced new land tenure systems intended to secure the production of cash crops and supplies the *métropole* needed. Indeed, the introduction of cash crops by the French was followed by the imposition of household taxes. This combination compelled the majority of Africans to produce cash crops at the expense of staple foods. Subsequent laws favored crop expansion and, thus, placed the interests of farmers above those of herders.[19] Second, colonial authorities carved territorial boundaries and districts based on administrative imperatives and the need to defeat resistance. The base redistricting tore apart previously integrated social groups along with the social systems that sustained them. Finally, the French implemented the new boundaries and economies through political cooptation and coercion.[20] These actions further strained relations among social groups.

Colonialism introduced "development" as an ideology and accessory to its modernizing project to secure raw materials, markets, and stability in colonies. The underlying agendas were initially linked directly to Western strategic and commercial interests: to stabilize colonial realms henceforth in the throes of anticolonial nationalism and (presumably) under the threat of communism. The stabilization included the eradication of poverty, disease, and, in the Sahel, desertification and attendant insecurities. Thus, prior to independence but long after Lord Lugard's declaration had tied progress in the colonial world to material advances in Europe, the World Bank Group, the United Nations Development Programme, and other

---

[15] Bennett et al., "Land Tenure and Livestock," 90–91.

[16] "Community Forestry."

[17] ibid.

[18] ibid.

[19] J. Gallais, *Pasteurs et paysans du Gourma: la condition sahelienne* (Paris: CNRS, 1975), 49.

[20] "Community Forestry."

international development agencies invested in extractive industries and agriculture. The initial goal was to guarantee European recovery from the ravages of war and stabilize restless colonies in the wake of pro-independence nationalist revolts. France contributed to this adventure through the Fonds d'Investissement pour le Développement Economique et Social (FIDES). This fund served to promote investment in infrastructure and agriculture in French colonies, from roads to agricultural extensions. The life of FIDES was extended after the independence of colonies with the creation of a ministerial cabinet designed specifically for relations with "friendly" French-speaking African countries. This achievement of the *ministry of cooperation* was the now famed *cooperation technique* and a bureaucratic infrastructure to provide technical assistance to the postcolonies. This bureaucracy was supported by formal training centers and policy institutes such as the Office de Recherche Scientifique et Technique d'Outre-Mer (ORSTOM).

The degree of development intervention depended on the assessment of the challenges faced by each region and colony. In the Sahel, the region bordering the Sahara desert from Senegal to Ethiopia and Somalia, France identified the main problem as social instability due to land conflicts, encroaching desertification, expanding populations, and harmful agricultural and herding practices. But their solutions only created greater social and political instability. Appropriate resource management did not accompany the colonial-induced expansion of crop cultivation into rangelands. This reluctance or inability of colonial authorities, and later the postcolonial government, to reserve areas for grazing, for instance, contributed to overgrazing around water points.[21] Starting in 1916, French authorities introduced measures that slowly destroyed the traditional political organization of the Tuareg, "pushing them away from their traditional lands, segregating them from farmers with whom they had good relations, and reducing the power of the traditional leader (*amenokal*) to that of a tax collector."[22] The result was that the Tuareg lost control over the range and associated territorial rights, preparing the ground for a gradual invasion by outsiders, such as the Fulanis.[23]

The nationalization of land by the independent Malian government and the accompanying land tenure system only compounded the problems created by the colonial administration. The land tenure code and the administrative division of the territory into semi-autonomous zones were intended to rationalize development according to regional specificity[24] and to end food deficiency and political insecurity. The new land tenure system was, thus, meant to replace supposedly antiquated institutions of land and property. The government also introduced new agricultural techniques and fertilizers through agricultural extensions in order to increase the production of foodstuffs and cash crops. These two long-term solutions were interspersed with punctual interventions in times of need—food aid in times of drought[25] and family planning interventions aimed at averting overpopulation in the Sahelian region.

---

[21] See, for instance, M. Horowitz and K. Badi, "Introduction of Forestry in Grazing Systems Forestry for Local Community Development Programme Series," Food and Agriculture Organization of the United Nations, 1981.

[22] E. Bernus, *Touaregs Nigeriens: unite culturelle et diversite regionale d'un peuple pasteur* (Paris : ORSTOM, no. 94, 1981).

[23] ibid.

[24] Gallais, *Pasteurs et paysans*.

[25] The U.S. government established its food aid program in 1954 as Public Law 480. Since then, the program, also known as Food for Peace, has allowed Americans to produce excesses without fear of depressing prices, based on the certainty that the government will commit agricultural surpluses to aid the developing world. Food for Peace also fed, literally, the appetite and capacities of U.S. philanthropic organizations—for example, Care, Save the Children, and Catholic Relief Services—who vied to bring aid to the poor.

These measures proved disastrous for the social, political, and natural environments. Specifically, the introduction of Western-based land tenure systems in Mali altered agricultural and herding practices only to open new avenues to social instability and conflicts. As indicated earlier, they also revived long-forgotten hostility between the Tuareg, a nomadic Berber Muslim people, and central authorities under Moussa Traore. This hostility led to a bloody conflict that lasted until the 1990s. The government and the Tuareg fighters have instrumentalized the plight of the Tuareg. Without supporting any cause or method of conflict, I want to make the important point that the nationalization of land and its subsequent privatization under the new land tenure system resulted in bitter fighting among clans, lineages, and individuals, as well as between regional collectives and two postcolonial governments that introduced Western-inspired land tenure systems and agricultural practices in the name of development. These policies gradually disrupted traditional systems and led to the depletion of resources, the degradation of the environment, and the intensification of social conflicts.

The New International Security Order

Prior to the events of September 11, 2001, there had been a growing recognition in the United States and Europe that land tenure experiments that sought to displace the *dina* had been disastrous. Studies by USAID had backed the view that Mali's *dina* could be reformed or improved upon as a mechanism for "advancing contemporary development policies."[26] A human rights activist and the first democratically elected president after Moussa Traore, Alpha Omar Konare also realized that colonial and postcolonial land tenure laws established land boundaries that often cut across complex pastoral routes, pastures, and agricultural systems.[27] The new system placed private wells, fences, and fodder where once stood a network of agricultural and herding implements used by all. This monopolization of resources by a few, especially traders and their allies in government, exacerbated the sentiment of social abandonment among the Tuareg when the 1970s drought hit. In this context, the attainment of peace and security required reconsideration by the government of development activities with due deference to prior local knowledges and institutions.

The pre–September 11 shift in perspectives concluded a long era of state interventions that either assumed institutional vacuum or inadequate local knowledge and practices in the regions of intervention. The optimists' view of an end to the era of official neglect or contempt for local institutions and practices did not last long. Once again, the question of security is posed in terms of territorial control, reminiscent of an era when the policing and pacification of populations took precedence over their ability to secure life and livelihood under conditions of mobility and flexible institutions.[28] Previously, under Moussa Traore, the Tuareg and the central government seemed to disagree over the extent of the Tuareg's territory. Even the superior military power of the central state did not bring about peace. Nor were its development programs, such as water resources development and disease eradication, sufficient for peace—read pacification. For the Tuareg, the greater issue was the inability of the central

---

[26] Bennett et al., "Land Tenure and Livestock Development," 7.

[27] "Community Forestry."

[28] H. Barral, Les populations nomades de l'Oudalan et leur espace pastoral (Paris : ORSTOM Traveaux et Documentation, no. 77, 1977); M. Benoit, Introduction a la géographie des aires pastorales soudanienne de Haute Volta (Paris : ORSTOM, no. 69, 1997).

government to align the constitutional order and national institutions on preexisting institutions and local knowledges, technologies of resource management, and organizational structures.

To be sure, agencies like the World Bank and the U.S. State Department continue to promote a progressive return to local knowledge and institutions in designing sensible development policies. But the overall U.S. foreign policy objective, in its fight against the forces of terrorism, depends on a return to the securitization of territorial boundaries and on reinforcing state capacities to monitor the activities of its citizens. Hence, USAID now promotes "foreign assistance" as "a key component of [a] comprehensive [U.S.] response to terrorism."[29] With specific reference to Africa, according to USAID, "the overarching goals of U.S. policy in Africa [are] to enhance African capacity to fight terrorism and create favorable conditions for U.S. and African trade and business opportunities."[30] Accordingly, the United States no longer seeks merely to promote "sustained growth, regional stability, good governance, a healthier population and responsible use of natural resources." Now, these objectives are to be combined with education and training of government officials in order to enhance their capacities to blend development and security concerns in ways that converge with U.S. interests and the fight against terrorism.

Having proclaimed African states to be fragile and many on the brink of collapse, Washington policymakers are now liable to interpret the condition of the "African state" as the source of global insecurity and, therefore, of threat.[31] Many Western policymakers have consistently redefined and expanded African development needs to include strengthening state capacity to manage and control political extremism, including terrorism. In order to link security and development, many increasingly hold the view that "insecurity, lawlessness, crime and violent conflict are among the biggest obstacles" to alleviating poverty and underdevelopment in Africa. Accordingly, these circumstances "create fertile conditions for conflict and the emergence of new security threats, including international crime and terrorism."[32] The United States has consistently buttressed the material and communicative capacities of army and police forces once thought in many parts of Africa to be irredeemably corrupt.

In the operation of U.S. national security, the responsibility for Africa falls to U.S. European, Central, and Pacific commands, as well as to the U.S. Special Operations Command and the army, air force, navy, and marines.[33] They "are responsible for conducting active military operations in Africa, including training exercises, humanitarian relief, peacekeeping, evacuating civilians from unstable countries, and other operations."[34] According to Daniel Volman, the United States also sells to most African countries arms and military hardware, including handguns, rifles, shotguns, electronics, police equipment, crowd-control chemicals, and explosives, "through the U.S. Defense Security Cooperation Agency, which falls under the authority of the Assistant Secretary of Defense for International Security Affairs. Some military hardware . . . is sold under a licensing program administered by the Office of Defense Trade Controls under the authority of the U.S. State

---

[29] Alice Hills, "Trojan Horses?" 633.

[30] ibid.

[31] See, for instance, Rita Abrahamson, "Blair's Africa: The Politics of Securitization and Fear," *Alternatives: Global, Local, Political*, 30.

[32] Alice Hills, "Trojan Horses?" 634.

[33] Daniel Volman, "U.S. Military Programs in Sub-Saharan Africa, 2005–2007," *African Security Research Project*, Washington, D.C., March 2006.

[34] ibid.

Department's Bureau of Political-Military Affairs."[35] Funds for peacekeeping training have been channeled until recently through the new Global Peace Operations Initiative (GPOI), "incorporating the African Contingency Operations Training Assistance (ACOTA) program and other U.S. aid channels."[36]

Indeed, according to the defenders of present U.S.-African policy, one the primary U.S. foreign policy goals on the continent must be to "increase Africa's counter-terrorism capabilities, prevent the creation of terrorist safe havens and, coincidentally, secure future energy and resources."[37] This means not only the institution of military training programs, but also the application of U.S. military power to civilian projects ("to dig wells and build schools and veterinary clinics") in order to give it "a record of positive public assistance." Thus, the U.S. military emerges both as a fighting force with intelligence and targeting capabilities and a friendly agent of development assistance.[38]

From the 1990s onward, the United States began to grow increasingly suspicious of groups that sought to overthrow or reform its allies. This suspicion was not limited to individual groups, whose political grievances could now be cast as manifestations of fundamentalism or radicalism, but extended to the institutions that sustained them.[39] These included market, security, and cultural organizations that relied on resources other than those of the state. The United States began to promote monitoring remittances and other money transfers to Islamic movements that they categorized as hard-line. Institutions of learning, like Quranic schools and madrassas, also increasingly came under the scrutiny of the security state. And the United States sought to provide direct military assistance to friendly regimes and establish "direct personal contact with African military leaders" through an effective military presence. The United States would provide a "security assistance program" to African militaries and would train and equip conventional and special forces for contingencies. Finally, the superpower would "stabilize" friendly states in a bid to "save them" from radicals and fundamentalists.

From the 1990s, therefore, U.S. policy would tilt toward the security and military organs of allied states and against elements of civil and political society that sought to transform them. It mattered little that the attempted transformation was constitutional (as in Algeria) or that it was extra-constitutional (as in Somalia). After September 11, countries like Mali were added to the list of those that deserved rescue and stabilization under the Pan-Sahel Initiative (PSI). Under this program, the United States has funded and deployed teams of U.S. Special Operations Forces (SOF) in Mali and has run joint military exercises. Further, the United States has provided equipment and counter-terrorism training to new Malian battalions and specialty units in order to ward off an array of internal and external enemies roaming the Saharan desert. These enemy groups include the Algeria-born Salafists and various al-Qaida groups. Chad, Mauritania, and Niger have benefited from the same programs under PSI and the larger Trans-Sahara Counter-Terrorism Partnership (TSCTP). In exchange, Mali has given the United States access to an airfield near Bamako, the capital of Mali. This facility complements others in several African nations; they are not permanent U.S. bases but serve American forces in crises.

---

[35] ibid.

[36] ibid.

[37] Alice Hills, "Trojan Horses?"

[38] *Jane's Defence Weekly*, 2005

[39] "Somalia's Fundamentalists Fear the Worst," *Guardian Weekly*, December 27, 1992.

Knowledge, Constitutionalism, and the Securitization of Life

It is hard to quarrel with a policy intended to stem political instability and "the rise of negative trends, including radical political Islam" anywhere in the Maghreb, Sahel, or the Horn of Africa.[40] Yet it is problematic that the United States does not try to win over violent Islamic insurgencies with its culture of tolerance and diversity. This is particularly troublesome when the United States is battling those who presumably only tactically support democracy. In the political contests that preceded the fall of the Soviet Union and continue to unfold today in the Muslim world, it is hard to discern democrats from anti-democrats, reformers from fundamentalists.[41] As in the Cold War, new security institutions, with their connections to development, offer pro-Western authoritarian regimes an opportunity to crush trouble-makers (often their political adversaries) while currying favor with Washington. The only requirement for the oppressing state is to present its political adversaries as radical Islamists or fanatics—a replay of yesteryear's epic struggle against communists in which nationalists everywhere could be cast as communists or fellow travelers for the purpose of repression.

Whereas anticolonial forces denounced the destruction of local institutions by the colonial administration, postcolonial arrangements did little to reverse the trend toward subversion of existing social orders and systems. In Mali, as elsewhere, the French-style land tenure system undermined the social order and the capacity of populations to deal with political crisis and famine. The disruption of the preexisting institutions and their instruments under Western-inspired constitutional arrangements contributed to food and social insecurity and near civil war in the 1980s and 1990s. Alarmingly, it also led to the sense of social abandonment and insecurity suffered by Tuareg and other excluded groups. The modern constitutional order alone was not at fault in this situation. The Cold War and French support for Moussa Traore, the Malian dictator, added to the instability of the country.

A Cold War–like scenario of political violence and the destruction of indigenous social orders are on the political horizon today in Mali, Niger, and other Sahelian states. The emergent representations of public safety and social well-being undermine local subjectivities, the exigencies of life in the Sahel, and the systems that ensured secure domestic production, distribution, solidarity, and justice. The norms of the global war on terror have already negatively affected the 1996 peace deal between the central government of Mali and the Tuareg. There is real dissonance between the domestic translation and implementation of the global war on terror in spatial conjectures as Mali and local conceptions of life, identity, and values. For instance, it is evident today in Mali and Niger that governments are not inclined to negotiate while they retain military superiority and international support for policies intended to literally wipe out resistance to the national order. The methods are not local innovations.

There are many casualties of the war on terrorism. First, local identities, subjectivities, and the knowledge that sustained social orders in entire regions are erased. Although the knowledge may remain ensconced in local memory, it is no longer operational in times of stress, such as political conflicts and droughts, because it becomes politically suspect. Nomadism in particular seems to be at odds with the new global antiterrorist regimes of surveillance and population control. For centuries, nomadic culture was founded on long-distance trade and herding, as well as on the ability to move in times of drought to neighboring regions with which nomads had forged sophisticated modes of

---

[40] ibid.

[41] Mai Yamani, "These Moderates Are in Fact Fanatics, Torturers and Killers," *Guardian*, February 6, 2007.

communication, solidarity, and conflict resolution. Common to this way of life were large armies and effective systems of taxation, but war was circumscribed at times due to harsh environmental conditions and the nature of economic activities in the Sahel and the desert. The ethos of the international order conflicts with this culture and the understanding between nomads and their neighbors. Indeed, whereas nomadism requires unconstrained mobility across large swaths of land encompassing many states, the war on terror depends on the ability of states to monitor their borders and the movement of populations within them in such a manner as to identify terrorist elements thought to thrive without borders in the freedom of the desert.

Africa and Africans do have stakes in global security matters, and they should not always chart a course of their own. But it behooves Africans to rediscover the social and symbolic imaginaries that underpinned the anticolonial desire for national independence and political autonomy. All constitutional questions and related issues of security and peace are tied to these imaginaries of society and social activity, solidarity and entitlements, and justice and ethics. Indeed, African elites confuse themselves and those they govern when they do not respond to the basic needs of their own populations in ways that support the kind of life that makes sense to their bases. Traditional life inscribed in social and other systems is even more important than imported constitutional models and the best institutions and practices that arrive with the latest fads from the West.

In short, successful social experiments come into being because they often correspond to the specific material and symbolic conditions of their environments. In the case of Sahel, the social experiments under attack are the result of centuries-old reflections on life, its purpose, and meaning. Their dismantlement, without proper understanding of the alternatives and successful transition, is bound to cause even more instability than currently exists. Further, if violent instability provides cover and fuel for terrorist recruitment and training, we must understand the difference between mobility as nomadism and instability as violent chaos. If we cannot learn to tailor our policies to address this difference, best-laid plans will only hasten our demise.

Conclusion

Political scientists may be correct to trace the causes of conflicts and insecurity in Africa to deficiencies in the constitutional and institutional orders. They may also be correct to point to the inadequacies of the Westphalia model, with its ideas of sovereignty, security, and political life, as the culprit. Indeed, the European models of state, sovereignty, and security—and their ethical norms—succeeded in Europe and the West because they were adapted to the environment in which they emerged. They were not suited for Africa—or at least regions of Africa—whose political trajectories (and, therefore, moral and ethical systems) differed greatly from those of the departing colonial powers.

Specifically, the "security question" in postcolonial Africa does not arise during conflicts. One precedes the other. The vast majority of postcolonial conflicts have their origins in insecurity created by the postcolonial enactment of the anticolonial vision. They arose from moral and institutional gaps between the constitutional orders (often inherited from the West) and the antecedent (anticolonial) visions of state, society, and justice. Indeed, while decolonization allowed for the transfer of the juridical attributes of sovereignty to postcolonial elites, few ruling coalitions aptly espoused a logic of government fitting the postcolonial conditions, whether these related to life, society, or the environment. African ruling elites merely embraced Western norms of constitutional order, power, and social relations. We have seen where that has led the continent.

The genealogy presented here does not just demonstrate that there are indigenous solutions. It also demonstrates that Africa is historical, i.e., that it can change and has changed. The *dina* is not a timeless or ahistorical institution; it developed through negotiation and practice. Colonial and postcolonial violence did not appear out of nowhere. That Africa is doomed to a cyclical and inevitable violence is simply not true. After all, if history repeats itself as this thesis asserts, Africa has many different histories. The question is which history will predominate; not all histories are alike. In any case, we must remind ourselves that the means to political stability and secure social order still reside in African moral systems and their base imaginaries of state, society, and ethics. It is hard to imagine more secure postcolonial orders until they are congruent with embedded visions of justice and equity. Only then, will mechanisms of duty, obligation, reward, and sanction be acceptable to all. This is the only path to peace in Mali, Niger, a reframed Africa, and the world.

REFERENCES

Abrahamson, Rita. "Blair's Africa: the Politics of Securitization and Fear." *Alternatives: Global, Local, Political* 30 (2005).

Barral, H. *Les populations nomades de l'Oudalan et leur espace pastoral*. Paris: ORSTOM No. 77, 1977.

Bayart, Jean-Francois. "Africa in the World: A History of Extraversion." *African Affairs* 99 (2000): 217–67.

Bernus, E. *Touaregs Nigeriens: unite culturelle et diversite regionale d'un peuple pasteur*. Paris: ORSTOM No. 94, 1981.

Benoit, M. *Introduction a la geographie des aires pastorales soudanienne de Haute Volta*. Paris: ORSTOM No. 69, 1997.

Bennett, John W. et al., "Land Tenure and Livestock Development in Sub-Saharan Africa." *Aid Evaluation Special Study* 39 (1986): 90–91.

Campbell, Bebe Moore. *Your Blues Ain't Like Mine*. New York: Ballantine Books, 1993.

Clapham, Christopher. *Africa and the International System: The politics of state survival*. Cambridge: Cambridge University Press, 1996.

Englebert, Pierre. "The Contemporary African State: Neither African nor State." *Third World Quarterly* 18 No. 4 (1997): 767–775.

Gallais, J. *Pasteurs et paysans du Gourma: la condition sahelienne*. Paris: CNRS, 1975.

Hills, Alice. "Trojan Horses? USAID, counterterrorism and Africa's police," *Third World Quarterly* 27 No. 4 (2006): 629–643.

Horowitz, M. and K. Badi. "Introduction of Forestry in Grazing Systems Forestry for Local Community Development Programme Series." Food and Agriculture Organization of the United Nations, 1981.

Hyden, Goran. *Beyond Ujamaa*. Portsmouth, NH: Heinemann, 1980.

Jackson, Robert H. and Carl G. Rosberg. *Personal Rule in Black Africa*. Berkeley: University of California Press, 1982.

Jackson, Robert H. "Juridical Statehood in Sub-Saharan Africa." *Journal of International Affairs* 46 no. 1 (1992):1–16.

Jackson, Robert H. *Quasi-States: Sovereignty, International Relations and the Third World*. Cambridge: Cambridge University Press, 1992.

Kaplan, Robert. "The Coming Anarchy." *Atlantic Monthly*. February, 1994.

Krasner, Stephen. "Realism, Imperialism, and Democracy." *Political Theory* 20 (1992).

Krasner, Stephen. "Structural Causes and Regime Consequences: Regimes as Intervening Variable."' *International Organizations* 36 (1982): 185–205.

Poulton, Robin E. and Ibrahim ag Youssouf. "A Peace of Timbuktu—Democratic Governance, Development and African Peacemaking," United Nations, 1998.

Scott, James C. *Seeing Like the State*. New Haven: Yale University Press, 1999.

Young, Crawford. *Ideology and Development in Africa*. New Haven: Yale University Press, 1982.

Volman, Daniel. "U.S. Military Programs in Sun-Saharan Africa, 2005–2007." African Security Research Project, 2006.

Chapter 12

THE GLOBAL ECONOMIC ORDER AND ITS SOCIOECONOMIC IMPACT

The African Perspective

Fantu Cheru

Africa is once again in the international development spotlight. In September 2000, with its attention on Africa, the international community signaled a renewed commitment to development and the mitigation of poverty and disease by adopting the United Nations Millennium Declaration and the Millennium Development Goals (MDGs). This was followed in 2001 by an agreement reached in Doha, Qatar, to launch, under the auspices of the World Trade Organization (WTO), a new round of trade negotiations, known as the Development Round, specifically to address the needs and concerns of developing countries. Moreover, at its summit held in Kananaskis, Canada, in 2002, the Group of Eight (G8) major industrialized countries adopted an action plan for Africa[1] and agreed that one-half or more of the additional resources pledged at the Monterrey UN Conference on Financing Development (2002) would be channeled to Africa. Again, in 2005, the Commission for Africa, set up by British prime minister Tony Blair, broadly mapped the outlines of what needed to be done to alleviate Africa's development crisis and emphasized the need for bold and extraordinary efforts.[2] All of these millennium initiatives called for special efforts to address the critical challenges confronting Africa.

Why has there been so much interest in Africa by the international community, which since the early 1980s has played a decisive role in dismantling many aspects of the African state in the name of market-oriented reforms? Do these recent initiatives signal a radical break from the past, thus allowing African countries to have the "policy space" to manage their own development independently and unconstrained by remote forces of globalization? Or are the new initiatives merely designed to perpetuate the subordinate position of Africa? The current chapter reframes the discourse on the international political economy of the continent by advocating skepticism regarding the renewed Western interest in helping Africa. Western aid must, in my view, be placed in historical context and should be scrutinized carefully. After all, the *raison d'être* of colonialism was also based on the premise that it is the responsibility of the civilized West to "save Africans from themselves" and help them transition from backwardness to modern societies.

In its contemporary form, many international programs for Africa's development adopted under the auspices of the United Nations in the 1980s and 1990s never lived up to their promises—or their potential.[3] Against the background of past failures, this chapter examines Africa's position in the new

---

[1] G8 Africa Action Plan, 2002 Kananaskis Summit, 2002.

[2] Commission for Africa, *Our Common Interest* (London: Penguin Press, 2005).

[3] United Nations. United Nations Program of Action for African Economic Recovery and Development 1986–1990 (UNPAAERD), Report of the Secretary-General, document A/42/560, New York, October 1, 1987.

global hierarchy. In this chapter, I also recommend the appropriate response that Africans themselves must develop at the national and continental levels to navigate successfully the cold currents of economic globalization. Reframing—understood as the need to explore an alternative to the neoliberal globalization of the "Washington Consensus"—has never been more urgent, given Africa's marginal position in the new global economy and the West's unwillingness to even the playing field of international economic relations.

Globalization and the African Condition

The last quarter of the twentieth century brought tremendous advances in the way human beings organize production, work, trade, and many other aspects of human activity. Accelerated advancements in science and technology, transformations in global trade and investment regimes, and the global compacts on environmental and social policies have been far reaching. These global economic and political shifts, with their contradictory tendencies, pose a great challenge to the African continent. Emerging from colonial subjugation, Africa has simply been ill prepared to adjust to complex global dynamics, exploit new opportunities, and manage internal and external threats, all at the same time.

Indeed, the global economic boom of the past two decades completely bypassed Africa and the continent has the lowest human development index in the world. A staggering number of Africans, at least 50 percent, live in absolute poverty on less than one U.S. dollar per day. And despite globalization, sub-Saharan Africa still plays a marginal role in world trade. Africa's share in world exports and imports has declined from 5 percent in the 1960s to a little over 2 percent in the 1990s.[4] Capital inflows have been low; Africa's share in foreign direct investment (FDI) is only 3 percent of the total, despite the fact that the rate of return to investment in Africa is between 25 and 30 percent, as opposed to 16 to 18 percent for all developing countries. This situation is in stark contrast to the industrialized countries, which have benefited enormously from globalization, and, to a lesser extent, some parts of East Asia and Latin America.

African countries have tried to respond to the challenges posed by globalization by simply "embracing neoliberal globalization" as a development strategy. Few countries have succeeded in defying the policies imposed by the institutions of the world system. "If you cannot fight globalization, you might as well join it" is the slogan most used by countries, such as Ghana and Mozambique. And since the 1980s, governments across the continent, either willingly or under pressure from the international financial institutions (IFIs) through "conditional lending," implemented far-reaching market reforms with few tangible economic benefits in the end. This strategy did little to reduce dependence and marginalization. Poverty and unemployment remain pervasive and the African continent will be the only region in the world that will not be able to achieve the MDGs by 2015. The number of poor people is expected to rise from 315 million in 1999 to 404 million by 2015.[5] For example, Uganda, Ghana, and Mozambique—dubbed Africa's post-adjustment success stories—remain dependent on foreign aid and loans to finance their development and annual social expenditures. The productive sectors of their economies remain stagnant, starved of investment inputs and supporting infrastructures.

Indeed, globalization can have a positive impact on Africa's development, but only if it is guided properly. This brings us face to face with the role of the state in national development. Successful developing

---

[4] Ibi S. Ajayi, "Globalization and Africa," *Journal of African Economies* 12, no. 1 (2003): 120–150.
[5] World Bank, World Development Indicators 2004.

countries have been, not the ones that have opted either for the primacy of the market or the state, but those that have shaped a constructive, mutually supportive relationship between the public and private sectors. The experience of China and India—along with Japan, South Korea, and Taiwan—shows that countries do not have to adopt liberal trade and capital policies in order to benefit from enhanced trade, to grow faster, and to develop an industrial structure to produce an increasing proportion of national consumption.[6] These countries actually grew faster under protective barriers, and only later did they begin to liberalize. In other words, developing countries require policy space to exercise institutional innovations that depart from the old discredited orthodoxies of the WTO, the International Monetary Fund (IMF), and the World Bank. Blind adherence to market integration is a prescription for disaster.

The "Golden" Years: Decolonization and the National Development Project

Africa's current economic and political predicament is intimately linked to its colonial past. Starting with the slave trade in 1650 and continuing under colonial rule after the Berlin Conference of 1884, the continent had been heavily drawn into the centers of capitalist accumulation but always as a subordinate partner whose primary role was to contribute to the development of rival capitalist powers.[7] Not only did the colonial system stunt basic economic and political structures, but it also shaped the nature of social and ethnic relations that continues to bedevil the continent until the present. Africa's subordinate role in the world changed relatively little in the postindependence period as the continent became the battleground in the Cold War between the West and the Soviet Union.

With the attainment of political independence, African countries embarked on programs of nation building and national development designed to bring the fruits of social and economic growth to all sections of the population. Over the next fifteen years, physical infrastructures were greatly improved, particularly in the areas of health, education, and communication. New universities, agricultural research centers, national transport networks, and local government structures were established to facilitate national development projects, often with resources coming from the departing colonial powers, which were intent on keeping their economic and geopolitical interests intact.[8] Investment was largely public because there was no globally competetive domestic private sector. Where such a private sector operated, it was usually foreign and exclusively in the extractive sector. All in all, during the first decade and half (1960–1975), African economies registered impressive growth rates, given initial conditions at the time of independence. Needless to say, the optimistic picture of the first decade after independence did not last long for reasons discussed below.

The nationalist project faced a formidable task from many fronts. Whether independence was achieved through direct negotiation or through the barrel of the gun, the nationalist leaders came to the world stage in a very unfavorable political and economic environment. The inherited colonial state was essentially an "empty shell," lacking the administrative structures, skilled personnel, and resources necessary for the efficient management of the economy and the affairs of government. Because of colonial

---

[6] Robert Wade, "What Strategies are Viable for Developing Countries Today? The WTO and the Shrinking of Development Space," *Review of International Political Economy* 10, no. 4 (2003): 621–647.

[7] Walter Rodney, *How Europe Underdeveloped Africa* (Washington, D.C.: Howard University Press, 1982); S. Amin, *Neo-colonialism in West Africa* (New York: Monthly Review Press, 1973).

[8] Prosser Gifford and William Roger Louis, *The Transfer of Power in Africa and Decolonization* (New Haven: Yale University Press, 1982).

neglect—poor infrastructure and support services and underdeveloped financial sector to support the emerging indigenous private sector—many countries came into independence poor, weak, and with little room to maneuver. Pragmatic accommodation to the inherited international system was thus preferred over "revolution" or delinking. Only a handful of countries—Tanzania, Guinea, Angola, and Mozambique—set out to transform their economies from external domination by promoting self-reliant strategies with limited success.

The majority of newly independent countries started out with an explicit recognition that economic growth was fundamentally dependent on the maintenance of pre-existing links with the former colonial powers. Buoyed by the enthusiasm and optimism of the times and guided by the thinking of such luminaries as economist Sir Arthur Lewis, African leaders pursued economic growth via the model known as "industrialization by invitation."[9] In addition to expanding export-led agriculture, countries were urged to take on numerous loans to finance large-scale infrastructure and import-substitution industrialization to kick-start their economies and pave the way to industrialization.[10] Underpinning this approach was the assumption that international market forces would allow the benefits of growth to trickle down to the small, poor nations of the South, reaching even the poor within these nations.[11] And as their economies grew, countries were expected to pay these loans without any difficulty.

Indeed, while some countries—i.e., Ivory Coast, Kenya, Nigeria, Ghana, and Zambia—initially succeeded in registering impressive growth by pursuing pragmatic "accommodation" with the West, the majority of countries did not. Even in these well-performing economies, the benefits largely went to local elites and Western interest groups and widened social inequalities. The overemphasis on primary export trade merely reinforced the inherited colonial division of labor, further condemning these countries to be suppliers of raw materials to industrialized nations while importing finished goods at much higher prices. This dependence on a narrow base of minerals and commodities has made African economies vulnerable to fluctuations in the terms of trade.[12] In the past three decades (1975–2005), export prices for much of Africa were twice as volatile as those of exports from East Asia and nearly four times more volatile than the exports of developed countries.[13] For example, between 1986 and 1989, the continent suffered losses, associated with price falls, of $56 billion or around 15 to 16 percent of GDP.[14] Persistent decline in commodity prices was further aggravated by mounting competition from substitutes, such as synthetics for cotton, aluminum for copper, and corn syrup for sugar. Attempts by African countries to offset lower world prices by increasing their share of the world market further drove down prices. Moreover, discriminatory tariffs continued to grow, whereby market access to African products remained limited.[15]

---

[9] W.A. Lewis, *The Theory of Economic Growth* (London: Allen and Unwin, 1955).

[10] Rene Dumont, *False Start in Africa* (New York: Praeger Publishers,1969).

[11] W.W. Rostow, *The Stages of Economic Growth: A Non-Communist Manifesto*, Cambridge University Press, 1960.

[12] Michael Barrat Brown and Pauline Tiffen, *Short Changed: Africa and the World Trade,* (London: Plutu Press, 1992).

[13] UNCTAD, Economic Development in Africa: Trade Performance and Commodity Dependence (Geneva: United Nations, 2003).

[14] Martin Khor, "Break the 'Conspiracy of Silence' on Commodities," August 30, 2004, www.twnside.org.sg, Third World Network, Global Trends.

[15] Economic Commission for Africa (2003), *The Doha Round and African Development: Turning Words into Deeds* (Addis Ababa: Trade and Regional Integration Division, 2003).

The economic crisis was also aggravated by poor economic governance at the national level as corrupt and unaccountable political elites, often supported by Western powers, let loose their predatory instincts and indulged in corruption, abuse of office, and repression. In an environment where civil society and a vibrant domestic private sector were suppressed due to colonial violence, and the new power holders themselves were vested with weak institutions to govern, it was not surprising that short-term considerations took precedence over long-term ones, power over welfare, personal interests over institutional considerations, and security over development.[16] Policies came to be determined solely by concern with the means, not the conditions of development. This gave rise to preoccupation with structures, leading to centralization and expansion of state bureaucracies, and encouraged a top-down approach to management of public affairs.[17]

The state thus became the market where office holders competed for acquisition of material benefits and maintained power through patron-client ties.[18] Conspicuous consumption at home and siphoning of funds in foreign banks became the predominant occupation of the emerging African bureaucratic elites. Moreover, ill-conceived projects, fiscal imprudence, and capital flight subsequently increased many countries' external debt burdens. Needless to say, the excesses of many corrupt African leaders did not raise eyebrows in Western capitals as long as these puppet regimes faithfully served the foreign policies of Western powers. Thus, barely half way into the second decade of independence, the vision of an independent Africa had started to fall apart, and the gulf between state and society widened considerably in the process.

More important, the postindependence international context was no more propitious than the colonial one. An attempt by a handful of progressive African leaders to chart a nonaligned position was not possible in a world that required alignment by necessity. Africa became the prime battleground in the East-West rivalry.[19] Conflicts between and within African states intensified as a result. Each side backed its "own" dictators, who abused their power to enrich themselves. As the African nationalist project came to be perceived by Western powers as synonymous with "communism," leaders who expressed any desire to chart an independent development path were either assassinated or overthrown by Western-sponsored military coups.[20] In their place, neocolonial regimes—civilian and military juntas—were imposed and often sustained by foreign aid.

As Africa entered the decade of the 1990s, which coincided with the end of the Cold War, the international community was finally expected to concentrate its attention on addressing Africa's development woes. The reality did not turn out that way. The new logic of global market integration instead demanded that African countries subscribe to the ideology of the "Washington Consensus" of market liberalization if they were to benefit from economic globalization, increased aid, and debt cancellations. Though this strategy dates back to the early 1980s, it received a major boost with the collapse of the Soviet Union in 1989, which some commentators characterized as the "triumph of liberalism."[21] Dire

---

[16] Claude Ake, *Democracy and Development in Africa* (Washington, D.C.: Brookings Institution, 1996), 42.

[17] Larry Diamond, "Class Formation in the Swollen African State," *Journal of Modern African Studies* 25, no. 4 (1987): 567–596.

[18] Patrick Chabal, *Political Domination in Africa: Reflections on the Limits of Power* (Cambridge University Press, 1986); D. Rothchild and Naomi Chazan, eds., *The Precarious Balance: State and Society in Africa* (Boulder, CO: Westview Press, 1988).

[19] Zaki Laidi, *The Super-powers and Africa: The Constraints of a Rivalry, 1960–1990* (University of Chicago Press, 1990).

[20] Samuel Decalo, *Coups and Army Rule in Africa: Motivations and Constraints*, (New Haven: Yale University Press, 1990).

[21] Francis Fukuyama, "The End of History?," *The National Interest*, Summer 1989.

predictions were made suggesting that African countries that failed to sufficiently globalize and embrace this "neoliberal" agenda were condemned to a future of anarchy, looting, and self-destruction.[22] The operative logic of the post-1990 political order has been that free market economies give birth to democratic rule, and the latter in turn contributes to a well-functioning market and prosperity in general. Following this logic, conditional lending became the main instrument to get African countries to open up their markets, dismantle many aspects of the African state, and institute minimal democratic procedures essential for the well functioning of the market.[23] Protection of vulnerable producers or infant industries was seen as detrimental to an efficient allocation of resources or to long-term competitiveness. And in the process, African governments increasingly became more and more accountable to external actors than to their own citizens. It is in this context that one has to examine the demand for democracy—often referred to as the second independence struggle—that began in the early 1990s. It is a reaction to the failure of the postcolonial state to realize the national project for genuine independence, national integration, economic development, and social justice.[24]

From Neocolonialism to Neoliberalism: The Shrinking "Policy Space"

As Africa entered the decade of the 1970s, the "national project" was threatened from within and without. With the intense drama of Cold War politics, democratic forces went into retreat as, in several countries, military regimes began to shape the nature and content of African politics in dramatic fashion. Two successive oil price hikes by OPEC further aggravated the economic crisis in Africa in the 1970s. Unable to keep their economies productive because of mounting oil bills and growing debt burdens, many African governments turned to Western multilateral institutions for more loans. As will be shown later, this dependence on multilateral institutions was to have a cataclysmic effect on African economies and shrink the policy space for African leaders to manage their economies independently.

It was Africa's foreign exchange problems and mounting debt that provided the main external reason for the introduction of structural adjustment programs (SAPs) across the continent from the late 1970s onwards. As more African countries ran into greater difficulty servicing their debts in the early 1980s, creditor governments and institutions insisted on implementation of an official neoliberal economic package—SAPs designed to "discipline" debtors as a condition for rescheduling the debt. The structural adjustment programs have reflected the liberalization of policies towards a particular type of package, mainly focusing on macroeconomic stabilization, public sector reform, and the liberalization of markets and trade. By the end of 1999, for example, out of the forty-seven countries in Africa, thirty were implementing adjustment programs, with eleven implementing ten or more programs. This process resulted in the adoption of one-size-fits-all economic policies, which were often poorly adapted to a country's specific needs, lacked broad popular support, and failed to make poverty reduction a priority.[25]

---

[22] Robert Kaplan, "The Coming Anarchy," *Atlantic Monthly*, February 1994.

[23] Fantu Cheru, *The Silent Revolution in Africa: Debt, Development and Democracy* (London and Harare: Zed Press, 1989).

[24] Bjorn Beckman, "Empowerment or Repression? The World Bank and the Politics of African Adjustment," in *Authoritarianism, Democracy and Adjustment*, eds. Peter Gibbon, Yosuf Bangura, and Are Ofstad (Uppsala: Scandinavian Institute of African Studies, 1989), 83–105.

[25] F. Cheru, *The Silent Revolution in Africa: Debt, Development and Democracy* (London: Zed Press, 1989); T. Mkandawire and C. Soludo, *Our Continent, Our Future: African Perspectives on Structural Adjustment* (Trenton, NJ: Africa World Press, 2002); SAPRIN, *Structural Adjustment: The Policy Roots of Economic Crisis, Poverty and Inequality* (London: Zed Press, 2004).

Two and half decades later, the role of the state in Africa has been significantly curtailed, the dominance of market forces set in place, and economies opened wide to external competition. Yet by the onset of the millennium, despite experiencing moderate growth of GDP compared to the crisis period, few African countries had achieved financial credibility in terms of any of the indicators that measure real, sustainable development. Instead, most had slid backwards into growing inequality, ecological degradation, deindustrialization, and poverty. Africa is the only region in the world where poverty has increased. In twenty-four African countries that implemented multiple adjustment programs, GDP per capita was less than in 1975 and in twelve countries, it was even below the 1960 level.[26] Adjustment was achieved by curtailing investment in social services and the productive sectors of the economy and by incurring more debt. This is in stark contrast to the newly industrializing countries (NICs) of East Asia that were able to engineer their development through careful investment in education, land reform, infrastructure upgrades, and developing indigenous technological capacity under the guidance of a strong and capable state.[27]

More important, the "adjustment decade" saw dethroning the state as the driver of development. By imposing particular policy choices on poor countries, creditors take away governments' sovereignty and accountability to their own people and make them answerable to unaccountable, external institutions for their choice of economic policies, level of spending on public services, and other crucial political decisions. This is recolonization, not development. The attempt to impose change from outside actually engenders resistance and gives rise to barriers to change.

In Africa, Globalization Is Neocolonialism

Proponents of globalization claim that integration of world markets creates growth and prosperity and enables governments to lift millions out of poverty. They argue that countries that have opened their economies to foreign investment and trade experience faster growth. Countries such as China, India, and the East Asian "tigers" are often used as examples of nations that embraced globalization, implemented proper reforms, experienced growth, and reduced overall poverty as a result.[28]

However, the real track record of neoliberal globalization unveils a rather different picture than the one presented by its proponents. Khor (2001) maintains that the same process links globalization, polarization, wealth creation, and marginalization. In other words, the very neoliberal economic recipes— financial, trade, and investment liberalization—that have created enormous wealth in the North have had cataclysmic effects on the South.[29] In places such as Africa and Latin America, the policies of neoliberalism are closely associated with economic regression, increased debt, the loss of social services, drastic inequality, declining terms of trade, and financial crisis. The mechanisms by which uneven development in Africa is transmitted and sustained include the following: debt structure, the official development assistance system, foreign direct investment, the unequal trading system, and capital flight.

---

[26] Branko Milanovic, "The Two Sides of Globalization: Against Globalization as We Know It," *World Development* 31, no. 4 (2003): 667–683.

[27] Robert Wade, "The Disturbing Rise in Poverty and Inequality," in *Taming Globalization*, ed. D. Held and M. Koenig-Archibugi (Cambridge: Polity Press, 2003); Walden Bellow and S. Ronsenfeld, *Dragons in Distress: Asia's Miracle Economies in Crisis* (San Francisco: Food First, 1990).

[28] D. Dolla and A. Kraay, "Spreading the Wealth," *Foreign Affairs*, January/February 2002.

[29] Martin Khor, *Rethinking Globalization: Critical Issues and Policy Choices* (London: Zed Press, 2001).

Africa and the World Trading System

One way in which poor countries can try to benefit from globalization is to increase their share of global trade. By providing access to foreign exchange, expanding markets, increasing foreign direct investment, facilitating the transfer of technology, and boosting domestic productivity, trade can create employment and increase domestic incomes. Needless to say, these supposed benefits from international trade have yet to materialize in Africa in a meaningful way. There are internal and external factors that contribute to Africa's low participation in international trade. The internal factors include: inappropriate domestic economic and social policies and the lack of progress in regional integration efforts, which have limited the region's ability to reduce transaction costs and increase competitiveness through economies of scale in the development of infrastructure. On the external front, costly and unfair trading practices of the developed countries have made it difficult for African countries to penetrate export markets in developed countries.[30]

According to the proponents of neoliberal globalization, openness to international trade is supposed to allow poor countries to alter the pace and pattern of their participation in the international division of labor and thereby overcome balance-of-payments problems and accelerate technical progress and economic growth to catch up with industrialized countries.[31] The Uruguay Round, launched in 1990, was expected to facilitate the process greatly. After all, it was argued that a strong rule-based system would benefit smaller and poorer economies by improving their access to Northern markets.

To the contrary, the benefits of trade liberalization, in terms of capital accumulation and productivity growth, balance of payments position, and manufacturing growth, tend to be distributed unevenly, and adverse forms of integrating into the global economy may actually increase rather than reduce poverty.[32] Despite the elimination of many of the barriers that have restricted international trade in goods, significant barriers to trade still persist—often to the detriment of the poorest countries. After decades of free market policies in Africa, absolute poverty is rising, Africa's share of world trade is declining, barriers to many African exports remain firmly in place in the United States and Europe, and the rate of FDI inflow to the continent remains abysmal.[33] As long as African countries export unprocessed materials, the tariff remains low. But for every step in the processing chain that adds value, the duties rise sharply, somewhere in the range of 300 to 400 percent. These tariff escalations undermine manufacturing and employment in industries where African countries need to be competitive.[34]

Developing countries, especially in Africa, have persistently complained that the current international trade regime works against them and have demanded major reform of the rules. In 2001, the developed countries agreed to a new round of trade negotiations, the Doha Development Round. The main issues of interest to developing countries include basic market access to industrial country economies, terms of trade between

---

[30] Oxfam, *Rigged Rules and Double Standards* (Oxford: Oxfam, 2002).

[31] J.D. Sachs and A. Warner, "Economic Reforms and the Process of Global Integration," Brookings Paper on Economic Activity (Washington, D.C.: Brookings Institution, 1995); J. Bhagwati, *In Defense of Globalization* (Oxford: Oxford University Press, 2004).

[32] Yilmaz Akyuz, "Trade, Growth and Industrialization: Issues, Experience and Policy Challenges," January 2005, Downloaded from Google Scholar May 15, 2009.

[33] UNCTAD, Economic Development in Africa: Rethinking the Role of Foreign Direct Investment (Geneva: United Nations, 2005).

[34] Yilmaz Akyuz, *The WTO Negotiations on Industrial Tariffs: What is At Stake for Developing Countries?* (Penang: Third World Network, 2005).

developing country exports and imports from industrial countries, commodity price volatility and trade patterns, phaseout of export subsidies and trade-distorting domestic support measures in agricultural exports by industrial countries (especially cotton), and special and differentiated treatment for poor countries.[35] Overall, the terms of trade losses offset about 70 percent of the official development assistance (ODA), while the loss of market shares in international trade cost Africa some $68 billion per annum between 1972 and 1997.[36]

Of all the topics in the current WTO agenda, agriculture has been the hottest. At the 2001 WTO summit in Doha, Qatar, governments agreed to create new, fairer trade rules for agriculture by March 2003 and even declared the Doha trade negotiations a "development round" to put fighting poverty at the heart of the global trade system. The promise was to eliminate unfair U.S. and European trade practices that locked African farm products out of rich country markets yet allowed wealthy countries to flood African markets with massively subsidized exports.

Agricultural subsidies by the developed countries, which are in excess of $350 billion a year, adversely affect the competitive advantage of African peasant farmers, further impoverishing them. The United States spends almost $4 billion on cotton subsidies to 25,000 cotton farmers who produce just $3 billion–worth of cotton.[37] The implications of this policy for some African countries that are heavily dependent on cotton exports have been well documented. These policies run counter to the principles of free trade. Their effect is to diminish developing country access to developed country markets, while driving down global prices of agricultural products by encouraging excess production.

It has been six years since the 2001 Doha Conference of the WTO, which set out to "rebalance" the imbalanced Uruguay Round agreements. Due to unrelenting pressure by developed countries, the Doha negotiations have veered from their proclaimed development orientation toward a "market access" direction in which developing countries are pressured to open their agricultural, industrial, and services sectors. In addition, the EU, Japan, and the United States pledged to grant duty- and quota-free market access to 97 percent of the fifty least developed countries' products by 2008, with the exception of some three hundred sensitive products (such as sugar and rice) that are of interest to African countries.[38] On the other hand, the United States, the EU, and Japan committed at the Hong Kong ministerial trade talks in December 2005 to eliminate export subsidies on agricultural goods by the end of 2013. Because these three giants wrote the WTO rules—creating loopholes that allow them to subsidize their farm economies—most subsidies have been "repackaged" under any new WTO rules. The farm lobby and their Congressional allies do not want to give up their existing subsidies, but they do want greater access to foreign markets, especially in developing countries. Considering that during the 2004 U.S. presidential election cycle, agribusiness industries contributed more than $52 million to political campaigns, it is not hard to see why.[39]

At the end of July 2006, the negotiations at the WTO on the Doha Work Program were suspended across the board. Six WTO members (the United States, the EU, India, Brazil, Japan, and Australia)

[35] Francis Perkins, "Africa's Agricultural Trade Reform and Development Options," *Trade Policy Briefing*, no. 1, South African Institute of International Affairs, 2003; Martin Khor, "Comments on the WTO's Geneva July 2004 Package," August 2004, www.twnside.org.sg, Third World Network Briefing Paper 22.

[36] World Bank, Can Africa Claim the 21st Century? (2000).

[37] "The Cancun Challenge," *The Economist*, September 6, 2003, 59–61.

[38] Bhagirath Lal Das, "Why the EU and US Offers on Farm Trade Are Not Good Enough," 2006, www.twnside.org.sg, Third World Network Briefing Paper 33.

[39] Kathy McNeely, "Food Security and Trade in Agriculture: Africa Keeps a Watchful Eye on U.S. Policy," *Washington Notes on Africa* 31, no. 1 (2006): 7.

failed to resolve their differences on the modalities of negotiations on two key areas: agriculture and non-agricultural market access (NAMA). Developed countries have succeeded in marginalizing "development issues," including the principles of special and differential treatment, less than full reciprocity in the agriculture, and NAMA negotiations, by not committing to reduce their total trade-distorting domestic subsidies beyond actual levels, and by introducing new modalities in services that make it potentially easier to pressure developing countries to liberalize while not making meaningful offers in areas that can practically benefit developing countries. In addition, they have succeeded in blocking progress in the TRIPS (Trade-Related Aspects of Intellectual Property Rights) negotiations on disclosure of genetic resources and traditional knowledge. As one frustrated and courageous African president put it, "It is better to have no agreement than to walk away with a bad agreement."

In the final analysis, achieving the MDGs in Africa would require, at the very least, the introduction of mechanisms to achieve fair and stable prices for commodities and improvement of market access for African exports. Without action on agricultural subsidies by industrialized countries, Africa's development will always be held in check. In addition to rewriting the current trade rules, new international measures are needed to strengthen the supply capacity of African countries in the commodity sector, especially in the areas of production, marketing, and diversification to enhance value-added through processing and manufacturing based on commodities.[40] This must be complemented by domestic measures to overcome structural impediments to production. Thus, even if there is market access for these countries, the "supply constraint" prevents them from being able to take advantage of it.

Trends in FDI Flow to Africa

One of the key elements of the new world economy is the volume of FDI, which has now replaced exports as the fastest growing component of the world economy. FDI can play an important role in the overall development process and in meeting the MDGs. First, FDI is a source of capital accumulation, both physical and human. Second, FDI can generate much-needed revenues for governments to spend on MDGs and finance infrastructure and services.

FDI to Africa has increased in recent years—from an average of $1 billion per year in the 1970s to $6 billion in the 1990s. With increased demand from China and India for Africa's energy and natural resources, FDI flows to Africa reached $20 billion in 2001 and $15 billion in 2003.[41] This impressive growth, however, is substantially lower than that for developing countries as a whole. In fact, Africa receives very little FDI outside of the mineral sector (Table 12.1). FDI concentrates in a small group of countries (and sectors), with East Asia and Latin America receiving more than 70 percent of total FDI directed to developing countries and China receiving almost 25 percent of the total. On the other hand, Africa's share, though growing in the extractive sector, has been extremely low. Three-quarters of annual FDI flows over the past two decades went to ten mineral-rich African countries.[42] This declining trend in FDI flows to Africa is very worrying in view of the crucial importance of FDI flows (as well as other sources of finance) for achieving the MDGs in the region.

---

[40] Martin Khor, "The Commodities Crisis and the Global Trade in Agriculture: Present Problems and Some Proposals," in *Millennium Development Goals: Raising the Resources to Tackle World Poverty*, eds. F. Cheru and C. Bradford (London: Zed Press, 2005), 97–117.

[41] UNCTAD, *Rethinking the Role of Foreign Direct Investment*, 5.

[42] ibid., 8, Table 2.

Table 12.1   FDI Inflows and Shares to Developing Regions, 1970–2003

	1970/79 average	1980/89 average	1990/99 average	2001	2003
FDI Inflows, World (millions of dollars)	24,124	93,887	401,028	817,574	560,115
Developing Countries	6,109	21,356	121,769	219,721	172,033
Africa	1,066	2,162	6,187	19,616	15,033
Latin America/Caribbean	3,269	7,438	44,432	88,139	49,722
Asia-Pacific	1,774	11,756	71,150	111,966	107,278
Developing Countries' Share of FDI (percentage)	25.3	22.7	30.4	26.9	30.7
Africa	4.4	2.3	1.5	2.4	2.7
Latin America/Caribbean	13.6	7.9	11.1	10.8	8.9
Asia-Pacific	7.4	12.5	17.7	13.7	19.2

Source: UNCTAD, Economic Development in Africa, Table 1.

In large measure, attracting high levels of FDI will require improving the domestic investment climate, with democratic governance as the overarching framework for guiding development.[43] This requires political stability and rule-based political order, mediated by an impartial and independent judiciary and particular emphasis on transparency, accountability, and greater citizens' participation in decision making. If a country provides a safe environment for its citizens and a climate in which resources can be used more productively, then flows will be strengthened and capital flight can be arrested.

A related issue is the role of infrastructure in attracting FDI flows. A recent World Bank survey of the executives of multinational corporations suggests that the state of physical infrastructure—such as energy, transport, information and communication technology, water supply and sanitation—is one key factor inhibiting FDI projects in Africa, along with high administrative costs, the tax regime, poor access to global markets, low levels of skills, and the regulatory and legal framework governing FDI, among others things. For example, unreliable electricity supply requires firms to invest in generators.[44] These disadvantages to FDI more than offset the low prices of labor in Africa. Therefore, the particular feature of the FDI flows to Africa call for an integrated approach to attract more FDI to the region.[45]

Financial Dependence: The Aid-Trade-Debt Nexus

Financial globalization has progressed significantly in the last decade and would seem to increase developing countries' access to international finance. Despite two decades of liberalization of domestic financial markets by African countries, they have little access to international financial markets and remain dependent on official development assistance (ODA). In this section, we examine the role of aid, debt, and capital flight.

As the table below indicates, ODA has assumed a significant role as private flows declined significantly from their peak in the 1970s. With the onset of the debt crisis in the late 1970s, African countries largely

---

[43] World Bank, *Doing Business in 2004: Understanding Regulations* (New York: Oxford University Press, 2004).

[44] World Bank, *World Development Report 2005: A Better Investment Climate for All.*

[45] D. W. Te Velde, "Foreign Direct Investment: Policy Challenges for Sub-Saharan African Countries" (Overseas Development Institute, 2002).

Table 12.2   Total Net Disbursements of Total Official and Private Flows by Type, 1971–2001 (as percentages)

ALL DEVELOPING COUNTRIES	1971–80	1981–90	1991–2002
Official Development Assistance (ODA)	36.7	50.8	43.6
Bilateral	29.0	38.3	30.9
Multilateral	7.7	12.5	12.7
Other Official Flows	8.7	6.6	4.3
Private Flows	50.7	38.2	47.7
Grants from NGOs	3.9	4.4	4.8
TOTAL	100.0	100.0	100.0
AFRICAN COUNTRIES[a]			
Official Development Assistance (ODA)	59.5	77.8	88.3
Bilateral	42.0	52.9	54.2
Multilateral	17.5	24.9	34.1
Other Official Flows	11.2	14.4	0.2
Private Flows	29.3	7.9	11.5
Grants from NGOs	n.a.	n.a.	n.a.
TOTAL	100.0	100.0	100.0

Source: OECD (2004).

[a] Does not include North Africa.

turned to multilateral institutions for loans. For example, Table 12.2 shows that ODA accounted for almost 90 percent of total flows to much of Africa during 1991–2002.[46] Aid levels are also high in per capita terms: in 2002, aid to Latin America was $9.80 per person; to South Asia, $4.70; and to Africa, $25–30.[47] This dependency brings with it high transaction costs for African governments because the conditionality associated with aid limits the policy space for governments to consider a range of policy alternatives.

In addition to the issue of excessive "conditionality," the unpredictability of donor funding and disbursements continues to hamper national efforts to improve the efficiency of public expenditure. Without predictable flows of external finance over the medium- to long-term range, African governments are unlikely to have the flexibility to make adequate budget allocations for poverty reduction.[48] Moreover, linking donor aid disbursements to purchases of donor country goods and services affects the quality of aid. A number of donors continue to provide tied aid, despite a recent OECD agreement (the Paris Declaration on Aid Harmonization) to untie aid to poor countries.

One critical problem for Africa's development has been the lack of adequate development finance. High level of capital flight from the continent and unsustainable levels of debt service payment to creditor countries further aggravate the scarcity of capital for productive purposes. Approximately 40 percent of the stock of African savings is held outside the continent, compared to just 6 percent for

---

[46] OECD, "International Development Statistics On-line" (Paris, 2004). OECD data does not include North Africa.

[47] World Bank, World Development Indicators 2004.

[48] J. Healy, M. Foster, A. Norton, and David Booth, *Towards National Public Expenditure Strategies for Poverty Reduction* (London: Overseas Development Institute, 2000).

Table 12.3 Comparison of Capital Flight from Africa and FDI Inflows into Africa

Country	Cumulative Capital Flight ($ millions in 1996)	FDI Inflows ($ millions)
Angola	17,003	3,103
Benin	−3,457	394
Burkina Faso	1,266	90
Burundi	819	34
Cameroon	13,099	1,097
Central African Republic	250	90
Congo, Dem. Rep. of	10,099	566
Congo	459	1,095
Côte d'Ivoire	23,370	1,837
Ethiopia	5,523	187
Gabon	2,989	258
Ghana	407	942
Guinea	343	155
Kenya	815	743
Madagascar	1,649	183
Malawi	705	217
Mali	−1,204	198
Mauritania	1,131	97
Mauritius	-268	293
Mozmabique	5,311	274
Niger	−3,153	364
Nigeria	86,762	15,658
Rwanda	2,115	233
Senegal	−7,278	379
Seychelles	567	351
Sierra Leone	1,473	8
Sudan	6,983	165
Tanzania	1,699	473
Uganda	2,155	398
Zambia	10,624	1,101

Source: Ndikumana 2004:357 and UNCTAD FDI/TNC database.

East Asia and 3 percent for South Asia.[49] While a portion of this capital flight is induced by a poor investment climate that forces citizens to take their savings abroad, a large proportion of capital held in foreign banks comes from the looting of public treasuries by corrupt and unaccountable leaders whose tenure in office is largely sustained by Western countries.

Adding fuel to the fire, rapid capital liberalization can result in economic volatility, unpredictability, and booms and busts in capital inflows. This has a serious impact on output and consumption, particularly in Africa where prudential regulation and sound domestic capital markets are weak or nonexistent.

---

[49] P. Collier, A. Hoeffler, and C. Patillo, "Capital Flight as a Portfolio Choice," *World Bank Economic Review* 15, no. 1 (2001): 55–80.

It must be understood that the conditions that gave rise to capital flight from the continent are the same ones that contributed to Africa's indebtedness since the mid-1970s. The policies pursued by both creditor and debtor nations are responsible for Africa's debt predicament and the associated economic collapse that followed it. While benefiting local elites and Western interests in the short-term, export-led development largely dependent on external borrowing has left the continent bankrupt and indebted. As mentioned before, poor economic governance at the national level also aggravated indebtedness, as corrupt and unaccountable leaders emptied the national treasury for their private gain. While measurable in dollar terms, the debt burden takes its toll on human beings with a brutality difficult to capture in words. Even with recent initiatives to lighten the debt burden, African countries still spend some $15 billion annually on debt service payments, thus crowding out critical public investment in human development.

At the end of 2005, African countries owed a total of $293 billion to creditor countries and institutions, of which countries in North Africa owed $84 billion. The debt grew from $120 billion in 1980 to $340 billion in 1995, the so-called structural adjustment decades when countries in crisis began to take more loans as per the IMF/World Bank–mandated structural adjustment programs. Almost 80 percent of Africa's debt was owed to official institutions, and about one-third of it was multilateral debt. At the same time, total debt service paid by the continent increased from 43.5 million in the 1970s to a peak of $26 billion in 1999. As the Economic Commission for Africa pointed out, for every dollar that Africa received in aid, nearly fifty cents went straight back to the developed world in debt payment.[50]

For twenty-five years, the guiding principle of the creditors' strategy has been to do the minimum to avert default but never enough to solve the African debt crisis. Their indifference was clearly evident in the piecemeal approach adopted by the G7 governments after the Venice G7 summit of 1987. The many initiatives that followed (e.g., Toronto, Trinidad, and Naples Terms) were set and reset arbitrarily, not based on serious assessment of the needs of each debtor country. In 1996, however, as a result of many years of persistent campaigning by a global coalition of NGOs, the IMF and the World Bank addressed the issue of poor-country debt by approving the Heavily Indebted Poor Countries (HIPC) Initiative.

Initially, few countries chose to apply to HIPC because of the stringent criteria that came with debt relief. By spring of 1999, only Uganda, Bolivia, and Mozambique had become eligible. At the 1999 G7 Cologne meeting, the leaders recommended that the prerequisites be relaxed in order to enable more countries to qualify for the debt relief initiative; thus, the Enhanced HIPC was born. Under the enhanced HIPC, debt relief became conditional on countries' preparing a poverty reduction strategy paper (PRSP) through a broad consultative process with domestic social actors.

While the decision to link debt relief to poverty reduction is a major step forward, the Enhanced HIPC is caught up in a complex web of IMF/World Bank eligibility conditions. Key economic policies continue to be imposed by the IFIs as a condition for receiving debt relief and new loans. The joint boards of the IMF and World Bank also retain veto power over the PRSPs. To enter the scheme ("reaching decision point"), a country must comply with an IMF program for three years. It then starts receiving interim relief; that is, it pays less service on a number of debts. The "decision point" is also when there are set "trigger conditions"—the list of conditions with which a country must comply in order to complete HIPC and get some of its debts canceled for good ("reaching completion point").

---

[50] Economic Commission for Africa (2005), 115.

At the end of March 2006, eighteen countries had completed the HIPC process and were granted nominal debt relief totaling $37.6 billion. Of the eighteen, fourteen were African countries.[51] Another ten (all from Africa) have reached their "decision points" and have received interim support of $18 billion. While the $37 billion in debt relief is no small change by any stretch of imagination, the initiative does not address the debt of the other forty poor African countries that still owe over $200 billion.[52] Based on Africa's huge financing needs to achieve the Millennium Development Goals (MDGs) by 2015, debt relief under the enhanced HIPC initiative has been neither sufficiently deep nor sufficiently broad to reduce the levels described by the World Bank as "sustainable." Greater effort is necessary by the international community to expand debt cancellation to all impoverished countries.

The New Orthodoxy of "Partnership": The G8 and Its Africa Action Plan

The years following the Monterrey Conference on Financing for Development (March 2002), witnessed strong support from the international community for Africa's development through significant debt relief, increased ODA, and bringing to a conclusion the Doha Development Round, which was expected to benefit developing countries. This section will examine the extent to which Western governments have been able to comply with the commitment they made at Monterrey, Kananaskis, and Gleneagles.

At the June 2002 Kananaskis Summit in Canada, the G8 adopted the African Action Plan (AAP) which contains a series of commitments in support of the objectives set by the New Partnership for Africa's Development (NEPAD). A major commitment made by the G8 was to increase ODA to African countries, in line with the consensus reached at the Monterrey Conference of 2002. To reach the global G8 target, set at $6 billion for 2006, most member countries committed to increase ODA to Africa, with some establishing new funds and most setting timetables for increases in ODA/gross national income (GNI) ratios, with a share of 50 percent of the increase allocated to Africa.

In May 2005, the European Union (EU) agreed to double its ODA between 2006 and 2010, with at least 50 percent of the increase earmarked for Africa. Specifically, after reaching the global ODA/GNI ratio of an estimated 0.35 percent in 2005, the EU was on track to achieve the 0.39 percent target in 2006. The EU has agreed to reach a new collective target of 0.56 ODA/GNI ratios by 2010, which would result in an increase in ODA of 20 billion euros between 2006 and 2010. At the European level, only Norway, Luxembourg, Denmark, Sweden, and The Netherlands met the 0.7 percent target.[53]

Japan agreed to increase its total ODA volume over the period 2005–2009 by $410 billion, while doubling its assistance to Africa between 2005 and 2008. Under its "Health and Development Initiative for Africa" launched in June 2005, Japan would provide $5 billion over the period 2005–2009. In addition, in partnership with the African Development Bank, Japan proposed an Enhanced Private Sector Assistance facility of $1.2 billion to be disbursed over five years. Following a tripling of net disbursements to Africa in 2000–2004, the United States intends to double its assistance to sub-Saharan Africa between 2004 and 2010. Canada continues to increase its ODA

---

[51] The fourteen African countries include Benin, Burkina Faso, Ethiopia, Ghana, Madagascar, Mali, Mauritania, Mozambique, Niger, Rwanda, Senegal, Tanzania, Uganda, and Zambia.

[52] Africa Action, "Debt is Not Done—The 2005 Debt Deal," September 21, 2005, africaaction.org/campaign_new/page. php?

[53] G8 Gleneagles, Progress report by the G8 Africa Personal Representatives on Implementation of the Africa Action Plan (2005), 20.

by 8 percent per annum to double its assistance by 2010, with half of the increase allocated to African countries.

Three years later, at its summit in Gleneagles, Scotland, in July 2005, the G8 announced that aid would increase by $50 billion over the next five years. And in conformity with the commitments made at the Monterrey Conference, the G8 decided to allocate at least half of the increase in ODA to Africa by 2006. The G8 leaders increased their assistance to the continent by an estimated $6 billion during the period 2001–2004. More important, the Gleneagles Summit endorsed the Multilateral Debt Relief Initiative (MDRI) for a 100 percent cancellation of debt owed to the International Monetary Fund (IMF), the International Development Association (IDA), and the African Development Fund (ADF) by fourteen African participants in the Heavily Indebted Poor Countries (HIPC) Initiative.

Despite the increasing volume of aid, there is a growing concern about publicized development aid figures that may include items that do not represent real resource transfers in support of development. For example, one-third of the ODA reported by the EU in 2005 did not include any new aid resources for poverty reduction in developing countries. A large amount of the stated aid spending was, in fact, allocated to finance housing for refugees in Europe and double counting of debt cancellations, despite the Monterrey Consensus agreement that debt cancellation should be additional to ODA. The NGO Action Aid reported that more than half of the aid remained "phantom"; and had been either poorly targeted, double counted as debt relief, tied to the purchase of donor goods and services, or badly coordinated and highly conditional.

The Monterrey Consensus on Financing Development gave special attention to the issue of poor countries' debt and recommended urgent action on two fronts: expedition of debt relief, including within the Paris and London Lenders Clubs, in order to free resources for development efforts and exploration of innovative proposals for a sovereign debt-restructuring mechanism to enable affected countries to manage the crisis effectively and debtors and creditors to share the burden equally. While the first approach deals primarily with the HIPC countries, the second set of proposals is aimed at resolving the debt problem of middle-income countries that fall outside the HIPC framework.

In July 2005, the Gleneagles Summit endorsed the Multilateral Debt Relief Initiative (MDRI) for a 100 percent cancellation of debt owed to the IMF and the World Bank by eighteen eligible poor countries, fourteen of whom were African countries. All eighteen countries were chosen because they had already completed the harsh Heavily Indebted Poor Countries (HIPC) initiative, which includes the full range of economic conditions required for debt cancellation.[54] But the agreement covers only fourteen African countries and excludes more than forty other deserving African countries whose economies are crippled by unpayable debts. The deal only cancels $40 billion of Africa's burgeoning debt stock of over $330 billion. The $40 billion debt forgiveness "represents less than ten percent of debt cancellation required for poor nations to meet the MDGs in 2015."[55]

One critical limitation of the current creditor-dominated debt relief strategy has been the continued interference in the policy choices of African governments. The conditions attached to debt relief not only undermine democracy, but also turn debt cancellation from a simple act of justice into a tool of

[54] These countries are Benin, Burkina Faso, Ethiopia, Ghana, Madagascar, Mali, Mauritania, Mozambique, Niger, Rwanda, Senegal, Tanzania, Uganda, and Zambia in Africa and Bolivia, Guyana, Honduras, and Nicaragua in Latin America.

[55] AFRODAD, "The G8 Debt Deal—A Half-baked Solution to the Crisis," 2005, www.afrodad.org/archive.

control. For example, of the twenty-nine countries that have gone through the HIPC process, nineteen have had to comply with onerous conditions, such as privatization of state enterprises and macroeconomic targets, in order to get debt relief. A number of African countries have their debt relief delayed for failing to meet set targets as part of their HIPC agreements.[56] The basic operative logic of G8 debt strategy is simple: the debt burden will be lightened just enough to keep the system going but not enough to remove its oppressive and distorting effects.

The development challenge in Africa is multi-dimensional, yet conventional development orthodoxies are ill suited to address them. For example, debt cancellation alone is not going to put African countries on a sound footing if there is little progress toward making the international trade regime fair. Similarly, it is meaningless to increase market access for African products if the gains from trade are lost by the unilateral action of a single developed country by changing global interest rates overnight, which would have a negative impact on the trading positions of developing countries. Debt cancellation can make a huge difference only when there is greater commitment on the part of developed countries to ensure that the trade-aid-debt-capital flow macroeconomic policy linkages are put in place and regularly monitored. But more important, for development to be sustainable, poor countries must have the option to choose among appropriate fiscal, monetary, macroeconomic, trade, and other economic and social policies without heavy-handed intervention by the IMF and the World Bank. Policy coherence is a good thing when the rules are just; policy coherence is bad when the rules are unjust. As we have demonstrated in this paper, there is a significant "coherence deficit" in the trade-debt-aid-investment policies of donor governments.

In Search of Genuine "Independence": A Roadmap for Africa's Development

As the preceding discussion has pointed out, the African continent is no stranger to globalization and its deleterious effects. More than any region in the world, Africa has paid a high price for the globalizing policies of rival capitalist powers as they strive to expand the geographic bounds of capital. Starting with the slave trade in 1650 and continuing under colonial rule after the Berlin Conference of 1884, the continent was heavily drawn into the centers of capitalist accumulation, but always as a subordinate partner with the primary purpose of contributing to the development of the metropolitan powers. The post–World War II international order has done very little to alter Africa's subordinate role. Economic coercion has largely replaced military coercion, with aid flows and debt structures as the dominant tools for ensuring the integration of African economies into the capitalist world economy.

Africa's marginal position in the new global hierarchy, therefore, provides us with a compelling occasion to redefine the "national development" project, to strengthen the continent's capacity to become more assertive in international affairs, and to defend Africa's sovereignty. If they are to reverse this economic decline, they must restructure the platform upon which these negative influences are made. To do so, African countries must be prepared to come up with alternative formulations and conditions under which they want to engage in global economic exchanges that are beneficial to them. This will entail adoption of key reforms at national and regional levels and greater economic policy coordination between them. The choice for Africa is neither de-linking nor uncritical embrace of neoliberalism. Experience shows that states that are able to guide the operation of the market in the manner that best

---

[56] Jubilee Debt Campaign, "Cutting the Strings!" (September 2006).

suits their needs and to establish their competitiveness tend to be the ones that experience the most success in the global economy. What nation-states do in regard to domestic wage levels, foreign investment, public services, and economic diversification can help determine, to a considerable extent, whether they develop or not. Although these powers are not always simple or easy to exercise, they have by no means completely disappeared from the national arena. The foundations for the African Renaissance should include the following:

Revitalizing Agricultural Production and Empowering the Peasantry

The first pillar of the African renaissance is agricultural transformation. The disappointing economic performance of the continent over the past three decades has been caused, to a large extent, by the failure of African governments to create the proper conditions for an agricultural revolution to take place, which would, in turn, propel the process of industrialization and social development. Agricultural revolution will remain a priority for several decades and is obviously complex and multifaceted. At minimum, it requires the presence of a strong and effective "enabling state" with the capacity to respond to the demands of rural producers. As experience from East Asia has shown, the state must play an active and supporting role by investing in agricultural research, extension, transport, communications, and storage facilities, which are essential for raising productivity and increasing income for farmers. Government-guaranteed prices and security of land tenure in particular are the most effective incentives for shifting peasant farmers from subsistence to production for the market.[57] These local initiatives will also require international support in the form of technical cooperation and assistance designed to build local capacity.

Investing in African Education and Basic Research

Africa cannot flourish unless the intellectual capital of the continent is developed and maintained. Education is a cornerstone of human development in every society. Through education, people can take advantage of the social and economic options available to them. At the moment, the state of education in Africa is depressing. Despite the tremendous gains made since the 1960s in increasing access to education, greater challenges lie ahead. Spending on each child is half what it was twenty years ago. Perhaps the most daunting challenge is that of promoting female education. Fiscal crisis, poor student participation, high dropout and repetition levels, and low academic achievements are widespread, destructive trends throughout the system.

Intellectual marginalization will occur unless Africa raises its educational levels and standards. The only way to narrow the knowledge gap is by investing in education, basic research, and development. Strengthening African universities and retaining Africa's best and brightest professionals are important. Investment in education should emphasize climbing the technological ladder and tapping into the global system of information and knowledge. Transforming the African educational system thus constitutes the second and most important pillar of the "transformation" strategy.

Strengthening Regional Economic Cooperation and South-South Trade

The emergence of three powerful trading blocs—NAFTA, EU, and APEC—poses a great challenge to African countries. Africa will find itself even more vulnerable and isolated if it remains a collection

---

[57] Cristobal Kay, "Why East Asia Overtook Latin America: Agrarian Reform, Industrialization and Development," *Third World Quarterly* 23, no. 6, (2006): 1073–1102.

of fifty-three small, competing exporters, dependent on regional giants to purchase their output and supply their needs. The Abuja Treaty, signed at the OAU Summit in June 1991, with the aim of establishing an economic community by 2025, shows African resolve to become an important player in global economic relations. Whether this ambitious goal can be achieved by 2025 is another matter. It will all depend on the ability and willingness of African governments to create an environment conducive to economic cooperation.

Clearly, sub-Saharan African countries cannot easily jump into ambitious market integration schemes involving detailed blueprints, rigid time frames, and formal institutional structures, because the administration involved would require technical and managerial capacities not often found in sufficient quantity in Africa. One of the lessons of the past is that less ambitious, more flexible institutional regional economic cooperation initiatives may have more potential because of their responsiveness to member states' priorities and interests. This implies less binding, project-oriented, and functional cooperation schemes, involving action on certain themes or in certain sectors that offer some immediate benefits. These types of pragmatic institutional arrangements with realistic and well-defined objectives responding to specific short-term needs may offer better prospects than ambitious initiatives.

Renewing Democracy and Improving Governance

Underlying the success of Africa's transformative agenda is the assumption that governments will make national development and poverty reduction their number one priority. The most reliable way of getting the citizens behind the national development agenda is through democratic structures and empowerment of people at the grassroots. Experience from Africa and elsewhere proves that government suppression of democratic expression, participation, and self-government of citizens has had limited success in creating conditions for economic growth and poverty reduction. The absence of democratic rule directly contributed to low productivity and low human development in the continent.

Notwithstanding remarkable progress in democratization since 1989, democracy in Africa is still in profound trouble and has not moved beyond holding multiparty elections. Entrenched and repressive structures continue to frustrate the process. This is partly because democratic institutions, including legislatures, local governments, electoral bodies, political parties, the judiciary, the media, and civil society, remain weak and are, therefore, unable to act as countervailing forces to an often-powerful executive branch of government. Moreover, for democracy to succeed in the African context there must be significant social reform and a reduction of inequalities, as well as decentralization of political power and decision making. By enlarging visions and raising consciousness, citizens can undermine the vicious circle of mass exclusion and marginalization. This will in turn increase the legitimacy of the state because the people will possess major decisions and feel involved in decision making and the promotion of economic reform.

Reinventing the African State

Successful development demands a greater role of the state in the economy than neoclassical theory has assumed. If the market is to function effectively, it requires elaborate state guidance. As the successful development experience of the Asian industrializing countries has shown, a competent state has a vital role to play in guiding national development, ensuring egalitarian distribution of resources, linking urban and rural production, and investing in human capital formation to provide equal opportunity and upward mobility for all. By contrast, the postindependence African state has acted as the servile executor of the policies of the Western powers. There is a strong correlation between the marginalization of Africa and the premature abandonment by the African state of its development role. In the process, the national development project and the political democratization agenda were abandoned against the wishes of the majority of Africans who had suffered immensely under colonial rule.

Central to Africa's renewal is the development of a strong, democratic, and activist state that would assert its development role within the context of a common national vision. Indeed, the lessons of the recent and distant past teach us that countries that experience faster rates of growth are not those that indiscriminately open their economies to foreign trade and investment but those that first develop their domestic markets adequately enough to compete in the world economy. The lessons from China and East Asia certainly demonstrate the importance of national policies that support strategic industries, develop internal infrastructure, invest in human capital, and control financial markets.[58] As Khor succinctly argued, "developing countries must have the ability, freedom, and flexibility to make strategic choices in finance, trade, and investment policies, where they can decide on the rate and scope of liberalization and combine this appropriately with the defense of local firms and farms."[59] If a government does not have freedom to control basic economic policy, it will be steamrolled by bigger, more efficient economies.

The Washington Consensus is simply wrong in its belief that dismantling trade barriers and removing government interference is a panacea for underdevelopment. On the contrary, an effective state is a prerequisite for a well-functioning market. Weak state capacity actually goes against the notion of "national ownership" of policy decisions. Brautigam (1996) identifies four areas of state capacity that are critical for guiding national development: regulatory capacity, which enables the state to set and enforce the rules of economic and social interaction, leading to greater predictability; technical capacity, which gives the state specialized abilities to assist producers and manage macroeconomic policy, leading to greater stability; taxation capacity, which allows the state to raise revenues to pay for its programs; and administrative capacity, which encompasses the management skills that provide effective government services.[60] In short, the development state is one that has the administrative, legal, and regulatory capacity to support the market and the private sector. Therefore, national economies need basic government institutions like courts, and bankruptcy provisions and standard weights and measures, to name a few, before they are ready to be successfully integrated into global, competitive economic activity.

At the international level, African countries must become more assertive in international negotiation by hammering out common positions rather than doing it alone. While the playing field in international trade is not level, African countries must take necessary steps towards the evolution and development of a coordinated trade strategy. The marginalization of African countries in international trade is due to the fact that most countries lack the capacity to engage substantially on the wide range of WTO issues. The Geneva-based delegations are often small and lack people with technical backgrounds. To overcome this weakness, African governments must do a lot more to strengthen analytic skills in a wide range of WTO issues, develop lobbying and negotiation skills, and establish an incentive structure to dissuade African specialists in trade, investment, and other relevant disciplines from leaving the continent.

[58] Jay Mazur, "Labor's New Internationalism," *Foreign Affairs*, January/February 2000, 11.
[59] Martin Khor, *Rethinking Globalization* (London: Zed Press, 2000), 37.
[60] Deborah Brautigam, "State Capacity and Effective Governance," in *Agenda for Africa's Economic Renewal*, in eds. B. Ndulu, Nicolas van de Walle et al. (Washington, D.C.: Overseas Development Council, 1996), 81–104.

This will also require African leadership in the G77 and other fora to come up with a solid third world position in major areas of international negotiations.

In conclusion, the international environment plays a key role in determining which countries are free to control their economic destiny. Those that can resist foreign pressure and implement independent development strategies are in a much better position to develop than those that cannot. Key for developing countries in today's world is trying to weave through the parameters set by the world economy and maintain as much independence as possible. In the process, they would do well to support efforts aimed at steering the current international system in a more just direction. Globalization is a man-made process. There is no reason to believe that it cannot be altered for the benefit of a broader section of humanity. Indeed, there are many movements working towards that end and advancing proposals on how to craft a more progressive and representative form of globalization.[61]

REFERENCES

Africa Action. "Debt is Not Done—The 2005 Debt Deal," September 21, 2005, africaaction.org/campaign_new/page.php?

AFRODAD. "The G8 Debt Deal—A Half-baked Solution to the Crisis," www.afrodad.org/archive.

Ajayi, S. Ibi. "Globalization and Africa," *Journal of African Economies* 12, Supplement 1 (2003): 120–150

Ake, Claude. *Democracy and Development in Africa.* Washington, D.C.: Brookings Institution, 1996, 42.

Akyuz, Yilmaz. "Trade, Growth and Industrialization: Issues, Experience and Policy Challenges," January 2005, Downloaded from Google Scholar May 15, 2009.

———. "The WTO Negotiations on Industrial Tariffs: What Is At Stake for Developing Countries?" Penang: Third World Network, 2005.

Amin, S. *Neo-colonialism in West Africa.* New York: Monthly Review Press, 1982.

Bhagwati, J. *In Defense of Globalization.* Oxford University Press, 2004.

Beckman, Bjorn. "Empowerment or Repression? The World Bank and the Politics of African Adjustment." In *Authoritarianism, Democracy and Adjustment,* edited by Peter Gibbon, Yosuf Bangura, and Are Ofstad, 83–105. Uppsala: Scandinavian Institute of African Studies, 1989.

Bellow, Walden, and S. Ronsenfeld. *Dragons in Distress: Asia's Miracle Economies in Crisis.* San Francisco: Food First, 1990.

Brautigam, Deborah. "State Capacity and Effective Governance." In *Agenda for Africa's Economic Renewal,* edited by B. Ndulu, Nicolas van de Walle et al. Washington, D.C.: Overseas Development Council, 1996, 81–104.

Broad, Robin. *Global Backlash: Citizen Initiatives for a Just World Economy.* New York: Rowman and Littlefield Publishers, 2002.

Brown, Michael Barrat, and Pauline Tiffen. *Short Changed: Africa and the World Trade.* London: Plutu Press, 1992.

"The Cancun Challenge," *The Economist,* September 4, 2003, 59–61.

Chabal, Patrick. *Political Domination in Africa: Reflections on the Limits of Power.* Cambridge University Press, 1986.

Cheru, Fantu. *The Silent Revolution in Africa: Debt, Development and Democracy.* London and Harare: Zed Press, 1989.

---

[61] Teivo Teivainen, "The World Social Forum and Global Democratization: Learning from Porto Alegre," *Third World Quarterly* 23, no. 4 (2002), 621–632; Robin Broad, *Global Backlash: Citizen Initiatives for a Just World Economy* (New York: Rowman & Littlefield Publishers, 2002); M. Edwards and John Gaventa, eds., *Global Citizen Action* (Boulder, CO: Lynne Rienner, 2001).

Collier, P., A. Hoeffler, and C. Patillo. "Capital Flight as a Portfolio Choice," *World Bank Economic Review* 15, no. 1 (2001): 55–80.

Commission for Africa. *Our Common Interest*. London: Penguin Press, 2005.

Das, Bhagirath Lal. "Why the EU and US Offers on Farm Trade Are Not Good Enough," 2006, www.twnside.org.sg, Third World Network Briefing Paper 33.

Decalo, Samuel. *Coups and Army Rule in Africa: Motivations and Constraints*. New Haven: Yale University Press, 1990.

Diamond, Larry. "Class Formation in the Swollen African State,"*Journal of Modern African Studies* 25, no. 4 (1987): 567–596.

Dolla, D., and A. Kraay. "Spreading the Wealth," *Foreign Affairs,* January/February 2002.

Dumont, Rene. *False Start in Africa*. New York: Praeger Publishers, 1969.

Economic Commission for Africa. *The Doha Round and African Development: Turning Words into Deeds*. Addis Ababa: Trade and Regional Integration Division, 2003.

Edwards, M., and John Gaventa, eds. *Global Citizen Action*. Boulder CO: Lynne Rienner, 2001.

Fukuyama, Francis. "The End of History?" *The National Interest,* Summer 1989.

G8 Africa Action Plan, 2002 Kananaskis Summit.

G8 Gleneagles. "Progress Report by the G8 Africa Personal Representatives on Implementation of the Africa Action Plan (2005)," 20.

Gifford, Prosser, and William Roger Louis. *The Transfer of Power in Africa and Decolonization*. New Haven: Yale University Press, 1982.

Healy, J., M. Foster, A. Norton, and David Booth. *Towards National Public Expenditure Strategies for Poverty Reduction*. London: Overseas Development Institute, 2002.

Jubilee Debt Campaign. *Cutting the Strings!* September 2006.

Kaplan, Robert. "The Coming Anarchy," *Atlantic Monthly,* February 1994.

Kay, Cristobal. "Why East Asia Overtook Latin America: Agrarian Reform, Industrialization and Development," *Third World Quarterly* 23, no. 6, 1073–1102.

Khor, Martin. *Break the "Conspiracy of Silence" on Commodities,* August 30, 2004, www.twnside.org.sg, Third World Network, Global Trends.

———. "Comments on the WTO's Geneva July 2004 Package," August 2004, www.twnside.org.sg, Third World Network, Briefing Paper 22.

———. "The Commodities Crisis and the Global Trade in Agriculture: Present problems and some proposals." In *Millennium Development Goals: Raising the Resources to Tackle World Poverty,* edited by F. Cheru and C. Bradford, 97–117. London: Zed Press, 2005.

———. *Rethinking Globalization: Critical Issues and Policy Choices*. London: Zed Press, 2001.

Laidi, Zaki. *The Super-powers and Africa: The Constraints of a Rivalry, 1960–1990*. University of Chicago Press, 1990.

Lewis, W.A. *The Theory of Economic Growth*. London: Allen and Unwin, 1995.

Mazur, Jay. "Labor's New Internationalism." *Foreign Affairs*, January/February 2000.

McNeely, Kathy. "Food Security and Trade in Agriculture: Africa Keeps a Watchful Eye on U.S. Policy." *Washington Notes on Africa* 31, no. 1 (2006): 7.

Milanovic, Branko. "The Two Sides of Globalization: Against Globalization as We Know It." *World Development* 31, no. 4 (2003): 667–683

Mkandawire, T., and Soludo, C. *Our Continent, Our Future: African Perspectives on Structural Adjustment*. Trenton, NJ: Africa World Press, 2002.

OECD. "International Development Statistics On-line," Paris, 2004.

Oxfam. *Rigged Rules and Double Standards*. Oxford: Oxfam, 2002.

Perkins, Francis. "Africa's Agricultural Trade Reform and Development Options," *Trade Policy Briefing*, no. 1, South African Institute of International Affairs, 2003.

Rothchild, D., and Naomi Chazan, eds. *The Precarious Balance: State and Society in Africa*. Boulder, CO: Westview Press, 1988.

Rodney, Walter. *How Europe Underdeveloped Africa*. Washington, D.C.: Howard University Press, 1982.

Rostow, W.W. *The Stages of Economic Growth: A Non-Communist Manifesto*. Cambridge University Press, 1960.

Sachs, J.D., and A. Warner. "Economic Reforms and the Process of Global Integration," *Brookings Paper on Economic Activity*. Washington, D.C.: Brookings Institution, 1995.

SAPRIN. *Structural Adjustment: The Policy Roots of Economic Crisis, Poverty and Inequality*. London: Zed Press: 2004.

Te Velde, D.W. "Foreign Direct Investment: Policy Challenges for Sub-Saharan African Countries," Overseas Development Institute, 2002.

Teivainen, Teivo. "The World Social Forum and Global Democratization: Learning from Porto Alegre." *Third World Quarterly* 23, no. 4 (2002): 621–632.

UNCTAD. Economic Development in Africa: Trade Performance and Commodity Dependence. Geneva: United Nations, 2003.

UNCTAD. Economic Development in Africa: Rethinking the Role of Foreign Direct Investment. Geneva: United Nations, 2005.

United Nations. United Nations Program of Action for African Economic Recovery and Development 1986–1990 (UNPAAERD), Report of the Secretary-General, document A/42/560, New York, October 1, 1987.

Wade, Robert. "The Disturbing Rise in Poverty and Inequality." In *Taming Globalization*, edited by D. Held and M. Koenig-Archibugi. Cambridge: Polity Press, 2003.

Wade, Robert. "What Strategies are Viable for Developing Countries Today? The WTO and the Shrinking of Development Space," *Review of International Political Economy* 10, no. 4 (2003): 621–647.

World Bank. Can Africa Claim the 21st Century? 2000.

———. *Doing Business in 2004: Understanding Regulations*. New York: Oxford University Press, 2004.

———. *World Development Report 2005: A Better Investment Climate for All*.

———. *World Development Indicators 2004*.

Chapter 13

THE NEW OIL GULF OF AFRICA
Global Geopolitics and Enclave Oil-Producing Economies

Okbazghi Yohannes

Africa's economic history has moved in tandem with the evolution, growth, and expansion of capital-ism. In this complex relationship, Africa has always played a critical role as a supplier of strategic resources to world capitalism. The discovery and production of hydrocarbon sources of energy in recent decades has given the continent, as a supplier of strategic resources, even greater geopolitical visibility in the global division of labor. These new developments are causing a reframing of African development. Africa's unique position in the global hydrocarbon belt, defined in terms of its geographic proximity to the United States and the superior quality of its petroleum, combined with the fact that the new oil fields lie outside the political influence of OPEC, have prompted policy makers and oil companies to designate the oil-producing regions of the continent as vital to U.S. national security interest. Oil, energy, and North-South political-economic relations represent core issues that dominate the contemporary global order in which the securitization of African energy sources is likely to make the continent even more integral to the global competition for access to and political influence over African oil-producing countries.

This chapter assesses the impact of Africa's expanding role in global capitalism as a strategic supplier of hydrocarbon energy on geopolitics, continental governance, and the internal dynamics of the energy-producing African countries. Particular attention will be given to the increasing importance of the Gulf of Guinea to the United States in the context of the geopolitical competition for energy sources. In light of the past record and present reality, the chapter concludes with evaluations of whether the production and export of oil and natural gas will substantially contribute to the mobilization and accumulation of capital for purposes of promoting African development, democracy, social stability, and intra-generational equity or whether it will foster rentierism, interethnic tensions, and ecological deterioration. The discourse is informed by a political economy approach.

The Epic Quest for Incremental African Petroleum

The quest for African hydrocarbon resources began right after the First World War. The French learned from the war experience that energy independence was a necessary precondition for national security. This orientation prompted France to establish state-owned oil companies, assigned to search for oil in its African colonial empire; the effort produced palpable results with the oil finds in Gabon (Yergin 1993, 525–526). The British were not far behind in adopting this orientation. In fact, Shell and British

Petroleum were among the first oil majors to begin their quest for oil in Nigeria in the 1930s. In 1956, oil was discovered in Nigeria, and two years later, it began flowing from the country to advanced industrial countries. In short order, Portuguese Angola, Congo Brazzaville, Gabon, and Cameroon joined Nigeria as suppliers of crude oil to Western refineries.

Even though Nigeria, as a member of OPEC, remained the major producer and supplier of crude oil to the West throughout the Cold War, the epic quest for African hydrocarbon resources did not begin until the 1990s. Several factors have driven the post–Cold War rush for African oil, the foremost of which involve international supply and demand conditions. Conventional economics textbooks tell us that the value of any commodity is determined by the intersection of supply and demand. A departure from the intersection of the two curves will signal changes in the value of the commodity.

Demand for oil and natural gas has been steadily rising in the last decade, owing to a combination of intensity of consumption by both the developed nations and the rapidly industrializing countries, especially China and India with a combined population of 2.5 billion. In 2006, China, for example, imported 47 percent of the oil it consumed, one-third of which came from Africa. China's dependency on imported oil is expected to rise to 67 percent of its total energy need by 2015, and China will account for 30 percent of total future world demand (Yergin 2006; Zweig and Jianhai 2005). Moreover, powerful geoeconomic forces will shape the evolution of hydrocarbon resources in favor of Asian industrializers. The proximity of the Middle Eastern and Central Asian oil-producing states to India, China, Japan, and South Korea give the oil-dependent Asian countries a strategic advantage over the United States. Cognizant of this fact, such countries as Saudi Arabia and Iran are already playing their "China card" under the pretext of diversifying their external customers. For example, in October 2004, China's oil giant SINOPEC struck oil and gas deals with Iran worth $70 billion (Zweig and Jianhai 2005). If Indian and Chinese energy deals with Iran are fleshed out, the two countries will spend up to $200 billion for Iranian hydrocarbon resources over the next twenty-five years (Pocha 2005).

None has been more aware of the changes in global demand conditions than the Bush administration. After just two weeks in office, President Bush established the National Energy Policy Development Group (NEPDG), chaired by Vice President Dick Cheney. According to the group's report, by 2020, demand in the United States for natural gas, electricity, and oil will rise by 50 percent, 45 percent, and 33 percent, respectively; deregulation and acceleration of domestic exploration and production figured prominently in the group's recommendations (Yohannes 2003). The group acknowledged that expanding consumption had intensified global demand for hydrocarbon resources. Indeed, Americans spent $38 billion more on gasoline during the first six months of 2006 than during the same period in 2005, raising U.S. oil imports to 66 percent of total energy consumption; U.S. daily oil imports reached 20.6 million bbl (barrels) in 2005 and is expected to rise to 27.6 MMb (million barrels) by 2030. Overall, global oil consumption, which rose from 63 MMb daily in 1980 to 84 MMb daily in 2005, is projected to rise to 118 MMb daily by 2030 (Wells 2007).

It is in the context of this rising global demand for energy that Africa has increasingly begun to receive the attention of oil multinationals and oil-importing countries. Indeed, the Cheney task force identified western Africa (including the eastern and southern Gulf of Guinea countries) as one of the fastest-growing sources of oil and gas to which the United States should turn its eye (Yohannes 2003). As part of its package of recommendations, the Cheney group advised that the United States upgrade its presence in oil-producing regions, strengthen its ties with such key oil-producing states as Nigeria and Angola, and enable U.S. oil companies to overcome obstacles to investment in foreign energy sectors (Yohannes 2003).

On the supply side, in 2000, the U.S. Geological Survey estimated current world reserves at 1.1 trillion bbl and potential reserves at 1.4 trillion bbl (Wells 2007). Other optimistic projections raise the figure even higher; however, petroleum projections are often unreliable because oil-producing countries tend to exaggerate the amount of oil they possess in order to attract foreign investment or to enhance their international credit worthiness. For example, Kuwait's total reserves estimate remained unchanged between 1991 and 2002 even though the country produced 8 billion bbl (BBL) and did not add new discoveries to its reserves (Wells 2007). Moreover, according to the International Energy Agency, it would require up to $1.7 trillion in fresh investment for new energy development over the next twenty-five years simply to keep present reserves from shrinking (Yergin 2006; Roberts 2004, 180).

The key principle determining the supply of oil is that natural depletion and disruption of the oil supply are crucial determinants of the international valuation of hydrocarbon resources. By definition, petroleum is nonrenewable and thus subject to the law of depletion. When old oil wells are exhausted, new ones must be found to keep oil flowing. In 1956, Shell Oil geologist King Hubbert developed a mathematical model demonstrating that potential disequilibrium between rates of depletion and discovery is inherent to oil production. Using this model, Hubbert accurately predicted the U.S. oil production peak in 1970, when the highest production rate of 10 MMb a day was followed by a downward decline to 5 MMb daily in 2005. His model, known as the Hubbert peak, continues to inform expectations of global oil production and supply, and growing disequilibrium in the discovery/consumption ratios does seem to punctuate its predictive value. For example, during the 1960s, global consumption stood at 6 billion barrels (BBL) annually, while oil finds ran between 30 and 60 BBL annually; between 1995 and 2004, the average yearly global consumption of oil was 24 BBL, compared to the yearly average of 9.6 BBL in new discoveries; and today, the world consumes 30 BBL annually, while new discoveries stand at less than 4 billion barrels (BBL) annually (EnergyBulletin.net 2006; Roberts 2004, 50–51). Oil production in twenty-four of the forty-four major oil-producing countries has peaked and is in decline.

Moreover, since hydrocarbon sources of energy are unevenly distributed globally, reliance on one region alone or on a limited number of suppliers entails vulnerability to political or social disruptions of supply. Measuring susceptibility to vicissitudes of political fortunes, the U.S. General Accounting Office estimates that 63 percent of global oil reserves are located in countries with medium to high levels of political risk (Wells 2007). The present global demand shock, triggered by a series of events, is a case in point. In late 2002 and early 2003, nationwide strikes and protests in Venezuela reduced the country's daily oil flow by 500,000 bbl. Similar events in Nigeria also reduced that country's oil flow by up to 20 percent: violence preceding the 2003 presidential election removed 800,000 bbl of oil a day from the market, and in early July 2004, a French oil multinational suspended production of 245,000 bbl daily and 187 million cubic meters of gas in order to preempt a strike by its Nigerian workers. The expectation that, following U.S. occupation, Iraq's daily oil production would return to its 1978 peak of 3.5 MMb also failed to materialize. In fact, Iraqi oil output is now below the preoccupation level (Yergin 2006; Goldwyn 2004).

Diversification of energy sources is the natural default option for energy-importing countries wishing to insulate their economies from potential perturbations. After all, major oil-importing countries have not yet forgotten the deleterious impact of the 1973–1974 Arab oil embargo on the United States and the Netherlands and the attendant politicization of petroleum. Mitigation of the potential impact of supply disruptions through diversification of producers and suppliers is a prudent strategy. In this context, West Africa offers two critical advantages to oil-importing countries.

First, West Africa is a non-Arab and non-OPEC oil-producing region. Excluding Nigeria, which is an OPEC member, West Africa has seven relatively big producers (Angola, Equatorial Guinea, Gabon, Congo Brazzaville, Cameroon, the Ivory Coast, and Mauritania) and three minor producers (Ghana, Benin[1], and Senegal[2]), whose collective supply of petroleum can enormously mitigate the effect of supply disruptions in the Middle East. In times of supply disruption, the region can serve as a swing supplier of oil. Furthermore, the major oil-producing area of West Africa (centered on the Gulf of Guinea) can be accessed, without natural obstruction or political interference, by oil tankers that can load their oil without having to pass through choke points. In this context, the expanding frontier of West Africa's deepwater oil production takes on added significance because oil produced in the ocean can simply be shipped directly to refineries in Europe and North America.

There are other reasons that make West Africa attractive to oil multinationals and oil-importing countries. First, by global standards, West Africa is generally regarded as a low-cost producing region. In 2005, for example, the cost of production in Angola, Equatorial Guinea, and Congo Brazzaville was $8.70 per barrel compared with the global industry average of $14.90 per barrel (Barkindo 2007). Moreover, the terms of the contractual relationship between the region's host countries and the oil multinationals is more favorable to the latter than anywhere else in the world. After fully recovering the cost of exploration and production, oil companies simply share the revenue with the governments. Second, because West African crude oil is light and sweet with low sulfur content, it is friendlier to the environment and cheaper to refine than the Middle East's heavy and sour oil. For this reason, West African oil is very attractive to refineries that must contend with stringent environmental regulations in Europe, North America, and Japan (Ghazvinian 2007).

Third, in so far as new oil finds are concerned, Africa is a relatively late bloomer. As of 2005, over 75 BBL of petroleum reserves were discovered onshore and in shallow offshore water in West Africa, 38.6 BBL of which have been produced (Barkindo 2007). The oil bonanza is likely to continue with the accelerated shift to deep and ultra-deep water exploration and production. Thanks to new oil finds in deep water, West Africa's proven oil reserves stood at 55 BBL at the end of 2005, 25 BBL of which were added since 1996 from 100 new finds in deep water and another 102 in shallow water (Barkindo 2007).

What distinguishes West Africa from other oil-producing regions is the fact that the success rate in oil discovery (boosted by deepwater exploration) in and around the Gulf of Guinea is unmatched elsewhere. Since 2000, a third of new global oil discoveries were made in West Africa; in 2001, 7 of the 8 BBL of new oil finds were in West Africa; by 2010, 20 percent of new global oil-production capacity will be in and around the Gulf of Guinea and deepwater oil will account for 50 percent of West African production, up from only 14 percent in 2005 (Ghazvinian 2007; Clark 2006). Moreover, the success rate in oil discovery in West Africa since the early 1990s has lifted the spirits of oil prospectors. While only twenty-nine giant fields (with reserves exceeding 500 MMb each) were found during the 1990s (down from 100 such discoveries in the 1960s), more than half of these (fifteen total) were found in

---

[1] Benin began producing a modest quantity of offshore oil in October 1982. Production ceased in recent years but exploration of new sites is ongoing. (CIA World FactBook 2009. Benin: www.cia.gov/library/publications/the-world-factbook/geos/bn.html.)

[2] Senegal is hoping to become the next African oil and gas success story. It is believed to possess many of the critical elements necessary for large-scale oil production. Recent work is focusing current exploration on higher potential play types in an effort to find significant reserve volumes believed to be present. See Kofi Akosah-Sarpong, "Senegal, Gambia and Guinea Bissau Join Vast New Oil Economies," in *Alexander's Gas and Oil Connections* 9, no. 5, Wednesday, March 10, 2004, www.gasandoil.com/goc/news/nta41087.htm.

West Africa, including six at a water depth of over 1,000 meters. In terms of volume, the new oil finds made in West Africa between 1996 and 2005 accounted for 21 percent of new global oil reserves and for 40 percent of the deepwater reserves. Consequently, the oil supply from West Africa (Nigeria excluded) rose from 1.6 MMb daily in 2000 to 2.3 MMb daily in 2005 with further expansion to 3.8 MMb a day expected by 2012. Nigeria's contribution rose from 2.2 MMb daily to 2.6 MMb daily, with a 4.2 MMb daily increase projected by 2012 (Barkindo 2007).

Given the rising expectations about undiscovered deepwater oil, West Africa's strategic location in the global hydrocarbon map is likely to attract more investment. In its 2000 report, the U.S. Geological Survey noted that there could be more than 400 BBL of undiscovered offshore hydrocarbon resources, representing 47 percent of total undiscovered oil worldwide. Before 2005, the world had discovered 503 BBL of deepwater oil, 204 BBL of which have been produced (Sandrea 2007). The West African portion of the undiscovered oil could be 70 BBL; this estimate appears to be credible since 12 BBL of oil were discovered in West Africa between 2001 and 2005; additional 5–15 BBL could result from further development of existing fields (Barkindo 2007). Such estimates have raised hopes and expectations, and West Africa's landscapes and ocean floors are now being drilled by big oil multinationals. The heartland of the hydrocarbon map in West Africa is obviously the Gulf of Guinea.

In the parlance of the oil industry, the hydrocarbon region of West Africa is divided into three petroleum provinces. In the middle (with the Gulf of Guinea as its vital center) is the Niger delta tertiary system, covering over 300,000 sq. km. With Nigeria as its heartland, this system encompasses Equatorial Guinea, Cameroon, Sao Tome, and the Ivory Coast. At the end of 2005, the Niger delta tertiary system was said to contain 38 BBL of proven oil reserves of which 9 BBL were in deep water (Barkindo 2007). Until quite recently, Nigeria's onshore oil fields in the Niger Delta supplied most of the province's petroleum. Since these onshore fields have long been exploited, many analysts forecast that Nigeria would be a mature oil producer, allowing Angola to surpass it because of its deepwater finds. However, with new discoveries and the promise of offshore possessions, Nigeria is roaring back into the game. Until 2003, the small Abo field had been Nigeria's only deepwater producer at 800 meters. But in January 2006, Shell's Bonga subsea oil field (constructed at $3.6 billion) began pumping 225,000 bbl a day; shortly thereafter, Erha field (jointly operated by Exxon and Shell) came onstream with 150,000 bbl a day. When the remaining new subsea finds come onstream by 2010, Nigeria's deepwater oil output will amount to almost 1.3 MMb a day, although even more is expected since Nigeria's deepwater region is generally regarded as relatively under-explored (Clark 2006).

Although Nigeria has been the hydrocarbon pillar of the Niger delta tertiary system for almost half a century, the addition of Equatorial Guinea as a major hydrocarbon producer has elevated the Niger delta system to a new status. Mobil first struck oil in the country in 1995 and came onstream a year later. Today, Exxon-Mobil's Zafiro oil field (holding 400 MMb) is Equatorial Guinea's jewel; 260,000 bbl a day are directly pumped into Exxon's floating production operation system on its way to the United States. In 1999, another U.S. oil company, Triton, discovered huge oil reserves at Ceiba. Ironically, the oil bonanza in Equatorial Guinea sparked a frenzy of mergers among U.S. oil companies: in 2001, Amarada Hess bought Triton Energy for $3 billion, and Exxon acquired Mobil. Equatorial Guinea has become the United States' petro-fiefdom as Exxon-Mobil, Marathon Energy, Amarada Hess, Noble Energy, and Devon Energy dominate the country's hydrocarbon sector. This is why Equatorial Guinea has become the premier destination for U.S. investment, attracting over $5 billion between 1998 and 2003, along with 3,000 U.S. oil workers (Frynas 2004).

Map 13.1   Africa's Gulf Oil States

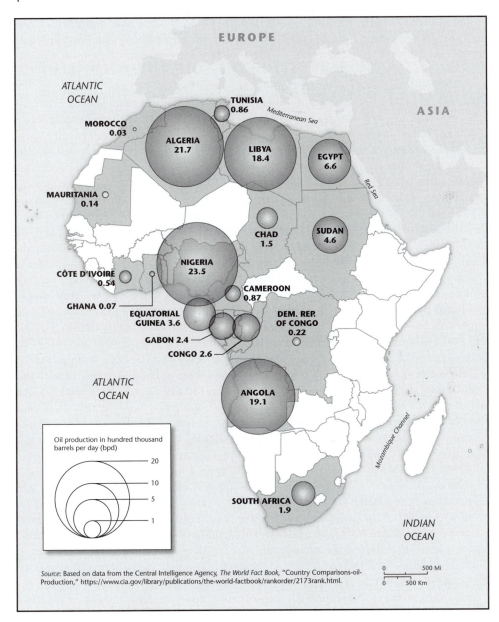

EUROPE

ASIA

ATLANTIC OCEAN

TUNISIA
0.86

Mediterranean Sea

MOROCCO
0.03

ALGERIA
21.7

LIBYA
18.4

EGYPT
6.6

Red Sea

MAURITANIA
0.14

CHAD
1.5

SUDAN
4.6

CÔTE D'IVOIRE
0.54

NIGERIA
23.5

CAMEROON
0.87

GHANA 0.07

EQUATORIAL
GUINEA 3.6

DEM. REP.
OF CONGO
0.22

GABON 2.4

CONGO 2.6

ATLANTIC OCEAN

ANGOLA
19.1

Oil production in hundred thousand
barrels per day (bpd)

20
10
5
1

Mozambique Channel

SOUTH AFRICA
1.9

INDIAN OCEAN

Source: Based on data from the Central Intelligence Agency, *The World Fact Book*, "Country Comparisons-oil-Production," https://www.cia.gov/library/publications/the-world-factbook/rankorder/2173rank.html.

0   500 Mi

0   500 Km

The second important West African hydrocarbon-producing region is the Gabon-Congo belt petroleum province, which lies south of the Gulf of Guinea with Angola as its vital center. This province had more than 16 BBL of proven oil reserves at the end of 2005, including 11.7 BBL discovered in the deepwater portions of Angola's maritime jurisdiction (Barkindo 2007). Congo Brazzaville's deepwater region has also shown potential; in March 2007, the French oil multinational Total announced the discovery of two oil wells in water depth of 2,000 meters some 80 km offshore of Congo. When the two wells came onstream in 2008, they were projected to produce 90,000 bbl per day, sustaining the country's 1.5 BBL reserves (*Les Echos*, April 3, 2007).

With its huge, untapped hydrocarbon resources, Angola remains the most coveted producer. As in Nigeria, a small quantity of oil was discovered in the 1950s and by the late 1990s, Angola was producing 770,000 bbl a day, mostly for the U.S. market. What made Angola particularly attractive to oil multinationals was the potential of its deepwater blocks. In 1999, Angola offered seventeen deepwater blocks and another four ultra-deepwater blocks for exploration. Exxon-Mobil has made seventeen discoveries since the late 1990s in Block 15, holding 4.5 BBL of oil; more discoveries are expected since Exxon-Mobil alone holds 12 million acres off the Angolan coast. Total has made fifteen discoveries in Block 17, including the Girassol field with thirty-nine subsea wells. Moreover, Total has eight discoveries in ultra-deepwater Block 32. For its part, BP has made twelve finds in ultra-deepwater in Block 31 (*Petroleum Economist*, May 1, 2007). The promise of Angola's deepwater fields was such that BP and Exxon paid $870 million in 1999 in signature bonuses, the nonrecoverable down payments for licenses, to drill oil in just three ultra-deepwater areas; this set an industry record because such payments had historically been in the range of $10 million to $100 million (Global Witness 1999). However, this sum pales in comparison with the $3.1 billion Angola received in signature bonuses plus $240 million for social projects in May 2006 from an Italian company and a consortium led by China's SINOPEC for licenses to explore in just three deepwater areas (Reed 2006).

The success rate of oil finds in Angola has been no less than spectacular. For example, between 1996 and 2002, the success rate in Angola's deepwater category was ten out of ten, compared with the global success rate of four out of ten (Yohannes 2003). In Angola, 100 subsea wells have yielded 8 BBL of oil compared to only 6.5 BBL from 450 such wells in the Gulf of Mexico (Clark 2006). As of November 2006, Angola had thirty-four deepwater blocks in various stages of development, including eighteen blocks already in production (Shankleman 2006, 103). All told, Angola anticipates $50 billion in fresh investment in its hydrocarbon sector over the next six years and is expected to raise its daily production from 1.5 MMb to 2.6 MMb by 2010 (Wingrove 2007). As a result, the windfall in revenue for the Angolan state would be $94 billion between 2002 and 2019, not including incomes from additional finds or price hikes (Shankleman 2006, 103).

The third component of the petroleum triangle, the Mauritania–Senegal–Guinea-Bissau province in the northern portions of West Africa, extends more than 600,000 sq. km. Although this region has yet to be fully explored, that Mauritania already has 500 MMb of proven deepwater reserves and that Senegal is said to have 800 MMb of oil yet to be proven are early indications of the region's great production potential (Barkindo 2007).

West Africa's role in the global natural gas sector is also important. As in the case of oil, the region's importance lies in its ability to meet incremental global demand for natural gas. As of January 2006, Nigeria alone claimed 185 trillion cubic feet of proven natural gas reserves compared to 193 trillion cubic feet for the United States. Natural gas production in Africa as a percentage of total world production is projected to rise from 5.5 percent in 2003 to 18.5 percent in 2025. The region's proximity to the U.S. market appears to elevate its importance, and although natural gas accounts for only 3 percent of total energy consumption in the United States today, this figure is projected to rise to 25 percent by 2020 (U.S. Department of Energy, International Energy Outlook 2006). After all, between 1999 and 2003 alone, many gas-powered plants with the capacity of 220,000 megawatts of electricity have been installed in the United States, with more to follow (Roberts 2004, 177).

U.S. companies are already gearing up to take advantage of future shortfalls in natural gas. Marathon Energy has created a natural gas liquefaction plant in Equatorial Guinea at a cost of $1.4 billion. The project began in 2000 when the Overseas Private Investment Corporation (a U.S. federal agency) offered Marathon $373 million (the biggest amount ever for the regions outside North Africa) in loan guarantees to leaven the dough (Yohannes 2003). The plant is expected to produce up to 3.8 million tons of liquefied natural gas annually, destined for the United States. Marathon's Alba field (with 5 trillion cubic meters of estimated reserves) will supply the feedstock for the plant (Quinlan 2007). To be sure, given that the world is expected to run out of gas in forty years, every incremental supply of West African natural gas will play a critical role in the global scramble for resources.

Geopolitics and Securitization of African Petroleum

From its moment of discovery, oil acquired geopolitical and security dimensions. Indeed, the centrality of petroleum to the economic prosperity and war-making capacity of nations is such that energy security and military security are treated as interchangeable in the geopolitical calculations of great powers. The enunciation of the Carter doctrine in 1980 illustrates the point. In the wake of the 1979 Iranian Revolution and the Soviet invasion of Afghanistan, President Carter warned that any threat to the oil-producing Persian Gulf region would be considered a threat to U.S. national security interests, entitling the United States to use military power to defend the oil-producing states from external aggression and internal subversion. In keeping with this declaration, the president created a rapid deployment force, eventually upgraded to the U.S. Central Command (CENTCOM) and tasked to defend the Middle East. Both the first Gulf War and the current U.S. occupation of Iraq have been conducted under the aegis of CENTCOM.

The Carter doctrine serves as a template for those seeking to incorporate the Gulf of Guinea into the U.S. sphere of influence. Since the late 1990s, U.S. oil companies involved in West Africa have been seeking the Africanization of the Carter doctrine. Their immediate concern then was the potential instability in the oil-producing states and the vulnerability of their offshore oil platforms and tankers to potential piracy. The oil multinationals sought the designation of the Gulf of Guinea as vital to U.S. national interest: this would allow them protection for their installations from the U.S. blue water navy and facilitate direct U.S. government involvement in the internal security of the oil-producing states, propping up the regimes by providing military assistance, training, and equipment.

The ideological foundation needed to achieve this objective has been framed primarily by private policy making institutions, chief among which are the Corporate Council on Africa, the Council on Foreign Relations, the Heritage Foundation, the Center for Strategic and International Studies, and the Jerusalem-based Institute for Advanced Strategic and Political Studies (IASPS). The ideological and political campaigns of these think tanks gathered momentum in the wake of the September 2001 terrorist attacks on the United States. In early 2002, for example, the IASPS organized a symposium, profiling the strategic importance of West Africa to U.S. energy and military security. The IASPS paraded an impressive panel of speakers from the oil industry, government, and academia. Janice Van Dyke Walden, vice president of Vanco Energy (whose holdings include 20 million deepwater acres in seven West African states), made a strong pitch on behalf of the oil industry for the urgent designation of the Gulf of Guinea as vital to U.S. security interest. As she put it, "Potential reserves number 8 billion barrels of oil just in Vanco. . . . If you were to take our acreage, and superimpose it onto the Gulf of Mexico you would see that it is about 75 percent of deepwater Gulf of Mexico, and that's one company alone. So clearly our interest is in Africa, and the deep water potential there is fantastic" (IASPS 2002).

Another speaker, Robert Murphy from the U.S. Department of State, elaborated on the comparative advantages West Africa offered to the United States over other oil-producing regions, "Africa has provided us with an excellent array of diverse oil exporters. Political discord or dispute in African oil states is unlikely to take on a regional or ideological tone that would result in a joint embargo by suppliers at once. Much of West Africa's oil is offshore, thereby insulated from domestic political or social turmoil, and can be delivered via open sea-lanes devoid of canals or narrow straits" (IASPS 2002).

The proliferation of task forces, advisory panels, study groups, seminars, and symposia (all calling for the designation of the Gulf of Guinea as vital to U.S. security) was unprecedented. Their descriptions of the strategic value of West Africa to the United States and of the security threats to this vital hydrocarbon region are notable for their extraordinary thematic consistency. The superiority of West African oil, proximity of the region to the U.S. market, exceptional productivity of West African offshore oil fields, hospitality of West Africa to foreign investment in the hydrocarbon sector, vulnerability of the Middle East to internal convulsion, potential deterioration in U.S.-Saudi relations, continued ability of OPEC to put a stranglehold on global supply conditions, and an increasing shift in Middle East oil supply towards Asia are the major themes raised in all think-tank literature as the presumably palpable reasons for the United States to place the Gulf of Guinea under its protective shield (Yohannes 2003; Gill 2007; Goldwyn 2004).

The backdrop against which the think tanks operated was the growing instability in the Niger Delta, the heartland of West Africa's hydrocarbon resources. Nigeria, the fifth largest oil exporter to the United States and the largest oil producer in Africa, has long held great potential as a cash cow for the multinationals if only the perils associated with petroleum exploitation in the country could be contained. Beginning in the early 1990s, communities in the Niger Delta increasingly became assertive, seeking redress against gross injustice, vandalization of their environmental resources, and deterioration of their ecology. Among the first to rise up in the early 1990s to reclaim their social authenticity and ecological autonomy were the Ogoni people who, after years of futile appealing to Shell and to the government for justice and equity, succeeded in chasing the company out from Ogoniland in 1993. For both the Nigerian government and oil multinationals, the Niger Delta presaged a nightmarish scenario because 90 percent of Nigeria's oil export revenue and 80 percent of government income mostly originate in the Delta. The Delta houses a mosaic of some forty ethnic groups and is one of the most densely populated regions with more than 27 million people crammed into just 27,000 square miles (Ghazvinian 2007). To stem a rising tide of communal opposition to the vandalization of the Niger Delta, the then Nigerian military leader Sanni Abacha publicly hanged nine environmental activists in 1995. But the cruel execution of the nine failed to yield the expected deterrent effect, and the struggle for social equity and ecological integrity that started in Ogoniland spread to other ethnic enclaves.

The number of cases involving damages to oil pipelines (officially reported as cases of vandalism) steadily increased from seven in 1993 to thirty-three in 1996, fifty-seven in 1998, 499 in 1999, and more than 600 in 2000 (Ghazvinian 2007). The result was immediately felt as Nigeria began to lose a substantial amount of oil output. What Western media and commentators characterized as vandalism was, in fact, a dress rehearsal for a Delta-wide social mobilization and political struggle. In July 2002, 600 women overran Chevron's Escravos export terminal (with a 450,000 bbl daily capacity) in what became a watershed event in the grassroots mobilization and struggle. The women confronted the company with twenty-six demands including the formation of a permanent tripartite body of representatives from the oil company, the government, and the communities; the creation of local jobs and income-generating projects; and the utilization of some of the oil revenue to provide social amenities, clinics, and infrastructure (Turner and Brownhill 2003). Following the Escravos example, twelve other occupations of oil terminals and flow stations took place in the Delta. In most cases, these were led by women who publicly disrobed themselves in order to shame them into action. Work stoppages, strikes, and seizures by oil workers of offshore platforms became a common occurrence.

The demands of the various communities in the Niger Delta are the same: restoration of the degraded ecology; reversion of ownership of their land; compensation for the social, economic, and environmental ills caused by the oil companies; and control of their resources. Although more than $350 billion have been siphoned off from the region since the late 1950s, the Delta communities still have no access to running water, proper sanitation, electricity, hospitals, or health clinics. Ironically, where communities have taken matters into their own hands, the oil multinationals (with the help of private policymaking institutions, the media, and even academia) have blamed the communities for these problems as well as for the vandalism, lawlessness, sabotage, and interethnic conflict that are said to create the gathering threat of supply disruption. On the other hand, wanton exposure of the communities to radioactive materials from gas flaring, respiratory illnesses, carcinogenic diseases, and the loss of environmental sources of livelihood are treated as legitimate consequences of doing business. Substandard oil production operations, blowouts and gas flares, frequent oil spills and leakage from old and poorly maintained equipment, and corrosion of pipelines and flow stations (which have eviscerated the sources of livelihoods for millions) hardly figure in the conventional literature.

In any event, the growing instability in the Niger Delta gave the oil multinationals and the private policymaking institutions further ammunition in their crusade to classify the Gulf of Guinea as vital to U.S. national security interest. By September 2003, 40 percent of Nigeria's oil production capacity was shut down, causing enormous economic losses (Turner and Brownhill 2004). The crisis in the Niger Delta was such that the U.S. Defense Department considered dispatching more than 5,000 U.S. troops from Germany to the region to help the Nigerian government quell the growing insurrection; instead, it launched a small contingent of U.S. forces in to assist Nigerian troops and oil security forces in battling the insurgents in the Delta (Turner and Brownhill 2007). The oil multinationals and the Bush administration began to present the Delta crisis as one triggered by ethnic and communal conflicts, rather than by corporate crimes and decades of privation.

Rather than stem the tide of insurgency, the misrepresentation of the Niger Delta crisis and the deepening U.S. involvement likely fueled grassroots activism. A number of groups began to roam the Delta in growing determination to reestablish their historic entitlement to their ecology. These groups have launched daring attacks on oil facilities and convoys and are well armed with machine guns, rocket launchers, and even speedboats. In June 2006, for example, the insurgents used speedboats to attack an offshore platform 60 kilometers from the coast, capturing six British, an American, and a Canadian and demonstrating their ability to paralyze even offshore oil production (Marqueardt 2006). The Niger Delta is a security nightmare for the Nigerian government, the oil companies, and the United States because the region's dense mangrove forests, swamps, and the labyrinth of waterways are more suitable for guerrilla warfare than conventional engagement. The oil installations, pipelines, and flow stations are strewn all over the Delta, making military protection of oil facilities without setting the whole Delta ablaze a formidable task. Shell alone possesses over 1,000 oil wells in the Delta, connected by a labyrinth of 6,000 km of pipeline (Marqueardt 2006). It is exceedingly difficult to mount an effective counterinsurgency.

Although oil multinationals and U.S. security managers are certainly alarmed by the growing insurgency in West Africa, their true fear is the establishment of an operational connection between global terrorism and the local insurgency. The fearsome image of global terror spreading to West Africa significantly boosted the position of those clamoring for the designation of the Gulf of Guinea as strategically vital to U.S. energy and military security. The Bush administration's answer to the security dilemma was to urgently put into place a West African security framework. One arm of the security framework would involve erecting security perimeters to the north of the oil-producing states to detect and deter global terrorists from entering the region. To this end, the Bush administration (after years of rehearsal) created the Trans-Saharan Counter-terrorism Initiative, inclusive of Nigeria, Senegal, Niger, Mali, Chad, Mauritania, Morocco, and Tunisia, which expanded the geographic scope and programmatic specificity to the effort to erect barriers against potential infiltrators from North Africa.

The second arm of the West African security framework would enable the petrostates to develop maritime capabilities in order to defend offshore oil facilities. In November 2006, the U.S. state and defense departments organized a conference in Benin of eleven West African states (including Angola, Congo Brazzaville, Gabon, Democratic Republic of Congo [DRC], Benin, Togo, Nigeria, Cameroon, Ghana, Equatorial Guinea, and Sao Tome) and representatives from Senegal and South Africa. In opening the conference, Admiral Harry Ulrich, commander of U.S. Naval Forces in Europe, declared that the petrostates were annually losing $1.5 billion of oil revenue to theft and hundreds of millions more to other illegal activities. However, the admiral reassured the ministers that "the United States and our European partners are committed to helping African nations build capacity to improve maritime governance. Our increased presence in the Gulf of Guinea is a sure sign of this commitment, and we aspire to do more. We are listening and learning from our African partners as we assist them in efforts to develop regional solutions to very serious regional maritime safety and security challenges" (Star News Service, November 16, 2006). The conference was declared a success when the eleven states signed a maritime security pact and agreed to meet twice yearly to review their shared maritime security concerns under U.S. stewardship (Star News Service, November 16, 2006). Their focus on maritime security collaboration was no accident. By 2020, when the United States will be importing 70 percent of its oil, an estimated 67 MMb of oil and 460 million tons of liquid natural gas will cross the world's oceans each day in tankers, making oceanic security a high priority (Yergin 2006).

United States–China Competition in Africa's New Gulf Oil States

The tipping point in the Bush administration's decision to eventually declare the Gulf of Guinea as vital to U.S. national security interests (warranting the formation of a separate Africa Command) was the arrival of China on the oil auction block. Until the late 1980s, China was a net oil exporter and was self-sufficient in oil as recently as 1993. Since then, China's oil import has skyrocketed. In 2005, China consumed 6.6 MMb of oil daily, almost half of which was imported; by 2030, China's daily oil consumption will reach 15.3 MMb (*Petroleum Economist*, December 1, 2006). According to a report by a Center for Strategic and International Studies delegation to China, Beijing views Africa as integral to China's effort to promote a multipolar reconfiguration of the global order. From this perspective, China needs Africa to furnish critical natural resources in order to continue its economic growth, to provide markets for its expanding industrial output, and for political support in its struggle to carve out a strategic niche in the global order (Gill et al. 2007).

To meet its growing energy need, China has deployed its three state-owned oil giants to the hydrocarbon trenches of the world. The China National Petroleum Corporation (CNPC) has purchased oil facilities in twenty-one countries and is planning to invest another $18 billion in overseas assets in the next fifteen years. Chinese companies have invested $8 billion in Sudan's oil sector, with the result that 60 percent of Sudan's oil output is now shipped to China. Nigeria, Equatorial Guinea, and Angola have now also become primary targets. In addition to owning exploratory rights in Equatorial Guinea (a country that ships 150,000 bbl a day to China), China National Oil Operating Corporation (CNOOC) has recently invested $2.3 billion in just one Nigerian oil field. China's investment in Angola's oil sector is even larger, transforming the country into the single-largest African oil exporter to China.

China's foray into the region's energy sector is lubricated by the extension of a $2 billion interest-free loan for infrastructure development by China's export-import bank (China Exim) to Angola and by a $1 billion soft loan to Nigeria after the latter awarded four exploration licenses to Chinese oil companies (*Petroleum Economist*, December 1, 2006; McGreal 2006). In 2006, China had standing pledges totaling $8.1 billion in soft loans for Nigeria, Angola, and Mozambique alone (Gill et al. 2007). In 2000, China agreed to write off $1.2 billion of Africa's debt and followed this with another pledge to forgive $750 million in 2003 (Gill et al. 2007). Because Chinese loans and debt write-offs are given without the usual attendant political conditions, the practice is disconcerting to the United States, which fears that the conditionality regime that has hitherto been imposed on aid recipients could be sent down the drain. The U.S. Treasury Department expressed its exasperation with this kind of behavior by labeling China a "rogue creditor" (Gill et al. 2007).

What is particularly alarming to Washington is China's vacuum-cleaner approach in its Africa policy. In 2000, China sponsored the creation of the Forum on China-Africa Cooperation (FOCAC) to ostensibly promote cooperation and consultation between African states and China on virtually everything. Since then, China has aggressively targeted the continent's energy, minerals, and markets. The mechanisms are trade, aid, investment, and debt forgiveness. China Exim (whose annual disbursable funds are in the range of $15 billion) disbursed $12.1 billion by mid-2006 for infrastructure development, mostly in oil- and mineral-producing states (Gill et al. 2007).

In November 2006, China hosted a summit of heads of state and government from forty-eight African countries with a view to furthering close relationships. According to the 2007–2009 cooperation plan, China has pledged to send 100 senior agronomists to Africa, to establish ten agricultural demonstration centers and to support heavy involvement by Chinese firms in the production and processing of African agricultural output. In order to boost Chinese investment in Africa, Beijing pledged to establish a $5 billion China-Africa development fund, primarily to enable Chinese corporations to invest in the continent and establish trade zones. Water conservation, power generation projects, telecommunications, transport, and other infrastructure projects are considered critical areas for investment. Moreover, China pledged to provide African states $3 billion in soft loans and another $2 billion in export credit to buy Chinese goods. In terms of human resources development, China will train 15,000 African professionals and will double the number of scholarships given to African students from 2,000 to 4,000 per year. China will add five more Confucius Institutes to the three that are already teaching the Chinese language to 8,000 Africans. China will also build hospitals, clinics, and schools in various African countries. Finally, in the security arena, China will help African countries to build counter-terrorism capabilities (Forum on China-Africa Cooperation, November 2006).

U.S.-China competition in Africa is not limited to the hydrocarbon sector. The search for external markets and sources of raw material has historically been integral to the expansion of capitalism. In a classic pattern, China has placed its covetous eye on African minerals. It is instructive to note that China's combined consumption of iron ore, aluminum, copper, and nickel as a percentage of total global consumption jumped from just 7 percent in 1990 to 20 percent in 2000 and is expected to reach 40 percent by 2010 (Zweig and Jianhai 2005). In order to meet this growing demand, Chinese companies are today aggressively mining platinum in Zimbabwe, copper in Zambia, diamonds in Sierra Leone, and cobalt in the DRC. Chinese logging firms have become active participants in the destruction of African forests in Gabon, Mozambique, and Equatorial Guinea (Walt 2005; McGreal 2006).

African markets are equally important for China. After all, the countries in the Gulf of Guinea together have 300 million potential consumers. More importantly, the pirate capitalists who control the flow of petrodollars are ideal customers for imported arms and luxury goods. Chinese trade with Africa has been on a steady rise, growing in value from just $2 billion in 1999 to $55 billion in 2006 and is projected to reach $100 billion by 2010, eclipsing Africa's trade with the European Union and the United States by a large margin (McLeary 2007).

China's competition for West African oil, minerals, and markets has a clear political dimension as China is openly challenging U.S. and European influence in Africa. China's strategy here is not only to provide the African states with fungible money, but also to offer them an alternative source of arms. For example, China sold Zimbabwe $240 million worth of military gadgets and supplied Nigeria with $251 million worth of fighter jets and other weapon systems and financed these transactions through China Exim. China even arranged for President Mugabe of Zimbabwe to receive a sumptuous $9 million home with a blue-tiled roof (Walt 2005).

China's competition in Africa has already complicated the Western response to the crisis of legitimation in the African petrostates. In the hope of thwarting the growing instability, the United States, the European Union, and international financial institutions have been waving the banner of transparency and good governance. This stratagem is meant to prod the national pirate capitalists to share some of the spoils from oil export with the population. Thus, transparency of receipts of oil revenue and accountability of public expenditure would serve as a measure of good governance. The prototypical model has been the much-touted Chad experiment. The discovery of oil in Chad in the mid-1990s put oil multinationals in a quandary for both political and ecological reasons. From the start, nongovernmental organizations (NGOs) raised serious concerns over the potential underground water pollution, loss of biodiversity, and displacement of indigenous communities as a result of petroleum development. Because of its multiethnic and multireligious character, Chad was very prone to the internal fragmentation and instability considered to be potential obstacles to the exploitation of the oil. Chad is also a landlocked country, meaning that a 1,100-km long pipeline had to be built to carry the crude oil to the

Cameroonian coast on the Atlantic Ocean, in the process displacing a large number of indigenous communities and destroying pristine forests. To overcome these political, social, and ecological challenges, the oil companies needed external support and cover. The World Bank volunteered to serve as intermediary between the oil multinationals, the Chadian government, and the nonstate actors. The Bank's position was that "poverty alleviation" was the primary aim of exploiting Chad's oil; to this end, the profits from Chad's oil would flow directly into an account controlled by the World Bank, which would then funnel the profits to Chad's central government, the oil-producing regions, and future generations, according to predetermined percentages (Pegg 2006; Shankleman 2006, 45–46; Yohannes 2003).

Exxon-Mobil, Chevron-Texaco, and Malaysia's Petronas formed a consortium and began drilling oil in earnest. A $3.7-billion pipeline was constructed all the way to the Atlantic coast. While the consortium provided $2.2 billion for the project, the World Bank mobilized the remaining $1.5 billion from commercial banks and its own affiliate, the International Finance Corporation. To bring the Chadian and Cameroonian governments on board, the Bank supplied $93 million of its own money to cover the Chadian and Cameroonian governments' stake in the project. Moreover, in order to assuage the concerns of indigenous communities and environmental groups, the Bank agreed to fund three schemes pertaining to environmental protection, sustainable petroleum production, and supervised distribution of oil revenue (Pegg 2006; Massey and May 2006; Yohannes 2003).

In so far as oil flow is concerned, the oil companies and the World Bank could not be happier. Between October 2003 and June 2005, the consortium exported almost 103 MMb of Chadian oil (Pegg 2006). But politics began to unravel the Chadian experiment; good governance became something of an elusive commodity. President Déby, in power since 1990, grew greedy and wanted more of the oil revenue for himself in violation of the agreed framework. In December 2005, he maneuvered parliament to unilaterally amend the standing regulatory framework. Hoping to intimidate Déby into compliance, the World Bank refused to funnel the oil profits to the government and even suspended disbursement of a $124-million World Bank loan already in the pipeline. Déby raised the ante and threatened to expel the oil companies; the Bank blinked first. Under pressure from Washington, World Bank president Wolfowitz accepted the amendment to the framework and ordered disbursement of the oil profits and the loan (Massey and May 2006).

The specter of terrorism and Chinese rivalry were certainly at play. The Bush administration identified Chad as both an ally in the struggle against international terrorism and a supplier of important incremental oil. As Déby sought to renege on the global, public-private partnership in hydrocarbon production, Chinese presence on the African continent afforded him yet another card to play against Western pressure for transparency and good governance. Chad's counter-elite, claiming to represent the ethnic groups excluded from the oil revenue, took arms against the central government; the rebels were said to be supported by Sudan and China. In the first six months of 2006 alone, Déby was rescued from three attempted coups by the 1,100 French troops that were stationed in the country with airlift capacity and supported by a squadron of French Mirage fighters (Massey and May 2006).

Thus, in the end, the Bush administration realized that the stakes for the United States in the African petrostates were big and the local proxy providers too weak to protect those stakes. The convergence of growing local insurgency, the specter of terrorism, and the Chinese challenge to Western domination of African markets and resources could be handled only by a robust U.S. engagement. It thus came to pass that on February 6, 2007, President Bush officially announced the creation of AFRICOM to protect U.S. energy interests in Africa while simultaneously keeping a vigilant eye on terrorists and

China. This is how the president framed AFRICOM's mission: "This new Command will strengthen our security cooperation with Africa and create new opportunities to bolster the capabilities of our partners in Africa. . . . Africa Command will enhance our efforts to bring peace and security to the people of Africa and promote our common goals of development, health, education, democracy, and economic growth in Africa" (White House News Releases, February 6, 2007).

In sum, the confluence of these three trends resulted in an unwelcome threat to U.S. energy security in Africa and unmistakably redefined U.S. orientation towards Africa. Now that the Africanization of the Carter doctrine has become a reality, with the declaration of the Gulf of Guinea as vital to U.S. national security interest, the oil companies and their partners in the private policymaking institutions can deliver their long-awaited valediction. Now that U.S. neo–Cold War orthodoxy is securely embedded in the neo-containment politics of the "global war on terror," U.S. troops under AFRICOM will do as imperial armies have done throughout history: protect trade routes, markets, and sources of hydrocarbon resources and minerals and prop up local proxy service providers.

Explaining the Petrolization of the State and the Effects on the Ecology, Polity, and Society

The dismal performance (if not the virtual collapse) of economies and the concomitant pauperization of the masses in resource-rich African countries once led to widespread theoretical speculation in the 1980s. After all, until the 1970s, development economists generally regarded national endowment in natural resources as a requisite source of primitive capital accumulation, allowing belated industrializers to generate sufficient foreign exchange revenues. These revenues were expected to facilitate importation of capital and intermediate goods, necessary to jump-start the industrialization process.

However, because resource-rich countries such as Nigeria, Angola, and the DRC have failed to match projected theoretical expectations, theory builders schooled in neoclassical economics and neoliberal politics now posit that resource abundance, rather than becoming a source of national capital accumulation, actually serves to decelerate (if not to completely derail) the development trajectory. Proponents of this orientation call this phenomenon a "resource curse." Using the petrolized Nigerian state as an example of this phenomenon, Sala-i-Martin and Subramanian (2003) are among the latest suppliers of the foundational text for the resource curse theory. The underbelly of the argument encapsulated in the so-called resource curse theory is that natural resource abundance, by likely prompting state elite and bureaucrats to develop rent-seeking behavior and corruption, becomes a determinant of state behavior with privileged causal priority.

By implication, this empiricist epistemology suggests that poor resource endowment (or reliance on agriculture or other non-oil primary resources) is likely to be conducive to "low-rent competitive industrialization," initially grounded in labor-intensive manufacturing, which would simultaneously trigger rapid rural labor transformation and urbanization (Auty 2007; Karl 1997, chapter 9; Sala-i-Martin and Subramanian 2003). In other words, having fewer natural resources compels governments to seek alternative sources of revenue to buttress their legitimacy and stay in power. This would presumably entail focused attention on the manufacturing sector to boost taxable national output. The upshot of this development trajectory is that the tax payer (civil society) and the tax collector (politicians) would enter into a dynamic interaction in which the right of the tax payer to demand accountability from the tax-collecting politicians and the latter's vested interest in nurturing their political legitimacy by providing public goods and services to the tax-paying civil society become mutual reinforcements of the industrialization process (Sala-i-Martin and Subramanian 2003; Auty 2007; Pegg 2006; Karl 1997, chapters 3 and 9).

In contrast, naturally resource-rich countries tend to pursue a high-rent development trajectory in which politicians (exclusively reliant on wealth found in nature such as oil and minerals) are likely to have little or no incentives to seek diversification of the economy in order to boost their tax collection capacity. In effect, as the argument goes, the rent generated by the export of natural resources would have four long-run results. The first is that the national elite's primary relationship is with nature and international buyers of the natural resources over which they have monopoly control. Consequently, the high rent from resource export tends to divorce politicians from civil society; because they would presumably have no need to collect taxes, they would not be obliged to provide public goods and services to civil society in order to ensure their political viability and legitimacy. The corollary is that civil society (not compelled to pay taxes) would feel no entitlement to demand transparency and accountability from government. Second, awash with high rent from resource export, politicians are positioned to accelerate and perpetuate the clientelization of resource distribution. Close allies are put in charge of state-controlled economic agencies, or parastatals, and actual opponents and potential challengers are co-opted through generous distribution of spoils derived from exports.

Third, petrolization of the economy could generate structural disarticulation among the various components of the economy. The steady flow of foreign exchange earnings from the export of oil would veritably bias investment in the oil sector, crowding out other sectors, such as agriculture and manufacturing. Fourth, in the event that clientelization of the economy or cooptation of challengers proves unable to sustain legitimation of the prevailing social order, the elite would have recourse to the application of unbridled coercion. This explains the deepening authoritarianization of African petrolized states and their gross democratic deficit. Dependency on oil rent thus retards democratic development and fosters institutional stagnation, regime decay, state disorganization, and widespread corruption. In sum, heavy dependency on oil not only undermines economic competitiveness, but also hinders democratization of the political order (Auty 2007; Sala-i-Martin and Subramanian 2003; Karl 1997, 189–191; Shankleman 2006, 43–45; Pegg 2006; Ross 2001; Jensen and Wantchekon 2004).

In her widely cited work, Terry Karl (1997, 205–208) attributes the growth of pirate capitalism, hyper-centralization of petrodollars, authoritarianism, disorganization of state institutions, ethnic and religious cleavages, political instability, and the stark poverty-wealth divide in Nigeria to the petrolization of the state and the economy. Data from Nigeria is used to demonstrate the relationship between petroleum dependency and the social and economic ills gripping petrostates. Nigeria's oil production (which was a mere 20,000 bbl per day in 1958) steadily rose to 2 MMb a day by 1973. As a result, government revenue from oil, which accounted for just 26.3 percent of total government revenue in 1970, rose to 82.1 percent in 1974. To maximize the flow of oil revenue to the treasury, the federal government established the Nigerian National Petroleum Corporation in 1971, which soon acquired 60 percent of the stake in the multinationals operating in the hydrocarbon sector.

The empirical evidence further shows that Nigeria received $350 billion over thirty years in oil revenue and yet has showed nothing for it. This amount does not include the profits collected by the oil companies. Despite momentous growth in oil revenue, income inequality in Nigeria worsened over time. For example, in 1970, the shares of the national income of the top 2 percent and the bottom 20 percent of the population were identical. Thirty years later, however, the share of the top 2 percent was equal to the aggregate income of the bottom 55 percent of the population. As a result, the number of Nigerians subsisting on less than a dollar a day rose from 19 million (36 percent of the population) in 1970 to 90 million (70 percent) in 2000. In addition to the negative impact of oil dependency on institutional quality and income distribution, petrolization of the Nigerian state has had a harmful impact on industry and agriculture, as agriculture's contribution to GDP progressively fell from 68 percent at independence to 35 percent by the early 1980s.

Looking at the quantitative relationships between the petrolization of the state and the economic performance of the West African petrostates, on the one hand, and the levels of political stagnation and corruption in these states, on the other, the resource curse theory appears to offer plausible explanations for the stark poverty, gross social injustice, and growing political instability in the region. A closer scrutiny of the theory, however, would present an entirely different picture. The theory is empirically flawed and epistemologically diversionary. On the empirical level, for every failed petrostate in West Africa, one could find two or more non-oil states in the continent that have miserably failed on all measures of development. Ethiopia, Somalia, Rwanda, Burundi, and many more would immediately come to mind. Furthermore, the ethnic and religious conflicts, political repression, and tremendous poverty in Sudan, Chad, and Equatorial Guinea predate the discovery of oil. By shuffling numbers around, it is almost infinitely possible to show spurious co-variability among any number of factors.

To remedy this empirical flaw, Thad Dunning (2005) offers what he calls the "equilibrium model" to demonstrate wide variation among resource-rich countries. Botswana, for example, judiciously exploits diamonds and equitably distributes the revenue from diamond export within a relatively democratic and stable political context, while the DRC does none of this; Indonesia does considerably better with its resources than the DRC yet not as well as Botswana. After examining such variations, Dunning comes to the conclusion that resource abundance by itself does not enjoy privileged causal priority. He thus opts for what he calls the "conditional theory" of the resource curse. While Dunning's "conditional theory" of the resource curse is an improvement on the static resource curse theory, it does not go far enough.

From epistemological considerations, the resource curse theory glosses over the social history, the temporal context in which the oil-producing African states find themselves and the particular division of labor to which they are assigned in late capitalism. The theory is also reductionist because the problems of poor performance and political stagnation are entirely indigenized. One cannot simply abstract the African petrostates from global capitalism and pretend that they are completely insulated from external manipulation and intervention. The resource curse theory actually peppers over the clear line of continuity between the colonial state and the postcolonial state.

It is worth recalling that the history of the West African petrostates began with the territorialization of nature. The colonial powers simply alienated vast natural resources from their owners and enclosed them into large commercial plantations and/or mineral reserves. This was in keeping with capitalism's first order preference for adaptation to preexisting modes of resource utilization when outright appropriation of nature was more profitable than the return on investment in new undertakings. In order to ensure stability of production and export of resources, the colonial powers put in place an authoritarian political structure. Thus, the colonial state was simultaneously rentier and authoritarian, through and through. What the Western-groomed "native" petty bourgeoisie inherited from the departing colonial powers was a rentier state. Indigenization of the state and nativization of formal ownership of natural resource by no means represented a qualitative transformation of the African economy, polity, and society.

Decolonization was the European response to a legitimation crisis, but the response was administered in such manner as to ensure continuity, not a structural break with the colonial past. What emerged from the decolonization of the African state was a dynamic realignment of classes with the bourgeoisified native elite now incorporated into the global class structure. The "native" state, appearing to possess sovereign autonomy, was actually transformed into an instrument of global capital accumulation. The postcolonial state would continue enclosing nature and more environmental resources; in oil-rich West Africa, petroleum was the determining factor in the enclosing process. The 1978 Nigerian Land Use Act illustrates the point.

In order to stimulate further oil exploration and production in the country, the federal government enacted a law in 1978 that was meant to make alienation of land easy for oil prospectors. Until 1978, the relationship between landowners and the oil companies was direct in that the latter rented or purchased the land from the owners and were legally bound to pay compensation to the owners for any changes, such as destruction of property or crops, made to the land. The 1978 Land Use Act, however, empowered state governors to declare any land public domain, designated as such for purposes of promoting the public interest. The land could be the object of oil exploration or could be used to construct pipelines and related facilities. In addition, whenever compensation payments were in order, the oil companies would direct the payments to the governor, not to the individuals or communities that were the original land owners (Frynas 2001).

Proponents of the resource curse theory are also prompt to indigenize corruption. The fact is that, contrary to conventional wisdom, corruption (as a social phenomenon) is integral to accumulation and is by no means confined to domestic social forces in the era of hyperglobalization. What makes corruption different in the African petrostates is not its magnitude but the manner in which it is used. Corruption in the petrostate per se is not the problem; African corruption becomes problematic when it is integrated into advanced economies. Whereas money embezzled or received in kickbacks in the advanced countries does not leave the circulatory arteries of capitalism in the global North, ill-gotten African wealth leaves the petrostates and enters the circulatory process in the global North via three routes.

First, in order to perpetuate political repression or contend with insurgency, the pirate capitalists in the petrostates are permanently dependent on international arms manufacturers for regular supplies. For example, Angola exported $31.4 billion worth of oil between 1992 and 1999, and the government's share of this value was $14.4 billion. Yet the government imported $5 billion worth of arms over the same period. Thus, militarization of Angola has (in no small way) been integral to the reproduction of capitalism in the arms-exporting countries. In 1997, 36 percent of Angola's national budget was spent on military goods and services, rising to 41 percent in 1999; yet the amount of spending on health, education, housing, and social welfare fell from 13 percent to 9.4 percent over the same period. Consequently, 82.5 percent of Angolans were in absolute and relative poverty; 59 percent of the general population had no access to safe drinking water, 60 percent lacked access to proper sanitation, and 76 percent had no access to health care (Global Witness 1999; Le Billon 2001).

The second route by which African petrodollars enter the advanced economies is through the hidden personal accounts of the pirate capitalists or the overseas accounts of petrostates' residents who lack faith in the domestic pirate capitalists. In 1999, for example, a reported 70 percent of Nigeria's private wealth (or $107 billion) was circulating in overseas economies (Jerome et al. 2005). Likewise, according to the IMF, $5 billion of Angola's oil money disappeared into offshore accounts from the national treasury between 1997 and 2002. The $1 billion that went missing every year was said to be equal to what Angola requested from the international community in 2002 in emergency and humanitarian assistance. In fact, despite earning $3 billion from oil exports that year, the World Food Program fed 2 million Angolans who were subsisting on leaves, insects, rats, and other wild animals (Anderson 2002).

The third route to integration is through the importation of consumer goods, ranging from perfumes to wine, beer, hard liquor, televisions, cars, and civilian aircraft. In effect, money generated by the export of oil is invested in the global North to subsidize the reproduction of capitalism. Corruption has never been entirely the affair of the oil-producing states. The major enablers and chief beneficiaries of African corruption have been oil multinationals and Western banks. The 2003 trial in a French court of a number of French officials (including a former interior minister and president of the French oil multinational) revealed the extent of foreign involvement in African corruption. The defendants were charged with skimming $410 million in kickbacks in Angola (Jerome et al. 2005). Moreover, the 2004 U.S. Senate investigation into the disappearance of Equatorial Guinea's oil money revealed that the dictator and members of his family had stashed more than $700 million in sixty different bank accounts with the Washington-based Riggs National Bank. Oil multinationals had been directly depositing oil money into these accounts on behalf of Obiang. Riggs was fined $25 million by the federal government for complicity in this money-laundering activity (Cue 2006). One of the dictator's sons also spent $35 million on a 15,000-square-foot mansion in California, which was fully serviced by a giant swimming pool, a tennis court, and four golf courses (Faul 2006).

Conclusion

Ever since the integration of Africa into global capitalism half a millennium ago, Africa's place in the international division of labor as a producer and supplier of primary resources has remained constant. The discovery and exploitation of hydrocarbon resources in recent decades have added complexity to the continent's historically determined assignment with long-term implications.

First, West Africa's growing importance as supplier of incremental petroleum is likely to fuel a continued scramble for the shrinking hydrocarbon resources among the major powers. The U.S. determination to keep West Africa within its sphere of influence and China's challenge to the status quo are likely to sharpen in the future. In this tug-of-war between the overstretched hegemon and the rising challenger, a visionless leadership in the West African petrostates will undoubtedly enjoy enough breathing space to ignore needed reforms. The external powers will have little or no incentives to push for reforms either, since the status quo will enable them to exploit the region's hydrocarbon resources without democratic control over the resources or a regulatory regime to protect the region's ecology.

As of this writing, neo–Cold War orthodoxy and the neo-containment politics of the "global war on terror" continue to supply the ideological justification for overlooking questions of human rights and social justice; this was the leverage and justification used so successfully by Chad's Déby, who threatened to cut off the oil supply to Western powers if they persisted in denying him full enjoyment of the oil revenue. Moreover, in 1995, the Clinton administration closed the U.S. embassy in Equatorial Guinea in protest of President Oteoro Nguema Obiang's poor human rights record. But when that country's hydrocarbon sector showed spectacular growth, the Bush administration reversed course and reopened the U.S. embassy in Malabo. Obiang was described in Washington as a friend of the United States, and the Corporate Council on Africa prepared a fifty-four-page booklet in honor of his visit to Washington, extolling Obiang's virtue as Africa's great reformer of the "latter day saint" variety (Yohannes 2003).

Second, in addition to deepening poverty, malnutrition, social injustice, and political repression, the region's ecology will continue to suffer further degradation. The ecological effects of oil exploration and production on the livelihoods and well-being of local communities will appreciably worsen in the future. The history of the Niger Delta does presage an unsavory future. The Delta was historically considered among the most pristine ecosystems, containing 7,000 sq. km., or three quarters, of Africa's remaining mangrove forests and providing the breeding grounds for some 60 percent of West African fish. Today, the Niger Delta is recognized as one of five most degraded and polluted places on earth (Hondros 2007). Shell by itself operates ninety fields in the Niger Delta with a network of 6,000 kilometers of flowlines and pipelines, seven gas plants, and eighty-six flow stations. A major source of pollution and contamination in the Delta has been gas flaring, a practice designed to remove from the petroleum what geologists call "associated" gas. In the West the associated gas is harnessed for electricity generation or reinjected into oil wells to maintain pressure; this way the environment is protected. In Africa, however, the associated gas is burned off by oil companies because they do not want to invest in modern pressure-maintenance systems in their oil wells.

More associated gas is flared in Nigeria than anywhere else in the world. More than 2.5 billion cubic feet of associated gas is burned off in Nigeria each day; this amount is equal to 40 percent of the total gas consumption in all of West, East, Central, and South Africa, and Nigeria's economic loss from flaring is $2.5 billion annually. This means that the opportunity cost to the country since the discovery of oil totals $50 billion (Friends of the Earth Nigeria 2005). Moreover, since oil drilling began in 1958, some 9.5 MMb of oil have been spilled in the Niger River Delta (Hondros 2007). When oil facilities and gas flare plants were built in the Niger Delta, villagers were promised employment, development, and compensation for any damage caused to their property or environment, yet they find themselves with ruined agriculture and fisheries, polluted water and air, and a contaminated environment. Although the oil companies and the Nigerian government promised to end the practice of gas flaring by 2004, it never happened; the promise was simply extended until 2008 (Hondros 2007).

The new focus on deepwater and ultra-deepwater production means that West Africa's sensitive marine ecosystems are dangerously vulnerable to unprecedented degradation. With no regulation and protection in place to restrain them, oil multinationals are poised to ransack the marine ecology. Today, West Africa's subsea sector is regarded as the hottest spot for the deployment of floating production operation systems, giant stand-alone vessels into which oil from subsea wells is directly pumped eliminating the need for pipelines or other infrastructure. The stored oil is then loaded onto tankers sailing to the United States or Europe. Of the $86 billion projected investment in floating systems in the next five years, the West African subsea market will capture $21 billion (Radler 2007). While oil multinationals and African pirate capitalists will enormously benefit from the spoiling of the marine ecology, the region's future generations will bear the brunt of destroyed fisheries and other marine resources. As long as the destructive consequences do not directly impact their countries, the home governments of the multinationals are likely to look the other way. For example, cognizant of the vulnerability of their marine ecology to unintended oil spills, the U.S. Congress enacted a law prohibiting oil companies from exploring in certain maritime areas, believed to contain approximately 76 BBL of undiscovered oil (Wells 2007).

What is to be done? Large numbers of scholars and commentators have composed gut-wrenching requiems about the dashed hopes for Africa. Obviously, describing what happened and explaining why it happened is easier than finding the right solution to a problem. The fundamental question confronting theory builders and policymakers today is partly one concerned with how to properly use African natural resources for the betterment and empowerment of the masses in the resource-rich countries. The answer to what appears to be the perpetual underdevelopment of Africa remains unchanged since colonial times, and it has to do with politics. Kwame Nkrumah's metaphorical invocation of the biblical injunction that Africans should first seek the "political kingdom" before enjoying material prosperity remains as true today as when he invoked it half a century ago. After all, we have for too long been forewarned that all economic decisions are, in the final analysis, political decisions. But political decisions cannot be understood in isolation from the prevailing social order and the existing power relations. In essence, all governments are political institutions, run by politicians (whether elected or self-anointed). The decisions that officeholders make are largely political in content to the extent that they have class bias. Where public resources (whether natural or produced) are monopolized by the political elite and bureaucrats, the veritable result is that those who control the state are likely to use such machinery to perpetuate existing maldistribution of resources in order to enrich themselves by depriving others.

What is needed in the West African petrostates is a radical transformation in orientation and direction. This would involve the articulation of a coherent counter-hegemonic narrative, the installation of countervailing institutions and the provision of intellectual infrastructure and leadership. The articulation of a counter-hegemonic narrative should start with a thorough understanding that the problem in resource-rich West African states is not resource abundance; it is systemic and political. The neoliberal presentation of capitalism as a social system for all times and places must be vigorously contested.

With respect to the second point raised above, the petrostates are often resistant to reform from within, but grassroots movements in the region might, with encouragement and guidance, construct countervailing institutions from below. The articulation of a counter-hegemonic narrative and installations of countervailing institutions will require the presence and activism of visionary intellectuals. By giving the grassroots movements a trans-communal, trans-ethnic, and transnational scope, as well as coherence and direction, public intellectuals can play a decisive role in the evolution of the disconnected and marginally linked struggles in the petrostates of the region.

REFERENCES

Auty, Richard M. "Natural Resources, Capital Accumulation and the Resource Curse." *Ecological Economics* 61, no. 4 (2007): 627–634.

Barkindo, Mohamed. "Undiscovered Oil Potential Still Large off West Africa." *Oil and Gas Journal* (January 8, 2007): 30.

Clark, Martin. "Deep Water: Nigeria Coming of Age." *Petroleum Economist* (October 1, 2006): 23–25.

Cue, Eduardo. "Dictator and Diplomat." *U.S. News & World Report*, September 25, 2006, 34–41.

"Deep-Water Discoveries Leap to 71, Producers 13." *Petroleum Economist* (May 1, 2007): 16–17.

Dunning, Thad. "Resource Dependence, Economic Performance and Political Stability." *Journal of Conflict Resolution* 49, no. 4 (August 2005): 451–482.

EnergyBulletin.net Peak Oil News Clearinghouse. "Peak Oil: Life After the Oil Crash," 2006, www.lifeaftertheoilcrash.net.

Faul, Michelle. "Son of Leader of Impoverished Equatorial Guinea Buys U.S. $35 Million California Mansion." AP Worldstream, November 8, 2006.

Forum on China-Africa Cooperation. "Bejing Action Plan (2007–2009)," November 16, 2006, www.cfr.org.

Friends of the Earth Nigeria. "Gas Flaring in Nigeria: A Human Rights, Environmental and Economic Monstrosity," a report published by Climate Justice Program and Environmental Rights Action, June 2005, www.climatelaw.org/gas.flaring/report/gas.flaring.in.nigeria.htm.

Frynas, Jedrzej, G. "Corporate and State Responses to Anti-Oil Protests in the Niger Delta." *African Affairs* 100, no. 398 (2001): 27–41.

———. "The Oil Boom in Equatorial Guinea." *African Affairs* 103, 413 (2004): 527–554.

Ghazvinian, John. "The Curse of Oil." *Virginia Quarterly Review* 83, no. 1 (Winter 2007): 4–27.

———. "Untapped: The Scramble for Africa's Oil." *Slate Magazine,* April 3, 2007, www.lexisnexis.com.

Gill, Bates et al. "China's Expanding Role in Africa: Implications for the United States," a report of the CSIS Delegation to China on China-Africa Relations, November 28–December 1, 2006, www.csis.org.

Goldwyn, David L. "The Gulf of Guinea and U.S. Strategic Energy Policy," testimony before the Senate Subcommittee on International Economic Policy, Export and Trade Promotion, July 15, 2004, www.senate.gov/~foreign/testimony/2004/GoldwynTestimony040715.pdf.

Hondros, Chris. "The Fire." *Virginia Quarterly Review* 83, no. 1 (Winter 2007): 28–33.

Jensen, Nathan, and Leonard Wantchekon. "Resource Wealth and Political Regimes inAfrica." *Comparative Political Studies* 37, no. 7 (September 2004): 816–840.

Jerome, Afeikhena et al. "Addressing Oil Related Corruption in Africa: Is the Push for Transparency Enough?" *Review of Human Factor Studies* 11, no. 1 (June 2005): 7–32.

Institute for Advanced Strategic and Political Studies. "African Oil: A Priority for U.S. Security and African Development," symposium proceedings, January 2002, www.iasps.org/strategic/africawhitepaper.pdf.

Karl, Terry L. *The Paradox of Plenty: Oil Booms and Petro-states.* Berkeley: University of California Press, 1997.

Le Billon, Philippe. "Angola's Political Economy of War: The Role of Oil and Diamonds, 1975–2000." *African Affairs* 100, no. 398 (2001): 55–80.

Marqueardt, Erich. "The Niger Delta Insurgency and Its Threat to Energy Security," August 10, 2006, www.jamestown.org/terrorism/news/article.php.

Massey, Simon, and Roy May. "Commentary: The Crisis in Chad." *African Affairs* 105, no. 420 (July 2006): 443–449.

McGreal, Chris. "Year in Review: Africa." *Guardian Weekly,* December 22, 2006, 6.

McLeary, Paul. "A Different Kind of Great Game," March 2007, www.cfr.org.

Pegg, Scott. "Can Policy Intervention Beat the Resource Curse? Evidence from the Chad-Cameroon Pipeline Project." *African Affairs* 105, no. 418 (January 2006): 1–25.

Pocha, Jehangir. "Rising China." *New Perspectives Quarterly* 22, no. 1 (Winter 2005): 50–55.

Radler, Marilyn. "Global Subsea Up." *Oil and Gas Journal* (March 12, 2007): 17.

Reed, Stanley. "Going off the Deep End of Oil." *Business Week,* June 26, 2006, 63.

Roberts, Paul. *The End of Oil.* Boston: Houghton Mifflin, 2004.

Ross, Michael L. "Does Oil Hinder Democracy?" *World Politics* 53, no. 3 (2001): 325–361.

Sala-i-Martin, Xavier, and Arvind Subramanian. "Addressing the Natural Resource Curse: An Illustration from Nigeria," IMF Working Paper No. 03/139, 2003, www.imf.org/external/publs/cat/logres.cfm?sk:16582.

Sandrea, Ivan. "Exploration Trends Show Continued Promise in World's Offshore Basins." *Oil and Gas Journal* (March 5, 2004): 34.

Shankleman, Jill. *Oil, Profits and Peace: Does Business Have a Role in Peace Making?* Washington, D.C.: U.S. Institute of Peace, 2006.

Star News Service. "Framework for Action Adopted at Ministerial Conference," November 16, 2006, www.lexisnexis.com.

Quinlan, Martin. "Oil, Gas and Uneasiness." *Petroleum Economist* (February 1, 2007): 15.

"The Scramble for Oil." *Petroleum Economist* (December 1, 2006): 16.

"Total Discovers Congolese Oil Reserves." *Les Echos,* April 3, 2007, www.lexisnexis.com.

Turner, Terisa E., and Leigh S. Brownhill. "Why Women are at War with Chevron: Nigerian Subsistence Struggles against the International Oil Industry." *Journal of Asian and African Studies* 39, nos. 1–2 (2004): 63–93.

———. "Climate Justice and Nigerian Women's Gift to Humanity." *Women and Environments International Magazine* 74–75 (Spring–Summer 2007): 47–48.

Wells, Jim. "Crude Oil: Uncertainty about Future Oil Supply Makes It Important to Develop a Strategy for Addressing Peak and Decline in Oil Production," testimony before U.S. House of Representatives Committee on Science and Technology, February 28, 2007, www.gao.gov/new.items/d07550t.pdf.

Walt, Vivienne. "China's African Safari." *Fortune,* February 26, 2006, 41–44.

White House News Releases. "President Bush Creates a Department of Defense Unified Combatant Command for Africa," February 6, 2007, www.whitehouse.gov/news/releases/2007/02/20070206-c.html.

Wingrove, Martyn. "Foreign Cash to Help Fund $50m Angola Oil Expansion." *Lloyd's List,* March 14, 2007, www.lexisnexis.com.

Yergin, Daniel. *The Prize: The Epic Quest for Oil, Money, and Power.* New York: Simon and Schuster, 1993.

———. "Ensuring Energy Security." *Foreign Affairs* (March/April 2006): 69–82.

Yohannes, Okbazghi. "America's New Frontier: Oil in the Gulf of Guinea." *Black Scholar* 33, no. 2 (Summer 2003): 2–21.

Zweig, David, and Jianhai, Bi. "China's Global Hunt for Energy." *Foreign Affairs* (July/August 2005): 25–38.

Chapter 14

THE POLITICS OF HIV/AIDS IN AFRICA
Representation and the Political Economy of Disease

Susan Craddock

Not only is AIDS one of the most critical issues facing the globe in the millennium, but the epidemic in Africa also tragically continues apace. At last count, approximately 22.3 million individuals were living with HIV in Africa; there were almost 2 million new infections and about 1.5 million deaths from AIDS (UNAIDS 2007). The only positive sign was a slight decrease—of 0.1 percent—in overall adult prevalence (ibid.).

But in this chapter I do not talk about what these statistics mean in terms of people's lives, experiences, and levels of suffering, except to say that statistics cannot begin to encompass the profound and devastating effects on everyday lives, relations, economies, and individual and collective futures. Consistent with the themes of the current volume, alternatively, I choose to reframe the discourse about AIDS in Africa to touch upon some of the controversies that AIDS has generated. Of significance is the range of appropriate responses from Western countries to an epidemic that has tested the status quo of geopolitical relations and highlighted the contradictions of subsuming public health within the regulatory structures of transnational economic practices and international governance. Space does not allow a full treatment of all the political "hot" topics that AIDS in Africa has generated in recent years, but two of the most contested issues pivot around the level and nature of funding for AIDS treatment in Africa and access to antiretrovirals.

The discussions that follow of these two issues are necessarily selective, less of a broad overview than a partial focus on those constituent parts that are representative of what is not only progress in responding, however belatedly, to a geographically and statistically massive epidemic, but also of the problems inherent when responses to disease become inextricably embedded within ideological agendas and the long-term geopolitics of "development," security, and economic inequalities.

Global Response and the Political Morality of AIDS Funding

The global response to AIDS in Africa has had a checkered history, from a sustained and confounding neglect on the part of the G8 and multinational agencies throughout the 1990s to more recent attempts at recognizing the importance and global impact of AIDS in Africa. As Kofi Annan commented in a speech given at the 2004 International AIDS Conference in Bangkok, "There must be no more sticking heads in the sand . . . there must be no more apathy" (July 12). Though levels of funding coming from Western governments and international financial institutions have risen in recent years, there remain problems in

Figure 14.1   HIV Global Trends

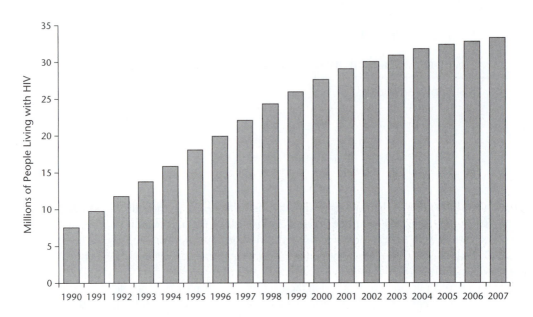

Source: The Avert Organization using UNAIDS statistics for 2007 published in July 2008: http://www.avert.org/worldstats.htm.
Note: The number of people living with HIV has risen from around 8 million in 1990 to 33 million in 2007 and is still growing.
Around 67% of people living with HIV are in Africa.

getting governments to fulfill their promises of increased aid, and levels can be regarded as still far from adequate. Equally important, however, is the point that funding in and of itself cannot lead to effective intervention into AIDS in Africa if too many contingencies, or the wrong kinds of contingencies, adhere to funding packages. Here, I depart from the more common critique that maintains that donations will be useless if they are mismanaged by African governments. I will focus instead on the motivations of donors themselves in the contention that inadequate scrutiny has attended the actions and consequences of U.S. administrations and transnational agencies regarding AIDS in Africa.

The primary sources of funding for HIV prevention and treatment today come from the United States under the President's Emergency Plan For AIDS Relief, or PEPFAR; the Global Fund; the Gates Foundation; and the World Bank. Though all are universally acknowledged for their efforts and acceleration of funding, they each have encountered criticism for the particular ways they structure their interventions and the ideological underpinnings of their financial donations. In the following discussion, I focus my attention on PEPFAR because it has now become one of the front players in the field of AIDS funding in Africa and because the most strident criticism of bilateral funding is directed at this program.

Responding to widespread criticism that his administration did not care about AIDS in Africa, President Bush in 2003 announced a new initiative "to meet a severe and urgent crisis abroad" (GAO

The cornerstone of all prevention programs funded under the President's Emergency Plan For AIDS Relief is the ABC approach—that is, Abstinence, Be Faithful, or use Condoms.

2006, 1). Pledging a total of $15 billion over five years, Bush's new Emergency Plan for AIDS Relief targeted fifteen countries primarily in Africa[1] with the aim of preventing 7 million new infections, caring for 10 million people affected by AIDS, and placing 2 million people on antiretrovirals by 2010 (ibid.; Gill 2006). After a relatively slow start, PEPFAR has stepped up its funding allocations in the last two years, increasing its prevention funding by 40 percent from $207 million in 2004 to $322 million in 2006 (GAO 2006, 4), even though the percentage of funding earmarked for prevention has actually decreased from 33 to only 20 percent of the total (ibid.). Since 2004, the Office of the Global AIDS Coordinator (OGAC) has created five primary categories of prevention: abstinence/faithfulness, "other prevention," prevention of mother-to-child transmission, safe medical injections, and blood safety. However, the cornerstone of all prevention programs funded under PEPFAR is the ABC approach—that is, Abstinence, Be Faithful, or use Condoms. In fact, as of 2006, at least 33 percent of all PEPFAR funds channeled into prevention must be spent on AB programs.

---

[1] Botswana, Côte d'Ivoire, Ethiopia, Guyana, Haiti, Kenya, Mozambique, Namibia, Nigeria, Rwanda, South Africa, Tanzania, Uganda, and Zambia. Vietnam is the fifteenth country, added in June 2004.

PEPFAR prevention funding has undoubtedly had positive effects in targeted countries, to varying degrees. According to its own accounts, antenatal clinics in host countries are increasingly offering HIV testing and counseling with PEPFAR funds, and attendance at these clinics has improved dramatically in ten of fifteen countries.[2] It has also supported provision of care for 2.5 million people living with HIV and 2 million orphans affected by AIDS, while disseminating a new "preventive care package" to those living with HIV to delay the need for treatment. Finally, it has stepped up provision of care for opportunistic infections, doubling its funding for treatment of tuberculosis between 2005 and 2006 and supporting treatment of 301,600 HIV-positive patients with tuberculosis in 2006 (PEPFAR 2006). Nevertheless, criticisms of prevention programs under PEPFAR have been multiple and widespread.

The most common criticism is of the insistence on ABC as the only means for tackling prevention and, more specifically, the increased focus on abstinence. Much of PEPFAR's emphasis on ABC comes from the apparent success of this strategy in lowering rates of HIV in Uganda. While this is undoubtedly true to some extent, the claim that ABC approaches alone curtailed HIV in Uganda is a controversial one, not only because diminishing HIV usually entails a multiplicity of factors, but also because the newer emphasis within PEPFAR funding on AB without condoms belies the fact that, according to Ugandan officials, condoms played a significant role in decreasing HIV infections through the 1990s (Gill 2006).

Second, the emphasis on abstinence as an effective strategy is dangerously misplaced, according to many public health and human rights officials. As Jonathan Cohen and his colleagues at Human Rights Watch claim, "U.S.-funded abstinence programs have a track record of censoring or distorting information about any other method of HIV prevention beyond abstinence" (Cohen, Schleifer, and Tate 2005). A Human Rights Watch study published in 2002, for example, found instances of misinformation and censorship in abstinence-only programs in Texas (Schleifer 2002), while other studies cited similar examples of misinformation in other U.S. abstinence-only interventions (cited in Cohen et al. 2005). Not surprisingly, this kind of misinformation has been exported to PEPFAR-funded programs in African countries, where messages on preventing either HIV or sexually transmitted diseases (STIs) focus on the unreliability of condoms by asserting they are too porous or too likely to break (ibid.). These messages, needless to say, threaten to actually increase rates of HIV, rather then decrease them, by convincing people that condoms do not work when in reality they are overwhelmingly acknowledged as the single most effective means of prevention apart from abstinence.

Though debates over the efficacy of abstinence-only programs continue in the United States, many studies present compelling evidence that these programs do not work in changing overall patterns of sexual activity, stemming sexual risk taking, or curbing rates of STIs. One overview of five years of abstinence-only programs showed that only one U.S. state out of eleven demonstrated short-term success in delaying first sex, while none of the reviewed programs showed success in long-term delays of sexual initiation among students participating in the programs. On the contrary, as the authors state, the negative impacts of abstinence-only programs included no decrease in sexual risk taking and a lower rate of contraceptive use during sex than those not participating in abstinence-only programs (Hauser 2004). Echoing this last finding, Brückner and Bearman in a large study of youths taking virginity pledges found comparable rates of STIs among pledgers and those never having pledged (2005). As the authors of both studies suggest, emphasis on abstinence only, rather than more comprehensive sex

---

[2] Exceptions are Côte d'Ivoire, Ethiopia, Nigeria, South Africa, and Zambia.

education, results often in adolescents who are less knowledgeable about condoms, less equipped to engage safely in sex when they have it, and less likely to seek testing for STIs.

Insisting on abstinence programming for adolescents and young adults under PEPFAR thus represents mandatory implementation of programs that at best show few improvements in delaying sex and at worst prove dangerous in withholding vital information about means of HIV and STI prevention. Nevertheless, PEPFAR regulations prevent governments and organizations from providing youth with condoms, insisting that condom provision be targeted only at so-called high-risk groups such as sex workers. In fact, PEPFAR money may not be used to provide information about condoms to youths ages 10–14 or to distribute condoms in schools even to youths over 14 (GAO 2006, 27). As Jodi Jacobson of the Center for Health and Gender Equity states, "The Office of the U.S. Global AIDS Coordinator has chosen a very narrow interpretation of a congressional directive. What we have now is money going to programs that have been disproved in the USA. There are high rates of sexual activity before marriage in almost all countries, and adolescents and young adults are now not getting the comprehensive tools and training that they need to protect themselves" (Nelson 2006, 194). Echoing these sentiments, one of the original congressional representatives responsible for launching PEPFAR commented, "HIV prevention policies should not be based in ideology. The U.S. government shouldn't be deciding who uses condoms and who doesn't" (ibid., 195).

Furthermore, though technically 33 percent of all prevention funding under PEPFAR guidelines must be dedicated to AB programs starting in 2006, in reality the emphasis on AB can lead to even greater allocations to this category at the country level. In the new restrictions, 50 percent of PEPFAR prevention funding must go to sexual transmission prevention programs (rather than those targeting mother-to-child transmission, safe injections, or blood supplies, for example), and of that 50 percent, a full two-thirds must go towards abstinence-until-marriage curricula (GAO 2006, 5). But according to a 2006 Government Accounting Office overview of PEPFAR prevention programs, sufficient confusion at the country level surrounding what is acceptable under PEPFAR guidelines and what is not regarding condom information versus promotion and marketing, especially to youths over 14, has lead many countries to err on the side of providing no information rather than risk abrogating PEPFAR regulations and future funding allocations (GAO 2006, 31).

The GAO report's main criticism of PEPFAR prevention approaches, in fact, centers upon the degree to which ABC guidelines, despite paying lip service to heeding the particular needs and primary HIV epidemiologies of each country, restrain HIV prevention teams from channeling funds into programs most appropriate to their populations. One team, for example, noted that most HIV cases in their country were transmitted between stable heterosexual couples, whether married or in monogamous relationships. Yet because such couples do not come under PEPFAR's definition of "high-risk" groups, condom information and provision could not be targeted towards this population, even though condoms would have been the most effective means of intervention (ibid., 32). Where HIV is primarily transmitted through non-monogamous sexual exchanges, such as sex work, or through injection drug use, such as in Vietnam, the rules on AB funding force countries to channel resources away from appropriate, effective prevention programs. In fact, PEPFAR funding does not support any programs that target injection drug use, and regulatory guidelines require groups receiving PEPFAR allocations to actively oppose any form of commercial sex work (Rubenstein and Friedman 2004; Gill 2006). The degree to which both of these restrictions on HIV prevention funding elide realities of everyday life in poor regions, as well as predominant transmission patterns, signals the degree to which PEPFAR formally inscribes "fundamentalist fervour into the area of sexual morality and public health" (Gill 2006, 2).

As many critics note even more explicitly than the GAO, PEPFAR's substitution of moral imperatives for the multivalent forces generating risk in many regions of Africa undermines much of the program's potential efficacy. Until significant progress is made in alleviating poverty and gendered economic inequity across many regions of Africa, for example, sex work will continue to be a significant means of resource generation for many women. If the particular coordinates of regional economies include substantial patterns of circular or short-term migration, then focusing on stable couples will be inappropriate. And pretending that same-sex relations do not exist in Africa, or even criminalizing them as in some African countries, drives same-sex exchanges underground and leaves participants ill informed about prevention (Cohen et al. 2005; Phillips 2004). Channeling funds into inappropriate arenas also leaves less to allocate to less visible, but important areas, such as campaigns to fight the stigma against those living with HIV and AIDS, to address the possibilities of violence against women should their husbands or partners find out they are HIV positive, and to maintain the supply and training of health care personnel in urban and rural areas (Rubenstein and Friedman 2004).

The degree to which PEPFAR regulations contravene realities within the countries it presumes to help raises questions about the motivations underlying U.S. aid, as well as the dangers of articulating ideological imperatives with health interventions. Intervening into public health crises as a means of imposing geopolitical interests is nothing new (Ingram 2007; King 2002; Keller 2006). It is no secret that the countries targeted for PEPFAR funds and the organizations implementing programs in each country were selected according to "the extent to which their priorities mirror those of . . . the U.S. government" (GAO 2006, 18). It might be more accurate, then, to suggest that PEPFAR money continues to shape foreign policies along trajectories already mapped by participating countries. Nevertheless, the degree to which PEPFAR regulations fail to prevent new infections under the imposition of a particular moral order has been noticed.

On World AIDS Day in 2006, the European Union issued a formal statement urging African governments to ignore the focus on abstinence under Bush's AIDS program, proclaiming that "we are profoundly concerned about the resurgence of partial or incomplete messages on HIV prevention which are not grounded in evidence and have limited effectiveness" (cited in Nelson 2006, 195). Echoing this sentiment, the former UN special envoy on AIDS in Africa, Stephen Lewis, during the Sixteenth International AIDS Conference in Toronto, stated that Washington was practicing "incipient neo-colonialism" in telling African nations how to fight AIDS and that "no government in the western world has the right to dictate policy to African governments around the way in which they respond to the pandemic" (complete citation BBC 2006). These sentiments in many respects are on target, and the specter of Western governments using AIDS as a tool for political rather than public health interventions needs recognition and scrutiny. Yet those recognizing the neocolonial reverberations of current U.S. interventions into African AIDS pose no alternative solutions for African countries hard hit by the epidemic. As Lewis himself admits, the Global Fund is chronically and acutely underfunded, even though it is considered by many governments and aid agencies to be a better mechanism for distributing prevention funds (ibid.).[3] Until other options are available, then, many African countries will have little choice but to accept PEPFAR dollars despite their counterproductive conditionalities.

---

[3] In 2006, the Global Fund received a total of $231,336,778 in contributions from all countries and agencies, a fraction of the $10 billion projected as necessary to adequately address the AIDS epidemic alone. The U.S. contribution was only $29,760,000—less than the contributions of The Netherlands and Sweden (UNAIDS 2007).

AIDS Treatment and the Politics of Antiretroviral Access

Access to antiretrovirals has become increasingly visible as another point of contestation throughout much of Africa and beyond over questions of how human rights, trade relations, technological capacity, and patent protectionism should be defined and delimited in the context of mortality rates from AIDS that in many African countries are on the rise or unabated. Though there are various dimensions to these debates, they pivot fundamentally around the financial inaccessibility of antiretrovirals to the vast majority of those who need them. In contrast—and thus adding impetus to the debate—antiretrovirals have become available to the majority of those in industrialized countries who need them, turning AIDS into more of a chronic disease and significantly decreasing mortality rates in these regions within the last decade. In this section, I will trace some of the complex terrain of antiretroviral (ARV) access in Africa today, covering some of the prime reasons why ARVs are not more prevalent and outlining what, so far, have remained unresolved contradictions in intervention, production, and regulation.

The primary mechanism governing distribution of new pharmaceutical products, such as ARVs, is the World Trade Organization's Trade Related Aspects of Intellectual Property Rights, or TRIPS. Like all other WTO agreements, TRIPS is virtually global in scope, having been "agreed upon" by all participating members of the WTO.[4] Its main function is to establish minimum standards for the global protection of intellectual property of all kinds, with the overt rationale of creating incentives for research and development of new technologies and mechanisms for their transfer and dissemination. As Correa describes, motivation for global regulation of intellectual property rights came in the wake of diminishing U.S. advantages in several areas of high technology and a growing trade deficit, the result of what was perceived to be a system too open to opportunities for piracy and profiting from U.S.-based innovations. As a consequence, "this perception was astutely and effectively promoted by industrial lobbies (particularly the pharmaceutical, software and phonogram industries), which convinced the U.S. government about the need to link trade and IPRs in order to increase the returns on R&D and to prevent imitation" (2000, 4).

The fundamental stipulations of TRIPS require all countries to eventually recognize patents on a wide range of commodities, including pharmaceutical products, and extend the legal limit of a patent to twenty years. The requirement of all WTO participating countries to recognize patents even on essential medicines is an especially significant departure from pre-TRIPS flexibilities exercised by individual countries. Many countries, such as India, chose not to patent medicines, for example, choosing to keep under government control products that have an impact on public welfare (Haakonsson and Richey 2007). Though there continues to be some debate about the actual effect of patents on the price of drugs in areas such as Africa (see Attaran and Gillespie-White 2001), there is widespread acknowledgment that patents in fact keep prices of medications such as AIDS drugs artificially high (UAEM 2007), in part because mechanisms such as TRIPS foreclose opportunities for generic production or competition among manufacturers.[5] The bottom line for

---

[4] For the closed-door and often coercive tactics characterizing WTO negotiations and favoring more powerful OECD countries, see Kwa (2003).

[5] Technically a patent itself does not preclude the possibility of "open licensing" or nonexclusive licensing—that is, conferring rights to more than one company to manufacture the product. In practice, however, pharmaceutical companies and universities that own patents tend overwhelmingly to stick with exclusive licensing models that confer rights to only one producer.

achieving universal recognition of patents in the case of pharmaceutical products is, therefore, that the pharmaceutical industry gains significant latitude in determining prices of patented commodities, including life-saving medications such as antiretrovirals, and, in turn, that all countries eventually be required to pay market prices for drugs whose patents have not expired. In the United States now, the annual price for a standard triple-drug regimen of ARVs costs from $10,000 to $20,000 per person. Though prices in most low-income countries are lower, they are still far beyond what the average individual, or even government, can afford to pay.

There are a few loopholes built into the TRIPS agreement, however, that complicate the picture to some degree. Because of the particularly harsh impact of TRIPS on low-income countries and their potential to supply needed medications to their populations, developing nations during 2001 negotiations in Doha pushed for amendments that would give "least developed" countries until 2016 to recognize patents on pharmaceuticals, including ARVs, and free them from the 2005 deadline for middle-income countries such as India. They also pushed for a stronger articulation of national interest in public health, which resulted in a statement that TRIPS "should be interpreted and implemented in a manner supportive of WTO members' right to protect public health and, in particular, to promote access to medicines for all" (cited in Barton 2004, 149). In practice, this means upholding the rights of countries to take advantage of flexibilities included within TRIPS, such as compulsory licensing of life-saving medications under conditions of national emergency[6] and rules for importing generic drugs. Despite these accommodations to public health and the implied recognition of inequitable burdens imposed by TRIPS regulations on low-income regions, it is widely acknowledged that TRIPS is a mechanism that largely favors the pharmaceutical and other industries, not the poor (see Curti 2001). One indication of this is that the vast majority of those needing antiretrovirals in Africa still do not have access to them.

However, as Haakonsson and Richey note in their overview of TRIPS and ARV access in Africa, TRIPS is not the only mechanism standing in the way of better access (2007). Technically, every country in Africa has the right to implement compulsory licenses to import generic versions of ARVs under TRIPS, but, so far, only Eritrea and Ghana have done so (ibid., 79). One reason for this, the authors suggest, is that many countries fear that even though they have WTO sanction to produce or import generic medications, they would jeopardize political relations with Western countries in doing so (ibid.). This fear is well founded. The United States in particular—and in direct contradiction of PEPFAR rhetoric—has been unrelenting in its position that TRIPS guidelines are too lenient and that bilateral or regional trade deals are the answer to what several U.S. administrations have considered too much latitude in circumventing intellectual property protection. Consequently, free trade agreements between the United States and several low-income regions and countries have so far included stipulations forcing countries to recognize patents even on essential medications such as ARVs immediately rather than in 2016, despite TRIPS specifications (Craddock, 2008). Even without active trade negotiations, countries dependent on Western aid are reluctant to take steps that might jeopardize continued assistance. As mentioned above, countries receiving PEPFAR funding were selected according to their alignment with U.S. political interests, a prerequisite that necessarily affects profoundly a participating country's

---

[6] In compulsory licensing, a government overrides a patent on a particular drug and allows manufacture of generics. Governments can and have broken patents and turned towards compulsory licenses under a variety of circumstances. For an overview, see UAEM 2007.

subsequent political actions. This is especially true when most countries in Africa depend heavily on donor assistance in maintaining or scaling up their access to ARVs.

In part, the inability of governments to purchase ARVs without external assistance derives from drug prices that remain too high despite recent price reductions and the increased availability of generics. In 2001, the Indian pharmaceutical company Cipla began offering generic antiretrovirals to South Africa and other countries for $600 per person, substantially below the $1,000–1,200-average price tag of patented ARV regimens.[7] Western pharmaceutical companies had no choice but to respond; most subsequently dropped the price of their ARVs or decided not to block generic imports (Curti 2001). In many cases, however, these price reductions were negotiated on a drug-by-drug and country-by-country basis rather than across the board, resulting in significant variability in price reductions across geographic regions and inordinate amounts of time spent on negotiations while people continued to die. And sometimes, promised price reductions simply did not come through. According to the organization Médecins Sans Frontières, for example, Gilead Sciences failed to follow through on its promise to lower the price of its AIDS drug Viread as part of the much-publicized Gilead Access program announced in 2003. As of 2006, Gilead had failed to gain regulatory approval in ninety-one of the countries it proposed to sell Viread "at no profit" (Elias 2006). Currently, the cheapest antiretrovirals cost $120 a year per person through a package negotiated by the Clinton Foundation, several Indian pharmaceutical companies, and AspenCare of South Africa for sixteen antiretrovirals and other medications to treat AIDS (www.clintonfoundation.org).

The Global Fund, Clinton Foundation, Gates Foundation, World Bank, and PEPFAR, among others, have been major players in either purchasing ARVs or supplying governments with funds for doing so. Though the increased availability of funds for treating AIDS in low-income regions is certainly heartening, the number of donors and their apparent lack of coordination create contradictions and problems for concerned countries. PEPFAR deserves particular attention for its controversial political jockeying between the corporate world and corporal welfare. Until 2005, the Office of the Global AIDS Coordinator insisted that only patented ARVs could be purchased by African countries and others receiving PEPFAR funds. This stipulation was especially disappointing given the $191 million made available for ARV purchases and $421 million for full antiretroviral treatment support in 2005—55 percent of total PEPFAR spending (PEPFAR 2006). The rationale for the office's stipulations was the supposedly insufficient oversight of production standards by Indian and other pharmaceutical companies already producing generic ARVs.

The FDA was subsequently designated the official regulatory body for approving safe generic ARVs, and it took until mid-2005 to approve the first round of generics. In the meantime, countries using PEPFAR funding were required to purchase only patented ARVs at up to four times the cost of generics, a rule many pronounced was designed to protect pharmaceutical company profits. It has also not gone

---

[7] This is related to a legal and human rights victory hailed the same year by AIDS activists. In a further example of the contested terrain of patent protection outside the parameters of TRIPS, in 1998 thirty-nine pharmaceutical companies brought suit against South Africa for legislation proposing an override of drug patents and allowing compulsory licensing of antiretrovirals in order to address one of the highest rates of AIDS in the world (Curti 2001). The Clinton administration, backed by strong pharmaceutical industry lobbying, threatened South Africa with trade sanctions if it did not back off of the proposed legislation, even though South Africa was within the limits of TRIPS. The combined actions of the thirty-nine companies and the U.S. government galvanized such a strong human rights response from public and NGO sectors that by 2001, the United States backed down from its threats, and the pharmaceutical companies dropped their suit (ibid.).

without note that Bush's choice to head PEPFAR efforts was Randall Tobias, the former CEO of pharmaceutical giant Eli Lilly. As Naomi Klein remarked in a 2003 Guardian article critiquing administrative support of Big Pharma over generic ARVs, "Tobias's appointment is a bit like trusting the CEO of ExxonMobil to lead a government effort to promote solar power" (www.guardian.co.uk).

As many AIDS activists and policy analysts noted at the 2004 International AIDS conference, the World Health Organization has provided strenuous oversight of production procedures and safety standards in the development and manufacture of generic ARVs. Insisting on FDA oversight, in addition to the existing system, served only to stall generic purchases, according to these critics, and give U.S.- and European-based pharmaceutical companies the upper hand. The desire on the part of governments and NGOs to purchase generics, however, can be seen in the rapid rise from 10 to 70 percent in the proportion of generics bought with PEPFAR money between 2005 and 2006 (PEPFAR 2006). Aside from the larger number of individuals who gain access to ARVs when generics are purchased, there is also the issue of adherence. Generic manufacturers have long since combined three-drug regimens of antiretrovirals into what is called a fixed-dose combination pill: patients can take one pill twice a day instead of multiple pills over the course of a day required by the complicated patented drug regimens.[8] Having access to a simplified, easy-to-follow, cheaper regimen explains, in part, the higher adherence rates recorded in several African countries compared to the United States, where a fixed-dose combination pill is still unavailable (Farmer 2001). Clearly, this is a critically important issue given the potential for developing multi-drug resistant strains of HIV with lower rates of adherence.

On a positive note, the result of increased availability of generic ARVs coupled with larger subsidies is that access has increased dramatically in the last several years. According to UNAIDS figures, coverage in low- and middle-income countries rose from 240,000 people in 2001 to 1.3 million in 2005, while coverage more than doubled across Africa to approximately 800,000 (UNAIDS 2006, 151). Several countries in northern and western Africa are reaching 25 percent or more of populations in need, and more countries, including Botswana, Ethiopia, Senegal, Tanzania, and Zambia, are offering ARVs free of charge in the public sector (WHO 2005). Perhaps even more heartening, in the face of significant obstacles to compulsory licensing, is the regional development of pharmaceutical industries in several African countries. South Africa's Aspen Pharmacare is manufacturing six generic antiretrovirals through voluntary paid licenses with Western pharmaceutical companies,[9] while Zimbabwe, Mozambique, Zambia, Nigeria, Kenya, and Uganda are also establishing pharmaceutical sectors with the assistance of Indian, Chinese, Thai, and Brazilian companies that are themselves seeking a way to extend their production of generic ARVs beyond the TRIPS deadline (Haakonsson and Richey 2007, 80). Given the amount of time it takes to develop a pharmaceutical industry scientifically and industrially, however, it might be questionable how effective these regional sectors can be in closing the access gap within the next few years, or even before 2016. What happens after 2016 when all low-income countries

---

[8] Because HIV mutates so rapidly, the recommendation is for individuals to take three (and sometimes more) antiretrovirals from different "classes," or modes of preventing the reproduction of HIV in the body. Until very recently, there were no fixed-dose combination pills on-patent because different pharmaceutical companies owned patents on the necessary combinations. Working together to combine pills required a degree of cross-corporate cooperation untenable for most pharmaceutical companies. In January 2006, however, Gilead and Bristol Myers Squibb announced that they should have a combination pill for U.S. and European markets by the end of the year (Gillis 2006).

[9] Voluntary licenses result when pharmaceutical companies owning patents or exclusive licenses on a drug voluntarily donate blue prints of specified drugs to generic producers for a negotiated percentage of profits from regional sales.

have to recognize patents also remains an open question. South Africa's model of seeking voluntary licenses is no doubt encouraging, but it has proven a slow way to gain manufacturing rights to ARVs.

Conclusion: Reframing the Discourse of the "Securitization and Sexualization" of AIDS in Africa

In recent years, the world has paid greater attention to the devastating and continuing effects of AIDS in hard-hit regions of Africa. Why it took so long to get the attention of Western governments and multinational agencies when the death toll from AIDS in Africa is in the millions has no reasonable answer. As this chapter also makes clear, the attention African countries are now finally receiving to help alleviate the suffering and mortality from AIDS in their countries does not come without its own set of political motivations, some of which almost certainly diminish the potential of local governments and organizations to intervene in the epidemic. And the upsurge in recent multinational responses does not elide the continued paucity of funds coming from European countries, Japan, and the United States for HIV and other categories of aid in Africa—a geopolitical failure gaining heightened visibility in the lead-up to the 2007 G8 summit in Germany (Elliott and Connelly 2007; Dugger 2005).

As recently noted (Ingram 2007; Elbe 2005, 2006), designating AIDS as a security and development issue arguably sets the stage for far greater financial and political attention on regions of Africa heavily affected by the epidemic. However, such designations also become important determinants of the types of intervention and the stipulations they carry. The fear that high rates of AIDS could cause destabilization of governments, worsen poverty, and incite discontent—the "securitization of AIDS"—has the potential, according to Elbe, to funnel interventions towards the military and away from other vulnerable sectors of civil society and to further stigmatize AIDS as a "threat" rather than to normalize it as a disease in need of humanitarian intervention (Elbe 2006).

On the other hand, Elbe also points out that designating AIDS as a security issue might be a more effective route to overriding patents on antiretrovirals in African countries because Article 73 in the TRIPS agreement stipulates that TRIPS should not stand in the way of a member country taking action to protect its essential security interests. Given the lack of success so far in designating AIDS a public health emergency in rationalizing patent overrides, Elbe contends that "it will be essential . . . to demonstrate that the AIDS pandemic constitutes an emergency affecting the security of states," if they want to win the case for low-cost AIDS drugs (ibid., 133).

Continuing the theme of treatment, other questions remain inadequately addressed and unresolved. As Haakonsson and Richey note (2007), the reliance on donors to fund purchase of ARVs and the fluctuation in levels of those donations mean that the supply, coordination, and dissemination of drugs remain precarious. Now that India has recognized patents, as stipulated by the TRIPS agreement, there is also widespread apprehension that generic antiretrovirals will become harder to find and that new sources will not be able to fill the gap left by the sizeable manufacturing capacities of Indian pharmaceutical companies. The newest antiretrovirals and second-line treatments, needed by those who do not respond well or develop resistance to first-line drugs, also remain prohibitively expensive, leaving even those in low-income countries with access to ARVs fewer options than is therapeutically advisable. For those countries without total access to ARVs, there are many dilemmas in the "social lives of AIDS medicines" (Whyte 2006), including who gets access to AIDS drugs and who does not, how access will be maintained once it is gained, and what sacrifices are made by families channeling disproportionate resources toward the purchase of ARVs to the detriment of other needs. Because often more than one family member is infected in high-incidence regions, there also comes the unconscionable choice of which family member gets access to life-saving medications if there is not enough money for all. In other words, AIDS drugs in countries with inadequate access take on material and symbolic significance as they introduce an interrelated set of ethical quandaries, social relations, hopes, calculated decisions, and burdens of suffering. They also stand as a symbol of the devastating reality of inequality at a local, national, and international scale (ibid., 242).

On one hand, G8 countries must be scrutinized for their failure to fulfill their 2005 promises to increase aid to Africa. According to the most recent report from the Organization for Economic Cooperation and Development (OECD), aid to Africa fell in 2006 for the first time in a decade, dipping 5 percent below 2005 levels (Dugger 2005). Though this includes funding for all categories of assistance, the impact on HIV in terms of poverty alleviation, school and health care subsidization, and infrastructure development is potentially profound.[10] Even with recent increased funding for AIDS in Africa, antiretroviral coverage is not what it needs to be. In all low- and middle-income countries, 80 percent of those in need of ARVs still do not have access to them, while in much of southern and eastern Africa—some of the hardest hit regions—coverage remains below 10 percent (UNAIDS 2006).

On the other hand, external funding for AIDS in Africa points to the seemingly intractable problems that inhere not only in an enormously complex epidemic, but also in the equally complex and inequitable geopolitical relations that shape it. The moralizing imperative encompassed within U.S. funding for AIDS in many African countries is but one illustration that AIDS lies at the nexus of several related issues of interest among Western governments, including global economic growth, national stability, and biosecurity. In its disciplining tactics couched as disease intervention, PEPFAR makes clear that decreasing AIDS in Africa necessitates coordinates that are not only drastically contradictory to the political economies governing some of the practices driving HIV transmission in Africa; they are also part of a larger political program. "Sexualization" of AIDS, in other words, overlaps directly the "securitization" of AIDS by dictating the social order at the heart of stable democracies and diminished HIV rates. Although African countries need financial donations from OECD countries to help them intervene in the epidemic, there needs to be far more scrutiny over the nature of the donations, the political designations that underwrite them, and the disciplining governmental practices they sometimes demand. This is especially important to ponder as the United States has committed another 30 billion dollars to fight AIDS in Africa.

REFERENCES

Annan, K. Opening speech, International AIDS Conference, Bangkok, Thailand, July 12, 2004.

Attaran, A. and L. Gillespie-White. "Do Patents for Antiretroviral Drugs Constrain Access to AIDS Treatment in Africa?" *JAMA* 286 (2001): 1886.

Barton, J. 2004. "TRIPS and the Global Pharmaceutical Market." *Health Affairs* 23, no. 3, (2004): 146–154.

BBC. "U.S. Criticized for HIV Aid Effort," August 16, 2006. news.bbc.co.uk (last accessed June 7, 2007).

---

[10] This is in no way to counter the critique of most "development" schemes targeted at Africa or to contradict my argument that increased funding is in itself necessarily effective or unproblematic. But geopolitical neglect is also unacceptable.

Brückner, H. and P. Bearman. "After the Promise: The STD Consequences of Adolescent Virginity Pledges." *Journal of Adolescent Health* 36 (2005): 271–178.

Cohen, J., R. Schleifer, and T. Tate. "AIDS in Uganda: The Human-Rights Dimension." *The Lancet* 365 (2005): 2075–2076.

Correa, C. *Intellectual Property Rights, the WTO and Developing Countries: The TRIPS Agreement and Policy Options.* London: Zed Books, 2000.

Craddock, S. "AIDS and the Politics of Violence," in *HIV/AIDS: Global Frontiers in Prevention/Intervention* edited by Cynthia Pope and Renee White. New York: Routledge, 2008.

Curti, A. "The WTO Dispute Settlement Understanding: An Unlikely Weapon in the Fight against AIDS." *American Journal of Law and Medicine* 27 (2001): 469–485.

Dugger, C. "Bono Faults: G8 Nations on Debt Relief to Africa," *International Herald Tribune, Europe,* May 15, 2005. www.iht.com (last accessed June 5, 2007).

Elbe, S. "AIDS, Security, Biopolitics." *International Relations* 19 (2005): 403–419.

———. "Should HIV/AIDS Be Securitized? The Ethical Dilemmas of Linking HIV/AIDS and Security." *International Studies Quarterly* 50 (2006): 119–144.

Elias, P. "Biotech Company Gilead Criticized for AIDS Drug Supply." Associated Press, February 8, 2006.

Elliott, L. and K. Connolly. "In 2005, G8 Pledged $50bn for Africa. Now the Reality." *Guardian,* April 25, 2007. www.guardian.co.uk (last accessed June 5, 2007).

Farmer, P. *Infections and Inequalities: The Modern Plagues.* Berkeley, CA: University of California Press, 2001.

Gill, P. "How Not to Banish HIV." *New Scientist* 190 (May 6, 2006): 2550.

Gillis, J. "Once-a-day Pill Could Be Ready Soon." *Washington Post,* January 19, 2006.

Government Accounting Office. "Global Health: Spending Requirement Presents Challenges for Allocating Prevention Funding under the President's Emergency Plan for AIDS Relief," Report to Congressional Committees. www.gao.gov/cgi-bin/getrpt?GAO-06–395 (last accessed May 3, 2007).

Haakonsson, S.J. and L.A. Richey. "TRIPS and Public Health: The Doha Declaration and Africa." *Development Policy Review* 25, no. 1 (2007): 71–90.

Hauser, D. "Five Years of Abstinence-Only-Until-Marriage Education: Assessing the Impact." www.advocatesforyouth.org/publications/stateevaluations.pdf (last accessed May 30, 2007).

Ingram, A. "HIV/AIDS, Security and the Geopolitics of U.S.-Nigerian Relations." *Review of International Political Economy* 14, no. 3 (2007).

Keller, R. "Geographies of Power, Legacies of Mistrust: Colonial Medicine in the Global Present." *Historical Geography* 34, 26–48.

King, N. "Security, Disease, Commerce: Ideologies of Postcolonial Global Health." *Social Studies of Medicine* 32, 763–789.

Klein, N. "Bush's AIDS 'Gift' Has Been Seized by Industry Giants: Now the U.S. May Block the Provision of Cheap Generic Drugs for Africa." *Guardian* October 13, 2003.

Kwa, A. *Power Politics in the WTO.* Bangkok: Focus on the Global South, 2003. www.publiccitizen.org/documents/powerpoliticsKWA.pdf.

Nelson, R. "Report Shows Mixed Results for PEPFAR." *The Lancet* 6, no. 4 (2006): 194–195.

Phillips, O. "The Invisible Presence of Homosexuality: Implications for HIV/AIDS and Rights in Southern Africa," in *HIV and AIDS in Africa: Beyond Epidemiology,* edited by E. Kalipeni, S. Craddock, J. Oppong, and J. Ghosh, 155–166. Oxford: Blackwell, 2004.

Rubenstein, L. and E. Friedman. "Human Rights and the President's AIDS Initiative." *Human Rights* 31, no. 4 (2004).

Schleifer, R. "Ignorance Only: HIV/AIDS, Human Rights and Federally Funded Abstinence-Only Programs in the United States." Human Rights Watch, hrw.org/reports/2002/usa0902 (last accessed 2002).

UAEM. "Closing the Access Gap: The Equitable Access License," www.essentialmed; www.publiccitizen.org/documents/powerpoliticsKWA.pdf; icine.org/EALPrimer.pdf (last accessed May 20, 2007).

UNAIDS. *Report on the Global AIDS Epidemic, 2006.* www.unaids.org (last accessed May 31, 2007).

———. List of Contributors, 2007. www.unaids.org (last accessed May 17, 2007).

Whyte, S., M. Whyte, L. Meinert, and B. Kyaddondo. "Treating AIDS: Dilemmas of Unequal Access in Uganda," in *Global Pharmaceuticals: Ethics, Markets, Practices,* edited by A. Petryna, A. Lakoff, and A. Kleinman, 240–262. Durham, NC: Duke University Press, 2006.

World Health Organization. "Fact Sheet: Countries Offering Free Access to HIV Treatment," 2005. www.who.int.

Part IV

POLITICAL AND POPULAR CULTURE AND THE DYNAMICS OF A CONTEMPORIZING CONTINENT

The fourth section of this book engages the spheres of political and popular culture, pathways into studying the vibrant dynamics that articulate voice, shape diverse identities, and defy the abuse of power across the continent. Mainstream postcolonial interpretations of the colonial construction of African culture illustrate ways in which the structural-functionalist anthropology of the Straussian[1] years distorted and preempted a dynamic understanding of politics and culture in Africa. Contemporary interpretations of African political culture, such as "the Big Man theory," "the neopatrimonial ruler," and the positing of Africans in a frozen "traditional versus modern" binarism have their roots in this anthropology, which lacked intellectual rigor, backed the colonial agenda to seek "order and stability," and supported material expropriation. It did not explore the dynamics of African sociocultural systems and institution on their own terms. Current writing on Africa is still guilty of a "reactionary cultural determinism" (Gusterson and Besteman 2005)[2] that ignores the immense historical and contemporary evidence of sociocultural accomplishments in the continent.

With this in mind, the analysts of African social and political culture in this volume draw distinctions between sociology and anthropology and infuse a new cultural studies methodology into the analysis of African public spaces. As one scholar has noted, analyses must move beyond the "ideology of African tribalism"(Mafeje 1971),[3] a theoretical lens still used by many to interpret events such as the Rwandan genocide. The authors of this section provide insights into the making and remaking of political theater within the ambit of artistic, literary, poetic, cinematic, and social traditions, identities, and roles. Their essays demonstrate that the excavation of cultural-political identities, "genderisms," cultural expressions, and ideologies in different African societies must engage key sociocultural, religious, and economic perspectives within a globalized historical continuum to yield meaningful interpretations of African polities.

---

[1] Leo Strauss (1899–1973), a charismatic political philosopher and professor at the University of Chicago, was born and educated in Germany and then emigrated to the United States in 1937 after a stint in the United Kingdom. Among other things, Strauss insisted that modern liberalism contained in its relativism, the seeds of both virulent nihilism and milder variants that tended to produce what he considered directionless egalitarianism and a loss of conservative and ancestral function in many Western democracies.

[2] Gusterson, Besteman, and colleagues deplore the vacuous writings of popular columnists and academic pundits because they subvert the role of serious anthropological studies. See Catherine Besteman and Hugh Gusterson, *Why America's Top Pundits Are Wrong: Anthropologists Talk Back*. California Series in Public Anthropology, 13. (Berkely and Los Angeles: University of California Press, 2005).

[3] Archie Mafeje, "The Ideology of Tribalism," *Journal of Modern African Studies* 9, no. 2 (1971), 253–261.

255

To begin, Pius Adesanmi, widely read poet, author of *The Wayfarer & Other Poems* (2001), and director of the Project on New African Literatures at Carleton University, takes on the Herculean task of capturing the contexts that birthed and shaped modern African writers and of addressing the questions that have driven their "struggles for meaning" in a changing climate of colonization, decolonization, and postcoloniality. In "Reshaping Power and the Public Sphere: The Political Voices of African Writers," he traces the protest traditions heralded by Maran's stinging indictment of colonial power, "you are the might that exceeds right. You aren't a torch but an inferno. Everything you touch, you consume." He then discusses the angst of later novelists and poets who unpack African realities and propel us on a voyage that links literary writings with sociopolitical developments in the continent and that spans francophone, anglophone, North African, Southern African, and Indian Ocean nations.

Adesanmi argues that while the African writer has been increasingly tied to the dual agendas of cultural nationalism and historical retrieval/revisionism, there has been a postindependence collapse of the marriage of convenience between creative writers, revolutionary theoreticians, and nationalist politicians. Creative writers have become radical and cynical since independence, and as Adesanmi reminds us in this passionate and extensive exploration, literature has had such a profound impact on our reading of Africa that we must understand writers' sociopolitical milieu and ideologies and how they frame our views of the continent.

In the second contribution to this section, "African Cinema: Visions, Meanings, and Measures," Jude Akudinobi, writer and author of the feature-length screenplay *Eze*, examines the emergence of the African film industry, which coincided with the struggle for political freedom.[4] Within Akudinobi's masterful grasp, the field of African cinema seems a delicious and seductive arena, teeming with sociopolitical discourses and vibrant ideological takes on Africa, past and future. The tension between cinema as political and cultural expression and as entertainment parallels the battle fought by some in the third world to retrieve control of their economies and cultures.

African, especially Nigerian, cinema, with its political and social messages and exuberant portrayals of diverse, constantly rearticulating sociopolitical realities, has become a powerful voice projected across the continent, the diaspora, and beyond. Akudinobi's handling of the contents, visions, and struggles of the world of African cinema reveals powerful landscapes of popular culture with which many "outsiders" are unfamiliar. Nevertheless, these are the voices that are themselves reframing and redefining how Africans and non-Africans alike engage in discourses of change that are increasingly free of Western hegemonic notions and political economies.

In the following chapter, Anene Ejikeme, author of "Let the Women Speak! And Listen," tackles the social dynamics of women's lives and the gender discourses in and about Africa. Her broad assessment of the growth and nature of literature on African women exposes popular perceptions, and tendencies to emphasize the roles and status of African women and to distinguish between their public and private lives. Speaking provocatively of the process of engendering African history—a tale of "sex, politics, and power"—Ejikeme moves from traditional models of framing to the reframing of gender by Ifi Amadiume, Oyeronke Oyewunmi, and others. These scholars have challenged the tendency to imagine African societies according to rigid Western typologies of women's subordination in patriarchal societies. Ejikeme analyzes matriarchy, linguistic and social categories, and differential worldviews to open the study of African women and expose the impact of colonialism.

---

[4] "African film-making is in a way a child of African political independence." See Imruh Bakari and Mbye Cham, eds., *African Experiences of Cinema* (London and Basingstoke: British Film Institute, 1996), 1.

Her powerful treatise confronts women's exploitation and socioeconomic crises and assesses women's agency and voice through study not merely of language codes, but also of the indisputable facts of their mobilization and enterprise. Ejikeme provides highly experienced Africanists, casual observers of Africa, and young scholars a critical intellectual frame and analytical language. As she insists, "Western-educated scholars have been trained to utilize Western typologies, yet their life experiences in Africa make them see that these typologies are not necessarily universal truths. Encountering Western scholarship through African eyes forces us to rethink the Western vision (and version) of Africa, and this can be vitally rewarding."

The feminist-womanist, young activist and scholar Kendra Sundal takes up where Ejikeme concludes with an intimate response and commentary, "Between Multiple Visions of Feminism." Her perspective as a young "outsider" emerges from her prolonged stay in Medie, Ghana, where she had a vision-altering experience with Ghanaian women. Her encounter gave her what Oyeronke Oyewunmi has described as an alternative "world sense"—a different way of seeing and understanding gender differences and roles.[5] Discovering traditional gender roles that contradicted Western conceptualizations of African women's oppression, subordination, and inferiority destabilized Sundal's construct of sex and gender and affirmed the relevance of the radical critiques of scholars such as Amdiume, Oyewunmi, and Ejikeme.[6]

The inclusion of Sundal's response is, of course, an unusual step in a book of this nature. In keeping with our search for new frames, she brings a critical dimension to the discourse on Africa, and her contribution speaks to the endless debates regarding the overly generalized notion of "Western feminism" and the multiple forms of female, or woman, philosophies that accompany the struggles for women's place and rights across the world. Sundal's is a personal reflection that affirms our feeling that writing must be a dialogue between key interlocutors. Its place in this volume is particularly poignant as more students from wealthy nations travel to Africa to expand their reading of the continent and as scholars seek feedback on the intersections of their personal and professional experiences. Her work is at once provocative and discomfiting, yet it illuminates, to some degree, the paradox that Soyinka-Airewele and Edozie discussed in the first chapter of this book: Sundal's encounter with female empowerment amid poverty and inequality in a small town in Ghana underlines the need to distinguish objective conditions of disempowerment from sociocultural and other factors that transform such "dis-enablement." Like Ejikeme, Sundal feels that applying new lenses on Africa can be intensely rewarding, and her essay reminds scholars that the analysis we proffer is part of a continuing discourse, or dialogue, that shapes identity, ideology, and understanding.

---

[5] See Oyeronke Oyewunmi, *The Invention of Women: Making an African Sense of Western Gender Discourses* (Minneapolis, MN: University of Minnesota Press, 1997).

[6] See Ifi Amadiume, *Male Daughters, Female Husbands: Gender and Sex in an African Society* (London: Zed Books, 1987).

Chapter 15

RESHAPING POWER AND THE PUBLIC SPHERE
The Political Voices of African Writers
Pius Adesanmi

I believe it's impossible to write anything in Africa without some kind of commitment, some kind of message, some kind of protest. In fact, I should say all our writers, whether they are aware of it or not, are committed writers. The whole pattern of life demands that you should protest, that you should put in a word for your history, your traditions, your religion and so on.

—Chinua Achebe

Beginnings: Of Extra-Creative Texts and the African Writer's Commitment

Nigerian poet and public intellectual Odia Ofeimun begins his essay "Postmodernism and the Impossible Death of the African Author" with a sobering evocation of the condition of the African writer in 1968, an epochal year marked by international convulsions and youth restiveness that had far-reaching consequences for framing the political in the domain of cultural production:

> In 1968, the year Roland Barthes, the French philosopher, announced the "Death of the Author," Wole Soyinka was in detention for opposing the prosecutors of the Nigerian civil war. The poet Christopher Okigbo had been killed in the early skirmishes of the war. Chinua Achebe was in exile, engaged in matters as distant from the literary as raising funds for and campaigning for the rise of the Biafran Sun. Mongo Beti was in Paris on a contested visa, his book soon due for banning in both his Camerounian homeland and France. Naguib Mahfouz's book *Children of Gebelawi* was banned in his country. Camara Laye was on the run from Sekou Toure's gendarmes. Can Themba had drunk himself to death in a Joburg shebeen. Bloke Modisane, overwhelmed by the depression of exile, was reported to have jumped down from a New York skyscraper. Alex la Guma was still incarcerated on Robben Island. And Dennis Brutus, freed from Robben Island, was in exile, as was Ezekiel Mpahlele and many other South African writers (24–25).

This continental, sadly inexhaustive, catalogue of writers at the receiving end of the brutal exertions of power in Africa, coming so soon after the euphoria of political independence in the 1960s, merely marks a phase in the continuous conflict between Africa's creative energies and the interweaving ideas of power and the public sphere, which the African literary process sought to refashion with a view to creating full human agency in a continent marked by colonial and postcolonial regimes of violence. The modern African writer emerged at the dawn of the twentieth century into a framework of anti-imperialist struggle. African writers and Black intellectuals operated in such ideological contexts as the Pan-Africanist movement, political nationalism, cultural nationalist movements, and Négritude, among numerous others. Their mission involved a struggle for meaning, spelled out in terms of the need for the African writer to create narratives that could contribute to a global process of Black conceptual decolonization and cultural self-fashioning against the backdrop of centuries of dehumanization by two negative aspects of modernity: slavery and colonialism.

To participate in the struggle for meaning was to enter into a contested political terrain that forced the first generation of African writers to produce texts essentially reactive to colonial power. These texts, which later fell under the critical rubric of African/negro-African protest literature, were indicative of an identity more or less forced on the new African writer as an *intellectuel engagé* (committed intellectual) along lines defined by Jean-Paul Sartre. The African writer's consecration as a politically committed artist started with René Maran's celebrated preface to his novel, *Batouala*, which won the prestigious Prix Goncourt in France in 1921.[1] The novel's preface has remained one of the most virulent textual indictments of the philosophical and moral matrix of the French colonial enterprise, summed up in one delusional expression: mission civilisatrice. Exposing the argument that European colonization aimed at civilizing the colonized as an elaborate farce, Maran's strident voice cut into the heart of the matter:

> Civilization, civilization, pride of the Europeans and their burying-ground for innocents; Rabindranath Tagore, the Hindu poet, one day in Tokyo, said what you were! You build your kingdom on corpses. Whatever you may want, whatever you may do, you act with deceit. At your sight, gushing tears and screaming pain. You are the might which exceeds right. You aren't a torch but an inferno. Everything you touch, you consume (16–17).

Coming in 1921, Maran's preface is significant on two accounts. First, it became the precursor of a protest tradition that was to bind subsequent generations of francophone African novelists to political engagements rooted in ideologies of decolonization. Second, it created a sense of urgency around acts of political enunciation that necessitated an extra-textual recourse to the preface in the tradition of the political novel in francophone Africa. A good number of the anticolonial novels of the late 1950s and the 1960s in francophone Africa had prefaces that signaled the increasing radicalization of the creative space and the increasing politicization of the writer. With the advent of political independence in the 1960s and the dawn of an era of postcolonial disillusionment, now infamously christened "the mourning after," the public sphere and the political space that inhere in it became hostage to the whims of a postcolonial state ruled by life-presidents and tyrants. In this context, the novelistic preface became a site of insidious subversion.

It would be a stretch to suggest a direct linkage between Maran's text and the subsequent emergence and combative nature of Négritude poetry in 1930s Paris, but it remains largely arguable that the cultural and creative space into which African Négritude poets—especially Léopold Sédar Senghor and David Diop—emerged was already profoundly marked by the angst of Black/African intellectuals and the promises of a textual dissidence that would be articulated as a desire to reshape history and recast

---

[1] Although René Maran was a Martinican who had served in the French colonial service in Oubangui-Chari, his novel was published into a tradition that lumped African and Caribbean writers together as "negro-african" writers. Hence *Batouala* has come to be regarded as the first text of the protest tradition in francophone African fiction.

the Black man's role in it. Within these dynamics was born the idea of history as a burden that the Black writer must unpack. The first major intellectual of the twentieth century to recognize and theorize the restorative/redemptive functions of the Black/African writer was Jean-Paul Sartre. His famous essay, "Orphée noir," is not only the chronological successor to Maran's preface in terms of the envisioning of a revolutionary role for the Black/African writer, it also signaled the beginning of critical tensions around the idea of the publics of the African writer.

After Sartre, the question of the Black/African writer's commitment would be persistently tied to the nature of the conflicting and overlapping publics for whom he was deemed to be writing. Writing in the context of a Black world that was still imperiled by the consequences of contact with Europe and modernity and an African world that was still bogged down by colonialism, Sartre surmised correctly that Black writing—a sort of rebellious gaze on Europe—addressed two "worlds" simultaneously: the White world and the African world. Although Sartre has been criticized for his recourse to European tropes and Graeco-Roman lore—the myth of Orpheus—in explaining the political mission of the Black writer, the point often missed is that Sartre offers the first philosophical positioning of the Black writer as a demiurge:

> The first revolutionary will be the apostle of the Black soul, the herald who will tear this negritude from himself to offer it to the world, a demi-prophet, a demi-advocate, in brief a poet in the precise sense of the word "vates." Black poetry has nothing in common with the effusions of the heart; it is functional, it answers a need which exactly defines it (17–18).

Thus began in the francophone cultural space the notion of the *écrivain-phare*, the writer as a socio-political prophet, a Moses whose pen would not only write his people out of the historical void into which post-Enlightenment European narratives had consigned them, but would also conscientize them for the impending struggle against colonial aggression and all forms of racist depredation. With Négritude as the encompassing liberationist ideology, poets like Léopold Sédar Senghor, David Diop, Bernard Dadié, Tchicaya U'Tamsi, Jean Tati-Loutard, Edouard Maunick, and Birago Diop went on to articulate a poetics of resistance based on a revaluation of an African cultural essence. Beyond the need to depart from the aesthetic sterilities of French poetry, Négritude poetry mined African oratorical, rhetorical, and narratological forms for deployment in the service of cultural renaissance and rebirth, an important aspect of a broader political struggle. It is in this sense that the first generation of francophone African writers—mainly Négritude poets—became speakers of truth to imperial power and architects of an emergent continental public sphere.

While the prefatory tradition did not announce the birth of the political angst of the anglophone African writer, the textual and political voices of the modern writer in anglophone Africa also emerged in what Omafume Onoge has described as "a hostile milieu"[2] marked by colonialism and a rapacious European capitalist expansion. In this context, it was also to be expected that the writer could not emerge as a vector of any neo-platonic tradition of pure art, given wholly to aesthetic explorations and immune to sociopolitical stimuli. Political protest and public critical interventionism were thus instrumental to the birth of modern anglophone African writing, if we are to go by conventional historiographical accounts that agree on the Ghanaian Joseph Casely-Hayford's *Ethiopia Unbound*, published in 1911, as the first creative text of modern anglophonic African literature.

---

[2] See his essay, "The Crisis of Consciousness in Modern African Literature: A Survey," 387.

Like Maran and the Négritude poets, whose commitment was to an Africa that was indissociable from a broader, global negro-African world and audience, Casely-Hayford's project of cultural renaissance in *Ethiopia Unbound* also adopts a global Pan-Africanist approach to the question of Black cultural renaissance. In the pages of *Ethiopia Unbound*, concepts such as nationalism, Pan-Africanism, and African Personality, which all became global frameworks for the Black man's aspiration for agency and self-determination, received their first fictional elaboration.

After the publication of *Ethiopia Unbound*, much of African writing remained of francophonic Négritude provenance until a generation of early anglophone poets emerged in the 1940s. This extremely weak poetry, best represented by figures like Nnamdi Azikiwe, Dennis Osadebay, Abioseh Nicol, Pita Nwana, Michael Dei-Anang, and Raphael Armattoe, was inspired largely by Christian hymns and functioned more as ancillary cultural propaganda tools for the nascent political nationalism of the era. Despite their failure as art, which has led Nigerian poet Amatoritsero Ede to consign them to the propagandistic basket of efforts with those he felicitously calls "the Bandung poets,"[3] this poetry provided a colorful cultural ambience to the forms of African nationalism that would eventually crystallize into the decolonization movements of the 1950s. It also created a precursive textual space for the far more accomplished anglophonic poetic effervescence of the 1960s spearheaded by writers like Wole Soyinka, Christopher Okigbo, and Dennis Brutus.

Présence Africaine and the African Public Sphere

It is thus evident that from *Ethiopia Unbound* to *Batouala*, from the first wave of Négritude poetry in the 1930s to the pioneer phase of anglophone African poetry in the 1940s, the idea of an African public sphere, vitiated by imperialist preferments and potentially amenable to textual refashioning by the creative writer acting as *vates* (honored seers or prophets), existed mainly as a tributary of a much broader global Black ideological push for agency and revalued selfhood. Thus, the political commitment of the African literary-intellectual elite of the first three momentous decades of the twentieth century had fuller meaning in the context of an interactive engagement with the politics and texts of such Black diasporic luminaries as Edward Blyden, Marcus Garvey, George Padmore, and W.E.B. Du Bois, on the one hand, and within the liberationist energies and currents of such political and cultural movements as the Harlem Renaissance and Pan-Africanism, on the other hand. So predominant was the diasporic inflection of the Black politics of this era that the historian Ayodele Langley has spoken of an amorphous "pan-negro sentiment" with "new world origins."[4] Although African nationalists and intellectuals, such as Casely Hayford, J.E.K Aggrey, Mojola Agbebi, and W.E.G Sekyi, had already gained considerable visibility during this period, their voices were weightier insofar as their intellectual dissidence reinforced what Langley calls a "commerce of ideas"[5] with activist Black diasporic intellectuals.

As works like Elizabeth Ezra's *The Colonial Unconscious* and Brent Hayes Edwards's *The Practice of Diaspora* remind us, interwar and immediate post-war France was the crucible of early twentieth-century global pan-negro sentiment as well as a centripetal cauldron of Black politics and art. A convulsive

---

[3] See Amatoritsero Ede, "The Bandung Poets," www.sentinelpoetry.org.uk/0707/editorial.htm.

[4] See his *Pan-Africanism and Nationalism in West Africa*, 37.

[5] ibid., 35.

political atmosphere, marked by the philosophical dissent of antiwar public intellectuals such as Sartre, Maurice Merleau Ponty, Simone de Beauvoir, and Raymond Aron, and by the anarchism of such artistic movements as surrealism and cubism, was further energized by the radical activities of Black students and intellectuals from the Caribbean, the United States, and francophone Africa. The result was a maelstrom of Black ideological activism, which eventuated in the Négritude movement. New World Black intellectuals still largely dominated even this phase, with Senghor being the most visible and influential African interjection in a process that found expression in such journals as *Légitime Défense* and *L'Etudiant Noir*. In this context, the African artist, no matter how committed, articulated that commitment to a negro-African or Black world.

The picture changed radically with the founding of the journal *Présence Africaine* in 1947 by Alioune Diop, a Senegalese literary intellectual and man of culture based in Paris. As the considerable range of the essays assembled in V.Y. Mudimbe's edited volume, *The Surreptitious Speech: Présence Africaine and the Politics of Otherness,* amply demonstrates, the literature on the origins, atmospherics, politics, and cultural impact of *Présence Africaine* on Africa and the Black world is considerable and beyond the brief of the present discussion. However, it should be noted that despite its location in Paris and the collaboration of virtually every progressive French (Sartre, André Gide, Michel Leiris, Albert Camus, Théodore Monod, and Georges Balandier) and Black diasporic (Du Bois, Richard Wright, Langston Hughes, George Lamming, Aimé Césaire, and Jean Price-Mars) intellectual of the twentieth century, *Présence Africaine* was the first cultural and institutional site where a truly African intellectual public sphere emerged and was consolidated. The specific African inflection that had hitherto been drowned by the global range and diasporic thrust of the pan-negro sentiment emerged forcefully in the pages of *Présence Africaine.*

The momentous decades of the 1950s and the 1960s were, perhaps, the journal's most decisive years in terms of providing a specific site for the expression of continental nationalisms by African writers and intellectuals and providing the philosophical stimulus for the continental decolonization movements that characterized the period. It needs to be recalled that by this period, the first generation of novelists had already succeeded the early poets in the francophonic and anglophonic traditions. Richard Rive, Alex la Guma, Peter Abrahams, Lewis Nkosi, Eskia Mphahlele, Can Themba, Cyprian Ekwensi, Amos Tutuola, T.M. Aluko, Wole Soyinka, Chinua Achebe, Sembene Ousmane, Ferdinand Oyono, Cheikh Hamidou Kane, Yambo Ouologuem, Mongo Beti, Ngũgĩ wa Thiong'o, and Camara Laye had all published works to critical acclaim. These writers, whose political commitment, protest, and struggle had by then taken national and regional inflections along lines dictated by the geographical boundaries imposed by the colonial masters, could break those artificial barriers to a truly continental liberationist agenda by participating in the commerce of ideas offered by *Présence Africaine*. In the first two decades of its existence, there was practically no known African writer who was not an active participant in the cultural and political project of the journal. Anglophone and francophone writers of western and eastern Africa rubbed minds with their counterparts from southern and northern Africa, Lusophone Africa, and the Indian Ocean nations.

Présence Africaine would go on to organize two highly successful international conferences of Negro Writers and Artists in Paris (1956) and Rome (1959). It is in the fulcrum of such intense cultural and artistic intellection that the first generation of African writers began to make some of the most articulate statements in terms of their perception of their role, functions, and obligations to their societies. Some of the statements that would become famous in future essayistic offerings by Achebe, Soyinka, Ngũgĩ, Beti, and a host of other writers first found initial expression in *Présence Africaine*. In such statements, best exemplified by Achebe's 1966 contribution to the journal, "The Black Writer's Burden," and Jacques Rabemananjara's 1956 piece, "Europe and Ourselves," the tripartite role of the writer and the real meaning of his commitment were articulated: educate the people, be their spokesperson, lead them in the march to freedom. In the case of Achebe, the offerings in *Présence Africaine* already contained the seeds of the major thematic thrust of an essayistic career that would produce such volumes as *Morning Yet on Creation Day, Hopes and Impediments,* and the more recent *Home and Exile.* Commenting on these three roles as defined by African writers themselves on the pages of *Présence Africaine*, Lylian Kesteloot asserts in her *Origins of the African Revolution* that "it is in these three ways—as teacher, spokesman, liberator— that the Black writer has considered himself "engagé," that is, "committed." His works have therefore been aimed at launching and sustaining a *program of action"* (26).

The journal ensured that these aims received a more Africa-specific tonality. It is worth noting that before *Présence Africaine*, so complete was the imbrication of the African political element within a much broader diasporic radicalism symbolized by Paris and Harlem that decades later, in the wake of rabid postcolonial theorizing, a Black Atlanticist strand of that area of knowledge, spearheaded by Paul Gilroy and his disciples in the North American academy, would operate something close to a discursive excision of Africa from the scheme of things.

Ménage à Trois: Writers, Nationalists, Revolutionaries, and the Invention of the African Public Sphere

Présence Africaine ensured that the program of action on the part of African writers and their commitment to the undermining of colonial power did not occur in a vacuum. A great deal has been written about the convergence of ideas and activities among African writers, revolutionary ideologists, and nationalist politicians in the buildup to decolonization. What is often left out, especially in anglophonic historiography, is the crucial role played by *Présence Africaine* in serving as a site for this convergence. The space that emerged for public critical interventionism after the independence of India in 1947 and the Bandung conference in 1955 was occupied by three categories of actors all belonging to the educated elite class: nationalist politicians such as Nnamdi Azikiwe, Obafemi Awolowo, Julius Nyerere, Kenneth Kaunda, Tom Mboya, Odinga Oginga, Milton Obote, Sékou Touré, and Kwame Nkrumah; revolutionary theorists and activists such as Frantz Fanon, Amilcar Cabral, Eduardo Mondlane, Albert Memmi, and Walter Rodney; and activist creative writers whose works of fiction would be so crucial to the elaboration of an anticolonial aesthetic in the pre-independence and immediate postindependence eras.

Although their interests were not necessarily coterminous, these various groups within the intelligentsia were united by the common aim of ending Europe's colonial stranglehold on the continent, and *Présence Africaine* served as the site for the meeting of minds. Two decades of committed anti-colonial discourse by these intellectuals created a continental epistemic environment in which the voice and the textual presence of the creative writer fed into what we may call a continental commonwealth of committed texts. The construction of this commonwealth was further reinforced by the constant blurring of boundaries between the known vocations of these groups of intellectuals. Thus, poets like Senghor and the Angolan Agostinho Neto were also nationalist statesmen and even earned the sobriquet, poet-politicians. Nationalist politicians like Azikiwe, Nkrumah, and Touré wrote suspect and artistically weak poetry.

Consequently, the political project of the novels of cultural nationalism and anticolonial resistance, such as Achebe's *Things Fall Apart* and *Arrow of God*, Beti's *The Poor Christ of Bomba*, Oyono's *Houseboy* and *The Old Man and the Medal*, and Cheikh Hamidou Kane's *Ambiguous Adventure*, cannot be understood outside of the commonwealth of dissenting texts they formed with such works as Chinweizu's *The West and the Rest of Us*, Fanon's *The Wretched of the Earth*, Rodney's *How Europe Underdeveloped Africa*, Cabral's *Unity and Struggle*, and Memmi's *The Colonizer and the Colonized*, on the one hand, and the memoirs and other political writings of Nkrumah, Kaunda, Azikiwe, and Nyerere, on the other hand.

In this current of continental combustions that heralded political independence, the African writer's role became increasingly tied to the dual agendas of cultural nationalism and historical retrieval/revisionism. Cultural pride and the invention of usable pasts were deemed key ingredients in the production and organization of foundational myths for the imagined, but as yet unrealized national entities. Achebe's *Things Fall Apart* and *Arrow of God* are the most frequently cited examples of the linkages between culture, history, and politics in the struggle to wrest the African space from colonial violation, preparatory to the emergence of national spaces peopled by enlightened citizenries. If Achebe's novels mobilize culture and history in the service of political emancipation, novels such as Peter Abraham's *A Wreath for Udomo* and Sembene Ousmane's *God's Bits of Wood* offer a more direct political perspective powered by socialist sensibilities and vision. Other novels, such as Oyono's *Houseboy* and *The Old Man and the Medal*, Beti's *The Poor Christ of Bomba*, and T.M. Aluko's *One Man, One Wife* and *One Man, One Matchet*, deployed devastating sarcasm, biting irony, and *humour noir* in articulating political insurrection against colonial power.

It is clear from this scenario that in the pursuit of an emancipatory political project, which left no room for pure aesthetic indulgence on the part of African writers in the 1950s–1960s, paratextual and extra-creative texts were not as prominent as they had been in the francophonic sphere of the first generation. The political novel and, to a great extent, South African poetry were the principal outlets for the political voice of the African writer of this period. In his classic *Politics and the Novel*, Irving Howe proposes a useful definition of the political novel:

> By political novel, I mean a novel in which political ideas play a dominant role or in which the political milieu is the dominant setting—though again a qualification is necessary since the word "dominant" is more than a little questionable. Perhaps it would be better to say: a novel in which we take to be dominant political ideas or the political milieu, a novel which permits this assumption without thereby suffering any radical distortion and, it follows, with the possibility of some analytical profit (19).

This apt definition allows for the inclusion of most of the novels of the immediate pre-independence era in the category of political novels. One fundamental textual strategy, common to almost all of the novels, reinforces the idea that these works are fictionalized expressions of the political sensibilities and voices of the authors: the unmistakable weight of authorial intrusions in the narrative process, more clearly discernible in novels of the omniscient narrative perspective. So audible is the writer's voice, playing the ostrich behind characters and contrived scenarios, that it almost mars the art in novels such as Sembene Ousmane's *O pays mon beau people* and *Le docker noir*.

The Divorce: African Writers and/in the Postcolony

Ghana opened the floodgates to African political independence in 1957. The phenomenon, memorably described by a British colonial as a "wind of change" blowing over Africa, gathered momentum in 1960, and by the end of that decade, many African nation-states had been born. This auspicious political development had serious implications for the nature and meaning of political commitment on the part of the African writer and also for the tone and nature of interactions between writer and nationalist politician, the latter now in control of a modern nation-state complete with its apparatuses of violence.

That the nation-state atrophied almost before it was born in Africa is no longer news. As early as 1962, in the full euphoria of political independence, French sociologist René Dumont cut short the celebrations with the publication of his controversial *False Start in Africa,* a book that not only inaugurated disciplinary Afro-pessimism, but also qualified as the precursor of later exposés on the tragedy of the state in Africa, such as Basil Davidson's *The Black Man's Burden* and more recent tomes such as Robert Guest's *The Shackled Continent* and Martin Meredith's *The State of Africa.* An expansive literature in the social sciences already accounts for the nature, character, and trajectory of the nation-statist postcolonial project in Africa, so we will not dwell on it here. Briefly, the failure followed three discernible patterns in case after case: despotic one-party states with an absolute monolithization of power in the person of a paternalistic life-president in much of francophone Africa; murderous military dictatorships spawned by successive coups d'état in anglophone Africa; and paradoxical and benign dictatorships exemplified by erstwhile progressive nationalists such as Kenneth Kaunda, Milton Obote, Julius Nyerere, and Sékou Touré.

One immediate symptom of the postcolonial malaise was the collapse of the affiliative and collaborative mechanisms that had brought creative writers, revolutionary theoreticians, and nationalist politicians together in a marriage of convenience, so long as the goal was political independence. It became clear soon after independence that the "common aims and aspirations" that brought these groups of intellectuals together were no more than an expedient patina beneath which lurked absolutely incompatible aspirations and visions of fundamental ideals, such as freedom, nationhood, civic responsibility, sovereignty of the people's will, and the very meaning of the state. The resultant clash of ambitions led to a "divorce," a complete collapse of the political *ménage à trois* among writers, revolutionaries, and politicians who, by now, had become rulers of the new postcolonial states. The tragic ramifications of this split were played out in the saga of Patrice Emery Lumumba in the Belgian Congo.

The divorce was, perhaps, predictable. While creative writers, true to the nature of their calling as dreamers of the possible, remain locked in the oneiric assumptions that had energized the African revolution in the pre-independence era, it soon became clear that the new political rulers were content with being permanent embodiments of Fanon's famous prediction that the aim of the colonized fighting the colonizer was to replace him, "sit at the settler's table, sleep in the settler's bed, with his wife if possible."[6] With these irreconcilable positions, the African writer's long march to prison and exile, which Ofeimun so vividly captures in his earlier cited essay, had begun.

The immediate consequence of what African writers deemed a tragic betrayal of the African revolution and the aims of independence by the new rulers was the radicalization of the political voices of the writers. So deep was the sense of betrayal and frustration on the part of the writers that Neil Lazarus's

---

[6] *The Wretched of the Earth,* 39.

description of the process in his essay, "Great Expectations and After: The Politics of Postcolonialism in African Fiction," is worth quoting in some detail:

> If we look at the literature of the immediate postcolonial era in Africa, we see that it did not take long, after independence, for writers to realize that something had gone terribly wrong. They had experienced decolonization as a time of massive transformation and opening up of options. Yet, looking around them in the aftermath, they quickly began to perceive that their "revolution" had been derailed (...). Some writers responded to these harsh realities of independent society with disillusionment and weary, "post-political" cynicism. The literature of disillusionment grew out of a feeling, experienced by many intellectuals, that they were becoming more and more socially marginalized as the drama of postcolonialism unfolded (51–52).

The political novel of the 1960s–1970s expressed this disillusion. In Ngũgĩ's *A Grain of Wheat, Devil on the Cross,* and *Petals of Blood;* Achebe's *A Man of the People;* Soyinka's *Season of Anomy;* Kofi Awoonor's *This Earth, My Brother;* and Ayi Kwei Armah's *Fragments* and *The Beautyful Ones Are Not Yet Born,* we encounter political terrains marked by the grotesqueness of politicians and the ruling elite. In all these works, the narrative emphasis lies not only in unflattering depictions of the ruling classes, but also in searing sociological evocations of the alienating effects of crude power.

Although anglophone Africa produced its own long list of tyrants and traducers of the democratic process, such as Kenya's Daniel Arap Moi, Uganda's Idi Amin Dada, Malawi's Kamuzu Banda, Liberia's Samuel Doe, Sierra Leone's Siaka Stevens, and Nigeria's succession of military despots, it is arguable that no other part of the continent came close to francophone Africa's theater of the absurd and the macabre in terms of the production of political despotism. Louis X1V's utterance, *L'état, c'est moi,* the most famous incidence of personalization of ruthless power recorded in history, found its most literal appropriation and actuation in francophone Africa's long list of life-presidents and fathers of the nation: Emperor Jean Bedel Bokassa of the Central African Republic, Zaire's Mobutu Sese Seko, Togo's Gnassingbe Eyadéma, Guinea's Sékou Touré, Cameroon's Ahmadou Ahidjo and Paul Biya, Côte d'Ivoire's Félix Houphouet Boigny, Gabon's Omar Bongo, Chad's Hisseini Habre, Congo's Dennis Sassou Nguesso, Benin's Mathieu Kérékou, and Mali's Modibbo Keita.

It is, therefore, no surprise that francophone Africa produced the most expansive corpus of militant political novels in the three decades following political independence. Although a variation of the political novel in anglophone Africa had explored the nuanced philosophical dimensions of power, as well as its psychological and sociological consequences, it became, in a more urgent francophone milieu, progressively whittled down—with few significant exceptions—to linear denunciations of the dictator, always at the center of the narrative and whose capacity for the grotesque is usually blown out of proportion for hyperbolic effect. In most cases, the writer makes little attempt to disguise the instrumentalization of these novels as texts of political dissent in an extremely carceral public sphere, emptied of even the most fundamental notions of freedom of expression. The most remarkable and artistically realized of these novels include Alioum Fantouré's *Le cercle des tropiques,* Henri Lopès's *Le pleurer-rire,* Sony Labou Tansi's *La vie et demie,* Williams Sassine's *Le Zéhéros n'est pas n'importe qui,* Tierno Monenembo's *Les crapauds-brousse,* Patrick Ilboudo's *Les vertiges du trone,* Emmanuel Dongala's *Les petits garçons naissent aussi des étoiles,* and Ahmadou Kourouma's *En attendant le vote des bêtes sauvages.*

Of francophone Africa's dictatorship novels, Labou Tansi's *La vie et demie* is the most ambitious and has justifiably attracted considerable critical attention. Through an effective transposition of the

Marquezian model of surrealism in *One Hundred Years of Solitude* to the African scene—a development that has brought echoes of plagiarism on the bad side and comparisons with Ben Okri and Dambudzo Marechera on the good side—Labou Tansi effects the most impressive use of the writer's militant voice as parody, caricature, irony, and hyperbole rather than the tract, manifesto, or whiff of propaganda we get from a good number of the dictatorship novels.

Although he has been criticized in some circles for using creative works as the basis for constructing broad theoretical paradigms for the African condition, it is noteworthy that Achille Mbembe's development of the idea of the postcolony in his now classic *On the Postcolony* derives largely from his magisterial reading of Labou Tansi's novel. Mbembe's reading of the postcolony as a site of excess is drawn largely from his reading of the dictator's performances of power, his ritualization of the public space, and rationalizations of the grotesque by the media in Labou Tansi's novel. Consequently, those who criticize him for his recourse to fiction to theorize the postcolony ignore the simple fact that at that crucial juncture in the postcolonial trajectory of francophone Africa, the dictatorship genre became the direct political voice of writers in societies where they had become an endangered species.

Anglophone Africa's response to the dictatorship genre as evolved by francophone writers came in the form of Soyinka's *A Play of Giants,* Achebe's *Anthills of the Savannah,* and Ngũgĩ *Matigari.* And by returning to that genre in his latest novel, *Wizard of the Crow,* Ngũgĩ has perhaps demonstrated that it is the writer's duty to sound a note of caution as Africa enters the second euphoria (the first euphoria after independence turned into bitter disillusionment) with the advent of simulacra of representative, electoral democracy all over the continent after the momentum generated by the end of apartheid in South Africa.

Looking Beyond Literature to Save Utopia

In a lecture delivered at the University of Leeds in 1996, Nigerian playwright Femi Osofisan reviewed the plight of West African writers since the 1970s and saw little difference between the situation of the writer in the decades of his focus and the earlier years Ofeimun had engaged in his own essay. Osofisan came to a somber conclusion: West African writers since the 1970s have run the risk of being nothing more than "warriors of a failed utopia."[7] Indeed, in the decades Osofisan considers, the famed propensity of African writers to deploy critical or socialist realism in art was becoming difficult to process as art because what passed for reality in much of Africa was consistently worse than the fiction that even the most gifted writer could produce. In his essay "Writing in a Continent under Siege," Sanya Osha extends Osofisan's arguments to the 1990s:

> That the African continent is truly under siege is no longer news. African intellectuals inevitably face the specter of both "internal" or "external" exile. By internal exile one means the prospect of enduring a disagreeable form of silence, banishment from the organic centers that activate society. One simply is forced to adopt a vegetative existence, something that no honorable intellectual would accept (174).

Osha fails to mention a third option available to writers—collaboration. Collaboration was the option tragically chosen, for instance, by Ferdinand Oyono, who was even used by the Cameroonian

---

[7] See Femi Osofisan, "Warriors of a Failed Utopia."

state to reinforce the woes of a fellow writer, Mongo Beti. Fortunately, most writers would neither collaborate nor be forced into internal exile. But the imperative of the moment dictated other strategies of expression that could ensure immediate public delivery beyond the hermeneutic requirements of a novel, a play, or a poem.

Thus, this period witnessed recourse to the extra-creative text by many writers in their manifold confrontations with power and the postcolonial state. Journalism, the essay genre, tract writing, and memoirs became the preferred modes of public critical interventionism, especially by anglophone writers. It is indicative of the dire straits in which the African writer was plunged by the postcolonial state that the prison memoir, or prison diary, an essayistic genre hitherto the near-exclusive preserve of writers from the communist bloc—Aleksandr Solzhenitsyn's *The Gulag Archipelago* and Adam Michnik's *Letters from Prison*—became a new addition to African writing. And the unfortunate genre became so expansive that Jack Mapanje, Malawi's famous poet and a veteran of Hastings Kamuzu Banda's prison dungeons was able to edit a gory harvest of prison narratives in his *Gathering Seaweed: African Prison Writing*.

Major examples of prison writing include Soyinka's *The Man Died*, Ngũgĩ *Detained: A Writer's Prison Diary*, and Saro Wiwa's *A Month and a Day*. South Africa has understandably produced the highest quantity of continental prison narratives. Although Breyten Breytenbach's *The True Confessions of an Albino Terrorist* is arguably the most famous South African prison narrative of the apartheid era, Paul Gready has offered one of the most compelling and expansive studies of the genre, citing numerous lesser-known texts in his seminal essay, "Autobiography and the 'Power of Writing': Political Prison Writing in the Apartheid Era."

An immediate theoretical question arises the moment one places prison writing in the context of political voicing and the public sphere: how to resolve the internal tensions and paradoxes resulting from the juxtaposition of the carceral world of the prison text and the public actuation necessary for an effective political voice to *be*. How does the writer constitute a public for his prison narrative from the space of incarceration, and how does the writer's "truth" interpellate an audience while it interrogates power? The answer lies in the evocative power of witnessing and testimony in the context of trauma, as Giorgio Agamben argues persuasively in *The Remnants of Auschwitz*.

Beyond its essence as collective or personal tragedy, trauma has value as spectacle. Trauma fascinates, and this fascination locks perpetrator and victim in a will to narrativize. This explains why the initial violence of incarceration imposes a frenzy of narrativization on the perpetrator—the state or the tyrant. Official positions and justifications, government communiqués, and statements from official spokespersons build into what Michel Foucault in *Discipline and Punish* calls the power of writing. Gready has noted, with specific reference to South Africa, that "apartheid's 'power of writing' served to isolate, to discredit, to destroy, to rewrite everything and everyone to serve a political end" (492).

By self-fashioning as witness and positioning the prison narrative as testimony, the African writer produces what Gready calls an "oppositional 'power of writing'" (493). Furthermore, the witness also self-positions as a subject in possession of a higher truth, an alternative truth capable of countering the oft-discredited "truths" of officialdom. This, combined with the spectral power of trauma, is what unites prison narrator and an enchanted public in a political communication that is enacted in defiance of official truths and in contestation of power, hence Soyinka's famous assertion in *The Man Died* that "the man dies in all who keep silent in the face of tyranny."

The prison narrative was not the only extra-creative instrument of public activism and political commitment African writers had to employ in their checkered relationship with the postcolonial African state. Essays in form of political propaganda tracts also came in handy as public denunciations of the alienation of African leadership from the people and the willingness of the ruling elite to serve as lackeys for neocolonial interests. In francophone Africa, Seydou Badian, notable Malian novelist and playwright, had published *Les dirigeants d'Afrique noire face à leur people* (African Rulers and Their People) as early as 1965. In acerbic prose, which betrays the earlier cited disappointment of African writers with the ruling class and the subsequent pall of disillusionment that enveloped them, Badian denounces leaders who are

more integrated in the economy of our former metropoles than in those of their own countries. Their needs, the habits that they acquired, their taste—all these constitute a weight that crushes our states. . . . But more disturbing than the style of life and "foreign" alignments that separate the organizational bourgeoisie from the mass of the population is the crushing burden of this bourgeoisie upon the nations' economies (89, my translation).

More than three decades after the publication of Badian's essayistic treatise, Soyinka returns to the same subject in eerily similar terms in his latest autobiographical offering, *You Must Set Forth at Dawn:*

The nationalists, the first-generation elected leaders and legislators of our semi-independent nation, had begun to visit Great Britain in droves. We watched their preening, their ostentatious spending, and their cultivated condescension, even disdain, toward the people they were supposed to represent. . . . While we dreamed of marching south to liberate southern Africa, they saw the nation as a prostrate victim to be ravished. . . . This strange breed was a complete contrast to the nationalist stalwarts into whose hands we had imagined that the country could be safely consigned while we went on our romantic liberation march to southern Africa. . . . Most of the time, however, as we ran eagerly to welcome the protagonists of the African Renaissance, we were bombarded by utterances that identified them as flamboyant replacements of the old colonial order, not transforming agents, not even empathizing participants in a process of liberation (42).

This extraordinary convergence of opinions and modalities of expression between Badian and Soyinka attests to the ability of political enunciation to cross Africa's notorious linguistic/ideological borders along lines defined by the pathologies and competing proclivities of British and French colonial processes. After Badian, francophone Africa was to wait till 1972 before another famous political essay was published, Mongo Beti's *Main basse sur le Cameroun* (The Rape of Cameroon). As the title indicates, Beti's text was a strident indictment of France's neocolonial stranglehold on Cameroon, facilitated in his opinion by the dictator Ahmadou Ahidjo and his cronies. So scared of this book were the French and the Cameroonian governments that they conspired to ban it simultaneously in France and Cameroon. It is significant that the book was banned in France at the request of the Cameroonian government through its ambassador in Paris, Ferdinand Oyono! Beti, however, remained committed to the struggle in Cameroon despite having spent more than thirty years in political exile in France. In 1993, he published another famous essay, *La France contre l'Afrique: retour au Cameroun* (France Against Africa: Return to Cameroon). By this time, the Cameroonian state had become so paranoid about Beti's political essays that it was dangerous to be associated with them: renowned literary scholar Ambroise Kom was once jailed for nothing more than subscribing to Beti's journal, *Peuples noirs, peuples africains.*

The essayistic tradition also flourished in anglophone Africa as the writers came to the inevitable conclusion, from the 1970s, that their utopia had indeed failed. In Nigeria, Achebe published his famous *The Trouble with Nigeria,* one of the most cogent analyses to date of the atrophy of the Nigerian state. Ngũgĩ *Writers in Politics* is another notable anglophone African example.

After Jail, Dissidence

In a seminal essay, *Intellectuels africains et enjeux de la démocratie: misère, répression et exil,* Ambroise Kom maps the path of African intellectuals to Euro-American exile. For many African writers, the journey to exile started very frequently from African jails. Beyond the familiar theorizations of the trauma of departure and deracination—around issues of home, loss, memory, the anxieties of arrival in diaspora—it must be stated that, with regard to numerous African writers, political exile in Euro-America also signaled a transition to dissidence and the birth of another genre of essayistic engagement of power: dissident narratives.

In "Dissidence and the African Writer: Commitment or Dependency," Oyekan Owomoyela has offered a comprehensive theoretical distinction between political dissent and dissidence. His reading of these distinctions is crucial to any understanding of the public careers of such African writers as Soyinka, Saro Wiwa, Ngũgĩ, Beti, Tierno Monenembo, and, of course, a swathe of North African and Southern African writers, down to the Swazi female writer Sarah Mkhonza. Owomoyela's study is particularly helpful in clearing hermeneutic problems occasioned by the widespread critical practice of characterizing African writers' political protest and militancy traditions interchangeably as dissent or dissidence. Speaking of dissent, Owomoyela says:

> It is the ultimate step that an individual takes in his attempt to bring about a change in the official conduct in his country. It is symptomatic of despair, of the conviction that the rulers will not voluntarily mend their ways or bow to popular pressure. As long as the dissenter works within the system he remains that, a dissenter. The moment despair induces him to take his campaign outside the country he becomes, technically, a dissident. In the second place, dissidence is predicated on the vulnerability of the dissident's country in one respect or another, and sympathy for the dissident's cause in other countries which have the resources, economic, political (or diplomatic), or military, to exploit the vulnerability and impose their will on the dissident's government. . . . In reality, however, dissidents rarely, if ever, seek sponsorship from governments friendly to their own. Inasmuch as they seek external pressure on their government that would force its hand or brand it an international pariah, their appeal must be to countries predisposed to hostility toward their own country (91).

What these distinctions make immediately clear is that the public careers of some of Africa's most famous activist-writers have always oscillated between dissent and dissidence. In the case of West Africa, the dissentient and dissident careers of Soyinka and Saro Wiwa are too well known to bear repetition here and so are the cases of Ngũgĩ, Jack Mapanje, and Frank Chipasula in East Africa. Soyinka and Saro Wiwa have scrupulously recorded the modalities of their respective oscillations between dissent and dissidence, leading, ultimately, to their much-internationalized confrontation with the murderous military regime of General Sani Abacha in the 1990s, a confrontation that eventually proved fatal for Saro Wiwa.

Soyinka's *The Open Sore of a Continent: A Personal Narrative of the Nigerian Crisis* is arguably one of the most formidable examples of the genre of African dissidence narrative. Far from being limited to an exposé on his clash with the Abacha regime, the text is a rallying cry, a call to arms addressed to the international community. This brings us to the question of the political value of the dissidence narrative. We know, from Owomoyela's study, that the audience of this genre is generally not intended to be domestic, produced as it were by an African writer who wants the international community to act and effect the changes he or she desires in his or her country. And in *You Must Set Forth at Dawn*, Soyinka goes to great length to describe his global peregrinations while trying to rally friendly and sympathetic foreign—mostly Western—governments to his cause against Abacha. It is also true, that for Shell and the Abacha regime, Saro Wiwa became a real threat and was consequently doomed, although he successfully internationalized his dissidence.

It follows, therefore, that the greater the fear of the international community, the more effective a dissident writer's voice and international political activism on behalf of his people could be. The downside of dissidence narrative and action lies in the contradiction of placing any African people's salvation in the hands of the so-called international community, a euphemism for the deleterious neocolonialist and imperialist interests of the West. Recently, Soyinka carried exaggerated and misplaced dissidence to the point of addressing the U.S. Congress on the farcical elections of April 2007 in Nigeria. Cajoling the Congress for action, in the context of full-blown U.S. will-to-Empire, is no more than an obsequious submission to the whims and interests of the said Empire.

The debate is still open as to whether the explosion of African women's writing and the various strands of feminism in which the writers thrive constitute the sort of political voicing we have described so far. This debate is further reinforced by the fact the continent's best known feminist works—Flora Nwapa's *Efuru*, Buchi Emecheta's *The Joys of Motherhood*, Mariama Ba's *So Long a Letter*, Bessie Head's *A Question of Power*, and Tsitsi Dangarembga's *Nervous Conditions*—are "personal" narratives of female subjects in the throes of patriarchal oppression in domestic situations. Thus, the debate has morphed into the familiar epistemological tensions between the private and public spheres. When is the private public and vice versa? And most important, when is the private political?

These questions are, unfortunately, not subject to easy, sacrosanct resolutions. What is certain is that African feminist/female action and writing have followed a trajectory of publicized political dissent and dissidence in North Africa, and this is amply illustrated by the careers of the Algerian Assia Djebbar and the Egyptian Nawal El Saadawi. Like Soyinka and Ngũgĩ, Saadawi's career and political activism have incurred the whole gamut of consequences: dissent, threats, intimidation, imprisonment, book banning, exile, and dissidence. Her books, especially *God Dies by the Nile, Memoirs of a Woman Doctor,* and *Woman at Point Zero,* have demonstrated the remarkable ability to crisscross several strands of political writing: the political novel, fictionalized autobiography, faction, dissidence narrative, and prison narrative. In her "author's preface" to *Woman at Point Zero,* for instance, Saadawi asserts that

> I wrote this novel after an encounter between me and a woman in Qanatir Prison. A few months before, I had started research on neurosis in Egyptian women and was able to concentrate most of my time on this work as I was then without a job. At the end of 1972, the Minister of Health had removed from me my functions as Director of Health education and Editor-in-Chief of the magazine *Health*. This was one

more consequence of the path I had chosen as a feminist author and novelist whose views were viewed unfavourably by the authorities. . . . The idea of "prison" had always exercised a special interest for me. I often wondered what prison life was like, especially for women. Perhaps this was because I lived in a country where many prominent intellectuals around me had spent various periods of time in prison for "political offences" (i).

Saadawi goes on to summarize the raison d'être of her political commitment and the internationalization of her voice: "the need to challenge and to overcome those forces that deprive human beings of their right to live, to love and to real freedom" (iv).

Conclusion: Globalization and the Death of Commitment

The last two decades have witnessed momentous transformations in the political landscape in Africa. The decade of the 1990s opened with a rash of national conferences in francophone Africa, which, in several cases, ended the long run of monolithic single parties and life-presidents. Today, Cameroon's Paul Biya and Gabon's Omar Bongo are the remaining relics of that old and sordid guard. In 1994, apartheid officially ended in South Africa; minimal processes of liberalization and expansion of the democratic space, though yet unrealized, commenced in North Africa. And in West Africa, multiparty liberal democracies emerged, the highpoint of which was Nigeria's accession to democracy in 1999. These seismic developments occurred in an era of unbridled globalization, transnational fluxes, the so-called undermining of the traditional boundaries and prerogatives of the nation-state, and, in the academy, the explosion of such discourses as multiculturalism, hybridity, diaspora, postmodernism, and postcolonialism. They also occurred in an era when African writing had come to be dominated by a new generation of writers, a third generation born mostly after independence who came to prominence since the mid-1980s.

The impact of these new developments on the idea and nature of the African writer's political commitment, dissent, dissidence, and public has been understandably considerable. From being nearly inescapable in the heady days of the African anticolonial revolution and the three decades after independence, commitment and protest writing have become jaded and quaint, and the writer who ventures into this terrain, especially among the new generation, is usually now easily dismissed as sacrificing art on the altar of sterile ideological posturing. This crisis of ontology was even more acute in post-apartheid South Africa. After decades of anti-apartheid protest writing and activism, the South African writer was suddenly deprived of the traditional idea of "the enemy" after 1994. This has resulted in what Amatoristero Ede has described as "tender" poetry as we see in the case of the poet Gabeba Baderoon.

Even in Nigeria, where the new generation started with a form of postcolonial protest poetry in the late 1980s, the nascent strand quickly petered out in favor of recherché artistry by such poets as Ogaga Ifowodo, Chiedu Ezeanah, Afam Akeh, Uche Nduka, Remi Raji, and Ede. For the new writers, therefore, the idea of commitment has come to settle on poetic or prosaic probings of their exilic or diasporic ruptures and conditions or broader international issues of postcolonial subjecthood in the context of the new Empire as we see in Ede's *Hitler's Children*. The traditional domains of continental political commitment, challenge of power and incumbency, and dissentient public intellection have remained, curiously, in the hands of the old guard, including Soyinka whose struggle to revive Nigeria's failed utopia has never wavered.

REFERENCES

Abraham, Peter. *A Wreath for Udomo*. London: Faber and Faber, 1956.

Achebe, Chinua. *Things Fall Apart*. London: Heinemann, 1958.

——. *Arrow of God*. London: Heinemann, 1964.

——. "The Black Writer's Burden." *Présence Africaine* 31.56 (1966): 135–140.

——. *Morning Yet on Creation Day*. London: Heinemann, 1975.

——. *Hopes and Impediments*. London: Heinemann, 1988.

——. *The Trouble with Nigeria*. London: Heinemann, 1983.

——. *Anthills of the Savannah*. London: Heinemann, 1987.

——. *Home and Exile*. Oxford and New York: Oxford University Press, 2000.

Agamben, Giorgio. *Remnants of Auschwitz: The Witness and the Archive*. New York: Zone Books, 2000.

Aluko, T.M. *One, Man, One Wife*. Ibadan: Heinemann, 1967.

——. *One Man, One Matchet*. London: Heinemann, 1964.

Armah, Ayi Kwei. *Fragments*. London: Heinemann, 1969.

——. *The Beautyful Ones Are Not Yet Born*. Boston: Houghton Mifflin, 1968.

Ba, Mariama. *So Long a Letter,* translated by Modupe Bode Thomas. London: Virago, 1982.

Badian, Seydou. *Les dirigeants d'afrique noire face a leur peuple*. Paris: Maspero, 1965.

Beti, Mongo. *The Poor Christ of Bomba,* translated by Gerald Moore. London: Heinemann, 1971.

——.*Main basse sur le Cameroun*. Paris: La Découverte, 2003.

——. *La France contre l'Afrique: retour au Cameroun*. Paris: Editions La Découverte, 1993, 2006.

Breytenbach, Breyten. *True Confessions of an Albino Terrorist*. London: Faber, 1984.

Cabral, Amilcar. *Unity and Struggle*. New York: Monthly Review Press, 1979.

Casely-Hayford, Joseph. *Ethiopia Unbound*. London: Cass, 1969.

Chinweizu. *The West and the Rest of Us*. New York: Random House, 1975.

Dangarembga, Tsitsi. *Nervous Conditions*. London: Women's Press, 1988.

Davidson, Basil. *The Black Man's Burden*. London: James Currey, 1992.

Dongala, Emmanuel. *Les petits garçons naissent aussi des étoiles*. Paris: Le serpent à plumes, 2000.

Dumont, René. *False Start in Africa*. London: Earthscan Publications, 1988.

Edwards, Brent Hayes. *The Practice of Diaspora*. Cambridge, MA: Harvard University Press, 2003.

Emechata, Buchi. *The Joys of Motherhood*. New York: Braziller, 1979.

Ezra, Elizabeth. *The Colonial Unconscious*. Ithaca, NY: Cornell University Press, 2000.

Fanon, Frantz. *The Wretched of the Earth*. New York: Grove Press, 1963.

Fantouré, Alioum. *Le cercle des tropiques*. Paris: Présence Africaine, 1972.

Foucault, Michel. *Discipline and Punish*. New York: Pantheon Books, 1977.

Gready, Paul. "Autobiography and the 'Power of Writing': Political Prison Writing in the Apartheid Era." *Journal of Southern African Studies* 19.3 (1993): 489–523.

Guest, Robert. *The Shackled Continent*. London: Macmillan, 2004.

Head, Bessie. *A Question of Power*. London: Davis-Poynter, 1973.

Howe, Irving. *Politics and the Novel*. New York: Avon Books, 1957.

Ilboudo, Patrick. *Les vertiges du trone*. Ouagadougou: Editions I.N.B., 1990.

Kane, Cheik Hamidou. *Ambiguous Adventure*. New York: Walker, 1963.

Kesteloot, Lilyan. *Intellectual Origins of the African Revolution*. Washington, D.C.: Black Orpheus Press, 1972.

Kom, Ambroise. "Intellectuels africains et enjeux de la démocratie: misère, répression, exil." *Politique Africaine* 51 (1993): 61–68.

Kourouma, Ahmadou. *En attendant le vote des betes sauvages*. Paris: Seuil, 1998.

Langley, Ayodele. *Pan-Africanism and Nationalism in West Africa, 1900–1945*. Oxford: Clarendon Press, 1973.

Lazarus, Neil. "Great Expectations and After: The Politics of Postcolonialism in African Fiction." *Social Text* 13 (1986): 49–63.

Lopès, Henri. *Le pleurer-rire*. Paris: Présence Africaine, 1982.

Mapanje, Jack, ed. *Gathering Seaweed: African Prison Writing*. Portsmouth, NH: Heinemann, 2002.

Maran, René. *Batouala: A True Black Novel*. Greenwhich, CT: Fawcett Publications, 1972.

Marquez, Gabriel Garcia. *One Hundred Years of Solitude*. New York: Harper and Row, 1970.

Mbembe, Achille. *On the Postcolony*. Berkeley: University of California Press, 2001.

Memmi, Albert. *The Colonizer and the Colonized*. New York: Orion Press, 1965.

Meredith, Martin. *The State of Africa*. New York: Public Affairs, 2005.

Michnik, Adam. *Letters from Prison*. Berkeley: University of California Press, 1985.

Monenembo, Tierno. *Les crapauds-brousse*. Paris: Seuil, 1979.

Mudimbe, V.Y., ed. *The Surreptitious Speech: Présence Africaine and the Politics of Otherness, 1947–1987*. University of Chicago Press, 1992.

Ngũgĩ wa Thiong'o. *A Grain of Wheat*. London: Heinemann, 1967.

——. *Petals of Blood*. London: Heinemann, 1977.

——. *Devil on the Cross*. London: Heinemann, 1982.

——. *Matigari*. Oxford: Heinemann, 1989.

——. *Wizard of the Crow*. New York: Pantheon Books, 2006.

——. *Detained: A Writer's Prison Diary*. London: Heinemann, 1981.

——. *Writers in Politics*. London: Heinemann, 1981.

Nwapa, Flora. *Efuru*. London: Heinemann, 1966.

Ofeimun, Odia. "Postmodernism and the Impossible Death of the African Author." *Glendora Review* 2.3 (2000): 24–47.

Onoge, Omafume. "The Crisis of Consciousness in Modern African Literature: A Survey." *Canadian Journal of African Studies* 8.2 (1974): 385–410.

Osha, Sanya. "Writing in a Continent under Siege." *Research in African Literatures*. 29.1 (1998): 174–178.

Osofisan, Femi. "Warriors of a Failed Utopia? West African Writers Since the 1970s." 2nd Annual African Studies Lecture of the Institute of African Studies Unit, University of Leeds, 1996.

Ousmane, Sembene. *God's Bits of Wood*. New York: Anchor Books, 1970.

——. *Le docker noir*. Paris: Debresse, 1956.

——. *O pays mon beau peuple*. London: Methuen Educational, 1986.

Owomoyela, Oyekan. "Dissidence and the African Writer: Commitment or Dependency?" *African Studies Review* 24.1 (1981): 83–98.

Oyono, Ferdinand. *Houseboy*. London: Heinemann, 1966.

Rabemananjara, Jacques. "Europe and Ouselves." *Présence Africaine* 8 (1956): 20

Rodney, Walter. *How Europe Underdeveloped Africa*. Washington, D.C.: Howard University Press, 1972.

Saadawi, El Nawal. *Woman at Point Zero*. London: Zed Books, 1983.

——. *God Dies by the Nile*. London: Zed Books, 1985.

——. *Memoirs of a Woman Doctor*. London: Saqi Books, 1988.

Sassine, Williams. *Le Zéhéros n'est pas n'importe qui*. Paris: Présence Africaine, 1985.

Saro-Wiwa, Ken. *A Month and a Day*. London: Penguin, 1996.

Sartre, Jean-Paul. *Orphée noir*. Paris: Presses Universitaires de France, 1948.

Solzhenitsyn, Aleksandr. *The Gulag Archipelago*. New York: Harper and Row, 1973.

Tansi, Sony Labou. *La vie et demie*. Paris: Seuil, 1979.

Soyinka, Wole. *The Man Died*. London: Rex Collins, 1972.

——. *A Play of Giants*. London: Methuen, 1984.

——. *The Open Sore of a Continent*. New York: Oxford University Press, 1996.

——. *You Must Set Forth at Dawn*. New York: Random House, 2006.

Chapter 16

AFRICAN CINEMA
Visions, Meanings, and Measures

Jude Akudinobi

Debates over the nature, function, and definition of African cinema underscore the need for establishing dynamic frameworks for engaging African cultural production and social realities, especially because the interplay between critique, society, and representation generate, from each successive wave or epoch, ample currencies for African filmmakers. Evoking social worlds fabricated from diverse sources, African filmmakers generally purpose their films as struggles to produce meaning about "realities." Films such as *The Narrow Path* (Tunde Kelani 2006), *Conversations on a Sunday Afternoon* (South Africa 2005), *Ezra* (Newton Aduaka 2007), *Bamako* (Abderrahmane Sissako 2006), *Africa Paradis* (Sylvestre Amoussou 2006), and *Les Saignantes* (Jean-Pierre Bekolo 2006) are not mere schemas of contemporary African social realities but derive from tendencies to juxtapose paradoxes with possibilities. They particularly offer substantive approaches to understanding certain dynamics and key developments, including the rise of "Nollywood" in Nigeria and the historic shifts in South Africa, thereby undergirding eclectic transformations in narrative styles, themes, and formats as complex as the continent.

Beginnings

Over the years, African cinema has attracted, first, condescending attention and, then, more discerning scrutiny, analyses, and debate. Hence, have come autonomous studies, such as Armes (2006), Barlet (2000), Diawara (1992), Gugler (2003), Harrow (2007), Thackway (2003), Ukadike (1995), Malkmus and Armes (1991), Murphy and Williams (2007); edited volumes, including Bakari and Cham (1996), Givanni (2001), Pfaff (2004); interview compilations, such as Ukadike (2002) and Bonetti and Reddy (2003); and any number of guest-edited, "special" journal issues, like Akudinobi (2000) and Okome (2007). These works show varying conceptual, critical, and theoretical frameworks that are inextricable from evolving cultural inquiry and artistic practice. Since its inception African cinema has often been formed within the axes of criticism. Given the emergence of African cinema in the ferment of anticolonial nationalism and postindependence, the pioneers saw themselves not as mere artists, but as activists in the vanguard of political, cultural, and ideological emancipation. Not surprisingly, they sought a relationship between cinema and politics, arguing in effect that cultural production need not be separated from politics but, instead, in constant dialogue. Central to this view was that ideology, subtle or not, especially in colonialist documentaries and, later, in dominant Hollywood films, anchors the relationship between Africa and its cinematic representations. In challenging normative interpretations of African social realities, the African cinematic pioneers favored an unapologetic, "utilitarian" cinema that grappled with "home truths" and sought remedies.

African filmmakers generally break with certain received wisdom about cinema, in so far as they want their works to be of purposeful consequence in the "real world." Within this framework, a cinema that is only entertaining and is divorced from the lived experiences of Africans is discounted. Hence, filmmakers use rhetorical flourishes to inspire their preferred African spectators to imagine new, more discerning relationships with prevailing social realties. Not surprisingly, insistence on the values and vitality of African cultural systems, appropriation of "oral tradition," inspirational narrative premises, and, in some instances—especially to avoid censorship—allegories of contemporary times feature prominently and contribute to an aesthetic strategy. Further, by fusing entertainment with enlightenment, they try to foster a model of cinema that does not cede their artistic impetus and critical authority to commercial calculations. In investing their films with critical power, they see cinema as a crucial site in the struggle to change or at least challenge various elements that give social realities their unwieldy textures and tangents. Juxtaposing certain "realities," *critically,* with the expressive capacity of the filmic medium has become the unwritten code. The premium, however, has never been on isolating esoteric features. *How,* rather than simply *what,* is important to filmmakers.

Right from its inception, African cinema was concerned with the negotiation of meanings, values, and identities through the formation of discerning spectatorhips. If Ousmane Sembene, as generally agreed (Gadjigo et al. 1993; Murphy 2001; Petty 1996; Pfaff 1984), is an insuperable pioneer, his compatriot, Djibril Diop Mambety, given to intrepid explorations of narrative forms and content, is an iconoclastic visionary and bridge to the present. Notably, in the contemporary configuration of African filmmaking, "the post-independent generation," as Armes (2006, 143–157) calls them, appears more interested in exploring narratives and aesthetics that express not only their individualities, but also the complexities of cultures, identities, positions, and issues that face the continent in the era of globalization. Much keener to work the international cinema circuits, they leaven their films' narratives with daring explorations of taboo subjects, like sexuality and gender politics, outside of erstwhile nationalist imperatives. Further, they favor rethinking social realities as the one-stop locus of inspiration and creativity and rely on social realism as the express vehicle for transporting their visions to the screen. Largely, the prevailing disposition is that "realities" should be engaged in any number of ways, including idiosyncratic ones, and that an African story should be told in ways that involve other cultural and artistic registers, fostering fecund juxtaposition and formulation of ideas.

The shift toward redefining identities, culture, artistic license, and province is largely about finding new ways to engage the complex dynamics of contemporary Africa. Hence, this development is neither necessarily at odds with the pioneering frameworks of representation, nor does it constitute a disavowal of the filmmakers' "Africanness." Arguably, it is a feature of the intrinsic dynamics of culture, a telling marker of the increasingly intricate hybrid cultural spaces the filmmakers inhabit and an invitation to ponder how certain representational inspirations may sprout more from the imagination than material "realities." So one finds casual references to art cinema and contemporary Western popular culture. This feature is important, too, for what it tells us about the relationship of African cinema to changing contexts of production, distribution, and consumption. We will now extend our inquiry by examining how Nollywood, Nigeria's irreverent video film culture, and South African cinema fit into and challenge previous frameworks for African filmmaking.

Transformations

Often associated with shoestring budgets, hectic production practices, theatrical acting styles, overwrought special effects, whimsical attention to character development, overt commercial inclinations, fascination with the supernatural, sensational narrative premises, trite moralizing, disparate aesthetic strategies, and idiosyncratic plot lines, Nollywood has grown from ostensibly "lowly origins" and novelty to global circulation through respected film festivals, academic circles, the African diaspora, unique niches in the popular cultural marketplace, and discerning documentaries in the West. Interestingly, it has confounded cultural critics like Moller (2004, 12), who describes it as a "homegrown hybrid cinema of outrageous schlock," scholars like Harrow (2007, xi), who (in arguing for new critical paradigms for African cinema) proposes "something trashy, to begin, straight out of the Nigerian video handbook," and other African filmmakers, some of whom acknowledge this new cultural formation with concern, contempt, or tentativeness. With its base in the vibrant sociocultural and economic milieu of southern Nigeria, the industry has been greeted by some reservations in the predominantly Islamic northern part of the country (see Adamu, Adamu, and Jibril 2004). Nevertheless, Nollywood marks a disruption in the dominant or generic paradigms of African cinema and is critical to the mapping of contemporary, "globalized," African cultural formations.

One cannot gain a firm understanding of Nollywood without attention to the dynamic of experimentation, entrepreneurship, mercantilism, and historical contexts that spawned and still drive it (see Haynes 2000; Okome 2007a and 2007b). Positioned between popular culture, art, and commerce, Nollywood redefined the commercial possibilities of African cinema principally by securing slim domestic capital, independent of European donors, funding institutions, and television channels that were hitherto critical to African filmmaking, promoting African stars, building self-sustained structures of production and networks of distribution, and expanding the parameters through which contemporary African experiences and narratives were engaged. Emerging from the economic crises, social anxieties, and political uncertainties of "oil-boom" Nigeria of the late 1980s, Nollywood, fueled in part by the rise of a popular, or tabloid, press in the country and new media technologies, blends indigenous belief systems, conventions of melodrama, and television serials (particularly in resisting firm narrative closures) with fragments of global popular culture into films that are usually shot in digital video, on location rather than in elaborate sets or studios, and have shelf lives of about three weeks before pirates move in. Whatever its features, Nollywood, given the relentless dynamics that drive it, is always in a state of flux, constantly reworking proven formulas and reformulating conventions of "popular" commercial (especially Hollywood and Bollywood) cinema.

In contrast to the founding phase of African cinema, Nollywood was not born of explicit political imperatives (a movement or consensus), intellectual affiliations, or aesthetic projects, such as imbuing narratives with "oral tradition." Its focus, shaped in part by technological developments, globalization, and the pervasive consumerist culture, is as local as it is global. Not surprisingly, Nollywood, with storylines inspired by news headlines, tabloids, rumors, and assorted urban and "folklore," has, through a dynamic of appropriation and reconfiguration, forged its own traditions, narrative conventions, and vernaculars of representation. Thus, in what may be termed an amalgamation of genres, Nollywood reformulated dominant film genres, particularly horror, melodrama, and comedy, to create distinctive styles and new genres. The seminal Nollywood film *Living in Bondage* with its pact-with-the-devil premise is a narrative about social ambiguities and cultural and moral fragmentation, juxtaposed with elements of Pentecostalism, simulated "indigenous" rituals, and critiques of materialism, laid the tracks for a popular cinema aesthetic. Following the film's success and the fledgling industry's search for winning commercial formulas, emphasis on "magic," ritual, and spectacle with supernatural overtones came to be, and still is for some, Nollywood's definition. This accent on the supernatural was a logical framework for articulating the various social contradictions circulating in the popular imaginary. In breaking with orthodoxies and commingling disparate elements of globalized popular culture, Nollywood inaugurated a nonprogrammatic film culture with novel registers to represent contemporary African social milieus, alternative "modernities," and frameworks to explore and negotiate previous marginalization of African cinema.

If Nollywood is artisanal, to the extent that it is based on loose production and distribution structures, South Africa is unique among African film cultures because it is plugged into the Hollywood paradigm of production and international circuits of distribution and exhibition. In addition to coproduction agreements with several Western countries (Italy, Denmark, Canada, the United Kingdom, France, New Zealand, and Australia, for instance), outstanding infrastructure, top-notch crews, cost-efficient incentives, and competitive currency rates, South Africa has been a veritable production hub for global film and media projects, chiefly commercials. It has also enjoyed great international success: its films have won awards at prestigious international film festivals. Charlize Theron, for instance, was feted nationally following her 2004 Oscar win, and Darrell James Roodt was recognized for *Yesterday* at the Venice Film Festival and the Oscars. In 2005, *Drum* (Zola Maseko 2004) won the Golden Stallion, the most prestigious prize in African cinema, at the Panafrican Film and Television Festival of Ouagadougou. *U-Carmen eKhayelitsha* (Mark Donford-May 2004) received the Golden Bear, the top award at the Berlin Film Festival, and in 2006, *Tsotsi* (Gavin Hood 2005) was awarded the Best Foreign Language Oscar.

Balseiro and Masilela (2003), Maingard (2008), and Tomaselli (1988) note that analysis of South African cinema must be situated within the context of debates about the nation's political history. At issue is not necessarily apartheid—or policies of racial discrimination—but how the nascent film culture grapples with the residual inequities and attempts to fill in the blank spaces and remedy the disjunctures of the moment. The latter are very important because the 1994 dismantling of apartheid initiated seismic shifts in the concepts of "nation" and national culture, as well as anxieties about how the unfolding narratives of nation and rebirth would play out. Hence, contemporary South African cinema is marked by retrospection (looking at the past, especially its implications for a national rebirth) and introspection (with eyes to the contradictions and complexities of the nation's present social environments).

Indeed, the nation's Truth and Reconciliation Commission worked to transform and redeem the past and sketch durable frameworks for negotiating contemporary realities. This largely exorcistic process, with its complex premises and narratives, understandably features in contemporary South African cinema, especially in how to project the nation and create spaces for emerging themes, voices, and talents. The process is especially important to Blacks who under apartheid were without the political, social, and economic platforms to tell their own stories or define their own identities. Thus, one of the unique developments of filmmaking in South Africa is a cycle of films inspired by the Truth and Reconciliation hearings—*In My Country* (John Doorman 2005) adapted from Antjie Krog's autobiographical *Country of My Skull; Red Dust* (Tom Hooper 2004) from Gillian Slovo's novel of the same name; *Forgiveness* (Ian Gabriel 2004); *Zulu Love Letter* (Ramadan Suleman 2004); and *Homecoming* (Norman Maake 2006). These films engage the culture of violence that supported apartheid and are, like the commission, geared towards critical historical inquiry. They air certain cluttered recesses of the national psyche, tie up as much as possible some loose ends from the apartheid years, and, very importantly, heal. In sifting through the rubble of history and facilitating intricate exchanges between personal and national histories, past and present, the films open necessary spaces for engaging the hitherto unspoken. In this way, the "Truth and Reconciliation films" are largely about transcending.

If transcendence is emblematic of the contemporary South African national culture, the government recognizes cinema as a medium through which discourses about the past, present, and future can find coherence. Currently home to FEPACI (Pan-African Federation of Filmmakers), South Africa bolstered its continental status when, under the auspices of its Department of Arts and Culture (DAC) and National Film and Video Foundation (NFVF), it hosted in 2006 the landmark African Film Summit and the Seventh General Congress of FEPACI, which examined the residual challenges to African cinema, the need for sustained cooperation among practitioners, and roles of the state, broadcasters, the African Union (AU), and the New Partnership for Africa's Development (NEPAD), with a view to developing the industry continentally. The summit resulted in the "Tshwane Declaration," which added substantively to African cinema's history of declarations and manifestos (see Bakari and Cham, 17–36) by calling for, among other things, the establishment of the African Film Fund and the African Film Commission.

Notably, too, in terms of government policy and institutional support for domestic production, South Africa fares much better than its continental counterparts. Coproduction agreements foster economic and cultural ties and bolster, if symbolically, the stature of the local industry, just as they enhance investor confidence, spread the risks among various constituents, and allow access to new talent, markets, and finances. Apart from the thriving documentary film culture, coproduction agreements through the country's Department of Trade and Industry (DTI) and the NFVF have "diversity" at their core. Worth noting is that the DTI's recent Revised Film and Production Incentive simultaneously aims to boost local production and attract international productions. Similarly, the NFVF's Funding Criteria emphasize skills and capacity development through grants for South African filmmakers to attend international film festivals. South Africa's international acclaim, however, comes with paradoxes in so far as it has not necessarily translated into domestic, box-office production boons and arguably puts the nation at risk of being a mere production facility, or outpost, for projects from elsewhere. We will now advance our analysis through use of three key frames: thematic (*The Narrow Path* and *Ezra*), aesthetic (*Bamako* and *Conversations on a Sunday Afternoon*), and conceptual (*Les Saignantes* and *Africa Paradis*).

Intersections

In *The Narrow Path,* which crystallizes Nollywood's possibilities, five nubile friends, Ajitoni, Lape, Peju, Ayoka, and Awero, from Orita Village weigh their marriage prospects. Two suitors, Odejimi, a hunter from Agbede Village, and Lapade, a goldsmith from Aku Village, vie for Awero's heart. Odejimi wins, and a wedding date is set. However, a smooth-talking hometown-boy-turned-city-slicker, Dauda, distracts Awero with gifts and, in an unguarded moment, rapes her. Awero, traumatized, becomes taciturn, depressed, and suicidal. Things are further complicated when Odejimi shoots Lapade in a hunting accident, and Awero is found on her nuptial night to be a "broken pot," a disparaging term for a non-virgin bride—taboo in Elerin. The prospective in-laws are anguished. The new school project in Orita, initiated by Abigail, a visiting government education official, is vandalized. Accusing fingers point to Agbede village, and the Orita community responds by setting fire to Agbede farms. With the villages on the brink of war, Awero, leading a women's procession, challenges the villages' warring men and averts catastrophe. Abigail confronts Dauda, now in prison for drug-related offenses, over Awero's rape and elicits an apology. The film closes with a *gelede* (a women's masquerade) in a recuperative ceremony.

Kelani articulates Awero's innermost turmoil about being "a broken pot" in two evocative scenes that link her struggles, extant cultural orders, and the metaphysical realm. Both scenes are also central in structuring the narrative's morals within indigenous belief systems. In one, Awero makes exonerative pleas to the River Atu, or its deity. In another, she curses Dauda, whose sneering visage, in an apparitional flash, materializes on the mirror he baited her with. Presenting herself to Atu is neither arbitrary nor temperamental. It expresses a culturally indexed way of settling certain inner conflicts, especially those with profound moral implications, to the extent that according to African and even universal systems of thought, sites like groves, rivers, and mountains span earthly and spiritual worlds (Mbiti 1969, 1991). Similarly, cursing Dauda is not a vestige of folkways. It carries a moral and potent force, all the more so because Kelani juxtaposes Awero's anguish with Dauda's smirks. This also stands with the near universal thinking that words, whether in incantations, prayers, or curses, can sometimes be imbued with mystical powers. So Dauda's imprisonment, with its intimations of retributive justice, is a powerful catharsis.

The film, therefore, is about violation and restoration. The violations here are not just physical, psychical, cultural, and moral. Importantly, they require a comprehensive framework for amelioration. In revisiting the issues of African women's position and prospects for agency within cultures, Kelani challenges the depreciatory assumptions about African womanhood and, just as important, cultures. In a way, Awero's dilemmas dramatize, to borrow from Clifford (1988), "the predicaments of culture" or, more specifically, the predicaments of patriarchal authority and privilege. While Awero's reticence following her rape is symptomatic of post-traumatic stress, it underscores the anguish of bearing an ineffable burden. Seen this way, the film is about breaking taboos, finding ways to engage and speak the unspeakable, and moving beyond the narrow limitations, unspoken expectations, and double standards of patriarchal codes of women's "honor" and "virtue." Arguably, a key question Kelani poses is, what happens when an innocent gets caught up in circumstances beyond her control? The dangling nooses that haunt Awero in her moments of distress speak not only to her contemplation of suicide, but also metaphorically to a fraught framework of gender relations and social worth.

Whereas the title suggests limitations, Kelani is more interested in exploring the tensions they generate and finding ways to transcend them. Awero's intervention, which singularly defuses an explosive situation, indicts patriarchal bravado and restores her to a sense of worth outside of restrictive prescriptions. It is this audacious act of self-assertion in spite of the abuse and humiliation she suffered, that constitutes her legacy, particularly if read in terms of identity formation and African womanhood's seizing and decisively exercising agency within extant cultural precepts. It is remarkable that the *gelede*, which in Yoruba cosmology is associated with mystical powers unique to women and motherhood, especially restorative capacities for social harmony and health (Drewal 1974; Lawal 1978), closes the film. By incorporating the *gelede*, in which men are usually dressed as women, the film's theme of social justice and restoration is given cultural specificity *and* a communal dynamic outside of the dominant criminal justice.

Even though Awero's fate is key to the narrative of *The Narrow Path*, to see the film's significance exclusively through one character would be mistaken because the film also explores the subtleties of progress within the discourse of development and in light of broad transformations within the society. Abigail, who compliments the film's women-as-agents-of-change theme may be a city sophisticate, but she is also a grassroots agent not affected by intellectual or class alienation. Through her routing of intimidating government officials from the village market by essentially transforming them into comic figures and tenaciously nudging Dauda into penitence, we see renegotiation of gender roles and African womanhood effectively taking on the challenges presented by circumstance and culture.

Although the film does not call for a radical change in the social order, the narrative is geared towards cultural reevaluation and reconstitution. Kelani's concern with Awero is not predicated on a sweeping repudiation of marriage but on exploring means for her to recuperate and articulate her own agency. Also, if Awero's travails show that gender permeates the constructions of individual, social, cultural, and communal identities, a critical thrust of *The Narrow Path* appears to be interpreting tradition in a new light. To a large extent, especially in exploring the tensions between tradition and change as they interact with various forms of patriarchal privilege, the exchanges between individual and social identities that fill Awero's path to healing show how Africans have used cinema to explore certain paradoxes of culture and reimagine their communities.

Ezra, which won African cinema's most coveted prize in 2007, similarly deals with social justice and restoration but through a narrative of societal fragmentation. The film spans a decade in the life of its eponymous character, Ezra, who at the age of seven was abducted one morning as he skipped to school by members of the People's Revolutionary Front (PRF), who transform him into a robotic killing machine. On the grueling march to the rebel's hideout, he witnesses a whimpering classmate's execution and later is inducted into the "Brotherhood," as the rebels prefer to call themselves, through nationalist inanities, hallucinatory drugs, brainwashing exhortations to forget his family, and assorted mayhem aimed at desensitization. Later at the Brotherhood, he sees the leader, Rufus, dealing in arms, drugs, and diamonds with shady Westerners and falls in love with and impregnates Mariam, the daughter of an assassinated Marxist journalist who is committed to her father's crusade against injustice.

As the film ends, Ezra is captured by a rival rebel faction, is humiliated, and envisages a new life in Lagos with Mariam, until she and the fetus are killed in crossfire that symbolizes the victimization of born and unborn generations. He is captured by government forces and brought before a Truth and Reconciliation Commission hearing aimed at engendering communal healing. The narrative shuttles from Ezra's life in the Brotherhood to his tormented soul and the testimonies of his sister, Onicha, whose tongue was mutilated by Brotherhood members and who implicates him in their parents' death following an attack on their once-idyllic village. Now amnesic, Ezra's traumatized and overburdened psyche stands in the way.

Ezra, given its dramatic, emotional intensity, is as much a psychological film as a coming-of-age narrative. It is remarkable, therefore, that history, personal and collective, occupies a critical position in the film's negotiation of reconciliation and nationhood, especially because putting the past to rest paradoxically involves its exhumation and public airing. Aduaka's insistence on revisiting history, a staple of African cinema, raises the question of whose experiences, voices, and interpretations should inform the writing of national trauma and, just as important, which considerations should guide the postwar healing process. With Ezra, Aduaka forsakes the binarism of sinner/victimizer and saint/victim, finding that such labels may not fully account for the complexity of history, human nature, and war that his character faces. Thus, Aduaka suggests that the nation's history is too riven with interstices, red flags, and disparate voices to be straightforward and uncontested. Ezra's testimonies, juxtaposed with Onicha's, become reflexive engagements with the construction of collective memory. The opening scene, in which the young Ezra obliviously skips to school, is critical because the film focuses on a generation whose lives and promising futures were mortgaged by the war (Zack-Williams 2001).

It is no surprise, then, that in one of the film's striking allusions, Ezra and friends, lost or trapped in circumstances beyond their control, liken their lot to Ikemefuna, a sacrificial victim of war, in Chinua Achebe's classic about communal disintegration, *Things Fall Apart*. With the characters' biblical names—Ezra, Mesach, Moses, Ezekiel, Rufus, Mariam, and Black Jesus—and Christian symbolism—Windsor Anglican Elementary, Ezra's former school, and a cross on the floor of the tribunal's office—Aduaka references the nation's colonial, Judeo-Christian heritage. Relocating the biblical personas—Ezra (a figure of reform in Israel's restoration), Mesach (a survivor), and Moses (a liberator)—to a contemporary African conflict brings up issues of religion, politics, and identity and recalls age-old narratives of persecution and quests for freedom. In Mariam, a religious figure is conflated through her nickname, Black Diamond, with nationalism and the mineral that stokes the conflict. Another character, Terminator, simultaneously references the ruthless cyborg of Hollywood's blockbuster film of the same name and a real-life Congolese renegade's nom de guerre (see "ICC"). References to "rebel music," through reggae/Rastafarianism, and hip-hop, through music icon Tupac Shakur, also speak of the group's revolutionary zeal and relationship to global popular culture. In all, these literary, cinematic, biblical, and pop-cultural intertextual references are enmeshed in far-ranging discourses that enhance the narrative's complexity.

Even though *Ezra* engages the pervasive and pernicious notion of Africa as war-torn and conflict ridden, it is not a "war film" in the service of nationalist sentiments or a "historical film" that excuses staging bittersweet, commemorative experiences. If anything, it explores the complicated, contradictory relationship between history and its representation. As the film shows, the aftermath of hostilities is closely related to the past, and to the extent that the film carries many unresolved issues from the past *and* the present, such as destabilized family structures, it inhabits a turbulent representational space. Also at issue in the film are the conduct, politics, and ideologies of war, especially in relationship to nationalism. Remarkably, a writing assignment for the pupils of Windsor Anglican Elementary, on the morning of the attack and subsequent abductions, is "Why I Love My Country." In this way, Aduaka makes Rufus's subsequent exhortations about bringing "our country to greatness" and "justice, for which you will live and die," ironically hollow like the child soldiers' instigated chant, "We are children of the revolution." Significantly, the Special Court for Sierra Leone upheld on May 28, 2008, the convictions for war crimes and increased sentences of former militia members in agreement with a Human Rights Watch memorandum ("Political Considerations" 2008) that argued that political motivations in armed conflicts are irrelevant in mitigating punishment.

Ezra is concretely about personal, familial, and national trauma. That being the case, a challenge of the film's Truth and Reconciliation hearings is how to mix the various truths, largely from testimonies and confessions, into healing salves. Interestingly, Aduaka frames this challenge around the particularities of memory and the dilemmas of facing a troubled past. Appropriately, the film's structure, which some like Anderson (2007) may see as disorienting, corroborates the difficulties of reconstructing the past and mimics the intrinsically fragmentary and non-synchronous nature of memory. Here, the key is that memory, like history, necessarily derives from disparate experiences, some of which may be traumatic, as in Ezra's case, and dependent on different registers for recollection and transformation into coherent units of meaning. So the film's oscillations between past and present offer various structures of experience and memory as critical sites from which composite truths can be gleaned. In engaging the burden of memory without cushioning, the film could, to borrow from Soyinka (1998), be read in terms of the requisite but arduous searches for "the muse of forgiveness."

Trajectories

Bamako takes place as a courtroom trial in the courtyard of a house in Hamdallaye, a working-class neighborhood of Bamako, the capital of Mali. A young couple (Mélé, a nightclub singer, and her unemployed husband, Chaka), whose marriage is on the verge of collapse, lives with other families. On trial, with Africa as the plaintiff, are the global financial institutions, the International Monetary Fund and the World Bank, who are charged with Africa's impoverishment. Debt, according to the prosecutor, "has brought Africa to her knees." Thus, the director, Sissako, underpins the implausible scenario, with portents of the continent's debt crisis. The court's proceedings tangle with random details of everyday life. Witnesses from assorted backgrounds stream in to give testimonies on behalf of Africa. In hers, Aminata Traoré, a former Malian minister of culture, attests, "I am against the fact that Africa's main characteristic in the eyes of the world is its poverty. Africa is rather the victim of its wealth." A schoolteacher is overcome with emotions and is lost for words on the witness stand, and an elderly farmer gives his anguished testimony, a cry from the heart in an untranslated lament. Household routines, small talk, and miscellaneous struggles for existence continue unperturbed outside the courtyard. Women dye fabric; a wife tends her ailing husband, who like Mélé's sick daughter has no access to medical care; the bailiff's gun goes missing (with Chaka as a suspect); a wedding takes place; would-be immigrants set off on a perilous journey across the desert; a man learns Hebrew; and a television western with allegorical implications, *Death in Timbuktu,* in which cowboys shoot up Africans, pops up on Malian airwaves. Chaka, whose troubled marriage is also an allegory for the continent's predicament, is aloof. Another character, Falaï, a forensic photographer who makes wedding videos, ironically prefers filming the dead because "they are more real." At one point, some disaffected men outside the courtyard wonder how long the trial will last and, in a defiant gesture, disconnect the loudspeakers set up to beam the proceedings.

In fostering affinities with the film's location, characters, and themes, Sissako challenges prevailing responses to and critical readings of Africa as an aggregate of "failed states." His concern informs the allegorical undertones and political currents that run through the film. Appropriately, a recurrent motif is the fragmentation of lives, loves, trust, community, and hope. The latter crystallize when *Death in Timbuktu* plays to the delight of a very tender audience. Here, globalization, as it relates to the traffic of cultures and relay of representations, is rendered dubious. Through this parody, dominant Hollywood cinema, its ideological baggage, and the western, a unique genre, are contrasted with *Bamako*'s distinctively humanist spirit. Crucially, it is not only that the gawking audience is inured to gratuitous violence, oblivious of the film's devaluation of African lives and the ideological relations informing their perception of the film's African victims as Others, but also that their prospects for self-definition, the future, and initiating counter-narratives, given their impaired vision, are severely compromised.

Bamako eschews the stereotypical courtroom drama in which the guilty are hauled to jail and the people's faith in the justice system is reaffirmed. In many ways, the film poses various questions about prevailing responses to what undoubtedly is a humanitarian crisis. Sissako appears more interested in morality than legality. For instance, Chaka, driven by despair, eventually commits suicide. On trial here are the detrimental effects on African economies and psyches of globalization, privatization, and official corruption. Significantly, the trial is a symbolic exercise that, in avoiding sanguine closure, gives no relief to the anxieties it raises. As a mock trial, the film's parodic overtones question The Hague's institutional worth, efficacy, and moral standing. In underscoring the need for reform by highlighting the Africans' alienation from and disillusionment with the court's proceedings, Sissako implicates the court as part of the problem rather than a viable institution for redress.

Sissako also seems to argue that the court should not be held outside of the material realities it purports to redress. Thus, the various intrusions, such as a goat charging at a judge, a man hawking tawdry counterfeit imports, and a neighborhood resident learning Hebrew, show aspects of lives often obfuscated by the formalities of the court and are clever ways to abrogate the intimidating distance of The Hague. Transposing The Hague to a nondescript courtyard in Hamdallaye, where the director grew up, is not an indulgent homage to origins or nostalgia. If anything, it brings the issues home, literally and figuratively, making the court a "people's court" of sorts, where previously subjugated voices and subjectivities form an oppositional, communal stance. Naming the film after the Malian capital, an ancient city suffused with history, is crucial, to the extent that cities usually have social, cultural, historical, administrative, economic, and even ideological significance. However, rather than offer a touristy excursion through landmarks, Sissako makes the city a paradigmatic staging ground for Africa's developmental impasse, with its vexing contradictions, institutional failures, and consequences. That Bamako is an ancient commercial center also invites critical rereading of the "inevitable progress," which, according to pundits of the global financial systems, would accrue through adoption of certain economic policies.

Of note here is that Bamako was in 1987 the site of a landmark conference that, under the auspices of the World Health Organization and UNICEF, produced The Bamako Initiative, a set of strategies to improve primary health care in the region. Hence, in the film, Sissako uses instances of inadequate health care and the untold sufferings they engender to refer ironically to another failed policy prescription by a global institution in concert with local authorities. Overall, the film's seemingly disjunctive, mundane details, juxtaposed with the proceedings, are in rhetorical relationship with each other, paint composite pictures of certain issues, and embody the aesthetic experimentation emerging in contemporary African cinema.

In *Conversations on a Sunday Afternoon*, a young writer, Keniloe, searches for lonesome Fatima, who fascinated him with stories she told in a Johannesburg park. (Interestingly, Keniloe is reading Somali writer Nuruddin Farah's novel *Links*.) Fatima, now a refugee in South Africa, had witnessed her brother's and father's murder and had herself been left for dead and made uncertain of her mother's fate. Troubled by Fatima's experiences, Keniloe is inspired to use them as the foundation for a book he wants to write about war, refugees, and displacement. As he looks for Fatima, he encounters a disparate population of refugees and immigrants—from Ethiopia, Kenya, Uganda, Serbia, Korea, the Democratic Republic of Congo, Palestine, Sudan, China, Malawi, and Zimbabwe—with unique histories and intriguing stories. Responding to Keniloe's questions, these real-life exiles, who have fled wars and difficult circumstances for brighter futures in South Africa, paint searing portraits of exilic life in Johannesburg's migrant neighborhoods.

According to Matabane, the film grew out of a chance encounter with a young Eritrean woman in a German airport lounge. As he recalls, "She and her family had run away from the war between Eritrea and Ethiopia. Her family was displaced across Europe and the U.S.A. When she heard I was a filmmaker, she asked me to make a film 'about people displaced by the stupidity of war.' . . . This is my love letter to her" (Harmanci 2007). The challenges for the director were how to register the cultural, emotional, historical, and social intricacies of the young exile's request; how to capture and represent with his character, Fatima, the trauma of loss and dislocation; and how to show the other refugees' redefinition of community and belonging. Even though the title suggests leisurely socialization, the film is about anything but that. Matabane aims at instituting critical dialogue by offering ways to explore the lives of people whom the average South African may never quite know. In this manner, the film is predicated on an aesthetic of social inquiry. Moreover, *Links,* which situates Fatima firmly within exilic narratives, is also a metaphor for the director's interest in drawing relationships between seemingly disparate social experiences and national histories. Significantly, the film, like an earlier South African short *The Foreigner* (Zola Maseko 1997), about the friendship between an immigrant street vendor and a homeless child, interrogates emergent notions of "difference" and Otherness in post-apartheid South Africa.

Hence, Matabane builds on tensions between a free South Africa and the restrictive realities of the country's various exiles, migrants, and refugees, all the more so because they have been inextricably caught up in the unfolding and contentious discourses of nation, rebirth, new cultural formations, and national identity. Thus, the film shows the paradoxes of constructing a "new" South Africa, and it particularly explores the cultural and political significance of South Africa's newfound status as a land of opportunity, where the world's exiles hope to dream anew. This is especially significant because South Africa, which was a pariah state under apartheid, is often seen today as a beacon of liberty. Much as the film is about displacement, it is also arguably about South Africa's attempt at self-definition, particularly as the Rainbow Nation. Aptly, the director gives human faces, deep humane emotions, and poignant personal histories to the abstractions and experiences of exilic life, which many South Africans were forced to endure during apartheid. Fatima's loneliness and tentativeness are as characteristic of exilic life as her decision not to speak with Keniloe at the end of the film is crucial for understanding the complexities of displacement, alienation, and marginality.

Matabane underscores the need to critically engage certain contradictions inherent in consigning the refugees to the limiting category of foreign Others, or *makwerekwere* in derogatory South African slang, which compromises their humanity and capacities for self-definition. Through the interviews, especially in elevating their subdued voices, he moves them out of the restrictive spaces or categories they have been made to occupy by circumstances and prejudice. By piecing together the fragmented lives and aspirations of the refugees and allowing them to speak in various languages and express themselves, certain realities borne of racial, religious, social, and national prejudices coalesce. Hence, the film's mix of documentary and other narrative forms is effective in registering the refugees' disparate experiences and South Africa's position in relation to global historical shifts.

On Sunday, May 11, 2008, Alexandra Township, north of Johannesburg, became the flashpoint for chilling, xenophobic acts of intimidation, abuse, assault, rape, arson, looting, murder (some victims were burned alive), and assorted human rights violations that spread across South Africa. The events substantiated *Conversations on a Sunday Afternoon* because the film shows a global assemblage of migrants, asylum seekers, refugees, and Black African foreigners (mainly Zimbabweans, Somalis, Mozambicans, Angolans, and Nigerians), who were, irrespective of South Africa's history of migrant settlement and integration, almost exclusively the targets and victims. The film's arguments against obdurate nationalist identities become especially prescient when in the "new nation discourse" of post-apartheid South Africa, the foreigner "stands at a site where identity, racism, and violent practices are reproduced" (Harris 2002, 169).

Thresholds

Set at night in 2025 in an unnamed African country, *Les Saignantes* opens with a female voice-over as a high-ranking government official dies in flagrante and ostensibly from a heart attack, while cavorting in bed with a much younger, very sexy partner, Majolie, who wants lucrative government contracts. Unnerved, Majolie calls on her friend, Chouchou, for help. They decide to dispose of the corpse by cutting it up but realize that a wake for such a key figure cannot be circumvented, so they hire a rogue mortuary attendant to stitch the body's head onto a cadaver from the morgue. Subsequently, they stage a WIP (Wake of Important Person), which turns to hobnobbing revelry, and no one, other than the widow, is suspicious of the corpse's physical discrepancies. Notwithstanding, the young women seize the moment to hustle another official for contracts. He, however, is ruthless and seeks to exploit their plight. Events lead to an inevitable showdown from which Majolie and Chouchou, like Ninja superheroes, emerge victorious.

Largely, the film chronicles the young women's grotesque escapades and intriguing characters, among them a matriarchal secret society, Mevoungou, which is endowed with supernatural powers. Cleverly, the director, Bekolo, poses, in the form of inter-titles inserted throughout the narrative, various provocative questions about the relationship of cinema and society. All told, the world evoked in *Les Saignantes* is an infernal sphere suffused with the excesses of power, corruption, money, and sex. Because of its very audacity, the film has been the object of censure, particularly for its highly eroticized content. There have been objections to its supposed pornography and prurient debasement of African womanhood (with Majolie and Chouchou as figures of renegade sexuality) and apprehensions about its depiction of a bleak African future haunted by death and debauchery. What has not been fruitfully explored, however, is the film's reformulation of women's power and role in society, especially in the film's representation of patriarchal relations driven by very aggressive libidinal impulses and in its raising questions about the values and morals of a future Africa. In so far as Bekolo situates Majolie and Chouchou on the margins of the prevailing culture, both characters could be said to represent the putative vulnerability of African womanhood and its potential for liberation. Arguably, it is this marginality that informs their dissident identities and leads to alternative paradigms of resistance to the regimes on which the dominant order thrives. It is, therefore, telling that the impetus and will to break with the status quo came from the gendered fringe.

In a way, *Les Saignantes* embodies extant anxieties about the future of Africa, especially, the fear of repeating mistakes of the past and present. Bekolo, however, does not reduce the future to instances of speculation or technological marvels but, in relating it to certain predicaments of the present, expands the scope of its conceptualization. Put differently, he appears less concerned with depicting the future per se than current life in a perverse, predatory social order. Diffuse narrative premises that mix the familiar with the strange by utilizing anomalies of the present to project a dismal destiny supplant verisimilitude. In many respects, Bekolo seems to argue that a tragic destiny is evitable by closing with the question, how can you watch this film and do nothing? This is a query, challenge, and call to arms through which the need for change is underscored. By using inter-titles to structure the film thematically and aesthetically, Bekolo hopes to instigate more intellectual than visceral engagement with the narrative. And in pushing for an active, not passive, spectatorship, he suggests that discerning Africa's future requires political and communal efforts, as well as unqualified repudiation of the ancien régime. Thus, the film's fragmented, brash style, which draws inextricable links between perversion, patronage, and politics, marks it as an overtly critical project and complements the subject matter.

Clearly, *Les Saignantes* returns to the long-standing search in African cinema, for the place of the arts in re/building the nation. Moreover, Bekolo adds to the vexed dynamics, renegotiations of power and gender roles, critical engagements with the continent's sociopolitical conundrums, and recognition of the intrinsic connections between seemingly disparate epochs as key to the search elements that may be used to fashion Africa's future. Through the film's bleak world, especially its charged psycho-spiritual atmosphere, Bekolo emphasizes struggles in a dangerous predatory culture in which ambiguities verge on the surreal. The film's political project is, in part, constituted by this culture: he plays Majolie's and Chouchou's femme fatale personas against the libidinal charges of their predators. Indeed, with Mevoungou literally and figuratively in the picture, Bekolo speculates on the future and roles of indigenous belief systems and, to the extent that Mevoungou is imbued with inscrutability and cultural authority, another paradigm of women's power. Not surprising, Mevoungou is introduced as a mystical force tied to the womb and a possible panacea for the pervasive turpitudes of the contemporary. Here, Mevoungou is not a force of cultural conservatism; it is imbued with critical nuances and, ultimately, with redemptive spirit. Thus, through a voice-over at the film's end, we are told that "Mevoungou dreamed in technicolor." This dream, arguably, is one of transcendence. In evoking mysticism, feminism, culture, and tradition, Bekolo proposes a fusion of "folk" with digital culture as part of a distinctively African future or modernity.

Interest in extending analysis of contemporary issues into the future also undergirds Sylvestre Amousssou's *Africa Paradis*, a futuristic satire on power relations, in which a once formidable European Union falls into ruin due to acute economic and political crises, and Africa, which has undergone an enviable transformation, has become the destination of choice for would-be European immigrants. In the film, Olivier, a French computer engineer, and his lover, Pauline, a teacher, both unemployed, decide to seek their fortunes in the United States of Africa, but, like other applicants, they are whimsically denied entry visas. Eventually, the couple uses the services of a smuggling ring to sneak into the continent. They are caught by the African border police and put in detention to await deportation. Olivier cracks the holding camp's security codes and escapes and lives as an illegal alien until he witnesses a motor accident in which a lawful European resident is killed. Olivier assumes the victim's identity by stealing his legal documents. Meanwhile, Pauline and other detainees grapple with the grim realities of undocumented migrants and eventually stage a protest rally that ends tragically. Olivier is deported, and Pauline's romance with the deputy minister of the Liberal African Party, Mr. Modibbo Kodossou, in whose household she works as a maid, blossoms. The minister's sister is an African cipher for Western racist attitudes.

Africa Paradis poses serious questions about what is generally perceived as an African predicament and offers unique ways for confronting familiar "realities." In using a reversal-of-fortune narrative framework, Amoussou appears not so much concerned with fostering a revenge fantasy or discovering new truths about generic discourses of immigration to the West, but with inspiring spectators to critically engage and reappraise their relationships to those they may see as denizens of distant worlds and as amorphous Others. By avoiding a trite, melodramatic narrative and cleverly repositioning Africans from their well-worn position as victims, the director presents the often-impassioned debates about immigration as a human, rather than exclusively African issue. Explicit in this, is a critique of the social relations the debates derive from and engender. Thus, the film is about the reversal of relations, not just of fortunes.

The preceding is very important because nullification of the immigrants' humanity by seeing them as *sans papiers* (without papers), "overwhelming numbers," "threats," and "problems" that require unflinching "solutions" requires their transformation into political fodder subject to manipulative electoral and cultural politics. Here, the lighthearted tones of the film become not only devices through which tensions are worked out, but also clever strategies for drawing awareness to the pervasive dynamic of humiliation and the compromising obstacle courses African immigrants face. Here, the film's satirical edges work to bridge the emotional distances between the various forms of stigmatized identities that the immigrants quite often have. Thus, to the extent that the director invites empathy through reconsideration of certain nationalist and generic prejudices, he appears more concerned with revealing popular mythologies about immigration and the rhetoric that feeds off them than with nuanced examination and nudging the spectators to identify with the often-outcast African Others.

The success of *Africa Paradis* in drawing parallels between the plights of African immigrants, marked as they are by abuse and exploitation, and those of the film's European characters, challenges the generic responses to and ambiguous positions in contemporary debates about immigration. Even though a protest march, led by European immigrants and African progressives whose rallying refrain is "equality and integration," ends tragically, one is moved to identify with the immigrants' struggles to redefine themselves, reassert their humanity, and explore avenues for political change. In drawing the spectator to view issues of the present through a different temporal and spatial frame, Amoussou insists on the recognition of a common humanity through the timeless, moral admonition "Treat others as you would like to be treated." Undoubtedly a political allegory, the film's inversion of the stereotypical immigrant and dominant narratives of immigration in the age of globalization resonates. And key to understanding the film is the clever play on what, in the view of skeptics, Africa may never be—progressive, economically stable, and functionally democratic. Here, Amoussou attempts to break Africa out of the various myths and stereotypical molds into which the immigration debates are quite often cast by presenting a more complicated picture of contemporary African immigration dilemmas in reverse. Modibbo's sister, for instance, inveighs that "Whites are lazy. All they want to do is play." Seen this way, alongside the analogous narrative premise, the film is about highly charged notions of racial difference intrinsic to the debates about nation and culture in contemporary Western immigration and cultural politics.

Notably, the film's title plays on the anachronistic image of an eternal Africa, replete with exotic scenery and wildlife. Also, the film's unified, prosperous Africa, an enduring dream of Pan-Africanists, gets a twist with the adaptation of a gaudy version of the American flag. The flag, not just a veritable nationalist symbol, is emblematic of the continent's emergent superpower status, which Amoussou uses cleverly to play on possible apprehensions about Africa's prospects, make comments about power and the balance of power, and critique certain manipulative features and trajectories of the immigration discourse in contemporary U.S. cultural politics. Running through this film, however, are love stories: one between Oliver and Pauline ends tragically, and another between Pauline and Modibbo, whose marriage destabilizes entrenched boundaries of class, race, and national identity. Whether or not the marriage is out of love or convenience, as reaffirmation of humanity and symbol of a hybrid cultural space, it is, given the pervasive acrimonious atmosphere, an emphatic political act.

Conclusion

To the extent that African cinema embodies dynamic cultural forms, tangled sociohistorical forces, complex interacting interests, and eclectic viewpoints, the preceding highlights the pitfalls of formulating a "standard" African cinema or "essential" approach to the study of African film. Moreover, globalization has ushered into Africa unique cultural forms that should not be categorized didactically or banally. New categories, expressive vocabularies, and representational registers are required. Marked by a push for more creative license and women directors, African cinema is concerned with exploring and utilizing emerging spaces and ways through which erstwhile representations of Africa can be updated. Even though contemporary African filmmaking deals with antecedents, its trajectories lie beyond particular schools of thought, and it leads to reevaluation of certain premises, more subtle political axes, and development in relation to new media technologies, the African diaspora, cosmopolitanism, and transnational identities, which have imbued contemporary Africa with distinct shades and shadows. So, the filmmakers insist, in various voices, on tweaking models of African cinema, especially because they see it as an artistic project, whose meanings accrue over time, and as capable of unapologetically taking on inspirations from elsewhere, not necessarily in response to exhortations from Western funders for African filmmakers to be more "universal" in their narratives and craft. Filmmakers question the stilted iconography of Hollywood's Africa and contest notions of African cinema as monolithic, unchanging, and without its own impetus. They are also ambivalent about the pervasive tendency, in and out of Western cultural circles, to see African films exclusively as sociological tracts, ethnographic capsules, or transparent windows on African societies. In this vein, African filmmakers interrogate aesthetic criteria, narrative premises, inspirational prerogatives, and dominant cinema's representations of Africa.

REFERENCES

Achebe, C. *Things Fall Apart*. London: Heinemann, 1958.

Adamu, A.U., Y.M. Adamu, and U.F. Jibril, eds. *Hausa Home Videos: Technology, Economy and Society*. Kano: Center for Hausa Cultural Studies, 2004.

Akudinobi, J.G., ed. *Social Identities: Journal for the Study of Race, Nation and Culture* 6, no. 3 (2000).

Anderson, J. "Ezra." *Variety*, February 12–18, 2007, 49.

Armes, R. *African Filmmaking: North and South of the Sahara*. Bloomington: Indiana University Press, 2006.

Bakari, I. and M. Cham, eds. *African Experiences of Cinema*. London: British Film Institute, 1996.

Balseiro, I. and N. Masilela. *To Change Reels: Film and Film Culture in South Africa*. Detroit: Wayne State University Press, 2003.

Barlet, O. *African Cinemas: Decolonizing the Gaze*. London: Zed Press, 2000.

Bonetti, M., and P. Reddy. *Through African Eyes: Dialogues with the Directors*. New York: African Film Festival, 2003.

Clifford, J. *Predicament of Culture: Twentieth-century Ethnography, Literature and Art*. Cambridge, MA: Harvard University Press, 1988.

Diawara, M. *African Cinema, Politics and Culture*. Bloomington: Indiana University Press, 1992.

Drewal, H.J. "Gelede Masquerade: Imagery and Motif." *African Arts* 7, no. 4 (1974): 8–19, 62–63, 95–96.

Gadjigo, S., R.H. Faulkingham, T. Cassirer, and R. Sander, eds. *Ousmane Sembène: Dialogue with Critics and Writers*. Amherst: University of Massachusetts Press, 1993.

Givanni, J., ed. *Symbolic Narratives/African Cinema: Audiences, Theory and the Moving Image*. London: British Film Institute, 2001.

Gugler, J. *African Film: Re-Imagining a Continent*. Bloomington: Indiana University Press, 2003.

Harmanci, R. "Mixed-up World." *San Francisco Chronicle*, February 15, 2007.

Harris, B. "Xenophobia: A New Pathology for a New South Africa?" In *Psychopathology and Social Prejudice*, edited by D. Hook and G. Eagle, 169–184. Cape Town: University of Cape Town Press, 2002.

Harrow, K.W. *Postcolonial African Cinema: From Political Engagement to Postmodernism*. Bloomington: Indiana University Press, 2007.

Haynes, J., ed. *Nigerian Video Films*. Athens: Ohio University Center for International Studies, 2000.

"ICC Seeks DR Congo's 'Terminator,'" May 28, 2008, news.bbc.co.uk/go/pr/fr/-/2/hi/africa/7372940.stm.

Lawal, B. "New Light on Gelede." *African Arts* 11, no. 2 (1978): 65–70, 94.

"Living on the Margins: Inadequate Protection for Refugees and Asylum Seekers in Johannesburg." *Human Rights Watch* 17, no. 15A (November 2005): 1–64.

Maingard, J. *South African National Cinema*. London and New York: Routledge, 2000.

Malkmus, L., and R. Armes. *Arab and African Filmmaking*. London: Zed Press, 1991.

Mbiti, J.S., ed. *Introduction to African Religion*. London: Heinemann, 1991.

Moller, O. "Nigerian Video Culture: A Homegrown Hybrid Cinema of Outrageous Schlock from Africa's Most Populous Nation." *Film Comment* 40, no. 2 (2004): 12–13.

Murphy, D. *Sembene: Imagining Alternatives in Film and Fiction*. Trenton, NJ: Africa World Press, 2001.

Murphy, D., and P. Williams *Postcolonial African Cinema: Ten Directors*. Manchester University Press, 2007

Nuruddin, F. *Links*. New York: Penguin, 2004.

Okome, O., ed. *Film International* 5, no. 4 (2007).

———, ed. *Postcolonial Text* 3, no. 2 (2007).

Petty, S., ed. *A Call to Action: The Films of Ousmane Sembene*. West Port, CT: Praeger, 1996.

Pfaff, F. *The Cinema of Ousmane Sembene: A Pioneer of African Film*. West Port, CT: Greenwood, 1984.

"Political Considerations in Sentence Mitigation for Serious Violations of the Laws of War before International Criminal Tribunals." *Human Rights Watch* (March 2008), 1–12.

"Prohibited Persons: Abuse of Undocumented Migrants, Asylum-Seekers, and Refugees in South Africa." *Human Rights Watch* (March 1998).

Soyinka, W. *Burden of Memory, Muse of Forgiveness*. New York: Oxford University Press, 1998.

Thackway, M. *Africa Shoots Back: Alternative Perspectives in Sub-Saharan Francophone African Film*. Bloomington: Indiana University Press, 2003.

Tomaselli, K. *The Cinema of Apartheid: Race and Class in South African Film*. Brooklyn, NY: Smyrna, 1988.

Ukadike, N.F. *Black African Cinema*. Berkeley: University of California Press, 1995.

———. *Questioning African Cinema*. Minneapolis: University of Minnesota Press, 2000.

Zack-Williams, A.B. "Child Soldiers in the Civil War in Sierra Leone." *Review of African Political Economy* 28, no. 87, 73–82.

Chapter 17

ENGENDERING AFRICAN HISTORY
A Tale of Sex, Politics, and Power

Anene Ejikeme

When Ellen Johnson-Sirleaf was campaigning to be elected president of Liberia, commentators were unanimous in the opinion that her greatest difficulty would be to persuade "traditional" African men, especially elders, to vote for a woman. Commentators agreed in their predictions of victory for George Weah, a former international soccer star, who was declared the front-runner in all the polls. It was, then, to the absolute astonishment of many that Ellen Johnson-Sirleaf did win the presidency to become the first African woman head of state. Unfortunately, Johnson-Sirleaf's victory was not followed by a rash of news reports and analyses examining why the pundits had been so wrong and why Liberian men apparently had no difficulty selecting a woman to steer their country. Certainly, inquiring minds want to know: Who or what persuaded African men to flout tradition and vote for Mrs. Johnson-Sirleaf? Why had the analysis of the so-called experts been so wrong? Could it be that African male elders were less troubled by the thought of a woman with extensive experience in the field of global finance leading their war-shattered country than by entrusting their fate in the hands of an inexperienced young man?

Unfortunately, the news reports about Liberia prior to the elections reflect a problem endemic in writing about Africa: journalists and putative experts substitute preconceived notions and received opinion for fact-based research. How many journalists actually asked Africans, male elders and others, whether they would vote for a woman and why (or why not)? How many bothered to study the history of the region? If neither public-opinion surveys nor historical analyses were conducted, on the basis of what were these journalists speaking so confidently about the power of African "conservatism" and "ancient traditions"?

The notion that Africans, particularly male elders, are "traditional" is so entrenched in the West and among African elites that this view is treated as such common-sense knowledge that it requires no further comment. The first question that should be posed is, what do we mean by "traditional"? But this very fundamental question is rarely raised. Journalists and other experts routinely express opinions about African women without bothering to conduct basic research, relying entirely on preconceived ideas derived from an evolutionist thinking, which takes as its point of departure the tenet that human societies all progress in the same direction and pass through the same stages of development. When it comes to issues related to gender and women, too frequently, commentators assume that the measures and yardsticks that apply in the West are universally applicable. Indeed, because Africa is "developing," the assumption is that African countries are at the stage of development that the West occupied centuries or decades ago, and these countries need to "catch up." According to this line of thinking, the West, with its economic hegemony, is at the forefront of religious, political, and social developments worldwide. Everyone else is on the road, or needs to be on the road, to achieving the "milestones" the West (has) achieved in all these realms. In economics, the very language of "development," which labels some countries "developed" and others "developing," underscores the tenacity of this belief. The reality, however, is that it is sloppy thinking to imagine that there is an automatic connection between a society's economic situation and other aspects of community (social, religious, political, etc.). But journalists and other professional observers routinely do this. "Backwardness" in the economic realm is translated to mean "backwardness" in all spheres—religious, political, and social.

These issues are at the heart of this essay's exploration of the ongoing and critical debates about how to frame African women's history. The goal here is not to catalog every work written on African women but to highlight some of the key connections between debates around the history of African women and their current status. First, I begin with a summary of the period since the late nineteenth century, and then I turn to the most hotly debated issues today with regard to how "to frame" African women. I look at the issue of development and aid because these are often the first—and sometimes the only—points of entry for U.S. students encountering Africa. The question of how to frame African women is critical because if categories developed in the West cannot be applied automatically to Africa, the question becomes, how should new categories be developed? It must be noted that what is at issue here is not to attempt to quantify how much of the writing about African women is "good" and how much "bad," but to underscore the need to be attentive to the categories with which we begin our analyses. It is important to recognize that what we think and the categories into which we organize that thinking shape the way we see new phenomena. One's location does play a role in what one observes because some things may be obscured, while others appear in sharp focus.

A Walk Through the Looking Glass

Framing Africa improperly is a practice of long standing, dating back to the armchair ethnographers of the nineteenth century and before. The early twentieth century saw the appearance of a new kind of commentator on Africa: the credentialed professional. The latter was often, though not always, employed in the offices of the colonial bureaucracy. As Hafkin and Bay complained in the introduction to their 1976 landmark collection, *Women in Africa,* the literature on African women in the first half of the twentieth century was written by European men, and there was a "concentration on African women as wives, lovers and mothers . . . [resulting] in [a] disproportionate attention to the sexual aspects of their lives."[1] These details about African women's intimate lives derived from sources written by people whose reliability, especially in gathering information of this nature, is now widely questioned. European men writing about African women interviewed African men, or more typically a single African man, and on the basis of statements from a single male "informant," they made sweeping statements, such as "women believe/do/desire, etc."

---

[1] Nancy J. Hafkin and Edna G. Bay, *Women in Africa: Studies in Social and Economic Change* (Stanford University Press, 1976).

During the colonial period, i.e., roughly 1880–1960, there were events that merited a broad reinterpretation of European understanding of women's status and gender relations in Africa, but these opportunities were not seized. For example, the regularity with which women challenged colonial authority and/or mounted resistance ought to have warranted a serious reappraisal of the common wisdom that African women were in effect beasts of burden, exploited and transacted by men, no better off than sheep and cattle. Women were among some of the most formidable resisters to colonial conquest and rule. In what is today Ghana, the Asante queen-mother of Ejisu (Edweso) led resistance against British encroachments at the beginning of the twentieth century. In Zimbabwe, the British hanged the Nehanda spirit medium for inspiring and spearheading a national war of resistance, or *chimurenga* in Shona. Even in "feudal" Ethiopia, the only African state to maintain its independence in the "Scramble for Africa," Empress Taytu marched at the head of her troops in battle against the Italians. Once European rule had become a fait accompli, the nature of resistance, naturally, had to adapt, too. Resistance now more typically targeted specific aspects of colonial rule. The most famous case of this type of resistance that involved women was the 1929 Women's War in Nigeria. During the 1940s and 1950s, women, as individuals and in groups, were active in the nationalist campaigns of the period.[2]

Most, but not all, of the writing on African women by Europeans in the colonial period was by men. Notable exceptions include Mary Kingsley, Sylvia Leith-Ross, Margery Perham, Audrey Richards, Mary Smith, and Deborah A. Talbot. The writings of European women were also often marked by prejudice about "primitive tribes," but some European women wrote very perceptively about the lives of African women. However, more often than not, those aspects of any writing that challenged long-held notions about African women were ignored. We can take the case of Sylvia Leith-Ross as an example. Leith-Ross was sent by the colonial authorities to investigate and report on Igbo women in Nigeria after the 1929 Women's War. The Women's War produced a rare acknowledgment by European colonial authorities that they did not "know" the "native woman," and the colonial government commissioned two British women to study and produce reports on Igbo women. While Leith-Ross's book was organized along the evolutionist model, categorizing Igbo women according to whether they were "traditional," "evolving," or "modern," she draws some conclusions that should have led to a serious review of the constant claims of the need to remake African society in Europe's image in order to "liberate" African women. She cautioned her readers that "there is no typical portrait one can draw and then say: 'This is an Ibo.' How much less then can one say, as is so often done, 'This is an African' or 'African women do this' or 'The women of Africa think that.'"[3] In a later work of reminiscences, first published in 1951, describing the market in Oguta, a town in Nigeria, Leith-Ross concluded that "the 'down-trodden African woman' is hard to find in Nigeria."[4]

---

[2] See, for example, Susan Geiger, *TANU Women: Gender and Culture in the Making of Nationalism, 1955–1965* (Portsmouth, NH: Heinemann, 1997) and Cheryl Johnson-Odim and Nina Mba, *For Women and the Nation: Funmilayo Ransome-Kuti of Nigeria* (Urbana: University of Illinois Press, 1997).

[3] Sylvia Leith-Ross, *African Women: A Study of the Ibo of Nigeria* (London: Routledge and Kegan Paul, 1939), 20. Another noteworthy book about one African woman is Mary Smith's *Baba of Karo* (1955) in which Baba's views challenge many of the assumptions about the powerlessness of African and Muslim women.

[4] Sylvia Leith-Ross, *Beyond the Niger* (Westport, CT: Negro Universities Press, 1971, first published 1951), 59.

In the postwar period, the pace of nationalist agitation picked up in the colonies, culminating in a long process of decolonization, beginning in about 1960.[5] Denise Paulme's edited volume, *Femmes d'Afrique Noire,* published in 1960 (1963 in English), heralded a new trajectory in the discussions about African women: the contributors to the Paulme volume were all professionally trained anthropologists who conducted research among women, and the papers paid much attention to women's political participation. In her introduction, Paulme proclaimed her project to have contributors focus on women in their "everyday life" and draw conclusions from that and not from "the usual preconceptions about the inferior position of women in a traditional African setting." One essay in particular, Annie Lebeuf's "The Role of Women in the Political Organization of African Societies," has been much cited because it represented a radical departure by focusing on the political life of women. From 1960 into the late 1970s, studies of African women in English often focused on elite women rulers and influential personalities. The works of Felicia Ekejiuba,[6] Kamene Okonjo,[7] Bolanle Awe,[8] Carol Hoffer MacCormack,[9] and Judith van Allen[10] rejected the notion that in "traditional" African communities women were excluded from political participation. Indeed, all these authors argued that, in precolonial African states, women could and did rise to high political office or had specific avenues to express their political will.

The 1960s were a major turning point due to the confluence of several events: the achievement by African countries of "flag independence"; in the United States, the advancement of civil rights; and the sexual revolution and women's movements throughout the West. All these developments would have ramifications in the academy and in the place Africa occupied in academic scholarship. In institutions of higher learning in the West, women, like Africans, had this in common: neither had a history, at least as far as the curriculum and the gatekeepers at these institutions were concerned. In graduate schools, women who were involved in the feminist movement complained that women were completely absent from the curricula. Once they graduated, some of these women scholars would focus on the study of women in their own research, often turning their attention to women in distant parts of the world. Margaret Strobel, one of the first group of historians of African women in the academy noted, "Before I became a historian of women, I became an Africanist. And while I was becoming an Africanist, I became a feminist, a historian, and an activist."[11]

As the civil rights movement insisted on equal rights for all in the American judicial system and in employment, advocates in colleges and universities also demanded the inclusion of Africa in university curricula. It was from this period that African history began to be included in the curriculum in

---

[5] Ghana and several North African countries were granted independence before 1960.

[6] Felicia Ekejiuba, "Omu Okwei," *Journal of the Historical Society of Nigeria* (1966).

[7] Kamene Okonjo, "The Dual-Sex Political System in Operation: Igbo Women and Community Politics in Midwestern Nigeria," in *Women in Africa: Studies in Social and Economic Change,* eds. Nancy J. Hafkin and Edna G. Bay (Stanford University Press, 1976).

[8] Bolanle Awe, "The Iyalode in the Traditional Yoruba Political System," in *Sexual Stratification: A Cross-cultural View,* ed. Alice Schlegel (New York: Columbia University Press, 1977).

[9] Carol Hoffer MacCormack, "Mende and Sherbro Women in High Office," *Canadian Journal of African Studies* (1972); see also Carol Hoffer MacCormack, "Madam Yoko: Ruler of the Kpa Mende Confederacy," in *Woman, Culture and Society,* eds. Michele Z. Rosaldo and Louise Lamphere (Stanford University Press, 1974), 171–187, 333–334.

[10] Judith Van Allen, "'Aba Riots' or Igbo 'Women's War'? Ideology, Stratification, and the Invisibility of Women," in *Women in Africa: Studies in Social and Economic Change,* eds. Nancy J. Hafkin and Edna G. Bay (Stanford University Press, 1976).

[11] See Margaret Strobel in *Voices of Women Historians: The Personal, the Political, the Professional,* ed. Eileen Boris and Nupur Chaudhuri (Bloomington: Indiana University Press, 1999), 175.

predominantly White colleges and universities in the United States. It must be noted, however, that historically Black colleges and universities had always taught African history.

Building on the foundations laid in the 1960s, the 1970s were a markedly productive period with regard to the study of women in Africa. In 1972, the venerable *Canadian Journal of African Studies* (CJAS) devoted an entire volume to African women; three years later, the African Studies Review did likewise. Both volumes included contributions by historians. However, it would be an error to equate quantity with quality or to imagine that as more attention was focused on African women, the value of the work rose in direct proportion. One example will suffice here: In the 1975 special volume of the *African Studies Review,* Jocelyn Murray reviewed a book that had been published just a few years previously, *Old Wives' Tales: Life Stories of African Women* by Iris Andreski. Murray noted that "college teachers embarking on new comparative courses on 'women in society' and the like will be making much use of this book." That the book, purportedly based on women's accounts of their lives, was going to be widely used as a source of knowledge about African women was no cause for celebration in Murray's assessment because she found the book decidedly not "useful for information." It is worth quoting from Murray's review:

> Mrs Andreski's almost totally negative view of Ibibio society seems to spring from *more* [emphasis added] than her reading of these narratives. . . . I do not deny that these aspects [i.e., the negative] of a society's life must be considered, and I am far from wishing to say that all customs in a society are good simply because they exist. But Mrs Andreski's comments often appear both racist and superficial.

Unfortunately, Murray's assessment of Andreski's *Old Wives' Tales* continues to be just as applicable to a good amount of widely read literature on African women in the decades since. And I would argue that much of the problem stems from looking at African women's lives through Western glasses.

Two other works published in the 1970s have proved extremely influential: Danish economist Ester Boserup's *Woman's Role in Economic Development* (1970) and the collection of essays gathered by Hafkin and Bay in *Women in Africa* (1976) which have already been mentioned. While a good majority of the essays in the special issue of the CJAS focused on urban women, Boserup turned her attention to rural women, who still constitute the vast majority of the African female population. For Boserup, colonialism did not liberate African women; it left them worse off. While agreeing with many of the historians who argued that African women were not the ciphers they had been portrayed by missionaries and earlier writings, Boserup focused on the contemporary challenges faced by women in Africa and elsewhere in the "third world." Boserup distinguished between "male" and "female" farming and argued that in Africa, where women did much of the farming, polygyny was economically rational. In Africa, where women were the primary cultivators in a continent that was overwhelmingly agrarian, Boserup argued that

> virtually all Europeans shared the opinion that men are superior to women in the art of farming; and it seemed to follow that for the development of agriculture male farming ought to be promoted to replace female farming. Many Europeans did all they could to achieve this.[12]

---

[12] Ester Boserup, *Woman's Role in Economic Development* (New York: St. Martin's Press, 1970), 4.

Boserup's book is typically cited as the point of departure for the emergence of the women-in-development (WID) movement.[13] WID was the strategy advocated by women scholars and activists who insisted on the need to consciously include women's needs in development planning. Notwithstanding her influence, Boserup has not been without her critics. She has been taken to task from many angles, from her failure to criticize capitalism to her "neoliberal" biases that fail to question the operating assumptions on which "development" is founded. Others have taken exception to Boserup's notion of distinct systems of "female farming" versus "male farming" and to her insistence that the gender division of labor is at the basis of all societies.[14] Although Boserup was an economist, her work was widely read by scholars in other fields, especially those self-identified as feminist.

Feminist was a label many of the women scholars studying African women's history, such as Margaret Strobel, embraced. The works of these early students of African women's history, who continue to be active, including Margaret Jean Hay (PhD, 1972), Iris Berger (PhD, 1973), and Claire Robertson (1974), are still widely read. The 1976 volume edited by historians Hafkin and Bay, which brought together scholars in various disciplines, including political science and sociology, remains a classic. The essays focus on women's activities in the "public sphere," examining changes in the economic, political, and associational lives of women. The editors' project was twofold: to focus on the mass of women rather than "exceptional" women and to focus on women as agents of change rather than on their relations to men. This was a clear attempt to move away from what the editors saw as the shortcomings of previous works on African women, which either focused on women only in relation to husbands and fathers or told only triumphant tales of female rulers. The authors consciously distinguished between "private" and "public" spheres, framing their studies around the latter.

The distinction between "public" and "private" spheres is also implicit in one of the most influential works to come out of this period, Karen Sacks's *Sisters and Wives* (1979). Employing a socialist-feminist approach, which integrates class and sex analyses, and drawing data from six African societies, Sacks argues that a woman's status and roles in society depended on two things, the first being whether she was a sister or a wife. The second factor, according to Sacks, was whether she lived in a class-based or non-class (kin-based or communal) society. Not treating women as a single category, Sacks rejects the notion that women's subordination is biologically determined and thus universal, arguing instead that women's status must be located specifically in time and place. In non-class societies, sisters fared well compared to brothers. However, as the role of kin diminished and the state assumed a more powerful role, only those with close ties to the power structures of state fared well, with neither sisters nor wives—unless they were elite—doing so well. Sacks's concern with the question of women's status and her arguments about its mutability have kept the interest of scholars of women in Africa and elsewhere.

The 1980s saw many works focused on "women's roles" and the "status of women" in society. Often, the underlying principle—sometimes stated, sometimes not—of books and articles on women's

---

[13] Other major developments in the 1970s include the 1975 World Conference of the International Women's Year in Mexico City and the United Nation's declaration of the Decade for Women (1976–1985). These activities were propelled by activists and scholars influenced by Boserup's thesis. USAID opened a WID section in 1973. See http://www.usaid.gov/our_work/cross-cutting_programs/wid/about.html.

[14] See, for example, Suellen Huntington, "Issues in Woman's Role in Economic Development: Critique and Alternatives," *Journal of Marriage and the Family* XXXVII (November 1975): 1001–1012. Probably the best-known critique of Boserup is in Lourdes Beneria and Gita Sen, "Accumulation, Reproduction and 'Women's Role in Economic Development': Boserup Revisited" *Signs* 7, no. 2 (Winter 1982): 279–298.

roles and status was the question of whether women were better off or not as a result of European colonial rule. Some authors argued that African women had low status in their societies, while others maintained the opposite. The more thoughtful authors pointed to the need to be attentive to the ways in which the structures of African societies may differ from the Western model, thus making the use of certain concepts and labels problematic. For example, in her study of women in nineteenth-century Lesotho, Elizabeth Eldredge notes that "domestic units in Africa did not resemble their counterparts in Europe: both men and women had obligations outside of the household and were less dependent on each other within the household."[15]

From the Colonial Past to the Present

In the twentieth century, women in southeastern Nigeria mounted a war against the forces of British colonial rule. More than fifty women lost their lives, and the number of those that sustained injuries was no doubt much higher. The women who participated in the Women's War of 1929 targeted all the symbols of the new political order—the offices and homes of colonial officialdom, as well as its representatives. The "disturbances" and the demands made by the women at the Commission of Inquiry, set up by the colonial government to investigate, surprised British officialdom, which insisted that part of its civilizing mission was the liberation of African women from the shackles of tradition. The women who testified before the Commission consistently demanded that women be represented in the new institutions that had been set up by the colonial government, but colonial authorities failed to appreciate the extent to which women felt aggrieved by colonial policies that rendered them invisible. Although the women organized and carried out this rebellion, it did not stop colonial authorities and missionaries from continuing to insist that African women were "no better than cattle and sheep" and completely lacking in agency.

Almost eighty years later, such assumptions about African women continue to prevail. Researchers and development workers invariably point to "tradition" as the reason for African women's inability to assert themselves in the public sphere. Take, for example, the statement issued by a recent international summit convened to address the economic crisis in Africa: "In Africa, the gender gap is even wider and the situation is more complex due to the cultural and traditional context which is anchored in beliefs, norms and practices which breed discrimination and feminised poverty. There is growing evidence that the number of women in Africa living in poverty has increased disproportionately to that of men." This was the conclusion of the Eighth Meeting of the African Partnership Forum (APF) in Germany in May 2007. The APF was founded in 2003 as a forum "to facilitate Africa's economic growth."[16] If "tradition" is to blame for the "feminised poverty" of African women, to what then should we ascribe the fact that there is "growing evidence" that the rate of poverty for African women "has increased disproportionately"? Is it to a growth in African traditions that we should attribute this? If "tradition" is a given to the APF and "development" workers, why then is the rate of poverty for African women increasing disproportionately?

---

[15] Elizabeth A. Eldredge, "Women in Production: The Economic Role of Women in Nineteenth-Century Lesotho" *Signs* 16, no. 4 (Summer 1991): 709.

[16] The members of the APF are Western donor countries that give more than $100 million in aid; multilateral institutions such as the UN, World Bank, IMF, WTO; African regional institutions such as ECOWAS, SADC, ADB; as well as the Pan-African NEPAD and AU.

There are practices in Africa that hamper women's ability to lead economically prosperous lives, but to point to "tradition" as *the* root cause of African women's poverty obscures more than it illuminates. First of all, there is no single "tradition" that exists all over Africa. Secondly, what is considered "traditional" in African communities is often of relatively recent vintage and was colonially generated. Foreign aid workers and African men are too eager to point to "tradition" when excluding women from development projects. For example, in Kenya, local men—and "development officers"—are often quick to insist that it is "untraditional" for women to own land. The truth is, of course, that individual land ownership is not "traditional" for anyone in Kenya; individual land ownership was usefully introduced by British colonial authorities keen to claim the most fertile lands for Europeans.

The idea conveyed when "tradition" is blamed for African women's economic predicament is that African beliefs and practices constitute part of an ancient, unchanging way of life, not easily amenable to change. The reality too often is that aid and development workers assume that the existence of "tradition" makes African women incapable of acting as authors of their own lives. Some activists and scholars point to the unwillingness or incapacity of development workers to engage African women in dialogue as a fundamental obstacle to the success of many so-called aid programs. Barbara Rogers's book, *The Domestication of Women*, shows just how futile and wasteful can be well-intentioned but ill-conceived projects devised by men and women who "go to help" without ever bothering to listen or even consult with those whose lives are supposed to be impacted by their projects. Brown's book is a catalog of failures spearheaded by various arms of the United Nations and other multilateral organizations. The point is not that large organizations are doomed to failure but that they must learn to listen and to acknowledge that poor people are not students only, but also teachers. Women at the so-called grassroots level must be heard because they have intimate knowledge of their lives and needs. Fundamental to any task of understanding Africa is the acknowledgment of the continent's diversity. Not even within a single country do sweeping generalizations hold. It is hard to imagine how grand schemes based on abstract ideas about African women and "traditions" are not destined for failure.

As we acknowledge that "tradition" cannot be the beginning and the end of any analysis of African women's economic realities, we must also acknowledge that the facts of African women's lives do not make for happy reading. The statistics, while they do not capture the reality of women's lives in all the different contexts in which they live, give an overall and pretty grim picture. Of all the continents, Africa has the largest percentage of people living in poverty, with signs that ever larger numbers will be threatened by poverty in the future. HIV/AIDS, for example, is making millions of African children AIDS orphans. The HIV/AIDS epidemic, which is recognized to be of significant consequence for economic development, affects women in notably higher numbers than men in some African countries. In Zimbabwe, Zambia, Kenya, and Malawi, this has resulted in a lower life expectancy for women than men, the reverse of what typically obtains. Although African women work longer hours, they own disproportionately less than African men. African women receive only 1 percent of credit facilities extended to agricultural producers. Yet, at least 70 percent of African women are involved in agriculture.[17]

Despite these disheartening statistics, aid is certainly not the panacea. In the first place, "aid assistance" and "development programs" have typically discriminated against women. In the second place,

---

[17] For the statistics, consult the annual reports issued by the African Development Bank.

attempts to incorporate women into development programs may be tempted to "bring women up to men's standards." The economic situation of African men is no model! But the strongest argument against aid is the fact that thirty years of "development aid" have produced little beyond huge amounts of crushing debt. In 2000, African external debt accounted for over 51 percent of GDP; by 2003, it had fallen to 49 percent of GDP. Such global figures obscure the particularly harsh reality for individual countries: for Malawi external debt was almost 200 percent of its GDP in 2006; for Sao Tome and Principe, it was 350 percent![18] For Africans, women and men, to become economically more prosperous, African economies have to be radically restructured. Most of the economies in Africa remain monocultures. There can be no prosperity for the majority of its citizens if a country relies on the exportation of low-value raw materials that are sent to other countries where they are processed and then returned to the world market with a much-increased price tag. Exporting copper or coffee will only make a few individuals or multinationals rich. Even high-value extractive commodities such as petroleum have proven, again and again, a curse rather than a blessing, bringing a lot of environmental degradation and little or no benefit to locals.

For several decades now, Africa has been the recipient of vast sums of money in the form of development assistance. Whatever one's views of the pros and cons of such aid, it is impossible to judge these programs, including WID and Gender and Development (GAD), a success, if the goal is poverty reduction or eradication. Today, there are more Africans in poverty than there were fifty years ago, and according to several indicators, the percentage of poor women is increasing disproportionately. The only viable avenue to "making poverty history" in Africa is for Africa to increase its share of the world market. Here, the role of African governments, and the foreign governments that sustain them, is paramount. Clearly, investors will invest only in places where profit seems likely and stability can be guaranteed. For too long, African regimes have failed to provide a climate attractive to investors. People cannot farm or run factories if they are dodging bullets or coerced to fight wars. Governments cannot invest in infrastructure if they use their countries' wealth to buy military equipment.[19]

Can Poor or Uneducated Women Speak?

In our contemporary world, formal education is seen as a prerequisite for success, and sometimes even the ability to think rationally. When formal education is deemed a neccesary a criterion for participation in discussions about one's life, the door is immediately shut to the recipients of aid and development efforts. It is unfortunate that too often formal education is treated by development professionals as a fetish. Being poor or "uneducated" should not be equated with being stupid. The success of the Grameen Bank in Bangladesh provides one example of poor, uneducated women who know what they

---

[18] For a critique of aid and development policies for Africa, see Ejikeme, "Aid for Money," forthcoming; Patrick Bond, *Looting Africa: The Economics of Exploitation* (Durban: University of KwaZulu-Natal Press and London and NY: Zed Press, 2007); William Easterly, *The White Man's Burden; Why the West's Efforts to Aid the Rest Have Done So Much Ill and So Little Good* (New York: Penguin, 2007).

[19] Britain's former prime minister, Tony Blair, was implicated in a scandal involving the government of Tanzania and the largest British arms manufacturer, BAE Systems. It appears Blair "convinced" Tanzania to sign a contract that the Tanzanians had initially rejected strenuously as overpriced and unnecessary. Claire Short, who served as Blair's international development secretary, called the deal "useless and hostile to the interests of Tanzania."

want and successfully implement it when given the opportunity (via credit, for example). In my own research on Onitsha, Nigeria, an important center of trade, where in the nineteenth century women controlled the marketplace, I found that their lack of literacy had been no barrier to women's ability to accumulate enormous wealth. Students of West African history are very familiar with self-help microfinance groups organized by women; such groups have a deep history, long predating the current "discovery" of microfinance in the West, due in large part to the award of the 2006 Nobel Peace Prize to Mohamed Yunus, founder of the Grameen Bank. The kind of aid with which we are most familiar, involving "experts" going from the global North to tell people in the global South what to do, cannot bring poor people permanently out of poverty; this is especially true for the ambitious and expensive projects based on government-to-government monetary transfers. On the other hand, assistance that is conceived as a partnership and actually involves the "recipients" in the planning and implementation can succeed.

The voices of African women themselves, whose lives are the targets of development and aid projects, must be heard. African women scholars, for example Felicia Ekejiuba and Achola Pala, who have been involved with development agencies and programs, have written important critiques interrogating the categories used to describe African women's lives, arguing that starting from incorrect assumptions harms the very women whose lives the projects are designed to assist.[20] In the context of the discussion here, it is worth noting that the UN Commission on the Status of Women declared its theme for 2008 as Financing for Gender Equality and the Empowerment of Women. In February 2007, the Commission convened an informal expert panel to discuss how to move forward on this agenda. It is disheartening— but, unfortunately, not surprising—that no African women were on the list of panelists; indeed, the only African—the minister of finance for Zambia—was also the only man.

Reframing the Categories, Rethinking Sex and Gender

Questions about the impact of colonial rule continue to be very contentious, impinging in important ways on national and international policies that affect the lives of African women today. African women scholars play a prominent role in these discussions: as soon as African women began to enter the Western academy, they began to speak against the ways in which African women have been framed in Western scholarship. Felicia Ekejiuba, Achola Pala, Nkiri Nzegwu, and Ifi Amadiume, for example, have written movingly about their inability to locate the real women they knew in their own communities in the books on African women they encountered as students pursuing graduate studies in the West. I turn now to two works that have been and remain influential in debates on "framing" African women. Published a decade apart, both are by African women.

Ifi Amadiume's *Male Daughters and Female Husbands,* published in 1987, radically challenges the ways in which African societies, and especially the lives of women in them, have been described by Western scholars and writers. Amadiume argues that the concepts and types derived from studying Western societies may be inapplicable to African ones. Whereas Kamene Okonjo, Felicia Ekejiuba, and Bolanle Awe had argued that a dual-sex system was the basis of political organization and the deploy-ment of power in some communities in Africa, Amadiume insists that in Nnobi Igbo society, the focus

---

[20] This is in line, of course, with the findings of Barbara Brown in *Domestication of Women: Discrimination in Developing Societies* (New York: St. Martin's Press, 1980).

of her study, the most important factor about the gender system was its fluidity, with sex and gender not always permanently aligned. Amadiume faults Okonjo, the best-known proponent of the dual-sex thesis, for having "fallen into the trap of classifying women into a single category," despite much data to the contrary.[21] Amadiume insists that in Nnobi individuals were able, indeed sometimes required, to cross the dominant lines of sex-gender. Both the gender system and language were flexible, allowing women "to be classified as 'males' in terms of power and authority over others."[22] Like Sacks, Amadiume points out that women's status varied depending on whether they were wives or daughters, with daughters enjoying superior status.[23] Going beyond Sacks, Amadiume insists that the classification "husband" was not biology-bound. "All Igbo daughters of a patrilineage are addressed as 'husbands' by the wives of the patrilineage. This, among other practices, negates any assumption of rigidity in the association of gender to sex in Igbo culture in general. More importantly, it poses the question of class and gender division of women."[24]

Amadiume attributes Igbo women's ability to achieve high power to the flexibility of the gender system, taking to task those scholars who posit a universal subordination of women "at all times in history and in all cultures." Indeed, Amadiume suggests that in certain African societies matriarchy, not patriarchy, has been the foundation of social organization.[25] She describes as prejudicial the anthropological insistence that only societies in which women rule completely are "matriarchal," yet the term "patriarchy" is used without the same qualifications: there are no societies in which men are completely in control, yet one labels many societies "patriarchal" without equivocation. Amadiume argues that African matriarchy was linked to maternity, which was seen as sacred, thus linking women's power to the spiritual-sacred realm.[26] She also asserts that Igbo women had a strong sense of solidarity, despite differences in economic class and in status as wives or daughters:

Igbo women's strong commitment to female solidarity was more advantageous in the period before electoral politics and the forming of political parties when, to a large extent, it could be claimed that there was a unity of purpose in women's struggles. This is in strong contrast to modern Nigerian history, which is typified by the exploitation of women's organizational ability and sense of female solidarity by male-dominated political parties and individual female political careerists. [Nina] Mba's conclusion is supported here by the evidence presented here; both show that women in Nigeria had more power under the traditional dual-sex political system, which gave them greater autonomy as women. I have, however, stressed the flexibility of the gender construct which modified the traditional dual-sex system. Mba's

---

[21] Ifi Amadiume, *Male Daughters, Female Husbands: Gender and Sex in an African Society* (London: Zed Books, 1987), 16 and 52.

[22] ibid., 185.

[23] As indicated above, this is an argument central to Karen Sacks's Sisters and Wives. See Helen K. Henderson, "Ritual Roles of Women in Onitsha Ibo Society" (PhD diss., University of California, Berkeley, 1969), in which the author also makes this point.

[24] Amadiume, *Male Daughters, Female Husbands*, 180.

[25] Ifi Amadiume, *Afrikan Matriarchal Foundations: The Igbo Case* (London: Karnak House, 1987).

[26] The idea that African women have or should organize on the basis of motherhood has been made by a number of African women scholars and activists. By contrast, in the Western feminist tradition, motherhood has often been seen as confining and at the root of women's subordination to men.

study also shows that Igbo women are politically disadvantaged by their lack of titles in comparison to Yoruba women, who can still buy chieftaincy titles during a political career, just as men can.[27]

Yoruba women are the focus of *The Invention of Women* by sociologist Oyeronke Oyewumi. The book's publication in 1997 was a landmark event because the author challenges the very foundations on which the study of African women was based. Oyewumi argues that "women" did not exist in Yoruba Oyo society prior to contact with Europeans. Although Yoruba recognized anatomical differences between men and women, Oyo society, Oyewumi maintains, did not make this a basis for social organization, and, thus, women were not constituted as a social category in Oyo Yoruba society. While Amadiume argues that women sometimes achieved power and took on male symbols of power, Oyeronke Oyewumi rejects the very notion of gendered power. Power is power is power, Oyewumi asserts.

Oyewumi argues that in Yoruba society, seniority occupies the place of sex in the West as a category of social organization. Because seniority can be determined only relationally, individuals do not have fixed social identities, Oyewumi insists. According to Oyewumi, while the factors that organized social life in Yoruba society prior to colonization by the West were polyvalent, seniority was the most important principle of social organization. Oyewumi is in full agreement with Amadiume that the categories used to analyze Western societies are not universally applicable. Importing categories from Europe into Africa, Oyewumi argues, make it impossible to apprehend the organizing principle(s) at work in African communities.

Language is at the center of Oyewumi's argument. She traces, for example, the recent history of two Yoruba words, *oga* and *aare*. These words originally were used to designate "boss," without regard to whether the boss was a man or woman. Now these words are reserved for men, and women bosses are referred to as "madam." According to Oyewumi, the language question is critical because Yoruba, like many other African languages, does not have a gender-specific pronoun, and titles and professions do not generally indicate the sex of the individual. As Amadiume noted with regard to Igbo, Oyewumi points out that in Yoruba the words "wife" and "husband" are not sex-specific: in other words, either can describe a man or a woman. Yet, when scholars encounter the word "husband," they assume it applies to males and use the English pronoun "he." Similarly kings are assumed to be male, without any attempt at corroboration. Since the word for "ruler" in Yoruba is non-gender specific, such assumptions are highly problematic. Oyewumi quotes the nineteenth century Yoruba missionary and linguist Samuel Johnson who stated that "our translators, in their desire to find a word expressing the English idea of sex rather than of age, coined the. . . . words *arakonri,* i.e., the male relative; and *arabrinrin,* the female relative; these words have always to be explained to the pure but illiterate Yoruba man."[28] Further, Oyewumi insists that in Yoruba speech because pronouns are ungendered, the pivotal distinction is not between "she" and "he," but rather between "older" and "younger." She notes, "It is possible to hold a long and detailed conversation about a person without indicating the gender of that person, unless the anatomy is central to the issue under discussion. . . . There is, however, considerable anxiety about establishing seniority in any social interaction."[29]

Oyewumi argues that Yoruba has a variety of ways to "locate" an individual, seniority being the most important, while in the West the result of the importance of sight is that the physical is elevated

---

[27] Amadiume, *Male Daughters, Female Husbands,* 183.

[28] Oyeronke Oyewumi, *The Invention of Women: Making an African Sense of Western Gender Discourses* (Minneapolis, MN: University of Minnesota Press, 1997), 41.

[29] ibid., 40.

over other realms, for example, the metaphysical. The "visual logic" of the West produces a "biological determinism." By this she means that the anatomical sex of men and women are thought to define their essence, and, thus, body-based categories such as "women" are privileged over non-body-based ones such as "traders." She goes on to state that

> from a Yoruba stance, the body appears to have an exaggerated presence in western thought and social practice, including feminist theories. In the Yoruba world, particularly in pre-nineteenth-century Oyo culture, society was conceived to be inhabited by people in relation to one another. That is, the "physicality" of maleness or femaleness did not have social antecedents and therefore did not constitute social categories.[30]

In the case of the Yoruba, Oyewumi asserts that "the frame of reference is based more on a combination of senses anchored by the auditory."[31] Given the primacy of the sense of sight in the West, Oyewumi says, it is logical to speak of a "worldview" with regard to Western societies, but she rejects the word "worldview" to describe the cultural logic of all societies, noting that the "world-sense" of some societies may not be predicated on the visual as in the West. Stressing the dangers of universalized categories, Oyewumi insists that "missing in many Western-derived analyses is the realization that more important categories may be at work, categories informed by and constituted from the indigenous frame of reference. . . . Other crucial categories could be those who were born under the full moon or the second child of the second wife. One could go on, but the point is that Western categories like gender are globalized and deployed as universally valid even as other more important local categories may have been rendered irrelevant and therefore inconceivable."[32]

Oyewumi stands unequivocally on the side of those who argue that colonial rule was a net loss for African women. Rejecting the notion of a sex-gender system as a universal, Oyewumi maintains that European colonizers introduced a gendered and racist worldview with overrule in Africa. Oyewumi catalogs the setbacks that Yoruba women experienced under colonial rule. Firstly, the colonial school promoted a system of scholarship that was gendered and discriminated against women. Secondly, the church also preached that women were less than men, and, indeed, the school and the church were intimately linked because much schooling was in the hands of the church. Thirdly, the coming of wage labor also led to further distance between men and women, with women largely excluded from wage labor, and the kinds of work that remained outside the system of wage labor became devalued at the same time. Fourth, the colonizers, with their own views on women and men, passed or enabled laws that discriminated against women, from the introduction of the alienation of land to so-called customary law.[33]

The thrust of Oyewumi's theses has led to much debate. Yet it is worth noting that, in its details, similar arguments have been put forward previously. For example, on the importance of seniority in Yoruba society, there is a great deal of agreement among those who study the Yoruba, and on that point, Oyewumi is in consensus with all major students of Yoruba. Indeed, there are many other points on which Oyewumi is in well-known company, for instance, the notion that African "customs" or traditions, often now

---

[30] ibid., 13.
[31] ibid., 30.
[32] ibid., 77.
[33] ibid., chap. 4.

enshrined in books of "customary law," are not as ancient as African males and the colonial authorities who wrote them down would have one believe. The best-known proponent of this argument is Neil Chanock, whose 1982 essay is widely cited as a positive contribution to the understanding and the study of Africa.[34] The argument that the West is ocular-centric is not new, having been made frequently by distinguished Western theorists. Speaking of this, the philosopher Hannah Arendt noted, "from the very outset, in formal philosophy, thinking has been thought of in terms of seeing. . . . The predominance of sight is so deeply embedded in Greek speech, and therefore in our conceptual language.[35] Whether one accepts some or none of the specifics of Oyewumi's arguments, she cannot be faulted for insisting that societies must be analyzed using categories that derive from the cultural logic of those societies.

Not a Pastime but a Priority: Reframing African Women

From women rulers to struggling peasants, the study of African women today ranges over a wide spectrum. Scholars of African women's history now generally agree that women in Africa, like those elsewhere, cannot be studied as a homogenous category. Class, religion, ethnicity, and race, as well as a host of other factors, must be taken into account.[36] Again and again, historians return to this question: did colonial rule have a negative impact or a positive impact on the status of African women? Some scholars point to the fact that during colonialism, women came in significant numbers to so-called native courts to sue for divorce as a sign that the new dispensation offered them choices that they did not have previously and afforded them greater agency. Writing about Nigeria, Nina Mba argued that although European colonial rule negatively impacted women in terms of political participation, in other ways, women benefited. Pointing to the marriage ordinance, Mba argues that colonial rule had a positive impact on women because it gave them the right to inherit from their husbands.[37]

While arguments continue about the status of African women in the past and the impact of European colonial rule on African women, the most heated debate in the study of African women, related yet distinct, is over whether the categories derived from the West are applicable to Africa. For example, with reference to the issue of gains made by married women as a result of colonial intervention, Oyewumi dismisses any suggestion that colonialism benefited women by allowing them to inherit from their husbands. She finds such a conclusion problematic because "the constitution of a new category of property called marital property meant that wives lost their independent property rights and that, by the same token, husbands could now take over their wives' property."[38] In line with her argument about the need to understand and analyze women in terms of their relational identities, Oyewumi adds, "the positioning of wives as the beneficiaries of husbands also meant that the rights of some other women,

---

[34] Neil Chanock, "Making Customary Law: Men, Women, and Courts in Colonial Northern Rhodesia," in African *Women and the Law: Historical Perspectives*, ed. M.J. Hay and M. Wright (Boston University, 1982), 53–67. See also Chanock, *Law, Custom and Social Order: The Colonial Experience in Malawi and Zambia* (New York: Cambridge University Press, 1985).

[35] Quoted in David Levin, *Modernity and the Hegemony of Vision* (Berkeley: University of California Press, 1993), 2

[36] See, for example, Margaret Jean Hay and Sharon Stichter, eds., *African Women South of the Sahara* (London and New York: Longman, 1984); see also Claire Robertson and Iris Berger, eds., *African Women and the Law and Women and Class in Africa* (New York: Africana Publishing, 1986).

[37] See Nina Emma Mba, *Nigerian Women Mobilized: Women's Political Activity in Southern Nigeria, 1900–1965* (Berkeley: University of California,1982), 54.

[38] Oyewumi, *The Invention of Women*, 128.

such as mothers, sisters, and daughters, were abrogated as well."[39] Thus, Amadiume's and Oyewumi's contribution is to challenge us to desist from relying on assumptions rather than inquiry. Whether or not, for example, one accepts the argument that the absence of male and female pronouns indicates a great deal about power across the lines of sex, surely it means something. The solution is not to ignore the absence of these pronouns but to interrogate fully this practice.

Do categories or conceptual frameworks really matter? They matter a great deal. Let us take, for example, a concept that remains quite hegemonic, despite challenges to it—the sexual division of labor. If women (and men) do not exist as social categories, there can be no sexual division of labor. If there is no sexual division of labor, this would have huge ramifications in terms of how societies and social phenomena should be studied. The question of how we frame our subject(s) of study is fundamental. We cannot import categories derived from elsewhere—no matter how hegemonic those places—and assume such categories are universally applicable. It is important to ask what it means if we now reserve a word (for example, the Yoruba oga, meaning roughly "boss") for men only when it was formerly used for men and women. It is important to understand that if we see communities as organized, as Felicia Ekejiuba advocates, on the basis of "hearthhold" (i.e., a woman and her children) rather than "household" (by which researchers typically assume a male head of household and his "dependents") this can have far-reaching consequences not only for the conclusions we draw, but also for the questions that we ask.

It is important to note that the battle lines of debate in African women's history are not drawn in any crude fashion—African versus Western scholars. Two recent books make this point. At the heart of Tabitha Kanogo's *African Womanhood* and Nwando Achebe's *Farmers, Traders, Warriors and Kings* is the question of the impact of European colonial rule on African women. While Kanogo traces the ways in which women exploited the spaces opened up by colonial rule to assert greater autonomy and agency, Achebe's sketch of the life of the only female "warrant chief" in colonial southeastern Nigeria argues forcefully for the need to attend to the question of appropriate "frames." In her discussion of the life and career of Ahebi Ugbabe, Achebe argues that studies of Igbo political life that fail to attend to the spiritual realm will necessarily be flawed. This pursuit of appropriate categories will continue to be an uphill struggle because we live in a political world in which the West is dominant. Western typologies dominate, and the West is the central site of production of knowledge about Africa. If hegemonic knowledge about Africa is produced primarily in the West, will the agenda not be set inevitably according to the concerns of those in the West? It is worth noting in this context that the African women scholars whose views have been discussed here have all spent considerable time—or live—in the West. Western-educated scholars have been trained to utilize Western typologies, yet their life experiences in Africa make them see that these typologies are not necessarily universal truths. Encountering Western scholarship through African eyes forces us to rethink the Western vision (and version) of Africa, and this can be vitally rewarding.

REFERENCES

Achebe, Nwando. *Farmers, Traders, Warriors, and Kings: Female Power in Northern Igboland, 1900-1960.* Portsmouth, NH: Heinemann, 2005.
Amadiume, Ifi. *Afrikan Matriarchal Foundations: The Igbo Case.* London: Karnak House, 1987.
———. *Male Daughters, Female Husbands: Gender and Sex in an African Society.* London: Zed Books, 1987.

---

[39] ibid.

Awe, Bolanle. "The Iyalode in the Traditional Yoruba Political System." In *Sexual Stratification: A Cross-cultural View,* edited by Alice Schlegel. New York: Columbia University Press, 1977.

Boserup, Ester. *Woman's Role in Economic Development.* New York: St. Martin's Press, 1970.

Boris, Eileen, and Nupur Chaudhuri, eds. *Voices of Women Historians: The Personal, the Political, the Professional.* Bloomington: Indiana University Press, 1999.

Chanock, Neil. "Making Customary Law: Men, Women, and Courts in Colonial Northern Rhodesia." In *African Women and the Law: Historical Perspectives,* edited by M.J. Hay and M. Wright, 53–67. Boston University, 1982.

Chanock ———. Law, Custon, amd Social Order: The Colonial Experience in Malawi and Zambia. New York: Cambridge University Press, 1985.

Ekejiuba, Felicia. "Omu Okwei." *Journal of the Historical Society of Nigeria* (1966).

Ekejiuba ———. "Down to Fundamentals: Women-Centered Heartholds in Rural West Africa," in Deborah Facy Bryceson, ed., *Women Wielding the Hoe.* Oxford: Oxford University Press, 1995.

Eldredge, Elizabeth A. "Women in Production: The Economic Role of Women in Nineteenth-Century Lesotho." *Signs* 16, no. 4 (Summer 1991).

Hafkin, Nancy J., and Edna G. Bay. *Women in Africa: Studies in Social and Economic Change.* Stanford University Press, 1976.

Hay, Margaret Jean, and Sharon Stichter, eds. *African Women South of the Sahara.* London: Longman, 1964.

Kanogo, Tabitha. *African Womanhood in Colonial Kenya, 1900-50.* Oxford: Ohio University Press, 2005.

Lebeuf, Annie. "The Role of Women in the Political Organization of African Societies." In *Femmes d'Afrique Noire,* edited by Denise Paulme. Paris: Mouton, 1960.

Leith-Ross, Sylvia. *African Women: A Study of the Ibo of Nigeria.* London: Routledge and Kegan Paul, 1939.

———. *Beyond the Niger.* Westport, CT: Negro Universities Press, 1971, first published 1951.

Levin, David. *Modernity and the Hegemony of Vision.* Berkeley: University of California Press, 1993.

MacCormack, Carol Hoffer. "Mende and Sherbro Women in High Office." *CJAS* (1972).

———. "Madam Yoko: Ruler of the Kpa Mende Confederacy." In *Woman, Culture and Society,* edited by Michele Z. Rosaldo and Louise Lamphere. Stanford University Press, 1974.

Mba, Nina Emma. *Nigerian Women Mobilized: Women's Political Activity in Southern Nigeria, 1900–1965.* Berkeley: University of California, 1982.

Murray, Jocelyn. Review of *Old Wives' Tales: Life Stories of African Women,* by Iris Andreski (New York, Schocken Books, 1970). African Studies Review 18, no. 3 (Dec. 1975): 131-132.

Nzegwu, Nkiru. "Globalization and the Jenda Journal." *Jenda: A Journal of Culture and African Women Studies,* 2001. http://www.africaresource.com/jenda/vol1.1/nzegwu1.html

Okonjo, Kamene. "The Dual-Sex Political System in Operation: Igbo Women and Community Politics in Midwestern Nigeria." In *Women in Africa: Studies in Social and Economic Change,* edited by Nancy J. Hafkin and Edna G. Bay. Stanford University Press, 1976.

Oyewumi, Oyeronke. *The Invention of Women: Making an African Sense of Western Gender Discourses.* Minneapolis, MN: University of Minnesota Press, 1997.

Pala, Achola. "Definitions of Women and Development: An African Perspective," *Signs* 3, no. 1: Autumn 1977.

Paulme, Denise, ed. *Femmes d'Afrique Noire.* Paris: Mouton, 1960.

Robertson, Claire, and Iris Berger, eds. *African Women and the Law and Women and Class in Africa.* New York: Africana Publishing, 1986.

Rogers, Barbara. *The Domestication of Women: Discrimination in Developing Societies.* New York: St. Martin's Press, 1980.

Sacks, Karen. *Sisters and Wives: The Past and Future of Sexual Equality.* Westport, Conn.: Greenwood Press, 1979.

Van Allen, Judith. "'Aba Riots' or Igbo 'Women's War'? Ideology, Stratification, and the Invisibility of Women." In *Women in Africa: Studies in Social and Economic Change,* edited by Nancy J. Hafkin and Edna G. Bay. Stanford University Press, 1976.

Chapter 18

BETWEEN MULTIPLE IDEALS OF FEMINISM
An Intercontinental Engagement with Womanhood
A Young Scholar's Response and Commentary

Kendra Sundal

This commentary explores some of the multiple meanings of feminism derived from my shifting position and my encounter with different gender constructs during my extended stay in Ghana. I write reflectively based on readings of the cultural critique of feminism by leading African scholars, including Anene Ejikeme;[1] personal struggles with the conflicted identities of my own adolescent constructs of feminist identity; and an abrupt realization of the varied notions of female identity and of gender roles and relations in Ghana.

My intent is partly to shed light, from the perspective of a young Western scholar, on the ways in which an impoverished hegemonial approach and assumptions about women's identity and agency in other parts of the world ultimately weaken the quest for meaningful change and gender rights. However, let me emphasize at the outset that this examination of difference and commonality within feminism can by no means capture the complexities of all locations or their varied histories of gender. Despite my exhilaration about the liberating lenses that allowed me to see the many ways to be feminist and empowered, I am not trying to glorify women in Ghana or be overcritical of Western or U.S. feminist thought and practice. Such a position would require a deliberate misrepresentation of the profound ideological and philosophical diversities in national and global communities of women and feminist activists.

A few more caveats are in order: I do not imagine that my story is universal or argue that my experience abroad necessarily revealed all the gender identities, roles, and relations that I describe here. Just as my own feminist experience is singularly my own in the broad context of U.S. society so, too, are the experiences and roles of women I met in Ghanaian society. Feminism is, indeed, "simultaneously an intensely personal and collective experience." (Soyinka-Airewele, 2006).

What I am driven to convey is how baffled I was when my stereotypes of Africa and African women were challenged and how the impact of my journey changed my search for a paradigm to guide my understanding of the world in which we live, with its global hierarchies and representations of the Other, particularly, the African Other. I may still be charged with reductionism or unwarranted generalization about feminism based on a relatively limited stay in Ghana. I hope, however, that my own

---

[1] Anene Ejikeme, "Let the Women Speak! and Listen," January 17, 2008, www.pambazuka.org/en/category/comment/45464.

reflections will help other young scholars form more nuanced views of gender and the complex realties of the African continent and provoke the human capacity for change that occurs when we open ourselves to the internal conflict that develops from challenging our prejudices.

A Personal Voyage Around My Feminist Identity: A Starting Point

Early in my education, I developed the impression that a strong woman was one who could compete on an even keel with any man. The epitome of feminist struggles was apparently women's equality. I, like any other woman, had not merely a right, but also *a duty* to be as educated, capable, creative, talented, skilled, and intellectual as any man I confronted in my lifetime. The critical term was *duty,* which placed the onus, or responsibility, and, ultimately, the guilt and blame for failure on the woman. Equality and equal rights in a gender context required males to be as capable of parenting, cooking, and cleaning as females. I certainly valued my right—again, my obligation—to be an independent and confident woman, yet in many ways, many of my peers and I thought that being strong meant acting like a man.

The most powerful and desirable role models were women who competed on an equal plane, almost indistinguishably, with men. Although the ascendancy of women in economic, social, and professional spheres was certainly a triumph, equality's effects on women's personal choices and identities seemed to diminish increasingly. For me, a member of a new generation and intellectual cohort, equality translated finally into masculinity because surely notions of masculinity—not femininity—defined women as equal, powerful, and capable competitors in the "world of men." Masculinity suggested strength, intellect, common sense, emotional toughness, and driving ambition.

Mine are not unique struggles. Numerous debates and ongoing discourses reveal that despite the undeniably exciting achievements of various sectors of the feminist vanguard in the States and Europe, many women took the challenge to succeed and perform competitively as a call to sacrifice the stereotypically feminine qualities they thought would hinder their career goals and equality in the eyes of male peers. The perhaps unintended effect of feminist struggles continues to be evident in the discomfiting debate between these women and women who valuate womanhood through motherhood. This conflict is understandable considering the manipulation of motherhood by many societies, including Western ones, in which it has been a ceiling women with alternative goals, visions, and life agendas must break. I certainly regarded motherhood as the antipathy of feminist success. This dilemma can best be analyzed through its impact on the generational connections that much of contemporary feminist thinking, enriched by the experiences of women in Latin America, Africa, Asia, the Middle East, and Euro-America, considers critical to the support structures that sustain female lives and struggles.

Certainly, my grandmother, mother, and sister did what they wanted, but what they, presumably for their children, sacrificed—high-powered professions and financial, social, and political independence— were far too great. Surely these three women, who were also three of the most important people in my life, had deprived themselves of countless possibilities for the sake of motherhood and had evaded the obligation to attain their potential as feminists. Such as they are, these personal stories are part of a political problematic at the heart of popular discourses, policymaking, and legislation on women's rights, choice, employer responsibilities, employee rights, divorce settlements, and parental responsibilities and autonomy. How are women's rights and identities defined when delimited by motherhood?

The idea that mothers were somehow less successful, less driven, and less capable than men or women in the business world seemed to me to be present in the cultural atmosphere in which I came of age. Over time, it became easy to recognize the historical patterns that had shaped feminist thought before me. Starting with the masculine conception of God, particularly in the English language and apparently not universally held throughout history, I became disillusioned in fairly short step with the world and my own feminist potential. The gulf between theory and practice was alarming: Where, I wondered, were the female presidential candidates? Where were the female CEOs? Why were women earning seventy-five cents of every dollar men made? Imagery from the *The Stepford Wives*—their frighteningly submissive, robotic existence—was not just on the screen, but also exaggerated a lifestyle that limited women's possibilities.

U.S. feminists have long sought to redefine gender roles to empower women and achieve ever more equality by changing ideals of "femaleness," despite vastly different concepts of feminism in the United States. But with the second wave of feminism (1963–1982) came a presumption that femininity and power could not go hand in hand. The stay-at-home mom continues to struggle against an image of motherhood as unenlightened, unprogressive, submissive, degrading, self-deprecating, and retrogressive. While the law could inscribe women's equality and lead to creation of supportive programs, it could not transform the perception that having masculine traits was tantamount to gender equality.

Contradictions between reality and perception of women's lives in the West should have prevented hasty assumptions about women in Africa. My mother is a bold, outspoken, and wholly self-possessed personality who elected to stay at home and raise her children, and my father is the reserved, precise, and gentle-natured male who demonstrated the utmost respect for his extroverted, confident, independent, and driven wife. Their relationship contradicted my notions of gender realties and relations in a fascinating way, which only began to make sense to me while I was in Ghana.

A Voyage Around Feminist Identities: The Mediated Image

While studying in Ghana from 2006 to 2007, I began to reexamine my concept of gender and feminism and the extent to which it framed my notions of the identities and roles of African women. It was not too hard, but was remarkably unsettling, to recognize how much my ideas were based on unsupportable stereotypes of African women perpetuated by popular Western culture. Most interestingly, however, these were not merely stereotypes of the African woman as racial Other, but also projected constructs of the failed woman in Western society and some feminist discourses. If female empowerment is deemed to result solely from professional competitiveness and accomplishments on par with those of men, then the grim data on inequalities permit us to assume, wrongly, that the majority of women can then be constituted and explained as passive failed victims of patriarchy, not as successes who make choices as my mother did.

In spite of the work of phenomenal African scholars such as Obioma Nnaemeka,[2] Ama Ata Aidoo, Ifi Amadiume[3] (author of the illuminating text *Male Daughters, Female Husbands: Gender and Sex in an African Society*), and prominent feminist and human rights activist Nawal El Saadawi,[4] much of the

---

[2] Obioma Nnaemeka, ed., *Sisterhood, Feminisms and Power in Africa: From Africa to the Diaspora* (Trenton, NJ: Africa World Press, 1998) and *Female Circumcision and the Politics of Knowledge: African Women in Imperialist Discourses* (Westport, CT: Praeger Publishers, 2005).

[3] Ifi Amadiume, *Male Daughters, Female Husbands: Gender and Sex in an African Society* (London: Zed Books, 1987).

[4] Nal El Saadawi, *The Nawal El Saadawi Reader* (London and New York: Zed Books, 1997).

Euro-American world of feminists has persisted in imagining African women as a beleaguered species of hapless and voiceless victims of the dominant African male. Indeed, Anene Ejikeme describes that persistent tendency and its motivations in this volume. Though a large number of Western feminists, whose international collaboration with women in other parts of the world has generated a radical rethinking of the concept of women's strength and sense of self in other parts of the world, some schools of feminist thought continue to hamper international understanding of African women.

Here, I refer to Western feminists who uncritically accept the U.S. women's movement as the universal standard. They assume that African women lack any concept of women's rights, identity, and struggle. Too often such feminist activists feel an obligation to speak on behalf of African women. For a time I felt the same pull, and though I was uncomfortable speaking for others, I often subconsciously attempted to do so by promoting a set of unrealistic and potentially imperialist measures. Now, as Nnaemeka writes, I understand that "we can lend our voices to or speak up against problems facing others without necessarily speaking for them."[5] This is hard for an activist or feminist to accept when confronted by women's suffering, abuse, and subjugation, but accept it she must to promote gender discourse around the world.

From this commanding frame of the Western, feminist, global activism grew a slightly more hesitant generation, molded in part by the misrepresentations of the Other in U.S. pop culture. Cinema and media images of women around the world lack depth and cannot convey the layered and complex realities of women's empowerment, strength, and identity that exist even in the traditional roles disdained by many in the West and other parts of the world. African women, in particular, especially the so-called Black African primitive and the North African subjugated, Islamic types are systematically captured in literature, news media, and cinema through misleading stereotypes that convey an imaginary of voiceless passivity and a lack of agency.

Many of my generation first became acquainted with Africa by watching *The Lion King,* which perpetuated a vision of Africa associated with safaris and animal kingdoms. When Eddie Murphy brought us *Coming to America,*[6] the animal kingdom imagery joined a plethora of other stereotypes about African people. An American comedy about an African prince who seeks an intelligent and independent wife in the United States, *Coming to America* bombards its audience with pictures of African women as submissive and sexualized robots—or "African Stepford Wives." When the queen-to-be is presented to the prince, he pulls her aside to ask her about herself, only to find that she has apparently been trained to serve only him and has no opinions or ideas of her own. In fact, she cannot even bring herself to disobey his order that she hop on one foot while barking like a dog. Though masked as comedy, this scene displays a deeply problematic stereotype of African women as submissive, brainless, obedient dogs, ready to bend to the will of their husband-masters. Rather than being nurtured as individuals, they are raised to be wives and mothers, or if they prove unsuitable wife material, to be mistresses or servants. Americans consume these stereotypes with little resistance and even exploit them in promoting activism and aid programs. Deepening the divide between stereotype and reality, the African prince comes to "America" to find an intelligent, caring, progressive, and fairer-skinned bride.

---

[5] Obioma Nnaemeka, "Urban Spaces, Women's Places: Polygamy as a Sign in Mariama Bâ's Novels," in *The Politics of (M)Othering: Womanhood, Identity and Resistance in African Literature,* ed. Obioma Nnaemeka (New York: Routledge, 1997), 164

[6] Eddie Murphy, David Sheffield, and Barry Blaustein, *Coming to America,* VHS, directed by John Landis. (Eddie Murphy Productions and Paramount Pictures, 1988.)

Although the obedient African queen-to-be in *Coming to America* is lavishly rich and beautiful, rarely is the image of African women this "prosperous." To the contrary, the most prominent image is of extremely impoverished women, wearing little more than rags, helpless to save themselves or their children from starvation, genital mutilation, genocide, or AIDS. Unfortunately, the imagery provides fodder for external aid organizations that work from the premise that African women cannot help themselves. Presumably, whether ashamed and despondent or eager and excited, African women are viewed as victims waiting for Western feminists to speak out for African women's rights.[7] While there is, indeed, a socioeconomic crisis whose impact has been defined by the feminization of poverty, such a reality and the images that convey it speak to objective conditions and not necessarily the complex construction of women's identities.[8] The divide between these distinct issues is often lost in the mediated image, as Soyinka-Airewele has noted, because "women's identities and gender relations are influenced by the roles and material circumstances that surround the group and individual but are ultimately determined by a complex of often invisible factors that include religion, historical trajectories, cultural philosophies, and ambiguous social spaces: unfortunately, these subterranean factors rarely make their way into the contractual discourses that determine how women are portrayed."[9]

One controversial influence is female circumcision, increasingly called genital mutilation. In Martha Grise's "'Scarred for Life?': Representations of Africa and Female Genital Cutting on American Television News Magazines," she notes that not only has the practice of genital cutting existed for more than 2,000 years,[10] but also that it is a cultural practice found around the world. Those who dismiss it as symbolic of the male phallic obsession and patriarchal ownership of women's bodies have rarely stood ready to address, let alone encountered, the diversities of contexts, symbolisms, and evidences of women's agencies that complicate efforts to eliminate the practice. Its conceptualization as an emblem of female empowerment through secret ceremonies that endow participants with spiritual power for life in some societies or as a counterpart to the coming-of-age circumcision rites of men in other societies makes it clear that it is not always a unilateral assault of African manhood against subjugated females.[11]

Indeed, it is fascinating that in at least one community in Chad, female circumcision is a newly adopted fad, a fashion among young girls who have to travel out of town because of opposition from town elders and parents—baffling perhaps but quite comprehensible when viewed against similar puzzling trends of multiple ear and body piercings among the younger generation in many Western societies

---

[7] See Peyi Airewele (Soyinka-Airewele) and Charles Udogu, "Gender Diplomacy at the Crossroads: Foreign Aid, Women and Development in Nigeria," in *Nigerian Women in Society and Development*, eds. Amadu Sesay and Adetanwa Odebiyi (Ibadan: Dokun Publishing House, 1998), 199–230.

[8] ibid.

[9] Peyi Soyinka-Airewele, "Engendering Change in Africa: Contradictions of Power, Desire and Oppression in Critical Spaces" (paper presented at the Oxford Round Table: Women's Leadership Oxford University, 2004).

[10] Martha S. Grise, "'Scarred for Life?' Representations of Africa and Female Genital Cutting on American Television News Magazines," in *Images of Africa: Stereotypes and Realities*, ed. Daniel Mengara (Trenton, NJ: Africa World Press, 2001), 249.

[11] Melissa Parker, "Rethinking Female Circumcision," *Africa* 65, no. 4: 517.

today.[12] Grise argues that the misrepresentative, culturally insensitive journalism on cross-cultural gender issues simply "exacerbates tensions between Western and African feminists" and, furthermore, "encourages clumsy intervention in African affairs, and thus exacerbates Africans' sense that their culture is under siege and deepens resistance to change."[13] To be certain, rarely do people who are misunderstood seek to adapt just to make it easier for outsiders to relate to them; the case of African identities, specifically with respect to gender, should not be any different. What is needed instead is a willingness to delve deeper into issues of cross-cultural representation, working towards Nnaemeka's distinction between speaking *for* and speaking *with*, or lending our voices to, the issues facing others.

A Voyage Around Gender Identity: The Ghanaian Junction

As a human rights activist, with a primary focus on the exploitation and violence against women around the world, I remain deeply concerned with these issues, but the opportunity to live with women in Medie, Ghana, has modified the methodologies I follow and ideological frames from which I see and seek these goals. Medie is a rural suburb of the Greater Accra region in the Ga West district close to the Atlantic beaches of Ghana. It has become one of the many rural destinations for folks wishing to pursue studies in traditional drumming, dancing, xylophone music, and visual arts (my original agenda), and many of its inhabitants pursue occupations in kente weaving, batik, tie-dyeing, drum making, and blacksmithing. In spite of this, Medie cannot by any stretch of the imagination be described as a wealthy or industrialized location. Indeed, a U.S.-based NGO recently announced plans to extend micro-credit loans to businesswomen in several villages of approximately 10,000 people in rural Medie, Ghana; to start a pilot project for a solar-powered well; and, finally, to introduce efficient, wood-burning stoves that will use 50 to 75 percent less wood than regular fires to help prevent deforestation.

> Interestingly, as a part of its women's microcredit scheme, the female beneficiaries in Medie are to be mentored by *international* students from the Institute of Professional Studies in Ghana, who will provide instruction in cost control, ethical business practices, customer care, basic bookkeeping and business planning. The value of these projects and mentoring budding entrepreneurs are not questionable. What is disturbing is the specific insistence that the mentorship come only from the international students at this institute in Ghana. Are they more competent or in need of encouragement to be philanthropic and serve globally? Whatever the case, it surely came at the expense of creating self-sustaining partnerships between Ghanaian citizens who share cultural, linguistic, and social knowledge (Soyinka Airewele, 2008).[14]

Anene Ejikeme, writing in this book, lambastes the tendency to assume poverty and lack of literacy can in any way be construed as "stupidity" or lack of self-determination and agency in personal and business matters. Mrs. Comfort, my first Ghanaian host-mother, was strong, assertive, and dedicated

---

[12] Peyi Soyinka-Airewele, "Hollywood Vaginas or Female Genital Mutilation?" (public lecture presented at the Delta Sigma Theta Sorority, Mu Gamma Chapter, Cornell University, Ithaca, NY, October 19, 2003); and "Engendering Change in Africa."

[13] Grise, "'Scarred for Life?'"

[14] Soyinka-Airewele, "Development and Social Transformation," 2008. See also Soyinka-Airewele and Ukeje, "Gender Diplomacy at the Crossroads"; and F. George, "Joy 2 the World Goes Back to Ghana," Landmark Education News, June 6, 2008.

to the pursuit of her needs and dreams and was as capable of achieving her goals as any man. With an incredible sense of resourcefulness and creativity, she, like every woman I met in Medie, Ghana, had skills to offer, and they worked together cooperatively towards achieving their goals and meeting their needs. Ifi Amadiume, in discussing the dual-sex organizational principles governing Igbo society, refers to the importance of such industriousness to women's accumulation of wealth and power in society.[15] While in Ghana, I saw a similar emphasis on women's economic bargaining power and women's agency in the household and community in determining gender roles and relationships of power. In contrast, of course, to the dominant images of African women existing passively in debilitating poverty, waiting for the munificence of their menfolk or the largess of foreigners, most of the women I met in Medie were engaged in entrepreneurship that contributed greatly to their status among other women, as well as men, and determined how much power they held in their relationships.

By accumulating diverse skill sets, the Ghanaian women I interacted with earned considerable communal respect, and the women with the greatest capacity to control their economic status gained a measure of authority over men and women in their spheres of influence. Interestingly, Medie also allowed me to have access to "women's associative power, " which we often hear about in the literature but rarely experience in the "disarticulated communities of an increasingly industrialized urbanism" (Soyinka-Airewele 2006).[16] The women I became close to (apart from my host mother whom I addressed as Aunty Comfort) were supportive of one another's endeavors, whether that meant referring a customer or providing child care. In the personal sphere, women looked out for one another concerning men; discussed health issues; warned each other about AIDS, STDs, and pregnancy; cared for one another's children; and helped each other through pregnancy. These are all instances I saw, heard, or was privy to in one way or another during my stay, and it was clear that these were common preoccupations in the women's daily lives, as they were in many other parts of the continent.

More importantly, in contrast to the struggle against the marginalization of women in the emerging global economy, for all intents and purposes, it seemed that women ran the markets. Market women often looked out for each other's stores, regulated prices to maintain fair competition even within the system of bartering, and sometimes controlled informal *susu* credit unions. Surrounded by women who were engaged in similar struggles for rights, development, and life dreams and whose feminism was constructed within a confident femininity and womanhood rather than masculine envy, I was surprised to find myself quite envious of the roles they had carved for themselves within a fairly patriarchal, postcolonial society.

Was it their confident sense of personal gender identity and definition of their collective and personal struggles and goals that allowed me to participate in tasks that I had never before known how to do—in part because I had never needed to and in part because I never wanted to in a resistance to stereotypical *feminine* activities that suggested resignation to domesticity and the very antithesis of my feminist goals? By the end of my second week in Ghana, I actively participated in hand washing everyone's

---

[15] Amadiume, *Male Daughters, Female Husbands,* 27–29.

[16] Peyi Soyinka-Airewele, "The Enigma of Yoruba Womanism" (guest lecture at the Women's Studies Center, Colgate University, February 17, 1998) and Peyi Soyinka-Airewele, "Gender Politics in Nollywood Cinema" (paper presented at the conference on "Transnational Challenges: Environment, Integration and Security in the Third World" at the Twenty-Fourth Annual Meeting of the Association for Third World Studies, Winston-Salem State University, Winston-Salem, NC, November 2–4, 2006).

clothes, cleaning, sweeping, assisting in kitchen duties, and caring for the children. I was washing thirty people's dishes with water I collected from the well and eventually balanced on my head (though not very well), dancing, and singing with a baby tied to my back, sewing without a pattern, and gossiping with the best of them. As others have said, "feminism is ultimately an intensely personal and collective identity.[17] It was in Medie, Ghana, that I first experienced the personal strength that comes from being an accepted member of a tightly knit band of women. In those weeks and over the months that followed, the kind of female camaraderie I observed in the community of women seemed to exemplify what I considered a missing piece of the puzzle for this generation, at least within the local arenas of women's activism and lives in which I had worked in the United States.

Gender relations were as illuminating: while the men in Medie were apparently strong, authoritative, income-earning males, they seemed to hesitate when it came to interfering with women's business. I found men cautious in the midst of complex female relationships and networks, not wishing to do or say anything against the wishes of the women. Though I certainly saw instances to the contrary, there were fewer than I had expected. The genderized role differentiations between young boys and girls were often less apparent than in many American homes: boys were raised to take care of the children, while the women went about their business, just as often as young girls were employed to carry their baby sisters on their backs. The same patterns obtained throughout life: it was common to see a man caring for his child when he was home or mentoring his son in his line of work to ensure the financial stability of the family, while young girls learned skills required to take care of a household or even an entire community.

The patterns of gender and marital relations I observed seemed to bespeak a form of equality, a genderized coexistence, or what Soyinka-Airewele has described as "that uncanny sense of being in the presence of an unquantifiable unequal equality."[18] I do not use the term coexistence to construct an African or Ghanaian difference or to evade the existence of inequalities and gender oppression but to cautiously reconstruct the meanings of equality even within an American or Western context in which so often equality still translates as the problematic equal right of a woman to achieve respect only through reconstructing herself within a "masculine" landscape or identity. Again, Soyinka-Airewele has spoken of the ways by which female politicians in many African societies typically and unapologetically deploy (and are understood as deploying) female rather than masculine strength through their head ties and other clothing, their language, and their religious, social, and other forms of female associative power, even in the face of male counter-political mobilization.[19]

A Voyage Around Gender: Ideology and Mediated Constructs

Returning to the United States, I discovered that this process of cultural critique had sensitized me to dominant stereotypes about African women, our sense of place in the world, intellectual and other global hierarchies, and the constructs of the hapless Other. Still concerned about the devastating violence in the Darfur region of the Sudan and incensed about the evidences of state complicity, I was troubled by the

---

[17] ibid.

[18] Soyinka-Airewele, "Engendering Change in Africa."

[19] Peyi Soyinka-Airewele, "The Enigma of Yoruba Womanism."

connotations of the slogan "Save Darfur." During a rally,[20] Western activists certainly spoke with compassion about going to refugee camps and seeing the Darfuri women in rags, but I was troubled by their bland sentiment, typically devoid of any frames of imaging, and by their defining the Darfuri women by the objective condition of their rags, instead of by their womanhood and humanity.

Indeed, "in this place of transition, it is hard to conjure the languages that can help define, capture, and guide ones activism or feminism, within the overwhelming awareness of the vast gulf that can easily exist between realities and the words of those who speak for others,"[21] as the women of Medie taught me. Disconnect with others of my generation occurred again when I participated in a college course entitled "Africa through Film: Representations and Reality," in which we critiqued various media representations of Africa—the very same representations that had originally shaped my conceptions of African women and that now seemed all too often misleading. Soon, it became clear to me that I was watching the films through a new lens, while many of my peers seemed unprepared for or oblivious to nuances of which I was now hyperaware. Tears stung my eyes as we watched the film *Bintou,*[22] and I reflected on the portrayal of the gender relationships in the film. The movie explores the debate between a mother and father over whether to continue their daughter's education. Filmmaker Fanta Regina Nacro examines the social considerations that weigh on their decision and the extent to which the father and mother each have a say in the decision. I was reminded of the iron will and fiery determination that I saw in the women I met, was again tickled by the awkwardness of men in dealing with the world of women and their cooperatives, pained by the threat to the young girl's education, and finally heartened by the loving mother who would not let her daughter be denied an opportunity. Happily, I can say that I know many women like this—Ghanaian and American—who have defended their right to opportunity while holding onto their identities as mothers, wives, and professionals.

My stay in Ghana—from Medie, to Accra, to Klikor, to Kumasi—allowed me to understand womanhood, femininity, feminism, and motherhood in new ways that are neither mutually exclusive nor defined by body image. "Strength is a fluid concept and rigid cultural notions of engendered differences should not limit our capacity to glimpse variants of feminist agency in other parts of the world. Gender equality is not yet universal in Ghana, the United States, or any other part of the world. The exploitation of women, domestic abuse, and institutional and media prejudices continue to prevail in both spaces."[23] And any Westerner would be gravely mistaken to assume that more industrialized, materially expansive societies have necessarily empowered Western women or that the communal affirmation, economic support, domestic respect, and personal esteem and confidence I encountered among Ghanaian women have produced a less gendered identity.[24]

---

[20] "Save Darfur" Rally, New York City (September 17, 2006).

[21] Soyinka-Airewele, "Gender Politics in Nollywood Cinema."

[22] *Bintou,* directed by Fanta Régina Nacro (Burkina Faso and France: Key Light, 2001).

[23] P.S. Airewele, "Women's Experiences of Childlessness and Sub-fertility in Nigeria" (paper presented at the Dissemination Seminar of the Women's Health and Research Center in collaboration with the Harvard University School of Public Health, March 15–16, 1995).

[24] Soyinka-Airewele arrived at such a conclusion in her analysis of the Yoruba of southwestern Nigeria. See Peyi Soyinka-Airewele, "The Enigma of Yoruba Womanism."

Perhaps I am no longer tempted to insist I know what full equality or "rights" should look like or how they should be achieved. Certainly, prejudices, assumptions, and stereotypes eliminate the space for a tangible discourse on how women experience and define oppression and subordination. Without doubt, these continue to exist, but "similar discursive spaces must be opened for relaying and accepting the ways in which women in African countries and elsewhere in the world are defining their needs, desires, struggles, and achievements on the basis of indigenous sociocultural institutions and/or transnational networks."[25] Again, I borrow from Ejikeme's conclusion in "Engendering African Women's History." She notes that "Western-educated scholars have been trained to utilize Western typologies, yet their life experiences in Africa make them see that these typologies are not necessarily universal truths. Encountering Western scholarship through African eyes forces us to rethink the Western vision (and version) of Africa, and this can be vitally rewarding."[26]

I conclude this voyage with Soyinka-Airewele's reminder that "our re-conceptualization of gender roles and identity must permit the continued struggle against gender exploitation and oppression while allowing space for understanding and for affirming the cultural norms, networks, mobilization strategies, and legacies of women across the globe"[27] who embrace different ideas of womanhood. We must actively dialogue across cultures and within them, seeking not to speak for others but to speak with them, to foster understanding of the value of difference and encourage full humanity of both men and women in whatever roles they pursue.

REFERENCES

Airewele, P.S. "Women's Experiences of Childlessness and Sub-fertility in Nigeria: A Review of Policy Implications and Agenda for Action." Paper presented at the Dissemination Seminar of the Women's Health and Research Center in collaboration with the Harvard University School of Public Health, March 15–16, 1995.

——, and C.U. Ukeje. "Gender Diplomacy at the Crossroads: Foreign Aid, Women and Development in Nigeria." In *Nigerian Women in Society and Development*, edited by Amadu Sesay and Adetanwa Odebiyi, 199–230. Ibadan: Dokun Publishing House, 1998.

Amadiume, Ifi. *Male Daughters, Female Husbands: Gender and Sex in an African Society.* London: Zed Books, 1987.

Bintou. Directed by Fanta Régina Nacro. Burkina Faso and France: Key Light, 2001.

El Saadawi, Nawal. *The Nawal El Saadawi Reader.* London and New York: Zed Books, 1997.

Ejikeme, Anene. "Engendering African History: A Tale of Sex, Politics, and Power." In *Reframing Contemporary Africa,* edited by Peyi Soyinka-Airewele and Kiki Edozie. Washington, D.C.: CQ Press.

——. "Let the Women Speak! and Listen," January 17, 2008, www.pambazuka.org/en/category/comment/45464.

Grise, Martha S. "'Scarred for Life?' Representations of Africa and Female Genital Cutting on American Television News Magazines." In *Images of Africa: Stereotypes and Realities,* edited by Daniel Mengara. Trenton, NJ: Africa World Press, 2001.

Murphy Edie, David Sheffield, and Barry Blaustein. *Coming to America,* VHS. Directed by John Landis. Eddie Murphy Productions and Paramount Pictures, 1988.

---

[25] Soyinka-Airewele, "Engendering Change in Africa."

[26.] Anene Ejikeme, "Engendering African History," in this volume.

[27.] Soyinka-Airewele, "Engendering Change in Africa."

Nnaemeka, Obioma. "Urban Spaces, Women's Places: Polygamy as a Sign in Mariama Bâ's Novels." In *The Politics of (M)Othering: Womanhood, Identity and Resistance in African Literature*, edited by Obioma Nnaemeka. New York: Routledge, 1997.

———, ed. *Sisterhood, Feminisms and Power in Africa: From Africa to the Diaspora*. Trenton, NJ: Africa World Press, 1998.

———, ed. *Female Circumcision and the Politics of Knowledge: African Women in Imperialist Discourses*. Westport, CT: Praeger Publishers, 2005.

Parker, Melissa. "Rethinking Female Circumcision." *Africa: Journal of the International African Institute* 65, no. 4 (1995): 506–523.

Soyinka-Airewele, Peyi. "Gender Politics in Nollywood Cinema." Paper presented at the conference on "Transnational Challenges: Environment, Integration and Security in the Third World" at the Twenty-fourth Annual Meeting of the Association for Third World Studies, Winston-Salem State University, NC. November 2–4, 2006.

———. "En*gender*ing Change in Africa: Contradictions of Power, Desire, and Oppression in Critical Spaces." Paper presented at the Oxford Round Table Women's Leadership. Lincoln College, Oxford, August 8–13, 2004.

———. "Hollywood Vaginas or Female Genital Mutilation?" Public lecture presented at the Delta Sigma Theta Sorority, Mu Gamma Chapter, Cornell University, Ithaca, NY. October 19, 2003.

———. "The Enigma of Yoruba Womanism." Guest Lecture at the Women's Studies Center, Colgate University, February 17, 1998.

Part V

CRITICAL QUESTIONS AND CHALLENGES FOR A GLOBALIZING AGE

The last section of this book reveals the complications of self-retrieval and political self-determination in Africa in an era of globalization. In Africa, as in other regions of the world, globalization influences the dynamic struggles for collective well-being and socioeconomic and political transformation, often in contradictory ways. Issues blithely characterized by outsiders as poverty, disease, authoritarianism, and corruption, in fact, intersect domestically and externally and affect the cultural, economic, political, and social landscapes of the continent. In this section, we present studies that shed light on internal debates and give voice to Africans undergoing global change. The chapters will challenge the image of a passive Africa—a suffering victim—and reveal the vibrant agency, resistance, struggles, and triumphs of Africans.

The 1990s set African affairs on a new trajectory. With the end of apartheid and the Cold War–era, political thought and practice were reconfigured. Engaging in critical debates were various African actors, including African political elites, civil societies, nations, communities, and regional organizations, as well as non-Africans, such as former imperial powers and international and non-governmental organizations.

While reflecting on the theories presented in previous sections, in this concluding section, the authors attempt to capture some of the most recent practices, processes, and debates. Many of the most essential issues have already been dealt with, including the African oil economy and the AIDS crisis. In this part, the writers focus on international relations and global governance, including African foreign policies, regionalism, and human rights in Africa.

Nobel prize–winning writer and author of *The Open Sore of a Continent* (Oxford University Press 1996) Wole Soyinka begins this section with a stinging commentary on the state of contemporary African affairs. The prominent African poet's frustrations with the continent's leadership, laid bare even in his essay's title "Millennial Challenges," propel him as one of the continent's progressive forces of change. Africa, whether the Sudan, Côte d'Ivoire, Nigeria-Cameroon, Ethiopia, or the African Union, is in flux, argues the Nobel laureate. Soyinka muses about Africans' attempts to address their problems by examining his personal involvement in resolving some of the continent's conflicts and economic development problems. Although he denounces the emergence of new nationalisms that invoke religion and boundary wars, Soyinka, nonetheless, believes that the reconstruction and reframing of African affairs is achievable. He asserts that the continent's welfare can only occur if Africans continue to actualize their capacities to transform the philosophies, institutions, and leaderships that determine social realities.

Injecting himself into what is clearly a raucous international debate about human rights in Africa, Makau Mutua, the author of *Human Rights: A Political and Cultural Critique* (University of Pennsylvania Press 2002), asks in the second chapter, "what are the limitations of liberalism in general, and human rights in particular, as transnational projects? How do we turn local claims into universal human rights claims? If it is desirable to put liberalism in the service of Africa, how does one do so? . . . how can human rights as conceived be of any help to the reconstruction and recovery of the African postcolonial state?"

Mutua suggests that the human rights project, dominated by Western-centric universalism and minimization of Africa's economic, cultural, and social dimensions, is very much conflicted, five decades after decolonization, because the continent is still haunted by crises of geographic, political, and moral legitimacy. However, the biggest challenges to the development of a viable African human rights agenda, according to Mutua, are the continent's protracted struggles with the legacies of postcolonial internal incoherence. He says, "At its dawn, the African postcolonial state was handed a virtually impossible task: assimilate the norms of the liberal tradition overnight within the structures of the colonial state while at the same time building a nation from disparate groups in a hostile international political economy." Mutua concludes that in order for the human rights project to be relevant to contemporary Africa, "African states must reconstruct their political orders, address ethnicity and group rights in political transitions, grow and nurture a vibrant civil society that is national in character, and expand the commitment of religious institutions to the full democratic project."

Following Mutua's chapter is Christopher LaMonica's analysis of international relations theory and African affairs. LaMonica is an American scholar resident in New Zealand and author of *International Politics: The Classic Texts* (Kendall Hunt 2004). In the current volume, he examines the overwhelming Euro-American dominance of African political discourse, which has contributed to Africa's marginalization in international relations (IR) theory. According to LaMonica, the discipline of IR remains parochially Western; African involvement in the discipline is sorely lacking; and the presentation of Africa as "different" leads to an essentializing and stigmatizing of the continent. LaMonica adds to our reframing Africa discourse by recognizing just how far we can go in describing Africa as a place of "difference."

He argues for identifying global "patterns" of human behavior that incorporate African experiences, an approach that will occur only when Africanists and other specialists in non-Western regions move away from monolithic, essentialist arguments towards more nuanced conversations that elicit truly global, respectful, and inclusive scholarship.

In the final chapter by Rita Kiki Edozie and Peyi Soyinka-Airewele, the authors present the utility of the emerging postcolonialist paradigm as a vehicle for the reconstructivist analysis of contemporary Africa. They argue that reconfiguring the study of Africa and re-imagining the continent require a consolidating, forceful intellectual platform, which helps "voice" and "represent" alternative and subverted expressions of formerly colonized peoples. Through a critical examination of select recent international policies regarding Darfur, the United States' AFRICOM, and Sarkozy's France-Afrique, the contributing editors of the book present a critical review of postcolonial theory as a way to frame not only new strategies for resistance and change, but also the lived experiences of African communities at the local and national levels.

Chapter 19

MILLENNIAL CHALLENGES FOR CONTEMPORARY AFRICAN AFFAIRS

Reconstructing from Within[1]

A Commentary

Wole Soyinka

The African continent is very much on the mind of the world these days, but that is nothing new. The number of conferences and working sessions that have been devoted over the years to the resuscitation of a continent assailed by multiple, seemingly incurable afflictions are many and often repetitious. I have myself participated in some three or four and could have made a tally of a dozen or more, had I so wished. However, perhaps in contrast with others with a higher threshold for that peculiar form of masochism that is associated with treading the same spoor over and over again, I found myself constantly inhibited by the sense of a Sisyphean curse. The problems are so obvious, the solutions sometimes equally obvious. Indeed, it would sometimes appear that, as remedial action is being taken in one spot or another along the paths meticulously set out by truly committed leadership—the result of informed considerations by both political and disinterestedly cerebral thinkers and planners for society—identical fires to earlier trouble spots flare up in another area, as if no serious thought had ever been dedicated to the causative issues.

This is certainly a continent in transformation, but whether its transformative trajectory is positive or negative is yet to be observed. The platform and context are also very different from just a decade ago. Like the rest of the world, African affairs today are shrouded in convoluted changes, so some ingenuity is required to rethink and reconstruct the entire continental circumstance.

Beyond Declarations for Change

I recall two sessions of a meeting of minds that I attended during the past decade: one was part of a series entitled "Audience Africa," an initiative of the immediate past director-general of UNESCO.[2]

---

[1] This chapter was adapted from an address originally released as "Millennial Challenges for the African Continent."

[2] In organizing Audience Africa in February 1995, the UNESCO director-general hoped to transform the organization's approach to Africa. For the first time, its headquarters hosted a meeting of African heads of state; senior officials from bilateral aid agencies; intergovernmental organizations (including the Organization of African Unity); the African Development Bank; various nongovernmental organizations; leading figures from civil society; and specialists from the worlds of education, science, culture, and communications. As noted in its report, the deliberations took account of the lessons of the past, the requirements of the present, and the demands of the future, to set down the terms of a self-reliant development policy that would secure the economic, social, political, and cultural progress of present populations and the survival in dignity, peace, democracy, and justice of generations to come. (See www.unesco.org/africa/VA/pages/africa/1a-an.html and Final Report, Audience Africa, www.unesco.org/africa/portal/finreportaudience.pdf.)

I even chaired some of these sessions. Among the participants were Graça Machel and Ahmadou Toure et al., and it was in "Audience Africa" that we tried and—I hope my memory serves me right here— actually succeeded in adopting the proposition that dictatorship is a crime against humanity, one that must be terminated before the end of the second millennium. Much good that has done the continent! I believe there had to have been some five or six successful military coups after the conference, Sierra Leone being the most notorious for its consequences.

However, it is to another and the last of such encounters that I would like to call special attention. It was called at the initiative of the then secretary-general of the United Nations, Kofi Annan, and con- sisted of several sessions that began in Abuja, Nigeria, continued south to Maputo, Mozambique, and ended in Ivory Coast. I found myself able to attend only the last of the series, and we shall have a bit more to say about its venue in a moment. What was remarkable about the series was that it was made up entirely of African intelligentsia, technocrats, and business entrepreneurs; it was uniquely compre- hensive. I believe we thought we had it in us to remake the African continent entirely and set its face resolutely toward a new millennium. The conference made a point of calling attention to the fact that this initiative was not new. It refused to ignore similar efforts in the past, stressing that it would only attempt to build on earlier reflections and calls to action, as reflected in the following excerpt from the preamble:

> The Commission has taken note of other efforts such as the Lagos Plan of Action, the Arusha Declaration, UNESCO's Audience Africa, MAP, OMEGA (I honestly do not recall what those final acronyms stood for) plus a number of other encounters, some of which have crystallized into The New Partnership for Africa's Development (NEPAD), whose principles were adopted by African Heads of State at Lusaka. The major economic objective of that document is a targeted 5.2 percent economic growth rate between the period 1995–2002 and from 6–7 percent by 2015.
>
> While lauding this, among other initiatives, the Independent Commission (that was us, the Millennial Commission) believes that this vision should be taken even further. We believe that the recommended growth rate falls below what is needed to eradicate the crushing poverty that has become the hallmark of the African continent. In addition, we believe that a concerted program is needed to mobilize our people, and especially women and youths, for a successful implementation of NEPAD.

Here are two more excerpts. They were subjectively selected because they reflect some of my own personal concerns. But they also indicate the seriousness of approach and detailed attention that almost exceptionally characterized these encounters—quite different from pre- and immediately post- independence gatherings where attendees almost uniformly expected an overindulgence in denuncia- tions of capitalism, colonialism, and neocolonialism. Those familiar and justly targeted scapegoats had served their purpose. The continent of Africa, it had become evident, was now confronted with herself, charged with the direction of her own destiny. Hence the Independent Commission declared:

> Scientific and technological education should focus on innovation and creativity. In this connection, we strongly recommend the creation of an African Millennium Institute for Science and Technology and call upon the African Development Bank and its partners to undertake a leading role in the realization in this initiative.

The passage goes further to demand

> an aggressive effort not only to stem the current brain drain from the African continent, but to woo back the scattered talents from the continent, who are presently devoting their genius to the development of over-endowed societies outside the continent. Again, we call upon internal resources, such as the African Development Bank, to assist with the necessary resources for those nations that put forward credible plans for creating the necessary conducive conditions for this repatriation of the intelligence bank of the continent.

I cannot overstress the crucial importance, and relevance, of such an agenda in the context of a meaningful partnership with the outside world. The NEPAD meeting took place in 1995, while our meeting of the millennium experts happened in 2001. And, yet, we may safely assume that these resolutions—as in the case of their predecessors—were forwarded not only to the initiator of these encounters, the secretary-general of the United Nations in the case of the latter meeting, but also to the African Union (formerly the Organization of African Unity) and heads of African states. It would be interesting to find out what the economic growth rate is today, whether it has achieved the 5.2 percent targeted by NEPAD, considered too low by us, the millennial/renaissance storm troopers. More concretely, I need not add that I remain unaware that one land slab has been set down for the creation of the African Millennium Institute for Science and Technology or that one single nation has taken the initiative to woo back the brain power that would be required for the creative productivity such an institute would require.

The issue of course is implementation. And it is easy to see why attendance at such gatherings soon palls. Not one, but several plans or blueprints for African resuscitation exist. They have been visited, revisited, debated, amended, adopted, revised, amplified, etc., and will be found with the accumulation of decades of dust on those shelves devoted to keeping the intellectual busybodies quiet yet busy, exercising their minds with the utmost solemnity but remaining totally ineffectual. Implementation is what is lacking, and, of course, the reasons for this vary from a lack of vision and enterprise in political leadership to the far more basic reality of lack of resources. Allied to these are the crippling external debts that continue to hamstring even simple national economic planning and management of resources, before we begin to venture remotely near the grandiose notion of those who insist on seeing that much-touted era—the African Renaissance—just round the corner.

Combating the Legacy of Conflict

Another reason, of course, is—conflict! The energies of the continent have been dissipated either by prosecuting wars or attempting to resolve them while dealing with their consequences, especially when wars spill over into neighboring nations. When this happens, the wars invoke fraternal allegiances that complicate solutions even further. This is why I chose to single out the case of the millennial encounter, the termination of whose labors took place, ironically, in Ivory Coast, that then-stable exemplar of the democratic ethos that would shortly after be engulfed in a civil war. Indeed, if we may forget the millennial utopians for one moment and simply examine a precedent plan of that government on its own for the mobilization of the intellectual quotient of the continent, we will come face to face with the subversive and terminal role of civil conflict in the disposition of well-laid plans.

President Gbagbo had actually invited a number of African scholars and technocrats to an inaugural meeting—twice postponed—for the establishment of an African Academy for Sciences and the Humanities. It was, indeed, on that very account that Professor Albert Tevodjare, the leader of the Millennial

Commission, chose Ivory Coast as the terminal point for the moving feast of brainstorming. How could one not be confident that in Ivory Coast we had at least a government whose plans coincided with the vision of the Millennial Commission? The government was one that would prosecute its propositions with total commitment, even into the corridors of the new African Union! Of course, not long after, Gbagbo's government was preoccupied with more urgent concerns than a long-term mobilization of the intellectual resources of the continent. It had first to secure its very survival and the survival of the nation. That is the real tragedy of civil wars. Beyond the human suffering—the traumatizing of individuals and communities—there is the very real stalling of projections that would, if faithfully executed, constitute in themselves at least some means of preventing conflicts. It is very much a vicious cycle.

Not surprisingly, therefore—since it is a scenario that has become commonplace nearly all over the continent—if I am compelled to select one phrase that, on its own, best captures the essence of the African dilemma today, I would unhesitatingly name it as the plague of exclusion. One of the greatest and most urgent challenges that confront us on the continent is how to establish inclusivity as a social principle. The tendency to exclude, for whatever reasons, one or another section of society from participation in regulating and managing its existence and the polity to which it clearly belongs undoubtedly undermines the cohesion of the polity.

That said, let me add that this problem is not peculiar to the African continent. Europe, the Americas, Asia, including the Middle East all the way south to Australasia, are themselves riddled with the affliction. The rise of extreme nationalism, often developing into outright xenophobia, barely disguised under legislative formalisms that never name their real goal—exclusion—are all symptoms of the increase, not decrease, of the we-or-they mentality that appears to be sweeping the world. It has resulted in wars of various degrees of bloodiness and duration, of which perhaps the most notorious have been the prolonged Irish low-intensity civil warfare and the killing fields of the Balkans into which even the North Atlantic Treaty Organization was drawn. These are all wars whose roots, however traceable to past histories of repression and economic impulses, are nonetheless products of the exclusivist tendency among peoples, and we should not pretend that they are based entirely on any more idealistic notions than this.

The events of the past decade or two make Africa a case for continental strategies, even as the Serbo-Croatian conflict was recognized, almost belatedly, as a challenge to modern Europe. I would go further to propose that the many social problems that can be categorized as originating from the exclusionist imperative, though less publicized, are on a par with the Middle East, a regional crisis that is tragically recognized as extending beyond its immediate region to threaten the very stability of the world.

In this context, then, was the case of Ivory Coast unexpected? Of course not. Even if, as we gathered for the conference for a millennial vision, we had been totally ignorant of the problems that simmered beneath the surface, we were not long denied knowledge that we had been plunged right into the center of the dangerous contradictions caused by exclusivist policy. We were bombarded with leaflets that charged, boldly, that the so-called democracy of Ivory Coast was a sham. For years, under President Houphouet-Boigny, that nation was lauded as a model of positive development and democracy. Yet it was nothing more than a one-party dictatorship whose political success—leaving aside its apron-strings attachment to France—was built around the very principle of exclusion masquerading under the seemingly innocuous designer label of *ivoirite*.[3] The uninformed outsider may be forgiven for thinking that

---

[3] Machel is the present wife of former South African president Nelson Mandela and the widow of the late Mozambican president Samora Machel. Ahmadou Toure is the president of Mali.

ivoirite is an expression of nationalism, but not the knowledgeable, among whom we must count the political class in Ivory Coast, foreign trading partners, and the club of the African Union.

The wealth of Ivory Coast—its successful self-reliance—was built partly on the sweat of those so-called foreigners, and—do note—these foreigners were fellow West Africans from neighboring countries such as Burkina Faso. Many of them had lived in Ivory Coast for generations, knew no other country, and claimed no other nationality. Yet purely for reasons of convenient political numbers, they were denied a voice in the very land that had achieved economic repute from their labor. This was a boil that was set to burst, and it did. Neither the actual conflict that resulted in the virtual division of the nation in two—North and South—nor the reverberations for the West African sub-region have subsided. And they will not subside any time soon. What we have is an uneasy lull, and the question that I ask myself is this: if those trading partners, for whom the stability of a political space is paramount, instead of cosseting the fallacies of successive governments, had exerted the right kind of pressure to effect a change in a flawed system, would we have been spared the agony of instability that has now overtaken the region? It is through honest answers to such questions that the foundations of productive partnership can be laid. Considering that it had just begun to stabilize two of its members—Liberia and Sierra Leone—the West African sub-region must have found it especially excruciating to lose so many lives and resources, not to mention a generation who grew up as child soldiers with a catalogue of atrocities, which were they adults, would have landed them in tribunals for crimes against humanity.

Soon after the doomed adventurism of General Guei, a retired general who was brought in as a stop-gap ruler after a revolt against an incipient civilian dictatorship, I made the following observation in "Encarta Africa":

> Let me remind you of what General Guei did. He attempted to execute that familiar scenario—manipulation of elections—in order to emerge the new president of the nation. There was a popular uprising, and he was put to flight. On this continent of ours, you learn to celebrate as quickly and as deeply as you can because although you may go to bed in a euphoric mood, when you wake up the next morning, it may be mourning time. And so it proved. The streets of Abidjan were still raging when I tuned into BBC Sky News ten hours after the flight of General Guei, and the hemorrhage of the city had become more pronounced. The blood of the victors of that immediate contestation was coursing the streets, but this time, it was not Guei against the rest, but the victor, Gbagbo, in a dubious game of numbers against a potential victor, Ouattara, who saw himself as having been deprived of the chances of victory.[4] The nominal victor of the nonexistent contest had failed to learn even from the dismal end of Guei.

I deemed the contest nonexistent because Gbagbo's victory had been made possible only through the politics of exclusion that went by the name *ivoirite*. And at the end, I posed a question, indeed, a challenge:

> a political contestant, Ouatarra, was suddenly robbed of his Ivorian citizenship or, in strict language, he was disqualified from contesting on account of his citizenship redefinition. This was what had precipitated the crisis in the first place, the sudden definition of a formidable challenger, Ouatarra, as a non-Ivorian. That law had been passed under the previous pre-Guei government to smooth the path of that incumbent to his second term. Guei was ousted in his turn and fled the country, the victim of inordinate

---

[4] "Côte d'Ivoire for the Ivorians" is invoked by southern Ivorian nationalists.

ambition. Elections proceeded, but the laws that had disqualified Ouatarra were *not* rescinded. Did the "winner," as I naively expected—in the company of quite a substantial number of African heads of state, I was relieved to learn!—call upon his unjustly disqualified rivals to plan a transition government pending new elections? Oh no, that would have been far too complicated. He was claiming "victory," outright victory, a victory that failed to tackle the flawed genesis of the electoral conduct itself. The "winner" conveniently forgot that Guei's manipulations had rendered the entire election a charade. No, this new "victor" did not immediately repudiate the process. The notion of a fresh election, properly conducted, was yet again unthinkable! Next-door was Liberia. Mr. Gbagbo failed to learn, not even from the lessons of that blood-soaked country, or fresher still, Sierra Leone.

Thus, a repeat bloodletting scenario! Forty-eight hours after victory chants and some two hundred Ivorians dead, including an evident massacre in cold blood of some forty young men in an isolated field, I watched our "victor" on television in a tepid embrace with his main rival, Mr. Ouatarra. Both had taken the mature step of calling on their supporters to stop the carnage. Did Mr. Gbagbo really expect that his claim of outright victory would go unchallenged?

That seeming reconciliation was of course—as we say in my part of the world—"simply for show"! A few months later, Ivory Coast was plunged into civil conflagration and, with it, all the utopian projections of the eggheads for whom the now-embattled Gbagbo had been confidently expected to serve as arrowhead. That scenario, of course, is only one of several such examples. I offer it here to take us beyond the battlefield and behind the ramparts, to remind us that, in addition to the humanity wasted on these killing fields, humanistic projects also die.

New Nationalisms and Boundary Redrawing

In all but name, Ivory Coast is redrawing its boundaries. There is a de facto division of that nation, one that may eventually be overcome. One hopes so, indeed. However, just like the Eritrean-Ethiopian and Sudanese conflicts, the tragedy of Ivory Coast leads us to address the very question of boundaries and ask if they have not contributed in large measure to the instability that appears to be the distinguishing characteristic of the African continent. It is true that these tainted seeds of guaranteed future conflicts on the continent were sown at the Berlin Conference, where a continent of many cultures and development traditions was divided piecemeal among the Western powers, with no consideration for history, languages, and economic linkages. However, what African leaders have so far failed to tackle in a systematic way is: What are the consequences of this quilt work? Can we trace some of the internecine conflicts to that moment in the history of the continent?

Nations are not merely multicolored patches on the atlas; they answer to some internal logic and historic progression toward cohesion or incompatibility. We all know the history of Eritrea and Ethiopia before the intrusion of the colonial powers. We know how the foundations of present-day Liberia were laid. Those periods differ drastically from what is now called the era of globalization. The hard question is not being asked: In the context of present realities, are African national entities still viable? Is there cause for their reexamination?

Now, when such questions are asked, there is a tendency to imagine that there is one answer, and one answer only—the disintegration of the present national entities, accompanied or unaccompanied by a reversion to the precolonial conditions of the rudimentary state. I have always found this response an unnecessarily negative preconditioning. Why, I now ask, should such an exercise not result in its opposite—the amalgamation of existing nation-states? One response to this might be that it has been tried before, and it failed in the Ghana-Guinea-Mali federation and in the never-consummated Egyptian-Libyan shotgun marriage. Yet the fact that this prospect only recorded failures in the 1960s does not mean that it will do so in the vastly changed socioeconomic realities and globalization of the twenty-first century. By the same token, one must concede that such a project could end in just another debacle. It is clear, therefore, that engagement in this exercise is presented only because some of the current civil conflicts, such as that of the Sudan, are legitimately traceable to a fusion that was forced upon peoples, one that did not proceed from their will and internal political ordering. Where that is seen clearly, common sense urges that, at very least, the basis for such amalgamations be revisited with a view to ascertaining where precisely lies the will of the people themselves, acting in freedom. The Ethiopia-Eritrea fires, no sooner doused than threatening new flare-ups, indicate that there is unfinished business in legitimizing the boundaries that we all take for granted. The impact of refugees on the economy of nations, even within the most internally stable, can no longer be ignored.

There is, however, one unsuspected benefit of this exercise. It must surely lead, in my view, to some concentration on the problem of exclusionism, to considering what the imperial powers chose to include or exclude within the artificial nations they created. Why was this populace and not that other included or excluded from a specific colonial territorial demarcation? The incidental answers, such as a treaty signed with a local chieftain or the arrival of one Western nation's exploration party and imperial flag seconds before another country's, should not distract us unduly. Of more profound interest is one factor that is common to all such appropriations of other people's lands and resources—self-interest.

That leads naturally to the next question: whose self-interest? And next: In whose interest precisely are the present boundaries retained, held so sacrosanct that the population of the continent is decimated routinely, millions are maimed and incapacitated for life, farmlands are rendered useless on account of liberally sown antipersonnel mines, as diseases, hitherto strangers to the environment are wafted from one nation to another on the winds of war, and youths are robbed of their innocence and humanity? In short, wherein lies the self-interest of the people who inhabit the continent, over whose spoils aliens have fought, and still fight, both directly and through surrogates that include, alas, some African power brokers? And what characterizes these surrogates? What creates them and guarantees their availability?

Once, the ready instrument was ideology. We have moved, however, beyond the panacea of ideologies. While they lasted, Africa was a plaything in the hands of communist and capitalist ideologues, or more accurately, of global power blocs that carried their banners. That was the season—the 1960s, 1970s, and early 1980s of the last century—when ideology quite understandably became a deified abstraction, a rarefied zone that seduced some of the best minds on the continent. It compelled them to fritter away their productive energies on behalf of alien interests that took no notice of the material conditions of the societies over which they sought to spread ideological banners of contesting hues. The intelligentsia also played into the hands of ambitious leaders, who were thus enabled to camouflage agendas of raw, naked power with the authority of ideological adhesion. Deviations from alien prescriptions for the governance and economic life of African society became crimes of life and death, and societies stagnated under numerous shades of ideological purism. We have only to recall the case of Sekou Toure's Republic of Guinea, with its infamous torture chambers, the diabolical electric boxes whose existence we all continued to deny as fabrications of the Western powers until confronted with stark evidence after his death. Under radical Pan-Africanism, allied with purely rhetorical, often deliberately perverted Marxist theology, even the first secretary-general of the OAU, Diallo Telli, was not spared and perished miserably in prison.

Do African nations require an ideology? Or, more accurately, do they need an ideological textbook? It is clear that many leaders of thought feel a distinct unease about the lack of one. What else, we might ask, leads to the promotion of concepts such as *ubuntu*,[5] this consciousness of a need for an ideological anchor for the many choices society is compelled to make? Ideology could take its root in rejection, and capitalism, having been generally found wanting in the cause of African liberation, communism, or sometimes socialism, was the sole candidate left standing. Now the African continent is going through a phase of skepticism: socialism appears also to have lost its allure, and capitalism, despite its victory in the struggle for the soul of Europe, has yet to be fully embraced as a viable answer. By whatever name—*ubuntu, ujamaa,* or whatever—the conscious search for an African ideology, one that will lead to the so-called African Renaissance, which, of course, is no ideology, appears to have taken hold of the reflective mind. Confronted with brutal civil wars, politics of marginalization, epidemics, failed economic measures, dubious foreign alliances, and, most of all, "incontinent" leadership, there is a sense of a vacuum or a plinth around which can be wrapped the mundane projects for the elevation of society, for articulating the relationship between individual, community, state, and, above all, sociopolitical identity.

Religion and Secularism

If we cannot yet agree on the content of an ideology, we can at least begin with the elimination of the unacceptable propositions that can be fed into its framework. Religion, for one, is as good a point of entry as any: whatever ideology we finally come up with, apart from guaranteeing religion as a fundamental human right, the secular nature of the state must be sacrosanct. I say this quite openly to those religious fanatics—or mere opportunists—who attempt not only to replace the province of ideology with their scriptures but go even further to declare that one scripture or the other is superior to a nation's constitution and, indeed, supersedes any secular ideology. Nigeria has not been spared this surge of theocratic imperialism, pronounced by no less a politician than a once self-declared Marxist. This, of course, is the most lamentable face of the exclusionist impulse. If religion must be the basis for ideology, all religions become viable contenders, and each one has as inalienable a right as the next to claim for its divine texts an ideological role. Strengthening African secular structures thus constitutes a priority in planning.

As an agent of exclusionism, theocracy ranks high on the list of menaces that confront the continent, compelling us to vote clearly for secularism. The current tendencies toward political control through territorially aggressive, power-lusting religious assertiveness can no longer be ignored and should be considered an urgent policy issue if Africa is to develop positively. The human potential of any nation is its

---

[5] Alassane Dramane Ouattara is an Ivorian politician and was prime minister of Côte d'Ivoire from 1990 to 1993. In 1995, just prior to the presidential elections, the National Assembly of Côte d'Ivoire passed an electoral code barring candidates who had not lived in Côte d'Ivoire for the preceding five years and had one parent of foreign nationality. The code was popularly regarded as an effort to prevent Ouattara from running for president. Although he produced a nationality certificate and had previously been prime minister, his nationality was annulled by a court after the incumbent president insisted that Ouattara was a citizen of neighboring Burkina Faso, even though that country's president Capt. Blaise Compaoré made it clear that Ouattara was not Burkinabe. After the prolonged political crises that engulfed the nation, President Gbagbo announced in 2007 that Ouattara was welcome to run for office in the next presidential election.

greatest resource, and it seems to me rather absurd to speak of development when backwardness shackles women, a substantial percentage of a nation, for any reason, be it tradition or religion. I have openly articulated my views on the place of religion in society and its place in a nation's politics; much that has taken place on the continent in the past decade has more than confirmed my conviction that the modern state has no choice but to separate religion from politics and socioeconomic strategies. Where religious claims interfere with the productive capacity and stability of any nation, individual freedom of choice, and the welfare of citizens, they must give way to the demands of the secular totality.

The logic in this is plain enough. It is the secular that unites, not divides; it is the secular that includes, not excludes. The secular is basically egalitarian, not privileged. It is the secular that guarantees equality of space and opportunity, irrespective of sex, ethnicity, *and* religion, even as it guarantees space and protection for rival faiths. The theocratic urge is, on the contrary, intolerant and constrictive. Religion has been responsible for some of the worst civil atrocities perpetrated in my own country, Nigeria—in peacetime. Let me quote again from the proceedings in Abidjan because I sometimes need reassurance that these notions go beyond my own personal inclinations:

> We deplore the opportunistic manipulation of "tradition" for the purpose of relegating the citizen on account of ethnic identity, sex, or religious inclination to a second-class status, of denying each citizen the right to self-fulfillment and integration into the full African community. . . . The marginalisation of the female sex on any grounds is a policy of retrogression that the African continent, with its need for the fullest mobilisation of human resources, can ill afford. More fundamentally, it is a gross act of injustice that is no better than the consignment of Africans to a sub-human status through centuries of the slave trade by other races. This millennium should be dedicated to the full emancipation of the African citizen, backed, we recommend, by a Citizen's Charter to which all members of the newly formed Africa Union should be signatories.

Here, evidently, is a critical arena for positive partnership, programs for the empowerment of the marginalized, outside of government intervention. Such programs naturally carry the burden of grassroots education for the marginalized sex so that women do not believe that empowerment is the provision of improved cooking utensils and streamlined pestles—though the latter might be useful for beating sense into the heads of some male atavists. True empowerment is the opportunity to access multiple skills, specialized professions, and diversified interests—logical developments for a social species. The potential of every member of society is unavoidably harnessed and maximized for social advance.

Economic Development

Now, as yet another brick may be inserted into the overall developmental edifice, I must address, in its own right, that new economic and development initiative that has been launched on the African continent—the New Partnership for Africa's Economic Development (NEPAD). I share with many genuine alarm about the initiative's critical dependence on foreign partnership for its development strategies. No one is preaching a policy of isolationism here, but because this initiative can be considered the economic arm of the new African Union, it strikes me that it encourages the continuation of the dependency syndrome that has bedeviled the continent, that it is not a radical move to break the shackles of economic indentureship. The OAU has itself been transformed into a new body—the African Union. Both Africans and the outside world are waiting to see if this is simply another instance of putting old wine in a new bottle, or a transfer of old tricks to a new cub by a debilitated lion that has lost is roar—if it ever had one. It is perhaps too early to judge. However, on the crucial issue of development strategies, it is never too soon to cry wolf, so let me use this occasion to reiterate the plea with which I ended my address to a meeting of technical experts at the NEPAD-initiated conference in Addis Ababa. It is a cry that is based on lessons from the roads hitherto taken, roads that have either ended in a cul-de-sac or taken quite a number of nations completely over the precipice, with the result that even the luckier ones are retarded by the grievous errors of others, rubbishing the paper magnificence of the many blueprints that have been drawn for lifting the continent out of the doldrums.

Experience, not theory, strongly suggests that what each nation needs is—if we may put it this way—a democratized economic development strategy. By this I mean a structured promotion of more and more microeconomic structures as opposed to grandiose projects that only land African nations in deeper debt and problems of sourcing. This economic approach is naturally dependent on spreading autonomy and control to the constituent units that presently make up our nations so that productivity becomes decentralized. Government policies that lead to the monopoly of power and resources at the center, while depleting its constitutive limbs, have proved detrimental to the full economic self-realization of the totality. An abandonment of the unsustainable mentality of the insatiable megalopolis, complemented by a pursuit of authentic federal structures over ossified centralization—these offer themselves as rational options for a continent that lags so woefully behind in technology. Such an approach would drastically transform the face of the continent in concrete terms. What has been tried till now reduces local self-reliance and promotes the inegalitarian phenomenon of obscenely affluent capitals squatting on top of and feeding off haphazard and ill-developed slum villages, whose neglected populations only drift toward the glitzy centers to perpetuate bloated, lopsided capital cities that burst open at the seams from the pressure on their service capacities. Those who wish to contest this have only to pay a visit to my own nation, Nigeria. We need, in short, new developmental models that result in unique *humanized* national landscapes, dynamic vistas of decentralization and democratization, living spaces rendered in the very architectural language that defines our physical existence.

Intra-Continental Foreign Relations

The other urgent plea that I made at that prior encounter, already identified in this contribution, is the note on which I wish to conclude. There is finally the necessity for a concerted strategy to terminate, as rapidly as possible, the cycle of wars that have been waged so murderously over colonially imposed national boundaries. The cycle includes the recently resolved Ethiopian-Eritrean bloodbath, an event of surely monumental inanity, perhaps unprecedented even in the checkered history of the continent. We know that few nations, as presently constituted, have it in them to actually prevent the outbreak of armed revolt within their borders, for reasons that may or may not be traceable to past acts or policies of state. It only takes a messianic surge in one sector of the community or the delirium of religious zealots, such as happened quite recently in Yobe, northern Nigeria, for a nation to find itself faced with an armed insurrection that defies rhyme or reason. However, surely two sovereign states—states that belong to the same association of sovereignties (the African Union)—must have it in them to opt for arbitration, rather than succumb to the ready jingoism that is so familiar to those who lack compassion for human beings who live within national boundaries of dubious origins that have, in part, led to the discontent.

The conduct of Nigeria and Cameroon, I believe, is one cheering instance of maturity. Both countries claim to own the Bakassi, an oil-rich island. Oil, rather than national kinship, has pushed the two nations closer to armed conflict more times in the last two decades than many on either side choose to remember. In the end, both parties agreed to submit their claims to the International Court at The Hague. As Verdict Day approached, the debate waxed fiercely on the pages of our newspapers, certainly on the Nigerian side. Dire predictions and incendiary commentaries flew all over the media. Left to the "patriots," Nigeria would simply have gone to war; nationalist zealots would not even have waited for the verdict to be pronounced. I found it most benumbing that we, who as colonized peoples had endured so much and for so long at the hands of aggressive foreign powers on our soil, should actually have urged what amounted to little more than colonial conduct. For that was all it was—colonization. You colonize a people when you impose a rule over them without their consent. And so I asked the question: has anyone ever ascertained from the people of Bakassi within just whose borders they prefer to be—the Cameroonian, the Nigerian, or simply the Bakassian? Any other course, anything short of a genuine referendum, would be an act of colonization. Well, as usual I earned myself a whole new set of names—most with an unpatriotic slant— but then, naming ceremonies are an integral part of the culture in which I grew up.

Another obvious course, needless to say, would be a partnership in the exploitation of the resources of the disputed slab of real estate. For this to happen, both sides would have to be conscious of a very banal reality; namely, the primary producer of wealth is, and thus the primary beneficiary of it should be, the humanity who invests in such a space, not the abstract entity known as a nation. Therefore, the primary wealth of a nation is its people, first, because it is the humanity that produces and, next, because any meaningful measure of a nation is taken, not in the extravagance of its monuments, but in the quality of life of its citizens. Neither Nation nor Society transcend abstraction; each is concretely defined by the humanity that animates and recreates the patch of dirt and foliage that many take to be the nation's reality.

I was more than consoled—if I was in need of any consolation—by the interjection of a much respected voice, indeed, a viable presidential aspirant in our last elections, who urged the people to beware—and he was very specific—of the voices that incited the government to reject the decision of the international court if it went against Nigeria. That commentator was in a position to disinter the not-so-disinterested motivations of one of the most belligerent voices, a Nigerian lawyer-politician. He revealed that the latter had, for several decades, done very well for himself on a lucrative retainer at The Hague. Naturally, such a patriot was not eager to see the conflict brought to a conclusion. Let me give you the flavor of the decorous, legal language of this agent provocateur, a "senior advocate of the state," and chairman of a former ruling party. When judgment was eventually rendered at The Hague, and it went against Nigeria, he damned the verdict as:

> fifty per cent law and fifty per cent international politics. . . . Blatantly biased and unfair . . . a total disaster and a complete fraud . . . a big joke . . . never in my entire legal career [have I] seen bias so blatantly displayed.

The advice of this legal luminary, once the nation's attorney-general, was to treat the judgment "with the greatest contempt it deserves."

There were other revelations from the contest for Bakassi. They need to serve as a cautionary lesson, to reemphasize that "nation" and "government" are not abstractions. Both are made up of people who have the power to make and undo either nations or governments. Education and mental reorientation are thus directed at individual minds, not at some vague construct somewhere out on the landscape. We learned, for instance, that yet another serving attorney-general had advised successive governments that the Nigerian case was very weak historically and was bound to fail at The Hague. He advised negotiations. The politician-advocate, however, advised otherwise and pressed the government to take the case to the International Court. There was also the earlier-mentioned formula, tabled by government advisers, for counseling bilateral agreement between two sister nations for a joint exploitation of the oil resources, which would have ensured that Nigeria did not end up as the outright loser. The prospect of a prolonged legal battle, however, with a juicy legal retainership spanning decades, fired the persuasive skills of the perpetual litigant, and his "patriotic" rhetoric carried the day.

The lesson is obvious. African countries have an opportunity to radicalize their existence by embarking on a policy of resolving boundary disputes—both internal and external—by ascertaining the wishes of the people who actually inhabit, develop, and produce their existence from the disputed areas. No mere territorial holding, including natural resources, is worth the life of any one of our fellow men, women, or children. If ideology has proved suspect in the past and is given scant place in national planning, we can at least embrace a profound humanistic philosophy that goes to the roots of societal formation. Models are not wanting in the realm of speculation, and what greater challenge could there be for us today than to construct a model based on the elementary unit of the human producer and to reject all forms of leadership that conflate its self-interest with that of the nation and fail to act as temporary custodians of a people's will, choices, and resources. When we speak of leadership, we must refer not only to governance, but also to the voices that have the ear of government, people who stand by to reap the benefits of a course of action, without ever having to carry the burden of responsibility that attaches to the visible government.

Disputed boundaries obviously are matters for negotiation, even where existing boundaries merely refute the pietistic notion that crime does not pay. Well, maybe not, but we do know that the crime of colonialism has proved most lucrative for the perpetrators, but at the very least, the tragedy of Africa's colonial territorial legacies behooves the victim to rise above the vices of its adversary. No legal system in the whole world condones the crime of robbery on the plea that the latest perpetrator was once a victim of robbery. And so, whether the contested space is no more than a piece of dirt that everyone agrees holds absolutely no marketable value, so that what is in dispute is no more than national pride or, as in the case of Bakassi, where the fire in the eye of national leaders is ignited by the sheer glint of greed, such contested spaces must be left open to discussion and negotiation by those involved.

Conclusion

Let me end with an earlier exhortation that attempted to capture the vision of the millennial utopians gathered at that time in Ivory Coast, a nation that, had we but known it, would shortly serve as the ironic, yet instructive initiation we moved into the new millennium. The vision, primarily and profoundly, is of a continent that is at peace with itself and with the outside world, where the mandates of a just liberation struggle that involved recourse to arms are transformed into an internal revolutionary process that empowers the citizen without recourse to an ethos of violence and militarism—in short, a vision that takes the welfare, the well-being, and the full self-realization of the citizen *as the end and primary objective of all social designs.*

Of course, it has all been said before, but that vision has not been invalidated. It is a horizon to keep before us, one that, at the very least, may instigate thoughts of practical strategies for its realization. In any search for ideology, let that declaration serve as the ultimate imperative and controlling principle. If there is to be partnership with others, the fundamental mandates of such a vision should constitute the defining philosophy that leads to collective action, one that, I hope, will move us all toward the evolution of new, truly refurbished, humanized nation spaces.

Chapter 20

HUMAN RIGHTS IN AFRICA
The Limited Promise of Liberalism[1]

Makau Mutua

I have chosen as my topic "Human Rights in Africa: The Limited Promise of Liberalism." I have done so for two reasons: first, to provoke, because that is partly our job description as thinkers, and second, to reflect the ferment of human rights in the context of postcolonialism. Fifty years is a sufficient time to gauge the utility of any ideology, creed, or doctrine. Human rights contain within them all three of these phenomena. The last fifty years represent the entire period of the African postcolonial state and give us a fantastic window through which to interrogate the performance of the human rights project in Africa. But first, I want to lay aside some misconceptions about the human rights corpus and movement. At the outset, though, I want to level with you about the subject of intellectual bias or normative location.

Even though objectivity is the name of our game, we are, nevertheless, products of the legacies and heritages that have forged our identity and philosophical outlooks. In that sense, true objectivity is an academic fiction because no one can be truly objective. In any case, if we were truly objective, we would be truly boring. And so, I want to plead my biases at the outset. But I also want to warn you that with respect to the subject at hand—that of the utility of human rights and liberalism in Africa—I adopt the view of an insider-outsider, an engaged skeptic who completely believes in human dignity but is not sure about the typology of political society that ought to be constructed to get us there (Mutua 2000).

Third world scholars, like myself, come to the study of human rights with a considerable degree of discomfort and an inbuilt sense of alienation. Neither human rights nor liberalism has been germinated in the African garden. To be sure, my native ears are not deaf to many of the substantive issues addressed by both disciplines. I have a keen interest in the relationships between states and citizens. My alienation comes not from these facts but from the particularized historical, cultural, and intellectual traditions and tongues in which both human rights and liberalism law are steeped. It is in that sense that I am an outsider. Though an outsider to human rights and liberalism, I am, in a very real sense, an insider to both. I am part of the international elite that benefits personally from the norms and structures of international liberalism. My reality is not that of marginal and downtrodden citizens in Latin America,

The original version of this article was presented as the M.K.O. Abiola Lecture at the African Studies Association fiftieth Anniversary Meeting, October 2007, New York City, and was published in *African Studies Review* 51, no. 1 (April 2008). This is an edited version and is reprinted with permission.

[1] Since 1992, the year it was established, the Abiola Lecture has been offered by fourteen speakers, including Wande Abimola, Jacob F. Ade Ajayi, Kofi Anyidoho, Bolanle Awe, Boubacar Barry, Abena Busia, Amina Mama, Mamphela Ramphele, James Robert Rubadiri, and Atieno Adhiambo. See www.africanstudies.org.

Africa, Asia, or, for that matter, North America. I do not strain under the daily avalanche of the cruelties of globalization, state repression, and abuse.

But I am also an outsider because of that other consciousness that I carry—the consciousness of the historical, political, and cultural realities of the Africa that I am a part of, indeed, of the third world to which I belong, as distinct from the West. In human rights, I see a system of ordering the world, of understanding the world, a system and normative edifice that makes me acutely aware of my subordinate and marginal place in it as the "Other." This is not to say that I completely reject the human rights project or dismiss its redemptive impulses and purposes. It is rather to say that human rights are not for me a final, inflexible truth or a glimpse of eternity, so to speak. That is to say that I do not see the human rights project as some kind of a sacred gospel with armies of missionaries poised to save savage cultures from themselves so that they can stop churning out victims (Mutua 2001).

Human rights do not have a holy writ, nor could they because like all rights regimes, they are just a genre of socially constructed tenets that have come to define modern civilization. Nor should human rights be, as its most dominant proponents have constructed them, a part of the colonial project that forms the unbroken chain of the Christian missionary, the early merchant of capital, and the colonial administrator. I guess these observations mean that I am not a true liberal, a label that I do not want to wear anyway. But I do not agree with those who say that the human rights project "is so over" that we must abandon it altogether. That is the view of a small number of postmodern, postcolonial thinkers who believe that nothing is really knowable or doable in a very complex world. There is a strain in some of these thinkers that objects to any reconstructionist project as a reintroduction somehow of oppressive values, structures, or institutions. For me, such a view is an abdication by some of us who are comfortable in our personal and professional lives and who seek to paralyze ourselves intellectually so that we can have a rational excuse for doing nothing. This is ultimately cowardly, opportunistic, or even anarchistic. I believe that Africans and Africanists ought to reject such nihilism.

But I want to suggest also that human rights are imprisoned in universality, one of the central proclivities of liberalism. This fact alone should give us pause about human rights because we ought to approach all claims of universality with caution and trepidation. I say this because visions of universality and predestination have often been intertwined throughout modern history. And that intersection of universality and predestination has not always been a happy one: With an alarming frequency, liberalism's key tenets have been deployed to advance narrow, sectarian, hateful, and exclusionary practices and ideas. So at the purely theoretical level, we are chastised to look not once—but twice and again—at universalizing creeds, ideas, and phenomena. This is not to suggest that universality is always wrongheaded, or even devious, although it has frequently been those things as well—but it is to assume that the universality of social phenomena is not a natural occurrence. Universality is always constructed by an interest for a specific purpose, with a specific intent, and with a projected substantive outcome in mind.

This critical view has special implications for Africa because it questions both the fit and utility of liberalism and human rights for the continent. If we agree that all social truths are initially local—even truths about the so-called natural attributes of human beings or the purposes of political society—what does that say about the assumptions of liberalism in Africa? If social truths are contextual, cultural, historical, and time-bound, how can one find the relevance of the human rights project in Africa? This is not to say that local truths cannot be transformed into universal truths. They can, but the question for students of Africa is how one gets from here to there—in other words, what are the limitations of liberalism in general, and human rights in particular, as transnational projects? How do we turn local claims into universal human rights claims? If it is desirable to put liberalism in the service of Africa, how does one do so?

Liberalism, Democracy, and Human Rights

Political democracy—no matter its iteration—is the most critical realization of the liberal tradition. Perhaps there is no better foundational articulation of liberalism and politics than John Locke's seminal works (1988 [1689]). Formal autonomy and abstract equality, its twin pillars, underlie the notion of the bare republican state, popular sovereignty, and ultimately a limited constitutional government (Steiner and Alston 2008). Even though Locke thinks of the individual as living in society, he nevertheless is the center of the moral universe (Strauss 1999, 248). This emphasis on the individual as an atomized artifact frames the development of political society in the West and forges a normative project that produces the human rights corpus. As I have argued elsewhere (1996, 601), in the "historical continuum, therefore, liberalism gave birth to democracy, which, in turn, now seeks to present itself internationally as the ideology of human rights."

It is granted that the theory and practice of political democracy are not static, nor can they be. Even so, both rise on several fundamental principles and assumptions. First, the individual, for whom the system ostensibly exists, is abstractly endowed with certain formal inviolable—sometimes called unalienable—rights. These are historically constructed from culture, religion, tradition, citizenship, and economic modes of production. There is nothing *natural* about such rights. However, such rights are normatively presented as the quintessence of human dignity, another elusive terminology that is loaded with cultural and political bias. Second, political society must be constructed in such a way that it protects and nurtures this vision of the ideal individual. Political democracy is the moral expression of human rights. Political democracy, as understood today, describes a normative typology of government that is characterized by certain procedural attributes. Even though it is a regime of institutions, political democracy is not consequentialist in substantive terms. Rather, some of its well-known theorists and proponents have defined it in purely procedural language (Dahl 1956; Schumpeter 1984 [1942]).

Democracy is at some level a *method* that yields a particular *system*. As Samuel Huntington puts it, the democratic method has two key dimensions: contestation and participation. It is through these dimensions that the "most powerful collective decision makers are selected through fair, honest, and periodic elections in which candidates freely compete for votes and in which virtually all the adult population is eligible to vote" (1991, 7). This definition does not problematize democracy and its proclivity for machine politics and the vested class interests that encumber the state through the media and other institutions of social control. But that is largely the point—democracy is mostly about process that on its face looks fair and ostensibly permits popular participation. What happens underneath the process, or its outcome, is not the major concern of democracy.

What is important is that contestation and participation—as critical pillars of the system—imply the existence of a number of vitally significant rights. These rights, which are referred to as *democratic* rights, are necessary for free and fair elections. Among others, these freedoms include the rights to speak, assemble, organize, and publish. But these rights only make a polity a democracy provided universal suffrage is granted, real political opposition is permitted, and the elections are free and fair. According to Huntington, therefore, "Elections, open, free, and fair, are the essence of democracy, the inescapable sine qua non" (1991, 9). This means that the elected leaders will be responsible for addressing—or not—the most pressing issues once they assume office.

It is not difficult to see why this limited vision of democracy is problematic. What if the elected leaders—or the political class—are not concerned about certain forms of powerlessness or assaults on human dignity?

Is the populace then doomed? This minimalist definition of democracy hearkens to liberalism's cardinal commitments—formal autonomy and juridical equality. Henry Steiner (1998, 109) has captured this commitment well: Under the traditional understandings of liberal democratic theory, the correlative duties of government do not obligate it to create the institutional frameworks for political debate and action or to assure all groups of equal ability to propagate their views. Rather, those traditional understandings require governments to protect citizens in their political organization and activities: forming political parties, mobilizing interest groups, soliciting campaign funds, petitioning and demonstrating, campaigning for votes, establishing associations to monitor local government, and lobbying.

Thus, traditional understandings of liberalism or political democracy are not concerned about the asymmetries of power among citizens or the ability of entrenched interests to maintain social control over politics. This *marketplace* approach to political democracy keeps impediments to actual equality and constrains the autonomous individual. Again, Steiner (1998, 109–10) has identified this question: Government makes many paths possible, but it is for citizens to open and pursue them. Choices about types and degrees of participation may depend on citizens' economic resources and social status. But it is not the government's responsibility to alleviate that dependence, to open paths to political participation that lack of funds or education or status would otherwise block. Steiner suggests, and I agree with him, that the basic human rights conventions and treaties provide for a regime of political participation that is virtually identical to political democracy (1988, 85–94).

There is little doubt that the drafting of these documents drew from a century of Western liberal pluralist doctrine and practice. Human rights texts provide elsewhere for other civil and political rights—such as due process protections, independence of the judiciary, and equality and nondiscrimination norms that are essential for a political democracy. Today, the spread of the liberal constitution—and constitutionalism—is deeply rooted in the human rights corpus and its discourse. Constitutionalism defines the genus of government that is envisioned by the human rights corpus. Its pillars are popular sovereignty, an idea based on the will of the people as the basis of government; genuine periodic elections in a multiparty system; checks and balances with an independent judiciary; and the guarantee of individual rights. The bills of rights in many post-1945 constitutions are central to the spread of this genus of government. William P. Alford (2000) has correctly written that after the end of the Cold War, the United States embarked on a campaign to export political democracy, even if it was done on a selective basis. European political democracies followed suit. In this civilizing orgy, human rights were often employed interchangeably with political democracy.

Ideology and Human Rights

Perhaps no other moral idea has exerted more influence over the internal character of the state than human rights in the last sixty years. As put by Louis Henkin, "Ours is the age of rights." To emphasize the point, Henkin states, without qualification, that "human rights is the idea of our time, the only political-moral idea that has received universal acceptance" (1990, ix). Such categorical statements from one of the most respected voices in the academy must be taken seriously. There is no doubt that the idea of human rights has proven seductive to many societies and traditions in the last half century, although Henkin's unequivocal statements appear to be aimed at critics of universalism. But whether cultures across the globe have given the idea what Henkin calls "universal acceptance" is a different matter. Distinction must be made between the ratification of human rights treaties by states and the internalization of the norms of the human rights corpus by the cultures on which those states stand. Even if one were to concede the point, the tension does not resolve the question about the politics of human rights.

It is my contention that the birth of the modern human rights movement during the Cold War irrevocably distorted the true identity and raison d'être of the human rights corpus. It is certainly true that human rights scholars and activists have been reluctant to ask uncomfortable questions about the philosophy and political purposes of the human rights movement. Such questions are often taken as a mark of disloyalty to the movement or an attempt to provide cover and comfort to those states that would violate its norms. Unfortunately, only a handful of critical thinkers have seriously engaged this debate. The result is a paucity of good critiques about one of the most powerful ideologies of modern times. At the very least, it is irresponsible for thinkers to avoid such conversations, precisely because human rights norms have become a blunt instrument in the hands of imperial states (Anghie 2005).

Of all the branches of international law, human rights scholarship appears to have suffered the most from zealous advocacy as opposed to critical analysis. In their role as thinkers, which ought to be largely compartmentalized and protected from proselytism, scholars have become unabashed advocates blurring the invisible line between thought and action. The failure of critical analysis is not accidental. While not conspiratorial, it is historical, strategic, and the unavoidable result of the internal logic of the human rights corpus. The founders of the human rights movement—most principally the drafters of the Universal Declaration of Human Rights (UDHR)—could only have succeeded by presenting the human rights idea as universal, nonpartisan, acultural, ahistorical, and nonideological.[2] Mary Ann Glendon attempts to show that the founders struggled with this dilemma, but in the end she concludes that "the principles underlying the draft Declaration were present in many cultural and religious traditions, though not always expressed in terms of rights" (2001, 73–78; also see Morsink 2000).

Nevertheless, the fact that they decided to cast the text in the Western idiom of the rights language is a telling choice. Surprisingly, there was not an extended discussion about the political nature of the society that would be yielded by the UDHR. Nor are there any extended philosophical postulates or ideological justifications in the UDHR or in any of the two principle human rights covenants.[3] These are glaring omissions, especially for the launch of a universal creed. Although the reasons for the failure to explicitly identify the human rights corpus with a particular political ideology, typology of government, or economic philosophy are complicated, the silence does not mean that such identification is completely absent.

A critical study of the corpus places it squarely in the liberal tradition and firmly in the genre of the state known as a political democracy. This is the floor below which human rights norms do not permit an observant state to fall. But within this iteration, where a bare political democracy is the minimum, a maximalist political society is a mature welfare state. In other words, a political democracy passes the human rights test for meeting the basic normative and institutional requirements for that typology of government. At their most rudimentary, these can be characterized by bare republicanism, as would be the case, for example, in some of the new democracies of Eastern Europe. At its most sophisticated,

---

[2] The Universal Declaration of Human Rights, G.A. Res. 217A (III), U.N. Doc. A/810, at 71 (1948).

[3] The International Covenant on Civil and Political Rights [ICCPR], G.A. Res.2200A (XXI), U.N. GAOR, 21st Sess., Supp. No. 16, at 52, U.N. Doc. A/6316 (1966); the International Covenant on Economic, Social and Cultural Rights [ICESCR], G.A. Res. 2200 (XXI), U.N. GAOR, 21st Sess., Supp. No. 16, at 49, U.N. Doc. A/6316 (1966).

political democracy is complemented by social democracy, or a "thick welfare state," as has been the case in most Scandinavian countries. In contrast, a political democracy could also be a "thin welfare state," such as the United States, in which marginalization is largely seen as an individual moral failing.[4]

In any case, both the *thin* and *thick* welfare states exceed the minimum normative standard set by the human rights corpus. My point is that no matter how biblical and humanist, the rhetoric of the human rights corpus is a project of political democracy. Whether wittingly—or unwittingly—the framers of human rights doctrine sought to vindicate values and norms that incubate political democracy. This should not be very surprising, given the identities of the conceptual framers of the UDHR. Virtually all were either drawn from, or steeped in, the liberal tradition (Donnelly 1990, 31; Leary 1990, 15). Africa, for instance, was not represented at the drafting table. Even though Glendon (2003, 27) has pointed to a significant contribution by Latin America to the UDHR, she is not referring to the input of native Latin American or non-European actors.

In the late 1940s, when the UDHR was formulated, the Latin American officials at the table were decidedly Eurocentric. But even Antonio Cassese, one of the most influential Western scholars and practitioners of human rights, has flatly admitted that the West was able to "impose" its philosophy of human rights on the rest of the world because it formulated the post-1945 international order and dominated the United Nations (1992, 31). It is true that later human rights texts, particularly after decolonization in the 1960s, were more participatory because of the entry into the United Nations of states from the global South. However, it would be a mistake to conflate inclusivity with a radical normative shift in the basic character of the human rights corpus. Subsequent texts built on the normative script of the founders. It is very strange that the founding documents of the human rights movement studiously avoided—did not even mention once—the most important words and terms of the past several hundred years. They still don't.

Is it not very curious that neither the UDHR, the ICCPR (International Covenant on Civil and Political Rights), nor the ICESCR (International Covenant on Economic, Social and Cultural Rights) uses the terms "capital," "market," "colonize," "imperial," "political democracy," "liberalism," or any of their derivatives? The exceptions are the oblique and dubious references to "democracy" in the UDHR and the ICCPR.[5] The UDHR appears to sanction political democracy as the presumptive choice of the human rights corpus, although it does not explicitly say so or explain why. The reference to "democracy" in the ICCPR is similarly vague. There are possible explanations for these omissions or the reluctance to identify the human rights movement with a particular normative tradition, philosophy, or ideology. Were any of these deficits deliberate or calculated? Whatever the case, the lack of extended

---

[4] I coined the term "thick welfare state" to refer to a state whose political, economic, and social norms and structures are designed to eliminate, to a large extent, glaring manifestations of poverty, exclusion, and privation. Usually, this is done through social security and other economic safety nets that prevent extreme forms of powerlessness. The term "thin welfare state," also coined by me, refers to a less generous welfare state in which government is more reluctant to support social programs for despised or marginalized groups.

[5] Article 29 (2) of the UDHR states: "In the exercise of his rights and freedoms, everyone shall be subject only to such limitations as are determined by law solely for the purpose of securing due recognition and respect for the rights and freedoms of others and of meeting the just requirements of morality, public order and the general welfare in a *democratic* society" (my emphasis). Article 21 of the ICCPR states: "The right of peaceful assembly shall be recognized. No restrictions may be placed on the exercise of this right other than those imposed in conformity with the law and which are necessary in a *democratic* society in the interests of national security or public safety, public order . . . , the protection of public health or morals or the protection of the rights and freedoms of others" (my emphasis).

theories and philosophical justifications for the human rights corpus has left the doctrine vulnerable to attack. Importantly, it has mystified and obfuscated the normative and cultural gaps in the corpus.

That is why I contend that the human rights corpus is a moral project of political democracy and that the failure of the framers to openly base the doctrine on this irrefutable premise has done more damage than good. First, it leaves human rights discourse as a project that orbits in space, not anchored in historical, cultural, and ideological choices. This abstraction is either debilitating, if you are a critic, or empowering, if you are a true believer. As a critic, one starts from the disadvantage of disproving a negative. But as a believer, all one has to do is deny the negative. Second, the distortion of the true identity of the corpus masks its deficits and makes it difficult to debate them in the open. It is an exercise that is akin to shadow boxing. The target is elusive, and the energy expended is not productively applied. Third, because of historical delinking of political democracy from human rights, a critique of the former is not necessarily the unveiling of the latter.

Soon the problem becomes obvious. The human rights corpus has a mercury-like quality: elusive and slippery. This is not a fingerprint that augurs well for a truth-searching inquiry. Nor does it render the corpus open to a reformist impulse. My argument is that identifying—*equating*—political democracy with human rights would provide us with a solid foundation for debating, articulating, and formulating an ideology that can better respond to powerlessness, human indignity, and the challenges of markets and globalization. The human rights movement is presented by its scholars and advocates as above politics. Even though its basic texts assume a genre of political and social organization, the literature and discourse of human rights are divorced from self-interest, ideology, materialism, and partisanship. Instead, movement scholars and activists paint it as a universal creed driven by nobility and higher human intelligence. The idiom of human rights is tinged with metaphors and language that suggest eternity or a final resting point in human history.

The basic human rights documents are not presented as either instrumentalist, utilitarian, experimental, or convenient. Rather, the authors speak as though such documents are the final truth. This elusive, yet lofty, idealism is almost biblical in its forbidding language. It implies that questioning its doctrine is perverse and unwelcome. The reality, however, is that human rights norms address mundane human problems and are routine politics. That is why the veneration of human rights, together with the attempt to clean the movement of partisanship, requires close and critical scrutiny. To understand why its proponents are shy to assert the ideological and historical signatures of the human rights corpus, one need not look further than their cradle. Admittedly, many of the ideas in human rights find analogies in other cultures and traditions, but this *particular* human rights corpus has its specific identity. It is that identity that yields certain societal typologies. As David Kennedy has aptly noted, the "human rights movement is the product of a particular moment and place."

He then indicts the origins of the human rights movement as "post-enlightenment, rationalist, secular, Western, modern, capitalist" (2002, 114). Kennedy talks about the ways in which these origins could be problematic for the movement—legitimacy in other cultures, the type of society that is created by the movement, and the social and other costs associated with this vision. Unlike most Western legal academics writing on human rights, Kennedy has no problem in identifying it with the politics of the modern, liberal, capitalist West, or political democracy. One can certainly conjecture as to why Kennedy is not invested in the general mystification of human rights that is the norm among Western writers and policymakers. The reason, as Kennedy himself suggests, is that he is not fully committed to the human rights project and he sees a movement in crisis: "The generation that built the human rights movement," he says, "focused its attention on the ways in which evil people in evil societies could be identified and restrained. More acute now is how good people, well-intentioned people in good societies, can go wrong, can entrench, support, the very things they have learned to denounce" (2002, 125).

Yet even in this article, much of which I agree with, Kennedy falls prey to the dichotomous matrix of the human rights movement in which the "good" secular West civilizes the "evil" or savage South, or "the other" (Mutua 2001). For what does he mean by "well-intentioned people in good societies"? Is that not the kind of language that excuses, legitimizes, and apoliticizes human rights without picking apart its political agenda? Ironically, though, I think this kind of language makes the point that the human rights movement *does* have a political agenda. After all, the "good society" is itself a normative project, and "well-intentioned people" are driven by the norms of the good society. What those norms are is what constitutes the political project of the human rights movement. Even so, Kennedy would probably object to the comments that Kenneth Roth, the executive director of Human Rights Watch, made in 1998 at a conference organized by the Carr Center for Human Rights Policy at the JFK School at Harvard.[6]

In response to my critique of human rights as a Eurocentric project, Roth likened human rights norms to antibiotics that must be administered to the sick, in this case the global South, even if they are unwilling to cooperate. For me, that was a revealing moment. Roth might as well have said explicitly that human rights were the antidote to political despotism, a regime of rules that would produce a secular, rights-based, modern political democracy. But he did not. The response by Roth betrays the deep-seated Eurocentrism of international law and its civilizing projects (Gathii 1999). But not all human rights activists refuse to own up to the political program of the movement. Ian Martin, a former head of Amnesty International, the one organization whose name is synonymous with human rights, called for the grounding of the movement in the "Universal Declaration of Human Rights and the two principal covenants on civil-political rights and social-economic-cultural rights." He was emphasizing the universality and equal importance of both sets of rights and arguing against a bias for the former over the latter. But he also warned that the human rights movement should not identify with the new Western rhetoric of "democracy, human rights, and the free market economy" (2002, 114).

But Martin's admonition appears to be tactical—if not strategic—although it is not based on principle or a sophisticated analysis of the relationship among human rights norms, democracy, and free markets. He seems to be saying that the movement should not be associated with the rhetoric of Western states. He is not saying that the rhetoric has no justification, philosophical foundation, or that it is wrong-headed. Rather, he is opposed to an *open* alliance between the human rights movement and the foreign policy objectives of the West. Nevertheless, he directly associates human rights norms with democracy: Of course, the human rights movement works to guarantee democracy. Universal human rights principles subsume democracy. They provide, however, a more precise definition of rights than can be derived from the hazier notion of promoting democracy, which itself can lead to too great a tolerance of human rights violations of governments that have been popularly elected—whatever the conditions and larger context for the elections (2002, 21–22). These assertions by Martin are unusual for a Western human rights crusader. They should be taken seriously and then further interrogated.

---

[6] The conference was the basis for an edited collection of essays on human rights. See Power and Allison (2000).

One might ask Martin to expand on what he thinks constitutes political democracy and where he sees a divergence, if any, between democracy and human rights. To the extent that he sees democracy as the *subset* of human rights, can he envisage other political systems, apart from political democracy, that are acceptable to human rights norms? Henkin seems to suggest this as a possibility, although he does not elaborate. In an apparent contradiction, Henkin (1990, 7) writes that human rights norms point to a particular political society, although not its form: The idea of rights reflected in the instruments, the particular rights recognized, and the consequent responsibilities for political societies imply particular political ideas and moral principles. International human rights does not hint at any theory of social contract, but it is committed to popular sovereignty. "The will of the people shall be the basis of the authority of government" and is to "be expressed in periodic elections which shall be by universal and equal suffrage" (Henkin 1990). It is not required that government based on the will of the people take any particular form.

It is not clear what Henkin is talking about when he uses the word *form* here. It appears that he is referring to different forms of political democracy, such as presidential or parliamentary systems, or different electoral systems (proportional representation as against a first-past-the-post system). These are types or iterations of the genre known as political democracy. As Steiner points out (1991, 930–31), and I think Henkin would agree, open political dictatorships, sham democracies, inherited leaderships, monarchies, and one-party states would violate the associational rights central to human rights and political democracy. A more direct and honest conversation about the political purposes of human rights can be had once these admissions are openly made. This would allow us to debate the values of human rights, its deficits, and ultimately the reformist project that must be undertaken to fully legitimize it. Whether that reformist project is really possible—as a pragmatic matter—is a different question.

What is important at this point in the history of the human rights movement is not whether its norms call for the installation of a political democracy. Movement scholars and activists should outwardly acknowledge this inherent conceptual and philosophical link so that attention can be focused on the meaning of that linkage. Are there, for example, some normative problems that are caused by this linkage? Do those problems deny the human rights movement—or political democracy—an opportunity to redeem its shortcomings? What are those shortcomings and can they be tweaked, or is there a necessity for a radical transformation of the human rights regime? It will be difficult, if not impossible, to get at some of these pressing questions if full disclosures are not made by the guardians of the human rights movement.

Human Rights and the African Reality

Assuming these basic philosophical difficulties, how can human rights as conceived be of any help to the reconstruction and recovery of the African postcolonial state? Five decades after decolonization, the African state is still haunted by crises of geographic, political, and moral legitimacy. It is beset by the protracted reality of national incoherence and the ills of economic underdevelopment. At its dawn, the African postcolonial state was handed a virtually impossible task: assimilate the norms of the liberal tradition overnight within the structures of the colonial state while at the same time building a nation from disparate groups in a hostile international political economy. Instead, the newly minted African postcolonial elites chose first to consolidate their own political power. We can blame them now, as I have, but we must also understand that the first instinct of the political class is to consolidate itself and concentrate power in its own hands.

In the Cold War context, this frequently meant stifling dissent, dismantling liberal constitutions, retreating to tribal loyalties or sycophantic cronies, and husbanding state resources for corruption or patronage purposes. In other words, any viable fabric of the postcolonial state started to crumble even before it was established. We know the rest—coups and countercoups, military regimes, and one-party dictatorships with the inevitable results of economic decay; collapse of infrastructure; the fragmentation of political society; bilious retribalization; religious, sectarian, and communal conflicts and civil wars; and state collapse in a number of cases. The achievement of political independence from colonial rule turned into a false renaissance as one African country after another experienced transitional difficulties. While the African state retained some form of international legitimacy, its domestic writ was wafer thin. It was a miracle that many African states did not implode altogether, given the challenges to internal legitimacy. Whatever the case, the liberal tradition failed to take hold as human rights were violated across the board (Zeleza and McConnaughay 2004).

However, the 1980s saw a resurgence of civil society and the reemergence of the political opposition. This started what has come to be loosely referred to as the Second Liberation. The entire continent was rocked by a wave of political liberalization not witnessed since the 1950s and 1960s. Virtually all states succumbed to some version of political reform. In all cases, the civil society and the political opposition sought a new social compact framed by the tenets of the liberal tradition. These were the rule of law, political democracy through multipartyism, checks on executive power, limitations on the arbitrary use of state power, judicial independence, directly elected and unencumbered legislatures, separation of powers, freedoms of the press, speech, assembly, and association—in a word, the whole gamut of civil and political rights or the full complement of so-called basic human rights.

It was as though Africans were asking to go back to the liberal constitutions imposed by the departing colonial powers. In some cases, new constitutional orders were established to respond to these demands. But a decade and a half after the frenzy to reintroduce the liberal tradition to the politics of Africa, we cannot count many blessings because the tumult of political liberalization has yielded very mixed results. Optimists see a steady progression, even though the reversals have been many and discouraging. Pessimists, or what one might even want to call realists, see an African state that is a stubborn predator, unable and unwilling to accept reform. For every one step forward, there seem to be several steps back. The near meltdown of Kenya in the aftermath of the December 2007 election is only one case in point. Is the African state impervious to human rights and the liberal tradition, or is the problem much more serious? The fault is variously placed on a bankrupt elite or political class; structural impediments within the state (ethnicity, religious zealotry, underdevelopment, the failure to establish a legitimate political order, social cleavages); an unyielding international economic order. Whatever the case, the jury on the current process of political liberalization, which is taking place simultaneously with economic globalization, is still out. It is still too early to say for certain whether the African postcolonial state is out of the woods.

The Limitations of Human Rights

The human rights corpus is defined by a variety of pathologies—both of choice and substance—that are limited and limiting. Many of these pathologies arise not only from the internal logic of the corpus, but also the tactical and strategic choices that its proponents have made over the past sixty years. One of these is the equation of the containment of state despotism with the attainment of human dignity. This "hands off" logic is an integral, if not the essential, signature of the corpus. Without going into a discussion about the critique of rights—indeterminacy, elasticity, and their double-edged signature—suffice it to note that the human rights project basically polices the space between the state and the individual and not between individual citizens. As put by Karl Klare (1991, 97), the dominant understanding of "the human rights project is to erect barriers between the individual and the state, so as to protect human autonomy and self-determination from being violated or crushed by governmental power." Yet there is nothing intrinsic to human beings that requires only their protection from the state and not the asymmetries of power among them.

This definition of the nature of human dignity, which draws heavily from liberalism and political democratic theory, has an atrophied understanding of the role of the state. Admittedly, the thick welfare state is an attempt to emphasize a more robust view of liberalism. In human rights doctrine, this fuller iteration of liberalism is ostensibly contained in the ICESCR. However, the flaccidity, impotency, and vagueness of the ICESCR are evidence of the bias of the corpus to the more limited vision (Bentham 1995, 41). As is the case with political democracy, the human rights regime appears to be more concerned with certain forms of human powerlessness than with others. This has certainly been the practice of human rights by the most influential human rights NGOs and institutions. In fact, there does not exist a major human rights NGO in the West that focuses on economic, social, and cultural rights. The problem is not simply one of orientation but of fundamental philosophical commitment by movement scholars and activists to vindicate "core" political and civil rights over a normative articulation that would disrupt vested class interests and require a different relationship between the state and citizens and among citizens.

It seems to have been convenient for human rights NGOs to shy away from questions of economic powerlessness during the Cold War because charities and Western governments frowned upon them. If so, it was a bias that was more than strategic—it was ideological. One of the more interesting pathologies of the human rights texts is their avoidance or reluctance to employ a certain vocabulary to describe powerlessness. What is striking about the key human rights documents is their failure to use some of the most important terms of the modern era to describe and formulate societal responses. In terms of power or lack of it, and the consequent violations, there are no more important words than "capitalism," "imperialism," "colonialism," and "apartheid." Yet the UDHR—the single most important human rights document—sanctions the right to private property (Article 147).

How credible is a document that calls itself a "common standard of achievement for all peoples and nations" (Preamble) if it does not recognize that at its writing most of the global South was under European colonial rule and subject to the vilest economic exploitation by the merchants of capital? It is difficult to believe that such an omission was an oversight. At the time, there was an epochal contest between socialism and capitalism. This too appears to have been conveniently overlooked in the basic texts. Or was it? My submission is that there was a surreptitious recognition of secularism, capitalism, and political democracy through the guarantee of the rights that yield a society framed by those systems. The failure to wrestle with the types of economic philosophies and systems that would best protect and nurture a fuller definition of human dignity has had a devastating effect on the human rights movement. From the start, the movement and its founders did not see themselves as charged with the responsibility to address economic powerlessness. Even though the UDHR addresses some economic, social, and cultural rights, it is clear that they are an afterthought and marginalized within the document.

Only the last six articles are devoted to these rights. But even so, the rights are not scripted in a way that directly confronts powerlessness and exploitation. The rights relating to work and labor assume, for example, the fact and legitimacy of capitalism and free markets (Articles 23–25). Working people are therefore expected to fight for their rights *within* those systems and structures. The same logic is the basis for the ICESCR, which presumably grants rights within a system of free enterprise that protects workers from the worst excesses of global capitalism. In this regard, the ICESCR should be understood as a normative project for a thick welfare state within a market economy. It is a document that seeks to mitigate the harshness of capitalism and give it a more human face. This failure of imagination and acquiescence to a free market vision of political democracy has robbed the human rights corpus and the movement of the impetus to think beyond markets and systems of exploitation that produce ugly social structures.

Fundamentally, the human rights corpus has no philosophy on money and whether, for example, the creation of a Bill Gates would itself be a violation of human rights norms. In political society, an absolute dictator would be impermissible under human rights norms and contemporary understandings of political democracy. Analogously, Bill Gates is the market equivalent of the political dictator, although that is not how he is understood in a political democracy or by the human rights corpus. In fact, Gates is a celebrated and venerated individual, the pinnacle of *success* in society. Yet the existence of his economic empire, which he holds personally, is a radical perversion of any egalitarian or equitable notions of human dignity. The multiplication of Gates by the number of other obscenely rich individuals and corporate interests yields a graphic overconcentration of power in the hands of a tiny majority. It is very difficult, if not impossible, to articulate a plausible argument of how a system that permits such vast differences among citizens does not violate basic notions of human dignity.

In an era of globalization, in which capital knows no borders and is virtually unaccountable, questions of economic justice and fairness should obsess the human rights corpus and the movement. It is not enough to decry, as human rights NGOs do, the worst excesses of globalization or the most shocking practices, such as sweatshops and cruel labor and slave-like conditions of work. The corpus must develop a defensible normative project to address economic and social arrangements and systems. Rather than treat the government simply as the regulator of markets—as is the case in a political democracy—human rights norms must do more. Perhaps one way of addressing this pathology is to reassess the place and role of the individual in society relative to the greater public good of the community and the environment. One of the problems here is the elevation of the individual and his placement above society. This runaway notion of individualism, which is a central tenet of liberalism, has retarded the capacity of human rights thinkers to moderate selfishness with community interests.

In other words, the individual should be placed within the society and constructed in such a way that he does not overwhelm his fellow beings or the society itself. There is nothing natural, inevitable, or frozen in time about how the individual ought to be constructed. Nor should a reconstruction of the individual necessarily wreak havoc with more defensible notions of popular sovereignty, individual autonomy, and political freedom. But this is an exercise that will require thinkers to look beyond Eurocentric lenses to build a more universal vision of the individual. The individual need not necessarily be placed at the center of the moral universe. Otherwise, the vices and abominations of globalization are bound to overcome the human race. Finally, the human rights corpus and movement focus too much on process and rights at the expense of politics and substance. This distinction is both a product of the rights idiom in which the corpus is expressed and tactical and strategic choices by movement activists. The movement sees itself as vindicating rights that are coded in positive law. In contrast, politics is partisan, sloppy, and lacking in neutrality. By casting themselves as doing the work of the law, movement activists perpetuate the myth of objectivity.

In fact, during the Cold War the human rights community in the West deliberately distanced itself from the overt promoters of democracy in the global South and the Soviet bloc (Carothers 1994). Instead, human rights activists presented themselves as a community interested in process and the rule of law, not politics or the ideological project of democracy. Partly, this was a reaction to the perceived danger of being seen as supporting the crusade of the West, particularly under President Ronald Reagan, of rooting out communism in favor of pro-Western market or political democracies. Even so, the human rights movement in the West relentlessly attacked Soviet bloc states and third world countries for their closed or authoritarian political systems. In this, they worked with prodemocracy human rights advocates in those countries. Objectively, human rights groups were pursuing an agenda very similar to that of the Reagan administration. Rather than playing such a game, human rights groups should only advocate consequentialist and outcome-based agendas instead of hiding behind process and rights. Such a full disclosure approach would demystify human rights and offer a clearer basis for critical thought.

There is little doubt that in the last half century the world has seen substantial progress in addressing state tyranny. Part of this success is clearly attributable to the human rights movement and its marketing of the liberal constitution and the values of political democracy. But the successful march against state despotism has been conducted as a cloak-and-dagger contest—pushing a value system without directly stating its normative and political identity. This is unfortunate and need not have been so, even if one were to allow for the tactical and strategic choices that the movement had to make. Lost in the translation was an opportunity to think more robustly about human rights as a political project and then question its broader prescriptions for the society of the future. This diffidence has been limiting to the human rights movement. Why hide the ball? Everything should be placed on the table so that we can openly debate questions of power and powerlessness and how to reformulate the human rights corpus to address pressing crises. Perhaps we will decide that human rights is not the right language for this struggle. Perhaps it is. In any case, we will never know until we take off the veil. What is clear today is that the movement will lose its relevance unless it can address—seriously and as a priority—human powerlessness in all its dimensions.

Can Human Rights Recover the African State?

The limitations that curtail the ability of the human rights corpus to respond to Africa's crises are conceptual and normative. The first limitation is simply one of the idiom in which the rights discourse is formulated. The language of rights, which is central to liberalism, is fraught with limitations that could be detrimental to the project of transforming deeply distorted societies. Inherent in the language of rights are indeterminacy, elasticity, and the double-edged nature of the rights discourse. All these characteristics open the rights language to malleability and misuse by malignant social elements, and they turn it into a tool in the hands of those opposed to reform. A case in point is South Africa, where a rights-based revolution has been unable to fundamentally transform deeply embedded social dysfunction and the perverse legacy of apartheid. The choice of the rights idiom as the medium of choice to unravel the ravages of apartheid has been less than successful in spite of continued economic growth (Matua 1997).

Another problem of the liberal tradition, which has been inherited by the human rights movement, is its unrelenting focus on individualism. This arises from liberalism's focus on formal equality and abstract autonomy. The human rights corpus views the individual as the center of the moral universe and, therefore, denigrates communities, collectives, and group rights. This is a particularly serious problem in Africa, where group and community rights are both deeply embedded in the cultures of the peoples and exacerbated by the multinational nature of the postcolonial state (Matua 1995b, 339). The concept of self-determination in Africa cannot simply be understood as an external problem: It must, of necessity, be understood as encompassing the many nations within a given postcolonial state. In reality, this means that individual rights of citizens within the state must be addressed in the context of group rights. Thus, group rights or the rights of peoples become important entitlements if the state is to gain the loyalties of its diverse citizens.

I do not deny that individualism is a necessity for any constitutional democracy, but I reject the idea that we can, or should, stop there in Africa. That would be a stunted understanding of rights from an African point of view. Indeed, for rights to make sense in the African context, one has to go beyond the individual and address group identities in the political and economic framework of the state. Even in South Africa, for example, one of the states with an avowedly liberal interpretation of the rights language, there was an accommodation of group rights to language, culture, and other forms of identity. One way political democracy deals with the question of multiple nations within one state is to grant autonomous regimes for groups or to devolve powers through forms of federalism (Steiner 1991, 1539). But the paradox for Africa is that autonomous regimes or federalist arrangements have not worked well wherever they have been tried (Matua 1995a, 1113). These schemes have been unable to stem the combustible problem of ethnicity and reduce the legitimacy of the state. Ethnic groups retain a consciousness that stubbornly refuses to transfer loyalty from the group to the whole nation.

Second, the human rights movement's primary grounding and bias toward civil and political rights—and the impotence and vagueness of economic, social, and cultural rights—is one of its major weaknesses in the African postcolonial context. Political democracy alone—without at least a strong welfare state or a social democracy—appears to be insufficient to recover the African state. The bias toward civil and political rights favors vested, narrow class interests and kleptocracies, which are entrenched in the bureaucratic, political, and business sectors of society and represent interests that are not inclined to challenge the economic powerlessness of the majority of postcolonial Africans. Yet the human rights movement assumes the naturalness of the market and the inevitability of employer-employee, capitalist-worker, and subordinated labor relations. It seeks the regulation of these relationships but not their fundamental reformulation.

By failing to interrogate and wrestle with economic and political philosophies and systems, the human rights movement indirectly sanctions capitalism and free markets. Importantly, the human rights corpus wrongly equates the containment of state despotism with the achievement of human dignity, so that it seeks the construction of a political society in which political tyranny—not economic tyranny—is circumscribed. But in so doing, it sidesteps economic powerlessness—the very condition that must be addressed if the African state is to be recovered. Clearly, political freedoms are important, but as South Africa has demonstrated, these are of limited utility in the struggle to empower populations and reduce the illegitimacy of the state. It is an illusion to think of powerlessness and human indignity in the African context in purely political terms, as the human rights movement does, and to prescribe political democracy and the human rights doctrine as a panacea.

Real human powerlessness and indignity in Africa—the very causes of the illegitimacy of the African state—arise from social and economic conditions. That is why the human rights movement's recognition of secularism, capitalism, and political democracy must be discussed openly to unveil its true identity so that we can recalculate its uses, and the limitations of those uses, to the reconstruction of the African state. To be useful to Africa's reconstruction, human rights cannot simply be advocated as an unreformed Eurocentric doctrine that must be gifted to native peoples. Nor can it be imposed on Africa like an antibiotic or be seen as a cure for the ills of a dark continent. I am afraid that this is how many in the West imagine what for them is a human rights crusade toward Africa. So far, this law-and-development model has not—and will not—work. Not only is it an imposition, but it would also deal mostly with symptoms, while leaving the underlying fundamentals untouched.

To be of utility to Africa and fundamentally transform the continent's dire fortunes, human rights must address economic powerlessness and the scandalous international order. Otherwise, it will promise too much while delivering too little, as it did in the case of Rwanda with the establishment of the International Criminal Tribunal for Rwanda and a false peace within the country. It will promise too much, while delivering too little, as it did in the wave of the so-called Second Liberation. The challenge for us is to figure out how we can retool and rethink the human rights project as one of the vehicles for the reconstruction of the African postcolonial state. I am afraid that this is a task for which we have been found wanting.

Conclusion

A half century is not a long time in the life of a country, much less a continent. That is how long Africa has been free of colonial rule. It is within that time span that the African postcolonial state has had an opportunity to revisit the project of modernity under the guidance of Africans themselves. There can be no doubt that the record of that period has been mixed, to put it hopefully. More often than not, the African state has labored under huge burdens of legitimacy and performance. In virtually every case, there have been huge disappointments. Rays of hope, whenever they have been possible, have been short and fleeting. Analysts have carried out numerous diagnoses of the African state. There is agreement on the general malaise, but not on the cure for it. At one level, there is consensus that the deficits of legitimacy, democracy, and development can be ameliorated by creating the open society. But is liberalism enough of a panacea for the African state, or do we need to imagine other solutions?

There is no doubt that the lessons of African history over the past several centuries have been discouraging. Since colonial rule, there has been a persistence and stubbornness to the crises facing the continent. There is a general consensus among proponents of liberalism that two variables, which are related, are at the center of these crises. The first, and perhaps the most important, is the African state itself. The illegitimacy and resistance of the African state to democratization are without question the key denominators in its dysfunction. Whether it is the repressive nature of the state, its disdain for civil society, its inability to perform the basic functions of statehood, or its proclivity for corruption, the African state stands at the center of the crisis. The second variable is Africa's relationship with the international legal, political, and economic order. International institutions, hegemonic states, and the culture of international law have been negligent at best, and they have been destructive at worst.

How do African states become effective and enabling actors in the lives of their citizens, instead of objects of charity and pity by the West and the rest of the world? In other words, how does the continent move from a humanitarian wasteland to developed, functioning, and democratic states? The suggestion is that the process of transformation has to be foundational and thorough. It is no longer tenable to simply prescribe cautious, band-aid, and unimaginative programs of the type that donors and multilateral organizations have historically promoted. Instead, African states must be reengineered from the bottom up. This is a task that must begin at home, with the Africans themselves. The citizens of each state, led by their elites, must consider the normative values and foundational compact on which the state is based and then either renegotiate them or restructure them to create a more viable and legitimate political society. Without such reform, the African state cannot be redeemed. Internationally, Africa needs debt relief, direct foreign investment, aid, and better trade terms to couple political reforms with economic renewal.

But there are no shortcuts for Africa. African states must reconstruct their political orders, address ethnicity and group rights in political transitions, grow and nurture a vibrant civil society that is national in character, and expand the commitment of religious institutions to the full democratic project. In some countries, the constitution-writing framework provides the perfect opportunity to begin the political renaissance of the state on all these fronts at once. There will no doubt be different entry points for a variety of states. And each of these variables will require contextual emphasis depending on the particulars of the state in question. But will these liberal prescriptions respond to the stubborn crises of the African state? Or do we need to reimagine liberalism to make it useful for the African reality? Based on historical evidence—and taking even the most successful cases such as South Africa into account—it is clear that even boilerplate liberalism under the guise of human rights is an insufficient response to African postcolonialism. My proposal, however, is not to throw out the baby with bathwater. Rather, it is to reconstruct the liberal project and its human rights expression in order to reclaim the tortured soul of the Africa state.

REFERENCES

Alford, William P. "Exporting the "Pursuit of Happiness." *Harvard Law Review* 113 (2000): 1677–1715.

Anghie, Antony. "Finding the Peripheries: Sovereignty and Colonialism in Nineteenth-Century International Law." *Harvard International Law Journal* 40 (1999): 1–81.

_____. *Imperialism, Sovereignty, and the Making of International Law.* Cambridge University Press, 2005.

Bentham, David. "What Future for Economic and Social Rights?" *Political Studies* 43 (1995): 1–9.

Carothers, Thomas. "Democracy and Human Rights: Policy Allies or Rivals?" *Washington Quarterly* (Summer 1994): 109–120.

Cassese, Antonio. "The General Assembly: Historical Perspective 1945–1989." In *The United Nations and Human Rights: A Critical Appraisal,* edited by Philip Alston. Oxford University Press, 1992.

Dahl, Robert. *A Preface to Democratic Theory.* University of Chicago Press, 1956.

Donnelly, Jack. "Human Rights and Western Liberalism." In *Human Rights in Africa: Cross-Cultural Perspectives,* edited by Abdullahi A. An-Na'im and Francis M. Deng. Washington, D.C.: Brookings Institution, 1990.

Gathii, James Thuo. "International Law and Eurocentricity." *European Journal of International Law* 9 (1998): 184–211.

Glendon, Mary Ann. *A World Made New: Eleanor Roosevelt and the Universal Declaration of Human Rights.* New York: Random House, 2001.

_____. "The Forgotten Crucible: The Latin American Influence on the Universal Human Rights Idea." *Harvard Human Rights Journal* 16 (2003): 27–39.

Henkin, Louis. *The Age of Rights.* New York: Columbia University Press, 1990.

Huntington, Samuel P. *The Third Wave: Democratization in the Twentieth Century.* Norman: University of Oklahoma Press, 1991.

Kennedy, David. "The International Human Rights Movement: Part of the Problem." *Harvard Human Rights Journal* 15 (2002): 101–125.

Klare, Karl. "Legal Theory and Democratic Reconstruction." *University of British Columbia Law Review* 25 (1991): 69–104.

Leary, Virginia. "The Effect of Western Perspectives on International Human Rights." In *Human Rights in Africa: Cross-Cultural Perspectives,* edited by Abdullahi A. An-Na'im and Francis M. Deng. Washington, D.C.: Brookings Institution, 1990.

Locke, John. *Two Treatises of Government,* edited by Peter Laslett. Cambridge University Press, 1988 (1689).

Martin, Ian. "The New World Order: Opportunity or Threat for Human Rights?" Edward A. Smith Visiting Fellow Lecture, Harvard Law School, 1993.

Morsink, Johannes. *The Universal Declaration of Human Rights: Origins, Drafting, and Intent.* Philadelphia: University of Pennsylvania Press, 2000.

Mutua, Makau wa. "Why Redraw the Map of Africa: A Moral and Legal Inquiry." *Michigan Journal of International Law* 16 (1995a): 1113–1176.

———. "The Banjul Charter and the African Cultural Fingerprint: An Evaluation of the Language of Duties." *Virginia Journal of International Law* 35 (1995b): 339–380.

———. "The Ideology of Human Rights." *Virginia Journal of International Law* 36 (1996): 589–657.

———. "Hope and Despair for a New South Africa: The Limits of Rights Discourse." *Harvard Human Rights Journal* 10 (1997): 63–114.

———. "Critical Race Theory and International Law: The View of an Insider-Outsider." *Villanova Law Review* 45 (2000): 841–854.

———. "Savages, Victims, and Saviors: The Metaphor of Human Rights." *Harvard International Law Journal* 42 (2001): 201–245.

Power, Samantha, and Graham Allison, eds. *Realizing Human Rights: Moving from Inspiration to Impact.* New York: St. Martin's Press, 2000.

Schumpeter, Joseph. *Capitalism, Socialism, and Democracy.* New York: HarperCollins, 1984 (1942).

Steiner, Henry J. "Political Participation as a Human Right." *Harvard Human Rights Yearbook* 1 (1988): 77–134.

———. "Ideals and Counter-ideals in the Struggle over Autonomy Regimes for Minorities." *Notre Dame Law Review* 66 (1991): 1539–1568.

Steiner, Henry J., and Philip Alston. *International Human Rights in Context: Law, Politics, Morals.* New York: Oxford University Press, 2008.

Strauss, Leo. *Natural Right and History.* University of Chicago Press, 1999.

Zeleza, Paul Tiyambe, and Philip J. McConnaughay, eds. *Human Rights, the Rule of Law, and Development in Africa.* Philadelphia: University of Pennsylvania Press, 2004.

Chapter 21

AFRICA IN INTERNATIONAL RELATIONS THEORY
Addressing the Quandary of Africa's Ongoing Marginalization Within the Discipline

Christopher LaMonica

In recent years, there has been a range of responses to the visible decline of interest in African area studies and the ongoing marginalization of Africa within the discipline of international relations. Some argue that there is no lack of scholarly interest in Africa (Bayart 2000; Taylor and Williams 2004), while others continue to suggest (Kitching 2000; Alpers and Roberts 2002; Hyden 2006) that the reverse is true. With a view to reframing the prevailing study of Africa in international relations theory, this chapter supports the latter view with a suggestion as to what scholars might do to alter present circumstances.

The chapter will argue that students and scholars of African affairs need to identify parallels of political experience and theory, rather than follow the prevailing norms of social science methodology, which stresses the importance of identifying Africa as "different." Among the recent trends in the literature is the suggestion that Africa is, in various ways, different from other regions, i.e., the language of international relations (IR) theory is inappropriate for the African political context due to the ambiguity of the African sovereign state. I believe that this position contributes to the process by which IR theory systematically marginalizes Africa with Western bias and assumptions (Dunn and Shaw 2001).

William Brown[1] has asserted that the notion that Africa is somehow different can only lead us down the path of "essentializing" Africa, in much the same way Orientalists have done to the Middle East (Said 1979). In this regard, Dunn and Shaw are right that African realities are marginalized and are, therefore, presented as different, and Brown is also right to say that there are limitations in presenting African affairs as "unique." The challenge, I suggest in this chapter, is that if we are to establish the right platform for a reconstructive analysis of Africa, we need to find ways to improve dialogue between Africanists and international relations theorists so that African political thought and experience can be better integrated into the main corpus of IR theory. Today, more than ever, the ongoing marginalization of Africa within the discipline is simply a matter of choice. We can do better.

Following a brief survey of the early intellectual debates within the field and the resulting "intellectual framework" of IR theory that Hans J. Morgenthau and E.H. Carr[2] established, I argue that there are mainly two

---

[1] William Brown, "Africa and International Relations: A Comment on IR Theory, Anarchy and Statehood," *Review of International Studies* 32 (2006): 116–143.

[2] E.H. Carr, *Twenty Years' Crisis,* first published in 1939, and Hans J. Morgenthau, *Politics Among Nations,* first published in 1948.

reasons why African political ideas have generally not been integrated into IR theory. Firstly, African theorists are forced to participate in global social science debates based on Western IR theory; and, secondly, the majority of IR theorists lack motivation to include African political thought and experience in the debates.

Political scientists, I suggest, are more fearful of looking naïve than other academics. Accordingly, caution and pessimism prevail, with a seemingly entrenched focus on the interests of the powerful. In other words, African studies have fallen victim to a range of Foucauldian challenges that link established "knowledge" with the interests of "power." I, therefore, consider the more "global" approaches used in other social science disciplines as possible models for future change in IR study. Finally, I consider some short-term ways by which African historical experience and ideas can be integrated into the ongoing debates within IR theory.

Recent Marginalization of Africa: Theory and Practice

In a remarkable June 2000 contribution to *African Studies Review,* Associate Professor of Politics Gavin Kitching from the University of New South Wales, Australia, remarked, "In a word, I gave up African studies because I found it depressing."[3] Kitching had entered the field at a time when "hope and optimism in and about Africa" had dominated; these had now been "replaced by pessimism and cynicism."[4] A whole generation of Africanists, now nearing the end of their careers, has reported much the same. Goran Hyden, for example, recently commented, "When I started my own career in political science in the early 1960s, Africa was the center of attention in the discipline."[5] And Immanuel Wallerstein provides a similar account:

> When I first set foot in Africa, in Dakar in 1952, I came in contact with an Africa in the last moments of the colonial era, an Africa in which nationalist movements were coming into existence and rapidly flourishing everywhere. I came in contact with an Africa whose populations, and particularly its young people, were optimistic and sure that the future looked bright. . . . In 1952, Africans were not alone in such sentiments . . . similar sentiments pervaded the peoples of Europe. And the general optimism was shared even, perhaps especially, in the United States . . . [yet] the optimistic, positive language the world used in the 1950s and 1960s was exceptional and, it seems, momentary.[6]

These were some of the sad testimonies available to me as a graduate student of African politics from 1995 to 2000, and they are indicative of the intellectual climate of that time. In fact, Kitching's piece entitled "Why I Gave Up African Studies" was made just months prior to my own doctoral dissertation defense on local governance in Zambia. During my *séjour* at Boston University's African Studies Center, it was hard not to notice the sleepy atmosphere that pervaded this once vibrant place of political science study. The words of Kitching, Hyden, and Wallerstein remind us that this dramatic turnaround, from center stage to today's almost complete disregard of African politics within political science study, is a remarkable event within the discipline.

---

[3] Gavin Kitching, "Why I Gave Up African Studies," *African Studies Review & Newsletter* XXII, no. 1 (June 2000): 21–26.

[4] ibid., 21.

[5] Goran Hyden, *African Politics in Comparative Perspective* (New York: Cambridge University Press 2006), 3.

[6] Immanuel Wallerstein, "What Hope Africa? What Hope the World?" in *After Liberalism* (New York: The New Press, 1995), 46, 48.

Somehow, there is not universal agreement among Africanists regarding the matter. Jean-François Bayart has commented, for example, "More than ever, the discourse of Africa's marginality is a nonsense [*sic*]."[7] Ian Taylor and Paul Williams similarly suggest that "Africa's predicament does not lack scholarly interest . . ." and that both extremes, of Afro-pessimism and Afro-optimism, "do a disservice to the study of Africa."[8] But there is a danger in making such arguments because students and young scholars can wrongly get the impression that there is no real cause for concern, i.e., "the issues are being addressed." For certain, as the world's few Africanists bicker among themselves over these matters, IR scholarship generally ignores African issues. A leading (Palgrave) IR text, for example, mentions Africa only once and in passing. The full sentence reads, "It is an argument that has been strengthened by recent transitions to democracy in Africa, East Asia and Latin America."[9] Another leading (Oxford) IR text of over eight hundred pages similarly mentions Africa in passing, briefly mentioning the issues of decolonization and regional cooperation in Africa.[10] Presumably, these texts deal with more important matters. So while there might be "scholarly" interest, as Taylor and Williams argue, it is not adequately reflected in the IR literature.

To the few students pursuing study in African politics today, some of whom are in the process of contemplating their future teaching careers, the messages are therefore mixed. For now, it seems clear that fewer students are pursuing this path of study than a generation ago. It is also clear that the broader context within which African studies take place has dramatically changed. Whereas the previous generation of scholars worked in an atmosphere of "optimism and hope," today's generation is presented with an Africa that is given the option to "participate or fall off the face of the Earth," if it is addressed at all. Whatever the exact reasons, many of the federally funded centers for African area studies throughout the United States (some of which were established in the 1940s and 1950s) are now virtually empty.[11] Some would argue that the ongoing business orientation of university teaching, which stresses the merit of individual interest, may have much to do with this trend. My point here is that, for the vast majority of today's IR theorists, professional interest does not include Africa.

Indeed, today, the very notion that a social scientist should take an interest in Africa for humanitarian interests, which may have motivated an earlier generation, is largely viewed as wrongheaded, patronizing, and foolish. Similarly, now that Cold War ties with Africa are no more, "aid" is largely viewed as detrimental to African interests.[12] In other words, "to help is to hurt" and it is in this new environment,

---

[7] Jean-François Bayart (2000) cited Ian Taylor and Paul Williams, *Africa in International Relations: External Involvement on the Continent* (New York: Routledge, 2004), 1.

[8] Taylor and Williams, *Africa in International Relations*, 1–2.

[9] Scott Burchill, *Theories of International Relations* (London: Palgrave, 2005), 56.

[10] John Baylis and Steve Smith, eds., The *Globalization of World Politics: An Introduction to International Relations* (Oxford University Press, 2006).

[11] While some would assuredly dispute this personal observation, there can be little doubt that these centers are far from "center stage" as Hyden (2006) describes. A full list of African Studies Centers in the United States and elsewhere is provided at africa.msu.edu/ascs.htm.

[12] Literature critically assessing the need for aid goes back to at least the University of the Chicago debates of the 1960s. See, for example, Hans Morgenthau, "A Political Theory of Foreign Aid," *The American Political Science Review* 56, no. 2 (June 1962): 301–309; and, more generally, the works of Milton Friedman, including *Capitalism and Freedom* (University of Chicago Press, 1962). These arguments gained tremendous popularity in the 1980s during the Reagan and Thatcher years and influenced policy. With regard to the recent and quite convincing critique of humanitarian aid see, for example, Fiona Terry, *Condemned to Repeat? The Paradox of Humanitarian Action* (Ithaca, NY: Cornell University Press, 2002); and Thomas G. Weiss, "Researching Humanitarian Intervention: Some Lessons," *Journal of Peace Research* 38, no. 4 (2001): 419–428.

hostile to what are now seen as patronizing investigations of Africa, that Kitching and Wallerstein reach their conclusions. There is also, and understandably, a growing number of African observers who are similarly dismissive of Western "aid," which they see as historically biased in favor of the powerful, as little more than a form of patronage.

There is no shortage of reasons for Africans to be suspicious of relations with the outside world: thus far, "inclusion" in the historical process of capitalist-oriented globalization has destroyed African kingdoms, undermined the checks and balances of indigenous political systems, challenged local norms and cultures, entirely transformed African economies, and generally dismissed the prospect for genuine African input. There were good reasons for nationalist leaders like Kwame Nkrumah or Patrice Lumumba to be critical of Western state involvement in African affairs, and as we enter the twenty-first century it is certain that such problematic relations will finally begin to fade.

Tragically, as the prospects for clearer thinking on Africa's historical role in the world should be improving, there remains a strong reflex of marginalization and difference. As is the case with so many other aspects of global relations with Africa/ns, the discipline of IR continues to reject African voices. To date, there is no real tradition of dialogue. Instead, what presides is self-interested exploitation, systematic debasement of all things African, and in the post–Cold War era, a remarkable fad of fingerpointing to newly found "corruption" and problems of governance. In other words, for a variety of reasons, the discipline of IR seems to say that Africa/ns cannot be listened to yet because they are "different," "not ready," "corrupt," or have no political ideas worthy of real consideration. The hypocrisies surrounding the support (if not the creation) of political "monsters" during the Cold War, contrasted with newly found "African problems," have not been lost on contemporary observers of African politics.

The Kenyan writer Mukoma Wa Ngũgĩ has argued, for example, "If a [British/Western] society continues to gain from a past atrocity, doesn't it have a duty to the children of the victims?"[13] In the current "save Africa" cauldron, as Ngũgĩ calls it, there are "two active ingredients missing: Africans and modern African history."[14] For those scholars who do take an interest in Africa, the problems "there" continue to be framed as "projects" for the powerful, in only the most pessimistic terms, and this almost invariably does not include Africans. Again, we can all do better.

Much of the pessimism towards Africa may well be based on many Africanists' new doubts over their long-held views on Africa and "solutions" to Africa's woes. Often remarked on, particularly in U.S. contexts, is that many of the Africanist professors who continue to work within these environments are, like Kitching, avowedly Marxist in their orientation. While these former advocates of nationalization and other politically leftist ideas are begrudgingly altering their lecture notes, any remaining Marxist logic used in the classroom tends to only further alienate the largely conservative student body that now seems to shun discussions of African politics.[15] In other words, this highly visible lack of interest—a remarkable reversal from previous decades—could also be due to the change in political orientation of many of the students themselves. In a post–Cold War atmosphere that suggests "Marxism is dead," the Marxist professor is suspect among many students.

---

[13] Mukoma Wa Ngugi, "To Save Africa: A Missing Step, Ex-colonial Powers Giving Africa Aid Today Should Also Right Past Wrongs," *The Christian Science Monitor*, November 13, 2007.

[14] ibid.

[15] Kitching's piece and the statement that he remained avowedly Marxist led to extensive debate on "a discipline adrift" in the years that followed. See chronicle.com/colloquy/2003/adrift.

The very fact that a Marxist orientation remains popular among Africanists past and present should not come as a surprise; it is difficult, upon reflection, to argue the merit of debating ideas when discussing African realities that seem so often dominated by matters of poverty, greedy elites, and other materialist concerns. Put simply, historical materialism strikes a chord for many in African area studies, whereas debating the merits of ideas in political philosophy seems like little more than the luxury of ivory tower elites. This is precisely what many Western students say of Marxist-Africanists in a post–Cold War world. As one observer put it on the *Chronicle of Higher Education* Web site, Marxists like Kitching are now "ineffectual, insulated and irrelevant."[16] And it is perhaps this opinion, more than any other, that explains Kitching's decision to move to other areas of political study. That is, it may have been more than just the subject that was depressing to him.

Throughout the 1990s, African leaders who had historically expressed support for Marxist views continued to believe that the pattern of Cold War patronage would continue in some form. In June 1993, for example, the still–presidential hopeful Nelson Mandela expressed his wish for some kind of Marshall Plan for South Africa. "What we expect," he told *Time* magazine, "is that the Western world, led by the US, should ensure that massive measures of assistance are given to the people of South Africa."[17] But, of course, this did not occur—least of all from the United States. For decades, U.S. aid patterns had been heading in the opposite direction from what post–Cold War African leaders like Mandela might have preferred. In fact, from 1960 to 2000, the U.S. stance on aid changed dramatically; similar patterns can be seen among virtually all of the Organization for Economic Co-operation and Development (OECD) "donor" states.

The logic for the United States' having 0.12 percent of GDP devoted to Official Development Assistance (ODA), while other OECD states have continued to provide ten times that percentage, is another clear demonstration of today's prevailing stance towards providing assistance to developing regions of the world, including Africa: "to help is to hurt." If anything, promoters of the Washington Consensus would like to convince other state donors of the need to reduce aid. According to this view, the Cold War African state had been a place of corruption and inefficiency; to remove the politically motivated flow of funds is the path towards better governance, less corruption, and accountability. Similarly, aid has only distorted economic development, reducing the drive and motivation of the local entrepreneur. All of these developmental distortions, and presumably Marxist logic, will ultimately wither on the vine, leading to a more prosperous Africa.

Table 21.1 Net ODA to "Third World" States as a Percentage of GNP (OECD): United States vs. Total (1960–2000)

	1960	1970	1980	1990	2000
United States	0.53	0.31	0.27	0.21	0.12
OECD Total	0.52	0.34	0.37	0.33	0.25

Source: OECD, *Development Cooperation* (various years) in Theodore H. Cohn, *Global Political Economy* (2006); Jeffrey Sachs, "The Development Challenge," *Foreign Affairs* 84, no. 2 (March/April 2005): 87.

---

[16] See comments posted on the above Web site by Brad Geltapfel.

[17] Nelson Mandela interview, in *Time*, June 14, 1993, quoted in Anthony Sampson, *Mandela: The Authorized Biography* (New York: Alfred A. Knopf, 1999), 507.

For those who bother to look, statistics on Africa's marginalization in world affairs are not difficult to find. Political economist Theodore Cohn reminds us that the developed market economies of the world still account for 92.1 percent of outward stocks of foreign direct investment (FDI) and 72.1 percent of the inward stocks. In other words, Cohn suggests, that in practice there exists a "triad including the European Union, North America, and Japan" as the main source and recipient of FDI.[18] In fact, mutual support within this triad was the stated objective of the highly influential Trilateral Commission, established in 1973:

> [To] seek a private consensus on the specific problems examined in the Trilateral analysis. Consensus-seeking must be a central element in the Trilateral process . . . the commission will seek to educate audiences in the three regions, so that public opinion in Japan, North America, and Europe will come to reflect private consensus.[19]

Much has been written on the self-interested motives of the Trilateral Commission vis-à-vis the developing world, so I will not repeat it here. Suffice to say that, since the 1990s, some use the term "triadization" to describe a new kind of hegemony, dominated by liberal policies and shared by three dominant countries/regional blocs: the United States/North America, Germany/EU, and Japan/East Asia.[20] Critics of developed-state dialogue within the Trilateral Commission, or a developed-state organization like the OECD, fear that this can only lead to the virtual exclusion of "the Rest," which includes Africa.

To Marxist-Leninists, disproportionate benefits in the global economy were often portrayed in terms of rich-poor or core-periphery, whereby a developed world had disproportionately benefited from the historical development of capitalism. In the 1980s—considered a "lost decade" for Africa—even proponents of laissez-faire capitalism began to question the direction of development in some regions of the world. In 1982, John Ruggie argued, for example, that the post–World War II period of decolonization was dominated by "embedded liberalism," which led to "lending and investment in the peripheral areas that has been both relatively lower [than under laissez-faire liberalism in the nineteenth century] and positively correlated with core expansion . . ."[21] In other words, liberal practices of the twentieth century were leading to a concentration of wealth in the core developed states, as the reverse was occurring in peripheral, underdeveloped states. And the statistics of the past few decades appear to back Ruggie's argument: when one considers inward stocks of FDI into Africa, as a percentage of the world total, they have declined from 6.7 percent in 1975 to 2.2 percent in 2000.[22] By contrast, developed market economies (Western Europe, the United States, and Japan) maintained between 72.7 percent and 80 percent of the world total during the same period.[23] The point here is that the practical realities of FDI flows within the triad, the three-decade-long pursuits of the Trilateral Commission, and the

---

[18] Theodore H. Cohn, *Global Political Economy* (2006), 309.

[19] Gerard C. Smith, cited in Holly Sklar, ed., *Trilateralism: The Trilateral Commission and Elite Planning for World Management* (Boston: South End Press, 1980), xii.

[20] Tim Allen and Alan Thomas, *Poverty and Development: Into the 21st-Century* (Oxford University Press, 2000), 252.

[21] John Gerard Ruggie, "International Regimes, Transactions and Change: Embedded Liberalism in the Postwar Economic Order," *International Organization* 36, no. 2 (Spring 1982).

[22] Theodore H. Cohn, *Global Political Economy*, 283.

[23] ibid.

Figure 21.1   Triadization and Africa

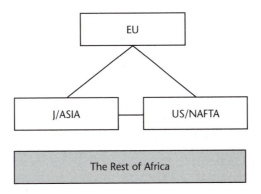

cooperative policymaking of OECD states have clear parallels in the theoretical discussions that take place in the political science classroom: interest in Africa is on the decline.

Economist Jeffrey Sachs, now leading the UN Millennium Development Goals (MDG) Project, has in recent years fought against the marginalization of African concerns in international affairs and, in particular, the idea that OECD development assistance should be kept to a minimum. In his best-selling book, *The End of Poverty,* Sachs provocatively states that the Marshall Plan provided "more than 1 percent of US GNP, on average, from 1948 through 1952 to rebuild Western Europe, around ten times the current effort as a share of GNP."[24] In a political environment focused on matters of security, Sachs also argues that Africa and other underdeveloped regions of the world are a crucial part of U.S. national interest. In a recent *Foreign Affairs* article, for example, Sachs states that "development aid is just as fundamental as military spending to US national security."[25] While cautious of overly zealous military expenditure and a vocal critic of the Bush administration, Sachs understands what has motivated the U.S. Congress to provide funding in the recent past—matters of national security. The ongoing "justifications" for a planned U.S. African Central Command (AFRICOM) use many of the same arguments.[26] It remains to be seen if these security-oriented (and funded) initiatives will have a positive or negative impact on Africa's relation to the global triad. Certainly, critics of Sachs's previous work on structural reform in other transitional economies of the world would likely argue that his new focus on Africa is misguided and, quite possibly, detrimental. Many free market economists like Sachs, who had

---

[24] Jeffrey Sachs, *The End of Poverty: How We Can Help Make It Happen in Our Lifetime* (London: Penguin Books, 2005), 342.

[25] Jeffrey Sachs, "The Development Challenge," *Foreign Affairs* 84, no. 2 (March/April 2005): 86.

[26] J. Stephen Morrison, "Exploring the US Africa Command and a New Strategic Relationship with Africa," testimony before the Senate Foreign Relations Subcommittee on Africa" (Washington, D.C.: Center for Strategic and International Studies, August 1, 2007).

previously focused on growth, are seemingly broadening their range of concerns, partly in response to UN MDG initiatives.[27]

The UN MDG effort—to increase ODA to 0.7 percent of OECD states' GNP—has, accordingly, met with much resistance. Aid in the form of Cold War patronage and structural reform loans has been rightly criticized by the political left. And, as discussed, the political right has similarly criticized aid, again, perhaps appropriately. Certainly Cold War forms of "aid as patronage" can corrupt, and aid has not always been used effectively. With the new anti-aid posture among the political left and right, the end result is that ODA remains well below 0.7 percent across the board, and the new emphasis (since the 2005 Paris Declaration) is "aid efficiency." In-line with the realist logic of IR, OECD state ODA also remains stubbornly focused on assistance to states of "national interest," for example Iraq and Afghanistan.[28] Today, if anything, U.S. policy towards Africa remains dominated by free trade initiatives through the (inappropriately named) African Growth and Opportunity Act (2000, 2004). The message is again "participate or fall off the face of the Earth."[29]

The Essentialists' Argument

One recurring theme among contemporary mainstream Africanists, especially those in the EU-North American-Japan triad, is that Africa is somehow different and can only be considered under alternative frameworks. This of course follows a long pattern of treating Africa and Africans as "exotic. This is what ultimately annoyed W.E.B. DuBois about the promoters of the 1920s–1940s Harlem Renaissance; in his view, their emphasis was ultimately on the entertaining differences of "the Negro." "Negrotarians" was Zora Neale Hurston's term for "Whites" who specialized in Afro-American uplift. They were divided between "earnest humanitarians and those who were merely fascinated."[30] It was in the midst of making all things African exotic and entertaining that the American writer Arna Bontemps observed, for instance, that it was now "fun to be a negro. . . . In Harlem, it was like a foretaste of paradise. . . . A blue haze descended at night and with it strings of fairy lights on the broad avenues."[31]

With visual reminders of Africans' exotic—presumably "tribal"—ways, patrons of the time were duly entertained by scantily clad women of African descent dancing amid "African" scenes. DuBois was among the first of the era to emphasize not only the vulgarity of the presentations, but also the wrong-headed spirit of the shows. There were many problems, but among his primary concerns was the dehumanization of the African through "Black stereotyping." Accordingly, in his many writings, DuBois

---

[27] As described in Jeffrey Sachs's most recent publication, *Common Wealth: Economics for a Crowded Planet* (London: Penguin Press, 2008), in which he considers a broad range of development issues, not simply economic growth. One could cynically argue that economists like Sachs are only now responding to long-standing critiques, political pressures, and the new directions in funding.

[28] In 2007, for example, the two top recipients of ODA from the United States were Iraq and Afghanistan. See www.oecd.org/dataoecd/42/30/40039096.gif.

[29] The "duping" of the U.S. political left, including many African Americans into the African Growth and Opportunity Act (AGOA) in the late 1990s, is a story that remains largely untold. Certainly, there were warnings, including "Oppose the Misnamed 'African Growth and Opportunity Act,'" *Public Citizen News* (May/June 1998), but U.S. politicians, from Charles Rangel (D-NY) to Jesse Jackson, Jr. (D-IL), ultimately supported the bill. In short, like the focus of all free market initiatives, the virtue of AGOA is in its possibilities for "efficiency" not "equity" or "fairness." The latter virtues do matter, particularly in the development of new relations with Africa and within the African context.

[30] David Levering Lewis, *When Harlem Was in Vogue* (London: Penguin Books, 1997), 98.

[31] Arna Bontemps, "Harlem the Beautiful," *Negro Digest* 15, no. 3 (Jan. 1965): 62; cited in ibid., 103.

focused on the problems of emphasizing difference and the continued marginalization of all things related to Africa. As late as 1946, he was still compelled to describe his "main issue" in the following terms, "black Africans are men in the same sense as white European or yellow Asiatics. . . ."[32]

While DuBois did not live to see the passage of U.S. civil rights legislation, he did witness the aforementioned moment of hope and optimism for postcolonial Africa. And this is when Frantz Fanon's work becomes especially important. What Fanon describes in clearer terms than most writers of the era is the seemingly dramatic "flip" in thinking about the African as colonized subject that, in his mind, would need to take place in the minds and practices of the former colonizers and formerly colonized. The "soul-less primitive" or former "slave" would now have to be treated as a "brother," and this, Fanon was among the first to argue, could be too much of an "ask." Notions of "difference" had become deeply embedded among colonizers and Africans alike.

Fanon understood that (in the Algerian context and elsewhere) it would be near impossible to shake off the various cultural, institutional, psychological, and other impacts that had accumulated; his inclination, which struck a chord with so many at the time, was to think in humanistic terms of true equality, as he wrote in his seminal *Peau noire, masques blancs.*[33] In the end, amid the horrors of ongoing torture in Algeria, news of which reached the popular press, Fanon forcefully advocated violence against the colonizer. A well-educated, intelligent, and charismatic figure, Fanon famously won over the support of many of the French, including the popular "public intellectual" Jean-Paul Sartre, in his quest for true African liberation.[34]

Interestingly, while Fanon has remained a divisive figure in French contexts, his legacy has largely faded within the Algerian.[35] Today's historical accounts of the Algerian revolution, suggests David Macey, do not generally give Fanon a leading role.[36] Concretely, considered "Black" and not an "Arab Muslim," Fanon is now thought of by many as being "different" himself. This is particularly ironic, and tragic, given that Fanon spent his life fighting against this kind of identity labeling! His life aim was to have people of all hues considered nothing but fundamentally human. He writes:

> Let us reconsider the question of mankind. Let us reconsider the question of cerebral reality and of the cerebral mass of all humanity, whose connections must be increased, whose channels must be diversified and whose message must be re-humanized.[37]

Yet he continues to be controversial, particularly among many French observers, for having advocated the African, i.e., for using darker "African" skin or origin in a kind of "reverse racism."[38] In other words, Fanon's message of humanism is lost among many caught in the predominant logic and resulting dialogues of "difference."

---

[32] W.E.B. DuBois, "Foreword," in *The World and Africa: An Inquiry into the Part Which Africa Has Played in World History* (New York: International Publishers, 1965), xii.

[33] Frantz Fanon, *Peau noire, masques blancs* (Paris : Seuil, 1975).

[34] Famously, by his writing a preface in 1961 to Fanon's *Les Damnées de la Terre* [The Wretched of the Earth].

[35] A point emphasized by one of his biographers, David Macey, in *Frantz Fanon: A Biography* (New York: Picador, 2000). On page 8, Macey comments, "Ever since its birth in the 1930s, modern Algerian naitonalism has been defined as 'Arab-Islamic,' and it is very difficult to absorb a black agnostic into that nationalism."

[36] ibid., 9.

[37] Frantz Fanon, The Wretched of the Earth (New York: Grove Press, 1968), 314.

[38] There are, of course, other controversies or disagreements with Fanon's work, including his apparent lack of interest in socialist politics and Algerian gender issues, among other things.

It is true that like so many others of the era, Fanon was deeply affected by the murder of Lumumba, and he sought solace in the future leadership of Africans, unified in a cause against the "colonial oppressor":

No one knows the name of the next Lumumba. There is in Africa a certain tendency represented by certain men. It is this tendency, dangerous for imperialism, which is at issue. Let us be sure never to forget it. . . . [39]

Postcolonial writing has often emphasized similar strategies and hopes; Fanon is, in that sense as well, a truly foundational figure. He understood that adverse personal experiences with the "colonial condition" could actually be an important and perhaps necessary counterforce to prevailing norms and attitudes.[40]

Beyond the popular, tactical, and perhaps primordial appeal of "difference," there do remain certain professional expectations among scholars to employ difference as an analytical device. In fact, it has been argued that it is an essential part of the Western mind-set and Cartesian approaches to all social science inquiry.[41] Within the discipline of comparative politics it is classically argued, for example, that "you cannot value or 'understand' circumstances in England without making a comparison to conditions elsewhere."[42] Alexis de Tocqueville similarly argued that "without comparisons to make, the mind does not know how to proceed."[43] The prevailing academic culture remains methodologically tied to emphasizing difference, and, accordingly, "all things African" are consistently placed in the category of the exotic "Other."

In the recent literature on Africa and IR theory, this is perhaps most vividly expressed by Kevin Dunn and Timothy Shaw in their book *Africa's Challenge to International Relations Theory*.[44] While the contributors say different things, a recurring argument in this important work is that Africa's primary challenge to IR theory is the "inappropriateness of the sovereign state" to the study of Africa. In other words, these IR theorists do not take into account the uniqueness of what they find on the African continent. Nevertheless, I agree with those who challenge Dunn and Shaw on this point and go on to argue that notions such as anarchy and sovereignty have been challenged and debated from the very beginning, within the IR discipline—not just in Africa. William Brown,[45] for example, suggests that Orientalists have made the same error in their observations of Middle Eastern politics; i.e., they have

---

[39] Frantz Fanon, *Toward the African Revolution,* translated by Haakon Chevalier (New York: Grove Press, 1964, 1967), 197.

[40] Writing after years of continued frustration with the lack of change in attitudes, Richard Falk reached a conclusion similar to that of Fanon. "One would," Falk argues, "expect that our Grotius, if he or she emerges, will come from the Third World rather than from the advanced industrial countries." Richard Falk, "The Grotian Quest," in *International Law: A Contemporary Perspective,* ed. R. Falk, F. Kratchowil, and S. Mendlovitz (1985), 36–42.

[41] A critique one finds among philosophers who emphasize, for example, the concept of "harmony" or of the dangers of "reductionism," etc. See, for example, Richard Tarnas, *The Passion of the Western Mind* (New York: Ballantine,1991), 357; and Alan Watts, The Way of Zen (New York: Vintage Books, 1957).

[42] As argued in the first chapter of Thomas Magstadt, *Nations and Governments: Comparative Politics in Regional Perspective* (Belmont, CA: Wadsworth Thomson, 2005).

[43] "Alexis de Tocqueville to Ernest de Chabrol," October 7, 1831, in *Alexis de Tocqueville: Selected Letters on Politics and Society,* ed. Roger Boesche (Berkley, CA: University of California Press, 1985), 191, cited in Gabriel A. Almond, *Comparative Politics Today: A World View* (New York: Pearson Longman, 2004), 31.

[44] Kevin Dunn and Timothy Shaw, *Africa's Challenge to International Relations Theory* (Basingstoke, UK: Palgrave, 2001).

[45] William Brown, "Africa and International Relations: A Comment on IR Theory, Anarchy and Statehood," *Review of International Studies* 32 (2006), 119–143.

tended to "essentialize" the Orient (Said 1979). Dunn and Shaw, in Brown's view, may well be leading us down an already well-trodden path when it comes to Africa.

V.Y. Mudimbe and others have already argued the historical treatment of Africa as different, but it seems to have had little effect.[46] Mudimbe employs the term "Africanism" to describe the development of a phenomenon similar to the Orientalism so famously described by Said. The suggestion here is that Africanists and IR theorists pay closer attention to writings that lead us down the path of Africanism (intentionally or not) than to those that help us identify patterns of political behavior found in all human contexts. In fact, the contributors to *Africa's Challenge to International Relations Theory* have actually expressed different points of view: on the one hand, "Africa is sui generis," i.e., entirely unique or different, and on the other hand, African political behavior is "rational" and, in many ways, similar to patterns of behavior found elsewhere.[47]

In reframing our discourse on Africa in international relations theory, we must recognize the limitations in describing Africa as a place of difference. In other words, like the Middle East, Africa is certainly not a monolith inhabited by anything other than human beings who share hopes, fears, and desires with people elsewhere. The prevailing method in all of the social sciences is, admittedly, to focus on difference. But as can be seen in the study of many other social sciences, there is also great value to identifying "patterns" of human behavior. Africanists F.W. Clark and Assis Malaquias clearly understood this and while acknowledging that the discipline of international relations is not truly international, wrote their contributions to *Africa's Challenge to International Relations Theory* to identify such patterns.

Among the social sciences, political science (of which IR is generally considered a subfield) has been the most resistant to the identification of recurring human patterns. How quickly we forget that all *Homo sapiens* came from the same place in northeast Africa only several tens of thousands of years ago; the study of Africa reminds us of this and of the fact that IR practice is little more than a renewed encounter with other members of our species.

Before contemplating possible avenues for identifying patterns of political thought and experience—to include Africa—I first consider a somewhat traditional discussion of the historical development and resulting framework of IR theory and follow with a brief survey of the more global approaches of other disciplines. What I aim to demonstrate is that IR theorists could learn from other methodologies, which emphasize similarities in human experience, thought, and behavior over differences.

International Relations Theory: Disciplinary Origins

International relations was originally a theory-based discipline.[48] Indeed, the continued prominence of theoretical discussions remains so central to the study of IR that the ever-popular "IR major" at university is often combined with other, more "practical" academic disciplines such as business, communications,

---

[46] V.Y. Mudimbe, *The Invention of Africa: Gnosis, Philosophy, and the Order of Knowledge* (Bloomington, IN: Indiana University Press, 1988).

[47] Book reviews acknowledge that there are varying arguments within the text. The suggestion here is that the emphasis on difference has its limits and dangers. In his review for the *American Political Science Review*, Clement E. Adibe writes, "Unlike Dunn (Chapters 1 and 4) and Assis Malaquias (Chapter 2), who argue willy nilly that Africa is sui generis, Grovogui and Clark contend that the content and outline of Africa's international relations are not nearly as different as those of Europe and other parts of the world as had been widely and erroneously assumed." See his review in APSR 96, no. 4 (December 2002): 878.

[48] See Scott Burchill, *Theories of International Relations*, 1.

environmental studies, languages, and the like. While a growing number of students clearly enjoy the study of IR and understand its practical relevance to various other fields of study, there remains a clear understanding of—and sometimes disappointment with—its theoretical "social science" orientation. When one considers the foundational texts that make reference to international relations, it quickly becomes clear that political theory predates international relations theory. In fact, early scholars of IR (notably E.H. Carr and Hans J. Morgenthau) drew on the lessons of political theory to make their arguments for what they considered to be the learned lessons of history.

Their immediate concern, and the concern of many politicians of the early twentieth century, was the growth of international cooperative ventures, such as the League of Nations and the United Nations, which some (moralists, idealists, or international liberals) argued should be based on shared normative values, ethics, or a sense of morality. Underlying the debate was the prospect of international organization and, most important, one global authority. As Brown argues, from the very start, the notions of anarchy and sovereignty had their proponents and challengers; African politics is, therefore, far from a new challenge to IR theory.

At universities around the world, the aforementioned issues are dutifully introduced to the growing number of IR majors as are the field's foundational texts, notably E.H. Carr's *The Twenty Years' Crisis* (1939) and Hans J. Morgenthau's *Politics Among Nations* (1948), albeit in an excerpted or summarized form.[49] What students are generally told is that the study of international relations, which, again, began as a theoretical discipline, is generally divided into two major schools, or "frameworks of analysis": Realism and Idealism.[50] The rift between these schools is also referred to as the first Great Debate.

These foundational IR texts introduced a framework of intellectual contributions to political realism that has since become known as the canon of Realism in International Relations Theory, i.e., the intellectual basis for supporting a global "system" of sovereign states. And it is this realist perspective that has, ever since, played a central role in the study of IR theory. Accordingly, the first chapter of any IR text will generally stress the centrality of realism to the study of IR; even a cursory look at IR textbooks will demonstrate this point. Political realists are portrayed as dominating IR practice throughout history, and although realist practice has always dominated state power relations, the Treaty of Westphalia (1638) is deemed by many to be the formal start of IR.[51]

It is this realistic argument in IR, based on the dominance of power politics, anarchical assumptions, and the role of sovereign states, that Dunn and Shaw appear to be most concerned with. But it is also important to remember that the "intellectual framework" for IR is entirely based on Western political thought and historical experience; that is, it remains "parochially Western." That foundation for IR theory can and should be challenged not solely on the basis of difference, but also in terms of inclusion for purposes of future dialogue. For now, the almost institutionalized exclusion of Africa within IR, coupled with the methodological emphasis on difference within political science, leaves virtually no room for the identification of parallels of political thought and behavior.

---

[49] E.H. Carr, *The Twenty Years' Crisis;* and Hans J. Morgenthau, *Politics Among Nations.*

[50] See Scott Burchill, *Theories of International Relations.* The term "Liberalism" is often used instead of "Idealism" because the latter is considered somewhat pejorative. Further, in the U.S. context, the term Liberalism is used to denote a more impractical Idealism, rather than what "classic" European thinkers such as Adam Smith and John Locke had in mind: Economic and Political Freedom, respectively.

[51] The Treaty of Westphalia established the principle of state sovereignty and is, therefore, considered by many to be the formal start of International Relations.

Importantly, while the intellectual ideas that Carr and Morgenthau referred to had hitherto been confined to the realm of Western "political theory," they now suggested that these political ideas could be applicable to the study of international relations. Ever since, the subject of international relations has been framed as an ongoing struggle between Idealists, what Morgenthau referred to as Moralists who emphasize the centrality of ethics, justice, and change to IR, and Realists, who remind us that the primary concern of any state is survival and who, therefore, focus on the centrality of power and order. By drawing lessons from history, what was especially important to Carr and Morgenthau was to demonstrate that traditional (usually military) strength, or power, was crucial to understanding outcomes of relations between states. Again, in doing so, these foundational texts relied on lessons from the West. The intellectual framework for the study of IR started with Thucydides (now considered the "Father of Realism"). It followed a pattern of Western intellectual thought, skipped the "Dark Ages," and continued with the writings of Machiavelli, Hobbes, and a handful of others, including perhaps Otto van Bismark, Kissinger, and the like.

Nowhere is there any serious consideration given to historical events in other parts of the world and, most important, to any political theory or practice from other parts of the world. To this day, the study of IR is presented as if the West had a historical monopoly on realist theory and practice. Like the "textual children" that Said argues European literature helped to create, the establishment of the discipline of IR led to institutionalized norms and language that, if anything, only led to generations of believers in Western uniqueness. They continue to proclaim: "we" have an intellectual story and history that is far too different for inclusion of the "rest." Those same textual children have continued to believe not only that "all things African" are different, but also in the "truths" that can be revealed through scientific comparison.

In the years that followed these foundational texts, the dominance of political realism in IR theory was ostensibly supported by state practice. Before the Second World War, for example, political realists had been successful in halting the activities of the League of Nations, established at the Paris Peace Conference in 1919.[52] By the 1940s, realists like Morgenthau were well aware, and weary, of new institutional arrangements made in the name of "international cooperation," as outlined in the United Nations Charter in 1945. Indeed, realists viewed as of little practical use—even potentially dangerous—the rapid declaration of UN resolutions, such as the Universal Declaration of Human Rights (adopted by the UN General Assembly in 1948).[53]

Such declarations, in their view, had to be backed by an ability to enforce, and this the UN lacked. The UN Security Council was hampered, in this regard, by the ability of any one UN Security Council member to veto a decision to use force. A more realistic and effective approach to international conflict was to have individual sovereign states take responsibility for their own affairs, including the "rational" pursuit of their defense, or "national interest." And this, again, required the acquisition and maintenance of state power. It is only when one understands this historic struggle, which can be thought of as a theoretical debate, that one begins to truly understand the arguments made by Morgenthau. His definitive list of the six principles of realism has been a classic of international relations ever since.[54]

---

[52] The League continued to function during World War II, although its security operations were halted in 1941. It was formally disbanded in 1946.

[53] This was certainly true of critics of the League, including Massachusetts Senator Henry Cabot Lodge. For a more recent Realist position on this point, see Henry Kissinger, *Diplomacy* (New York: Touchstone, 1995); or Patrick Buchanan, *A Republic, Not An Empire* (Washington, D.C.: Regnery Publishing, 2002).

[54] Hans J. Morgenthau, *Politics Among Nations*, Chap. 1.

Idealists, Moralists, or Liberal Internationalists (often pejoratives) present the opposing view by contending that cooperative international arrangements are the best path to world peace. If anything, in their view, the establishment of new networks of communication, possible through transnational endeavors (such as the League of Nations or the UN), is one of the best guarantees of avoiding future conflict. Of course, the debate over the virtue of such transnational organizations continues to this day. The conservative American politician and columnist Pat Buchanan recently went as far as to suggest that the United States should kick the UN headquarters out of the country, adding, "if you have trouble leaving we'll send up 10,000 U.S. Marines to help you pack."[55]

By contrast, in the 1970s, Richard Falk considered transnational networks of communication to be so important to the prospects for world peace that he helped establish what he termed the World Order Model Project (WOMP), through which he and others published a great many articles and books.[56] Like Morgenthau before him, Falk argues that the other group—the political realists—is wrongheaded, and their focus on power, possibly dangerous. Not only does Falk believe that realists "do not understand," he further argues that someone from the southern hemisphere might well need to lead the way. In his view, we in the West are simply too entrenched in our discussions of power to consider other models. When there is examination of alternatives to power politics, it takes place in a kind of "shadowland" on the academic margins, where, for those of us in the industrialized West, it can mean "dangerous intellectual work that often engenders rejection. . . ."[57] Some would say that certain Western scholars, notably Noam Chomsky, have built their entire careers on critiquing power politics.[58] Nevertheless, in his admiration of Hugo Grotius's forward-looking vision of the seventeenth century, Falk argues:

> Grotius came from an independent state in the Protestant north of Europe that was the setting for revolt against the holistic domination of all Europe by the Catholic south. One would similarly expect that *our Grotius, if he or she emerges, will come from the Third World rather than from the advanced industrial countries* [emphasis added]. The shadowland is more accessible to those who are victims of the old order, apostles of the new order, but who yet see that the hopes for a benign transition depend on the success of an ideological synthesis.[59]

In one way or another, the political idealist is generally concerned with wrongs associated with the existing order and looks for answers. Interestingly, the needed perspective will likely come from a citizen of the oppressed third world, according to Falk.[60] For Plato, it will come from a "philosopher

---

[55] "UN Dismisses Pat Buchanan's Call for US to Kick Them Out," Associated Press, September 20, 2000.

[56] See, for example, Richard Falk, *A Study of Future Worlds* (New York: Free Press, 1975).

[57] Richard Falk, "The Grotian Quest," cited in Burns H. Weston, Richard Falk, and Anthony D'Amato, *International Law and World Order* (St. Paul, MN: West Publishing,1990), 1087.

[58] See, for example, Noam Chomsky, *The Umbrella of US Power: The Universal Declaration of Human Rights and the Contradictions of US Policy* (Publishers Group West, 2002); *For Reasons of the State* (New York: New Press, 2003); *Rogues States: The Rule of Force in World Affairs* (Cambridge: South End Press, 2000); and his ever-popular *Deterring Democracy* (Hill and Wang, 1992).

[59] Falk (1985) in Weston et al. (1990), 1091.

[60] Since the end of the Cold War, "third world" has become somewhat dated, although some still use it. During the Cold War, the "first world" referred to the politically free world (the United States and its allies); "second world," to the communist states (the USSR and its allies); and "third world," to the remainder, the generally underdeveloped states.

king."[61] But in all cases, the idealist argues that answers to global woes usually necessitate change, often in the name of "justice."

The result of the aforementioned debates among IR scholars is an intellectual framework that, to this day, scarcely includes perspectives from non-Western regions of the world. If Africa is mentioned, it is rarely mentioned as a source of political ideas. In fact, in his book *But Not Philosophy: Seven Introductions to Non-Western Thought,* George Anastaplo surveys the political literature from non-Western parts of the world to argue this very point.[62] Based on Carr and Morgenthau's use of preexisting political philosophy to intellectually ground IR theory, one could easily conclude that without non-Western political philosophy, there could not possibly be any positive development of international relations theory in the non-West. Accordingly, the growing consensus among international relations theorists seems to be very much like that among many political theorists; both are presented as entirely Western intellectual enterprises. The resulting framework is typically presented, as in Table 21.2.

Perhaps Richard Falk is correct—that the force of change will come outside the West, but even within Western academic institutions, there is a growing recognition that this approach to the study of IR is clearly Western-centric and that something needs to be done to alter this form of scholarly presentation. To say that African political ideas and practice have no relation to the aforementioned paradigms of IR is inappropriate, inaccurate, and alienating to a growing number of students from Africa and the non-West.

That said, yes, among individuals and groups there are, and always have been, differences, but identification of those differences is not the only intellectual challenge available to social science researchers. That would be akin to the age-old reaction to the proverbial tribe on the other side of the hill: "they" are different. It is, perhaps, the "first" human reaction, much like the first literature that emphasized only the exotic nature of the Other. The ongoing emphasis on difference has proved to be a powerful and evocative analytic tool; as Claude Lévi-Strauss has argued, it may even have a biological basis—something that helps us to feel more secure, to "understand" our surroundings. Yet we all know that we are capable of more than simply identifying differences in our encounters with "strangers."

Scholars of IR must first seek parallels among the arguments within African (indeed, non-Western) political thought and find historical examples of African political practice. This could be a starting point for making the subject of international relations more internationally oriented, rather than dominated, as it is now, by the priorities and perspectives of the triad.

Lessons from Other Disciplines?

The Western dominance of political theory has become increasingly apparent to the growing number who read the "traditional" texts in popular and academic contexts.[63] Among their reactions is that

---

[61] This famous argument is made in Plato's *Republic.* Some have argued that this aspect of Plato's work can, therefore, be interpreted as the intellectual basis for the formation of a vanguard and/or communism. George H. Sabine, for example, contemplates this question in *A History of Political Theory* (New York: Henry Holt, 1937; 1966). Certainly, this is not the general conclusion drawn by Western readers of Plato's work. His quest for an "ideal state" can also be viewed as an Idealist pursuit. See, for example, the discussion of Plato in Brian R. Nelson, *Western Political Thought: From Socrates to the Age of Ideology* (Princeton, NJ: Prentice Hall, 1996), Chap 2.

[62] George Anastaplo, *But Not Philosophy: Seven Introductions to Non-Western Thought* (Lanham, MD: Lexington Books, 2002).

[63] The Nigerian political scientist Claude Ake, for example, has suggested that the current structure of the social science disciplines is nothing short of an extended form of imperialism. See Claude Ake, *Social Science As Imperialism* (Ibadan: University of Ibadan Press, 1979); Edward Said, *Culture and Imperialism* (New York: Vintage Press,1994); and Ella Shohat and Robert Stam, *Unthinking Eurocentrism* (London: Routledge, 1994).

Table 21.2 Paradigms of International Relations

	REALISM	IDEALISM	LIBERALISM	HISTORICAL STRUCTURALISM	CRITICAL THEORY
Focus	"What is"; History; Status Quo	"What ought to be"; Alter status quo	Freedom (Political and Economic); Gradual evolution of status quo	Exploitation	Includes: Feminism; Race and Ethnicity; Green Perspectives; Postmodernism; etc.
Assumptions	Belief in *universals*: Self-Interest; Power; Order is desirable.	An objective understanding of morality is possible and worth striving for (international law); Unless the existing order is just, change is warranted.	Comparative Advantage (we all have something to offer); Principle of Self-determination	Limited global wealth; individual workers (proletariat) and LDCs are poor due to the exploitative behavior of elites (bourgeois).	May alter all other perspectives on IR theory and practice
Key Terms	Power; Order	Justice; Change	Laissez-faire; Individualism	Historical Materialism; Determinism; Imperialism; Class struggle; Core-Periphery Analysis	Gender; Discrimination; Tragedy of the Commons; Discourse; etc.
Solutions	Balance of Power; State Sovereignty	Philosopher Kings (Plato); International Cooperation; International Law; Transnational solutions	Free Market; Bretton Woods Institutions: IMF, WB, WTO	Revolution; UNCTAD and other UN General Assembly aims; NIEO demands	Education; Policy Change; Methodological Change
Critique	Does might make right? In a world where weapons of mass destruction, i.e., "power," can be hidden in a vial in someone's top pocket, is this still a good organizing principle?	Proposed solutions are too far removed from actual political practice, i.e., "impracticality"; Fundamentalism; Religious fanatics; Utopian goals	Distributional flaws	Zero-Sum Logic	Often as in Idealism; Neglecting the subject of politics—"life and death"
Contributors	Thucydides Hobbes Machiavelli Bismark Morgenthau Kissinger	Ancient Greeks Hugo Grotius Wilson Falk	Locke Jefferson Rawls Smith Ricardo Friedman	Marx Lenin Prebisch Dos Santos Wallerstein	Tickner Said Foucault

expressed by Claude Ake, who argues that the present structure of academic inquiry is directly linked to the priorities of capitalism (e.g., greed, selfishness, and competition). Like John Ralston Saul, writers like Ake appear to argue that human societies hold other values dear, but Ake seems to blame all of the West, and the Western domination of the social sciences, for the degradation of "other" values, such as caring, compassion, and community.[64] The 2006 letter from Iranian president Mahmoud Ahmadinejad to U.S. president George Bush suggested that the West challenges the values that other, non-Western societies cherish.[65]

These are powerful messages that, for a full range of reasons, have struck a chord. Lost in this discussion, however, is that there are Westerners who are similarly fearful of the exact things about which Ake and Ahmadinejad write, namely, loss of a sense of community and a decline of family values. As Said suggests in his works, these generalizations are also unfortunate in that they promote an essentialist "us versus them" understanding of differences. All human societies have valued caring, compassion, and community throughout history; that is, there are universally recognized virtues among human societies that social scientists should consider more closely. Western sociologists, for example, such as Robert Putnam, have famously emphasized the importance of such values to the proper functioning of democracies.[66] These values are not unique to the non-West or West; they are human values. This is the kind of cross-cultural thinking that most social scientists seem to completely forget, and thus constructive avenues for dialogue are blocked.

"Non-Western" ideas, if they are considered at all, are usually relegated to "area studies." Accordingly, the IR student interested in pursuing Asian or African ideas is left with little alternative but to enroll in area studies, and, understandably, this leaves many students with the clear impression that such ideas are essentially "different" and peripheral to the subject of IR and that Western ideas matter most. Further, none of the aforementioned responses to Western dominance in the social sciences (notably Ake's) aims at integrating intellectual ideas; that is, the dominant stance is one of essential difference. When compared to other academic disciplines, political science is not unique in this regard, but it is especially unambiguous.

For example, cross-cultural psychology, a growing subfield of psychology, accepts the idea that human beings in different cultural contexts share similar psychological experiences. Among the many aims of this emerging field is to identify areas of common sympathy and understanding in an effort to engage in more effective therapies.[67] In fact, it is in this common human spirit that the *Diagnostic and Statistical Manual of Mental Disorders* (DSM) was established, and although some critics argue that the current DSM-IV is unscientific, insurance companies in the United States typically will not pay for psychiatric care unless a DSM-IV diagnosis accompanies the insurance claim. What is particularly significant about such initiatives is that they argue that human experiences, albeit within the realm of mental health, are similar.

---

[64] Claude Ake, *Social Science As Imperialism*. Similar arguments have been made by many "Non-Western" state leaders, such as Fidel Castro and, most recently, Iranian president Mahmoud Ahmadinejad in a letter to U.S. president George W. Bush. In the letter President Ahmadinejad wrote, "The people of many countries are angry about the attacks on their cultural foundations and the disintegration of families. They are equally dismayed with the fading of care and compassion."

[65] The full text of this letter can be seen at www.informationclearinghouse.info/article12984.htm. Reference to these "other" values is on the last page of the eighteen-page letter.

[66] Robert Putnam, "Bowling Alone," *Journal of Democracy* 6, no. 1 (1995): 65–78.

[67] There are many debates within this growing subfield of psychology. See the *Journal of Cross-Cultural Psychology*.

Among the first psychologists Carl Jung is considered one of the pioneers of "psychology types" and, perhaps most famously, "archetypes." Again, and not without controversy, Jung suggested that there are parallels in human experience that lead to similar outcomes. For anyone who has read the works of Jung, rather than secondary interpretations of them, it is clear that Jung wanted to demonstrate that certain archetypes existed throughout the world, not only in the West. Indeed, Jung may well have been influenced by arguments made within the study of mythology, an area of great interest to him. Mythologists had long contemplated mythological patterns among disparate cultures across the globe.

The less-known Otto Rank, another of Sigmund Freud's entourage, who, like Jung, was cast out, also argued that patterns of myth had, as their origin, the human mind. While other writers on mythology promoted "diffusionist" theories, i.e., the idea that all myths had a common geographic source, Rank argued in his writings that the hopes, fears, and desires—the common experience—of human beings was the ultimate source of parallels among existing myths.[68] Indeed, the study of comparative mythology might be considered a pioneering discipline in identifying the "universal" patterns of human thought. This is very different from the "universals" to which IR realists (such as Carr and Morgenthau) referred. Recall that the universal behavior of man was to be inherently "self-interested"; political behavior was best understood in those terms.

By contrast, mythological literature did not demonstrate that all human beings shared one thought but that there were clear patterns in their thought that emerged among peoples from entirely different geographical regions and cultures. A lifelong student of world mythologies and literatures, Joseph Campell concluded, after decades of study, "the main result for me has been [the] confirmation of a thought I have long and faithfully entertained: of the unity of the race of man, not only in its biology but also in its spiritual history, which has everywhere unfolded in the manner of a single symphony. . . ."[69]

The writings of at least some mythologists and psychologists demonstrate a willingness to contemplate parallels of thought, based on a common human experience. It is when one begins to venture into the realm of political philosophy that the resistance seems to be strongest. Nevertheless, there have been pioneers within this domain as well. Specifically, in an age when IR theory was still in its development, German philosopher Karl Jaspers made an important contribution to the development of a global framework for the study of political philosophy. IR theorists have entirely neglected his idea of an Axial Age (800–200 B.C.) when philosophical thought was intense and similar in Africa, China, India, and the West (Occident).

Even within the limited realm of philosophical inquiry, Jaspers's idea, though contentious, has gained popularity among writers on comparative religion, including Karen Armstrong.[70] In her works, Armstrong regularly uses the term "Axial Age" to draw important parallels among the religions of the world. The crucial point is that the very idea that human beings experience similar hopes, fears, and desires in life is certainly less controversial in many academic disciplines than it is within political

---

[68] Tragically, many of Otto Rank's writings have not been translated from the original German. A brief overview of his work, which addresses Rank's careful attention to mythical writings, is Philip Freund, ed., *Otto Rank: The Myth of the Birth of the Hero and Other Writings* (New York: Vintage Press, 1964).

[69] Joseph Campbell, *The Masks of God: Primitive Mythology* (New York: Viking Press, 1959). See the foreword of the 1969 edition.

[70] Her best-selling book, *A History of God: From Abraham to the Present, the 4000 Year Quest for God* (New York: Knopf, 1993) and her other works for the use of the term "Axial Age." A recent publication, *The Great Transformation* (Conshohocken, PA: Atlantic Books, 2006), frames the "Axial Age" as a kind of Idealist—usually religious—response to the recurring problem of violence.

thought. This is especially important because IR was originally "informed" by Western historical experience and political thought.

Perhaps most controversial of all, yet also relevant here, is the ongoing argument presented by Martin Bernal in his series entitled *Black Athena: The Afroasiatic Roots of Classical Civilization*.[71] Bernal argues that European writers, influenced by anti-Semitic and anti-Black (African) attitudes entrenched by the seventeenth and eighteenth centuries, developed the Western tradition. He claims, countering the establishment "classics," that the writings of the Ancient Greeks were not isolated. According to what he calls the "Ancient Model," Ancient Greeks understood the contributions to their culture from their Mediterranean and African neighbors to the south.

By looking at archaeological and linguistic evidence, in addition to his own interpretation of many of the Greek classics (notably Herodotus), Bernal suggests that the historic links are more than clear. If true, this would bolster the existing arguments that the Western inclination is to separate "inconvenient" information and emphasize difference in a Cartesian fashion. What is most controversial about this, of course, is that Bernal is arguing that the reasons for excluding the non-West, including Southern and Eastern Europe, were fundamentally racist.[72]

At various times in recent history, perhaps in an effort to correct the marginalization of others in history, it has been fashionable to contemplate other, mostly "Eastern" philosophies.[73] The transcendentalist movement in nineteenth-century America, for example, was fascinated with Eastern cultures and philosophies. The founder of transcendentalism, Ralph Waldo Emerson, was especially interested in a branch of Hinduism, known as Vedanta philosophy.[74] Indeed, throughout the West, there have been countless phases of Eastern influence on Western literature and art. Another example is the European Romantic movement, which included Goethe, Wordsworth, and Carlyle and advocated Neoplatonic and mystical traditions inspired by the East.[75] And with the wave of nationalist movements across the globe in the mid-twentieth century, styles and ideas from Africa, Latin America, and Asia swept across the West in countless ways. These influences have generally been dismissed, passing as periodic fads or fashions might and leading to today's prevailing notion that Western ideas are what matter most.

Outside of anthropology, the few preliminary efforts to understand African political thought were conducted during the period of postindependence optimism, and, tragically, much of this inquiry was influenced by the prevailing logic of the Cold War. Writing for *World Politics* in 1966, for example, Kenneth Grundy suggested that "judged by volume, the most frequently discussed subject in the analytical literature is African economics, particularly socialism."[76] For decades, scholarly contributions to

---

[71] Martin Bernal, *Black Athena: The Afroasiatic Roots of Classical Civilization* (New Brunswick, NJ: Rutgers University Press, 1987). Bernal has just published the third of five volumes of this book.

[72] See the critiques of Mary Lefkowitz, for example, *Not Out of Africa* (New York: Harper Collins, 1996).

[73] An interesting discussion of the "phases" of scholarly interest in non-Western ideas in Western contexts is offered by J.J. Clarke, *Oriental Enlightenment: The Encounter between Asian and Western Thought* (London: Routledge, 1997). He explains on page 19, "one of the most common explanations for the West's persistent enchantment with the East can be summed up in the word romanticism."

[74] ibid., 84–85. Vendata philosophy, clearly more universal or holistic in its approach to political problems, would likely fall under the heading of an Idealist contribution. As has been the case with others who have been labeled "Idealist," this may be seen as pejorative; nevertheless, it would be a step towards inclusion.

[75] ibid.

[76] Kenneth W. Grundy, "Recent Contributions to the Study of African Political Thought," *World Politics,* XVIII (July 1966): 679.

journals on African studies including the *Journal of African History* and the *Journal of Modern African Studies* were, in one way or another, dominated by investigations of socialism on the African continent. Similarly, when African politics was mentioned at all in the leading journals on international affairs, such as *Foreign Affairs*, it was to emphasize the role of Marxism-Leninism in Africa and, in particular, the influence of the Soviets or the Chinese.[77] Fear of communism on the African continent clearly seemed to influence a great many writers on African politics in the postindependence period. Zbignieuw Brzezinski, for instance, political adviser to several U.S. presidents during the Cold War, published a 1963 study on the policy aspects of communist influence in Africa.[78]

During most of the Cold War, then, African political thought was clearly viewed as sympathetic to various forms of Marxism-Leninism or socialism. To government leaders such as Brzezinski, Kissinger, and others, this mattered because it might have affected the global ideological battle to defeat communism. Grundy, however, goes further than simply focusing on the predominance of socialism on the African continent; he also asks, "Is there such a thing as a distinctive African personality and distinctive African patterns of thought?" As in his survey of African political thought, he concludes, "Those who have tried to analyze African ways of doing things invariably answer these questions positively."[79]

As V.Y. Mudimbe has stressed, there is a long history of scholars who view Africa as essentially different, and their perspective is the norm. While Dunn and Shaw appear to offer a unique insight into Africa's place in the world, in fact, large sections of the book argue much the same. That, in their view, is Africa's overarching challenge to the debates of international relations theory.

Conclusion: Challenges and Prospects

Remaining Challenges

At a meeting that I attended in Zambia in 1997, where matters related to public health were discussed among "development practitioners," a Zambian participant suggested that what was forgotten in the discussion was "love" and that if all of those in attendance could prioritize this feeling, all would go well. The majority in attendance was thrown by this suggestion, and after a period of awkward silence, the discussion continued as before. Had there been more acknowledgment of the popularity of Zambian Humanism, a philosophy that former president Kenneth Kaunda introduced, perhaps there would have been room for inclusion of his idea. Although it is a philosophy that recognizes the real and practical hardships that most Zambians are facing as local cultures and traditions are challenged, it goes largely ignored by outsiders. The overarching idea—"we are in for a hard time, so let us be nice to each other . . ."—which upon reflection makes some sense in a subregional context, would likely be placed under a heading such as Idealism. At least, it would be acknowledged.

Examples of the use and maintenance of power, in order to achieve desired results, can also be found in sub-Saharan African and historical contexts throughout the world; these should also be understood,

---

[77] See, for example, Walter Z. Laquer, "Communism and Nationalism in *Tropical Africa*," *Foreign Affairs*, XXXVIII (April 1962): 152–169.

[78] Zbignieuw Brzezinski, *Africa in the Communist World* (Stanford, CA: Stanford University Press, 1963), cited in Grundy (1966): 682.

[79] Grundy (1966): 683–684.

included, and acknowledged. To argue that Realism and Idealism are solely Western phenomena is clearly wrongheaded. Moreover, it runs counter to historical facts and the very nature of the subject, which is, after all, global in reach.

The portrayal of Africa and much of the non-West as Marxist (Historical Structuralist) and little else is similarly not especially helpful. Latin American *dependencistas*, Maoists, and a great many African politicians have been structuralist in their orientation, but to conclude that the all non-Westerners engage in international politics with only structuralist ideas in mind would be false. Realist and Idealist, or conservative and radical/progressive, ideas are always part of one's "intellectual tradition" and political practice, even if they are not stressed within the prevailing literature. The ideas need only to be identified and documented because they are patterns of thought that have been around since time immemorial. If anything, the intellectual battleground of the future may well be over various interpretations of liberalism.

Kim Dae Jung, for instance, has argued that "long before Locke," the classic writers of Asia had notions of liberalism.[80] Now, if only quietly, works such as *The Liberal Tradition in China*, by William Theodore de Bary, are discussed in university classrooms.[81] Assuredly, there are liberal ideas on the African continent, perhaps as interpretations of "freedom." Yet this task, from what I can tell, remains largely incomplete. In the table below, I suggest that Nelson Mandela could be thought of as a leading proponent of democratic liberalism on the African continent; Jomo Kenyatta, Yoweri Museveni, Houphouet-Boigny, and others have remained open to capitalism or free market liberalism but should not be portrayed as classic political liberals. The same can be said of the South African government during the apartheid era: it was economically liberal, yes, but certainly not politically liberal. The point here is that these are the distinctions that matter in discussions of IR theory, but the dominant political voices and practitioners within the discipline of IR remain mostly Western; virtually none are African.[82] Again, this remains a matter of what scholars choose to include in their IR syllabi.

Scholars who endeavor to introduce non-Western political ideas alongside Western political theory "classics" are met with a host of challenges. Even a cursory look at the texts leaves the observer with the clear impression that political theory remains a very Eurocentric area of academic inquiry, which might make some sense for the standard course on political theory in Western universities were it not for their pretense of offering a comprehensive survey of political ideas. Time and again, university courses of the kind survey the Ancient Greek classics, followed by European Enlightenment thinkers and other Western writers. In an effort to preserve this method of teaching political theory, many universities have introduced "core curricula" that emphasize only Western classics. Eastern, Southern, and other influences on the Western tradition are scarcely, if ever, contemplated. The few writers who do are systematically marginalized.

On the whole, progress towards becoming more geographically, culturally, and linguistically inclusive has been painfully slow. Even the most basic task of identifying Realists and Idealists in non-Western contexts remains elusive. For a variety of professional, practical, logistical, and other reasons, most of the world's population has not yet successfully challenged the dominance of the Western classics. Several scholarly exceptions have been mentioned in the current chapter. Some have fought against

---

[80] Kim Dae Jung, "The Myth of Asia's Anti-Democratic Values," *Foreign Affairs* (November/December 1994).

[81] William Theodore de Bary, *The Liberal Tradition in China* (Hong Kong: Chinese University Press, 1982).

[82] Africanist Peter Schraeder is among the few who make distinctions of this kind in the African context, but he uses "Liberal vs. Critical" traditions and speaks predominantly of Western contributors to these ideas.

the notion of separation; others have emphasized the importance of remembering our common human experience. Yet despite their calls for change in the social sciences, the job of globalizing the subject of international relations remains.

Students who are aware of the problem are understandably more concerned with completion of a course or degree than with combating it, and university professors are hardly awarded for inclusion of non-Western texts. The links between power and knowledge have been documented by writers such as Antonio Gramsci and may well have merit because few of us dare to step out of the traditional IR framework. Do we fear being thought naïve or, as postmodernists might contend, do we stick to the "right" classics for reasons of professional credibility?

Regardless, the problem of Euro-American dominance of IR theory remains overwhelming to most. Africanists, and all specialists of non-Western thought and practice, can help by moving away from monolithic essentialist arguments towards more nuanced discussions of conservative, progressive, and other ideals (with parallels in IR theory) within their chosen areas of study.

Prospects

The first, most visible and perhaps logical option is for African scholars to continue along the path established by earlier generations of the twentieth century. While they have expressed a range of views, the overwhelming majority of Africanists have emphasized the subversive role that capitalism played in African history. Upon reflection, this makes perfect sense. Yet, as elsewhere, Marxist-Leninist ideas are now less popular in Africa. The increasingly visible choice of liberalization is generally portrayed as a positive step for African development. The policies of the past, including nationalization of industry, are quickly being dismantled.

From this socialism versus liberalism perspective, leaders like Mandela are heralded as African heroes leading other African citizens down the path of liberalization. Yet IR theory is not only about socialism and liberalism; the fundamental rift, as the founding IR theorists Carr and Morgenthau presented, is between Realists and Idealists. These are the categories used in IR theory. The prevailing question in IR was never: are you communist? As Brown argues, IR theory from the start was preoccupied with such notions as anarchy, sovereignty, and the challenges of international organization. Yet this Cold War legacy remains influential in how we think of African political thought and practice.

Twentieth-century scholarship on African politics has also celebrated and glorified a long-threatened African past based on age-old traditions (e.g., Mobutu's Zairinization), empathy for other human beings, and sharing and community (e.g., Nyerere's *ujaama*). It has also advanced capitalist culture and values in politics, the social sciences, and other fields, although I feel that Africans and Africanists should be careful when making essentialist generalizations lest they lead us down the path of Orientalism and us-versus-them thinking. For example, in his book *Social Science As Imperialism* (1979), Ake makes a strong, but essentialist, case that the social sciences are dominated by capitalist values such as selfishness, greed, materialism, and exploitation. But essentialism of this kind can prove to be a barrier to an engaging, inclusive dialogue, regardless of its source.

One must also strive to understand (as, admittedly, many Africanists did in the 1960s) the postindependence appeal of Marxism-Leninism in Africa. Without doubt and upon reflection understandably, a great many Africanists viewed the historical development of capitalism as harmful to the weak. Like the *dependencistas* of Latin America, many Africanists emphasized the underdevelopment of Africa and the structural biases of the global economy that kept the African continent, like other underdeveloped regions of the world, in their dependent or peripheral state. Accurate or not, such perspectives are likely to remain popular in underdeveloped regions, including Africa. Accordingly, there will not be a shortage of Historical Structuralists to add to the table of IR paradigms, below. But it is just as likely that there will be more variants of Realists and Idealists in African politics, as has happened in all political contexts at all times in human history.

For political theorists throughout the world, the future battle will be over the theory and practice of liberalism. Interpretations of what freedom entails may well be influenced by local geographies, histories, cultures, and priorities. But this is an intellectual conflict well worth waging. African political thought is, and always has been, much more nuanced than is commonly supposed. The traditional categories of political thought, as they inform IR theory, can be excellent places to start. But the establishment of a more open global dialogue on political ideas just may require some of us within the West to reach out with mutual respect and the aim of scholarly inclusion. Further, we cannot assume that all attempts to describe the dynamics of international politics have been completely useless or uniform. Debates among IR theorists continue to be the norm. As Brown suggests, the notion that all principles of IR do not apply to Africa blocks constructive engagement with African scholars. There are historical and other differences that might well appeal to both Western and African social scientists; however, we should be wary of those who emphasize only difference.

It has been said that "knowledge is invented, not discovered," and systematic exclusion is presently the state of Africa in IR theory. All who engage in IR scholarship do not uniformly accept purported IR knowledge, which is rightly debated and will continue to be so. What is certain is that the discipline of IR remains parochially Western; African involvement in the discipline is sorely lacking; and there are limits to the usefulness of methodologies that emphasize difference because individuals, societies, and

Table 21.3   Paradigms of International Relations: African Political Thought/Historical Experience

	REALISM	*IDEALISM*	*LIBERALISM*	*STRUCTURALISM*	*CRITICAL THEORY*
Focus	"What is"; History; Status Quo	"What ought to be"; Alter status quo	Freedom (Political and Economic); Gradual evolution of status quo	Exploitation	Includes: Feminism; Race and Ethnicity; Green Perspectives; Post-modernism; etc.
African Political Thought: Historical Experience:	"Successful military leaders" "Political survivors of the Cold War"	Zera Yacob, Walda Heywat Kenneth Kaunda (Humanism)	Political Nelson Mandela, Steve Biko Economic Jomo Kenyatta, Houphouet-Boigny	African Socialism Julius Nyerere, Kwame Nkrumah, Amicar Cabral, Patrice Lumumba	Negritude Black Consciousness Samir Amin, Frantz Fanon

cultures while different are also similar. In saying that one or another political reality is "different" we must never lose sight of our true subject—humanity. To do so, as Said suggested, leads to objectifying or dehumanizing others. Like their counterparts in other disciplines, IR theorists should discuss parallels in human thought and experience. Only then will they engage in truly global scholarship.

REFERENCES

Bayart, Jean-François. "Africa in the World: A History of Extroversion." *African Affairs* 99 (2000): 217–267.

Taylor, Ian, and Paul Williams. *Africa in International Politics.* New York: Routledge, 2004.

Kitching, Gavin. "Why I Gave Up African Studies." *African Studies Review & Newsletter* XXII/1 (2000): 21–26.

Alpers, Edward A., and Allen F. Robers. "What is African Studies? Some Reflections." *African Studies Association* XXX/2 (2002): 11–18.

Hydén, Göran. *African Politics in Comparative Perspective.* New York: Cambridge University Press, 2006.

Dunn, Kevin C., and Timothy M. Shaw. *Africa's Challenge to International Relations Theory.* New York: Palgrave, 2001.

Said, Edward. *Orientalism: Western Conceptions of the Orient.* New York: Penguin, 1991 (first published 1978).

Carr, Edward Hallet. *The Twenty Years' Crisis, 1919–1939.* London: Macmillan, 1940.

Morgenthau, Hans J. *Politics Among Nations.* New York: Knopf, 1948.

Ake, Claude. *Social Science as Imperialism.* Ibadan, Nigeria: Ibadan University Press, 1979.

Chapter 22

REFRAMING AFRICA IN THE GLOBAL ERA
The Relevance of Postcolonial Studies

Rita Kiki Edozie

Peyi Soyinka-Airewele

Throughout this book, we have presented the crucial need for a "re-framing" and "re-representation" of African affairs. For us, the current volume constitutes but one scholarly product that captures a genre of intellectual thinking about Africa. It is written by Africanist authors who in diverse ways have been involved in two main tasks: Firstly, in analyzing African global histories, politics, economics, societies, and cultures, we have revealed popular misrepresentations by commentators who have posited the continent in skewed constructions that deepen the impact of colonialist power in defining the configuration of contemporary Africa. Secondly, our style has generally been oppositional and critical of this totalizing Western historicism regarding Africa.[1] In presenting discourses that interrogate the West as much as try to understand Africa, we cite the concerns of the British scholar of African politics Patrick Chabal who writes that "the general handicap under which 'we' labor is 'our' heritage- by which I mean the accumulated weight of what 'our' culture says about Africa."[2]

Our concluding chapter, therefore, not only reaffirms the themes and practices already presented, but also ties them together using the intellectual framework generally described as postcolonial theory. The contributors to this book do not necessarily categorize their scholarship within the corpus of postcolonial theory, which is still new and often suspect. In fact, in the late 1990s, some scholars argued that postcolonial theory might be suitable for India and other regions of the third world but not for Africa's recent colonial encounters.[3] Most contributors to this volume have simply written from a critical perspective rooted in empirical research that nonetheless parallels postcolonial theory in that they concern themselves with providing epistemological agency to Africans in the broad field of African affairs.

That is why as editors of the volume we will conclude by speaking to the relevance of the postcolonial paradigm for a rigorous analysis of Africa's past, present, and future. Importantly, we feel that the

---

[1] Stephen Slemon, "The Scramble for Postcolonialism," in *The Postcolonial Studies Reader,* ed. Bill Ashcroft, Gareth Griffiths, and Helen Tiffin (London and New York: Routledge, 1995).

[2] Patrick Chabal, "The African Crisis: Context and Interpretation," in *Post-colonial Identities in Africa,* eds. R. Werbner and T. Ranger (London: Zed Books, 1999), 29–54.

[3] Adebayo Williams, "The Postcolonial Flaneur and Other Fellow-Travelers: Conceits for a Narrative Redemption," *Third World Quarterly* 18, no. 5 (1997): 821.

multiple perspectives and revised interpretations of African affairs in this book call for a theoretical platform capable of demonstrating critical areas of convergence.

Note that there is nothing new about postcolonial theory in African affairs; after all, what we call today "postcolonialism," which used to be known as "third worldism," merely reengages the theory and practice of Africa with its post–World War II roots. At that time, newly independent African nations were aligned with other newly independent nations in the Caribbean and Asia: These regions all shared a history of imperialism, colonialism, struggles for anticolonialism and independence, nationalism, sovereign nation building, and economic development. In our mind then, postcolonialism is simply the refashioning of this history in the post–Cold War period and in the no less ambiguous era of globalization.

Reframing Contemporary Africa's introductory sections have already illustrated how the negative "image" of Africa dominates and hurts global interactions with Africans. We cited Kenyan writer Binyavanga Wainaina's satirical article on "How to Write about Africa," Célestin Monga's critique of mainstream Africanist analysis of the continent as an "El Dorado of wild thought," Shobat and Stam's call to challenge "Eurocentrism" regarding the crisis of scholarship in Africa, and Mahmood Mamdani's keynote summons to "reconfigure the study of Africa." If we are to realistically take up these ambitious goals, scholars must contest the negative images, framings, and representations of Africa to contribute to an alternative discourse, scholarship, and practice of African affairs.

Similarly, our introduction highlighted the importance that post-structural theories of "representation" play in underscoring the negative constructions about Africa established during colonial encounters; certain signifiers that classified Africa in the past have been sustained in the contemporary discourse of African affairs. Representation theory identifies the concept of "nodal points," which are ideas that have been accepted as indisputably true and are thus used as anchors for creating a much larger framework that facilitates making predictions about the behavior of something without having to fully understand it. [4]

In the current chapter, consistent with the fifth part's critical debates about Africa's international relations, we offer yet another manifestation and distinctive critique of the negative framing of Africa by signifying nodal points such as "genocide," "collapsed," and "outside of history." We will show the ways in which structures of meaning about the continent continue to be associated with hegemonic international relations practice and new initiatives in global governance. In doing so, we demonstrate ways in which Africa is still discursively represented by policy makers, scholars, journalists, and others in the international arena in ways that complicate African affairs policy in the millennium.

To this end, we revive the conceptual frameworks of postcolonial Africanist scholars, Valentine Mudimbe and Bill Ashcroft. Mudimbe has often referred to the concept of "Africanism," which the erudite Congolese scholar derives from Edward Said's classic concept "Orientalism," or the Western practice of marginalizing, even subjugating the Middle East by controlling its representation and constructing a supposedly inferior identity for the region. Similarly, Africanism[5] is a European (externalist) construction and representational analysis of Africa and Africans premised on Europe's historical hegemonic encounter with the continent and the West's continuing attempt to control Africa.

Postcolonial theorist Bill Ashcroft (1997) provides us with an additional analytical tool that he has referred to as the "new internationalism." Ashcroft argues that Africanism's Orientalist-type ideology has

---

[4] See Roxanne Doty, *Imperial Encounters: The Politics of Representation in North-South Relations* (Minneapolis, MN: University of Minnesota Press, 1996).

[5] Valentine Mudimbe, *The Invention of Africa* (Bloomington, IN: Indiana University Press, 1994).

been incorporated broadly into contemporary international relations theory and practice towards Africa. As discourse and practice, the new internationalism absorbs Africa into a global, transnational, cultural, and economic reality in a way that is not very different from the Europe-Africa colonial relationship in which representations of Africa undergirded the West's hegemonic control of the continent.

Empirically, contemporary events present abundant evidence of the continuing use of the frames critiqued in Mudimbe's Africanism and Ashcroft's new internationalism. These events include, for instance, the heated debates surrounding the discourses and practice of "genocide" in the Sudan, the concerns about the remilitarization of Africa with the establishment of the controversial U.S. AFRICOM command inaugurated in 2008, and protests among francophone Africans of neocolonialist discourses embedded in French–francophone African relations. It is such seemingly disparate events that awaken the quest for an intellectual framework capable of challenging the tyranny of the discourse that shapes Africa's historic and continuing representations (Ashcroft 1997) and reinserting excluded and marginalized societies into contemporary global conversations.

Africanism and the new internationalism conceptually connect discursive practices towards Africa to similar practices elsewhere in the world, in a manner that is consistent with Edward Said's position in his book *Culture and Imperialism*, in which he elaborates on the ways the world has come to be located firmly within the West's orbit (1979). Further, in *Provincializing Europe: Postcolonial Thought and Historical Difference*, Dipesh Chakrabarty observes that in the academic discourse of history, Europe remains the sovereign, theoretical subject of all histories, including those of India, China, and Kenya.[6]

Thus, in these final pages, while engaging in a critical review of postcolonial theory and weighing its potential to help us rethink international approaches to events and issues that are currently the focus of African policy debates, we hope to provide an intellectual platform for investigating African affairs through the responses of African countries to political, economic, cultural, and social issues. As we advocated in our introduction, we must move beyond a mere Euro-Africa deconstructionist confrontation and generate new frames through which the complex contemporary realities of Africa can be resituated, connected, and explained, and with which new strategies of resistance and change at the local and national levels can evolve in the context of the disempowering effects of contemporary global hegemonic processes.[7] Pal Ahluwalia signifies the importance of such a venture when he classically asserts in *The Empire Writes Back* that a postcolonial theory offers to *formerly colonized Africans as well*,[8] the ability to "write back."[9] This is how we utilize this theoretical framework to share our re-imaginings of Africa.

Defining Postcolonialism

Postcolonial theory emerged from a hermeneutical, post-structuralist tradition brought to the fore with Edward Said's classic 1979 analysis of the Middle East. Said based his study of Orientalism on what he

---

[6] D. Chakrabarty, "Provincializing Europe: Postcoloniality and the Critique of History," *Cultural Studies* 6 (1992): 337–357.

[7] Bill Ashcroft, "Globalism, Postcolonialism and African Studies," in *Postcolonialism: Culture and Identity in Africa*, eds. Pal Ahluwalia and Paul Nursey-Bray (New York: Nova Science Publishers, 1997).

[8] Italics represent the authors' emphasis.

[9] Quoted in Pal Ahluwalia's *Politics and Postcolonial Theory: African Inflections*. See Ashcroft et al., *The Empire Writes Back: Theory and Practice in Post-colonial Literatures*, 2nd ed. (London and New York: Routledge, 1989), and Edward Said's *Orientalism*.

perceived to be the subtle prejudice against Arab-Muslim peoples and their culture.[10] Since then, numerous postcolonial scholars from the Indian school—Homi Bhaba, Gyan Prakash, and Gayatari Spivak—and from an Africanist cadre—Valentine Mudimbe, Mahmood Mamdani, Pal Ahluwalia, and Oyeronke Oyewumi—have expanded upon and consolidated Said's insights by critiquing the positivist Western discourse of the non-Western world. These scholars have been critical of the West's tendency to analyze formerly colonized regions from culturally determined and often limited Western historical perspectives.[11]

Since the early 1980s, postcolonial theory has presented five major streams of analysis of dominant discourses of non-Western peoples. Firstly, third world postcolonialists argued that normative Western discourse of the non-Western world lumped countries in southern regions together in geographical blocks, which resulted in overlooking vital differences in history, views, and cultural practices among and within countries in the third world. Secondly, postcolonial theory has also criticized the hegemonic use of "colonial" languages—English, French, and Portuguese—which, its proponents argue, has marginalized and subverted the richness and complexity of non-Western languages, social practices, cultures, and histories.

Thirdly, postcolonial theory has exposed global inequality. Some claim that its ideological force helps to counter the economic and political coercion of the hegemonic North, which denies developing countries use of their own resources and fair access to global markets.[12] Fourthly, borrowing from the post-modern and post-structuralist paradigms of Otherness, postcolonial thinkers argue that non-Western peoples have been defined by their European former colonizers as the Other, an inferior subject to the superior Western "self." Postcolonial thought references this Freudian psychoanalytical conceptualization of Self and Other to posit resistance among peoples considered Other. It promotes agency among once-colonized peoples resisting their past and invites them to cast off despised, negative colonialist attitudes.

Fifthly and most important, postcolonial theory has evolved a critique of colonialism itself that expands our understanding of the continuities of the colonial experience. The authors of *The Empire Writes Back* (1989) are unequivocal in proclaiming that postcolonial theory covers the moment of colonial contact to the present to underscore the continuity and persistence of colonizing practices, as well as the critical limits and possibilities they have engendered. Gyan Prakash's definition of postcolonialism is similarly instructive in this regard. He states that postcoloniality does not represent either the transcendence or the reversal of colonialism. In fact, he says significantly that postcolonial theory is inclined to sidestep the language of beginnings and endings. Linked to the experience of colonialism, but not contained by it, postcoloniality, argues Prakash, can be seen as a realignment of the contemporary developing-world state-society, which constantly and critically undoes and redraws colonialism's boundaries.[13]

Because of its increasing popularity and interest across disciplines, postcolonial theory has come to be defined pluralistically as a medium for the voice, representation, and agency of formerly colonized peoples. Darby and Paolini (1994) argue that postcolonialism is the attempt by the third world intellectual, the progressive Western academic, and the subaltern native to reclaim the moral and emotional

---

[10] Edward Said, *Orientalism*, 1979.

[11] George Landow, *Contemporary Postcolonial and Postimperial Literature in English*, www.scholars.nus.edu.sg/landow/post/index.html.

[12] Friends of the Third World, www.friendsofthethirdworld.org.

[13] Gyan Prakash, "Who is Afraid of Postcoloniality?" *Social Text* 14, no. 4 (Winter): 187–2031. Also see *After Colonialism: Imperial Histories and Postcolonial Displacements* (Princeton University Press, 1995).

high ground through interrogating the impact of Western modernity. Further, Ali Rattansi has called postcolonialist studies the investigation of the mutually constitutive role played by colonizer and colonized, center and periphery, the metropolitan and the "native" in forming, in part, the identities of the Western powers and the non-Western cultures that they forged.[14]

An important way to understand postcolonialism, for the purposes of the current chapter, is by its interdisciplinary methodology. Founded in literary and culturalist critical theory, postcolonial theory's current explorations are of the complex political, economic, and cultural relations and conjunctures of the contemporary global era. Moreover, there is a sub-discipline of postcolonialism emerging in international relations. Using the themes of representation, cultural politics, resistance, and agency, Geeta Chowdhry and Sheila Nair (2002) argue that a postcolonialist international relations theory acknowledges that colonialism still influences independent countries and that postcolonial societies are continuously responding in myriad ways to the experience of colonial contact.[15]

Postcolonial international relations theory seeks to disrupt what it argues has been the tendency by Western scholarship to present these independent states in "imperial binary" classifications (Doty 1996) of tradition and modernization, or even in simplistic dualisms pitting West against non-West. Contrarily, postcolonial scholars investigate the interstitial space arising out of the postcolonial condition, raising the possibility of the complexity of the postcolonial subject, who is not on a "failed linear trajectory to modernity" but is a hybrid subject whose interactions with other countries—especially former colonizers—need to be problematized.

Self-proclaimed postcolonialist Himadeep Muppidi has argued, for example, that there are two poles in the new world order. One is the colonial, characterized by antidemocratic and authoritarian processes that are increasingly employed to dominate the international politics of "difference"; the other is the postcolonial, distinguished by the predominance of democratic procedures.[16] A democratic, global governance of security relations, according to Muppidi, is not one that excludes equal membership of third world states or that invokes negative epithets characterizing the third world as "disorderly, failed threats," or other such constructs of colonial governance.[17] Alternatively, in positing a perspective that he calls postcolonial governance, Muppidi envisions an international community that is governed by a meaningful, shared imagination of the world.

In his own definition of postcolonial theory, David Slater has also shown how it is beginning to shape current theorizations of global change in favor of marginalized regions, countries, and communities. Postcolonial dialogues of the sort discussed in our introduction (the debates on African civilizations and their places in world history) have fostered new encounters between Western and non-Western agents of knowledge, enabling scholars to rethink issues of globalization.[18] Slater shows that postcolonial theory already bridges these encounters because it is an alternative to the many paradigms of globalization.

In this regard, postcolonialism counters and complements narrow mainstream political theory by integrating local, national, and transnational perspectives, as well as economic structures that critically

[14] Ali Rattansi, "Postcolonialism and its Discontents," *Economy and Society* 26, no. 4 (November 1997): 480–500.

[15] Geeta Chowdhry and Sheila Nair Power, *Postcolonialism and International Relations* (London and New York: Routledge, 2002).

[16] Himadeep Muppidi, "Colonial and Postcolonial Global Governance," in *Power in Global Governance,* eds. Michael Barnett and Raymond Duvall.

[17] (Cambridge University Press, 2005).

[18] Michael Barnett and Raymond Duvall, eds., *Power in Global Governance* (Cambridge University Press, 2005), 276.

influence the internationalization of the developing world. In effect, as an intellectual tradition, postcolonialism also counteracts global change by reversing internationalization that marginalizes peripheral regions of the world like Africa. In doing so, it helps to renew the true subject-agent voice(s) of African sociopolitical forces. Geeta Chowdhry and Sheila Nair (2002) confirm this objective of postcolonial international relations theory when they claim that its strength rests in exposing the multiple interpretations, voices, and struggles employed to examine and understand international affairs.

Critiquing Postcolonialism

Like most grand theories of international relations, including Realism, Liberalism, Marxism, and Constructivism, postcolonialism is an extremely contested intellectual domain as well. Many progressive Africanist scholars, while indirectly and unconsciously engaging postcolonialism, either silently promote it or outright reject its relevance to contemporary Africa. There are four arguments against postcolonial theory:

Firstly, it is argued that postcolonial theory is post-modernist and post-structural and, thus, belongs to literary studies concerned primarily with a "discourse" and "textual analysis" that minimize "materialist" political-economic processes. Secondly, and paradoxically related to the first, postcolonialism is ostensibly seen as a more acceptable theory to the subjects of its critique—former colonial powers—because it does not employ radical discourses of imperialism and other structuralist, traditional Africanist, Marxist theories of dependency and neocolonialism.

Thirdly, many complain that postcolonialism is not rooted in the regions that it professes to represent and that it is a fad among third world scholars in Western academic institutions. Fourthly, some scholars reject postcolonialism by arguing that colonialism and its effects are no longer relevant to independent countries or that postcolonial theory merely critiques countries' abilities or inabilities to move beyond colonialism. These Africanists feel that "neocolonialism" better captures the African experience.

Let us examine each critique in detail in order to determine postcolonial theory's applicability to contemporary Africa.

Postcolonialism and Debates on Coloniality and Modernism

There exists a vibrant debate regarding the relationships between post-structuralism, post-modernism, and postcolonialism (Ahluwalia 2001). Postcolonialism is often assumed to belong to the same school as post-modernism and post-structuralism. Arif Dirik has argued, for example, that postcolonialism is postmodernism's progeny.[19] Others, however, including Aijaz Ahmad, critically distinguish the three "posts," insisting that postcolonialism is superficial because of its overdetermined focus on the condition and representation of postcoloniality as opposed to Africans' lived material experiences. Such scholars view postcolonialism mainly as an exclusive "intellectual" discourse relevant primarily to the intelligentsia. According to this critique, the post-modern orientation of postcolonialism propels it down a blind tunnel with identity struggles. Consequently, critics such as Anne McClintock are inclined to regard postcolonialism as an intellectual fad riding on a wave of global popularity.

Ashcroft and his colleagues address these concerns, acknowledging that both postcolonialists *and* post-modernists attempt to break down the binaries of imperial discourse. The authors not only

---

[19] David Slater, "Postcolonial Questions for Global Times,"*Review of International Political Economy* 5, no. 4 (Winter 1998): 647–678.

recognize the literary roots of postcolonialism in their own and the works of Edward Said, but also draw attention to the heterogeneity of postcolonialism and its application outside of the humanities, especially in the social sciences. While welcoming this heterogeneity, Stephen Selmon says that postcolonial theory was adopted by nonliterary disciplines for pragmatic reasons that have to do with the nature of colonialism. The fact that colonialism is an economic and political structure of cross-cultural domination has occasioned a set of debates, and at the heart of these debates, claims Selmon, is a "literary" and, thus, post-structural discourse ideology that views colonialism as an apparatus for constituting subject positions through representation.

Postcolonial theory's heterogeneity—its interdisciplinary weaving of humanities and social science disciplines—is accompanied by a new "inter-discipline" known as cultural theory through which numerous postcolonialists speak. However, critics maintain that the integration of disciplines such as political economy, literature, sociology, history, and anthropology has yet to occur because most postcolonialists merely poke around in these disciplines.[20] Peter Childs and Patrick Williams disagree, arguing that postcolonialism maintains a level of interdisciplinarity that few disciplines could emulate.

From our point of view, we welcome Childs and Williams's interdisciplinary outlook and offer this book in the same spirit. Even though we are political scientists, our contributors come from an array of disciplines in the humanities and social sciences. In *Reframing Contemporary Africa*, we have navigated literatures, histories, politics, economics, popular culture, anthropology, and international relations. Our contributors do more than poke around African political affairs; they use their different disciplinary perspectives to bring to politics a deeper, more rigorous analysis and understanding.

Debates About Relevance to African Political Economies

Many third world structuralist scholars contend that because of its post-modernist allegiance, postcolonialism sidesteps the most important issues of postcolonial societies, including underdevelopment, global inequality, dependency, and the growing erosion of third world countries' national economic sovereignty. David Scott has argued that a major weakness in postcolonialism is its inability, thus far, to provide a sophisticated "political-economic" framework that promotes teasing out the relationship between colonialism and socialism in formerly colonized regions. Scott claims that postcolonialism implicitly rejects the Marxist narrative and thereby fails to make the critique of capitalism its foundational principle.[21]

A proponent of this view, Arif Dirlik, further argues that denying the critical role of capitalism in postcolonial theory reveals the culturalist bias of postcolonial theory, which Dirlik maintains, has important ideological consequences. It results in Eurocentrism that blurs power relationships and reinforces world hegemony. Postcolonialism within such a context, according to Dirlik, fails to explain why Eurocentrism was able to define modern global history.[22]

Postcolonialist theorists have a mixed response to this criticism. Some, like Kwame Appiah, employ a brand of postcolonialism that supports capitalism and rejects anticapitalist socialism and welfarism. Appiah argues that postcolonialism ought to be defined in terms of post-nationalism, post-socialism, and post-essentialism

---

[20] Dirlik 1994, 348, cited in Ahluwalia 2002.

[21] Jacoby, cited in Moore-Gilbert 1997, 14.

[22] David Scott, "Colonial Governmentality," *Social Text,* no. 43: 101–220.

in both Marxist and liberal terms (Appiah 1997).[23] David Scott supports this contention when he argues that postcolonialism ought to distance itself entirely from the Enlightenment—liberalism and Marxism. Pal Ahluwalia also fashions himself as a post-national postcolonialist when he criticizes the Tanzanian *ujaama* economy and points to the failure of former president Julius Nyerere's socialist and nationalist project. Supporting Scott, Ahluwalia claims that postcolonialism requires a different political modernity than that offered by Nyerere's brand of socialism. By implication, this school of postcolonialism generally agrees that the foundationalist and universalist assumptions of Marxism need to be rejected to further a genuinely non-Eurocentric (and non-Marxist) history (Gyan Prakash 1997).

Other postcolonialists take a different view. They believe that postcolonialist discourse has emerged from Marxism, especially from the neo-Marxist scholarship of Antonnio Gramsci. These scholars present postcolonialism's subaltern school, with its focus on the political-economic struggles of the oppressed, class stratification, and ideological formulation among elites, as an illustration of the integral relationship between Marxism and postcolonialism. Indeed, postcolonialists of this genre suggest that their debates about "representation" are not simply ideational. Said's and other postcolonialists' works, for instance, have emphasized the relationship between Western representation and knowledge, on the one hand, and Western material and political power on the other (Moore-Gilbert 1997, 34). These postcolonialists are interdisciplinary because they foreground the interconnections between culture, discourse, and material practices, especially in their constructions of the continuing inequalities in North-South relations.

Teresa Ebert has revealed that there are two different ways of understanding postcoloniality in this respect. The first is Foucauldian (post-structuralist) and culturalist and seeks to show the relationships between power and regimes of knowledge; this is what makes postcolonialism focus on "representational" issues. However, a second highlights the international division of labor and poses the problem of the economics of untruth in the relations of the metropolitan North and the peripheral South. Ebert claims that postcolonialism suggests that the politics of representation cannot be understood separately from the international political economy.[24] Contributors to the current volume are also sensitive to the connections between African cultures and identity struggles, as well as to the structural materialism manifest in the continent's underdevelopment and poverty.

Debates About Conceptual Origins

A final and important critique of postcolonial theory, especially among progressive Africanists, is that it is not indigenous to Africa and Asia, the postcolonial regions that it professes to represent. In India, this view is enshrined in the seminal article of Gayatri Spivak, "Can the Subaltern Speak?"[25] Her work is sympathetic to the postcolonialist project to give voice to "suppressed" colonial subjects whose experiences have been written out of the colonialist record. Spivak is wary of her own "representational" status as an Indian woman living in New York City; she grapples with whether postcolonial elites like herself can truly represent the "subaltern" in English, a "foreign" language in postcolonial India. Spivak

---

[23] A. Dirlik, "The Postcolonial Aura: Third World Criticism in the Age of Global Capitalism," in *Dangerous Liaisons: Gender, Nation and Postcolonial Perspective,* eds. Anne McClintock, Aamir Mufti, and Ella Shohat (Minneapolis, MN: University of Minnesota Press, 1997).

[24] Kwame Appiah, "Is the 'Post' in Postcolonial the 'Post' in Postmodern?" in *Dangerous Liaisons: Gender, Nation and Postcolonial Perspective,* eds. Anne McClintock, Aamir Mufti, and Ella Shohat (Minneapolis, MN: University of Minnesota Press, 1997).

[25] Teresa Elbert, "Subalternity and Feminism in the Moment of the Postmodern: The Materialist Return," in *Order Partialities: Theory, Pedagogy and the Postcolonial,* eds. K. Myrsiades and J. McGuire (Albany, NY: SUNY, 1995).

is concerned about her Westernized representational positionality as she tries to advance the cause of the Indian peasant. She says that, ironically, her work may reflect the manner that Britain—now without an empire—maintains cultural authority in postcolonial societies (Ashcroft et al. 1989).

While many Africans believe that postcolonial theory originated in the Indian school—and that despite its claims to cross-cultural legitimacy, it does not speak to African experiences—Spivak's ruminations are evidence that the debate over the indigenousness or culturalist authenticity of postcolonialism invokes Eurocentric assumptions about race, nationality, and literature over and over again to haunt postcolonial writing in all postcolonial regions, not just in Africa. In our introduction, we also raised the need to address similar paradoxes as phenomena of African human relations. After all, African writings have also been sites of imperial representation, language, and ideological control. Chinua Achebe's *Things Fall Apart* is a case in point. Interestingly, for example, some interpret this classic novel as an authentic postcolonial work that illustrates the human and cultural agency of Nigeria's Igbo in resisting British Empire.

There are other interpretations, however. One examines the tragic fall of the book's main character, Okonkwo, who is represented as an Igbo cultural artifact of an archetypical colonized African "state-society." There is an emergent interpretation of Achebe's novel that argues that Okonkwo's character suggests Africans need to succumb and adapt to colonial legacies, hence to postcolonialism. Such a message, advocated by the intellectual progeny of former colonizers—the nationalist elite—suggests that Africans must absorb changes introduced during the Euro-Africa encounter in order to progress and advance their newly independent nations. Nevertheless, this message feeds into a Eurocentric hegemony, imposing on Africans the superiority of Western over African values and experiences. Critics of this way of interpreting postcolonial Africa argue that English-speaking indigenous, postcolonial writers and thinkers who have constructed this representation of Africa do so because they have imbibed the cultural biases of English colonizers. Such critics claim that Achebe, like Spivak, is a product of English colonialism and that through *Things Fall Apart,* he presents a nonindigenous rendering of a postcolonial culture.

Similarly, some critics maintain that postcolonial theory is an elitist debate among third world and diasporan scholars who reside in the West. Indeed, they criticize Kwame Appiah for not even apologizing for being elitist. Appiah refers to his relatively small, Westernized group of postcolonial writers and thinkers as a "comprador intelligentsia" who mediate the trade of cultural commodities of world capitalism at the periphery.[26] In rejecting these Westernized, alienating claims, Nigerian historian Adebayo Williams denies any relevance of postcolonialism to Africa. He views postcolonialism as a project of the Indian intellectual aristocracy whose equivalent does not exist in Africa. Calling Gupta's and Spivak's subaltern studies "nativized" Marxism and bemoaning the "collapse" of African states, Williams argues that neo-colonialism, not "postcolonialism," dominates contemporary African state-societies.[27]

However, as African postcolonialist Pal Ahluwalia insists in his defense of the postcolonial paradigm for Africa, Williams misreads postcolonial theory. Ahluwalia argues that Williams is incorrect to categorize postcolonialism as Indian and focused merely on the experiences of third world state-societies "after" colonialism. To rebut William's first misconception, Ahluwalia presents postcolonialism's multiregional origins in the Middle East (Said, Memeh), Caribbean (Lammy), Africa (Fanon, Mudimbe), and South Asia (Spivak, Prakash). As for his colleague's other concerns, Ahuwalia points to the numerous

---

[26] Gayatri Chakravorty Spivak, "Can the Subaltern Speak?" in *The Postcolonial Studies Reader,* eds. Bill Ashcroft, Gareth Griffiths, and Helen Tiffin (London and New York: Routledge, 1995).

[27] Cited in Ahluwalia (2002).

steps that postcolonialists have taken to demonstrate that their scope begins with the colonial encounter and, therefore, covers the centrality of colonialism and its influences on present-day postcolonial states.

Regarding the explicit origins of postcolonial theory, the authors of *The Empire Writes Back*, for instance, have been especially sensitive to the question of cultural legitimacy, given their location in Australia, a postcolonial British settler-colony (1989). The authors refuse to be limited by their own postcolonial cultural experience and, instead, seek to demonstrate that the Australian colonial experience extends to other Commonwealth nations, the United States, and other colonized and colonizer nations. From such a position, postcolonial authors begin to understand the many ways in which the postcolonial experience is a truly global experience. Ahluwalia quotes Said who demonstrated that imperialism brought the world together in its insidious and unjust separation of Europeans and natives and argues that postcolonial theory regards the experience of empire as a common one.[28]

In reply to Williams, who feels that "neocolonialism" is a more adequate framework for examining African affairs, Pal Ahluwalia asserts that the "neocolonial" experience comes under the rubric of postcolonialism and is not just relevant to Africa. Postcolonial theory continues to be relevant to contemporary African states and societies for the very reasons that Williams argues that it does not. To drive home his point, Ahluwalia cites the works of Kwame Nkrumah and Franz Fanon and categorizes them as postcolonialist because they recognize colonialism in neocolonialism. What is more, according to Ahluwalia, all third world postcolonial societies, not just African ones, share similar characteristics of ethnic and cultural pluralism, uneven underdevelopment, political instability, and civil conflict or what Williams describes as features of "collapse," which in reality are perverted byproducts of colonial nation building. Thus, postcolonial discourse recognizes "neocolonialism" and critically analyzes it by focusing on global inequality and North-South issues. Postcolonialists also pay attention to the pernicious control of the IMF and the World Bank, which wield unilateral economic, political, and cultural control over the continent.

Given the neocolonial realities in Africa, *Reframing Contemporary Africa*'s editors and contributors have also highlighted the relevance of understanding coloniality in Africa, especially as a way to counter the pervasive externalist discourse and reading of colonialist history. Because colonialism and neocolonialism have perhaps been more destructive and recent in Africa than in other regions, the postcolonial framework is even more legitimate to Africa.

Postcolonial Applications and Contemporary Africa in the New Internationalism: Darfur, AFRICOM, and Zoe's Ark

Despite its heterogeneity and contested premises, there are tangible reasons why postcolonial theory is relevant to the analysis of contemporary African affairs. The important events discussed below demonstrate that current internationalist policy prescriptions for the continent tend to be driven by globalist interests, rather than by local, national, and regional ones.

Illustrated in news headlines in the Western press and in academic conference titles, such as "Saving Africa," "Aiding Africa," "Whither Africa," "Africa's Second Genocide," and "Educating Africans," contemporary international relations primarily attributes Africa's problems to the continent's presumed incompetent

[28] Adebayo Williams, "The Post Colonial Flaneur and Other Fellow-Travelers: Conceits for a Narrative of Redemption," *Third World Quarterly* 18, no. 5, (1997): 821–841.

and immoral leadership, as well as to the developmental and cultural backwardness of its peoples. The West/non-West representational binaries established as a result of the colonial encounter—real versus collapsed states, democracies versus dictatorships, modern versus traditional nations—are generally sustained in contemporary analysis of African issues. Negative, discursive, representational signifiers that present Africa as a site that is "prone to genocide" (Sudan-Darfur), that marginalize the policy initiatives of African foreign policy actors (African Union versus AFRICOM), and that construct foreign policies in Africa by presenting Africans as the inferior Other (French-Africa relations), provide important lenses through which to examine current trends in the new internationalism.

Darfur: Africa as the Site for "Moral" International Relations

The Sudan-Darfur conflict has generated the most substantial recent attention in international policy initiatives and debates. It symbolizes disputations between African countries and top-tier powers constituted as the "international community" (EU, the United States, and the UN Security Council) over a range of representations concerning Africa. The conflict in the country's western province first appeared in international headlines in 2004 on the heels of the peace agreement that ended the Sudan's twenty-year civil war between the northern Islamic and southern non-Islamic regions. However, peace did not come so easily. Just a few months after the signing of the consequential peace agreement, Darfur's Justice and Equality Movement (JEM) and the Sudanese Liberation Movement took up arms against the government to claim an equitable share in the country's national resources.

The five-year conflict (2004 to present) rekindled debate in April 2009 when the International Criminal Court (ICC) issued an arrest warrant—the first ever for a sitting head of state[29]—for Sudanese president Omar Hassan Ahmad al-Bashiron. While the ICC cleared the Sudanese president of the "genocide" indictment, the Sudanese president remains accused of criminal responsibility for his role as a coperpetrator of war crimes and crimes against humanity. The indictment accuses the Sudanese president of intentionally directing the murder, extermination, rape, torture, and forcible transfer of large numbers of civilians and of pillaging their property. Jean Ping, chairman of the African Union Commission, called the indictment a "threat to peace in Sudan" and claimed that he felt that the rules of conflict were not being applied fairly. He used Iraq, Gaza, Colombia, and the Caucasus as examples. His position was shared by Senegalese president Abdoulaye Wade, who said the ICC seemed to be "only after Africans."

Numerous statements by African Union (AU) leaders, however, focused on other implications of the arrest warrant. For instance, Tanzanian foreign minister Bernard Membe, speaking to the press on behalf of then-chair of the African Union, President Jakaya Kikwete, explained that "if Bashir is indicted and taken, there will be a power vacuum in the Sudan and that risks military coups and widespread anarchy reminiscent of what is happening in Iraq. We in the African Union do not condone impunity, genocide and violence because we believe in due process of the rule of law . . . but what we are calling for is a deferment in indicting Bashir because there is a risk of anarchy in a proportion we have not seen in this continent."[30]

---

[29] Ahluwalia (2002), 10.

[30] ICC Press Release: 04.03.2009, "ICC Issues a warrant of arrest for Omar Al Bashir, President of Sudan," ICC-CPI-20090304-PR394, http://www.icc-cpi.int/NR/rdonlyres/0EF62173-05ED-403A-80C8-F15EE1D25BB3/279934/Press_ARA3.pdfwww.icccpi.int/Menus/ICC/About+the+Court/ International Criminal Court (Press and Media).

The ICC indictment was certainly supported and even hailed by many African democracy activists and human rights organizations, with activists calling on their governments to refrain from supporting the AU's criticism of the ICC indictment.[31] But even from within the ranks of some of the human rights lobbies emerged strongly voiced complaints that included issues such as the inadequate attention given by the ICC to the recommendations of local human rights groups on handling the timing of the indictment, concerns about its possible impact on the peace process and refugee welfare, and continued concerns about the inscription of difference in Western constructions of human rights issues in Africa and elsewhere in the world. [32]

How then should we interpret the varied African perspectives on the Sudan-Darfur conflict and areas of divergence with the ICC decision? Mainstream Africanists and international public opinion tend to attribute the African Union's opposition to the indictment of President Omar al-Bashir to a number of factors, including the notion that African authoritarian values tend to normalize what might otherwise be described as state terrorism and violence. Other explanations for the AU position have traced it to political pressures from the North African or Arab-African states, which had indeed made it clear they would brook no intervention in the Sudanese conflict. Other commentators have argued that few leaders wish to set precedence for indictments that might be used against their own governments by external powers. In response to the first conjecture, we must note that the strident criticisms of the Sudanese president by many African scholars, African human rights groups, and media, and the role played by several African leaders seeking to engineer a democratic Sudanese peace process make it evident that so-called authoritarian values do not resonate in the complex African responses to the crisis.[33] Contrarily, however, we must inquire whether the African position can be understood through the lenses offered by postcolonial theory, while the various international policy decisions and framings of the Darfur conflict are rooted, to some extent, in the practices critiqued as the new internationalism and Africanism.

Debates over the appropriate classifying of the Sudan crisis began in 2004 with what some scholars have called the West's political-economy of knowledge production of formerly colonized nations by which negative signifiers deployed during the colonial period are reconstituted to achieve similar strategies of domination and control in the contemporary global era (Doty 1996). To the consternation of some, this discourse debate seemed to be symbolized in what one Africanist scholar has referred to as "the political-economic uses and abuses of the term genocide"[34] in classifying the Sudan-Darfur conflict.

The first to classify the conflict in Darfur as genocide were U.S. journalists and nongovernmental organizations. In the forefront was Human Rights Watch, which announced that it had evidence of "ethnic cleansing," with up to 250,000 deaths.[35] These announcements were followed by a U.S. Congressional resolution to protest the Sudanese government's "genocide" in Darfur. Until pressured

[31] "AU warns of Coup, Anarchy if Sudan President Indicted," www.sudan.net/news/posted/16105.html.

[32] See Ghanapolitics, wwwghanapolitics.blogspot.com/2009/03/ghana-must-not-support-aus-position-on.html.

[33] Peyi Soyinka-Airewele, "Navigating Realities, Illusions and Academic Impulses: Displaced Scholars at Large," SSRC, programs.ssrc.org/gsc/gsc_quarterly/newsletter6/content/peyi.

[34] See, for instance, Peyi Soyinka-Airewele, "Divided We Stand? Darfur, The Sudan and the Struggles for the Rights of Humanity" (public lecture delivered on International Human Rights Day, Textor Hall, Ithaca College, December 10, 2004).

[35] Mahmood Mamdani, "The Politics of Naming: Genocide, Civil War, Insurgency," *London Review of Books*, March 8, 2007.

by the U.S. Congress and numerous human rights organizations, the U.S. State Department, at the request of President George W. Bush, shied away from using the term "genocide" to define the Sudanese-Darfur conflict. Moreover, after a fact-finding investigation, the United Nations Security Council (UNSC) ruled in 2005 that the conflict was not genocide but a war with gross human rights violations by individual government officials and Darfurian rebels. By this time, the UNSC ruling met with protest in many parts of the world including media and human rights groups in several African countries who raised the specter of the reenactment of Rwanda and Bosnia. African leaders represented through the African Union however generally maintained that the Sudanese conflict was not a genocide per se but a civil war whose resolution required a diplomatic, not a military or a non-African interventionist solution.

The African Union's position was consistent with the body's rejection of the ICC indictment, in which some leaders had seen the international proclivity to focus a lens on Africa and apply double standards in addressing abuses conducted by more powerful countries. Indeed, while few serious observers would deny the evidence of gross state violence and abuse in the Sudan and the attendant human tragedy, the ICC indictment of the Sudanese leader raises urgent questions about the selectivity of "justice" and naming of global villains, given that the Burmese military, which mercilessly shot and killed Buddhist monks who peacefully protested against the regime, and the still-communist Chinese state, which recently crushed an armed rebellion in Tibet, have still not received the same kind of international attention as the Sudan. Indeed, when U.S. President Barack Obama announced that he was conflicted over the Chinese clampdown on Tibet, he said it was a "complex" situation, not easily discernible from the perspective of human rights.[36]

Why have these conflicts not been classified as "genocidal," and why has the ICC not indicted these countries' leaders? Africans ask whether justice can be served if war criminals from powerful nations are free to walk and non-African regimes guilty of similar uses and abuses of "state power" are not similarly targeted by international enforcement institutions. One news source reported that Africans felt that they were again being humiliated by the former colonial powers.[37]

From the perspective of representation studies, mainstream discursive narratives that describe the Sudan-Darfur conflict demonstrate that the international community is inclined towards simplistically reducing the conflict's complexity to what one scholar describes as a "morality tale unfolding in a world populated by villains and victims who never trade places and so can always and easily be told apart."[38] Darfur is represented as a place without history and politics, as international human rights organizations mobilize the international community by representing the Sudan-Darfur conflict as a place of "horror, without context."[39] Significantly, since the conflict is presented as devoid of political context, it thereby fails to construct Africans in variable, complex, and rational terms.

A postcolonial analysis of the Sudanese-Darfur crisis is unequivocal in its assertion that the Sudanese regime presided over by President Omar al-Bashir is authoritarian, militaristic, and has deployed state

---

[36] Nicholas Kristof, "Mass Murder in Slow Motion," January 25, 2006, www.AlbertMohler.com.

[37] *MSNBC Online*, "Obama Says He's Conflicted on Olympics, U.S. Participation Questioned Because of China's Human Rights Record," April. 2, 2008, www.msnbc.msn.com/id/23916733.

[38] Michael Keating, "African Leaders Reject the ICC Bashir Indictment," March 5, 2009, *World Politics Review* (WPR) Blog, www.worldpoliticsreview.com/blog/blog.aspx?id=3395.

[39] Mamdani, 2007.

terrorism to quell a legitimate insurgency led by Darfur's grieved political movements agitating for national democratic inclusion.[40] Beleaguered since the 1980s by communal and cross-border conflicts with Chad over land and resources, in their original claims, Darfur's Justice and Morality Movement and the Sudanese Liberation Movements have justifiably argued for equitable national resource distribution for their province. By recognizing the complexity of Africa's underdevelopment in the context of the continent's racial, ethnic, and religious pluralism within its arbitrarily colonially constructed national territories, a postcolonial framework leads us to identify and critically examine the depth and scope of the conflict, which reveals the historical, sociopolitical, and economic roots that have thrown up the current circumstance. In doing so, the intersections by which the conflict is located in local, national, and international networks of interest are also exposed.

A postcolonial discourse analysis also recognizes the inclusion of African voices and perspectives on this conflict without prejudging that same position as authoritarian and corrupt. As a representative regional organization, the African Union's position and policy initiatives on the conflict are as legitimate and complexly formulated as the United Nations' position on Afghanistan or the European Union's position on Chechneya. While individual African countries do have strategic national interests tied to the Sudan—and seek to secure those interests—the African Union as a collective body does not condone genocide among its members. In fact, the regional organization has been instrumental in fostering a consensus among its members to solve the Sudan crisis with equity and justice. The African Union despite some divergence in its ranks has chosen to classify the Sudanese-Darfur conflict as a civil war that has emerged as a result of a chronic political crisis of a deeply divided nation.

While such a position might appear milder than the tragedies of human suffering demand, it must be noted that the AU has been involved in multiple interventions in Sudan's problematic colonial social formation for many years and has devised several diplomatic initiatives and decision points to assist the Sudanese government in recognizing the country's ethnic and religious pluralism similar to other multi-ethnic African nations. Since the Darfur crisis was preceded by a prolonged civil war rooted in the struggles of identity and political rights (between a predominantly Arab-Muslim Northern region and a Black African–Christian South), as early as 1986 for example, the sub-regional organization IGAD (Intergovernmental Development Association of the Horn of African Countries) established a Declaration of Principles (DOP) in which it set forth the premises for Sudanese "unity" on the resolution of the national democratic question. Sudanese regimes were asked to recognize self-determination, racial, ethnic, cultural, and religious diversity, as well as legal, political, and social equality in a secular and democratic state that fosters freedom of belief and worship.[41]

The African Union has also been proactive in contributing to a peaceful resolution of the Sudan-Darfur conflict. It has sponsored several conflict resolution conferences that have been negotiated, signed, and broken by all parties to the Sudanese conflict, including the armed rebels. These Darfurian movements have recently splintered into several factions that resumed their armed rebellion despite a peace agreement with the Sudanese regime signed in Abuja, Nigeria, in 2007. The AU has also contributed peacekeeping troops to the Sudan-Darfur conflict. The African Union Mission in the Sudan (AMIS) originated in early July 2004, when both the African Union and European Union sent monitors to observe the Darfur crisis cease-fire. In August 2004,

---

[40] David Rieff, *A Bed for the Night: Humanitarianism in Crisis* (New York: Simon and Schuster, 2002), 33.

[41] Rita Kiki Edozie, "Sudan Identity Wars and Democratic Route to Peace," in *Perspectives on Contemporary Ethnic Conflict,* ed. Santosh Saha (Lanham, MD: Lexington Books, 2006).

the African Union sent 150 Rwandan troops to protect the cease-fire monitors. Again, during April 2005, after the government of Sudan signed a cease-fire agreement with the Sudan People's Liberation Army and the Justice and Morality Movement, the AMIS force was increased by six hundred troops and eighty military observers. In July 2005, the force was increased by about three thousand three hundred and in April 2007, AMIS was increased to about seven thousand.

The fact is that the international response to the Sudan-Darfur conflict is represented in new internationalist frameworks. Doing so marginalizes both the political-economic and sociocultural contexts of the conflict while ignoring the contributions of Africans to its resolution and constraining the agency of Africans in addressing these issues using their own strategies. Sudan-Darfur and other African conflicts need to be analyzed with the same kind of scholarly scrutiny as comparative insurgency wars in the global era when state paramilitary counterinsurgency strategies are *wrongly* used to quell militant insurgencies in the context of the so-called global war on terror. As stated by the African Union, a postcolonial method unequivocally condemns the authoritarianism, state terrorism, and all aspects of violent identity politics of exclusion and oppression in the Sudan and elsewhere and encourages a democratic route to peace.[42] Nevertheless, the route to peace must be achieved by a comprehensive scholarly representation of the political-economic context of the conflict—one that is also constructed and represented in ways that include the self-determined foreign policy voices of African institutions and leaderships.

AFRICOM: The Re-securitization of Africa

External influence over African affairs is not merely representational and discourse oriented, as the Sudan-Darfur case suggests. Africanism and the new internationalism also hold sway in the influence that hegemonic, militarily powerful Western states now have on the political-economic and social development of Africa. In 2009, complex material transformations in Africa are fostering what some are proclaiming is the recolonization of the continent, politically, economically, and militarily. This trend could not be more apparent in current U.S. policy towards Africa than in the launching of the U.S.-Africa Command (AFRICOM) as a unit of the U.S. Defense Department. AFRICOM is designed to run all U.S. military operations in Africa. According to a Pentagon press release, the new command will eventually be responsible for U.S. military relations with fifty-three African countries, which, the United States claims, will welcome AFRICOM's goal to bring peace and security to the continent because of decades of violence and civil strife.[43] Former U. S. president George W. Bush announced that the new base would not only improve the continent's security, but would also promote Africa's health, education, democratization, and economic growth.

AFRICOM is an example of unilateral U.S. foreign policy, not a bilateral or multilateral one. The Bush administration did not negotiate its plan to establish AFRICOM with Africans and thus ignored their self-determination and national sovereignty.[44] Africans insist that they were not appropriately consulted about U.S. decisions regarding Africa. In November 2007, U.S. deputy secretary of state John Negroponte paid a courtesy call to Abuja, Nigeria, to notify the Nigerian government that the United

---

[42] Robert Collins, "Africans, Arabs and Islamists: From the Conference Tables to the Battlefields in the Sudan," *African Studies Review* 42, no. 2 (September 1999).

[43] Rita Kiki Edozie, "Sudan's Identity Wars."

[44] David Gordon, "The Controversy over AFRICOM," *BBC World Service's Analysis*, October 3, 2007, news.bbc.co.uk/2/hi/africa.

States would establish AFRICOM. According to a daily newspaper, this trip was a diplomatic courtesy, not for negotiation.[45] Furthermore, because AFRICOM is a military initiative fusing hard and soft power initiatives, African nations fear a new trend to militarize economic development initiatives. Humanitarian work previously conducted by the State Department and the U.S. Agency for International Development (USAID) would now fall under the U.S. Department of Defense (DoD).

Many African leaders and democratic constituencies worry that AFRICOM's new internationalist objective is to resecuritize U.S.-African affairs by extending to Africa the Bush Doctrine, which is premised on the Global War on Terror and oil/energy interests.[46] Except for Liberia, which has been the only African country to express public support for AFRICOM, most African governments, regional organizations (such as the Economic Community of West African States, the Southern African Development Community, and the African Union), and African civil society organizations reject AFRICOM on several grounds. Many recognize that a country that hosts AFRICOM could become a target of anti-U.S. terrorism, thereby increasing instability in Africa and threatening further destabilization of an already fragile continent.

The most important criticism by Africans of this new U.S. foreign policy initiative is that its goals, structure, and operationalization could well subvert African sovereignty. By 2009, almost fifty years after much of the continent was freed from colonialism, African countries feel the need to develop their own foreign policy capacities to protect their national sovereignties. Thus, in defiance of U.S. foreign policy, many in Africa continue to resist AFRICOM because it thwarts the self-determined collective will of African countries represented by the African Union. African leaders are apprehensive about the extent to which AFRICOM will take the place of the AU force, which has also been established to defend the continent.

Postcolonial analysis offers important insights into the new U.S.-Africa contention over AFRICOM. While the United States promotes AFRICOM as the "savior" of Africa, Africans fear it will put into place structures of global interest and power tantamount to the "recolonization" of the continent.[47] This is a typical postcolonial response. Africans are concerned that contemporary international policy towards the continent is a new internationalist throwback to the nineteenth-century "civilizing mission" and the racist Western insistence that Africa is unable to govern itself. AFRICOM's establishment limits the likelihood of vibrant U.S.-African relations based on consensual and self-determined development.

Sarkozy and Zoe's Ark

A final event that underscores the limitations of the new internationalist approach towards African affairs can be found in contemporary French-African relations. Since the election of the controversial French president Nicholas Sarkozy, French-African relations feature elements of an Africanism that appear to resuscitate colonial discursive practices towards Africa. In his book *Testimony: France in the Twenty-First Century*,[48] in which Sarkozy outlines foreign policy towards France's former African colonies, his prescriptions have all the symptoms of the new internationalism.

---

[45] "AFRICOM," *US Policy World*, uspw.org/index.php?title=AFRICOM.

[46] Obi Nwakanma, "AFRICOM—The Invasion of Africa?" *Vanguard*, November 19, 2007.

[47] Abdoulaye W. Dukule, "AFRICOM: A New Paradigm in US-Africa Relations," *The Perspective*, September 17, 2007.

[48] Nwakanma, "AFRICOM—The Invasion of Africa?"

Sarkozy prefaces his proposals by insisting that France prioritize Africa and rethink its Africa policy—both apparently laudable recommendations. However, Sarkozy then promptly reveals the historic paternalism that underlies his new French-Africa policy as he goes on to proclaim that the French could best show their respect for Africans by *not* excusing them from all responsibility for the under-development of their continent. Blaming Africa's failure on the consequences of colonialism, Sarkozy states, is contrary to reality and denies a pragmatic diagnosis necessary for Africa's recovery.[49] Of course, African analysts, citizens, and governments have not been unaware of and have not failed to speak to the many internal and external problems that feed the continent's ongoing struggles. But of concern is that the French president's racialized imaginary could be so gravely in denial of his nation's continuing interests and role in the structural crisis of the continent that he determinedly conjures imagery of the slothful, irresponsible African who subverts the good intentions of European interventionists. Alarming also is that he could use the current economic struggles in Africa as occasion for absolving and cleansing the colonial past and reestablishing favored binaries.

Subsequent to the publication of *Testimony* and six months into his regime, Sarkozy made several statements that caused Africans to classify new French policy towards Africa as simply "racist." During a trip to Senegal, his first visit as president to Africa, Sarkozy went as far as to state that the tragedy of Africa lay in the fact that Africans had never really entered history. Like most African commentators, the AU chairman issued a stinging condemnation of Sarkozy's speech by saying that it reminded Africans of another age.[50]

The Zoe's Ark scandal crystallized worsening French-francophone African relations. In October 2007, President Nicolas Sarkozy was forced to fly to Chad to win the release of seventeen European—nine of them French—employees of the French charity Zoe's Ark. Chad had jailed the workers for allegedly kidnapping 103 children and flying them to France for adoption by French citizens. Before Sarkozy's visit, the Chadian government had arrested twenty-one people in relation to the crisis, which began when Zoe's Ark planned to fly the children out of the eastern Chadian city of Abeche on October 25. In pleading not guilty to charges of kidnapping children, the nine French workers claimed that the international charity had been rescuing children who were orphans of the bloody conflict in neighboring Darfur.

However, upon investigation, the Chadian government, UN humanitarian agencies, and the International Red Cross discovered that most of the children were actually Chadian, not Darfurian. They were found not to be orphans at all; several parents had been promised that their children would be educated locally in Chad. The parents claimed that they had never given anyone permission to take their children out of the country, let alone put them up for adoption. There were several protests in the town of Abeche and in the Chadian capital, N'Djamena, denouncing the French president and referring to him and other French citizens as "kidnappers of African children." Protesters demanded that the alleged French perpetrators be tried in Chad.[51]

Many Africans and Chadians saw as demeaning and pathetic the utter powerlessness of Chadian president Idris Déby Itno in preventing the interference of the French president in the internal affairs of Chad. Sarkozy's "rescue" was, to their eyes, yet another high-minded attempt by the French to undermine

---

[49] Nicolas Sarkozy, *Testimony: France in the Twenty-first Century* (New York: Pantheon Books, 2007).

[50] ibid., 229.

[51] Chris McGreal, "Mbeki Criticized for Praising Racist Sarkozy," Guardian, August 2007.

Chad's judiciary and sovereignty.[52] In fact, a week after securing the release of six prisoners, in what Africans viewed as another paternalistic act by Sarkozy, France announced that it would send troops to the Chadian-Sudanese border to prevent new violence in the region.

France's current policy towards Africa is similar to that exhibited in the Bush administration's establishment of AFRICOM. In *Testimony*, Sarkozy argues that while it is important for French citizens to debate French-African relations, they should understand that maintaining a French military presence on the African continent is vital for promoting peace and preventing genocidal clashes and tension in the continent.[53] In pronouncing such a policy position, France arrogates to itself the role of sustained intervention in Africa, without consultation with those who stand to be affected by its decisions. This genre of discourse is characteristic of France's broader policy towards Africa. Again, in *Testimony*, the French leader proclaims that the horror in Darfur is reminiscent of the worst tragedies in the continent. Then, paradoxically, Sarkozy proceeds to contend that it is the "skin color" of Darfurians that has prevented "great democracies" such as France and the United States from intervening in the conflict thus far. The French president not only continues to invoke identity discourse that provokes a crude ideology of Africanism, but his policy also remains at the discursive representational level. If France agrees that "horror" characterizes the Sudan-Darfur conflict, why has it not appropriately intervened in concert with Africans to end the conflict?

French-Africa policy under Sarkozy suggests key elements of the new internationalism and Africanism. Sarkozy's speeches and actions towards Africans are quite patently paternalistic and self-serving. This type of policy reifies colonialist discourses of France, which frames itself (a former colonial power) as a superior "Self" and its former African colonies, such as Chad, as inferior "Others." Chadian and other francophone Africans consider Sarkozy's opinions and actions towards Africa to be "neo-colonialist," a sentiment common in the postcolony and consistent with a postcolonial reaction.

Contemporary francophone-Africa relations and UN and U.S. policy in Africa, as manifest in the Darfur and AFRICOM cases, underscore the limitations of the new internationalist approach. They demand urgent consideration of an alternative representation of Africa, as well as a more viable international relations study and policy-practice for the continent. The current way of representing African affairs is inclined to justify external interventionist policies that are applied in ways that skew real knowledge of African problems. These approaches tend to preclude a rigorous interrogation of the specific political-economic and comparative culturalist contexts of sovereign African nation-states.

Instead of formulating policies in consultation with legitimate African political regimes and organizations, international policy responses to African "crises" are often represented simplistically in "humanitarian" frames constructed to mobilize global moral sentiment around Africa, permit the West to indulge in reification of its moral magnificence while ignoring its own failures and interest-driven role. In this regard, postcolonial theorists are right to reject the various specters of the new internationalism that dominate the study, discourses, foreign policy practice, and interventions in contemporary Africa; these are all too often unilateral, externally derived, simplistically constructed and analyzed, and subjectively implemented.

---

[52] Stephanie Hancock, "Anti-French Riot Erupts in Chad," *BBC World News Service,* October 2007.

[53] Sifelani Tsiko, "Sarkozy's Racist Africa," *Black Star News,* November 13, 2007.

Conclusion: Reframing África in a Postcolonial Global Era

The discourses presented throughout *Reframing Contemporary Africa* have demonstrated that there remains an inextricable link between international practices that construct social, economic, and political power and Africa's contemporary identity, on the one hand, and, on the other, practices of representation that continue to frame a negative meaning of Africans. The current chapter has shown that in the global arena as well, misrepresentations of Africa have contributed to the shaping of the continent's bottom-tier hierarchy, which, in turn, has influenced how African actors are perceived negatively by other international actors.

Critical intellectual traditions, such as those embodied in postcolonial studies, offer scholars a more rigorous body of knowledge about Africa. Even more significantly, the ideological precision imbued in postcolonial discourse may indeed help mobilize a shift in the analysis of African affairs so that an emerging Africanist scholarship can similarly challenge the geopolitics of mainstream hegemonic international relations in its many streams.[54] In presenting a comprehensive, sensitive, transformative analysis of African politics, economics, societies, and cultures, policy practitioners and scholars of Africa alike may be served with a different way of investigating the diverse and complex ways by which African societies are responding to the demands of a globalizing world. The analysis undertaken here adopts a method of framing that has the potential for revealing and allowing for self-determined policy solutions at national and local levels where societal goals ought to be constructed and contested.

Non-African Africanists have already begun to recognize the need for such a scholarly restructuring. David Slater, for example, argues that international relations needs to move beyond viewing Africa as simply a "place" that produces "cultures" to be studied by Western ethnographers and contemporary "Africa specialists." Instead, African scholars must be seen as generating knowledge and theories about their cultures. This has been our book's foremost goal.

In closing, it is important to underscore to our readers that our quest for methodological, theoretical, and ideological platforms to reframe Africa is widely supported not just by scholars like Slater, but also and importantly, by African policy practitioners and their constituencies. Consider, for example, the posture by African governments and the AU at the December 2007 EU-Africa Summit in Lisbon, Portugal. The then-chair of the African Union Commission, Alpha Oumar Konaré, spoke on behalf of the continent at the summit. In a public critique of the World Trade Organization, he informed the EU, "Africa doesn't want charity or paternalism. We don't want anyone doing things for us. We want to play in the global economy, but with new rules."

REFERENCES

Ashcroft, Bill. *The Post-Colonial Studies Reader.* London and New York: Routledge, 2006.

———. "Globalism, Post-Colonialism and African Studies." In *Post-Colonialism: Culture and Identity in Africa,* edited by Pal Ahluwalia and Paul Nursey-Bray. New York: Nova Science Publishers, 1997.

———, Gareth Griffiths, and Helen Tiffin. *The Empire Writes Back: Theory and Practice in Post-colonial Literatures.* 2nd ed. London and New York: Routledge, 1989.

Ahluwalia, Pal. *Politics and Post-colonial Theory: African Inflections.* London and New York: Routledge, 2001.

---

[54] Sarkozy, *Testimony,* 230.

Appiah, Kwame Anthony. "Is the 'Post' in Postcolonial the 'Post' in Postmodern?" In *Dangerous Liaisons: Gender, Nation and Postcolonial Perspective*, edited by Anne McClintock, Aamir Mufti, and Ella Shohat. Minneapolis, MN: University of Minnesota Press, 1997.

Chakrabarty, D. "Provincializing Europe: Postcoloniality and the Critique of History." *Cultural Studies* 6 (1992): 337–357.

Chowdhry, Geeta, and Sheila Nair Power. *Postcolonialism and International Relations*. London and New York: Routledge, 2002.

Darby, Phillip, and A.J. Paolini. "Bridging International Relations and Postcolonialism." *Alternatives* 19, no. 3 (1994): 371-397.

Duvall, Robert, and Himadeep Muppiddi. "The Politics of Care." Paper presented at the International Studies Association, 2007.

Dirlik, A. "The Postcolonial Aura: Third World Criticism in the Age of Global Capitalism." In *Dangerous Liaisons: Gender, Nation and Postcolonial Perspective*, edited by Anne McClintock, Aamir Mufti, and Ella Shohat. Minneapolis, MN: University of Minnesota Press, 1997.

Doty, Roxanne. *Imperial Encounters: The Politics of Representation in North-South Relations*. Minneapolis, MN: University of Minnesota Press, 1996.

Elbert, Teresa. "Subalternity and Feminism in the Moment of the Postmodern: The Materialist Return." In *Order Partialities: Theory, Pedagogy and the Postcolonial*, edited by K. Myrsiades and J. McGuire. Albany, NY: SUNY, 1995.

Kristof, Nicholas. "Mass Murder in Slow Motion." January 25, 2006, www.AlbertMohler.com.

Landow, George. "Contemporary Postcolonial and Postimperial Literature in English," www.scholars.nus.edu.sg/landow/post/index.html.

Mamdani, Mahmood. *Saviors and Survivors: Darfur, Politics, and the War on Terror*. New York and Toronto: Random House and Pantheon Books, 2009.

———. "The Politics of Naming: Genocide, Civil War, Insurgency." *London Review of Books*, March 8, 2007.

Moore-Gilbert, Bart. *Postcolonial Theory: Contexts, Practices, Politics*. London: Verso, 1997.

Muppidi, Himadeep. "Colonial and Postcolonial Global Governance." In *Power in Global Governance*, edited by Michael Barnett and Raymond Duvall. Cambridge University Press, 2005.

Mudimbe, Valentine. *The Invention of Africa*. Bloomington, IN: Indiana University Press, 1994.

Prakash, Gyan. "Who is Afraid of Postcoloniality?" *Social Text* 14, no. 4 (Winter): 187–2031.

———, ed., *After Colonialism: Imperial Histories and Postcolonial Displacements*. Princeton University Press, 1995.

Rattansi, Ali. "Postcolonialism and its Discontents." *Economy and Society* 26, no. 4 (November 1997): 480–500.

Rieff, David. *A Bed for the Night: Humanitarianism in Crisis*. New York: Simon and Schuster, 2002.

Said, Edward. *Orientalism*. New York and Toronto: Vintage Books and Random House, 1979.

Sarkozy, Nicolas. *Testimony: France in the Twenty-first Century*. New York: Pantheon Books, 2007.

Scott, David. "Colonial Governmentality," *Social Text*, no. 43: 101–220.

Slater, David. "Post-colonial Questions for Global Times." *Review of International Political Economy* 5, no. 4 (Winter 1998): 647–678.

Stemon, Stephen. "The Scramble for Post-Colonialism." In *The Post-Colonial Studies Reader*, edited by Bill Ashcroft, Gareth Griffiths, and Helen Tiffin. London and New York: Routledge, 1995.

Spivak, Gayatri Chakravorty. "Can the Subaltern Speak?" In *The Post-Colonial Studies Reader*, edited by Bill Ashcroft, Gareth Griffiths, and Helen Tiffin. London and New York: Routledge, 1995.

Tiffin, Helen, Gareth Griffiths, and Bill Ashcroft. *Key Concepts in Post-Colonial Studies*. London and New York: Routledge, 2001.

Williams, Adebayo. "The Post Colonial Flaneur and Other Fellow-Travelers: Conceits for a Narrative of Redemption." *Third World Quarterly* 18, no. 5 (1997).

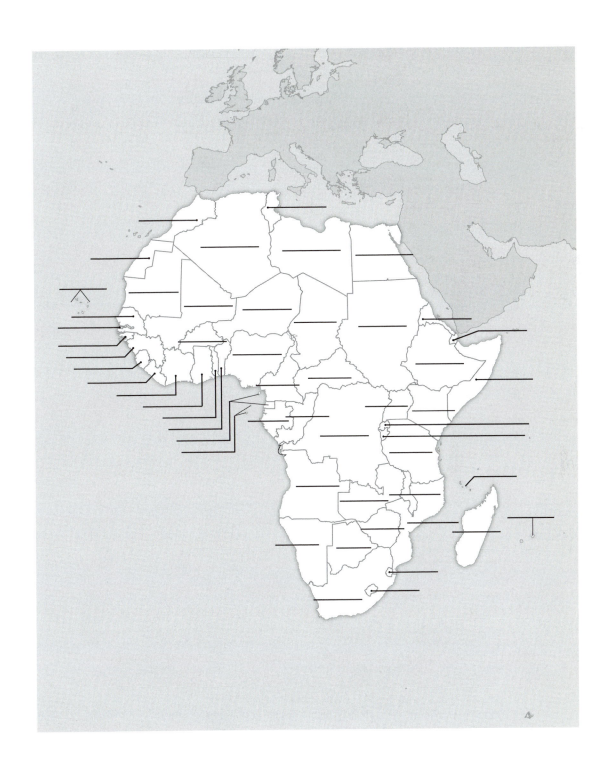